TRIBAL LAW AND JUSTICE

About the Author

W.G. ARCHER (1907-78) carried his passion for poetry and interest in art into his administrative career spread over sixteen years in the Indian Civil Service in Bihar. His interest in folk art in the remote jungles of West Bihar was reflected in the publication of *The Vertical Man : A Study of Primitive Indian Sculpture* (1947). He also published two volumes on Oraon poetry, *The Blue Grove* (1940) and *The Dove and the Leopard* (1948), translated with a poet's sensitivity. In December 1942 he was appointed Deputy Commissioner of the Santal Parganas where he continued as Special Officer to record and codify Santal Law. He produced a three volume report on Santal Laws and Justice in June 1946 which has so far remained unpublished. Before he finally left India on premature retirement, he worked as Additional Deputy Commissioner, Mokokchung in Nagaland from November 1946 to February 1948. After 1949, Archer emerged as an eminent specialist on Indian painting, culture and poetry, becoming Keeper of the Indian Department of the Victoria and Albert Museum, London.

K.S. SINGH (1935-2006), a senior member of the Indian Administrative Service has spent many years serving and studying backward communities in middle India. He was fellow, Indian Institute of Advanced Study, Simla (1970) and Jawaharlal Nehru Fellow (1970-72). As Director of the Anthropological Survey of India (1976-77), he planned and organised many all-India surveys to generate the profiles of tribal society. He has written two books : *Birsa Munda and his Movement in Chotanagpur and The Indian Famine 1967 : A Study in Crisis and Change* which have been well received. He edited *Tribal Situation in India* (1976) for the Indian Institute of Advanced Study and two volumes on *Tribal Movements* for the Anthropological Survey of India (Manohar 1982). He has also introduced W.G. Archer's *Tribal Laws and Justice* (Concept 1982).

TRIBAL LAW AND JUSTICE

A Report on the Santal
(In Three Volumes)

W.G. ARCHER

With an Introduction by
K.S. SINGH

Published under the Authority of
the Bihar Government

CONCEPT PUBLISHING COMPANY PVT. LTD.,
NEW DELHI-110059

Kumar Suresh Singh *(1935-2006)*

ISBN-13 : 978-81-7022-127-2 (H.B)

ISBN-13 : 978-93-5125-049-4 (P.B)

Reprinted 2014
First Published 1984

Published and Printed by

Concept
Since 1974

Concept Publishing Company Pvt. Ltd.
A/15-16, Commercial Block, Mohan Garden
New Delhi-110059 (India)
T: 25351460, 25351794, *F*: 091-11-25357109
E: publishing@conceptpub.com, W: www.conceptpub.com
Editorial Office: H-13, Bali Nagar, New Delhi-110 015, India.

INTRODUCTION

THE Santal have probably been the most written about, if not the best studied, tribe in middle India. There is an impressiverange of published material on them. An even larger body of material lies buried in the official archives, and a good many of the political and mission papers remain unpublished. Apart from the Santal theme in Bengali literature, an indigenous Santali literature has also developed. One reason for the favourable notice of the Santal could be that only a few tribes in middle India have been as militant, handsome and mobile; the Santal are justly described as the largest, most integrated and possibly the most resilient tribe in eastern India. They made the Santal Parganas their home early in the colonial period and spilled over the Ganga into Purnea. Few tribes have so pervaded the agrarian system of the eastern India region and played such a crucial role in it as reclaimers of land, agricultural labourers—they are excellent at the transplantation of paddy—and sharecroppers. Many streams of writing have contributed to our understanding of the Santal. The administrators, though chastened by the experience of the *hul*, the Santal insurrection of 1855-56 in which about ten thousand Santal fell, tended to romanticize Santal life. Some like R. Carstairs sought to strengthen the special system of administration for the Santal; other like E.S. Hoernle valiantly resisted attempts by the Government of Bihar in the 1930s to assimilate the special system in the Santal Parganas into the general administration, and questioned the assumption that the constitutional device of "partial exclusion" evolved under the Government of India Act of 1935 was only a temporary expedient. They wrote excellent reports on the Santal Parganas and Carstairs even wrote a novel on Santal life. The missionaries were even more prolific, they compiled grammars and dictionaries and described Santal customs and manners.

P.O. Bodding was easily the most outstanding of them, accounting for the largest literary output on the Santal and their country—suggestively called Santalistan; the original are preserved at Oslo, which probably constitute the largest collection on any tribe outside its country. Swami Vivekananda and Rabindranath Tagore waxed lyrical about the Santal; Jamini Roy painted them larger than life; Tarashanker Bandopadhyaya described the *hul* in *Aranyabahni*; Satyajit Ray could not help bringing a Santal character into the film, *Aranyer din ratri* and Mrinal Sen made a full-length movie *Mrigaya* on Santal life. Historians and anthropologists have been active in this area of study, though a full-length monograph on the Santal, in the great tradition of tribal monographs, and a more detailed and critical study of the *hul*, about which more information is now available are overdue.

II

W.G. Archer (1907-79) carried his passion for poetry and interest in art into his administrative career in Bihar which spanned a period of sixteen years from 1931 to 1946. As an administrator, he was given assignments that ordinarily came one's way in those days. Archer used his postings in rural areas of Bihar to cultivate his interests in Indian art and literature and to develop new dimensions of interests in Indian ethnology and anthropology. His first posting in the rural district of Arrah (now Shahabad) stimulated his interest in the cult of Birnath, the god worshipped by the Ahirs whose wooden image he saw while on a Christmas tiger shoot in Rohtas. The investigation continued until 1939 when he visited, accompanied by good aides, the entire Ahir belt lying across the Sone and Ganga rivers and the Chotanagpur and Shahabad forest regions. He studied the regional styles in wood of this Ahir cattle god, Bir Kuar also known as Birnath. The story of this cult and of its hero in wood and stone is told in *The Vertical Man, A Study in Primitive Indian Sculpture* published eight years later in 1947. This cult has since gained in popularity as part of the deepening consciousness of Ahir. Close to Chattarpur in Palamau, visited by Archer, I saw in 1978 a magnificent statue of Bir Kuar in a temple like structure recently constructed. The sanskritisation of this cult of the cattle god is under way.

A visit to Puri in 1932 put Archer in touch with the Puri painters, and a stint as Subdivisional Officer of Madhubani (1933-34) aroused his interest in the famous folk art of Mithila, revealed within the houses struck down by the devastating earthquake of 1934. However, it was his many years of service in tribal Bihar that shaped his interest in tribal poetry. As Assistant Settlement Officer on training at Ormanjhi in Ranchi district, he had his first exposure to the tribes. Later as Sub-divisional Officer of Gumla, predominantly inhabited by the Oraon tribe, he learnt the Oraon language as part of his official duties, and went beyond the normal range of interests permitted of an administrator in those expansive days to collect Oraon poetry, marriage songs and riddles through process-servers who during their visits to villages would collect and write down for him the words of the songs. These were published later in *The Blue Grove* (1940) and *The Dove and the Leopard* (1948). Verrier Elwin described the first as a "work of the greatest significance and importance, which set a new standard in translation from Indian poetry and opened a new doorway in the anthropological investigation of the Indian tribes". While working as District Magistrate of Purnea district, Archer came in contact with the Santal tribe for the first time. However, he was more fascinated then by the painted lanterns made by the Mali community. Back in Chotanagpur as Census Superintendent of Bihar (1939-41) at Hazaribagh, he travelled all over the province and collected a mass of anthropological material, all of which could not be published owing to wartime economies, though a good deal of tribal poetry in the vernacular collected with the aid of many tribal young men was published in tribal languages, Oraon (*Lil Khora Khekhel*), Ho (*Ho Durang*) and Kharia (*Kharia Along*) during 1941 and 1942. The Census Report of 1941 turned out to be a controversial document; it was generally supposed that the estimate of the tribal population given in the 1941 Census was exaggerated as compared to that of the 1931 Census and as revealed by the 1951 Census data. The possible reasons for this have been explained recently as follows:

> Archer was very unhappy about the form in which questions had been put by the Census staff to the villagers in the 1931 Census. They were so angled that many tribals, even when their life was essentially tribal, got listed as Hindus. He took great trouble to devise questions—very simple ones—which led to a much more realistic and anthropologically correct view of the situation. This of course did not please Hindu politicians and I am sure that by 1951 there was a return to the old forms. [Personal communication]

This phase with a brief interruption in Patna as Collector reached a climax in a four-year stay in the Santal Parganas, first as Deputy Commissioner (1942-45) and then as Special Officer of the Judicial Department to record the Santal Laws (1945-46). Archer also become Joint Editor with Verrier Elwin of *Man in India* founded by S.C. Roy, of which many issues were devoted to specific administrative and literary themes; the two together also gave it a poetic and aesthetic bias. Archer had close links with scholars and administrators who were active in the area of tribal studies and welfare, Sir W.V. Grigson, Christoph von Fürer Haimendorf, Philip Mills and Verrier Elwin. Of all of them, he seems to have come closest to Verrier Elwin who was in the process of formulating his approach to tribal problems in the 1940s. Again as part of his official duties he learnt Santali. He continued to take interest in tribal poetry and organised the collection of Santal poetry which was published in three volumes, *Hor Soren*, *Don Soren* and *Hor Kudum*.

These also provided the material for the *Hill of the Flutes: Life, Love and Poetry in Tribal India, A Portrait of the Santals* (1974), published almost thirty years later. This book does not belong to the category of traditional monographs. It does not deal with the material traits or the mode of production; it does not describe the range and dimensions of culture contact, though the Santal have been among the most acculturated tribes. It takes up only some aspects of Santal life, life-cycle ceremonies and festivals, sex and love. Although there is little that is original about the material used to describe Santal life and institutions, except the poetry, the account derives strength from the case histories adduced to support the traditional accounts of the Santal customs and from Archer's personal experience. The narrative begins with a description of the ideal, happy setting, the village, the clan system and the world of spirits (*bongas*); this is followed by a portrayal of the life-cycle. The delineation of Santal love and sex is excellent, and almost equals Verrier Elwin's in *The Muria and their Ghotul* (1947). Archer's is probably the most remarkable collection of Santal poetry, particularly erotic poetry. Transcreated with great sensitivity on the model of Arthur Wayley, this "simple, sensuous and passionate" poetry "shared with that of Kalidasa and Jayadeva, explained the early Indian attitude to sex". This conceptualization of the linkage between the little and great traditions of India has considerable merit. Unquestionably a classic on the Santal, it is based on the material collected in the early 1940s, and describes those sections of the Santal tribe, which were to a great extent unaffected by either Hindu or Muslim practices. However, it does not describe how the Santal had also become restive and an agrarian movement in the mid-thirties swept across the Santal areas of Bhagalpur, Monghyr and Hazaribagh.

III

Archer's duties as Deputy Commissioner of Santal Parganas (December 1942 to June 1945) brought him into close contact with the Santal. He had to decide cases involving the Santal and had thus the firsthand opportunity to observe the points of conflict that arose out of the application to the Santal of the statutory laws (the Indian Penal Code, Civil and Criminal Procedure Codes) and the Santal's adherence to his customary laws. Many others before him had commented upon the disastrous impact of the imposition of the colonial laws and judicial system on tribes and watched with dismay the erosion of the tribal system. Attempts had been made to enclave many tribal areas and introduce the single-line administration in which the officers combined judicial and executive functions to provide quick relief for tribals, and to consult the tribals before disposing of the cases involving them. But such experiments remained like islands and elsewhere the tribals had been assimilated into the administrative and judicial system of the *raj*. In the mid-1930s many administrators and anthropologists had commented upon the dichotomy of tribal and colonial legal systems and pleaded for the recognition of tribal law. It was this recognition of the autonomy of the tribal system and laws which could best be administered in the interest of the tribals themselves that lay behind the codification of Santal laws. It was expected that this would help the courts understand Santal laws and dispose of the cases involving tribals in the light of their own customary laws. Such a measure was recommended in very general terms by the Santal Pargana Inquiry Committee in its report (1937) which suggested framing of a self-contained Tenancy Act, updating of the Santal Parganas Manual, compilation of the rulings of courts etc. The Committee observed in its report:

> There is a real danger that an attempt at complete codification may result in a rigidity and fixity of law which would remove the elasticity of the system which is so essential in dealing with a district that is gradually advancing from a state of backwardness. This must be avoided. . . . The main outlines of the rights of landlords, pradhans, raiyats etc., should be incorporated. . . . Generally, therefore we do not wish to alter the law but to state it as clearly and as fully as possible (Para 70).

The Committee spoke of the agrarian laws in particular while recommending codification of the laws in general. Archer described pointedly the genesis of the inquiry to codify the Santal laws under his supervision as Special Officer as follows:

> For many years prior to the appointment of the Santal Parganas Inquiry Committee, the absence of a complete statement of Santal law had been a notable defect in the district administration. It had always been assumed and rightly assumed—that in all civil matters the Santal had a tribal law of their own and that this should be applied by the courts in the decision of their civil suits. It had also been assumed that officers trying such suits would know what the law was. This latter assumption, however, was

> often belied by facts and there can be little doubt that in the absence of a full statement numberless wrong decisions were given in the past. The matter was further complicated by the fact that during the present century the law regarding the rights of women appeared to be changing. Officers holding Santal Courts were, therefore, frequently at a loss to know what principles to apply. It was with a view to remedying this state of affairs that the Santal Parganas Inquiry Committee recommended that a memorandum should be prepared stating the present position of the law and it was with a view to implementing that recommendation and rectifying a very serious weakness in the civil administration of the district that I was placed on special duty to prepare the present report. [Archer papers]

The objective of Archer's Inquiry, therefore, was that "the Santal courts should have a statement of Santal law for without that it is quite impossible for them to do justice. If my book is published they will have the work of reference they need." There was also a deeper and more remote reason for this:

> Regulation III of 1872 had definitely provided for a record of Santal law, the need for such a record had been conceded by McPherson in his Settlement Report in 1909. . . none the less all the settlements had neglected this point. I also pointed out that such a knowledge of Santal law was very necessary for the settlements since without it a number of incorrect entries were made. In this connection I have referred to a remark by McPherson who stated that when the Settlement Courts became acquainted with Santal Law they ceased to record women as the successors to jotes (cultivated land). [Archer papers]

Archer also describes the mode of inquiry into the Santal laws followed by him over the period from June 1945 to June 1946 in the last paragraph of his preface to civil laws. A band of young Santali-knowing officers, "independent magistrates", whom he mentions, helped him, along with Santal informants, to collect, check and crosscheck the material on the laws at twenty centres in the Santal Parganas, to make sure that the account was as complete and authentic as possible.

> All the principles recorded in the report were ascertained, checked and attested at 20 centres all over the Santal portions of the district. These enquiries were made by14 officers, 8 of whom were Hindus and 6 Santals and they showed that there was now a clear and coherent body of Santal law accepted and applied by Santal throughout the district. To describe this law as "customary law", is completely to confuse the issue while to deny that a Santal law exists is to ignore all the results of a long and thorough investigation. [Archer papers]

The evidence was fully checked all over the Santal Parganas. The book was thus "neither invented by an Englishman or a *Diku* (alien) but was an account accepted and attested by the Santals".

As regards Archer's own competence to conduct and supervise an operation of this kind, he recalled his experiences as Munshiff and in various other capacities in Chotanagpur.

> From 1934 to 1937 I was Subdivisional Officer at Gumla in Ranchi district and was ex-officio Munshiff. As Munshiff in Chota Nagpur I certainly had considerable experience of civil justice in another tribal part of the Province. . . . In addition to my service as Subdivision Officer—Munshiff I have had six months' experience of the Ranchi Settlement in the Sadar Subdivision. I toured in Chota Nagpur at my own expense for four months while on leave in India in 1938-39. I lived at Hazaribagh [from 1939-41] and toured widely through Chota Nagpur. [Archer papers]

The end product of the labours was the three volume report on the Santal laws which gave a complete and authentic picture of the state of the Santal laws in the mid-1940s as they existed in the Santal Parganas. The inquiry did not cover the non-Santal (*Diku*)—or deal with their perception of the law—and extend beyond the administrative jurisdiction of the Santal Parganas. As a definitive work on the Santal, it went beyond

Kolean Haram's *Horkoren Mare Hapremko Reak' Katha,* which was published in 1887 but written in 1872. It gives a vivid account of many Santal institutions but it is in no sense a complete or systematic account. Nor does it deal with Santal practices with the precision necessary for the civil courts. There is no proof that it was in fact correct. It was never checked or attested. This account was so incomplete that it could not usefully serve as a basis for a coherent and clear statement of the Santal law.

Archer emphasised that his reports were not an account of the customary law but a statement of the "present law" as practised by the Santal and not as interpreted by the courts.

> It will be obvious from the very fact that Santal law has changed in the last 50 years that the law cannot be called *customary.* A custom must by its very nature be ancient, unaltered and constant and that Santal law is not. The only possible definition, therefore, which bears any relation to tribal life or which is of any use for the purpose of administration is one which Santals of the Santal Parganas now accept as defining their civil rights and duties. It is current principles rather than obsolete customs which constitute their law. That such a law exists was fully substantiated by my inquiries. (Archer papers)

IV

The material emerging from this exercise was initially organised into two volumes (i) Civil Law in Santal Society, and (ii) Bitlaha, A Report on Santal Criminal law. The accompanying third volume, Civil Justice in Tribal India with special reference to the Santal Parganas was mostly based on this material, though it drew upon other sources of information, too. However, the last volume stands apart from the other two in that it deals with larger issues and became the most controversial of the three volumes.

The first report highlights the unique features of the Santal civil laws. Custom is only a part of the tribal laws, a guide to attitude, and therefore it does not constitute a final definition of law. Tribal law is in fact a set of principles a tribe accepts and applies. Santal law is actually a synthesis of tribal attitudes expressed through a hierarchy of tribal courts ranging from the village court to the Court of Five Manjhis. Like the administrators of his generation, Archer regarded the Santal agrarian system, with its institution of public ownership of land, as socialistic. In fact it was clan ownership under which the right over land vested in the male agnates of the family. Private rights in land were also emerging, which were recognised by the survey and settlement operations much to the chagrin of those administrators who wanted to preserve the communal character of land ownership. Disputes over land led to theft, abuse and affray, as Archer observed.

One of the redeeming features of Santal society was that it did not have to deal with the problems of illegitimate children. Apart from the checks on Santal bastardy enforced through infanticide and abortion, the illegitimate children were readily absorbed into the Santal community. The Santal servants enjoyed a measure of equality with members of the family. They were Santals first and servants later and could even end up as *ghar jawae* (the serving son-in-law). However, while Santal women did enjoy a measure of freedom, they were "things" and had no right to property. A widow could claim only maintenance. The daughter or sister had no right to ancestral property if she had a brother. In case of the death of a father having no male issue, the daughter married to a *ghar jawae* could inherit the property.

The patrilineal system is now under stress. Archer himself had noticed the growing trend towards change whereby a childless widow inherited her late husband's land until she remarried. He had also observed how the settlement operation in deference to local customs recognised the rights of the women by recording them as owners, as a matter of fact. Thus the settlement conferred rights on widows and daughters who were thus acquiring rights beyond the customary law. (Paras 45 and 46 of Gantzer's *Settlement Report*.) Probably the most notable judgement upholding the right of a widow to bequeath property to her daughter, ignoring the interests and rights of male agnates of the family was delivered by the Commissioner of Bhagalpur, A.J. Mainwaring (the Santal Parganas Civil Appeal No. 22 of 1940). The widow's right had been duly recorded in the settlement proceedings. Since Archer noted this, the daughters and widows have increasingly asserted their rights to property not only among the Santal, but also among the Ho and Munda tribes. Those Santal who accept the Hindu Succession Law insist on their daughters or sisters getting rights. Those who have become Christians also recognise the right of their daughters by transferring land through gift or sale. Those who are without any male issue, insist on the transfer of rights to their daughter even without a *ghar jawae*. There are today any number of case laws on the rights of the daughters. Right to transfer land to wife and daughter has been upheld in many judicial decisions after 1947. The Santal Parganas Tenancy Act (Supplementary Provision) Sec. 1949 upholds the right of a widow or a minor to make over the landholding temporarily on trust for cultivation. Proviso to Section 24(2) stipulates that a gift to the husband or to the wife of the donor or to a son adopted under the Hindu law or to the daughter, sister, adopted son or adopted daughter of the donor under the Santal law or to a relation by consanguinity within three degrees of such donor shall not require any registration fee to be paid to the Government or in other words shall be automatically recognised. Similarly transfer of a raiyat holding by sale, gift, will or exchange in accordance with the provisions of this Act and records of right shall be recognised. The Act also recognises the Santal's right to make a gift in favour of his sister or daughter where this is permitted by the local custom—and this has to be established in case of a dispute—and to make a grant in respect of his land not exceeding one half of the area of his holding to his widowed mother or to his wife or her maintenance after his death. However where local custom does not so permit, widows having no sons or daughters with a *ghar jawae* have only a life-interest, unmarried daughters without brothers lose all interest in land in the event of their marriage, and the right of male agnates prevails over that of a female. The temporary rights of the females of the two categories mentioned above are duly recorded in the settlement proceedings. However, the movement in favour of the recognition of the right of women is growing as also the resistance offered by the male agnates to this on the ground that the land belongs to the lineage (*khunt*) which reclaims it (*katti*) and therefore transfer of interest to women will undermine the very foundation of the social organization of the tribe.

While in the north-east the tribals were by and large left free to be regulated by their own conception of the law and by their own machinery, elsewhere they were assimilated, islands apart, into the judicial system of British India. Differences between a tribal perception of a crime and the Indian Penal Code's concept of a crime as interpreted by the courts came out sharply. Adultery, kidnapping and abduction are not crimes in a tribal society unless they are committed against prescribed relations. Marriage by capture is common, rape is not a major sin, punishments are generally awarded in the shape of fines or feasts within one's means. Assaults are not taken seriously. Even murder under provocation and in certain circumstances is not condemned. A tribal law takes a more humane view of human failings. Rehabilitation of convicts is easier and poses no problems. Tribals have their own system to punish offenders. The Santal have their *bitlaha*, the much impressive, much dreaded form of Santal punishment of incest which polluted the tribe and threatened to destroy tribal integrity. It was a unique Santal institution. Archer has handed down what is probably the most vivid account of this institution.

> The ritual of the ceremony is one of the most impressive in the whole range of Santal life. It is performed by an enormous crowd. It is done to the thunder and roll of drums. The crowd advances on the house in long surging lines. Finally a ceremony of symbolic defilement is performed in the heart of the courtyard. In its disciplined expression of revolted disgust, its intense assertion of tribal values, its savage dignity, the ceremony is unique in tribal India.

And yet this institution was almost dying as Archer wrote about it. He himself recorded only 18 *bitlahas* during the period 1920-1945 and pleaded for its continuance and regularisation as it posed no major threat to property or life; it also did not provoke communal or agrarian riots. It was a more civilised way for securing justice than communal riots; it substituted symbols for action and a dance for an outrage. But neither the colonial nor the post-Independence government agreed with such a romantic notion of the *bitlaha*. Incidence of loss of property, no matter how minor, did occur. With the agrarian situation rapidly deteriorating in the Santal Parganas, the *bitlaha* could well be the spark that could set the whole region ablaze. Therefore, the *bitlaha* continued to be treated as a 'law and order' matter.

There were 8 cases of *bitlaha* in the heart of the Santal land between 1955 and 1963, mostly among the Santals or between the Santal and another tribe, the Paharia. The *bitlaha* performed against the non-Santal could take a serious turn and revive latent animosities. Thus the *bitlaha* performed at village Kharibari (Maheshpur) on 27 June 1956 turned out to be a very serious affair. About 20,000 Santal armed with weapons came in to perform the *bitlaha*, burnt down the house of the non-Santal offender and clashed with the police. As a result of firing 10 Santals died on the spot. The *bitlaha* ended in a massacre, as Archer had apprehended. The institution has been on the decline. It is not idle to speculate whether or not the present phase of Santal militancy is a continuation of the spirit of *bitlaha* in another form.

The third volume on civil justice in tribal India with special reference to the Santal Parganas, as mentioned earlier, appears to have been written independently of the first two volumes. It deals with the structure of the judicial system in tribal regions and shows up the erosion of tribal customary laws and their supercession by statutory laws. Archer suggested, like many others in the 1930s, the setting up of a chain of tribal courts to administer justice in tribal areas because, as he observed, the modern law courts and their procedures and practices were unsuited for the tribals. Much the same views had been expressed by missionaries and anthropologists many years before. But the colonial administration had rejected this policy of exclusion of tribal areas in middle India from the operation of the general laws. Exclusion or partial exclusion of tribal areas from such laws as envisaged in the Constitution of 1935 was only a temporary expedient, the ultimate aim being their assimilation with the larger system of administration and justice. Archer himself as Deputy Commissioner of the Santal Parganas in December 1945 supported the recommendation made by the Santal Parganas Inquiry Committee to end the special status of the Santal Parganas and of its Deputy Commissioner in matters of control over civil and criminal justice and to transfer his functions in this respect to the jurisdiction of the High Court except in matters coming under the preventive provisions of the Code of Criminal Procedure. This official stance was at variance with his later views that there should be only one set of courts to administer the law for the Santal or that the Santal tribal councils should be associated with the Santal civil court to advise the latter in matters concerning the Santal. Archer also went further and suggested that the tribal should be excluded from the provision of the Indian Succession Act and put beyond the pale of Mitakshara and Dayabhaga schools of Hindu law and the jurisdiction of Muslim law. The question whether the tribals were bound by Hindu law or tribal law should according to Archer be settled once for all. The only concession he was willing to make *a la* Verrier Elwin was that the tribal law should be recognised as the "aboriginal school" of Hindu law.

V

Archer submitted his reports in June 1946, and proceeded on four months' leave. On return from leave he was posted as Additional Deputy Commissioner of Mokokchung in Nagaland at the instance of Philip Mills, Governor's Adviser in Assam. Meanwhile, his reports had been examined by a senior colleague, Nilmani Senapati, a former Commissioner of Bhagalpur, who had also worked as Deputy Commissioner of Manbhum where a good number of Santal lived and who was considered some sort of an expert on the Santal. Senapati found the reports lacking in many particulars and containing criticisms of the officers and the official policies and he recommended that they should be filed. Archer who was at Dumka in December 1946 sent two letters marked "private and personal" to Binodanand Jha, Minister of the Local Self Government Department which had commissioned the reports. These constituted Archer's spirited rejoinders to Senapati's criticisms. Since these exchanges involve substantive issues, the diatribes of a personal nature apart, it will be necessary to present a summary of these.

Senapati contested Archer's thesis that there was a Santal customary law because there were so many variations to suit the local circumstances that it was impossible to conclude that any custom existed. Archer while rebutting this argument pointed out that there were a number of equally valid ways of dealing with situations which pointed to commonly accepted principles by the Santal. These, he insisted, represented a very clear body of tribal law. Knowledge of the principles and a statement of the law were required for all, otherwise the civil courts may do great injustice. Secondly, Senapati thought that the Santal would resent the impression created by certain statements in the first report that that lived in a state of loose morals and that any Santal could have the sexual act with any Santal girl, married or unmarried, provided they were outside the restricted relationship. Archer pointed out in reply that the moral code of the Santal was governed by certain rigid tribal conventions and remedies were prescribed which in no way justified the inference that crimes were being continually committed. Archer also denied the charge that the appointment of a woman as Manjhi would lead to chaos. He explained that his comparison of Mahatma Gandhi with the tribal priest (*dihri*) could not be interpreted as intentionally disrespectful, which he readily agreed to delete from the final draft. This was "a half-humorous witty remark which Senapati took overseriously" (Mildred Archer).

Senapati's criticisms of Archer's thesis in the third volume were more strident as were Archer's rebuttals. Senapati appeared to have taken a serious view of an Englishman's and that too of a civil servant's criticism of the judicial system of Chotanagpur, of his references to the officers' and judges' ignorance of the tribal languages and tribal customs etc. Archer explained that much the same criticism had been levelled by the anthropologist, S.C. Roy against the British system and that it was not the officers but the system that was to be blamed. If the British Government had done nothing there was no reason why a popular government should not take up the matter. Senapati also found Archer rather too critical of the handling of the Santal laws and Santal suits by regular sub-judge courts and of the High Court's ruling brushing aside the appeal to Santal law, which Archer thought was wrong. However, Archer was on strong grounds when he tried to refute Senapati's argument that the settlement operation records only the existing right and does not create a right. The settlement operation in the Santal Paraganas to this day is unique in that the Settlement Officer and his officers function as civil court and unlike their counterparts elsewhere can thus decide points of title and create title. The jurisdiction of the civil court is specifically barred, and the entries in the settlement records are the conclusive proof of right and custom and have the force of a decree. The Santal Pargana Regulation of 1872 (Regulation 3 of 1872) which provides for these was shaped by the historical experience of preserving the Santal identity.

However, it appears that Senapati's recommendations prevailed despite Archer's clarifications, and the three reports were filed. Twenty-six years later Senapati still found Archer's position untenable :

> I found some serious faults in the book and recommended that Government should not publish it. My most serious point of disagreement with Mr. Archer was that he was prepared to allow ex-communication of a non-Santal by a thoroughly disgusting ceremony called Bitlaha. While Santal custom can apply to Santals it cannot apply to non-Santals. I have some recollection of a judgment by Mr. Justice B.K. Ray of the Patna High Court in this connection. I did not hear any more about Mr. Archer's book even though we met several times both in India and in England. (Personal communication)

With this died Archer's suggestion that the Bihar Government should pass a short Act prescribing that in all suits in which both the parties were aboriginals they should be bound by the law of the aboriginals concerned.

VI

There could be other factors behind the burying of these

reports. Partition of the country was in the offing. The Adibasi Mahasabha was becoming militant, in close league with the Muslim League, even though it had lost at the polls. Archer's view points could be misunderstood and provide grist to the political mill. However as one looks back at the debate, there will be little disagreement today in the light of our experiences of the regular courts functiong in tribal areas that there should be better understanding of the tribal customary laws in deciding cases of a civil nature involving tribals and that the codification of tribal laws is intrinsic to tribal welfare. There was thus a great deal in Archer's suggestion that the regular courts of law should show a better appreciation of the tribal custom in deciding cases involving the tribals. This is possible only if the tribal laws are codified. Unfortunately there has been little progress in the codification of tribal laws in our country except in the northeast. Archer's report could serve as a model for codification of tribal law in middle India. In spite of its limitations, it remains a definitive account of Santal laws in the mid-1940s, a notable piece of social research.

Codification of tribal laws together with the provisions for legal aid should go a long way in meeting the tribals' grievances against the working of the present day legal systems. When I was in the Anthropological Survey of India, I had drawn up in 1976, a scheme to conduct a survey of tribal customary laws. A seminar was held in November 1978. A format of a larger survey is still to be worked out, because while studies of tribal laws have been confined to homicide (Elwin, Verma), the canvas of tribal laws is much wider and covers the entire gamut of tribal life. Archer's work in this regard is an important contribution to the anthropology of law which is emerging as a major sub-discipline of anthropology. As Hoebal says :

> Modern Anthropology has its special contribution to make to the understanding of law for two reasons. The first is that the anthropologist, who has traditionally concentrated his studies on small societies with single cultures, has been in a position to comprehend such societies, each

> in its entirety and so to deal with cultures as integrated working wholes. This has made possible the development of comprehensive theories of cultural dynamics embracing legal phenomenon as but one aspect of culture. The second arose from the fact that anthropology is first and foremost a comparative science. It draws its data from all orders of society, primitive and civilised, pre-historic and contemporary and from all portions of the globe. It makes it possible to move such closer to the realisation of a genuine and empirical science of law. Such an approach to law through anthropology is one of functional realism by means of comparative legal dynamics. [Introduction]

It is relevant to our need not only to explore the many dimensions of law and society but also to evolve a system which should make understanding of the relation of law and society and of tribal laws easier and administration of justice to the tribal quicker, less expensive and more effective.

VII

Finally, a few words about how this manuscript on the Santal laws came to be retrieved and published. When I was Director, Anthropological Survey of India, the late Mr. Archer enquired through a common friend if I could seek the permission of the Bihar Government to publish his reports. This set the ball rolling. I took up the matter with the Bihar Government immediately, who accorded the permission to publish the manuscript in May 1979 on the following conditions:

(i) that the royalties accruing from the sale of the book shall be credited to a fund to be created in the Bihar Tribal Research Institute for the promotion of the Santal language, literature, law and development ; and

(ii) that there shall be an acknowledgment that the book has been published under the authority of the State Government.

When I took up the manuscript for examination later, many chapters were found missing. The Indian Council of Social

Science Research very kindly came forward in September 1981 to provide financial assistance to secure the xerox of the master copy of Archer's manuscript kept in the Indian Office Library and towards its printing. I have made the changes in the manuscript as suggested later by Archer himself but have not omitted Part VI on trial of Santal suits which he had included on his successor's request. Dr. Mildred Archer has touchingly pursued the publication of her husband's work on the Santal, which is yet another token of their affection for India. The Concept Publishing Company took up the printing with enthusiasm and did it very competently. My thanks are to all those who helped at at different stages towards the publication of the manuscript.

K.S. SINGH

NOTES AND REFERENCES

In writing this introduction, I had the benefit of personal communication with Nilmani Senapati who is happily still with us, Dr. Mildred Archer who commented on it, Shankar Prasad, Settlement Officer of the Santal Parganas, and many other officers some of whom had worked with Archer. The Bihar State Archive has a couple of files on the Archer manuscripts and the Santal issue (File No. 220 Judicial Branch, Judicial Department 1946 and File No. 49-56 Judicial Branch, Judicial Department August 1947) but the main file relating to the decision on the clarifications furnished by Archer is not traceable. The Archer papers were made available to me by Dr. Mildred Archer. These mainly included two letters dated 1 & 6 June, 1946 from Archer to Pandit Binodanand Jha, Minister of Local Self Government, Bihar, replying to the criticisms of his reports by his colleague N. Senapati, who was Commissioner of Bhagalpur in the 1940s. Archer's comments on the criminal section are not available : these were probably not called for in view of Senapati's views and the Government's known position on the *bitlaha.*

Mildred Archer, A passion for India, *Roopa Lekha*, Vol. LI, Nos. 1 & 2, 17-21.

Archer, W.G., *The Blue Grove : the Poetry of the Oraons*, London 1940; *The Dove and the Leopard*, London, 1948; *The Vertical Man : A Study of Primitive Indian Sculpture*, London 1947; *Hill of the Flutes : Life, Love and Poetry in Tribal India, A Portrait of the Santals*, London 1974.

Elwin, Verrier, *The Muria and their Ghotul*, Oxford University Press, 1947.

Gantzer, J.F., *Final Report on the Revision Survey and Settlement Operations in the District of the Santal Parganas*, 1922-35, Patna 1936.

Hoebel, E. Adamson, *The Law of Primitive Man : A Study in Comparative Legal Dynamics*, Atheneum, New York, 1976.

Report of the Santal Parganas Inquiry Committee, 1973.

Singh, K.S., Book review of W.G. Archer, *The Hill of Flutes : Life, Love and Poetry in Tribal India, A Portrait of the Santals* (George Allen and Unwin 1974), *The Indian Historical Review*, Vol. II, No. 2, January, 1976, pp. 1-7.

Verma, S.C., *The Bhil Kills*, King Publishing Home, Delhi, 1978.

CONTENTS

PART FOUR

THE LAW OF MARRIAGE AND DIVORCE

PART FIVE

THE RITES OF CRISIS

PART SIX

VOLUME TWO

BITLAHA
A REPORT ON SANTAL CRIMINAL LAW

PART ONE
THE SETTING

PART TWO

THE SANTAL LAW

PART THREE
THE FUTURE

VOLUME THREE

CIVIL JUSTICE IN TRIBAL INDIA WITH SPECIAL REFERENCE TO THE SANTAL PARGANAS

APPENDICES

GLOSSARY

I

Ag muk	The funerary ceremony of touching the mouth of a corpse with fire
Agu hatar	A ghar jawae by anticipation
Agu mit'	A son-in-law brought back to be a ghar jawae
Ak' yuric'	The leading girl assistant at a wedding
Anna	One-sixteenth of a rupee before the present metric system was adopted in India
Apangir	Elopement
Ara	Sixteen pais (i.e., 8-9 seers)
Asul badha	A foundling, reared but not adopted
Asul duruc' ic'	A servant engaged by a master for life-long maintenance
Asul sangha	Marriage with an elder brother's widow
Ato bapla	'A wedding by the village', symbolic term
Babre era	'The Brahman's wife', a Santal girl who assists at a wedding
Babu jawae	'Bride and bridegroom', also the leaf emblems depicting the sexual organs
Baha saoha	Putting a flower in sangha marriage
Bahu	Bride or wife
Bahu bande	Presenting the bride's cloth
Bahu daura	The basket in which a bride is lifted
Baisi	Council, meeting
Bande onodon	'A cloth to cover her nakedness', part of chadaodi or divorce money

Bapla kora	Married boy
Bapla maeji	Married woman
Bare itat'	The brother's due or bullock at the marriage of his sister
Bariat	Bridegroom's party
Batki	Senior of two or more wives
Bhagwa	A strip of cloth passed between the thighs and tucked into the waist-string
Bidhua	Bastard
Bir sendra	Annual hunt
Bitlaha	A mass punishment for major tribal offences
Bhandan	Final funerary feast
Bhitar	Private shrine
Bitol	Outcaste
Bohok' bancao	'Saving the head', a fee taken by the manjhi for averting punishment by execution
Bohok' chadwi	A girl who has had iputut' done to her and has refused to be the boy's wife
Bonga	Spirit
Bonga budhi	A bride's father's mother
Bor horo	Paddy loaned in aid of a wedding
Caco chatiar	Initiation ceremony
Camda	Wedding shed of an inferior type
Candla dangra	Money in lieu of a bullock for bare itat'
Caro	Hire of cattle
Celan gitil	'Scouring the pot', compensation for adultery
Chadwa	Divorced boy
Chadwi	Divorced girl
Chadaodi	Divorce money
Chakladar	Pargana's orderly

Chatai taka	'Mat money', the costs of a meeting
Chutki	Junior of two or more co-wives
Cak	Part of the courtyard where the bridal pair sit
Cak khunti	Central pole in a marriage booth
Cak purauni	Present for painting the cak at a wedding
Condka	Pole with branch of straw indicating a staked claim
Culha	Earthen hearth
Culha jharaoni	Present to the wedding cooks
Cupi chadwi	A girl who is known (1) to have miscarried or (2) to have lived with a boy as his wife without receiving sindur and after that to have been divorced
Curuc' Cawale	Land set aside for agnates and worship of ancestral spirits
Dai budhi	Midwife
Dan	Witch
Dandom	Fine
Dangua	Unmarried
Daram dak' enec'	Welcome dance at weddings
Dard mitauni	'Easing the pain', compensation for injury
Deshmanjhi	Pargana's deputy and assistant
Dharwak'	Branch : Sending round a dharwak', a summons
Dihri	President of an annual hunt
Disom nor	Men of the country, the Santal of the area
Dol bapla	Full dress wedding
Dunger	Dance by nude jokers at bitlahas or annual hunts
Enec' halan te	'Gathering it at a dance', pregnancy due to illicit intercourse
Enga itat'	Mother's share of the bride price

Gamcha	A small cloth worn at the waist or neck
Ganji	Vest
Gate kuri	A boy's village girl, at a wedding the bridesmaid
Ghar jawae	A permanent serving son-in-law
Ghardi jawae	A temporary serving son-in-law
Gidi cumaura	Waving ceremony at a wedding when presents are given
Godet	Headman's orderly or messenger
Golaeti	Marriage by exchange of sons and daughters
Gongo salaka	Present to the bride's paternal uncle
Gonon	Price
Gonon pon	Bride-price
Gonon taraoni	Return presents to the bride groom and his party
Gupi paisa	Jogmanjhi's fee for 'shepherding' a girl between her betrothal and the wedding
Hanapuri	The afterworld
Here budhi	Bride's mother's mother
Hirom baiha	Indemnity to a senior wife on her hus band's marriage with a co-wife
Hirom cetan bapla	Marriage of a co-wife
Hilit'era sangha	Marriage with an elder brother's widow
Horok' cikhna	'Recognizing by clothes', a stage of betrothal
Iputut'	The forcible application of sindur to a girl
Jaher	Sacred grove
Jan guru	Witch-finder
Janum chatiar	Birth ceremony
Jarge palat'	A change of clothes for the rainy season
Jawae	Bridegroom or husband
Jawae dhuti	The bridegroom's dhoti

Jawae kirinok' bapla	Marriage by purchase of a bridegroom
Jhili ladu	Large ball-like sweets
Jobrani	A fine for using force
Jogmanjhi	Children's protector
Jog paranik	Jogmanjhi's assistant
Jom jati	Feast for re-admission to the tribe
Jonam bitol	Permanent outcaste
Karpa kudi	'Wearing out the shoes', a fee to the match-maker
Khajari	Parched rice
Khanda	Women's cloth
Kharailak' taka	'For getting ready the threshing floor', part of the food expenses at a wedding
Khasi	A gelded goat or pig
Khil	Name of sub-sept
Khiti puran	Compensation
Khunt	Sub-sept
Kisar bonga	Brownie
Kombro	Thief
Kora bariat	Bridegroom's party
Kudam naeke	Assistant priest
Kulhi	Street
Kulhi durup'	A street sitting, a village meeting
Kuman	Husband of father's sister
Kundal napam	'Meeting when lying down', marriage by intercourse
Lajao marao	Outrage to modesty
Langta	Nude
Lasar tengoc'	A 'share axe' or village pleader
Lumti budhi	Bride's chaperon
Lumti kora	Younger cousin of the bridegroom, 'the best man'
Maila	Polluted
Mama salaka	Present to bride's maternal uncle

Mandal	Striker's share of an animal or bird
Mandla	A fee of one rupee paid to the manjhi of the bride's village by the bridegroom's father
Mandwa	Marriage booth
Mandwa chadwi	A girl whose wedding is abandoned after the marriage booth has been erected
Manjhi	Village headman
Manjhithan	Shrine to the village founder
Mon rofa	'Calming the mind', a gift to a co-wife
More hor	The village council
More sika	Five four-anna bits, commonly, the cost of a village sitting
Naeke	Priest
Nim dak' mandi	Rice water mixed with nim leaves and served at the birth ceremony
Nir bolok'	Marriage by intrusion
Nunu taka	'Price of the milk', gift to a mother by her son at his wedding
Ojha	Medicine man
Or ader	'Pulling in', marriage by capture
Orak' duar nel	'Seeing the household', a stage in the wedding talks
Pai	Half a seer
Palki	Litter
Panca	A small temporary loan without interest
Panci	Cloth worn by men as a loin-cloth and by women over the breasts and shoulder
Pante begar	'Separation from the line', the minor form of excommunication
Paranik	Deputy headman
Pargana	Leader of a group of villages, president of the council of five villages
Parhand	Short petticoat

Penda dopot' chadwi	'A cracked base', an unmarried girl who has miscarried or has had a child out of wedlock
Phucia kaudi	Jogmanjhi's fee for 'shepherding' a girl between her betrothal and the wedding
Pichauri	A cotton over-cloth made by sewing two pieces of cloth together
Pitha	Cake
Pon	Bride-price
Porodhol	The first ancestor
Raebaric'	Match-maker
Rahi	Wedding litter
Randi	Widow
Rin	A permanent loan with interest
Rongo thutkut	Charred piece of wood
Rum	Ecstatic 'possession'
Sadai bapla	Normal wedding, 'the standard form'
Sake bonga	An ojha's tutelary spirit
Sakri sakam	A soiled leaf plate
Sangha bapla	Marriage of a widow or divorcee
Sariat	Bride's party
Sendra	Hunt
Sindurdan	Public smearing of the bride's forehead with sindur at a wedding
Sindur urani	A payment for 'wiping off the sindur' after iputut'
Si-tora	Servant's contract by which land is cultivated in lieu of wages
Son chadaoni	A parting present
Susun sasan chadwi	A girl whose marriage is abandoned after she has been smeared with oil and turmeric for her wedding
Taben jom	A gift of land for 'eating taben', maintenance

Takal cal	Paying the bride-price
Taram gande	'Stepping over the elder sister', a fee at wedding
Tel nahan	'Washing with oil', part of the funerary rites
Tenan	Elder sister's husband
Tetre kuri	Maids of all work at a wedding
Todor	A metal wristlet worn by men
Thutki jonok'	Worn-out broom
Tuar	Orphan
Um narka rakap'	The return from bathing at a funeral
Uric' utin'	Servant's contract by which bullocks are loaned in place of wages

VOLUME ONE

CIVIL LAW
IN
SANTAL SOCIETY

Man in society is naturally just,
because society, if it is real, is
a bond of mutual consideration.
Common law is essentially the
common feeling of what is right and
just, as between the members of a
community.

Herbert Read, On Justice

PREFACE

IN this report I have set out the principles of tribal law which Santals of the Santal Parganas now accept as defining their civil rights and duties. These principles cover such widely differing subjects as the rights of Santal men and women, the law of marriage and divorce, the claims which arise at the crises of birth, sickness and death. Moreover, the tribe as a whole is also an important subject for law and besides explaining the rights of the village community, I have described the functions of the tribal courts and the duties of village officials. In a last chapter, I have turned from principles to administration and have commented on the trial of Santal suits.

In making this survey, I have necessarily been influenced by the nature of tribal law itself and there are various points to which I should draw attention.

The various principles I have recorded are current Santal law in the sense that it is these and these only which Santals now observe in deciding their civil disputes. I have not attempted an historical reconstruction for we have neither the means of codifying early Santal law nor is it true that the law is the same now as what it once was. On the contrary, with their increasing contacts with caste Hindus, Muhammadans and Christians, Santals have gradually altered certain of their major legal views. To state Santal law as what it was fifty years ago would be to give to Santal justice a form both obsolete and fictitious.

It is for this reason also that in any discussion of Santal law it is necessary to use the term 'principles' instead of 'custom'. In ordinary litigation, custom always implies a measure of antiquity. 'The legal. . . . title of customs to recognition depends on their certainty and antiquity'. 'What the law requires before an alleged custom can receive the recognition of the court and so acquire legal force, is satisfactory proof of usage so long and invariably acted upon in practice as to show that it has, by common consent, been submitted to as the establishing governing rule of the particular family, class, district or country and the course of practice upon which the custom rests, must not be left in doubt, but be proved with certainty'. 'A custom must be proved by strict evidence that what is sought to be established has existed unaltered and uninterrupted from time immemorial'. 'A custom to be binding must be unaltered, uniform, constant and definite'. 'A custom to be valid must have been continued and acquiesced in and must be reasonable and certain'.*

In Santal decisions, on the other hand, custom is only one of several ingredients. In adjusting disputes or punishing offences, a tribal court is moved not only by the ways in which similar disputes have been adjusted formerly or offences punished but also by contemporary tribal attitudes. Normally, the latter will reflect a whole body of local usage but at times, a gradual change in tribal attitude slowly displaces 'the rules of the ancestors' and in turn gives rise to a new tradition of tribal practice. As more and more cases oust the earlier practice, the new 'custom' gathers force until finally a new period is reached in which recent usage again expresses tribal values. In such periods, the final basis for decisions is never solely custom. The ultimate canon is the tribal view of what is just.

But besides its incompatibility with vital growth, there is a further reason why 'custom' is not in itself a final definition of Santal law. In certain cases the issues in question may never have been raised before. Custom in the sense of a body of approved precedents will be completely lacking and if the only standard of reference were previous usage, Santals would have no way of deciding new disputes. Yet in practice no dispute is ever unadjudicated and the reason is that even if no previous custom can be cited, the principles of Santal law are known. Custom, where it exists, is only a guide to attitudes. It is the

*M.C. Sarkar and S.C Sarkar, *Law of Evidence in India* (Calcutta, 1932), 103-4.

set of principles which a tribe accepts and applies that constitutes its law.

If custom is only a part of tribal law, it none the less exerts a dominant influence on its principles. Santal law like Santal poetry is a projection of all that the tribe values. Behind all Santal decisions is a sense of the Santal tribe as a whole and the effort of all tribal courts is to do justice in a manner that is vitally Santal. This ideal can be achieved only by a deep respect for previous decisions and traditional practice and in fact when a village council meets it does not sit alone but 'sits with the ancestors'. Moreover each area is acutely conscious of neighbouring regions and in giving it decisions, a tribal court does not consciously flout the values of the region. Although, therefore, contemporary tribal attitudes are ultimately the source of Santal law, there is often, at any one time and for the greater part of the law, little or no difference between recent usage and present principles.

Equally when tribal attitudes begin to differ from custom the breach is not deliberate or conscious. The fissure first shows itself not in actual decisions but through changing usage. If we take only one example—the law that a childless widow inherits her husband's land for life or until she remains or leaves the village—it is evident that this important change was not accomplished solely by conscious decisions. The change first began by consent in a few families. From this it became the voluntary usage of a village. The practice of some villages influenced others and only as local practice became regional usage, the tribal attitudes which had unconsciously inaugurated the change began to be conscious and deliberate. Indeed to many village courts decreeing a widow these new rights, recent usage may well have seemed the only known custom. Far from committing an act of revolution, they believed they were only respecting the recent ancestors. It is because respect for previous practice and regional attitudes are consciously valued that Santals throughout the Santal Parganas have a single incgrated law.

Since this report must necessarily claim authority, I should explain fully my methods of enquiry. I joined at Dumka as Deputy Commissioner of the Santal Parganas in December 1942 and began to learn Santali the day I joined. This had one immediate consequence—that Santals came to see me everyday and I had thus the advantage of hearing at first hand a host of Santal disputes and recording notes on custom and principles. During long tours which took me in 1943 and 1944 into the heart of the district I extended these contacts and witnessed festivals and ceremonies, in 1943 I associated others with my investigation and in 1944 I attempted to draft a comprehensive statement of Santal law. Other duties however made detailed drafting impossible and after Sir Robert Russell, Adviser to the Governor had visited the district in February 1945, the Bihar Government placed me on special duty in the Judicial Department to compile this present survey. I joined as Special Officer on 1 June 1945 and with the exception of December 1945 when I again acted as Deputy Commissioner, I remained on special duty until 15 June 1946.

Since the authority of my record hinges on its sources, I will note in detail the various steps which preceded the final drafting. I first compiled each chapter on the basis of my own notes and the reports of the officers and non-officials who had supplemented my enquiries in the two preceding years. The essential portions of thirty-five chapters* were then analysed in terms of questions and eleven officials and non-officials were asked to attest the chapters at twenty centres.**

To secure the widest possible differences of approach I selected both educated Santals as well as officers who had learnt Santali. Centres were chosen representing all the main Santal areas in the district and the officers then carried out three successive attestations. In arranging these enquiries I bore in mind Section 32(4) of the Indian Evidence Act and the High Court ruling, 'on matters relating to the existence of any general custom or right, opinions of persons who would be likely to know of its existence, is relevant, as such evidence is the best possible under the circumstances. The persons contemplated by this section are, so to speak, the depositaries of customary law, just as the text books are depositaries of general law'. I therefore requested the Sub-divisional Officers

*Chapters 1—12, 14—18, 21—22, 24—38.

**I have given full details of officers, centres, attesting manjhis and dates in Appendix III.

to secure at each centre the attendance of twenty intelligent and experienced manjhis or headmen whose duties as presidents of tribal courts and whose continuing knowledge of Santal law would enable them to attest the drafts. The procedure at each centre then followed a prescribed pattern. Each group of manjhis was put each question and their answers were checked with the statements in the draft. If their answers differed, their statements were carefully noted. As far as possible local cases illustrating the law were also recorded and where points of law were in doubt the questions only were put and answers were noted. I then reviewed the drafts in the light of these reports, added many further examples, and made final corrections. Where there were differences in local law I noted these in the text. It is the views of the attesting manjhis which constitute the authority of the record.

The scope and limitations of this report will now perhaps be clear. It is an attempt to record Santal law at a certain time and in a certain place. It is, as it were, an act of measurement, a reading of a glacier. Its claim to authority is its approval by the tribe and the reinforcement of this approval by recorded instances of recent practice. I have stated accepted principles and wherever possible have cited instances which show that such principles have in fact been applied. To insist that Santal law is neither obsolete nor stationary, that it represents vital methods of adjustment and that it changes with the tribe itself, is to define the limitations of this survey but not, I think, to deny its value. When I began this enquiry, it was evident that between Santal principles and recent usage there was, in fact, a close identity. It is now unlikely that Santal law will undergo further major changes, though to ascertain their possibility might prove a fruitful subject for further enquiry. But for twenty years at least only a revolution in the economic status of Santals is likely to modify the present law.

To the many who assisted me in the work of enquiry and attestation I am deeply grateful. In the first two years I was much aided by Gopal Gamaliel Soren and by Solomon Shankar Murmu while from Stephen Hidim Murmu I had the advantage of almost daily help. This young Santal is the nearest equivalent I know of to Verrier Elwin's Sunderlal. If

'Sunderlal certainly knows more about the Baiga than any man living', there was a time when Stephen Murmu knew more about Santal village ritual and practice than any other educated Santal. For the last two years he has been working outside the Santal Parganas. But during the two years he was with me his skill in enquiry and his alert intelligence made him an invaluable assistant.

I must also mention Chotu Ramu Murmu of Amtala, Ranjit Hembrom of Kusma, Bijai Hembrom of Kalajor, Dhudu Ranjit Hembrom of Haripur, Ramdas Soren of Jhili and Meghrae Kisku of Kalajor. These experienced and intelligent village officials informed me of the principles of law current in the Dumka Damin and it is to their ungrudging collaboration that I owe the elucidation of many complex issues.

If it was these Santals who enabled me to understand many points of law, I was also much aided by discussion with the Rev J. Gausdal and the Rev R. Rosenlund. To the Rev J. Portelli, the Rev Grech, the Rev B. Ernst and the Rev B. Cauchi—all of them members of the Society of Jesus—I am also indebted for confirming various principles in these earlier months.

During the third year of my enquiries and in the actual preparation of the report, a crucial part was played by that small band of officers who carried through the arduous work of attestation. Stephen Hari Tudu, Sashi Kant Sinha, Ram Dutta Pande, Ajit Kumar Chatterji, James Hembrom Kumar, Jacob Hembrom, Sushil Soren brought to this work much patient care while behind the frail physique of Keshava Nandan Sahay lurked astonishing powers of sympathetic investigation. I must also mention the work of Doman Sahu. This young clerk who alone of his Hindu colleagues had passed the Matriculation in the First Division with Santali as a subject attested my report at Rajabhita and submitted comments of uniform value.

But besides these officers whose work confirmed principles, there are three others of whose assistance I must make detailed mention. Besides attesting the report in three centres of the Rajmahal subdivision Seth Choron Hansdak' assisted me in many local enquiries, clarified many points of Santal law and with great patience assisted me in elucidating Santal texts.

Rameshwar Nath collated for me the various attestation reports and his quick appreciation of issues and grasp of Santal law not only saved much of my time but rendered much easier my final drafting.

Above all I had throughout the advantage of discussion with Syed Muhammad Naqavi. Before I joined the district this officer had already made a preliminary analysis of Santal law and had mastered all that had then been written on the subject. As my enquiries went on, he extended his own investigations and our knowledge grew together. Finally when I had begin to draft this book, his insistence that Santal justice presupposed expert knowledge and that this could only be achieved by the taking of enormous pains—such astringent views were more valuable than many tonics. I must also acknowledge the ungrudging labour of Uma Prasad Das and Sachindra Nath Moitra is preparing the typescript.

Finally, I must record my indebtedness to Sir Robert Russell. As Deputy Commissioner of the Santal Parganas from 1922 to 1926, Sir Robert Russell was an example of "the ever-touring Englishman" and in some of my remotest tours I found his name as the last Deputy Commissioner who had visited these lonely spots. During his stay in Dumka he was known as "Russell the just" and when later as Adviser to the Governor, he visited Dumka his understanding of the Santals led ultimately to the decision to *record* their law. To his example as an administrator and his understanding as a friend, this report is an inadequate tribute.

Dumka W.G. ARCHER

1 June 1946

PART ONE

1

THE MACHINERY OF SANTAL JUSTICE

I THE TRIBAL COUNCILS

SANTAL LAW, as it now exists, is not an arbitrary creation of individual Santals. To command obedience, to exist as law at all, it must of necessity be a collective product, the creation of the tribe itself. If in one sense it is the highest common factor of recent village decisions it is equally the mature outcome of regional reviews. In giving it a logic and a pattern, each grade of tribal council plays a part. Santal law is actually a synthesis of tribal attitudes expressed through a hierarchy of tribal courts.

I will begin therefore with an account of these tribal councils, their function in Santal life and the rights and duties which arise from their working.

The first of these assemblies is the village community. This body is the original court of tribal justice and in all disputes it is the first to intervene. Its duty is to see that the rites of birth, initiation and death, the conduct of the year's festivals, the laws of exogamy, and the canons of sex are duly observed. It ensures that the principles of law are followed, it maintains civil rights and in many cases it acts as a court of registration. It revolves round seven village officials and while in point of law these are only its servants, the administration of the village, the maintenance and making of its law depend on their integrity and influence.*

II VILLAGE OFFICIALS

The chief official is the manjhi or village headman. In villages where rent is payable by the village as a whole it is the manjhi who collects it and makes payment. All abandoned holdings, and waste land are in his charge. He is the custodian of village property—the communal wells, roads, bandhs and grazing grounds and is empowered to requisition village labour in order to repair them. His duty is to maintain the manjhithan or founder's shrine and to administer the jaher or sacred grove. If the grove is getting thin and there is no other grove in the village, he must have it planted up with saplings. If a bonga tree dies, he must arrange for the naeke to shift the bonga to a new tree and if necessary, to change the grove. He is also charged with disposing of the dead timber. If the manjhithan requires a new pole, he can allot the wood for this purpose. Otherwise he can allow a member of the village to use it after due sacrifice. Besides maintaining this religious property, he must also see that the year's festivals are duly performed, that every householder contributes and that in the ceremonies of birth, death and marriage the whole village participates. If sickness breaks out in the village, he must summon a meeting and arrange special sacrifices. When a dispute arises or a tribal offence is committed he must summon the village meeting and preside at its discussions. At the end of the meeting he interprets the sense of the village and announces its decision. Finally if a major criminal offence is committed he must arrest the offender and inform the authorities.

His position in fact is that of a genial disciplinarian, a communal custodian. Because of his vital role in the life of the village, he commands general respect. Indeed the common Santal attitude is to regard him as the father of the village :

*In certain villages, two or more of these posts are sometimes held by one official and it is by no means uncommon for the manjhi to be also naeke and godet.

"Manjhi Baba, you are our father". At his death there is often genuine grief for until the new manjhi has established his influence, the village may face disruption.

Next to the manjhi the most important official is the paranik. This man is virtually a deputy manjhi and is sometimes so closely allied to him in his general duties that Dalton confused him with the headman himself. He officiates for the—manjhi in the latter's absence and if the manjhi dies without heirs, or his relations are absent, he is sometimes appointed manjhi instead. One of his main duties is to act as the manjhi's patwari or rent receiver.

The headman's second assistant is the jogmanjhi. 'This official' says Bodding, 'acts as custos morum to the young people of the village. His duty is not to prevent sexual intercourse between the two sexes when unmarried (except when they are non-marriageable relatives) but to see that no scandal arises. If a girl becomes pregnant, the jogmanjhi has to find out who is responsible. If he does not, the village people take him to the manjhi's cow-shed and tie him with a buffalo's rope to a pole, scold him before the panchayat, who will deal with the culprit. During the Sohrae festival the village boys and girls live for five days and nights with the jogmanjhi, who is responsible for their behaviour. At the birth of a child and at marriages he is master of the ceremonies; he is also in a way responsible when the village youths attend certain night festivals which are always accompanied by revelry. Formerly the jogmanjhi was stricter and had a very important position in the village. Now-a-days he has less authority, but the young people still use him as a safe depository of their secrets. If a girl has a liaison, she may, as a precaution, tell the jogmanjhi of it in confidence and give him handi to purchase his silence. The young men also try to bribe him.[1] 'When they do this', Kolean Haram adds, 'the jogmanjhi says, take care. You will have to keep your girl or I shall flog you white.'[2]

Dalton remarks, 'His most important duty is apparently to look after the morals of the boys and girls and if he is at all straightlaced, they must often lead him a hard life of it'.[3] These accounts accurately review his present duties.

After these three officials are two others—the jog paranik who officiates for the jogmanjhi when he is absent and the godet 'who acts as the manjhi's orderly,—calls the villagers together at his command, and also collects sacrificial fowls for the village sacrifices.'[4] He removes dead animals from the village and if villagers do not obey his orders he reports them to the manjhi. 'The godet is called the big manjhi' says Kolean Haram 'In the village his word is law. He is like the police.' The ancestors say 'Maran Buru was Thakur's godet.'[5]

Finally, there are two officials who minister to religious needs. These are the naeke or principal village priest and his assistant the kudam naeke or 'field' priest. The naeke officiates at all the public festivals and performs the sacrifices while the kudam naeke offers his own blood to the pargana bonga and the bongas of the outskirts. He pricks his thigh with a thorn, squeezes out a little blood and drips it on rice. Besides doing this at the Sohrae festival he also offers his blood before a hunt so that no one may be hurt or killed.*

III CONDITIONS OF APPOINTMENT

The term of appointment of all these officials is in theory for only one year. At the Mag festival, the manjhi says 'Now it is Mag—Mag for thieves, Mag for cultivators, Mag for boy servants and maid servants, Mag for manjhis and paraniks. The year is at an end. I am laying down my office. Let him take it who will.' The other officials say the same. 'We too are tired of serving'. But a week or ten days later the manjhi calls the villagers. He gives them each two leafcups of rice beer. They ask him, 'What beer is this?' 'It is of broken rice picked in bits'. 'But what is it for?' 'I laid down my office. But it seems you will not leave me. I am taking it up again.' Then the villagers reply, 'We were waiting for this word. There is no one else we want.' It is said, 'The old rulers and the old bongas—these alone are good'. 'You only are our manjhi. Where can we find the shade of a tree with such thick branches?' After that they drink more rice beer and the manjhi continues for another year. The other officials hold similar meetings and each resumes his office.

*In the Rajmahal subdivision, there is occasionally a third priest—the susaria naeke. This naeke officiates at Jatra festivals and Kalipuja and sacrifices to the Jatra and Kali bongas.

This annual renunciation of office is naturally far more nominal than real. It is assumed that all officials are appointed for life and unless they give up office voluntarily or so neglect their work that the village suffers, they are entitled to retain their functions until death. The significance of the Mag festival is that it emphasises village approval as the basis for office and provides an annual occasion for the expression of grievances.

If an official neglects his work, the villagers first remonstrate and then either wait until the Mag festival or hold a village meeting. At this meeting they review the charges and either give the official a final warning or remove him. Jolha Soren was godet of Daldali. He did not carry out the manjhi's orders, call the villagers to meetings or collect the fowls, so the village dismissed him and appointed Khade Murmu in his place.

Domon Soren was Jogmanjhi of Ranga. At weddings he always stole utensils, so the village dismissed him. Since other members of his family were also thieves Sankho Murmu of another family was appointed in his place.

In Hororaidih the jogmanjhi was dismissed by the village for misbehaving with the village girls—while in Tardiha, the jogmanjhi was always drunk and neglectful of his duties, so the villagers dismissed him and appointed Khenkha Marandi in his place.

If the official holds service lands, he can be deprived of his office by the villagers but if his successor is to get the lands, the order of removal must be confirmed by the Deputy Commissioner and followed by an order of eviction.

Similarly, if a manjhi is responsible for the village rent, the Deputy Commissioner must approve his dismissal. For these reasons, if a manjhi is not giving satisfaction, the usual practice is for the village to move the Subdivisional Officer, direct and then to dismiss him with the Deputy Commissioner's approval.

The villagers of Dumria got tired of their manjhi who was also the pargana and moved the Subdivisional Officer of Godda to dismiss him. 'He has not been starting the annual festivals', they said 'he has not been holding village meetings for ending village troubles. He has settled waste land with outsiders. He has neglected the manjhithan and jaherthan.

We put all our trust in our manjhi but he never gives us his wisdom'.

In Gadiganj the villagers complained 'The manjhi does not give us rent receipts. At the Baha and Sohrae festivals he gives us neither rice beer nor rice for making it. He has become a Christian and drinks it all himself'.

In Baca, Surai Kisku, the manjhi, also forfeited village confidence. His brothers encroached on roads and waste land and his servants took his cattle and grazed them on standing crops. In the end the villagers dismissed him and the man lands of twenty-four bighas went to his successor.

IV METHODS OF APPOINTMENT

When an official dies, resigns or is dismissed, his successor is appointed by a village meeting. If the official is a pardhan*, the meeting is presided over by the Subdivisional Officer and the appointment is approved by the Deputy Commissioner. Otherwise it is the village which decides. All offices are hereditary and the eldest son is, therefore, usually appointed. But if the official has been dismissed or his heir is unsuitable, someone else can be chosen.

Daria Soren of Daldali was paranik but when he died the villagers passed over his son and appointed his younger brother.

In Khejurkhal Manjhi Soren was the eldest son of Kasun Soren, the pardhan. When his father died Manjhi was suffering from leprosy, so the villagers passed him over and appointed his younger brother.

For all appointments beyond the family, village discretion is usually unfettered but in the case of naekes and kudam naekes appointment is more complex. A kudam naeke for example can be drawn from certain sub-septs only. A nij Murmu, nij Soren or nij Marandi is disqualified. Moreover, if the naeke is a Murmu, Soren or Hembrom, the kudam naeke cannot be taken from the khil Murmu, khil Soren or khil Hembrom sub-septs. Subject to these restrictions, however,

*A manjhi charged with the duty of rent collection.

any Santal is eligible and his appointment is by village selection.

A new naeke, on the other hand, must be chosen by the bongas themselves. The villagers gather at the manjhithan. Three new winnowing fans and rice are set out on the plinth. Then a villager, who need not be manjhi, invokes Maran Buru, Jaher Era and More ko Turuc' ko and requests them to make their choice. Each of the bongas then possesses a man and during their frenzy they seize a villager and declare him to be priest. If there is doubt the choice of Jaher Era prevails, but whoever has been captured is obliged to serve and can neither refuse nor renounce the office.*

V WOMEN MANJHIS

Hitherto for all these appointments, men only have been eligible but for a number of years, women also have sometimes proposed themselves as manjhis and provided the village concurs there would seem to be nothing in Santal law to forbid their appointment.

> 'One of the first cases', says Carstairs, 'that came before me was that of a headman who had died at a very advanced age—over eighty whose son, a grey-haired elder of sixty, was proposed as his successor. But another claimant stepped in the person of the widow, an aged but vigorous dame. I mildly represented that she, as a woman, was hardly qualified for the post. One of the duties was to arrest thieves and she could not be expected to do that.
> 'Can't I!' exclaimed the old lady fiercely. 'Try me'.
> Again I pointed out that obviously the right man for the post was her elderly son, already mentioned.
> 'That boy!' cried the dame, 'He's far too young to be trusted!'
> She was passed over, nevertheless, and the son was appointed.'[6]

* This practice is followed throughout the district except in the Pakaur subdivision where it has fallen into disuse and the post is filled by village selection.

In Paharpur the manjhi died in 1942 leaving no sons. All the villagers wanted his widow, a firm and masterful old lady to be manjhi in his place, and they moved the Subdivisional Officer of Dumka accordingly.

In Khejuria the manjhi went to the war and left his wife Kari Hansdak', in charge. Kari performed the social duties of the manjhi but found the work of rent collection too heavy. She then asked the Subdivisional Officer to let the landlord take charge of rent collection until her husband returned while she herself did all the rest.

Up to the present, the Revenue law of the district has not permitted a woman's formal or permanent appointment. In the draft Tenancy Regulation however, Subdivisional Officers have now been given discretion and if this ultimately becomes law we may expect a gradual growth of female appointments.

VI FEES OF OFFICE

All these offices are posts of honour and prestige. 'It is not the money but the pride', said Chotu Ramu 'which makes us serve', and there are always far more candidates than vacancies. At the same time the work is never merely honorary and in return for faithfully discharging their duties, the village officials receive certain lands, fees and privileges and the only condition is that on succession or appointment each new official must give the village a goat or five rupees.*

If there are no service lands, it is usual for the officials to receive certain fees in their place. These are sometimes paid in cash and sometimes in kind. There is not, however, any regional usage and while in many villages all the officials receive certain fees, in other areas some officials are given and others not. When they are paid in cash such fees range between eight annas and five rupees per year, but the exact sums are decided by each village. When they are paid in paddy or maize, their value is about the same. The fees are paid by village levy at the Mag festival and in return for lands or fees, each official must give the villagers a pot of rice beer.

*In the Rajabhita and Boarijore areas, money or a goat is given if there are man lands and a pot of rice beer if there are fees.

But besides fees certain offices carry with them perquisites and privileges. When the manjhi is in charge of rent collection, he is entitled to realise one anna per rupee on the rent collected from each raiyat (in addition to the rent due from them) and also one anna in the rupee from the landlord. At all festivals he is privileged to visit each house and receive leafcups of rice beer and on the occasion of a wedding and the meetings which precede it, rice beer is again due. In addition, if the wedding is in his own village, he can claim a manjhi mandla of one rupee but must sometime share it with the other manjhi and must give the party a pot of rice beer. He is also entitled to a turban at the first and last wedding in a family. If a dispute involving marriage or divorce arises with another village, he receives kharailak' or chatai taka of one rupee. This is given to him by the outside party as a fee for summoning a village meeting. Moreover, he can require the villagers to assist him in cultivating his own lands but must give them in return a mid-day meal of rice and some rice beer. He is entitled to settle waste land with himself but must do so with village approval. He has also the first claim to a dead tree in the sacred grove provided he gives the necessary goat for sacrifice. At a hunt and in the division of a dead animal he receives a specified share of the carcase. If a pig is shot in a field with crops, the head and a foreleg are taken to him and after cooking them with rice, he is entitled to a third of the spoil. If a Santal commits adultery, the manjhi also receives a personal fee of five rupees for intervening and 'saving his head' and if a man or boy forcibly puts *sindur* on a girl's head, the penalty fine may include a similar award to the manjhi. Finally, when a fine or costs are spent on a feast, the manjhi is given a portion of food double that of an ordinary villager.

In return for all these perquisites, the manjhi must present the villagers with at least one pot of rice beer at both the Sohrae and Baha festivals in addition to the pot of rice beer which he gives them at Mag.

The remaining six officials are somewhat less favoured but some of them have extra dues. The paranik and godet each receives a double share of food from fines and costs. In addition the godet can collect a bunch of four maize cobs from every house each year and in some villages he is also given four to five pais of paddy. In the Raksi area, he is given half a pai of paddy by each family after each of the Sohrae, Baha and Erok' festivals.

The naeke and kudam naeke get the major share of sacrificial meat and the jogmanjhi is reputedly the biggest recipient of rice beer. Like the manjhi he receives a turban at the first and last wedding in a family and is also given certain dues at every marriage.

These extra privileges do not greatly swell the incomes of the posts but add considerably to their honour and status.

VII THE FUNCTION OF THE VILLAGE COUNCIL

If much of the daily administration of tribal law vests in the village officials, these are in no sense substitutes for the village community, but are merely its agents and representatives. If tribal law is broken, if disputes arise or if action requires approval, a village council is necessary. This council is known as the more hor or five men—the approximate number who constitute its quorum.

The procedure of each meeting is usually determined by circumstances. If a tribal offence has been committed, the facts are placed before the villagers, witnesses are heard, the accused is examined. Anyone who likes can give an opinion and a lasar tengoc' or sharp axe is allowed to plead. This lasar tengoc' is sometimes a 'clerk of the court' sometimes a 'Judge Advocate' and sometimes a 'private pleader'. He gives precision to the discussion and his advocacy is often responsible for the final agreed decision.

At these meetings, every male rent payer is entitled to participate and all are equal. In practice, younger male members of the families also attend and the village community is thus virtually synonymous with all the adult male Santals of the village.

When the discussion is over the manjhi interprets the sense of the meeting and announces the decision. If the offence involves injury or damage to property the offender is fined and either the whole or half the sum is allotted to the sufferer as compensation or dard mitauni. If the whole is given the sufferer must allot a share to the council. If no damage or injury is in issue the offender is fined for breaking tribal law and the whole amount is appropriated by the meeting. The village share is then either spent at once on goats, salt or liquor or if it is less than five rupees, it is often kept with a trusted villager until other fines have increased it to a sum large enough to spend. In the distribution, all the villagers except the manjhi, paranik godet and lasar tengoc' get a single equal share. The lasar tengoc' is given a slightly larger helping while each of the three officials receives a double portion.

If the cause of the meeting is a civil dispute, such as a claim for lajao marao, celan gitil, damages or divorce, both parties explain their cases, other villagers give their views and the manjhi announces the decision. At such hearings each side must pay the meeting the local rate of fee. If both are equally to blame, each must pay the same fee, but if one party is not at fault, a half fee only is charged. In the southern parts of the district, the standard fee is five four anna bits but in the Rajmahal and Pakaur subdivisions, although the prevailing fee is called more sika or five fouranna bits, only one rupee is charged. The fee is the same irrespective of the number of meetings and is paid immediately the meeting ends. The manjhi must then spend the money on a goat, salt, rice beer or liquor, and whatever is bought is shared by everyone in the same proportions as for fines. At the end of the proceedings the matter is 'buried'. This is now-a-days only a verbal expression but Bodding records that in earlier days a small hole was dug in which both parties and the manjhi each placed a lump of cow dung and a lump of earth, the hollow was filled up and a stone placed on top. After that no one could bring the matter up again and if he did so he was fined.[7]

But besides adjudicating offences and settling civil disputes, the village meeting acts also as a court of registration in all the following cases :

(i) adoption of a son or daughter,
(ii) induction of a ghardi jawae,
(iii) conversion of a union into a ghar jawae marriage,
(iv) induction of a ghar jawae by agu hatar,
(v) bringing of a married daughter's husband as a ghar jawae by agu mit',

(vi) gift of land to a daughter sister or niece as taben jom,
(vii) gift of land to an asul badna, and
(viii) exchange of land.

If a villager desires to take any of these actions, he must inform the manjhi and request a village meeting. At this meeting, he gives the villagers rice beer. The people say 'What beer is this? Why are we drinking?' The Santal announces his intention, the meeting accords its approval and rice beer is drunk as formal ratification.

Such meetings are held only when village approval is a foregone conclusion and if the 'greater family' opposes the action the matter is first treated as a civil dispute and decided accordingly. If the council overrules the agnates, the decision amounts to registration and no further rice beer is necessary. On the other hand, if the Santal himself is overruled, the manjhi declines all further liquor and 'registration' is disallowed.

In addition to these matters village 'registration' is also required in cases of marriage, birth, death and divorce.

But besides matters for which registration in a formal meeting of the whole village is necessary, there are other contracts and gifts for which registration is demanded but to a lesser degree. Such cases include :

(i) the showing of bare itat' and its receipt,
(ii) the payment of the bride price,
(iii) the grant of presents at bahu bande and jawae dhuti,
(iv) the conveyance of land to a custodian, and
(v) the engagement of a servant.

In all these cases, a meeting of the whole village is unnecessary but some of the village officials or in certain cases only the villagers must witness the transaction and register it on behalf of the village.

A further subject for village action is partition of family property. This is sometimes done privately but more usually in a formal meeting. The wishes of each person are considered and the village then makes the fairest division. If a father or a son is in conflict with his family, the village decides what shares will be appropriate. The community in fact is not only an arbitrator of claims but an informal distributor of private property.

Finally, it is the village community which allots communal property. If a Santal desires settlement of waste land or land which has reverted to the village either by abandonment or by the death of its owner without heirs, he approaches the manjhi and gives him rice beer. The manjhi summons a meeting and if the villagers approve, the settlement taker gives a goat and the allotment is ratified with a feast.

At all these meetings the joint drinking of rice beer is not merely a reward for mental exercise but a symbolic sealing of the decision. It proclaims the solidarity of the meeting. It infuses the members with goodwill. It blurs the ferocity of opposing points of view and 'ratifies an order in the heart'.

VIII THE COUNCIL OF FIVE MANJHIS

While the first tribal assembly is the community of the village, the second Santal court is the council of the neighbourhood. This body is known as the council of the five manjhis and consists of village headmen drawn from the vicinity. Its function is to settle extra-village disputes, to adjudicate in all matters which the villagers themselves fail to decide and to act as an appellate court from village-decisions. Like the village community, the council is the final source of local power but there are two ways in which it is constituted and functions.

(1) In the Damin, the local unit for Santal law is a bungalow or group of ten to thirty villages and these are focused on a rest house. Each bungalow has its council of manjhis which in turn is assisted by three permanent officials. The chief of these is the pargana* who besides being a standing president of the council is also a Government officer with a variety of functions. He is primarily responsible for the efficient collection of land revenue and acts as a superior tahsildar who stimulates and supervises village collections by the manjhis.

*'Also called paraganait, though the latter is not a Santali word' (*Gazetteer*, 132).

He exercises the powers of a Sub-Inspector of Police and except in serious cases where the investigation is done by a Sub-Inspector of the General Police Department, he administers his neighbourhood, as if it were, a police station. As a Sub-Inspector of Police he has the power to arrest and this official status in the administration gives him a personal prestige and authority which is over and above his position as a tribal leader. Moreover on behalf of government he has the general duty of seeing that all forests, schools and government institutions in his area are kept in good order and that the Damin—bungalow or rest house is properly maintained and guarded. He is also actively associated with the administration of Damin grain golas and is in fact the official link or medium of communication between government and the village headmen and raiyats.

In carrying out these duties, he is assisted by a deshmanjhi and a chakladar. The deshmanjhi is virtually a paranik who assists in revenue collection, takes an active part in hearing disputes and is generally the pargana's deputy. A chakladar is a regional godet who summons the manjhis, calls the parties and assists in executing the decisions of the council.

Since these two officials are more the personal assistants of the pargana than the executives of the tribal council, they are not elected by the council of the neighbourhood. Their appointment and dismissal is made by the pargana subject to control by the Subdivisional Officer.

In view of the pargana's place in local administration, each appointment is made by the Subdivisional Officer. As with village officials the post is normally hereditary but in view of the expert police work which a Damin pargana must now do, the need for securing educated officers has in recent years overridden the claims of the family. The relations of a dismissed or retired pargana are first considered, the opinion of the local manjhis is taken but ultimately the candidate whom the Subdivisional Officer considers most competent is selected for the post. In a similar way the power of dismissal now rests with the Subdivisional Officer and although the council of the neighbourhood, can express dissatisfaction with a pargana, it has no longer the power to discharge or replace him.

This dual position as servants both of government and of

the neighbourhood is reflected in the emoluments of parganas. Every Damin village which pays a total rent of more than fifty rupees is required to pay the pargana three rupees while villages which pay total rents between ten rupees and fifty rupees pay him an annual sum of one rupee eight annas. When three rupees is paid the pargana retains one rupee ten annas for himself and gives fourteen annas to the deshmanjhi and eight annas to the chakladar. When the annual fee is one rupee eight annas the pargana keeps thirteen annas and pays the deshmanjhi seven annas and the chakladar four annas. When the total rent of a village is ten rupees or less no payment is required. In addition each pargana in the Damin gets commission for land revenue, chaukidari tax and grain gola collection and under orders of government passed in 1945 he is now entitled to receive an extra allowance calculated on the difference between his maximum land revenue commission with village dues and twenty, thirty and forty rupees per month according to the size and importance of his area. His position in fact has now become that of a government officer who presides at the local council rather than that of a tribal chief who is now a government officer.

It is in this setting that the manjhis' council meets in the Damin. Where the pargana is sensitive to local opinion he respects and values the council and is in turn respected and valued by it Where, however, he unduly stresses his importance as a government officer there is often friction between the two and the five manjhis sometimes meet in spite of rather than at the instance of their president.

In areas where the pargana works smoothly with his council an appellant pays him a personal fee of one rupee for summoning the council. The pargana then assembles the manjhis of his bungalow and at the end of the meeting the parties pay the same costs as in a meeting of the village. Half of this is taken by the pargana and the remainder shared by the meeting. If one of the parties has been injured or his property damaged, the fine is awarded and distributed as in a meeting of the village. If a person is fined for an offence and no injury or damage is in issue, the entire fine is taken by the council. Each member is entitled to a single share and the pargana is not entitled to anything more. The fine is shared as soon as it is realised and is usually spent either on a goat or liquor. In such meetings, all manjhis of the bungalow are entitled to attend. There is not however any strict quorum and while there should normally be at least five manjhis present a council can meet and discharge its duties with either less or more manjhis present.

(2) Outside the Damin, the Manjhis' councils are also associated with parganas and there are two types of appointment. In the Pakaur subdivision, 'the serial arrangement of villages is based on pargana's jurisdictions,[8] parganas function as tribal leaders and are assisted by deshmanjhis and chakladars. They are recognised and controlled by the Subdivisional Officer in the same way as parganas in the Damin but they do not possess any revenue, police or executive powers. Their sole functions are to act as—presidents of the manjhi's councils and as spokesmen of their areas. They receive annual village fees but apart from shares in fines and costs, no other remuneration.

In the remaining Santal areas of the district, in the Rajmahal, Godda, Dumka and Jamtara subdivisions the unit of villages is the Sardari circle and within each circle the pargana is the local Santal leader. If the Sardar is a Santal he is sometimes the pargana also but the two offices are quite distinct. The Sardar is elected every five years and can also be a Diku. The pargana is the permanent president of the manjhis' council, and is appointed for life. His post is normally hereditary but each pargana is subject to removal by the manjhis' council. In all these areas, the post does not carry any village fees but the pargana can realise from a party one rupee for summoning the council and can also appropriate his usual share in fines and costs. His name is entered in the office of the Subdivisional Officer and at the instance of the manjhis' council can also be mutated.

IX THE ANNUAL HUNT

The final authority in Santal society is the disom hor or people of the region. This body meets once a year at the lo bir sendra or 'hunt in the burnt forest'. The hunt is given this name 'as the jungle is fired in March to clear the undergrowth' and 'we burn offences there'. It is said that originally there was only one hunt for the whole tribe but now every region has a hunt of its own. These hunts do not follow administrative units and often overlap. They take their name from the central mountain over which the hunt passes and villagers within ten or twenty miles of the mountain come to attend it. The Nunu Buru Sendra near Nonihat attracts Santals from Ramgarh and Nonihat police stations. In Jhandaburu, first one dihri and then another organises a hunt and people from overlapping areas in the Godda Damin attend the two.

The hunt falls into three distinct parts—the hunt itself, the recital of sexual songs and narratives and finally the council of the people itself. Each of these stages is presided over by the dihri who is at once a priest, a master of the hunt, a president of the ballet, a leader of the house and a chief justice. He is not however, a permanent official. Just as the local people relapse into collective obscurity once the hunt is over, the dihri is ruler of the region only for the period of the hunt. For two days he is the lord of the parganas and manjhis but after that he resumes his own quiet place in the life of his village.

This intimate connection between the council of the region and a hunting celebration is due to various causes. A hunt is obviously much the most effective way of assembling the Santals of a region. 'Very few would come', said Barka Besra, a dihri of Jhandaburu, 'if I invited them only for a council'. The sexual recitals which are ritually necessary for the hunt's success provide a vital corollary to the code of sexual conduct. Similarly, the secrecy of the forest, its remoteness from villages, its seclusion from women creates the necessary conditions for a free discussion of sexual rules. Finally, the constitution of a forest court is sanctioned by myth. When the first Santals, Pilchu Haram and Pilchu Budhi, divided their family into septs and laid down the rules of exogamy, they assembled in the forest. 'It is because Pilchu Haram said this in the forest', a Santal told me, 'that we go there to preserve our blood'.

This connection between hunting and the council explains the dihri's method of appointment, the perquisites of his office and his function in the assembly. His first duty is to control the hunt, to ensure that animals are killed, to save the hunters from danger. He must be able to placate the bongas for the council can succeed only if the hunt itself is a success. Unless he can do this his tenure of the post is insecure. Equally it is his power to control the hunt, his demonstrable ability, that secures him his appointment. Before Dhunu Hembrom became dihri of the Nunu Buru Sendra, he worked under Khade Kisku, the dihri of the Dumka Damin. He first mastered the art from this famous dihri and then founded in 1938 a new hunt near Nonihat. The father of Karan Tudu acted as dihri of Jhandaburu and Karan assisted him. When his father died, the villagers said to Karan, 'Your father was dihri, Will you not take us hunting?' As his father had always got them animals, they believed that Karan would also have the power.

It is for this reason that certain sendras employ Paharias as dihris. 'They know the animals and can lead them to us'. The ancestors of Gangu Paharia conducted hunts in Sawalak-pahar. Then the hunt lapsed and after some years the pargana of Bokrabandh asked Gangu to restart it. He underwent instruction from two Jan gurus and since then he has been controlling the hunt and presiding at the council. For this reason also if a dihri dies the post goes to any qualified successor. His son may succeed him provided he is competent. Otherwise the people choose a new dihri with the necessary skill.

Sadgo Kisku of Kolakondha was dihri of the Terma Buru Sendra for many years. When he died his son and grandson both refused to act. One day when all the family were together the grandson was suddenly possessed by the Buru sendra bonga and began to shout the hunting calls. He then assumed office for two years and after that his uncle acted.

Since the dihri exists only in and for the hunt, the perquisites of his office are only those which the hunt itself can provide. He is entitled only to the neck of a large animal such as a deer, leopard, bear or wild pig and he receives nothing if the spoil is a bird or a small animal like a hare.*

But the dihri's skill in magic not only explains his appointment. It also determines his relation to the council. He pre-

*In certain areas however he is also given service lands and Allanson records that in parts of Pakaur, service lands were found in certain dihris' enjoyment.

sides at the meeting only because of his controlling powers in the hunt. He is not necessarily a persuasive leader—a mob orator. Khade Dihri has a gentle voice that barely issues from a majestic flowing beard. Barka Soren of Jhandaburu speaks in tones which could scarcely startle a bird. His duty in fact is to be guided by the council. He is there not to dominate but to record. He places matters before the people. He hears their speeches. He is less a spokesman than an interpreter. It is true that certain dihris take a more active view of their functions. Dhunu Hembrom, for example, dominates the Nunu Buru council by the flow of his eloquence. But it is not his oratory that has made him dihri or maintains him in the appointment. In 1944, he was in danger of losing the post as people said he had driven the leopards from the hills to the villages and had thus protected the hunters at the expense of the cattle. The dihri's function in fact is to bring the hunt safely to the council, to inaugurate its meeting and then to allow the council to take its own democratic course. He is at his truest when he is least noticed.

Once the council has started anyone may speak however lowly and the officials of the village and the neighbourhood are in temporary eclipse. 'The council', said Bodding, 'is an example of literal and true democracy'.[9] 'The forest council', said Kolean Haram 'is our High Court.' There the parganas, deshmanjhis and manjhis cannot keep us down. The people, both small and great, decide everything. If they find that the big and greedy have acted unjustly, they punish them severely. In the forest no injustice is allowed. Only justice is done. In the village manjhis and parganas snub and scold us. But in the forest they cannot silence us. There they hang their tails like timid dogs.[10] The extent of this demotion naturally varies from official to official. In the Godda Damin the Jhandaburu sendra owes much of its present vitality to the support it received from Rai Sahib Ram Marandi, the pargana of Sundarpahari. The Sawalakpahar Sendra, we have already seen, was revived by the pargana of Bokrabandh. In many sendras, the dihri refers quarrels back to the manjhis and parganas and freely takes their views. At the same time it is not unusual for parganas to regard the hunt with an air of unwilling tolerance. Not all the parganas in the Dumka Damin attend Khade Kisku's sendra and Sagram Hembrom, the leading pargana of the Dumka Damin, has always made a point of taking out the licence in his own name. Although, therefore, hostility is always disguised, it is sometimes latent. The council of the local people is in fact the poor man's rostrum, the assembly where delegated power is at a discount and where for one night the final authority is the people themselves.

Since the assembly is a great crowd that meets at night—'their fires', said Kolean Haram 'are like a forest fire'—it follows that discussion is disultory and often ranges from the major to the petty. Much time, for example, frequently goes in deciding hunting disputes and it is only when these are settled that the dihri says 'If you have any more disputes, tell me'. 'After that', says Kolean Haram, 'each man tells his grievances. One man will say that the village manjhi and the five have fined him without cause or that the pargana and five manjhis have not decided properly the dispute about his land or his quarrel with his wife, or that they have without reason called him a witches' man, or that he has been outcasted for some reason or other or that the villagers without any cause have blocked his door with thorns. They make a thousand complaints'.[11] It is in the hearing of these appeals that the first function of the council rests. When the assembly has given its views the decision is final.

It will illustrate the scope of a hunting council if I now record some examples of cases which were recently decided.

In the Terma bir sendra of 1943 Suphal Marandi of Kolha appealed against a decision of the village council fining him Rs. 15 for illicit intercourse with a married girl who was related to him as niece. In the council, he concealed the fact of relationship but after the dihri had questioned the villagers of Kolha the council held that Suphal could not marry the girl and his fine was enhanced to forty rupees.

In the Bhusko bir sendra held in March 1945 the villager of Kanchanbera complained that a dispute with Barka Hembrom concerning his sister's divorce had not been settled. The facts were placed before the hunt and the council granted a divorce and ordered Barka Hembrom to return the bride price.

At the Saptola Buru sendra for 1945, an appeal was heard

from a decision of the villagers of Khatangi and Jorkokba relating to divorce.

In addition to hearing appeals the council can also act as a court of first instance and if the account of Kolean Haram is followed it is likely that all cases involving a breach of exogamy were at one time taken direct to the hunt and bitlaha followed as a sequel to the hunt itself.[12] At the present time, the accepted usage is to take such matters first to the village council and then to the five manjhis but if the matter is detected immediately prior to a hunt it can also be taken direct to the people themselves. At the Bhuski bir sendra of 1945, Sukhal Murmu of Jorbita was proved to have had intercourse with the wife of his younger brother. He was given the option of paying a fine of one hundred and forty rupees or suffering bitlaha. He paid the fine and no bitlaha was performed. At the same hunt a boy and girl of Murgabani who were both of the Marandi sept were reported to the council as having contracted illicit relations and to have set up house together. The council held the matter proved and they were sentenced to bitlaha.

But besides acting as an important check on local justice the council is also concerned with regional grievances and general principles. At the Jhandaburu sendra in 1943, it drew my attention to forest grievances, the lack of wells, bandhs and schools and the incursions of thieves. It also complained bitterly of the illegal alienation of land. 'When we first came', they said, 'the forests were everywhere. It was we who reclaimed them. But the best lands have gone to Dikus'. At the Nunu Buru sendra in 1944 the council decided the bride price for widows and divorced girls. At Jhandaburu in 1945, it discussed the problem of witches, their profound malevolence and the apparent lack of all solution.

It is in fact in the expression of general principles and the ventilation of regional grievances that the council has its greatest significance. It not only co-ordinates the decisions of the village and the neighbourhood and thus ensures that local practice corresponds to tribal rules. It has the supremely important function of reviewing usage and of asserting and extending the ancestral law.

'At Tore Pokhori Baha Bondela', says Kolean Haram 'the

ancestors met under a sal tree, an atnak' and a mahua.' They spread out lotus leaves and for twelve years or twelve days they drank the water of Kere dadi. They reviewed their customs and decided the rites of birth, initiation, marriage, sickness and death. When all was over they went across Tore Pokhori Baha Bandela either on the bank or over the water on the lotus leaves. The men came up and gathered by an icak' bush and the women met in the shade of a mahua. Then they saw that the red dye on their feet was not wet and that the lotus leaves were neither crushed not bruised. So they said, "We have decided well. May these rules and customs stay as now for ever."[13]

In reviewing usage the hunting council parallels the actions of the ancestors. It affirms the wisdom of the general meeting. It re-determines the tribal pattern. It gives continuing approval to the basic principles of tribal law.

REFERENCES

1. L.S.S. O'Malley, *Bengal District Gazetteers: Santal Parganas* (Calcutta, 1910), 110.
2. L.O. Skrefsrud and Kolean Haram, *Horkoren Mare Hapramko reak' Katha* (Third edition, Benagaria, 1928), 131.
3. E.T. Dalton, *The Descriptive Ethnology of Bengal* (Calcutta, 1872), 213.
4. *Gazetteer*, 135.
5. op. cit., 132.
6. R. Carstairs, *The Little World of an Indian District Officer* (London, 1912), 320-1.
7. *Gazetteer*, 139.
8. H. Ll. L., Allanson, *Final Report on the Survey and Settlement Operations in the District of Santal Parganas (1898-1910)* (Calcutta, 1912), 81.
9. P.O. Bodding, *A Santal Dictionary* (Oslo, 1936), V, 241.
10. op. cit., 161-2.
11. Ibid., 161.
12. Ibid., 104.
13. Ibid., 14.

2

THE VILLAGE COMMUNITY

I THE OWNERSHIP OF LAND

IF WE seek an analogy to the Santal village community, we shall find it, surprisingly in the English modern state. Each presents a blend of ultimate democracy with influential leaders, of private ownership with moderate socialism, of citizens with claims and a community with rights.

The first aspect of Santal socialism is the public ownership of land. At the founding of a new village, each Santal receives land not by individual seizure but by village decision, and it is only when he has brought his holding under cultivation, that he acquires a permanent right to remain in possession. If he desires to exchange his land with another Santal, he can only do so with village approval and this must be ratified by the Subdivisional Officer. He cannot otherwise transfer the land out of his family.

He must also pay his share of the communal village rent. This rent is calculated on the basis of land but it is actually a joint tax which Santals pay as a community. If a Santal fails to pay his rent, the land is first held by the headmen until the arrears are cleared from its produce and then it is restored to him. If he dies without heirs or finally deserts the village, the land goes back to the village stock. The village land in fact is partitioned among individual Santals only as functioning members of the community and it is the community which is the final owner.

This public ownership is not confined to arable land but

also covers waste land, village roads, grazing ground, the beds of streams, irrigation channels, cremation and burial sites. These are administered by the headman and are held by the village as a whole. A Santal can not encroach on land reserved for communal use and if he overploughs its limits or brings it under cultivation, he becomes a trespasser who is liable to eviction. Similarly, if he reclaims waste land, he must take the approval of the village. Without that sanction, his labour may well be in vain for if the community or individual Santals object, the Deputy Commissioner can approve his eviction and order the settlement of the plot with other members of the village.

II RIGHTS IN TREES

To this important principle there is only one exception. In the case of land with trees the needs of the region override the ownership of the village. In the Damin and other Khas Mahals, government is regarded as a superior trustee and the cutting of trees is controlled by forest rules, the Forest Settlement and the record-of-rights. Similarly, the zamindar, although actually only a rent receiver, is accorded under the record-of-rights, certain superior claims to trees and also to land either recorded as khas forest or excluded from the village for forest purposes. Even then, however, certain types of tree fall within the scope of the village. The produce of all mahua trees whether on waste land or in the forest is regarded as communal property and is distributed among its members. A Santal can thus collect the fruit and flowers from all mahua trees within his share and the exact distribution of trees can at any time be revised by the community. Leaves, brushwood and small unreserved trees can be freely taken from waste land for fuel and domestic purposes. Similarly, out of the stock of sal trees under the proprietor's control, the villagers can demand trees between 9″ and 18″ in girth, for the construction or repair of their houses and the proprietor can only cut sal trees below 9″ and 24″ in girth if the cutting does not prejudice the present or future supply of the raiyats of the village. Finally, if a Santal has fruit-bearing trees on his own land, he is entitled to the fruit.

III RIGHTS IN WATER

Besides controlling land, the village is also to a great extent the public owner of water. Streams and rivers are technically the property either of government or the superior landlord and if tanks and bandhs have been made by the landlord's agency, the village has no rights. Fishing rights, for example, are usually reserved if they are capable of exploitation. Where, however, such control is difficult, the village is for practical purposes a free user. Similarly, if a Santal makes a well, a bandh or a small tank on his own plot, the village acquires no general right to user. But in all other cases, it is the village which is the owner. All wells, bandhs or tanks made by the community itself belong to the village. It is these which the manjhi can require the villagers to repair and which each member of the community is entitled to use. If a Santal is outcasted he ceases to be a member of the community and one of his greatest deprivations is the loss of village-owned water.

IV THE MANJHITHAN

This principle of public ownership also extends to religion. In medieval England, the village church was at once a place of communal worship and a public assembly hall and in a Santal village the same function is fulfilled by the manjhithan. This shrine should normally consist of a smoothly cemented plinth of mud with two stones, to represent the founder manjhi and his wife, a centre pillar of sal wood, a second and smaller pillar supporting a pot of water and finally a roof of thatch or tiles. There are, however, many local variations. Sometimes the manjhithan is only a small plinth with a stone and sometimes a plinth with a stone and post. At Katikund, the plinth is of smooth grey mud-moulded with beautiful precision and with a moulded grey post rising from it like a smooth menhir. A little stone, to mark the founder, lurks at its base. At Bhaura there are no stones but carved heads. At Talberia, the manjhi's own house is large and spacious with a roof of corrugated iron while the manjhithan has a thatched roof with a piece of tin dangling from the pole. 'Whatever the manjhi has the ancestors must have also'. Elsewhere if the manjhi's house is tiled, the manjhithan has often either a tiled roof or tiles imbedded in the plinth.

This shrine is intimately associated with the manjhi's office. It is the village court of justice where Sherwill noted in 1851 'the headmen (elders) of the village meet, talk over the affairs of the village, threaten the unruly, punish the guilty, collect the rents and sometimes make small votive grain offerings to the defunct Manjhi'.[1] It is regarded both as a memorial to the first founder and as the abode of recently deceased manjhis. 'We recall the Manjhi's father and grandfather, but not beyond that'. These recent ancestors sit with the living and their presence gives continuity to tribal decisions.

Because of this intimate union the shrine is normally situated opposite the manjhi's dwelling and if the headmanship passes from one family to another, the manjhithan is shifted to a site by the new headman's house. In March 1944, when the manjhi of Sibtala was removed a new manjhithan was put up by the house of Chanda Soren, the new headman. A hole was dug 'until the earth from it was as high as a man's ear when he touches the ground'. Then a sal pole was put in. Manjhi Haram 'possessed' an old man from another village and the new manjhi said, 'We want to bring you here. Are you willing?' 'If they wish it, I am ready'. Then the villagers went to the old manjhithan, took out the two stones, imbedded them in the new plinth and the new headman sacrificed a goat.

At Thengadih the new Dumka-Jamtara road was due to over-run the old manjhithan, so villagers were given compensation and in May 1944 I watched the change of site. They first put up a spacious shed with thatch, decorating it lavishly with cream-coloured flowers and straw tassels. Then the manjhi was 'possessed' and dug out the old post and stone. After that he set the stone and the posts' fragments in the new plinth and the naeke's wife plastered it with cowdung. Later in the morning he again sat at the new shrine with a winnowing fan in his hands. Once more he went into a frenzy, jerking the fan wildly to and fro. Then he cried out, 'He is content', poured rice into the naeke's hands and the frenzy left him. The naeke beheaded two goats, put their heads on the shrine and again the Manjhi was possessed. He clasped the posts, gnawed the bleeding heads and writhed backwards and forwards over the plinth.

Then his struggles slowly eased. Water was poured on him and he became himself. After that we all went down to the jaher or sacred grove where four goats, a sheep and a pig were sacrificed and when we had returned to the village the manjhi offered rice beer at the hew then, and so ended the ritual.

In this latter case, a change of site was forced on the villagers owing to the new road and the cost was met by the District Board. In other cases when a change in site is due to a new headman, it is the latter who must bear the cost of the rice beer, and of the animals for sacrifice. The villagers may help him if they like but contributions are not compulsory. Similarly, it is the manjhi's duty to keep the manjhithan in order, to thatch or tile it every year, and to keep a stately pole firmly rising from its plinth. For this purpose the naeke acts as his mentor, and if the shrine collapses or gets untidy it is he who should remind the manjhi to set it right. If the naeke says nothing, the manjhi himself must take action but he can reprove the naeke for not drawing his attention. To meet the cost of the materials the manjhi can levy a village subscription and may requisition labour but when the villagers repair the shrine he is expected to give them a pot of rice beer. The manjhi's duty in fact is to co-ordinate the operation so that the village dignity and his own prestige are preserved.

V THE JAHER

The other public shrine is the jaher or sacred grove. This consists of a clump of sal trees with one mahua standing near. Three trees in a line are dedicated to Maran Buru, Jaher Era and More ko Turuc' ko, another to Pargana Bonga while the mahua tree is reserved for Gosae Era. At the base of each of these trees, a stone is imbedded and all five are known as bonga trees. The remaining trees in the grove are not reserved for particular bongas but form a kind of annexe where other bongas of the hills and forests may dwell if they wish. All the trees in the grove whether living or dead, belong to the village community. While a tree is living, no one may chop it with an axe as otherwise 'the bongas will burn his house'. The villagers will also intervene and punish him. Similarly, when a tree in the grove is struck by lightning or dies from other causes, it can only be cut and taken away after the naeke has sacrificed a goat. If a Santal needs the timber and the village approves, the goat is given by whoever takes the tree. Otherwise if the tree is a bonga tree a goat is procured by village subscription and after it has been sacrificed, the bonga is transferred to another tree. If a dead bonga tree is not removed at the time of sacrifice, but is taken later, the person taking it must provide an extra fowl for the naeke to sacrifice. In the case of Pargana bonga and Gosae Era, any tree in the grove is eligible as a new site and the exact tree is chosen by a Santal in 'possession'. With Maran Buru, Jaher Era and Moreko Turuc' ko on the other hand the choice is less easy. All these must stand in one line and if one tree dies, either a new sapling must be planted in the line, another tree in continuation of the line must be found or if neither can be done all three bongas must be moved to a fresh line of trees. If no other trees of the grove form such a line the jaher itself must be changed and all the bongas taken to a new separate site.

Such a case occurred at Birajpur in 1946. The tree of Maran Buru died. No other trees were in a line and although the grove contained much tall majestic timber, the site was abandoned and a copse of young saplings was chosen in its place.

Once a grove has been deserted, the trees are purged of their bongas and become like other sal trees on waste land. They cease to be the reserved property of the community and are governed by the ordinary rules for other trees.

VI THE SANTAL HOUSE

Finally the ownership of houses vests only partly in individuals and the larger Santal community has certain rights of user and control. A Santal can not for example sell his house since no land in a Santal village can be sold under law. He may however pull it down and sell the materials.[2] If his roof encroaches on another Santal's, the village can compel him to adjust it. If he occupies the house, he must allow Santal's admission for all tribal purposes, and if he is subjected to bitlaha, he must permit defilement of the verandah and courtyard.

He holds his house in fact as a member of a Santal village and his individual rights are overriden by the tribal privileges.

VII DUTIES TO THE VILLAGE

But besides acting as a public owner, the village community is also a source of taxation and conscription. As a member of the village each householder must pay the prescribed officials' fees and contribute to the festivals. He must also give his labour in repairing village roads, bandhs, and tanks, assist in making communal wells and tanks and play his part in repairing the manjhithan. He must attend village meetings, assist in village councils and if appointed an official, he has the duty to serve. Moreover, he is, as it were, a member of a mobile militia. If a hunt or fishing expedition is organised, he is expected to join it. If a boy weds a girl of another village in dol bapla, he must go in the marriage party, share in the drinking and dancing and offer the customary presents. If a death occurs in the village he must observe the ritual pollution, assist the mourners in the disposal of the body and attend the final feast. At a birth, he must attend the naming ceremony either in person or by proxy, and submit his cheeks to shaving. He must be present at initiation ceremonies and must also attend all festivals. If there is an epidemic he must join in sacrifice at the manjhithan. He must in fact conform to the whole pattern of conduct which life in the community imposes.

REFERENCES

1. W.S. Sherwill, 'Notes upon a tour through the Rajmahal Hills', *J.A.S. Beng*. (1851), 500.
2. The statement in the *Gazetteer* (second edition, 132) that the timber of a house belongs to the village is no longer correct.

PART TWO

THE RIGHTS OF SANTAL MEN

3

THE INNER AND THE GREATER FAMILY

I INTRODUCTION

IF THE village is a first focus for Santal law, it is the Santal in his family who evokes the greater portion of its rules. This family is one of the most flexible institutions in Santal society and in considering how best to state the claims of near and distant kinsmen, I was at first inclined to adopt Geoffrey Gorer's phrase 'the immediate and extended family'. In the end I decided to refer to 'the inner and the greater family' and I propose to distinguish these two groups in the following manner.

By an inner family I mean the household of a man and his wife if they are living alone or the family of a man and his children so long as they are joint. All other paternal relations not covered by these groups comprise the greater family. The inner family determines a Santal's routine. It is the setting in which he lives, works, eats and sleeps. His outer family on the other hand exists in reserve. It intervenes at times of crisis and possesses a number of residuary claims. Both families derive ultimately from the status of the father and I will therefore begin by describing the rights and duties of fathers and sons.

II FATHERS AND SONS

In an undivided household, the father is as it were the director of his children. He is the owner and manager of the family land and movables. He directs the family cultivation and presides at the family festivals. If any of his sons or daughters earn wages they must pay them to him and no son has the right to withhold them for himself. Similarly, the bare itat or brother's due which the sons receive at their sister's marriage becomes a part of the family property. If at any time an unmarried son quarrels or disobeys his father the latter can decline to keep him and can drive him from the home. Such action is taken with village approval and a son has no remedy until he either marries or his father dies. His only course is to go away and earn his living by day labour. In his old age, the father relinquishes control but can demand that his sons should maintain him.

In return for this despotism the sons have certain precise rights. They can demand food and clothes for themselves and their families out of the joint family stock. They can demand the expenses of all the ceremonies for their children including all the rites of birth, initiation, marriage and death. If they are unmarried, they can demand to be treated in sickness and married on maturity. With their father's approval sons can treat as their own certain movables such as ploughs, flutes, and drums. Above all provided they are major, they are their father's first heirs.* At their father's death, major sons inherit equal shares in his land and equal shares in the movables.** They must meet the expenses of his funeral, continue to support their mother, maintain their unmarried sisters and finally arrange their marriage. But subject to these charges they inherit all their father's property.† For this purpose every son is on a parity with any other son and it matters nothing whether a son's mother is alive, dead or divorced or whether the son was expelled in his father's lifetime. If a son is minor, his share is kept for him until his majority.

Finally, married sons have an equal right with their father to effect a partition of the family land and movables. When

*For their rights when minor see Chapter 18.

**If there are co-wives with separate household, each son inherits the movables in his mother's household and not the pooled movables of the entire households.

†For the purpose of inheritance a daughter married to a ghar jawae has also the status of a son (see Chapter 22).

this latter right is exercised the original despotism of the father shifts to a series of little despotisms by the sons and a fresh family cycle is started.

III PARTITION

So long as it is humanly possible Santals desire that a family should remain united. In Santal folk-tales 'the futility of family quarrels and the folly of partitions is a common theme'. In 'The Oilman and his five sons' (Bompas IX) the sons wish to set up separate households as their wives have quarrelled. The father takes a large log, and asks them to break it up. They fail. Then he tells them cut the log up into six pieces with their axes. They do so and he gives them each a piece of the wood. Then he tells them to break these pieces up into sticks with their hands and the sticks easily snap'. 'We are like the whole log', says the father 'we have plenty of property and are strong and can overcome attack but if we separate we shall be like split sticks and easily broken.'[1]

There are however, certain circumstances which make partition unavoidable. 'The envy of brothers' wives withers like leprosy'. Similarly, as the sons grow up they often develop wills of their own. 'Five brothers five wills', 'as many men as many wills' are common Santal proverbs. Friction of this kind has usually no other upshort, except a separation. Again, if the father has lost his first wife by divorce or death and marries a second time his second wife often quarrels with his sons' wives. This also is a frequent cause of family bitterness and is only resolved by partition. Finally, as the father gets old and his sons get grandchildren a single household becomes unwieldy. The father loses his general grip on the family affairs and a partition becomes advisable in the interest partly of space and of general control. In such cases a partition is made without any bitterness, for all the members agree it is the best thing for the family.

When the need for partition arises, the initiative can be taken by the father himself or by any of the married sons. If either of these desires a separation a partition can be demanded and no one can refuse it. A married son, however, who insists on separation against the general will of the family can be penalised by being given a small and temporary share.

In Amtala, the eldest son of Chotu Ramu Hambrom demanded partition. Chotu Ramu and his second son were unwilling so in the end Chotu Ramu gave him ten bighas as jom hatar—to keep him—and kept sixty-two for himself and his son.

Lodo Soren of Modikola had three sons all of whom were married. The first two demanded a partition but Lodo was strongly opposed. In the end each of them received 3 bighas by way of preliminary division and Lodo and his youngest son kept fifteen.

In Kukurkata Chandrai Hansdak' had three sons. The wife of the eldest did not like living in the same house as her husband's younger brothers, so Chandrai was asked to partition the property. He and his other sons did not want a partition so in the end the eldest son was given a fifth share in the lands.

Similarly, when friction arose in the family of Lakhan Hembrom of Saltala his two married sons demanded partition. Their father was opposed but ultimately he gave them each three bighas and kept ten bighas for himself and his wife.

If adopted sons are married they also can suggest partitions but cannot demand them. If their suggestion is accepted, however, they share like other married sons. Similarly, a daughter married in ghar jawae form can suggest but not demand a partition and after separation will either get a similar share to that of her married brothers, something less, or half such shares according as the village decides.

Once a partition has been decided on, it is done either by private family consultation or by a public act of the village. The first is resorted to when there is general agreement among the family. It does not, however, bind the members or the village officials and if there is any dispute it must be taken to the village and the whole partition ratified. A public partition by the village is, therefore the usual course. Everything in the family house is taken out and stacked in a field and with the villagers assisting, it is then divided out among the members. The land is also discussed and suitable allocations are made. No one except the father can claim a particular article or piece of land as of right but individual preferences are humoured when there is no opposition. At the end of the proceedings the villagers are given rice beer in the house and if the family means allow the leading villagers get a feast in the evening. This ratifies the partition. If the partition is preliminary to a final partition later, or is a partial one enforced against the general will, it holds good until old age compels the father to make a final distribution. If the partition is made in his old age, there is no further revision and the matter cannot be reopened. If the father subsequently acquires property, it is shared at his death.

In making such partitions the village community usually allots the father and each son an equal share. As between the sons the shares must be equal but the father sometimes gets a larger or a smaller share according to his needs. If a man and his wife are still active, the major part of the land and movables is kept by them and the sons are given only small shares. It is only when they have grown too old for having further children and can no longer work in the fields that a full and final partition is made. At a final partition, there, is therefore, no need to make provision for unborn sons or daughters. If on the other hand the partition is only preliminary to a later and final one, any subsequent sons will get their share from the property remaining with their father. Movables are similarly divided giving each son an equal share and allotting the father whatever he reasonably demands. In the case of unmarried sons their shares are given in trust to married brother or are kept by the father and in addition to their shares as sons, a little land or some movables or sometimes both are reserved for meeting the expenses of their marriage. When the marriage has been performed any of the reserved movables which remain unsold are either partitioned or remain with the father till his death. Similarly, if the land has been set aside for meeting the wedding expenses from its produce division will take place either when the weddings are over or at the death of the father. In all such final partitions, all sons of a father who desire to separate receive equal shares provided they are not expelled from the household. The fact that three sons are of one mother and one is from a second makes no difference to their claims. Each receives the same share, for each is a son of the same father. If a son has been expelled and is still unmarried he can claim no share but if he is married after expulsion and before the partition he can demand and get a share. If a son is absent at the time of partition a share is reserved for him and placed in charge of the father or a brother.

In Chhota Dhamni Jairam Hembrom had three sons. After the eldest was married a partition was effected. The father kept 5½ bighas of land, two buffaloes and two bales of paddy. The remaining lands were shared equally by the three sons but one bigha extra was allotted to the two sons who were still unmarried. In addition each son received one buffalo and six sulis of paddy.

When Mangal Tudu of Latberwa partitioned his property he gave his three sons equal shares and himself retained a fourth share with 10 bighas extra. He kept for himself sixteen goats, eight cows, a pair of buffaloes and a pair of bullocks and gave each son eight goats, one cow, and a pair of bullocks.

In Gargaria Siru Marandi had three sons. He set aside two bighas to cover the wedding expenses of the son who was unmarried and the remaining lands were divided equally between three sons and himself. When the youngest brother is married the two bighas will be divided among the brothers.

In all such partitions unless a daughter is married to a ghar jawae she cannot claim a share in land as of right. If, however, she is wedded to a ghar jawae her share whether by inheritance or partition is decided at her marriage.

Basta Hembrom of Latberwa had a daughter and two younger sons. The daughter was married to a ghar jawae and when the property was partitioned the daughter received land with an annual rent of six rupees four annas while the two sons were each given land with an annual rent of eight annas more.

In Kalidaspur Ratna Tudu had a daughter and a son. He brought a ghar jawae for the daughter and also married his son. After Ratna and his son both died there was a family partition. The daughter received half the lands and movables while her brother's son received the other half.

If a daughter is married, but not to a ghar jawae, the

family may in its discretion give her a little land as taben jom. Citwa Hansdak' of Lakhanpur allotted four bighas of land as taben jom for his married daughter when the family lands were partitioned.

If the daughter is unmarried certain lands or movables will be earmarked for her wedding expenses and provision will also be made for maintaining her till marriage.

Randhan Soren of Tengadih had two brothers. When her father died and she was unmarried they set aside one bigha of land for her maintenance. By family agreement Randhan cultivated this land for 7 years even after her wedding, but after that her brothers took it back.

In Amrapara Tilkai Murmu had a lame daughter. As there was no chance of getting her married two bighas of land were allotted to her at the family partition and she lived with her elder brother until she died.

Besides making this provision for daughters the family may sometimes give each daughter a cow to add to her private property. This however is possible only when the family is well-to-do and when the village thinks it reasonable.

Bhondo Hembrom of Amjora had two sons and two daughters. All were married and at the family partition each married daughter was given a cow.

Finally, a widow living with her sons is entitled to a share sufficient to maintain her and the same applies to a wife who is past the age of divorce, and is living separately from her husband.

Mangar Murmu of Susania died leaving a widow and two sons. There was then a partition. Each of the sons received two-fifths of the land while their mother received one-fifth.

In Dalu Rupai Marandi died leaving a widow, two married daughters and three sons. At the family partition, the married daughters received nothing, the widow was given four bighas and the remaining 56 bighas were divided equally between the three sons.

Once a family is separated each son becomes the sole owner of his land and movables in the same way as his father was the sole owner prior to the partition. But unless friction or bitterness have led to the partition, there is no social separation. Each son acquires a 'greater family' in his brothers and nephews. These help him in birth, illness and death. They rally to his aid at weddings—each bearing part of the expense. If one brother gives rice for rice beer, another pays for the Dom drummers or the litter. When his children are due for initiation, ceremonies of several brothers' children are often done at one time. Similarly, if one brother has no children, his other brothers assist him in cultivation and if he desires to adopt a son, marry a daughter in ghar jawae form, he usually does so in consultation with them. The 'greater family' is in fact a supplement to the 'inner'. It remains a form of insurance against calamity and it is only if hostility or hatred arise that the greater family ceases to advise and aid.

IV THE FIRST HEIR AFTER MAJOR SONS: WIDOWS

If a Santal's land and movables are separate and he dies leaving only minor sons or no sons at all his property goes first to his widow. The widow acts as a substitute for her husband* and keeps his land and movables till she either remarries, leaves the village or dies. This principle is now everywhere accepted but I will give three examples from widely different places.

Kalu Murmu of Haria died leaving a widow and one brother who was separate. All the property remained with the widow.

In Kusumpokhar Bodoc' Marandi died leaving a widow and no sons. The widow remained in possession of his lands and when she died it was shared equally by her husband's brothers.

Matla Tudu of Kalidaspur died leaving a widow, his two sons having predeceased him. The widow holds all his lands and Matla's three brothers will only inherit them on her death, second marriage or departure from the village.

V THE FATHER

When the rights of a widow lapse or if she has died before

*See Chapter 18.

her husband the property passes to her minor sons if she has any and if there are none to her husband.

If the minor sons inherit, their guardian administers the property for them while if the father is the heir, he either adds the lands to his own share and keeps them for his lifetime or makes a fresh partition and divides them between himself and his other sons. During their father's lifetime the latter cannot demand that this extra share should be partitioned neither have they any claim to the deceased's extra movables.

VI BROTHERS

If the father is already dead, the next heirs are the brothers. These inherit equal shares in the land and movables. If a brother is dead but has left sons, his share is inherited by them to the same extent as if he had been alive. Similarly, if a brother has had two sons and one of them has died leaving sons, these latter jointly inherit their father's share. In the following table, *A* is the dead Santal, *B* and *C* are his brothers *D*, *E* and *F* are their sons, while *G* and *H* are the sons of a son.

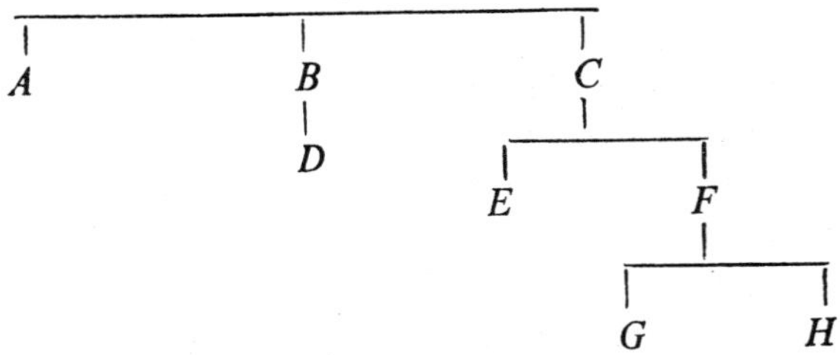

In these circumstances if *B* and *C* are alive, they each inherit a half share in *A*'s land and movables. If *B* is dead, *D* fills his place and shares equally with *C*. If *C* is dead, *E* and *F* inherit *C*'s half share. Finally, if *E* is alive but *C* and *F* are dead, *G* and *H* inherit the share of *F*.

Tibu Marandi of Modikola was one of three brothers. He died leaving two married daughters and his widow. Subsequently the widow became a co-wife to his younger brother and his two brothers inherited his land.

In Bichkora Baghrae Soren had three sons all of whom were separated at his death. One son died without issue and another died leaving one son. The land of the first son was then shared by his surviving brother and the nephew.

This right to inherit is not confined to uterine brothers but extends to all brothers who are the sons of one father. If *A* is a Santal, *B* and *C* are his brothers by the same mother and *D* is the son of his father but by a second wife, *B*, *C*, and *D* all inherit equally *A*'s land. If however, the households were separate, movables are shared on a household basis.

This right to inherit is subject to the duty of performing the funerary rites*, of maintaining unmarried daughters and performing their initiation and marriage ceremonies.**

VII MOTHER, GRANDFATHER, PATERNAL UNCLES AND GRANDMOTHER

If there are no brothers, the next reversioner is the mother, after her the grandfather, after him the paternal uncles or their sons and finally the grandmother. If a paternal uncle is dead but is survived by a son or grandson these inherit to the extent of the share he would have got if he had been alive. Both mother and grandmother inherit subject to their not having re-married and to their residing in the village.

Baset and Basia were two brothers in Sitasal. Baset died leaving two sons who in turn died before they were married and had children. Basia their paternal uncle then inherited their lands.

Kandan and Ramsai Murmu were two brothers in Nipania. Ramsai died leaving two sons who in turn died without widows or children. Kandan and his son also died—the latter leaving a daughter who was married to a ghar jawae. The son's daughter has now inherited both Kandan and Ramsai's lands.

VIII DAUGHTERS AND SISTERS

Finally, if there are no male agnates, daughters whether

*See Chapter 39.
**See Chapter 14.

married or unmarried inherit.* In the case of a single unmarried daughter, it is not infrequent for the village community to arrange her marriage in ghar jawae form. Pending this arrangement the land and movables are kept for her by a village guardian. If an unmarried daughter has married sisters, all inherit equally and the share of the unmarried daughter is kept in trust for her by the sisters until she is married.

Durgu Murmu of Chutia died leaving a widow, a son and a married daughter. Sometime later, the son died, the widow remarried and the married daughter has now inherited the land.

In Jitalpur Baghrae Murmu died leaving no son, widow or agnates. He had a married daughter and it was she who inherited.

Bariar Tudu of Sundarmaur died leaving two daughters. His sons were already dead and his cousins had left the area and made no claim. All his daughters were married in the standard form and on his death all of them inherited the property, the daughter who had nursed him in his illness getting a slightly larger share by family consent.

In Bokrabandh Bhaia Besra had three daughters and two sons. He married his daughters in the standard form and then his two sons died. When Bhaia himself died his properties were divided between his three daughters, the daughter who nursed him during his illness being given one plot of land more than the others.

Equally if there are no daughters but granddaughters, similar principles apply. A granddaughter by a son, however, will exclude a daughter since the son is the first heir. A granddaughter by a daughter on the other hand will share equally with a daughter. If there are no daughters or granddaughters, sisters inherit and similar principles apply.

Matla Hembrom of Litipara died leaving no widow, child or male agnate. He had a married sister and she inherited all his lands and movables.

In Modikolha Kanhu Tudu died without any male heirs.

*The position of a daughter married in ghar jawae form is that of a son in relation to a father and that of a brother in relation to brother.

He also had an elder sister and all his land was inherited by her.

Singrai Soren of Nimakalan died leaving no widow, sons or daughters. His paternal uncles had migrated to Bengal and did not claim his land. He had four married sisters and when he died his sisters jointly performed his funeral ceremony and received equal shares in his land.

Once a woman has inherited, her own children take precedence over her sisters and their sons. Her first heir is her son, after him a grandson through a son, then a granddaughter by a son, then a daughter, then a grandson by a daughter, then a granddaughter by a daughter and so on; and even though all her sisters have sons and grandsons none can claim her property until her own line is finished.

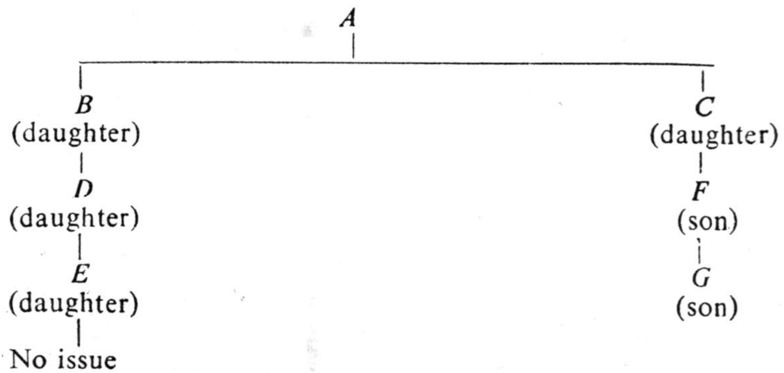

In this table, *B* and *C* inherit equally the property of *A*. The heir of *B* is *D* and after *D*, *E*. *F* and *G* succeed *E* only when she has died without issue.

IX CONCLUSION

Out of this intricate 'system of mutual rights and duties' we may now summarise certain salient principles. Inheritance of male property is normally male but in the absence of sons a widow in a separate family has now the first claim to her husband's lands. Her position is safe not merely for her husband's lifetime but her own. As against daughters, the greater family, if male, normally takes precedence but marriage to a ghar jawae gives a daughter the right to inherit like a son. If there are no male heirs, inheritance is permissible through females. The inner and the greater families, in fact, whether as male or female groups have now priority over the village. The lands of a Santal are in last analysis the lands of a family and it is only when a whole family is exhausted that the community resumes possession.

REFERENCE

1. Mildred Archer, The folk-tale in Santal society, *Man in India*, XXIV, 228.

4

ADOPTION

I INTRODUCTION

IN HIS paper on Santal rules of succession, Campbell says: 'Adoption is not practised by the Santals'[1] and Bodding while dissenting remarks, 'I have heard of one or two instances'.[2] Sir Robert Russell, on the other hand, made enquiries in 1924 from 'an assembly of parganaits in the Dumka Damin, the parganait of Amrapara, the Sardars of Sikaripara, Rajbandh, Banspahari, Masanjor and a number of others'[3] and found that such a custom existed from very early times. At the present day there is no uncertainty for the practice is not only a Santal custom but is a common expedient in Santal life.

The most usual situation which results in adoption is when a Santal has no son. 'It is for love and joy that we want sons' said Salku Soren, deshmanjhi of Durgapur. But beyond this delight in male children is the knowledge that a son is the main support in old age. A Santal ploughs so long as his health and strength remain but sooner or later these must end and then if he has no son there is only the decrepitude of old age, its weak helplessness, the plight of 'an old man, a dull head among windy spaces'.

It is in circumstances such as these that a Santal often resorts to adoption—sometimes only to secure a son but more usually to gain a prop in his fading years.

II ADOPTION WITHIN THE FAMILY

When a Santal needs a son whether for solace or for maintenance the first and most usual course is to take a youth as posu putra from his own 'greater' family. Within this unit his choice is wide—though not as wide as we might at first expect. He cannot, for example, adopt a brother, the son of a paternal or maternal uncle, a granduncle, a paternal or maternal uncle, or the son or grandson of a granduncle. He is in fact debarred from adopting anyone who is on the tribal level of a brother, father or uncle. But there is no objection to the taking, among others, of the son or grandson of a brother, the grandson or great grandson of a paternal uncle, or the great grandsons of paternal granduncles. Similarly although it is rare to adopt a man whose age is more than thirty, adoption at any age from birth to early manhood is often done.

In such cases, the boy is of the same sept as his adopting father. If the latter dies he can already offer water to him.* He has already full access to his bongas. All that is necessary is village approval and even if certain of the agnates disapprove, the decision of the village is final. When the village has approved, the adopted son moves over from a place in the 'greater' family of his adopting father to a place in the 'inner'. Unless any rights are specifically reserved for him at the time of his adoption, he loses all rights in his own father's 'inner' family. He can no longer demand partition on marriage or claim a son's share on his father's death.

If a share is given to him, it is merely by grace and not of right.

When Kishun Marandi of Saharpur adopted one of his brother's three sons, it was specifically agreed that the son would retain his share in his natural father's land. Accordingly when the natural father died, the son who had been adopted as well as his two brothers each inherited a third.

In Jokpahari, Bodi Hembrom who was one of two brothers was adopted by his father's sister. When his adoptive mother died, he inherited all her lands and on the death of his natural father, he was given a half share in his lands as well. In this case, there was no reservation of a share at the time of adoption but as an act of grace and by mutual agreement, his

*See Chapter 39.

brother allowed him to receive it. If he nad not agreed, Bodi would have had no claim.

Similarly if his natural father dies, an adopted son can no longer claim his land and if he inherits his property, it is only because he is a next reversioner. He becomes, in fact, the son of his adopting father—with almost all the privileges of a natural son. He cannot claim partition after marriage, for—this would destroy the raison d'etre of his induction. But in all other ways it is as if he had been born into his new family. If he is unmarried, his adopting father will arrange and pay for his marriage and the first grandson will be named after him. If the adopted son is married and has children, the next son will take the adopting father's name. His death expenses will be borne by the new family. If sons are born to his new father after his adoption, he will share equally with them. If brothers of his adopting father die with no sons he inherits like any other reversioner. Equally if he dies without a son or wife and had separate lands at the time of his adoption, his adopting father becomes his nearest heir.

Muchia Hansdak' of Karmatanr was one of three brothers. He himself had no sons but his elder brother had four. He therefore adopted one of the sons as posu putra. On Muchia's death this son inherited all the lands of Muchia except an eighth which he gave up voluntarily to his brothers. His brothers inherited all his natural father's land and the adopted son named his children as if Muchia was his actual father.

In Dalu, Karan and Dugu Tudu were two brothers. Karan had three sons while Dugu was childless. Dugu therefore adopted Karan's second son as posu putra and on Karan's death only the two remaining sons inherited his land.

In Lakrapahari, Barka Chore was adopted as posu putra by his paternal uncle. Barka got all his uncle's lands but his brothers took his father's.

III ADOPTION OF OUTSIDERS

A second course is to draw a youth, not from the adopting father's 'greater' family, but from a family with no previous relationship to him. This may occur when the brothers are on bad terms or the 'greater' family is short of boys; or what is even more common, when the adopting father has married a widow with children and adopts a stepson.

In such cases, village opinion is decisive and while the agnates can voice objection, their views do not have the force of vetos. The village weighs the whole situation and if it thinks adoption is necessary it sanctions it irrespective of whether the agnates agree or disagree.

Lodo Hansdak' of Khajurm̐a married a widow with a son. His brother had several sons, but as they were not on good terms, Lodo took village approval and adopted his stepson instead.

A boy who is so adopted is also known as posu putra. He severs all connection with his natural father's 'inner' family and unless rights are specifically reserved, he loses all claims to his former father's land. He changes his sept and is completely absorbed into his adopting father's family.

This absorption into the adopting family is by the ceremony of bonga tala—'inducting into the bongas'. It is an almost exact replica of the janam chatiar or original naming ceremony. The adoptive son and the village men are shaved and go to a tank for bathing. Flour is put on the chests of both men and women. After that a midwife announces the sept of the adopting father and the new name the adopted son will bear. Finally rice water with nim leaves is drunk and the meeting ends. From then onwards the boy has access to the man's own bongas. He shares in the family's sacrificial meat and can assist his adopting father in all the services of his bongas. He can, if necessary, be married in his former sept. With bonga tala, he becomes the man's own son.

Jadu Kisku and Jasai Kisku of Taljhari were two brothers. Jasai died leaving no one. Jadu married but his wife and children all died. He then married a widow with a son. He adopted his stepson and bonga talaed him. At the bonga tala, having named his dead son after his father, he gave his stepson the name of his father's brother. He moved me to place this on record so that later on no one might dispossess him.

IV ADOPTION WITHOUT BONGA TALA

Yet a third type of adoption is when the adopted youth is

either the son of a sister, the son of a daughter of a paternal or a maternal aunt or uncle, the son of a stepchild the son of a wife's elder sister, or indeed of anyone with whom sexual relations by the adopting father are tabooed.

In such cases not only the bongas but the sept of the boy will be different and in that respect he will be the same as a stepson or outsider. He will not, however, be bonga talaed. The reason for this is that bonga tala would put his adopting father in an incest relation to the boy's mother.* When therefore, the boy's mother is such that intercourse with her by the man would lead to outcasting the boy is adopted only by a declaration in the village. He becomes the same as a posu putra but he inherits like a daughter married to a gharjawae. Some land is set aside for curuc' cawale and the worship of the bongas is done by a male agnates of the father. In all other respects, his rights are same as if he had come from his adopting father's family.

Anpa Murmu of Banspahari had no sons so he adopted a son of his sister. The boy's name, Munshi Marandi but since his mother was Anpa's sister, no bonga tala was possible and Munshi retrained his own name and sept. Anpa then arranged Munshi's marriage and his first son has been named Anpa after his adoptive father. On Anpa's death, Munshi will inherit all his lands.

Similarly when Bando Murmu of Ero adopted Kanhu Hembrom, Kanhu was the son of Bando's grandfather's sister's son and Kanhu's own father was younger than Bando. Accordingly Bando stood in an incest relation to Kanhu's mother, bonga tala was impossible and Kanhu was therefore adopted as posu putra by a declaration with village approval.**

V THE ADOPTION OF GIRLS

There remains a fourth type--the adoption of a girl. When this occurs, it is usually a brother's daughter or brother's granddaughter who is selected but an outsider, a stepdaughter,

*For a detailed discussion of tabooed relations, see my account *Bitlaha*.

**This case which came before Mr. A.R. Adair was of great interest for if Kanhu's father had been older than Bando the incest relation with Kanhu's mother would no longer have existed and bonga tala would have been essentially necessary.

the daughter of a sister, the daughter of a stepchild, or a girl from the family of the adopting mother are among those who are commonly adopted.

If such a girl is already married, her husband may be converted into a gharjawae by agu mit' while if she is still unmarried, her wedding may be done in gharjawae form with village approval.

When the girl is drawn from a brother's family, her name and sept continue as before but if she is a stepdaughter or outside the father's family her adoption is done by bonga tala. If, however, she is the daughter of her adopting father's sister or the daughter of a stepchild or if sexual relations by the new father with her mother would amount to incest, bonga tala is dispensed with and she acquires the status of a posu putra by a village declaration.

Bardo, Larpa and Kisum Murmu were three brothers of Brindaban. Bardo had no children, Larpa had a son and Kisum a daughter. Bardo wanted to adopt his brother's son for life long maintenance, but the son did not agree. So Bardo adopted Kisum's daughter and brought her with her husband. He set apart two bighas of land as curuc' cawale for Larpa's son and the remaining ten bighas he kept for himself, and his adopted daughter.

In this case the daughter's husband became a gharjawae by agu mit' and the girl, after adoption inherited like an actual daughter married to a gharjawae.

Ram Murmu of Bandorkonda was married to Solma. They had no children and later Solma left him and lived with Pandu Hansdak'. A daughter—Khandi Hansdak' was born to them but after Pandu's death, Solma came back to Ram Murmu and brought Khandi as a stepdaughter. Ram then adopted her by bonga tala and named her Raimat Murmu. Raimat was the name of his mother and Murmu was his sept. When Raimat grew older Ram married her in gharjawae form and later Raimat inherited his lands.

In a case from Bandarjuri Thakura Hembrom had a single daughter and no son. The girl had a love affair with a Dom and but for the fact that she left Bandarjuri and "became dead" the village would have bitlahaed her. Thakura then married a widow with two daughters. He got husbands for the two daughters and a step-granddaughter was born later. The child's father died and her mother re-married in another village. Thakura then adopted his step-granddaughter but since relations with her mother (Thakura's stepdaughter) would have amounted to incest bonga tala was impossible and the adoption was completed by a village declaration. After that Thakura took village approval and married the girl to a gharjawae. The gharjawae died and in 1942 Thakura brought a second gharjawae. When at last Thakura himself died his own daughter tried to get her father's land but a little later not only the village but a meeting of five manjhis all awarded the lands to the adopted girl.

VI OTHER CONDITIONS

When adoption is proposed, a Santal usually selects a spare son or daughter from a fairly large family. But there is no bar to the adoption of only sons. If only sons are taken, however, they are usually chosen from among the brothers' sons and grandsons and then usually when the adoption does not deprive the brother of a vital assistant. An only son from an outside family is seldom adopted since this would deprive the father of a son to offer him water after his death. Moreover the father would lose all hope of a grandson to carry on his name. Adoption of an only son from a brother is free from these weaknesses. The adopted son can still name a son—though not his first—after his natural father and he can still offer him water. It is for this reason that when an only son is adopted it is almost always from the sons of brothers.

Pandu and Ramu Tudu of Gopaldih were two brothers. Pandu had no children while Ramu had an only son. Pandu is older than Ramu and has since adopted Ramu's son.

Narain and Dhudu Hembrom of Rajabandh were two brothers each with separate lands. Narain had no children while Dhudu had one son and five daughters. Narain then adopted Dhudu's son as posu pitra and on his death the son inherited his lands. Some years later Dhudu went to live with him and in 1944 when the son was drinking himself into debt, he tried to oust him from Narain's lands. The village held however, that the adoption had given the son full rights in Narain's land and Dhudu had no claim.

Similarly, although the existence of natural sons and daughters is not in itself an absolute bar to the adoption of a posu putra, the only circumstances in which village approval is given is when a man has been abandoned by all his children, or his sons or daughters agree to the adoption, or an only son is a cripple or infirm. In such circumstances the adoption of posu putra will not be invalid and the village may approve.

In Karmatanr Ledho Murmu was one of four brothers and had a daughter but no son. A brother had three sons so Ledho adopted one of them. The boy has named his children as if Ledho were his father.

Jhulu Hansdak' of Tesaria brought his sister and her son to his house after the woman's husband had died. He himself already had several sons but as none of them objected, he adopted the nephew as a posu putra and at a family partition he gave him a son's share in his lands. As bonga tala would have put the boy's mother in an incest relation to him, his name and sept were not changed and the adoption was effected by village approval and a declaration in a meeting.

VII ADOPTION OF ORPHANS

But besides adoption for getting a son or securing maintenance in old age, there is a third type—the adoption of a tuar or orphan out of pity. 'In the olden days', says Sido deshmanjhi 'during the rebellion, they adopted many sons.' 'Even now an abandoned child or an orphan is rarely left to die. It is taken into a family and brought up like other children of the village.

There are, however, two possible lines of action. If its foster father wishes, he may formally adopt it, give it his own sept and bring it into his bongas. In that event the child becomes his own and its rights are the same as those of any child adopted by bonga tala.

Kurumlaya Hansdak' of Goskolha had no sons. He consulted his brothers and as they had no objection, he adopted an orphan. The boy was bonga talaed, and given the name of Kauralaya Hansdak'. When Kurumlaya died, the boy inherited all his land.

Similarly during the famine of 1938, Rendhu Soren of Agua found a baby boy abandoned on the road. He himself had no children. He consulted his two brothers who approved and he then bonga talaed him in the presence of the village. At this bonga tala he named the child Torya Soren after his father.

Later, Rendhu arranged his marriage and although at Rendhu's death the two agnates, objected the village five held that the boy alone had any rights to Rendhu's property.

, In Gosainpahari Bagan Soren and Banki Hansdak' had an only daughter whom they married to a gharjawae. Their daughter died leaving an only son and the gharjawae wanted to go home. Bagan did not like this so he adopted an orphan girl from Gedial. Her name was Kapra Hansdak' and at the bonga tala he named her Somia Soren, after his wife's mother. He then married her in gharjawae form to his son-in-law and her son has now inherited equally with the son by his daughter.

Not all orphans however, are destitute and in certain cases, an orphan may already have inherited lands. In such circumstances, adoption is contingent in the conduct of the agnates. If these are duly performing their duties no occasion for adoption arises, since the orphan will be brought up by them and given his lands when he comes of age. If however, there are no agnates or they neglect the orphan or ill treat him, the village itself can assume the guardianship and sanction an adoption. In such cases, the agnates lose all rights as reversioners in the orphan's land and the orphan's heirs are first his son, then his adoptive father, after that his foster brothers and their sons and finaliy his adoptive father's agnates.

VIII ASUL BADHA

An orphan who is given shelter is not however invariably adopted and if bonga tala is not performed. He is known as asul badha. Badha means literally a foundling and asul badha, a foundling who has been brought up or reared. This circumstance does not in itself give him any rights as a son and he can only get 'what is given to him'.*

In Kusma Gukul Murmu who already had two sons took pity on an orphan. He consulted his family and then in the presence of the village he said 'if this child obeys me like a son, I will give him a hut and a stick a little land (mit pati jumi) and a pair of bullocks'. Since then the boy has been in his house. He has not however been bonga talaed and has acquired no other claim.

Early in the 20th century Ban Singh Murmu, who was on his way back from Assam found a boy baby abandoned on the road. He took it to "Tomtom Sahib", the Subdivisional Officer, Dumka who induced Jolha Marandi of Sibnagar to rear it. Jolha already had three sons so he did not bonga tala the baby. Instead he gave him the sept of Hembrom and called him Badhu. When the boy grew up Jolha gave him some land which his gharjawae married sister had abandoned.

In Kalidaspur Sabhan Marandi reared the orphan son of his sister. The boy's name was Mangal Murmu and when he grew up, Sabhan gave him 15 bighas out of his 175 bighas and divided the rest among his sons.

Similar action was taken in a well-known family of the district. The Rev Chaitan Hembrom Kumar took pity on an orphan treated him like a son named him Badha Hembrom and reared him in his family. He did not however formally adopt him and when he partitioned his lands, his two sons received the major shares while the orphan got five bighas out of kindness.

IX ADOPTION BY WIDOWS

In almost all cases adoption is done only by men but there is

*Bodding is not entirely correct in stating that 'badha may give the full right of inheritance to a boy taken in and make him a lawful heir' (*A Santal Dictionary*, I, 165).

Similarly Sido Deshmanjhi does not exactly state the entire position. 'People sometimes take in and rear children and orphans. On growing up they get an equal share of the lands, money and cattle with real sons' (*Hor Korem Mare Hapram ko reak' Katha*, 256-7).

Such rights only accrue after a formal adoption by bonga tala.

no bar to a widow adopting a son or daughter 'for her dead husband'. As in all cases of adoption village approval is a necessary condition but such cases almost always occur only when there are no agnates to oppose or where the husband's brothers fully approve. Moveover it is generally accepted that if a widow so adopts she will do so from her husband's greater family. There have so far been no cases in which the village has overruled the agnates and has allowed adoption by a widow against their will.

The widow of Sital Soren of Raghunathpur adopted the son of her dead husband's brother's son.

In Jhanjhko the widow of Bhondo Murmu took a son of her husband's brother as posu putra and the same was done by the widow of Tilak Marandi of Dahua and the widow of Jiban Soren of Litipara.

In a case from Birgaon the widow of Chandra Soren adopted an outsider. Her dead husband had left no agnates and the boy was adopted from outside the family with the approval of the village.

X CANCELLATION

In all these cases, adoption is for 'the mutual help' the one of the other and for this reason it is always a permanent relationship which is intended to end only with death. Occasionally however, friction develops between the adopting father and the adopted child or circumstances change. When this happens a number of adjustments are necessary.

If an adopted son is a posu putra and has come from the greater family, the adopting father can appeal to the village and with village approval can either expel him from his house or cancel the adoption. If he resorts to expulsion and the adopted son is married the latter can claim sufficient of his land to maintain himself and his family. If however, the adopted son is unmarried he must work as a labourer until his adoptive father dies. If an adoption is cancelled, the adopted son returns to his natural father's house, his rights in his adopting father's house terminate and he reverts to the position which he held previous to his adoption.

All his previous rights revive and it is as if no adoption had ever taken place.

If he has separate lands of his own prior to his adoption these will not have merged in his adopting father's property and accordingly if he is expelled or his adoption is cancelled his possession is unaffected.

In the case of a girl taken from the greater family, the same principles apply, but if she has been married to a gharjawae her adoption cannot be cancelled and all that her adopting father can do is to partition his land and movables and live separately.

In Malipara Biswas Marandi and his brother Bisu had no sons. Biswas therefore adopted as posu putra a grandson of his father's brother. Later Bisu got three sons and then by family settlement the adoption was cancelled and the adopted son was returned to his father.

In Raghunathpur Lala Besra adopted Deo Besra as a posu putra. The adopted son began to neglect him and then with village approval Lala cancelled the adoption and expelled him from his house.

These principles govern the adoption of posu putras from within the family. If however, a son or daughter has been brought from outside and adopted by bonga tala, the adoption cannot be cancelled and if friction arises the only remedies are partition and separation or the adoption of further children to off-set the recalcitrant one.

XI 'FALSE' ADOPTION

Finally, there is one further circumstance in which adoption is occasionally procured. If a boy and girl fall in love but their septs are the same they are normally debarred from marrying and if their intimacy is detected, they are liable to excommunication. In such circumstances, a 'false' adoptive father is sometime permitted. A Santal agrees to take the girl in to his bongas and to give her his sept. Bonga tala is duly done and the boy and girl are then allowed to marry. The adopted child acquires no rights in the adoptive father's family property and the adoptive father secures no right in the person of the child. The arrangement is merely an adoption 'for convenience' and apart from enabling the girl to marry in her previous sept it has no other significance.

In Talwa Dhorba Soren eloped with Khendle Soren. When they returned the boy was fined twenty rupees and the girl ten. The village jogmanjhi then performed a 'false' adoption. The girl was bonga talaed and given the sept of Tudu and after that they were allowed to live together.

In Bordoha Mansingh Soren fell in love with the daughter of Dugga Soren. The village tried to part them but the two insisted on being married. When the villagers saw that there was no alternative, a Murmu man was paid to act as a 'false' adopting father. He took the girl into his bongas, named her Hisi Murmu and the boy and girl were later married.

REFERENCES

1. A. Campbell, Rules of succession and partition of property as observed by the Santals, *J.B.O.R.S.*, I (1915), 21.
2. P.O. Bodding, Some remarks on the position of women among the Santals, *J.B.O.R.S.*, II (1916), 249.
3. R.E. Russell, Judgment in Deputy Commissioner's Title Appeal No. 42 of 1923, Lachu Hansdak' and others versus Mangal Hansdak'.

5

THE ILLEGITIMATE CHILD

I INTRODUCTION

AMONG the tribes of Middle and Eastern India, the bastard or illegitimate child is so scarce that in many monographs its possibility is not even considered. In *The Kharias*, *The Birhors* and *The Mundas*, Sarat Chandra Roy makes no mention of the problem while in *The Oraons*, after discussing premarital relations, he adds 'Such companionship seldom ends in marriage. Marriage between boys and girls of the same clan is strictly prohibited, and even when the boy and the girl are of different clans, a marriage between a boy and a girl of the same village is not considered desirable. Community of clan is, however (in practice though not in theory) often no bar to premarital intercourse. Cases of abortion though they seldom come to light, are not rare. To prevent conception, an Oraon maiden either reverses her loin-cloth for the nonce by wearing it with its front side to the back or ties to her loin-cloth just over the abdomen the false plait of hair sometimes worn as a coiffure. When notwithstanding such precautions, inconvenient consequences follow such premarital connexion, the girl is given a glass or two of phuli or mahua liquor to drink, and this, it is said, generally serves to cause abortion. If, however, this fails of the desired effect, the help of a Kusraon or midwife, generally of the Ghasi caste, is sought to cause abortion through medicines. In a very few cases, this course is not adopted, but either the affair ends in a marriage if the boy and the girl belong to different clans, or if they happen to belong to the same clan, they live together as husband and wife. In the latter case, the young man has to provide a feast to his co-villagers to legalise the union and avoid excommunication. Sons by such a marriage inherit their father's property.'[1]

In his *Descriptive Ethnology of Bengal,* Dalton gives a similar testimony. 'Long and strong attachments between young (Oraon) couples are common. Dhumkuria lads are no doubt great flirts, but each has a special favourite amongst the young girls of his acquaintance and the girls well known to whose touch or pressure in the dance each maiden's heart is responsive. Liaisons between boys and girls of the same village seldom end in marriage. Yet whilst hardly ever failing to present their husband with a pledge of love after marriage, instances of illegitimate births are rare though young Oraon girls remain unmarried for some years after reaching maturity'.[2]

The problem is equally absent among *the Maria Gonds of Bastar.* W.V. Grigson states that if premarital intercourse results in pregnancy, the girl states the name of the man responsible and goes to live in his house without any ceremony, the union being described as ottur (taken away). If the child is born without even ottur it is considered as belonging to its father's clan and the father is expected to take the mother and the child to his house, the union being known to Hill Marias as ahene hattu (thus went). Grigson adds that 'no stigma attaches to such unions and the children have exactly the same position and rights as the children of a formal marriage'. He does not state what happens if the father declines but it is obvious from his account that such refusals are unknown.[3]

Among *the Reddis of the Bison Hills,* Christoph Von Fürer Haimendorf notes 'Though a couple eloping in order to escape parental opposition incurs no lasting malice, not all lovers avail themselves of this simplest way of overcoming their difficulties, and many young people enjoy secret intrigues with the result that sometimes an unmarried girl finds herself with child. Then the old men of both communities concerned call the man responsible and insist on his marrying the girl. Even if the parents of either side view the match with disfavour they will often be persuaded to give their consent. My informants thought that if the girl had a reputation for promiscuity she might be driven out of the village and her child given the clan name of any of the potential fathers. They admitted, however, that they had never heard of a concrete instance and suggested that a girl's parents would never allow matters to come to such a pass, but would marry her off to anybody willing to take her into his house'.[4]

There is a similar situation among the Baiga and Verrier Elwin states that 'Illegitimate children are almost unknown'. There is in any case no stigma attached to bastardy. The names bhula for the child and bhuli for the mother are only given when the father is not known and when no other man is willing to accept the responsibility for the paternity. This happens very rarely. In his long life Mahatu can remember only one example.

The bhula child suffers from no disabilities. 'I would marry my daughter to him', says Mahatu 'we do not think him bad. It was his mother who was bad. But she too did nothing'.

When the mother marries and has other children, the bhula child has almost equal rights with them. If it is a boy, he can inherit, and shares with the other brothers but he gets a little less than they do.

No bastard figures in any of the myths, legends or songs and the word is not used in Baiga gali.[5]

Moreover, the lamsena or serving son-in-law, is a common Baiga way of disguising a bastard and absorbing him into society.

'Sometimes if the lamsena is old enough and the girl is willing, they are married first and the boy does his work later. This is done when the girl is suspected of an intrigue with some one, or when she is made pregnant by an unknown lover. The lamsena is the official refuge of the unmarried mother. His duty is to save a girl's reputation'.[6]

Among the Chenchus, 'The seducer of an unmarried girl who has become pregnant is usually persuaded to take her into his house. Should he refuse, he has to pay a fine which is 'eaten' by the elders, and the child is brought up by the girl's family, but belongs to the father's clan'.[7]

This apparent absence of a problem is also true of Santals and Campbell writing in 1915 went so far as to declare that 'no illegitimate children are born into the Santal community'.[8]

This statement is not entirely correct but it nonetheless approximately summarises the position.

What are the reasons for this state of affairs?

II INFANTICIDE

A first and significant check on Santal bastardy is infanticide.[9] This is now-a-days very rarely practised but Bompas has recorded a Santal view that 'often if a father will not acknowledge a child the mother will strangle it at birth and bury the body. Men who practise sorcery dig up the bones of such murdered infants and use them as rattles when doing their sorceries and are helped by them to deceive people'.[10]

In the myth of the Sikhar Raja, abandonment is an integral part of the story and in the version recorded by Bompas, 'A certain woman was with child but could not say by whom she was pregnant so she fled into the jungle and at the foot of a clump of bamboos gave birth to twins, a boy and girl; and then went home leaving the children lying in the jungle'.[11]

As recently as 1944, a case of infanticide led to two Santal women hanging themselves in jail. A young Santal girl, Mundu Marandi, had been married to a Santal and then divorced. She was working as a servant in the house of a Muhammadan of Gopalpur and after some time became pregnant by him. At the village meeting she declined to say who was the father and matters hung fire until the time of birth. In September 1944 she gave birth to a girl and the same night her mother took the baby and after smothering it to death buried it in a small hill near the house. The girl's aunt had advised her to do this and when the matter came to the police both the old women were arrested and lodged in jail. A few days later they hanged themselves by tying their cloths to the bars of the cell. In this case, the shame arising out of their daughter's misconduct with a Muhammadan proved too much for the women and after disposing of the child they killed themselves to avoid the agony of a trial.

III ABORTION

Next to infanticide the most obvious check on Santal bastardy is abortion. This is by no means uncommon, and the stock Santal term for a girl who has had a child outside marriage includes the case of a girl who has miscarried. She is a penda dopot chadwi,* a pot with a cracked base, or a cupi chadwi, a split tail. Her status is better than an ordinary girl who has been divorced, she can still be wedded as an unmarried girl, and she can still receive *sindur* at her wedding. But her status is slightly lower,** and her father can demand only the bride price of a girl who has been divorced.

It would be a mistake, however, to suppose that every unmarried girl attempts abortion. The main circumstance in which abortion is tried is when a girl is pregnant and the boy is debarred from marrying her. He may possibly be a boy of her own sept or even a kinsman, a brother's son or an uncle. He may even be a Diku, a Kamar boy, a Paharia. In such cases discovery will mean punishment and possibly, bitlaha. A marriage with him will be out of the question. The actual father will never be accepted as the legal father. Abortion is then the only way and it is significant that in all the bitlahas which occurred in the last five years I have not heard of one in which the guilty woman was pregnant.

IV MARRIAGE

Abortion however is at most a check. It is not always successful and it is not always tried. A girl may hope that her boy will marry her and she may let her pregnancy develop until the child is born.

> Mirza, you had and had me
> And now a boy is born
> O my love
> Wait and hear
> The name of the boy

*The term also includes a girl who has lived with a boy as his wife, has not been given *sindur* and is then divorced.

**In the Karbindha, Nonihat, Poreyahat and Chandna areas she is treated as a *chadwi* and can only receive *sindur* on a flower.

As soon therefore as a girl is visibly pregnant and the news of her condition spreads through the village, her parents question her about it, and the matter goes to the jogmanjhi.

In Silingi village, when Melco Marandi became pregnant, the jogmanjhi said to her 'Your parents tell me you are not looking the same. Have you got anything?' 'Yes, I have found something.' 'Where did you get it ?' 'From a boy of the paranik's.' 'Why did you do it ?' 'He said we would keep each other.' 'How many months ?' 'Two'.

The jogmanjhi then interviews the boy and a village council sits to settle the matter.

If the boy accepts the paternity and agrees to marry the girl, the solution is fairly simple. He pays a fee or fine of two goats to the manjhi, the pon or bride price to the father and the girl goes to his house. She becomes his wife by order or pulling in. While the child is in the womb full dress wedding is forbidden but once the child has been born, a dol bapla can proceed and the girl can be lifted in the basket and given *sindur*. There is only one qualification. The baby itself cannot enter the basket with its mother and must not be present at the wedding.

In such cases, the fact that the child is born in marriage nullifies the fact that conception occurred outside it. The child is no different from any child conceived and born months after a wedding.

V THE NAMING CEREMONY

Not every boy, however, agrees to marry and in certain cases the father is unknown. In such circumstances, the child may be born out of marriage and the naming ceremony by which it enters a family will be endangered. This ceremony of nim dak' mandi I will now briefly describe.

When a Santal is born in a Santal house, the village becomes impure and information must at once be sent to the naeke or village priest. The naeke impersonates the village on its ghostly side and is the means by which it senses its pollution. When the news reaches him, he at once goes and bathes. With the news oil is also sent but if the child's father is unknown, the naeke says 'In whose name can I wash ?' He then refuses the oil and washes for an unknown child. But if the father is known he washes in water and rubs himself with oil 'in the name of the father and the child'. This rids him of his personal pollution and the naming makes clear the impurity from which he is absolved. When this is done he can again take food. Later, on the third, fifth or any uneven day, the owner of the house summons the villagers* and the ritual of nim dak' mandi is held.

In this ceremony, there are five essential participants—the priest, the child's mother and father, the midwife and the child itself. If the naeke is absent the kudum naeke or the naeke's son officiates. And if these are also absent, either a villager acts as a naeke by proxy or a dummy naeke is made by planting a stick in the ground. Without the naeke's presence whether factual or symbolic—the ceremony cannot go on. Similarly, the child's parents must attend and if the known father is absent, the girl's father, a relative or a proxy must act as substitute.

The ceremony begins with the shaving of the naeke. This is done by a villager who is made the barber and is confined to dressing the cheeks and chins. After this, the manjhi and the other villagers are shaved, and finally the child's father. When this has been done the barber shaves a little patch on the child's head, carefully collects the hair in a leaf-cup, pours some oil on it and gives it to the midwife. The midwife then rubs the child's head with some oil, some washing earth and finally some turmeric. The men then go to a tank for bathing and the naeke is the first to take a bath.

While they are away the midwife takes the arrow which cut the umbilical cord, winds two threads of cotton round it, takes the leaf-cup with the hair and goes with the women for bathing. At the ghat she plants the arrow in the water, makes marks of *sindur* and lamp black on the ground and then 'buys the ghat' by putting the child's hair and a thread in the water and letting them float away. The women bathe and go back to the

*The summoning is by the owner and not by the godet. If a birth occurs during the ten days of Sohrae, only the naeke and manjhi attends and only they and the child's father have flour put on their chests.

house and the midwife then soaks the other thread in *haldi* and ties it round the child's waist.

The mother now sits on the verandah with the child in her lap and some atnak' leaves in her hand. The midwife mixes cowdung in water and then lets it trickle into the left hand of the mother. The mother dabs it on her head and sips a little. After that three leaf-cups of the same mixture are handed to the midwife who punctures each with a finger and tosses them away. The child is then taken inside. Here two little cakes of pitar are pressed against its cheeks, legs and chest. After that the midwife makes a thick white paste from rice flour. She first marks the four legs of the mother's cot and then goes round the courtyard marking first the chest of the naeke and then the other villagers in the order of shaving.* She ends with the child's father. When the men are finished she begins with the naeke's wife and marks the other women in the same order as their husbands.

The child is then formally named. Its sept is always that of its father and if the marriage is not in gharjawae form, a first son is always given its first name after its father's father and a girl after its father's mother. When the known father boycots the ceremony, the name is decided by the girl and her father.

The midwife then comes out and announces the name. She salutes the naeke and after that, the other villagers. Rice is boiled with nim leaves and after the head of the house has offered to his immediate ancestors the village drinks the rice and nim water. With the end of the ceremony, the village bongas are purified and the village as a whole is cleansed. The child is now part of a family and has a father.

VI THE UNMARRIED MOTHER AND THE KNOWN FATHER

For a boy who agrees to marry a girl, the naming ceremony offers little embarrassment. The child is shaved in his name, he gives it his sept and in fact the situation is the same as if the child had been conceived in wedlock.

*In certain areas it is only children whose chests are marked—the flour paste being sprinkled at the feet of adults.

While accepting the paternity, however, a boy may refuse to marry the girl.

Prem Kumar Murmu of Kusma admitted before the village that he had made Kapra Tudu pregnant, but as his father was against the marriage, he refused to marry her.

Similarly the boy may deny the paternity but the village may fasten its responsibility on him.

In Bordaha Bale Hembrom fell in love with a girl of his village. He first met her in the jungle and then came to her almost every night and slept in her house. After a few months, the girl became pregnant and Bale hurriedly married another girl. The matter was referred to the jogmanjhi and although the boy denied the connection, it was common knowledge and the village overruled him.

In both these circumstances, the village requires the boy to maintain the girl during the later stages of the pregnancy from the date the village meets to the time the child is born. He must also compensate her for suckling the baby. After that he either takes the child into his house or goes on maintaining it.[12] He must also pay the girl's father a correct bride-price as well as the brother's due, and must meet the expenses of the naming ceremony. If the boy is married whether before or after the conception, he must pay the bride-price of a married man who marries an unmarried girl. When the girl can work again she gets no further maintenance and must keep herself.* If she ultimately marries, she will marry as a dangua or unmarried girl but her bride price will be that of a girl who has been divorced.

On the social side, the known father is accepted as the real father and at the naming ceremony the child is named as if the parents had been married. If it is a boy he is named after the boy's father and if its known father does not attend the ceremony the child is given its father's sept by proxy. The attitude of the known father is therefore, immaterial and once the village has decided the matter the child's paternity is assured.

Lakhi Kisku of Dhaka became pregnant by Hopna Murmu.

*In the Taljhari, Boarijore, Raksi and Rajabhita areas, the boy must also pay the girl chadaodi or divorce money.

The case went to the village council and Hopna admitted the connection. It was then arranged that he would take of the girl to his house. His father however, kept postponing matters and at last the girl's father called another meeting. The boy's parent who was handi-manjhi came and a quarrel ensued. The villagers then appealed to the sardar who came to the village three times. Each time the boy's father avoided meeting him and after the third failure the villagers resorted to the minor form of excommunication known as pante begar. The girl's father was still hoping that the boy would marry her, and made no attempt to arrange another husband. The boy's parent did nothing and in January 1943 a child was born. On its birth the villagers pante begared the girl and her father but took them back after the naming ritual when they paid three rupees. At this ceremony the girl named the child Dukhia Murmu after the boy's father and her own father officiated in place of the boy. A little later Dukhia arranged another girl for his son and the wedding took place the same hot weather. Finding no other way, the girl's father then went to court and the magistrate awarded her five rupees a month as maintenance for the child. This was obviously only a temporary solution, and when the matter came to me in revision, the question was how to adjust it permanently. All the villagers said that the boy must take the child since the latter would inherit his land. Lakhi's father did not press for the brother's dues or the costs of the naming. It was decided therefore, that after suckling the child another three months, Lakhi would hand it over to Hopna. Twelve rupees would be paid as bride price and twenty rupees as cost of the milk. This was all that could be done but the girl wept at losing the child.

In cases such as these, the child may be born out of marriage but it is only in this sense that it is illegitimate. It is not called a *bidhua*, a bastard, for its father is known and its naming ceremony has been performed. It has scarcely any disabilities. Its mother and father do not live together but the child is not without a father. In fact, in most cases, the child is brought up in its father's house. If the child is a girl, the father arranges her marriage. If the child is a boy, he is as much a son as a boy born in marriage. He can demand a partition and can inherit his father's land and movables in equal shares with any other son. Even if he is living with his mother his right to his father's land and movables does not cease. Moreover, he is part of Santal society. He has access to his father's bongas. He possesses his father's sept. His sole tragedy is that to go to his father he must leave his mother but even then his case is no worse than that of children in any marriage which fails.

VII THE UNKNOWN FATHER

There remains the case in which paternity is denied and the village holds that the matter is not proved.

> O my love, come inside
> Like yours the hands and feet
> Like your the eyes and face
> O my love a child has come.

But other evidence may be lacking. The girl's friends may know of her friendship but no one may have actually seen the boy and girl together. Or the boy may have promised the girl everything but given her nothing, which connects him with her. At the same time, the girl's pregnancy may cause a revulsion in the boy.

> While you were keen to have me
> You were always about
> But now I am having a baby
> You keep away.

The boy may wildly deny any kind of intimacy and if they have been careful lovers, it is only the girl's word against the boy's. Occasionally the circumstances may be such that even the girl does not know which boy is to blame.

Dukhni Kisku of Nipania was a half witted girl who had been with many boys. No one knew who was the father of her child and Dukhni herself could not say.*

*The Santal proverb—'A thousand ojhas and the patient dies'—refers to the plight of an unmarried girl who is pregnant by many lovers.

In these circumstances, the true father can neither maintain the child nor give him his sept. He is an unknown stranger who is beyond the scope of village control. Yet the child is not necessarily illegitimate. A substitute father is permissible and there are two ways in which this is arranged.

VIII THE FALSE FATHER : THE BOUGHT HUSBAND

The first type of false father is one who is secured by marriage. When the pregnancy is unadjusted, the girl's father and his household are pante begared or semi-outcasted and they can only return to caste by arranging a father for the child and either giving a small feast or paying some rupees.

If the child's father is known but his relations with the mother amounted to clan or kin incest he is debarred from marrying her or giving the child his name. He must therefore arrange a false father by—obtaining for the girl a bought husband.*

In such circumstances the girl's parents look round for a boy who will marry the girl and accept the child as his own. In some cases they offer to take him as a ghar jawae, in others they remit the bride price and the brother's due or if no boy is obtainable on lesser terms, they purchase a husband by paying him cash, giving him cattle, or even if the village approves by giving him some land.

Dulhan Tudu of Dhanbad did not know who was the father of her child, so her father bought a husband for her by exempting him from payment of bride-price. The husband accepted the child as his own and the boy has now inherited his land.

In Majdiha a girl became pregnant enec' halante 'by gathering it in a dance'. The father was not known, so Phoce Tudu was brought from Lukhipur. He was bought for ten rupees, exempted from a bride price and married the girl before she gave birth. He is living in her house. The child was born but died later.

In Damakol a girl became pregnant and the boy could not be proved. Her father, therefore, bought Dukhia Hansdak' of

*For examples of this form of adjustment, see my report, *Bitlaha*.

Belpahari. He gave him ten maunds of paddy and a pair of bullocks and exempted him from a bride price and all the other dues. Dukhia lived in the girl's house until the child was born. He then went back to his home taking his wife and false child with him.

In Kalhachak Ningli Hembrom became pregnant by an unknown lover. Udai Besra was therefore brought from Bansberwa. He was given a pair of bullocks, twelve maunds of paddy and twelve rupees and excused the customary payments. He then took the girl to his house and wedded her in sangha form.

In Bara Lakhmi, the daughter of Sankho Kisku became pregnant and Dhano Tudu of Ulatari was purchased as a husband. He was given eight bighas of land with the approval of the villagers and the child has since been named after his father.

When the terms of purchase are discussed, it is settled who will pay the costs of the naming ceremony. These are often met by the girl's father and when Rengta Kisku of Dumdumi was purchased for a girl of Garduara he was given ten maunds of paddy, a dhoti and a pair of bullocks, was exempted from all other payments and had all the costs of the naming ceremony borne for him.

In Kajikend on the other hand, the father of Sugda Hansdak' purchased a husband more cheaply. He gave him a pair of bullocks and exempted him from the bride-price and other payments but when the child was born, the husband paid the cost of the naming.

In all these cases, the boy became the girl's husband, took over full responsibility for the child, named it as if he were the true father and the child acquired all the rights of a true son or daughter.*

IX THE BOUGHT FATHER

Not all families, however, can arrange a bought husband.

*In Ranidih Parbet Baske was bought a husband for twenty-five rupees. The child was a girl and when she grew up her false father even married her in ghar jawae form and she has since inherited his lands.

Moreover, if the child is a boy, a false father may not always want him to inherit his land. Another method is therefore tried. Instead of linking the false father to the girl by marriage a man or boy is produced who becomes the child's father but without any civil responsibilities. At the naming ceremony he is the last to be shaved, to receive the marks of flour on his chest and to drink the rice and nim water. He acquiesces in the midwife's announcement. He gives the child his sept. But he does not marry its mother. The child acquires no rights in his land. He is not required to maintain it. He becomes a 'god-father' rather than a father and his obligations are neither civil nor economic. But his action saves the child. The girl's father pays a few rupees or gives a small feast and the family is re-admitted to the tribe.*

In Baramasia the daughter of Odga Tudu became pregnant by a boy of the Tudu sept. Her father did not purchase a husband but paid another Santal twenty-five rupees for naming the child.

In Malipara the daughter of Fudan Marandi gave birth to a child and Charan Hansdak' of her village was induced to give the child his sept on payment of twelve rupees.

In such cases, the child is a bidhua, or bastard, only until its naming has been done. After that no one may call it a bidhua, and if a villager does so, he is sharply fined. The child stays on with its mother. It possesses and inherits only her own land. If its mother marries later her husband may, if he

*In certain cases although a boy may refuse to be bought as a husband he may be willing to accord the child the full rights of a son. If, for example, he is married but without children, and is anxious for a son, he may agree to be bought as a full father but on the distinct understanding that he does not marry its mother. In such cases, he names the child as if it were his own, takes it to his house and accepts full responsibility. He does not however take the girl and she is treated as if she had been married and then immediately divorced.

In Harma Dheba Kisku was purchased as a husband of Theme Baske of Patro. The girl's father gave him a pair of bullocks, a bale of paddy and twelve rupees in cash. Dheba Kisku took the boy to his house, named him after his father and has since treated him as his true son. But the girl has remained with her father and Dheba Kisku is not acting as her husband.

likes, adopt it but he need not do so. Otherwise, if it is a girl, she will be married when she grows up. But, if it is a boy, he has to live by day labour. The child's disability is not its lack of permanent father. Its main disability is its lack of land.

X THE MULTIPLE LOVER

If the father is sometimes unknown because the actual lover is not proved, cases also arise in which several boys admit a joint connection. When this happens the true father remains equally unknown but the responsibility can be declared and fixed. In such cases the boys are fined and with the money either a Santal is paid to give the child his sept or a husband is purchased for the girl. Part of the money goes to the girl and some of it is kept by the village.

The daughter of Dharma Hembrom of Ladapathar became pregnant and proved before the village that three boys had relations with her. The boys admitted the connection and were fined seven rupees each. In this case, the village did not take any of the money but gave it all to the girl's father. The girl's elder sister's husband was then purchased and the girl became a co-wife.

In Panchuara the daughter of Surai Soren became pregnant and implicated three boys. All were fined on proof and each had to pay four maunds of paddy to the girl's father and ten rupees each to the village. After that, the girl's father purchased another man and he took the girl to his house as a wife.

When the daughter of Matru Tudu of Kundli became pregnant and four boys admitted responsibility. In this case all the boys and the girl herself were each fined ten rupees. The money was taken by the village but the village itself purchased a father for the child and the girl's parents took him as a ghar jawae.

In a case from Amjhor Phugri Pauria became pregnant and six boys admitted joint responsibility. Each of the boys was fined fifteen rupees and out of this sum, the village kept six rupees for a feast and the girl's brother-in-law was given the five rupees for giving child his sept. The rest of the money was given to the girl.

In cases where a girl has had relations with several boys

but one is more involved than the others the latter is sometimes required to pay a larger fine. In Mohulpahari the daughter of Sukri Marandi had intercourse with three boys and became pregnant. All three admitted responsibility but one of them had been with the girl more frequently than the others. He was, therefore, fined ten rupees and the others five rupees each. In addition, the three boys and the girl each gave the village a goat. All the money was paid to the girl's father. When the child was born it was given the sept of the boy who was fined ten rupees but he did not become the girl's husband.

In a final case which vividly expresses the Santal attitude the daughter of Dalu Marandi of Guhiajuri became pregnant and on being questioned by the villagers she named Lodo Hembrom as responsible. Lodo denied all relations with her but the villagers forced the paternity on him. Twenty days later labour pains started but for two days the child was not delivered. When the midwife saw the obstruction she told the girl that the baby seemed to be of several fathers and she must know their names, so that a mark of *sindur* might be given for each and the delivery of the child secured. Thereupon the girl named fourteen boys, the midwife gave fourteen marks and shortly afterwards a girl baby was born. When Lodo heard that the girl had admitted intercourse with fourteen boys he obstinately refused to have anything to do with the child or its mother and the village too could obviously not abide by its former decision. There was a deadlock for a month during which no naming ceremony was performed and finally the girl and her parents left caste and became Christians.

XI THE MARRIED MOTHER AND THE ABSENT HUSBAND

There is yet one further situation, when the girl is unmarried, divorcee or a widow, a true or a false father can be settled and the naming ceremony can proceed. But it is not only these who can have bidhua children. A married girl can also give birth to an illegitimate child.

A Santal of Godda went to the war. He came home on leave in September and returned in October, and the following September his wife gave birth to a child.

In Manoharchok Randhon Marandi stayed with her

husband only a few days and then returned to her father. About a year later she became pregnant. The villagers said to her father 'How is it that without staying at her husband's house her body is full?'

In such circumstances, the adjustment depends on whether the girl has been living in her husband's house and whether her husband has a younger brother. If a girl becomes pregnant in her husband's absence and her father-in-law considers a young son responsible, the matter is not taken to the village and either the woman's husband is treated as the child's father or the child goes to the younger brother. Similarly if on his return the husband raises no objection no further steps are taken. If he does not wish to keep his wife the younger brother takes her.

Suna Manjhi of Rangasola had a wife and two children. He went away to the collieries and did not return. His wife remained in his house and after four years gave birth to a girl. Her husband's younger brother admitted paternity and was fined two rupees and gave a feast. After that the woman and the child continued living with him as if nothing had happened.

It is not however in every case that the woman is with her father-in-law and circumstances also do not always implicate her husband's younger brother.

When a family connection is ruled out a meeting is called and the village adjudicates. If the boy is 'tracked down' he must take the child and give him his sept. If the boy marries the girl he must pay the husband double the bride price and if the marriage is recent, the cost of the wedding. If the husband keeps her he can claim celan gitil for 'cleaning the pot'. If neither the husband nor the boy keeps her the boy must indemnify the husband as if he had taken her and also give the girl chadaodi or divorce money. He must also pay the girl the 'cost of the milk', maintain the child and give it his sept. He also pays the manjhi five rupees for 'saving his head'.

In the case from Manorchok, the girl named Bhudu Tudu as the father. The boy at first denied it but later admitted it. He then married her and paid her husband a double bride price.

In Simaldahi Khendec' Murmu had gone to the war and

while he was away his wife gave birth to a child by the son of Sham Soren. At the village meeting the boy paid a double bride price and took the child and its mother.

In other cases, when the father is not proved or is unknown the responsibility devolves either on the husband or the girl's father. If the child is born in the husband's house, it is this house which becomes impure. The husband, if he is still away, a brother must then either give the child his sept or arrange a false father. If a false father is given, the wife is then divorced and sent back with the child to her father. But if the child is born in the house of the girl's father, it is he who must secure a father for the child and until he does so his house is pante begared. The married mother with an absent husband is then no different from the unmarried mother who has no husband at all.

XII THE BIDHUA CHILD

But if all these expedients fail, what then is the situation?

If the unmarried mother is away from her village, working in the tea gardens or as a labourer in Bengal, the child is born and remains a bidhua. Because it has no father, neither true nor false, it has also no sept. It cannot worship any family bongas. It inherits no land. It can live only as a labourer. So long as it is known to be a bastard it cannot even marry. It is not even a Santal but a mere nobody with neither a tribe nor a sept. In such a situation the child lives with its mother until it grows up. After that it goes away. It leaves the area and settles where no one has ever heard of it. It assumes a sept and keeps its bastard origin a secret. Such cases, however, are so rare that I know of no examples. Santals talk of cases but no one can remember any. 'They have all left the country'. Today the permanent bidhua is a possibility rather than a fact.

If, however, the unmarried mother is still in her village other factors intervene. Until the naming has been done, the whole village is maila or unclean and no wedding festivals or sacrifices can take place. At Mahuatanr a child was born during a wedding in May 1944. The boy's party had arrived but the wedding stopped as the village at once became polluted. Although, therefore, the child was only a few hours old, the naming was done forthwith and only then did the wedding proceed. Since the giving of a name and sept to the child is an essential part of the purification the village remains polluted until a father is secured. The inconvenience is so great that everyone wants to end it quickly and there is a general interest in getting a father promptly. Accordingly if the girl and her parents fail to arrange a father, the village itself intervenes. 'To save the child's head' they either fine the family or subscribe for bringing the household back into the tribe and they compel the jogmanjhi or another villager to act as the father.

In Manglapara a widow, Lukhi Soren, had a baby girl. No one agreed to be bought, so in the end the villagers intervened. They chose an old man and against his will they forced him to give her his sept of Hansdak'.

In Mahuadangal a widow had a child. The alleged father absconded, so the family was pante begared. As the father was not proved, one way or the other, the naming ceremony was not performed and the village remained impure for seven months. Finally, the alleged father appeared, admitted his connexion and named the child. This purified the village, but because of the delay, the widow was fined a large goat.*

*In a folk-tale recorded by C.H. Bompas, a similar delay in identifying the father results in a fine and a penalty feast. 'Once upon a time there was a girl whose parents took the greatest care that she should not be familiar with any of the young men of the village. But in spite of their precautions she formed an intimacy with a young man and was presently found to be with child. When this became known the villagers held a panchayat to enquire into the matter, but the girl flatly declined to give any information and her father and brothers were unable to point out the offender. So the village elders decided to let the matter stand over till the child was born.

When the birth took place the question arose in whose name its head should be shaved; as its father was still unknown, the villagers decided that this should be settled when the child was old enough to talk. So when the child was two or three years old and could prattle a little, the girl's father went to the headman and paranik and asked them what was to be done. They said that he must pay a fine to them and another to the villagers because he had made the village unclean for so long, and give a feast to the villagers and then they would find out the father of the child and make him marry the girl; and if he refused to do this, he would be outcasted. The unfortunate man agreed and then the jogmanjhi and the godet were sent to call all the men of the neighbourhood to a meeting. *(Contd.)*

In Kusumpukhur a girl gave birth to a son. She claimed that Gurwa Hansdak' was the father. Gurwa denied it and the village did not feel it was proved. But the girl was not satisfied. She refused to arrange a false father and at the naming her father officiated and named the child after Gurwa's father, Shyam. The girl has not married since—'she has no abode'—and the boy who is eight years old is still with her.

In this case the village did not approve of the naming but neither did it reject it. The naming father acquired no responsibilities. He was no different from a father who had been bought or compelled to give a name. The child inherited no land and received no maintenance. But its mother's insistence made it a Santal and by its acquiescence the village ceased to be impure.

Finally, if no one in the village is constrained to give the child his sept and all efforts by the village fail, the girl's father is made to give a goat and the girl and the child are expelled from the village. The goat is then sacrificed at the manjhithan and the village is purified. This is the last resort when all else fails but I do not know of any case in which this has been done.

XIII CONCLUSION

In creating this situation, three factors are obviously of prime importance. There is first the religious role of the father. He is the agent who inducts a child into the bongas and as a corollary into the family and the tribe. If a child is to be a Santal he must, therefore, have a father. Secondly, all Santals are loath to lose a Santal for the tribe would obviously be weakened if the children of Santal mothers were not all

---

They assembled in their best clothes and pagris and sat down in rows, and in the middle a circle was drawn on the ground; then prayers were offered to Chando and the child was set in the circle and told to find its father. The child began to walk slowly along the lines of men but it did not stop till it came to its real father, who was sitting a little apart, and then it threw itself into his arms. Thus the truth was discovered and the man married the girl and as he was very poor went to live in his father-in-law's house.' (Bompas, 172-3)

Santals. Lastly, there is the intimate connexion between removing the pollution of child-birth and admitting the child to the bongas. In Santal practice, the two go together, and to perform the one, the other is necessary. It is due to these three factors that the illegitimate child is almost unknown in Santal society.

REFERENCES

1. S.C. Roy, *The Oraons* (Ranchi, 1915), 247-8.
2. Dalton, op. cit., 248.
3. W.V. Grigson, *The Maria Gonds of Bastar* (Oxford, 1938), 248.
4. C. Von Fürer Haimendorf in collaboration with Elizabeth Von Fürer Haimendorf, *The Reddis of the Bison Hills* (London, 1945), 129.
5. Verrier Elwin, *The Baiga* (London, 1940), 288.
6. Verrier Elwin, op. cit., 288.
7. C. Von Fürer Haimendorf, *The Chenchus* (London, 1944), 174.
8. A. Campbell, 'Rules of Succession and Position of Property as observed by the Santals', *J.B.O.R.S.*, Vol. I (1915), 23.
9. Gorer records a similar practice among Lepchas—'It is a very great disgrace for a girl to produce a bastard and it is believed that possibly some girls bear their bastards in field-houses or the forest and kill them rather than confess to the act' (Geoffrey Gorer, *Himalayan Village* (London, 1967), 173.

   Shamrao Hivale similarly records of the Pardhans. 'The one unforgivable sin for an unmarried girl is to conceive. The first thing is to attempt an abortion. If this fails and the baby is actually born, it is sometimes quietly put out of the way. I heard of one case long ago where such a baby was left in the house by the mother and in her absence the grandmother mixed a little ash in water, gave it to the child and thus killed it'. [*The Pardhans of the Upper Narbada Valley* (Bombay, 1946), 161].
10. C.H. Bompas, *Folk-lore of the Santal Parganas* (London, 1909), 416.
11. Ibid., 405.
12. In Lakher society, 'As soon as the riathama (bastard's price) has been paid a bastard belongs to its father, but the mother is responsible for it till it is three years old'. [N.F. Parry, *The Lakhers* (London, 1932), 279].

6

THE STEPCHILD

I INTRODUCTION

IF THE illegitimate child is quickly absorbed by Santal society, the stepchild also benefits from the attitude of Santals to their children. Second wives may occasionally neglect the children of their predecessors but a stepfather is usually kind and indulgent. Indeed the fact that his wife has already had offspring may sometime give her an added value and surround her children with reflected favour. If a Santal himself has had no children his wife's fertility affords him ground for hoping that for him also she may bear a son, and even if this hope is not fulfilled his stepchildren give life and vigour to his days.

II THE DUTIES OF THE STEPFATHER

When a house has stepchildren, their rights are determined by the circumstances in which they have gone to their stepfather. The accepted principle is that if a Santal marries a divorced girl or a widow and then takes her children to his house, he becomes responsible for maintaining them in food and clothes, treating them in sickness and performing their initiation and marriage ceremonies. In return his stepchildren must accept his discipline, and assist him in the work of the house and the fields.

They must pay their stepfather all their earnings from day labour and only if they leave his house can they keep their wages. A stepson will not be given any wages for his work in the family but a stepdaughter is allowed gleanings from the time she helps in harvesting. If a stepson is married and remains in the house, his wife also can claim. If a stepson is quarrelsome or disobedient his stepfather can expel him after obtaining the approval of the village.

Jeth Murmu of Latberwa married a wife with three daughters by her former husband. He brought all of them to his house and has since performed the marriage of the two eldest. The youngest has not as yet been married and is still in his house.

In Telni, Champai Tudu married a widow with four children. He kept them in his house and when three of them fell ill, he met all the expenses of their treatment. On one occasion the eldest daughter was ill for two months and her stepfather gave the ojha a goat, four pigeons, two fowls and a dhoti for making the sacrifices.

All these expenses must be met by the stepfather from his own resources but in certain circumstances he derives assistance.

If his stepchildren have no paternal grandfather, uncles, or cousins but their father has left land their mother remains their legal guardian but until a stepson is adult, their stepfather can assist her in its cultivation and keep the children from its produce.

A Santal of Sahri married Ratni Murmu of Simaldhab. Ratni was a widow with a son by her first husband and no agnates. When she married she took her son to her second husband's house and the stepfather is now cultivating the stepson's land.

In Phulsahri, Chandrai Hembrom married a widow with two sons by her former husband. As the boys were young and their father had no brothers, Chandrai took them to his house and supervised the cultivation of their lands. Later, one of them died and Chandrai has since performed the marriage of the other and his stepson has now taken charge of his lands.

In such cases a stepfather does not himself acquire any right in the land. He is at most a custodian for his wife and stepchildren. When his stepson grows up, he must make over the land to him and should the latter die without legal heirs, the land reverts to the village community. But the cultivation of extra fields lightens his burden. Their produce swells the family stock and in many cases it may more than cover the cost of keeping the children and their mother.

III AID BY AGNATES

If the act of keeping stepchildren normally charges their stepfather with full responsibility for their welfare, arrangements are also made by which the rearing of the children is done by their mother and stepfather while the agnates arrange for their marriages and supply part or all of their keep.

Kalidas Tudu of Beoa married a widow with a son and daughter by her former husband. By agreement with the children's paternal uncles he took the stepchildren to his house while their uncles took charge of their lands. When the stepson grew up his marriage was performed by his paternal uncles and he was given back his land.

In Dalu, Suphal Marandi married a widow with a son and daughter by her former husband. As the daughter was very young the widow took her to Suphal's house and Suphal has since been maintaining his stepdaughter.

In such cases the duties of the stepfather were modified by family agreement. If this had not been done the stepfather himself would have had to meet the cost so long as the children were with him.

IV GIFTS TO STEPCHILDREN

Finally, although, a stepfather is in many ways an assistant guardian of his stepchildren he can only become their true or legal father by a formal act of adoption. Just as he himself has no right of inheritance in his stepson's land or movables, a stepchild only acquires rights his stepfather's land or property after the ceremony of bonga tala. Without adoption, a stepchild is not an heir and it is only by a duly sanctioned gift that he can acquire any of his stepfather's land. For securing such a gift village approval is necessary and this can be accorded only when there is no greater family of the stepfather, or his nearest agnates agree. If there is opposition the accepted principle is that the village cannot and does not agree.

In Sahardal Naran Murmu consulted his agnates and with their consent and the approval of the village community he gave his stepson one and a half bigha of land.

Jolha Hansdak' of Boro Chapor gave his stepson three bighas of land with the approval of his agnates and the villagers. Jolha has a son from his second wife and also a brother.

In Jamua Narayan Core had seven sons by his first wife. He then married a widow with a son by her former husband. His holding was large and with the approval of his sons and the villagers he gave three paddy fields and one upland to his stepson.

In all these cases, gifts of land were made with the consent of the agnates and with village approval and if these had not been forthcoming, the stepson could not have obtained any of his stepfather's land.

In Murgabani Muchia Marandi married a widow with three sons by her first husband. He took his three stepsons to his house brought them up and performed their marriages. He did not, however, give them any of his land. Two of them are now living at the house of their wives while the third has received settlement of some vacant land from the village community.

V CONCLUSION

The stepchild in Santal society does not therefore receive exceptional privileges. His true place remains always in the family of his father and a limit is set to the duties of his stepfather. But his claims as a child are fully conceded. He is guaranteed maintenance. His marriage is performed and when he grows up he is accorded a normal place in Santal society.

7

GUARDIANS

I THE SANTAL CONCEPTION OF MINORITY

SO LONG as Santal children are small their first requirements are training in tribal ways and the protection of a guardian. There are not, however, any rigid ideas concerning when a child becomes a major. Until the age of sixteen children are usually not regarded as responsible for their actions but once a girl is married, and goes to live with her husband she is usually not thought of as a minor. Similarly when a boy has had his initiation ceremony performed, has begun to plough and is capable of earning his living ceases to be a gupi kora, or 'cowherd' and becomes for all practical purposes adult. Until this stage is reached every boy and girl must have a guardian.

II THE ORDER OF GUARDIANSHIP

For determining a child's guardian the most important factor is the structure of the family. If the child's father is joint with his father, brothers or paternal uncles he will have only a subordinate or residuary role and the head of the joint household will be the final guardian. Similarly, if the child's mother is married to a ghar jawae and is joint with her father, brothers or paternal uncles, the mother will remain a parent but the actual function of guardianship will vest in the head of the household.

On the other hand, if the child's parents are separate, the order of guardianship will be determined by the nature of the marriage. In all marriage except those in ghar jawae form the father is the final guardian and the responsibility for keeping the child, administering his land and performing his ceremonies descends in the following order :

Order	Name of relation
1.	Father
2.	Elder brother if major
3.	Mother if not remarried
4.	Elder sister if married to a ghar jawae
5.	Ghar jawae husband of an elder sister if remaining on the land
6.	Stepmother if not remarried
7.	Father's father if still active
8.	Father's brother*
9.	Father's brother's son
10.	Elder sister if married
11.	Father's sister if married
12.	Mother's brother
13.	Mother's father
14.	Mother's mother
15.	Mother if remarried
16.	Stepfather

*Bodding states that, 'As between elder and youngerbr others the younger brothers most commonly act; a possible cause for this may be the relationship often found between a man and his hili i.e., elder brother's wife'. (P.O. Bodding, *Santal Folk Tales* (Oslo, 1925), I, 40, note.)
In the event of dispute, however, an elder brother will take precedence.

If the guardian is a man, he is also responsible for the child's conduct while if a woman is the guardian, her husband will act as her assistant or deputy in all matters concerning the minor's behaviour. If she has no husband, the next male guardian will perform this function for her. If the child's guardian is its mother (serial 3), the person responsible for the child's conduct will be either serial 5 (the ghar jawae husband of an elder sister if living in the village), serial 7 (its father's father if still active), or serial 8 (its father's brother, if neither serials 5 or 7 are available). This male guardian will be in charge of discipline while the child's female guardian will decide all other matters.

If the marriage is in a ghar jawae form, the mother takes the place of the father and the order of guardianship is radically altered.

Order	Name of relation
1.	Mother
2.	Father (if not remarried without family approval and if remaining on the land)
3.	Elder brother if married
4.	Elder sister if married to a ghar jawae
5.	Ghar jawae husband of elder sister if remaining on the land
6.	Stepfather if not remarried and remaining on the land
7.	Mother's father (if active)
8.	Mother's brother
9.	Mother's brother's son
10.	Mother's mother
11.	Elder sister if married
12.	Mother's sister if married
13.	Father if remarried without family approval
14.	Father's brother
15.	Father's father
16.	Father's mother
17.	Stepmother

These orders of preference assume that the child will have at least one living relation.

If a child is left a complete orphan with no near kinsmen on either side, a villager is appointed guardian by the community and the child is brought up in his house.

Munsi Kisku of Durgapur was left an orphan with no relations of any kind in the village. She was 14 at the time so

Arsu Hansdak' of the village took her into his family as a maid servant and became her village guardian.

In Sitakahabar Rauta Marandi took pity on an orphan girl and brought her to his house. He did not adopt her but became her recognised guardian. In 1944, a Gwala boy of the village was caught in intercourse with her and since Rauta was the girl's guardian, he was deemed responsible for her conduct. He did not pay the fine, and was bitlahaed.

III FAMILY ADJUSTMENTS

These orders are the accepted orders of preference. If, however, the minor child prefers one guardian to another two guardians sometimes officiate. The legal guardian will then be in charge of the minor's land while the chosen guardian takes care of the movables and the minor himself. If the legal guardian has approved of the arrangement he will send half the produce of the minor's lands each year as contribution to his maintenance or if he waives his claim to the custody of the land this may also pass to the chosen guardian. It is necessary however, that the arrangement should be amicable and if a relative of the minor keeps him against the will of the legal guardian the latter can either insist on his return or decline to give the movables or send the produce.

Ratu Hansdak' of Nimakalan died leaving a minor son and aughter. The children were unhappy with their paternal uncles so by family arrangement their mother's father was chosen as their guardian. The family land was cultivated by their father's brother and every year half the produce was sent.

In Phapnad Debi Soren died leaving two minor daughters. Their mother deserted them and by agreement with their father's relations their father's sister became their guardian. The lands of Debi did not, however, go to his sister but were cultivated by his brother. Every year he sent his sister half the produce and in 1944 when the elder daughter was married to a ghar jawae he gave the lands to her.

Raju Hansdak' of Ero was left an orphan when his father died. His maternal grandfather then became his chosen guardian while his legal guardian, Kaila Hansdak' cultivated his lands. Kaila was his father's brother and each year he sent the chosen guardian half the produce.

If the families are well-to-do and the arrangement is amicable the actual guardian may even forego the produce and leave it with the technical one.

Bijai Hembrom of Kalhajor took his sister's son after his sister and her husband had died. His father's brothers cultivated his lands but did not give any paddy as Bijai did not need it.

IV THE DUTIES OF GUARDIANS

Once a guardian has assumed charge he becomes a trustee for the minor's welfare. If he is in charge of the minor's person, he must keep him in food and clothes, tend him in sickness and perform his initiation and marriage ceremonies. While he is not debarred from selling his movables, he can only do so in the minor's interest and if he has been appointed by the village community, he must take village permission before he sells. When the child becomes of age, his guardian must account to him for all the movables he received. Similarly, if he is in charge of the minor's land he must see that the fields are cultivated and must make them over to him when at last he comes of age.

In Dalu, Munshi Tudu was left an orphan on the death of his father. Chotka Tudu of the same village was then appointed his guardian and took charge of his movables which consisted of paddy, rice and three cows. When the boy grew up Chotka Tudu arranged his marriage and returned him all the cattle along with their increase.

In Kharimati Jetha Marandi became the ward of his father's brother's son. When his father died, there were two cows, a calf, and some metal utensils in the house. His guardian took these over and when the child grew up all the utensils were returned to him. The calf and one of the cows had died of smallpox but all the surviving animals and the calves which had later been born were given to the boy.

V VILLAGE REVISION

If a guardian neglects his duty or misappropriates the minor's property the village community has full power to intervene and if necessary to appoint another guardian in his place.

In Nayadih, the sister's son of Barka Soren was originally under the guardianship of his father's brother. The guardian did not look after him, so the villagers called Barka Soren and the boy was removed from his guardian and placed in Barka's charge. With the village approval Barka then assumed charge of the boy's lands and arranged for their cultivation by Santals of the village. Half the produce was given to him and with this paddy the boy was maintained.

Jugla Marandi of Jaipani died leaving a minor son. His mother's brother Barka Hansdak' became his guardian but as he neglected the child the villagers intervened and placed the boy and his land in charge of Domon Kisku. The latter was not related to the boy in any way.

In Jili the father of Salkhu Kisku was left an orphan. His maternal uncle became his guardian but began to beat and ill-treat him in the expectation that the child would run away. The villagers then intervened and the minor son with his movables and lands was placed under the guardianship of Baijnath Hembrom of the village. Baijnath brought the boy up, arranged his marriage and then returned to him the lands and the balance of his movables.

In Boromani Kandna Tudu died leaving a son Pitho and a widow Bale. Sometime later, his widow remarried and the paternal uncles of the boy then became his guardian. The boy was not happy with them and his uncles then allowed him to stay with his mother's eldest sister. They made over his land to her and allowed her to take his movables. A little later she let out the land to some dikus for cultivation on half produce and on this the boy's paternal uncles intervened, resumed charge of his land and themselves sent half its produce for the child's maintenance. This worked well for sometime till the boy's aunt sold some of his cattle and hired him out as a servant. On this, his paternal uncles again intervened and refused to send the produce. The boy's aunt then complained to the pargana who decided in consultation with the neighbouring manjhis that the boy should not be hired out as a servant and should be given the price of the sold cattle. His aunt has since stopped hiring him out and his paternal uncles are again sending half the produce of the land.

8

CUSTODIANS

I THE CAUSES OF CUSTODIANSHIP

WHEN a Santal has only a small holding in the village he sometimes migrates to the Tea gardens in Assam or to parts of North Bihar or Bengal where there is either scrub jungle to be cleared or living can be got by day labour. If he finds a village unhealthy he sometimes changes his residence while a widow sometimes leaves her husband's village and takes her children to her father.

In such cases the owner may abandon his holding by telling the Manjhi that he is not returning. The village then settles the land with another Santal and even if the original tenant changes his mind and returns he can not get the property. If, however, he goes away with the possibility of returning he can leave his property in the care of a custodian.

II THE ORDER OF PREFERENCE

When a custodian is to be appointed the members of the greater family have the first claim to the custody. If the brothers or agnates agree a married servant is sometimes allowed to act and a co-villager (not a relative) is sometimes permitted to take charge. Such arrangements, however, are entirely subject to the approval of the greater family and if a custodian is appointed against their wishes or without their approval the greater family can appeal to the village and themselves take charge.

In Khajuria Thakra Murmu decided to go with a labour gang for work on the railway and arranged with Suphal Marandi of his village to look after his lands while he was away. Suphal was not related to him and thereupon his cousin objected and called a village meeting. The villagers decided in favour of the cousin and Thakra had to adopt him as custodian.

Fuchu Murmu of Kheribari went to the tea gardens leaving his lands with a villager named Bhao Murmu. Fuchu's elder brother heard of it and called a village meeting. In the meeting the village decided that the elder brother was the correct custodian and Bhao was made to leave the property.

In certain cases the members of the greater family acquiesced in the appointment of a co-villager (not a relation) if they think that the period of absence is likely to be short. But if they subsequently decide to assert their rights, there is no time bar and they can claim custody whenever they choose.

Jhalga and Barka Murmu of Muchiadih went to Bengal leaving their lands in the custody of Budhrai Marandi of their village. Budhrai kept them for 4 years, but after that the cousins of Jhalga and Barka asserted their right and took possession.

In Bilmi Hathimara, Ram Marandi left his lands with Sugda Hansdak' of his village. His brother allowed the custodian to cultivate the land for one year but after that, with village approval he dispossessed him and himself took it over.

Larka Tudu of Indpahari went to Bengal leaving his lands in the custody of his wife's brother.

He had three brothers and after the custodian had cultivated the lands for 3 years and paid rent, the brothers asserted their rights and assumed charge.

If there are no members of the greater family either in the village or its vicinity, a Santal may appoint a co-villager to act as custodian and failing a co-villager may place his lands and cattle in the custody of the Manjhi.

In Borwa, Chandrai Murmu went to Bengal leaving his land in the custody of Siba Hansdak' of the village. Chandrai had no heirs or agnates. For two years he sent the rent of the lands from Bengal and when he returned the custodian returned the land to him.

In appointing a custodian, the owner need only 'register' his action with the manjhi but if there is a dispute, it is the village community which must finally approve.

III TERMS OF CUSTODIANSHIP

When a custodian is appointed the terms of the charge are settled by private agreement and in the light of certain accepted principles.

The custodian is firstly responsible for cultivating the owner's lands, maintaining their quality and preventing deterioration and encroachments. If the owner sends the rent by money order or by hand, the custodian keeps half the crop and reserve the rest for the owner. If the custodian pays the rent on behalf of the owner, he either appropriates all the produce or keeps a share according as the two decide.

A Santal of Ramkol left his land in the custody of Baghrae Kisku of his village. Baghrae cultivated his land, keep all the produce but paid the rent.

In Telni, Pando Murmu left his village and with the approval of his uncles kept the lands in the custody of Durga Hembrom. The arrangement is still in force and Pando is paying the rent and Durga is giving him half the produce.

In the second place, a custodian is responsible for all the owner's animals and cattle. He can appropriate their dung and use them in cultivation but he is not entitled to sell them and must account for them in toto when the owner returns. He cannot also claim any of their increase but at the time of settling the terms of custody, some animals or cash are usually allotted to him by way of remuneration. These are payable when the term of custody is ended.

Jagan Soren of Dharampur went to the tea gardens leaving seven goats and one calf with Jetha Soren. While he was on the garden, Jagan got married and sent a letter to the custodian directing him to give the calf as the customary present to his wife's brother. Shortly afterwards Jagan and his wife returned and the girl's brother came and took the calf away. The custodian received two goats as remuneration for his work.

Finally a custodian is expected to maintain the owner's house and keep it in repair.

Chita Murmu of Kheribari went to the tea gardens leaving his house and land with his uncle. When he returned he found that his house had fallen down and the custodian was obliged to build him another.

IV DEFAULTS AND THEIR ADJUSTMENT

If a custodian pays the rent but neglects the land, house or cattle, the owner can demand compensation for the damage and can also dismiss the custodian and appoint another.

Lilu Tudu of Rakh left his land in the custody of his elder brother and went to Bengal. When he returned after seven years he found that the ridges of his fields had been damaged and the drainage affected. Lilu appealed to the village and the custodian was made to give him five rupees.

In Telni, Pirthi Kisku went across the Ganges leaving his lands in the custody of Peru. Two bighas were damaged by a rush of water and some other lands were left uncultivated. When Pirthi returned he complained to the village of the conduct of the custodian. The village declined to give him any compensation for the two bighas damaged by water as they held that the custodian was not at fault. But they awarded two maunds of paddy in respect of the land which had remained in good order and which the custodian failed to cultivate.

If the custodian is a member of the greater family, but neglects his duty the owner can bring his grievances before a village meeting and with village approval can eject his relation and appoint a co-villager (not a relation) in his place.

Handi Tudu of Dalabar left the land in the custody of his two brothers. When he returned after one year he was not satisfied with the produce and with the village approval he removed his brother and kept the land with a co-villager Lachhu Murmu.

Moreover if in the absence of the owner, a custodian fails to look after the land or defaults in paying rent, the manjhi can intervene and in the owner's interest discharge the custodian and either himself take charge or appoint another as a new custodian.

In Chitlo, Khade Hembrom went to Assam leaving his lands with his father-in-law. The custodian died and his sons took over in his place. They failed to keep the lands under cultivation and to pay rent so the village manjhi intervened and himself acted as custodian. If and when Khade returns the Manjhi will return the lands to him.

The manjhi, in fact, is the final protector of the owner, the guardian of his interests, and the supervisor of custodians.

V RESUMPTION

Although custodianship is fully recognised, a Santal who leaves his land is expected to keep in touch with the custodian or the village. If nothing is heard of him for twelve years, the manjhi can assume the holding to be abandoned and if there is no heir the villagers can settle it with another tenant. If after twelve years the owner comes back, he cannot claim the land as of right and can get it only if the settlement taker gives it up without objection.

In Baramasia, Lakhan and Fudu Hembrom went to Bengal leaving their lands in the custody of Lodo Murmu of their village. Nothing was heard of them for fifteen years and the village then settled their lands with the custodian.

Sometime later Fudu returned but did not get his lands.

A Santal of Chaparia went to the tea garden leaving his lands in the custody of the village manjhi. Nothing was heard of him for twelve years and the manjhi then settled the land with Bhado Murmu of his village. Two years later the Santal returned but it was too late, nothing could be done and the lands remained with Bhado.

Tunglu Tudu of Sukhbaria went to Assam leaving his lands with his maternal uncle who was also manjhi of the village. Nothing was heard of Tunglu and the villagers then insisted on settling the lands with various Santals of the village. The manjhi custodian objected to the settlement but was overruled by the village. A long time afterwards the grandson of Tunglu returned and by village agreement and with the consent of the settlement-takers was given back his grandfather's lands.

VI INHERITANCE

When the owner dies, the fact of custodianship does not affect succession and if there are heirs they inherit the land and movables and can eject the custodian.

Bhogon Baske of Tilaki went to Bengal leaving his land with his uncle, Baghrae. Sometime later Bhogon died without issue, Bhagrae then inherited a third share not as custodian but as Bhogon's uncle while the remaining two shares were taken by Bhogon's other uncles.

In Bhadodih, Mansa Kisku went to Bengal leaving his land with Hatha Marandi of his village. Sometime later Mansa died without issue and his brother's two daughters claimed his land. The custodian objected but the village gave the land to the two girls.

If a man dies heirless and his land is in the custody of another, the fact of long possession does not entitle the custodian to inherit but may influence the village in settling the land with him.

Jairam Baske of Chhota Sindri went to Bengal leaving his land with Bhado Marandi a co-villager. Jairam had no agnates and when he died the village settled the land with the custodian.

In Muchridih, Sujan Marandi went to the tea gardens leaving his lands with Khare Murmu of his village. Sujan had no agnates and when he died seven years ago the villagers allowed the custodian to take his lands.

VII CONCLUSION

In Santal society therefore the aim of custodianship is to ease a temporary difficulty. It affirms the responsibility of the owner to cultivate his own land. It allows him time to meet a crisis and to adjust his family to new conditions. When this has been done, it demands a positive decision, it links the ownership of land to active participation in village life and if the owner becomes permanently 'dead' to the village, his ownership lapses and custodianship ends.

9

GUESTS AND CREDITORS

I GUESTS

WITHIN the village, the life of a Santal is determined by the rights and duties of his family and by the needs of the community. But the village is only a cell of the main tribe and beyond the immediate calls of the family is the wider obligation to assist a tribesman at any time of need.

The first of these duties is to aid a stranded traveller. If a Santal is a stranger and needs a night's lodging, he goes to the manjhi, introduces himself and asks for the use of a verandah. The manjhi then offers him a night's meal. He does this as headman of the village as guardian of its prestige. He cannot however levy anything from the village by way of sumptuary allowance and must treat all strangers as his private guests. In the morning, the guest departs—sometimes with a little tobacco to chew on the road—but normally not with the day's rations. In return for this service nothing is demanded or taken.

If a stranger arrives in a sick state, the manjhi sends a man to fetch his kinsmen. After that the sick man is put in a litter and his kinsmen carry him away. While the man is lying in his house the manjhi feeds him and neither claims nor accepts anything in return.

This etiquette is so generally observed that I know of no cases in which a manjhi failed to shelter a stranger. If a manjhi turned a traveller away it would give the village such a bad name that sooner or later the villagers themselves would remove the manjhi for his lack of tribal feeling.

A second case is that of a match-maker. In most cases he

is already known to someone in the village but if he is not, the jogmanjhi is expected to offer him a night's hospitality. In such cases the jogmanjhi deputises for the manjhi since the visit is concerned with boys and girls.

But besides travellers and envoys, relations are frequent visitors to a village. 'Apart from their parents', says Kolean Haram 'a married pair respect the wife's relations most. They are attached most to the wife's maternal uncles and her brothers and see them frequently. When they go and visit them these relatives kill fowls and pigs for them and give them plenty of food and rice beer.' The married pair are equally hospitable in return. They are also very fond of the husband's brothers and maternal uncles and show them hospitality but on a smaller scale. There is a story that once a child's maternal and paternal uncles came to visit his parents. When the mid-day meal was over, the sky became dark and threatened rain. The mother put her son on her hip and played with him in the courtyard. 'Son', she said 'there are dark clouds on the side of your mother's brothers but it is clear on the side of your father's brothers. Then the husband's brothers came out, looked around and saw that the sky was everywhere the same. They understood that she was sending them away so that she might entertain her brothers. Then with one excuse or another they quietly went away. The wife's brothers also got ready to go but she said 'Brothers do not go, there is still a little rice beer, stay a while longer'. At night she poured out the rice beer and made her husband kill a pig. She gave them meat, rice and beer and feasted them to the full.'

'In every Asin', Kolean Haram continues 'a married pair go round visiting their relatives, even if they are at a great distance, so long as they are known. If there is a grown up son at home, both of them go. Otherwise the husband goes alone. The purpose of visiting relations is in order not to lose them. If they are on good terms, and times are bad the wife's relations and the husband's help the pair with food or plough cattle'.*

On such visits the current convention is to give food and lodging for two or three days and demand nothing in return.

**Horkoren Mare Hapramko reak' katha*, 120-21.

After that the kinsman must help in the house or the fields and so for practical purposes earn his keep.

All these conventions of hospitability are of great importance for they enable Santals to live without anxiety and they assist in integrating the tribe.

II CREDITORS

Visitors from other villages are not however the only Santals who require help. Within the village itself, families vary greatly in size and prosperity and the large family with little land is only one of various cases which sometimes need assistance.

If a person is old and weak, and has neither relations nor land, Santals often verge on the callous. They feel that his days as an active member of the community are over. There is no family which will absorb him. He is nor a drag on village life. He may sometimes be given scraps of food but once his power to work has gone no one has any obligation to feed him. His duty is to die.

If a person on the other hand is still active but is temporarily in want, the richer Santals of the village are expected to advance him loans. These loans are of two kinds—panca, or a small loan to tide over a sudden difficulty and rin, which is a much bigger loan to cover a longer period. A panca loan carries no interest and must be repaid within one or two days or at most within a week. A rin on the other hand is for any length of time and carries interest. This interest varies according as the loan is in cash or in kind. For loans in cash, twenty-five per cent is the normal rate but this is simple or compound according to local practice or agreement. For loans in kind, fifty per cent interest is usual when the paddy is taken for food but a hundred per cent is often charged for seed paddy or loans of rice. Loans in kind are normally repayable out of the next crop.

Since most Santals are still illiterate, almost all these loans are oral and are either made in the presence of the parties or before the manjhi. If a debtor cannot repay when the term is up, he gives cattle in lieu of the cash or paddy. But it is only his own movables that he can thus expend. He cannot sell or give away the movables or cattle of his wife. Similarly if his sons or daughters have any private property these are also exempted from appropriation. If he dies before the debt is paid, the heir who inherits his movables becomes responsible for its payment. It is necessary, however, that the heir or the village should have full knowledge of the debt. If no one in the village knows of it, the heir is not liable. Similarly if the debt was incurred but repayment never demanded, the creditor can get from the heir only the principle and not the interest. Moreover while in most cases the heir regards repayment as a point of personal honour, if the creditor has finally to sue, it is only the debtor's own movables that can be sold in execution. The crops raised by his son or the produce of his son's separate property are beyond the scope of legal process. Similarly land is throughout unaffected, for neither by tribal practice nor the revenue laws of the district can land be given, leased or sold in liquidation of a debt.

10

SERVANTS

I THE ASUL DURUC' IC'

IN SANTAL families, servants are a common phenomenon and there are three circumstances which lead to their engagement.

The first is when a Santal has no son and there is no one to support him in his old age. In these circumstances he engages a servant for 'asul duruc' or life-long maintenance. The servant becomes a pseudoson 'by contract'. He enters his family, he cultivates his master's lands, looks after him and keeps him in food and clothes. He does not however change his sept or bongas or lose his rights in his own father's family. He is not adopted and does not gain the status of a son.

In return for life-long service, he is given food and clothes and should he fall ill, all the expenses of his treatment are borne by his master. He does not however receive any annual money or movables but in certain cases his master may perform his marriage and in the Karbinda area, it is customary for masters to give their permanent servants a bale of paddy and either a cow or a bullock at the end of ten years.

In certain cases also, a master may obtain village approval and then allot certain lands to a servant for use in his lifetime and for inheritance at his death.

Apart from these concessions or unless the right to inherit lands or movables is made clear at the time of his engagement and this concession is ratified by a village meeting, a life-long servant cannot be an heir. When there is no reservation but much family land, the agnates may give him a little land 'from kindness', but such a gift is invariably an act of grace and can never be claimed as of right. If his master dies and the agnates do not give him anything he must go back to his father's house.

In Kukha Kalidas Kisku had no sons but a large tract of land. He therefore, engaged a married servant and with village approval he allotted him some land. When Kalidas died this land was inherited by the servant.

Similarly when Bhima Tudu had been converted into a ghar jawae by agu mit' his wife brought Maha Hembrom for asul duruc'. Their lands were in Kusum and under the original contract it was agreed that the servant would inherit all the lands at their death. The contract was approved by the village and the servant has since inherited.

On the other hand, when a Santal of Telabani engaged Degra Core of Bhagnadih for his life-long maintenance, only clothes and keep were stipulated. When the pair died, the agnates intervened and he was made to leave the land.

Jitu Baske of Mangru migrated to Assam. His mother remained in the village and brought a servant, Sankbo Baske, for her life-long maintenance. When the mother died, her daughter claimed the land and since inheritance, was not a part of the contract the servant was ejected.

Doman Soren of Dhamni kept Udai Hansdak' as his life-long servant. Udai served both Doman and his son and grand-son but when he died he had been given nothing except his food and clothes.

In Chak Lakhanpur, Chunka Marandi kept Shankar Soren as a life-long servant. The contract was only for food and clothes but when Chunka died, his son gave the servant five bighas as an act of grace.

II SERVANTS WITH LAND

A second circumstance is when a boy has land of his own but no one to cultivate it. In such cases, he can hire himself to a rich Santal on si-tora and contract to work as a servant in return for clothes and keep. In lieu of annual money, however, his master gets his land cultivated. When such arrangements are made, the servant gives the seed, the master provides all the labour and the servant is given the whole crop. In some cases the master acts as his unofficial guardian. He administers the property, holds its produce and even performs the servant's marriage. In other cases, the produce is held until the servant is of age and after that plough cattle are purchased and the servant starts on his own.

Mijha Tudu of Ralipathar had seven bighas of land but no cattle. He therefore went to work as a servant and made the lands over to his master on si-tora. He did not take any produce for three years but at the end he bought a pair of bullocks and a plough from it.

In Kolyan, Kusum Murmu and his elder sister were left orphans. The boy had twenty-five bighas of land but no ploughs or cattle. He and his sister therefore went as servants in the house of Partu Kisku of Gaichand. Partu cultivated his land and gave the boy and girl their food and clothes. He performed the girl's marriage once and the boy's three times. All these wedding expenses were met from the produce and at the end of nine years the boy himself took charge.

In Khatangi, a rich Santal, Bhalku Soren, was in need of servants. Bodoc' Murmu had died leaving a widow and a small son and daughter. The widow could not cultivate her lands, so she and the two children entered Bhalku's service. Bhalku gave them a room to live in, cultivated their lands, gave them the produce and kept them in food and clothes. In return the widow and her daughter helped in the house and the boy grazed the cattle. When he grew up, some bullocks were purchased out of the produce, a new house was built and the boy started cultivation.

III ANNUAL SERVANTS

The third and most common circumstance is when a Santal's holding is large and help is needed either in cultivation, tending cattle or doing house work. A life-long arrangement is unnecessary and a boy or a girl are hired on an annual contract. These contracts are very common and are made in the days immediately following the Mag festival in February. At this festival the year's engagements are terminated, accounts are squared and the way cleared for new contracts. If a man requires a boy servant he makes enquiries and when he hears of a suitable boy he discusses with his father or guardian the amount of maintenance, clothes and annual money which he requires in return for daily work in the house throughout the year. He also settles the circumstances in which the boy may take a few days' leave and who will treat him if he falls ill. In most cases a servant does not get leave unless there is serious illness in his family.

Similarly, if the servant himself falls ill, the master is expected to treat petty ailments but to return him to his home if the illness is serious. In the latter cases the cost of treating illness is met by the servant's father or guardian and is not a claim on the master.

Sibu Murmu of Baramasia was a servant in the house of Ragda Hansdak' of Damru. The servant was ill for five days and during this time his master treated him. As the period was short, the servant was not sent home neither was the cost of treatment realised from his parents.

In Amdiha Manidas Murmu kept a servant for two years. He renewed the contract but in the third year the servant fell ill and was carried to his parent's house. As the servant was semi permanent, his master not only met the cost of the ojhas and the servant's food, but spent one rupee four annas on sweets, two annas on pan, and six pice on betel, as extra comforts ten annas on ten pigeons for sacrifice and one rupee on a cloth.

On the other hand when the servant of Peru Tudu of Telni fell ill, he was in the first year of his contract and was sent to his parent's house. There was no agreement that his master would treat him and after he had sent him food for a fortnight, he gave him nothing more and the parents met all the expenses of his treatment.

When these details are settled, the guardian of the boy brings him to his master rice beer is brewed and some neighbours are called. The purpose of the rice beer is then announced. The boy's induction into the family is published and often either all or half the wages are given to his guardian. In the case of a girl servant a similar procedure is followed and there is normally the same ratification of the arrangements by a formal drinking of rice beer with the neighbours.

If the contract is renewed after a year, a fresh meeting with rice beer is unnecessary. The guardian merely meets the master and arranges for the boy or girl to stay. If no advance money was part of the original agreement, the servant either stays on with the tacit understanding that the contract is the same or new terms are settled. Occasionally, as at Poreyahat, the servant's wishes are ascertained through symbol. On the day after *sankrant* when the servant has gone out with the cattle his master keeps ready two pots of food—one hot and the other cold. If the servant argees to stay, he eats both sets of food but if he wishes to leave he eats only one. If the master is a Santal of prominence, the calling of the neighbours at the original contract is sometimes dispensed with and the word given to the guardian is accepted as sufficient guarantee.

The terms on which these annual servants are engaged usually follow regional custom. In the Katikund area, in 1945, the standard terms were six to twelve rupees in cash, with food and keep throughout the year and clothes at the following intervals:

The commencement of the rains	1 jarge palat
The Dasae festival	1 dhoti
	1 ganji
	1 gamcha
The Mag festival	1 panci
	1 pichauri*

In the Taljhari area no cash was being paid but five to twelve maunds of paddy were being given, the terms for clothes and keep being the same.

In Fatehpur in the Jamtara subdivision the standard rate was twelve rupees with clothes as follows :

The commencement of the rains	1 pichauri
The Dasae festival	1 dhoti
The Sohrae festival	1 pichauri
At need	1 gamcha
	1 bhagwa

*See Glossary.

Elsewhere in the district terms ranged from two to eighteen rupees in cash, three quarters of a maund of paddy to twelve maunds and from four to six pieces of cloth—according to the area and the contract.

A variation of these terms is known as uric' utin'. By this contract the master gives the servant his clothes and keep but instead of paying any annual money, he loans the parent or guardian a pair of bullocks for the period of service.

Besides these payments, it is often understood that the boy's master will give him one or two annas for buying tobacco or pan at a *mela* and in certain areas the agreement between the families may also provide for one or two rupees to the boy over and above the fixed annual sum.

In the case of girl servants wages are rarely paid in cash but are usually given either in the form of ir arpa or as paddy. In the latter case the amount ranges between one and six maunds, the girl receives her food and keep, as well as clothes at the following intervals :

The commencement of the rains	1 panci
	1 parhand
The Dasae festival	1 sari
The Mag festival	1 khando

IV CLAIMS

Once a boy or girl have been engaged they are expected to work hard and do whatever their masters say. In Santal experience it is much easier to lose a servant than to get one and well-to-do Santals who need servants usually remove them only if they are lazy or incompetent. If a servant is turned out but not through his own fault any advance wages that may have been given to his guardian are not returnable, but if he is removed owing to his laziness or any other fault full or proportionate wages can be claimed by his master.

Lal Hembrom of Haripur had a servant from Bichapahari and had paid his annual wages of six rupees, at the time of the engagement. The servant was always slack, so after a month Lal Hembrom sent him home and the servant's father repaid the six rupees.

In Amtala, Chotu Ramu also engaged a boy on a contract of seven rupees as annual money. He paid an advance of three rupees but after a few months the boy ran away. When Chotu Ramu demanded his money back the boy's father gave a small goat in its place.

In such circumstances, the return of the advance money is all that can be claimed and once a master has given a servant clothes he cannot take them back. If a master is dissatisfied with a servant his only remedy is to return him to his father and when I asked the manjhis at Katikund whether a master might not sometimes postpone giving clothes at the due times as an act of discipline they scouted the suggestion as fantastic, 'if a servant does not get his clothes at the Dasae',* they said 'how can he go out with the Dasae boy? He will leave at once and the master can claim nothing'. A servant, therefore, will either work tolerably well and stay, or work badly and leave.

But besides working well, a servant is also required to be careful with his master's property. If he is negligent with the family animals his master can claim compensation from the servant's guardian.

In Amtala, Chotu Ramu kept a cousin's son as a servant. He met the expenses of his wedding and it was agreed that he would work for five years without any annual money to pay the money off. One day he was grazing his master's buffalo when the buffalo died. Chotu took the matter to the village. It was decided that the animal was worth thirty rupees and that the servant must work another six years to pay it off. He started to work and then decamped to Assam with his wife. But in 1945 when he returned he paid Chotu twenty rupees.

In such cases, the village meeting decides the amount of the damage and the responsibility of the servant and assessees the amount payable to the master. Since the servant's guardian received his wages it is against the guardian that the claim lies and this may finally be settled by extending the period of service.

Similarly, if by the negligence or misbehaviour of a servant

*The festival when the pupils of gurus, graduate and go on a begging expedition.

damage is caused to other villagers, the master is held responsible but can recover any costs from the servant or his guardian.

Thakur Kisku of Kherwa had a servant who picked some sugarcane from another Santal's field. The village fined the servant five rupees and Thakur had to pay it.

The servant of Ram Murmu of Dalabar was in charge of his cattle when they grazed a Santal's paddy. The Santal took them to the pound and when Ram Murmu had paid for their release, he told his servant that if it happened again, he would recover all the money from him.

In Tilaki, a servant of Dhonkistu Murmu allowed his cattle to damage some maize. The servant was fined two rupees by the village and although Dhonkistu paid the fine, he warned his servant that he would recover all the money if he was ever fined again.

V STATUS

Once a boy has entered a master's house as a servant, he becomes a temporary member of his family. He is regarded less as a menial than as a friend. He is often allowed the greatest intimacy with his master's daughter and if he proves a good and obedient worker, his master may even encourage the two to sleep together. Such a union is known as kundal napam bapla—a meeting at bed time, and in many cases the son-in-law is subsequently converted into a ghar jawae.

In Chirapathar, Manoda Tudu brought Munshi Murmu as a servant. While he was working in the house, Munshi became intimate with Manoda's daughter. They 'met at bed time' and the girl had two children. Their marriage was recognised as kundal napam and later Manoda converted Munshi into a ghar jawae.

But besides entering their master's family, boy and girl servants also become temporary members of the village. They join in the village dancing and festivals. Boy servants 'laugh and joke' with girl of their temporary village as if they had been born there. A girl of another village who comes to a house as a servant becomes the 'property' of the village boys as if she were any other girl of the village. Since however, their master is a provisional rather than a final guardian, their behaviour has often a greater wildness and daring than that of boys and girls who are living in their homes and in the tales and songs which are recited at hunts, it is almost always a serving boy or girl who fills the violent roles.

I

To the upper village, mother
I went for food
The manjhi's serving boy
Was grazing buffaloes
Oh No, No, No, I told him
But he caught my hand
Oh don't, Oh don't I said
But by force he took me.

II

Girls, do not stroll
By the banks of the rivers
The manjhi's serving boy
Is like a buffalo in rut
By the spring with the tamarind
He is rolling in the mud
Tie his legs with a fly whisk
Fix him with a hair pin
Hammer him with a bangle.

III

In the jungle where the village ends
There roars a tiger and a bear growls
No it is not a tiger
It is not a bear
The manjhi's maid
Is howling with a child.

IV

Midnight
And the manjhi's servant
The paranik's maid
Have run away together
Sound the drums
Blow the trumpets
Like a silkworm moth in a thicket
They have linked their lives together.

If their misconduct is of a petty nature, their master is expected to reprimand them but if the matter is serious, he must either himself bear the consequences or send at once for the servant's father or final guardian.

Babai Marandi of Majdiha had a boy and girl as servants. One day the boy suddenly married the girl by putting *sindur* on her. Babai sent words to her parents and they came and blamed Babai. Babai then took them to the boy's village. There they made the boy's father mortgage some land for the goats and the brideprice. Two goats were given by the boy's father but the third was given by Babai to help the boy's father. The servants then went back and stayed the year out with Babai.

In this case, the decisive action was taken by the fathers of the boy and the girl but the master acted as a go-between and assisted at every stage.

Lodo Marandi of Dalu had a servant who one day brought a girl of the village to his house. Lodo surprised them together and in the village meeting it was decided that the servant and the girl should be married. Lodo himself paid the brideprice to the girl's father and later it was arranged with the boy's guardians that the servant and the girl would work for Lodo for a term long enough to pay him back the money.

In Paharpur Nimbai Murmu put *sindur* on a daughter of his master. The boy's father was informed and after paying the fine and the brideprice he took the boy and girl to his house. The younger brother of the servant was then sent back as substitute.

When as sometimes happens the servant has no relations; his master is not merely a proxy but a final guardian.

In Jokpahari a servant of Mirol Soren was caught in intercourse with a girl of the village. The servant had no guardian and Mirol paid the cost of the meeting and the brideprice and also bore the expenses of the wedding.

VI

The position of servants in fact is one of democratic equality. For daily life they are as much members of the family as its sons and daughters. They are Santals first and servants later. Their standard of living is the same as the rest of the house. It is only when death intervenes that the position changes. It is then that the family asserts its rights and the claims of service go down before the rules of kin.

11

OWNERS OF LIVESTOCK

AMONG a Santal's property, livestock is often a principal possession. A litter of pigs or a goat with kidling redeems his diet from monotony, while the cow, bullock and buffalo are as indispensable to cultivation as the ploughs and levellers which they draw when he possesses bullock, then, Santal's first duty is to see that his animals come to no harm while to the village he bears the responsibility of ensuring that none of them cause harm or damage.

If goats or cattle graze a standing crop, they are taken to the manjhi who estimates the extent of the damage. The owner of the animals must then pay the cost and if he does not, he is made to suffer begar or minor outcasting.* If the damage is deliberate the owner is also fined and if the offence is repeated the fine is doubled.

Similarly, if an animal harms or gores another, its owner must pay whatever compensation is decided by the villagers. If the attacked animal is killed, another of equal value must be given or its price paid in money. Similarly, if an animal is rendered useless, it must either be replaced or paid for. The only exception is when two owners agree to a contest. In Chandarpura for example, Bhado Marandi and his sister's husband had each a rutting buffalo. Af er baiting the cattle at Sohrae, they thought that a buffalo fight would be good sport, so they set the buffaloes on each other. After a long clash one

*For the special law regarding pigs, see my report, *Bitlaha*.

buffalo killed the other and the two owners jointly replaced it with another for twelve rupees.

Ramchand Hembrom of Ranidih and a Santal of Shampur had each a fighting ram. They arranged a contest and during the fight the ram of Ramchand killed the other.

There was joint meeting of the two villages and it was decided that the man whose ram, was killed must bear the loss.

In such cases where the risk is willingly undertaken the practice is that either the owner bears the loss himself or his opponent shares it.

If a Santal is responsible for his own cattle, he is, also responsible for cattle in his charge. A servant who injures a buffalo can be made to indemnify his master. Similarly, a Santal who has taken loan of cattle on the caro system* must return them free from injury. In the Dumka Damin, the rate in 1945 for hiring plough cattle was eight rupees for two bullocks and twelve rupees for a pair of buffaloes. The hire is for a season (May to January) and when the ploughing time is over the animals are given back. If an animal dies from disease or is killed by a leopard, the owner is given the head, skull and hide and cannot claim replacement. If, however, the animal breaks its leg, gets its tail broken, or dies from an injury, the hirer must replace it with one of equal value.

Sometimes cattle are not hired to another villager but are merely kept with him for stalling. In such circumstances, the custodian gets the dung and is sometimes paid some money. He is responsible for injuries in the stall, but unless there is a contract to the contrary, the owner is responsible for the animal while it is at work or grazing.

Ondrac' Murmu of Taljhari had 20 cattle all of which he stalled with Karam Hansdak' of Mangrutikur (Banjhi), besides taking the dung Karam was paid eight rupees a year.

Finally, when a cow, bullock or buffalo dies the village shares its flesh. If the carcass is outside the village, the man who carries it in is given the neck while the owner gets the head but shares it with the villagers. He is also entitled to the

*A system of annual hire.

tiki, the loins and back legs. The rest is split into three—the owner getting one share and the village the rest.

Such meat is not taken into the village or the house but is cooked and eaten outside. If it is given to the female members of the family they are called outside the village and after they have eaten they wash before returning. The pot used in cooking the dead meat is also not brought to the house.

12

HUNTING AND FISHING

I THE SANTAL ATTITUDE TO HUNTING

FOR SANTAL men, hunting satisfies a wide variety of needs. It is not only a way of varying a dull and tasteless diet. It is an exciting amusement, a test of manhood. 'The crisis of a woman's life is child birth, the crisis of a man's is the hunt'. To village girls the hunt is always a source of anxiety for they themselves are debarred from going to it while the long passage through the forest exposes their young lovers to unknown dangers. Yet a boy would feel himself a woman if he stayed away.

The mountain and the Karam, my love
You may not let me see
But do not keep me from the hunt
There are bears and tigers
Bison and stags
O my love
Your body is still young
And you do not know
How to meet them.

But in spite of these dangers a boy must join a hunt for it is only when he has done so that he feels himself a man.

II TECHNIQUE

The process of hunting follows a simple routine. The hunters do not lie in wait for quarry but merely advance in a long line combing the forest as they go. At the great annual hunts, the village is one of many units and must keep together in its passage through the hills. At other hunts on the *Sankrat* day of Sohrae or when three or four villages combine for a jarpa or local expedition—the village again hunts as a unit but covers only the nearby jungle. In the big regional hunts, it is the dihri who decides the course and averts danger by making sacrifices while in the local hunts, the manjhi directs operations and the kudum naeke scratches his thigh for blood and appeases the bongas.

III HUNTING RULES

The hunting rules are few. In general any bird or animal may be attacked but the following are important exceptions.

No Santal may kill any kind of monkey, the *jhirni* and cercetee' kinds of lizard, a hanuman, a wild dog or the duludun snake while among birds it is wrong to kill a parrot, weaver bird (hisi), an oriole, a kutis bird or an uric'. Certain septs and khunts have prohibitions of their own. No Murmu may kill a Murum or Nilgae and no Hansdak' may kill a hans or swan. Jihu Hansdak' are forbidden to kill the Jihu bird or Babbler, Kahu Besras the Kahu or crow and Cilbindha Hansdak' the cil or kite. If these rules are broken, various consequences follow.

In Sarkandal some boys killed a monkey and the next year all the crops failed. In certain areas, the village itself does not take any action but the act is regarded as very ominous and certain to bring bad luck. To kill a kutis bird for example may cause an attack of goitre for the bird has swelling on its neck. To kill an oriole or a uric' bird may doom a marriage to failure, for these two birds are regarded as match-makers. In other areas the killer of a tabooed bird must observe certain ritual. In Rajabhita and Narainpur he must perform a funerary feast for the dead animal and give a small feast to his kinsmen. In Poreyahat and Basetkundi, he must give a feast to whatever members of his sept are in the village. In Kundahit it is sufficient if he purifies himself with water. In Pathna and Raksi, he must offer sacrifices to the orak' bongas and observe the abge bonga feast. While in Pakaur, a man who kills a hanuman is fined five rupees. Apart from these restrictions all birds and animals are lawful quarry, and anyone may aim at any bird or any animal.

In the case of regional hunts, the man who either first hits a bird or an animal with his own weapon or whose dog first mauls it is entitled to the mandal or first spoil. For animals such as a deer, bear or leopard, this consists of one hindquarters and a half share in the head, and liver. The thigh contains five muscles and each sister of the first striker is entitled to a muscle with its flesh. Out of the head and liver the striker makes a pudding and offers it to his ancestors. After the first striker, the spoil is divided as follows :

The village manjhi	the other hindquarters
The final killer	a foreleg
The main hunt	a foreleg
The dihri	the neck
The other hunters of the striker's village	half the head and liver and the rest of the carcase.

Out of the hindquarters the manjhi keeps only a third and for this he must give the hunters five pais of rice and some salt. After the hunters have returned to the village, the other two thirds, half the head and the liver and the rest of the carcase are cooked with the rice and eaten by the hunters in equal shares. A little is set aside as capo joro 'for those who did not go' and the man who carries the carcase gets a double share.

In the case of peacocks the striker's mandal is the tail feathers half the breast and one wing* and in the case of hares both the hindquarters. The killer gets one leg of a peacock and one foreleg of a hare. The rest goes to the hunters

*In the Raksi area the striker's mandal is the whole breast, one wing up to the socket, one wing up to the first joint and two thirds of the tail feathers. The remaining feathers go to the dihri.

of the village. As the spoil is small, the dihri, and the disom hor get nothing and the manjhi shares like other hunters.

When the hunt is merely local, the division of the spoil is considerably simpler. One hindquarters of a big animal, both the hindquarters of a small one and half the breast and one wing of a bird go to the striker while all the rest is shared by the hunters of the striker's village. The manjhi, the killer and the bearer of the spoil get single shares and the manjhi is not required to give the hunters rice.

In both types of hunt, the striker takes the hindquarters or the wing the moment the bird or animal falls and the rest of the carcase is then brought back either to the manjhi's camp or the village.

IV HUNTING INJURIES

If in the course of a hunt a man is shot by accident, the early practice was to award summary retribution. The village five conferred and repaid the murder. 'They made the man who had done the killing stand at the place where the killed man was shot and a kinsman of the person who was killed stand at the place where the shot man had been.' If from that place the kinsman could in one shot kill the man who had shot the other, well and good, otherwise he was set free. Similarly, if a man was killed by an arrow after it had pierced an animal, an animal was taken and the shooter stood at the same distance as the killed man. If he was killed after an arrow had pierced the animal, well and good, otherwise he was set free.* Now-a-days, if an accidental murder happens in the Damin it is reported to the pargana or if outside the Damin, information is sent to the police. If a man is merely wounded, the hunt itself decides what should be done.

V DISPUTES

If quarrels arise concerning spoil, these must always be kept within temperate limits and however much a hunter may think himself wronged, he may on no account threaten or injure any

**Hor Koren Mare Hapramko reak' Katha*, 167-8.

person. In the Jhandaburu hunt in 1943, a Santal wounded a peacock and another hunter killed it. The latter rushed to claim his wing and in the excitement he wrenched out the tail feathers. These are greatly prized as they are used for decorating drums. The first striker was enraged at his action and at once fitted an arrow and made as if to shoot. At the council in the night, the killer was held to have taken the feathers by a bona fide mistake but the first striker was fined a rupee for threatening him.

All disputes in a regional hunt are heard by the council and the dihri. 'The whole crowd of hunters' says Kolean Haram, 'sit round the dihri like a halo round the sun'. The important men sit close to him. The dihri says 'Countrymen let us know if anyone is in trouble, or has a quarrel. Is everyone well or not?' The countrymen reply 'Through your good wishes our lives are safe'. Then the dihri replies 'By the good wishes of Thakur we shall get what is good'.

Then everyone in turn tells his grievance to the dihri. One says 'we have a quarrel about a hare with such and such'. The dihri says 'How'. One man says 'I hit it with a stick.' Someone else says 'My dog caught it'. The dihri says 'Have you witnesses?' They reply 'Yes, they are of such and such villages.' The dihri summons the witnesses and hears the two sides. Whoever is proved to have first struck the hare gets it. The people help the dihri in his decisions, but the dihri gives the final word. If there are no witnesses, or if they are bribed and make conflicting statements, the dihri waits till next day at dawn. He then plants two arrows in the ground—one for the complainant and one for the accused. He puts the *sindur* on the arrows and standing with water in a lota, says 'O Thakur, God of the sky, by your mercy we have decided, but they have not listened. You fill the sky and we have settled this on earth. Since our words have failed, hold us not to blame. Both of them you know. Decide for them'. Then the dihri and the people say to the complainant and the accused 'Bow to the Sun Bonga and pick up this arrow. If harm befalls you, we share not to blame. Pick up your own arrows and fear us not. Only fear Thakur.' Then they make them say 'O Thakur, if I have done wrong may the tiger of the forest kill me and if I have spoken the truth may I come safely to my home.' The other man if he is equally bold says the same thing. Otherwise he withdraws. The dihri pours the water from the lota at the place where the arrows had been planted. Then bowing low he says 'O Thakur, decide which of them is right'. After they have taken the vows the people make them keep together in the hunt. In the forest a tiger roars. It suddenly rushes on the two men. It springs on one who has spoken truth and does him no harm. Then leaving him it kills the man whose act was bad.*

This trial by ordeal is no longer current in the district as tigers no longer roam its forests. If the matter is difficult therefore resort is either had to other special oaths** or the dihri finally decides.

In the case of local hunts, the manjhi and the village meeting decide all disputes.

VI FISHING

But besides their joy in hunting, Santals have also a zest for fishing. This does not rank as a major amusement. It is rather a diversion which varies the diet and provides a little sport. Unlike hunting women also can fish though they cannot use a rod and line while in parts of the district they can only bail out water.

The most common form of fishing is to set traps in a rice field. These consist of the saera or trap of split bamboo and the torodan or long bag of plaited reeds. A little opening is made in a ridge, the trap is stuck in position and as the water trickles through it sweeps the fish in. When traps are set up in a man's own field, he takes all the catches for himself but if he has put them in another's field he shares the fish with its owner.

Angling with rod and line is also done towards the end of the rains. For this kind of fishing there is no ownership of water and the angler takes all the catches.

When water collects in a shallow pool, it is often bailed out and the mud examined for fish. Before this is done the owner of the land must give permission and settle the terms.

*Ibid., 159-161.

**See Chapter 1.

For fishing in shallow pools or streams a mucu is often employed. This is a conical bamboo basket open at both its ends—the top end being a good deal smaller than the bottom. The fisherman wades through the water, plunging the mucu into the sand or gravel as he goes. When a fish is trapped he puts a hand in through the top and secures the fish which is writhing at the bottom. If the water is fairly deep, a number of nets are employed. The gitoe is a net with floats for use in still water. The lebda is a casting net while the cabhi has a wide circular opening fixed to a ring of bamboo which is pressed down when a fish is caught. The ganari is round like a handnet but without a handle while the hunda which is the most common form has a long tapering bag attached to a triangular framework. The fisherman enters the water, pushes the net along the bottom and sweeps the fish into the bag.

If the river is small and shallow the usual method is to raise a small dam of stones where the banks narrow and instal a stout saera below the stones. The fishermen then wade upstream feeling under the banks with their hands and either gripping the fish or sending them rushing downstream to the trap.

When a bandh or pond is to be fished, the terms are settled with its owner. The catch is divided in three and usually two shares are taken by the owner and one by the fishers. Similarly, if a river is leased, the lessee grants permission and settles the exact terms with the manjhi. If the river is public, the village fishes within its own limits but must give the manjhi of the next village a third share if it crosses his boundaries. At the end of the day, the catch is divided equally among the fishers—the village manjhi getting a double portion.

PART THREE

THE RIGHTS OF SANTAL WOMEN

13

THE SANTAL VIEW OF WOMAN

I

IF A first object of Santal law is to define the rights of men, a number of provisions give precise status to the rights of women. These principles reflect prevailing Santal attitudes and I will, therefore, preface an account of female rights by describing the Santal view of woman.

II

A first Santal attitude is expressed in the phrase, jinis kanako—'they are things'. But by this phrase, Santals do not imply the lifeless boredom of stones nor the placid utility of ploughs or pots. They express rather the view of woman which has survived from the hunting period of their tribal life. In this period with its constant migrations and dangers in the forest woman may well have seemed a form of baggage—an appendage to the hunter, a domestic animal rather than a being with equal rights and powers. Moreover, even today while a Santal woman is muscular and robust, she is none the less a member of a weaker sex. Throughout her life she is attached to men. As a child, she is linked to her father; as a wife, to her husband; as a widow, to her husband's family, her father or her sons and as a sister to her brother. She is in fact the property of men—not in the sense of mere servility but as one whose functions and needs can only be fulfilled in association with men themselves.

'A very common word used to describe a wife', says Shamrao Hivale of the Pardhan woman 'is *mal*, property. Woman herself is perhaps the most valuable piece of property that a man can own. This should not, however, be understood as meaning that the Pardhan has a low opinion of woman or looks down upon her. We do not generally, as a matter of fact, despise our most valuable possessions. The feminist may think that it is derogatory for a woman to be possessed by man but where a woman is free and independent as in Pardhan society the sense of being possessed is something treasured even by woman herself'.[1] This description of the Pardhan woman might apply with equal force to Santal women.

If at bottom, woman is property, it is only to a slight extent that she is treated as such. Until a girl is married, she is the property of her father but in the sense that he protects her person and is responsible for her conduct. If she has a lover and he is publicly detected, her value for marriage is impaired. It is, therefore, the father's rights which are infringed. If an unmarried girl commits an offence, her father is fined or outcasted 'for his property has gone astray'. Similarly, when a girl is married she becomes the property of her husband. But here also the term has certain close limits. In acquiring a husband, a girl becomes 'a child-producing housekeeper'. She bears children for her husband and it is his household which she manages. If she gives her body to another, it is her husband's household which is deranged, while if a wife commits an offence, her husband must bear the consequence. A wife is, therefore, her husband's property because he alone possesses her person and is ultimately responsible for her actions.*

*Bodding comments on this situation as follows :
'If a Santal woman commits an offence against the laws of Santal communal life the matter is brought before the village "Five" and adjudicated, and sentence is passed. It is, however, always the husband or father or brothers, etc., who will have to pay. The punishment is always a fine, when the misdemeanour is not so heinous that the women is driven away. Until this happens, the responsible male relative has to pay. It is not of very frequent occurrence, but it happens that a man complains to the village "Five" against his wife. The matter is taken up; the wife is found guilty and sentenced to a fine. But the husband has to pay.' (*Santal Folk-Tales*, I, 222).

But beyond these limits, a Santal woman is hardly property at all. As between the sexes labour is divided but this arrangement is based not on inferiority but on convenience and propriety. For certain acts, men are more fitted than women while in others performance by women would suggest a sexual deviation. Women for example, cannot plough, thatch a roof or use a leveller. They may not shoot arrows, use a razor, chisel holes, strike with an axe or fish with line and hook. They can not weave cloth or string a cot. They cannot wear male clothes or play male instruments. All these actions are recognisable diagrams of the male sexual act. Moreover, women are debarred from sacrificing animals as well as from witnessing sacrificing. They can assist in certain ceremonies but can share only certain portions of the sacrificial meat. In certain circumstances, certain women may not enter the bhitar or private shrine. This is because the sex of women will contaminate the bongas. All these actions, men only are competent to do. On the other hand the collection of fuel and the daily drawing of water is almost exclusively a woman's task and cooking also is normally the function of women only.

In other respects, a Santal woman is virtually as free as a man. She can go about alone. Like a Baigin, 'she may dance in public, she may take her wares to the bazaar and open her own shop there, she may drink and smoke in her husband's presence'.[2] In household matters she has as big a say as her husband. In arranging marriages her voice and influence are often decisive. Even in village meetings, women are virtually on a par with men. 'You cannot argue with a skirt.' 'A woman's words are like an arrow in the shoulder blade.' Moreover, she is not debarred from owning land and can also own certain types of movables. In by far the greater spheres of life, a Santal woman is as free to be a woman as a Santal man may be a man.[3]

It is only in one respect that Santal women diverge sharply from men. In Santal society, only women are witches while men are witch-finders and healers. For this reason women do not use drums go to Manjhithans or accompany a corpse. All these things are done by witches and to do any of them would expose a woman to village suspicion. It is the role of witch which invests her with a slightly sinister mystery and in the last analysis assures to Santal woman a respected place in tribal affairs.

REFERENCES

1. Hivale, op. cit., 149.
2. Elwin, op. cit., 235.
3. Among Chenchus, 'In theory women are legally inferior to men; they cannot inherit any substantial property although they can own property, they are dependent on their relatives in concluding marriages and have to abide by their husbands' decisions in regard, for instance to place of residence. But actual life presents a different picture. There we see the Chenchu woman as the equal companion of Chenchu man, doing as much if not more of the work in maintaining the common household, and consequently considering herself and being considered by her husband, as joint possessor of the family property insofar as it is acquired by their concerted labour. In all her daily tasks she acts exactly as she thinks right and her husband seldom interferes in the domain which is hers.'
   (Haimendorf, *The Chenchus*, 143-4).

14

UNMARRIED DAUGHTERS

At the spring and tank
I laughed aloud like green
O you big brother
I am tall and slim
I shall laugh and smile
Until they marry me.

I THE DUTIES OF UNMARRIED DAUGHTERS

IN SANTAL law, the rights of daughters presuppose a number of duties. A girl is brought up in her father's house. Her mother teaches her to husk rice in the early morning, sweep the house and courtyard and smear them with cowdung, to balance a pot and bring water from the spring and make plates and cups of sal leaves. She learns to cook and wash clothes with ashes. At times of cultivation she assists in uprooting and transplanting the seedlings of paddy and in harvesting the crop. She also goes to the jungle with other women and girls for fire wood, tooth twigs and leaves. She often grazes the cattle. In the evening she attends the village dancing.

Moreover, at festivals, she must join the village girls in dancing and village worship, she helps her parents in certain religious acts. As a girl whose head has never received *sindur*, she is still 'in her father's bongas'. She may clean the bhitar or private shrine and cowdung a place for offerings. She can fast and make the flour for the offerings. She can cook the pitar or flour cakes offered in the cowshed at Sohrae. She can cook all the sacrificial meat except the head and can share in eating any meat offered to all the bhitar bongas except the abge. The only exception is that here also she cannot eat the head. She is in fact a member of the household on both its economic and religious sides.

During this period and until she grows up or is married, her father is responsible for maintaining her in food and clothes, paying for her tattooing, performing her birth and initiation ceremonies, treating her in sickness and finally for arranging her marriage. He is the owner of her person and is responsible to society for both her conduct and her marriage. If she offends against the tribal code, her father must pay the fine or suffer excommunication. During this time a Santal daughter must do as her mother and father say but even if she is lazy and disobedient her mother can only slap or spank her and cannot drive her from the house. It is only if she is intimate with a Diku that her parents can expel her. Until she goes to a husband, in fact, a young Santal girl has a wild exciting freedom :

> Big sister
> How long will your cloth flutter?
> I am my father's wealth
> My mother's love
> I shall flirt for ever.

II RIGHTS IN MOVABLES

If the girl's father is the 'owner' of his daughter, an unmarried girl is also the owner of certain kinds of movables. So long as she is with her father or guardian any wages that she earns are given to the head of the household and are never kept by the girl herself but there are six types of property which she herself may keep.

The first of these consists of ir arpa. This is a share in any crop which she has helped to harvest. If her family is fairly well-to-do this is always allowed and it is only in very poor families that ir arpa is not given. If the crop is of paddy it consists of one sheaf and in the case of maize, of one small basket of cobs for every day of work. She also gets a similar share of gundli and other crops. Each day's share is kept in a corner of the threshing floor and after threshing is taken home. The grains which are amassed in this way are then either sold for cash or exchanged for an animal or are loaned out on interest. As a Santal girl assists in reaping from about the age of puberty she usually earn ir arpa for three or four years, and thus acquires earrings, necklaces, bangles, or anklets and even a stock of goats, chickens, pigs or cattle. Barki Hansdak' of Chandna had acquired a cow, a goat and some fowls from her ir arpa at the time she was married and when I visited her father's house in 1944 her two sisters who were aged 16 and 15 and were still unmarried had each a goat, a cow and some fowls besides some ornaments.

A second type of property consists of any animals which her maternal uncle may have given her on account of *gahna* chadao or ending a solar or lunar eclipse. The girl goes to her maternal uncle and says, 'The sun was eclipsed. I called out '*gahna chor ponea katha barea katha*'. Then it ended.' As a present for ending the eclipse the maternal uncle gives the girl and her brothers and sisters a cow, a goat, a pig or a fowl. This is shared between them and the girl's share becomes her private property.

There are thirdly a number of occasions on which a young girl receives customary presents. If her grandfather, her elder sister's husband or her father's sister's husband come to the house she washes their feet and they give her either a rupee or two, four or eight annas. Similarly, if she meets them at a *mela* she can demand a present from them. At the wedding of her elder sister she acts as leading girl or ak' yuric' and at the time of washing the bridegroom she is given four pice. She also gets an anna or so when the bridegroom enters the house. If she cowdungs the place where the bride and bridegroom sit for the present-giving she receives four annas from the bridegroom's father and at the present-giving itself she gets an anna from her mother and a pice or so from some of those who give the presents. If she herself gives the pair a rupee, she can demand a calf from the boy's father. If she is an elder sister and a younger sister is married before her in dol form, she can claim two rupees from the bridegroom's father as taram gande. If this is not given to her at the wedding she can force herself into the basket and insist on being given *sindur* also.* All these presents are the girl's own property.

But besides these ritual gifts she is given certain things by way of family routine. She receives her clothes from her father and these are her own and not the family property. In a well-to-do household she may also have a looking glass, a comb, a brass pot for fetching water as well as thari bati (plates and bowls) of her own. These must be expressly given to her and without such a gift they are ordinarily part of the general household property. The same also applies to the girl's ornaments. All ornaments bought from her own ir arpa or from cash given as a customary present belong to her but all other ornaments unless expressly given to her by her father, a relative, an employer or a friend are part of the family stock. If the girl has a village friend and he wishes to give her an ornament she usually takes it in the form of money, keeps it a secret, gives out that it is a part of her ir arpa and then has something made.

A fifth type consists of all the property which she may have inherited on the death of her father or mother. If her mother is already dead and she has no brothers she gets her father's movable property on his death and retains it till her marriage. If she is a major she can dispose of it as likes. Otherwise it will be kept for her by her guardian until she is married or attains majority. If her mother dies, she will have no claim to her movables so long as there are brothers but if there are no brothers, she inherits all her mother's movables, and her father's agnates have no claim.

Jadu Hembrom of Kalidaspur died leaving an only daughter

*Barsa Murmu of Kurumpaghar had two daughters. Barka Tudu chose the younger for marriage with his son and Barsa offered his elder daughter a cow in lieu of taram gande. The girl refused to take it and said that if Barka himself did not give her taram gande, she would enter the basket. Barka at first declined but after the wedding had been held up for a day he paid it and after that the younger sister's marriage was performed.

who was still unmarried. His own brothers were alive but the girl inherited all his movables.

Finally, if there is a partition in the family before the girl is married she will not be given any formal share but if the stock of cattle is sufficient a cow will be given to her. She will go on living either with her father or with a brother but the cow will remain part of her private property and will go with her when she marries.

III RIGHTS IN LAND

These types virtually exhaust the property which an unmarried daughter can hold. She has ordinarily no rights at all in land. She cannot ask for a partition and if her brothers separate, some land may be kept by her father or a brother for financing her marriage and maintaining her but that is to fulfil their duties towards her and does not confer upon her any rights. At the partition she is given no share.

At the same time her right to maintenance continues and if she is adult and her father, brothers or father's agnates do not fulfil their duty, she can claim enough land for keeping her till marriage. Moreover, it is not impossible for her to acquire land of her own out of her ir arpa. Such land is then her absolute property.

Similarly, in certain circumstances an unmarried daughter can inherit land. If her father dies leaving no widow, sons or agnates she will get his lands until she is married. If later she is married in ghar jawae form, the land remains her own. If, however, she has married sisters and her marriage is not to a ghar jawae her sisters will share equally with her as soon as she is married. If she has no sisters, the village community puts the land in charge of a villager who cultivates it for the girl until she is married. The girl is then almost always married in ghar jawae form and her village guardian arranges and performs the marriage.

IV INHERITANCE OF UNMARRIED DAUGHTER'S PROPERTY

If a daughter dies before marriage who inherits her property ?

If she has any land, the order of inheritance is the same as for a son. The father inherits first, after that her brothers or their sons then her mother and then her own paternal uncles and finally in the absence of all male agnates, her sisters or their heirs. In respect of movables the principles are somewhat different for in this case the person who is maintaining her is entitled to succeed. For this purpose no distinction is made between poultry, pigs, cattle, and utensils on the one hand and feminine articles on the other. None of this property is specifically appropriated to her funeral expenses but whoever inherits her movables will be charged with the duty of performing her funeral.

V LA JAO MARAO

What are the rights of an unmarried daughter in her own person? We have seen that until her marriage she is the property of her father and it is he rather than the girl who is responsible for breaches by her of the tribal code. If she is the victim of force, however, it is either the girl herself or her father who can claim damages. These are known as la jao marao and are normally fixed at five rupees. This money is given to the girl but is often kept by her father while the culprit is also fined any sum up to ten rupees.

Lofar Hembrom of Dholkata had intercourse with the daughter of Pirthi Murmu of his village against the girl's will. The matter went to the village and he was fined ten rupees and had to pay five rupees as la jao marao.

In Modikolha Dipai Hembrom was in love with a girl of his village. One evening the boys and girls were dancing in a *mela* and Dipai pulled the girl out of the dance and dragged her to a field. In the field he forced her to have intercourse. The girl complained to the village and the boy was made to pay ten rupees as fine and five rupees as la jao marao.

Malho Murmu of Jhimuli was watching a field of arahar. When her brother went to the field, he found a boy of the village with her. The boy rushed away but although the girl's brother ran after him he failed to catch him. Other villagers saw the chase and at the meeting the girl proved that the boy had gone to her by force. This boy also was fined ten rupees and had to pay five rupees to the girl.

Similarly, in Balajhore Fongo Hembrom caught the daughter of Naro Murmu in a paddy field. The boy forced her down and when he had finished, the girl went weeping to her father. The village manjhi was informed and at the meeting the boy said that he had done this as he wanted to keep her. The girl said that if he had wanted to marry her there was no reason for doing it against her will. The village fined the boy ten rupees and he too had to pay five rupees to the girl as la jao marao.

The same principles apply when two or more boys combine and force a girl together. In such cases, la jao marao of five rupees is realised from each. They are also fined and if the village so decides part of the fine is given as extra compensation.

Banda Hansdak' and Harma Baske of Khatangi had intercourse with the daughter of the manjhi of Silingi. Each boy was fined ten rupees and each paid five rupees to the girl.

In Kharagdiha Churka Tudu and Pandu Soren caught the daughter of Budhna Hembrom one day at dusk. The girl struggled but the two boys overpowered her. During the encounter the girl snatched the cloth of one of the boys and tore out the pocket of the other's shirt. When she got back to the village she told the manjhi and at the meeting each boy had to give her five rupees as compensation.

Missir Murmu, Jugu Murmu and Kisto Tudu of Parerkola caught the daughter of Bhaju Hansdak' of their village. The girl had no objection to Kisto but the other two had their way by force. At the village meeting each boy paid five rupees and out of this ten rupees was treated as la jao marao and five rupees went to the village.

In a case from Beldiha, the daughter of Gondo Besra was caught by two boys. One of them held her down while the other had relations with her. The girl complained to the village manjhi and at the meeting the boy who did the act was made to pay fifteen rupees and his companion ten. In this case, the whole sum of twenty-five rupees was treated as la jao marao and was given to the girl who gave it to her father.

But besides actual intercourse infringements of modesty also give rise to claims and if a boy makes free with a girl he can be made to give her a similar amount.

In Ilaki Barki Murmu was caught by three boys who pushed her under a cloth and spread it over her like a tent. They did not do anything else but as the girl was very much annoyed she complained to the manjhi. At the meeting the village fined—the principal boy fifteen rupees and the others ten rupees each. Out of this, the girl's father was given twenty rupees as la jao marao, while fifteen rupees was kept by the villagers for a feast.

In all these cases, la jao marao was awarded because the girl herself complained. It is not, however, necessary that the girl herself should always voice the matter or that the act of sex should be against her will. If the girl is willing and either elopes with a boy or is brought to his house by or ader and then for any reason, the boy resiles from marriage, the girl or her father can demand the same indemnity.

In Aswari Rabia Soren took the daughter of Khenka Besra to his house. The girl was willing to marry him but the boy's mother did not like the match. In the end, the boy went back on his promise and five rupees was paid as compensation.

Similarly, if a boy and girl are publicly detected in an act of sex the girl herself may not complain but unless she has incited the boy and is to blame for the encounter, her father can demand la jao marao. The reason for this claim is that the exposure has damaged her reputation. If, however, the girl has compelled the boy to go to her, compensation is sometimes not awarded at all and both the boy and girl are fined instead.

In Kalidaspur Kishun Tudu was caught with the daughter of Dasmat Marandi of Sanola. The boy and girl were in love but because of their public exposure the boy was made to pay her five rupees.

Ratan Marandi of Udalbani was caught with Batki Kisku in an act of sex. The villagers fined the boy ten rupees and made him give a further five as the girls' indemnity.

On the other hand when Barka Marandi of Baghmara was caught with a girl of Ilaki, the boy said that the girl had insisted on his going to her. The meeting fined him fifteen rupees but none of this was given to the girl. On the contrary she was warned that if she went to the boy again she herself would be fined. Sometime later the girl went to the boy's village and the two were caught again. On this occasion, the girl's father had to pay fifteen rupees and out of this, ten rupees were kept by the villagers and five rupees was paid to the boy.

15

MARRIED DAUGHTERS

I RIGHTS IN MOVABLES

WHEN a Santal girl is married her legal position is at once altered and she acquires a double status. On the one hand she secures the rights of a wife while on the other she retains the privileges of a daughter. These latter rights are partly modified by her marriage for she leaves the custody of her father and becomes the property of her husband. Her claims on her father for maintenance accordingly lapse and it is only if she is married to a ghar jawae or her father has left no widow sons, brothers or other male agnates that she can keep possession of his land or movables.*

On the other hand all utensils, articles, ornaments, cash or cattle possessed by her as an unmarried daughter remain her own and their ownership is unaffected by her marriage. The harvest gleanings or ir arpa which have accrued before her marriage stay with her and no one but herself has any claim to them. If after marriage she returns to her father to assist him at harvest, she earns fresh gleanings and these are added to the original stock. If the ir arpa consists of fowls, pigs, goats, cattle or cash it is usually kept at her father's house until she has finally settled at her husband's and in many cases, the property is not removed until a child has been born. Once, however, she has settled down with her husband the property from ir arpa as well as her other movables is shifted

*For the rights of a daughter married to a ghar jawae see Chapter Twenty-two.

to his house. Any increase remains the property of the married daughter and so long as she is alive no one else has any rights.

Similarly, unless any of them are expressly reserved for her father all gifts which a daughter receives at her wedding remain her property.* These consist of cash, utensil and sometimes of clothes and like ir arpa, they are at first kept with her father and taken to her husband's house when the marriage has become stable. Similarly, if at the time of marriage her father gives or promises her a calf this becomes her property. In the case of promises, the claim does not lapse with the father's death and provided the promise is proved, it constitutes a claim which can always be enforced. If a particular animal is promised only that animal and its offspring can be claimed and if the animal dies before the promise is redeemed no other animal can be demanded in its place.

Ratu Marandi of Dulu promised and showed a cow to his daughter at the time of her marriage. When he died his three sons partitioned his property and the cow which had been shown remained with the eldest in trust for the girl. Eight years after the partition the girl demanded the cow and her brother gave it to her along with the 9 cows and bullocks to which it had given birth.

In Kusma Sendra Murmu promised a cow to his daughter at the time of her marriage. He died some years later. As the girl had not born any children she had deferred laying claim to the animal. Sendra's sons at first contested their sister's claim but on the intervention of their uncles who were also aware of the promise they redeemed their father's pledge.

Bikram Soren of Balajhor showed a calf to his daughter at the time of her marriage. When he died his daughter had already given birth to several children and she claimed the cow and took it with its calves to her husband's house.

*See Chapter 24. In the Karbindha area, a brass plate (thari) is placed before the girl. Presents which are put in her hand remain her property. Those which are put on the plate go to her father.

II RIGHTS IN LAND

But besides possessing movables a married daughter may in certain circumstances possess her own land. If her father has died leaving no widow, sons, brothers or male agnates, she either shares his land with her sisters or if there are no sisters, she inherits it entire.

Lakhan Hansdak' of Baristand had two daughters and a son and no agnates. After his son's death he married his two daughters and at the time of his own death the two married daughters shared the land.

In Barwa Bikram Hansdak' had a distant cousin Fuchu and no other relations. Fuchu died without issue and when Bikram himself died his married daughter inherited all his lands and those of Fuchu also.

Durgu Murmu of Chutia died leaving a widow, a son and a daughter. After the daughter had been married the boy died and the widow remarried. There were no agnates and the married daughter inherited all the lands.

Moreover, just as in very rare circumstances an unmarried daughter can possess self-acquired land, a married daughter can also on occasion acquire similar land by taking separate settlement. If she has taken settlement of land prior to her marriage, the land continues to be her private property even though she has a husband.

In Baghmara Raisen Murmu had three daughters. While the youngest was still unmarried 5 bighas of fauti land were settled with her, the cost of the settlement being met from her ir arpa. When she was married she continued to exercise possession.

Panu Murmu of Dulu had a sistee who took settlement of 15 bighas of land out of her ir arpa, before her marriage. She kept the lands but after she and her children had died they were inherited by the sons of her brother.

III TABEN JOM

If lands are sometimes settled with a daughter from the village stock, an even more common form of possession is the grant of family land for taben jom or maintenance. Such land may be given to a married woman either by her father, brothers, or her father's agnates. It usually consists of not more than 10 bighas and is often little more than two or three. It is given sometimes on the occasion of the girl's wedding and sometimes after she is married. Although the gift is generally made of affection, an underlying idea is often a sense of obligation to a daughter or sister and it is this which is emphasised in the myth which sanctions and vitalises the custom.

'A wife made her husband a curry from the after-birth of a goat. The husband ate it. Then she said 'You have eaten living meat. Tell me what it is or I will kill you.' The husband could not guess so he sent for his sister. As the sister came, she heard the young ones of a vulture talking to their mother 'Mother, we are starving'. The vulture replied, 'Never mind. Tomorrow I will give you flesh. A woman is killing her husband. She gave him the after-birth of a goat and he ate it without knowing'. The sister reached the house and said to the wife, 'How will you kill my brother?' The wife showed the weapon. Then the sister took it and killed her saying, 'You made my brother eat the after-birth and now you will kill him'. Then because she had saved his life, her brother gave her land as taben jom. Since then brothers are giving taben jom to their sisters.'

In other cases the gift may be a kind of insurance for the early years of the girl's marriage. A brother may say 'Perhaps her marriage will not turn out well. We will keep some land for her in case she needs it. She may have to come back later'. Or again, if the girl is a favourite sister and her brother is not yet married he may be anxious that she should visit him regularly. He may argue, 'I am getting married later. My wife may not treat her well when she comes to visit us. But if she has some land she can claim good food'. Moreover, although a sister may be happy with her husband, conditions in his village may not suit her. A girl of Jitpur was married in Kalhajor to Morha Marandi. The water did not suit her so the girl's father gave them a little land as taben jom and she and her husband moved to his village.

In Sundarpahari Budhrai Murmu had four sons and two daughters. One daughter was married in Jabarda. As her children kept dying in that village she and her husband came back to Sundarpahari. When they arrived, he gave them some land as taben jom.

In certain circumstances, the grant of taben jom is an alternative to converting a son-in-law into a ghar jawae. Instead of bringing back a married daughter by agu mit' or marrying a daughter to a serving son-in-law, a father gives her a little land as taben jom and secures her help and presence.

When a gift for taben jom is made it is usually done by the father with the approval of his sons or if the father is dead by the girl's brothers or paternal uncles acting in agreement. A girl married in ghar jawae form may similarly give taben jom to a sister, aunt or niece. All such gifts are made in a village meeting and if a relative objects, the village decides whether the gift is proper. Even if a man is separate from his sons, brothers or uncles, the latter can protest and the village decision will be final. At the village meeting it is made clear whether the gift is to the girl for life, jiwet bhor lagit' or whether jao jug lagit', for ever. If there is no express statement at the meeting or if no formal meeting is held the assumption is that the gift is only for the girl's lifetime and when she dies the land will go back to those who gave it.

Bhagmat Hembrom of Haripur gave 2 bighas of land in Chandarpura to his sister as taben jom, but only for her lifetime. When she died she left a son but he did not get it and the land returned to Bhagmat.

Matla Marandi of Chota Ranga gave some land to his sister who was married in the same village. He gave it to her only for her lifetime and when she died although she had children he took the land back.

In Dahari Santali Doso Soren had a married daughter and a brother's son. Doso fell ill and his daughter and her husband came to look after him. Then Doso died and his nephew did ag muk and performed the funeral. After that, the nephew got the lands but for taben jom, he gave 5 bighas to Doso's daughter for her lifetime on the understanding that it would revert to him at her death.

When the land has been given 'for ever' all rights of the girl's father, brothers, or agnates as the case may be are extinguished and it becomes her property in as absolute a manner as ir arpa. 'It has been given to be eaten' 'We have spat on it'.

In Kalhajore, Ranjit Hembrom, the grandfather of the present manjhi had 150 bighas of land. When his sister married Dharmu Murmu of Baliadih he gave her 5 bighas. He made the gift 'for ever' and when his sister died, her 3 sons inherited it.*

IV HEIRS

During her lifetime a married daughter has full rights of ownership in all these types of land and movables. What then is the procedure at her death?

In the case of movables her property is not inherited by her husband but is divided equally between her sons. If the sons are joint, the property remains in the joint family stock but is 'reserved' for the sons. If she has no sons her daughters whether married or unmarried inherit it. If she has sons and daughters it is only the sons and not the daughters who will share it. If the woman dies childless her property goes first to her father, then to her brothers, and then to her mother.

The wife of Baiju Murmu of Baghmara possessed a necklace, two gold earrings, a gold mandoli and two armlets as her private property. When she died her only child, a daughter, inherited the ornaments and when shortly afterwards the daughter also died, the woman's father took them all away.

Phatu Murmu of Barabandh married a girl of Ilaki. The girl had three cows, and 8 goats of her own but then she died without any children, her brothers shared all the animals and gave one goat to her husband. They also took back all their sister's ornaments.

In Bokrabandh Ragda Hansdak' had one son and three daughters. At the time of her marriage one daughter possessed two bales of paddy. When she died soon after her marriage her father claimed the two bales and took them both away.

*For the circumstances in which rights in taben jom land are forfeited, see my report, *Bitlaha*.

The daughter of Bhagan Kisku of Murbhanga was married at Karanpura. Her ir arpa amounted to ten cows and 5 bales of paddy and when she died without any issue, her father claimed the animals and paddy and took them to his house.

If she has no children her husband may be given one or two animals as an act of grace but he cannot claim them as of right. Such inheritance usually covers only animals, utensils, clothes and ornaments. 'Who can say where money has gone?' If, however, some cash has been left it will be inherited like other movable property.

In the case of land, inheritance varies according to its character. If the land has been acquired, 'for ever', as taben jom the children by the married daughter inherit it. If there are sons they receive it and if there are no sons, daughters, whether married or unmarried, will get it. The husband or his agnates will not, however, have any claim 'for the land was never theirs'. If the woman does not have any children, the land will return to her father, brothers, mother or male agnates.

In the case from Sundarpahari in which Budhrai gave his daughter taben jom, he gave the land 'for ever' and when the girl died, her son, Kam Hansdak', inherited it. Kam has since died and one of his surviving sons is cultivating it.

In Tetaria, Sibu Tudu, the grandfather of the present manjhi had a sister who was married in Jitpur. As Sibu had more than sufficient land of his own he gave some fields as taben jom to his sister. Her husband built a house in Tetaria and he and his family lived in the two villages. The gift was for ever and the girl's children have since inherited it.

Similar principles apply if the land is self-acquired. The acquisition is equivalent to starting a new family stock and only if there are no children will it go to the woman's father, brothers, mother or male agnates.

Bogoc' Soren of Bhimpahari was married in Karjuri. As her children began to die she left the village and returned to her home. When her husband died Bogoc' took settlement of 12 bighas of land in a village meeting the cost being met from her ir arpa. On her death her four daughters inherited and not her brothers.

Finally, if the land has been inherited, the heirs will be her sons and failing any sons, her daughters. Since the land will have come to her originally only through the failure of male agnates or the death or remarriage of her mother, the question of reversion to a father, brother, mother or uncle cannot arise. If she has no children, her sisters and their sons inherit and after them their daughters.

16

WIVES

O you true one,
In front of men and God
You gave me cloth and sindur
Now you must give me
Food and drink.

—*Don Seren*, 3212.

I STATUS

FOR almost every Santal girl, a first ambition is to be a wife. This is not because marriage will necessarily bring immediate happiness, for in most cases it will mean the loss of the parents' home. Moreover, it will almost invariably involve a parting from a lover. But it gives a Santal girl a new status. It is the first step to independent charge of a household. It is the accepted condition for being a mother. It completes her position in society and gives her adult respect.

II CELAN GITIL

The first result of this new status is that she ceases to be the ward of her father and enters the custody of her husband. She retains the land or movables which she owned as a married or unmarried daughter but the rights in her person now pass to her husband. If 'her skin is stolen' it is he who must be compensated and there are four ways in which a claim may lie.

When intercourse has occurred but neither the husband

nor the wife desires to separate, the husband can claim from the adulterer a sum of money known as celan gitil—'for scouring the pot' and the culprit must also pay the manjhi of his village five rupees 'for saving his head'. This latter payment is now regarded as a fine and is a survival from a time when an adulterer could be slain by the woman's husband. It is kept by the manjhi as his private perquisite. The sum 'for scouring the pot' is either five, ten or fifteen rupees according to the custom of the area. In the greater part of Dumka subdivision and much of the district, it is five rupees but in the Pakaur subdivision, it is almost always fixed at fifteen. In addition, each party must also pay the cost of the sitting—the adulterer at full rate and the injured husband at half rates.

Sital Hembrom of Murgibani reached home one night at nine o'clock. It was the day of the Mag festival and his wife and children were dancing in the village. Sometime after midnight they came home and Sital who was sitting in his cowshed saw his wife go out again. He could not understand why she should do this, so a little later he got up and went to look for her. He found her on a verandah in the act of intercourse with Samu Murmu. Samu got up and ran away but left behind his cloth. Sital gave chase but failed to catch him. He then took his wife and the cloth to the manjhi and left them with him. Sital did not want to lose his wife neither did his wife want to change her husband. Sital therefore claimed celan gitil of fifteen rupees from Samu. Samu paid it and also gave a further five rupees to the manjhi for saving his head.

In Nawadih Dula Marandi and Ragda Marandi were married men with children. One night when Dula was out in the village Ragda suddenly entered his house and went to his wife. She cried and protested but Ragda forced her down and against her will had intercourse. While this was happening her husband heard the noise and coming back found Ragda with his wife. Ragda ran away but although Dula chased him he made good his escape. The next day Dula called a village meeting and Ragda admitted that out of passion he had gone to Dula's wife. Ragda paid five rupees to Dula 'for scouring the pot' and five rupees to the manjhi 'for saving his head'.[1]

A second circumstance is when intercourse has occurred and the husband does not wish to keep his wife. When this happens he cannot claim a sum for 'scouring the pot' but the adulterer must pay him double the brideprice and if the marriage was recent he may also have to pay the expenses of the wedding. In addition, the adulterer must pay the manjhi of his village the usual five rupees for 'saving his head' and give the village the cost of the meeting which sometimes also includes a fine. If he does not wish to keep the woman he must also pay her the local rate of divorce money.

Haji Tudu of Sundrapalan ran away with the wife of Raska Hembrom during the Sohrae festival of 1940. Raska Hembrom did not wish to keep his wife, so Haji paid the double bride price of twenty-four rupees to Raska. The manjhi could have levied a fee for 'saving his head' but on this occasion did not take it.

In Ghagri the wife of Choto Murmu committed adultery with Jara Marandi of Amarpur. Choto was very angry and divorced her and the adulterer had to pay a double bride price to the husband, five rupees to his own manjhi 'for saving his head' and five rupees to the village.

In Beoa the wife of Nuna Kisku was detected in intercourse with Sikhar Murmu. Nuna divorced his wife and Sikhar had to pay sixth rupees to the husband as double bride price and the expenses of the wedding, a fine of ten rupees to the village and five rupees to the manjhi 'for saving his head'.

If, as sometimes happens, several men or boys have intercourse with a married woman one after another, and if the woman's husband declines to keep her and none of the boys accepts her, all of them are jointly liable for paying a sum which may include a double bride price and the expenses of the wedding to the husband and divorce money to the woman. They must also pay the village a fine and besides this give a further sum of five rupees each to the manjhi for saving their heads.

If one of the boys accepts her as his wife the divorce money is excluded from the sum. The others, however, must share in the payment of double bride price unless the boy who takes the woman agrees to bear it all. If the husband divorces his wife and she declines to go to any of the boys, they must pay her joint divorce money. If the husband does not divorce his wife each of the boys or men is liable for a separate celan gitil as well as for a fee to the manjhi for saving his head and a fine to the village.

The wife of Dheba Marandi of Taldih had intercourse with two men one after another. Dheba agreed to keep her but each man had to pay a sum of fifteen rupees as celan gitil.

In Garra the wife of Bodon Hembrom was caught with two men. Each of these paid fifteen rupees—half being treated as celan gitil and the rest being taken by the village.

In Kosidih the wife of Bhattu Marandi had been to a *mela* with other boys and girls of her village. On the way back at night she stayed under a tree with three boys and all of them had intercourse with her. Later they were detected and at the village meeting the three boys between them paid sixty rupees to the girl's husband and one of the boys married her.

Finally, a man may be caught with another's wife in a manner which compromises the woman and leaves her chastity in doubt.

In such cases the gesture is held to have implied the deed and the same adjustments are made as if the two had been surprised in actual congress.

Jogon Soren of Lodhna found his wife talking with Bhogon Hembrom in a lonely place. Jogon suspected that they had had relations and took the matter to the village. The village held them guilty and Bhogon paid five rupees as celan gitil.

In Tilaki Rajain Kisku found his wife inside the house with a boy of the same village. The village presumed sexual intercourse and the boy was made to pay celan gitil of fifteen rupees to the husband.

In all such cases the guilty parties must be captured and produced before a village official. In the alternative, some tangible evidence must always be produced, the man himself must confess his complicity, or some independent unconnected witnesses must prove the happening. If the man escapes leaving nothing behind and also denies his part and if no one except the other party has seen him it is only one word against another and the claim is rarely conceded.

In Pathna a Santal and his wife had been drinking country liquor and the husband was drunk. They were sleeping on separate cots when a Santal of the village crept into the house and began to go to the woman. She woke in a start and seized him by the hand. Then her husband woke in a dazed state and helped to hold him. The two tied him with a cloth and began to walk him to the manjhi. On the way the man stopped to make water and while he was stooping down he untied the cloth and was off before they could catch him. In this case the man denied that he had done anything and as he escaped and left nothing behind and no one else had seen him the villagers took no action.

III LA JAO MARAO

If sexual intercourse with another man is primarily the infringement of a husband's rights, a wife is also entitled to la jao marao or private damages if the act is done to her by force. In such cases the amount is the same as for unmarried daughters and is payable in addition to whatever may be awarded as celan gitil or as divorce money. If several boys are involved, each is liable for this extra sum.

In Chotochuan a Santal was friendly with a married girl named Paku. One day when the girl's husband was away he went to her house and proposed intercourse. For some reason Paku did not want him that day and told him not to do it. The boy did not listen and went to her by force. Paku screamed and the boy's wife and other villagers arrived. They gave the boy a beating and in the village settlement he was made to give Paku ten rupees as la jao marao as well as other payments to the village and her husband.

Similarly, when Kandu Tudu of Subhbari forced the wife of Sagram Tudu to have intercourse, he was made to pay a fine to the village and to give celan gitil to Sagram and la jao marao to the girl.

IV RELIGIOUS CONSEQUENCES

A second consequence of marriage is that a woman acquires a new religious relation. This is conditional on her husband putting *sindur* on her and arises only in the forms of marriage in which *sindur* is given.* If the girl was previously un-

*See Chapters 23-32.

married and her husband puts *sindur* on her she becomes his wife not only for the present world but also for the next. She is now disqualified from performing any religious function in her father's house and becomes competent to assist her husband in the service of his bongas. If she was divorced or a widow and had not received *sindur* previously, she acquires the same new relation in her husband's house. If however, she has received *sindur* prior to her marriage she is debarred from assisting her husband in any religious act, and even if *sindur* is given to her later by the process of baha saoha* this is only a dummy *sindur* which merely enables her children to have *sindur* at their weddings.

V ECONOMIC

But besides providing a girl with a new set of bonga, marriage also gives her a new domestic focus. Instead of working for her father the wife must now work for her husband. She becomes the member of a new household and it is this which now has full claim on all her energies. Her work consists of an exacting routine from early morning until night and Kolean Haram has given a description which is still to a great extent true of Santal life :

'Women', he says, 'work continuously. In the early morning they get up and pound the paddy in the dhinki.** As it dawns they clean the courtyard with cowdung. They draw and bring the water. They give the men and the children the watered gruel which is left-over from the day before. When they have eaten the women eat. Then they put the midday meal on the fire to cook, they prepare rice and curry, they make leaf cups and leaf plates, they take out the cooked rice from the pot. At noon they give the midday meal to the men and the children and then eat themselves. From midday until evening they do other work. They go and pick pot herbs, they bring leaves, and if a forest is near, they bring fuel. When it is dusk they go to draw water and prepare the supper. When it is two hours after dusk they eat. The women eat last. They rarely eat

*See Chapter 27.

**This is now-a-days often done in the evening.

meat. They generally eat rice with dal and pot herbs. Then they talk about various domestic matters and then sleep. During the days of planting and harvesting, the women transplant paddy, they harvest maize, when the paddy is ripe they reap and thresh it. In the month of Pus they make the house clean and smooth. These are the duties of women.'*

So long as her husband is joint with his father the wife's position differs little from what it was in her father's house. She is equally subordinate to the senior women and must work according to their bidding. When, however, her husband sets up a separate house of his own, she moves into a position of great responsibility and becomes a trustee for all his possessions. All expenditure must have her husband's approval and she cannot commit her husband to any action without his express consent.

'Some men and their wives' says Kolean Haram 'live very happily. The husband lightens the burden of his wife and the wife lightens the burden of her husband. In the evening the husband and wife consult each other about their work. The husband speaks to the wife when times are hard. 'Now-a-days water the rice carefully, these are times of scarcity.' The wife also says, 'Exert yourself to get food for us. Our stock is running short. The clothes of the children are torn. How will you make clothes for them? The boy has grown up, will you look for a daughter-in-law? Perhaps he may get into trouble and get us into trouble also. The children are not listening to me. How many times shall I tell them to do things and scold them? The children are ill. Feel their pulse'. In this way good husbands and wives heed each other, work with heart and soul, and live in peace together.**

VI ETIQUETTE

This sense of partnership is at the root of a wife's status but to achieve and maintain it, she must regulate her conduct by certain rules of behaviour. She must observe certain ritual conduct with her new relations and she can leave her husband's

**Horkoren Mare Hapramko reak' Katha*, 113.
**Ibid., 115.

house on visits only with his permission. If she wishes to see her parents a brother must either come and fetch her or her husband, his sister or his mother must take her to her home. If she goes without an approved escort, her act amounts to desertion and her husband can divorce her. It is only when she has had two or three children that an escort can be dispensed with but her husband is expected to know and approve of where she has gone.

VII CHILDREN

Finally, there is one aspect of her status which stresses her subordination. As a corollary to her husband's possession of her person, all children that are born become his and if her marriage fails a wife has no claim to their control or custody. If she is suckling a child she can claim to keep it until it is two years old and is weaned but if she does so, she retains it in trust for her husband. It is for her husband and not herself that a Santal wife bears children.

If, however, the marriage is permanent, she exercises equal powers of discipline and it is only in the eye of law that the children are not hers.

VIII RIGHTS

In return for all these obligations a Santal wife has certain rights. Her husband must clothe her according to the accepted village standards and whatever he eats and drinks he must share with his wife. If her husband leaves home, he must make arrangements for her maintenance and if he is joint with his brothers or father and friction developes, she can claim sufficient lands to keep her. If she falls ill her husband must make arrangements for her medical attention, and unless she gives him provocation he must not ill-treat or beat her. Equally he must give her opportunities of visiting her family. Apart from times of family crisis, such as sickness, births, deaths or weddings, married daughters are particularly welcome at the Sohrae, Baha and Erok' festivals. When they come they are expected to bring a pot of rice beer with them and it is the husband's duty to place no obstacle in his wife's observance of this custom.[2]

Finally he must respect her property and if they are estranged after the age of divorce, he must give her sufficient land for maintenance and allow her to live apart.

Suphal Hansdak' of Pokharia began to waste all his household goods on drink. He had a wife and three children. His wife did not want divorce as she would then have lost the children and she feared that her drunken husband would neglect them. The matter went to the village and the Pargana and Suphal's lands were divided into three. The wife received two shares for the children and herself and the husband got one.

In Bostadiha Barka Kisku and his wife became estranged and Baika wanted a divorce. As his wife was old and stood no chance of marrying again she did not agree so the two were separated and Barka gave her six bighas of land for her maintenance.

In Moti Lachmi, Suna Murmu quarrelled with all his sons and separated from them. Later he quarrelled with his wife also and since they were beyond the age of divorce, he gave her some lands and they lived apart.

REFERENCES

1. Among the Lepchas, 'discovered adultery is not a cause of enmity either between husband and wife or between husband and lover; only in the case of persistent adultery, and of the woman showing a really marked preference for the lover would the marriage be broken up'.
(Gorer, *Himalayan Village*, 138).
2. Verrier Elwin has drawn attention to the important place of these visits in the life of aboriginal girls. 'After marriage', he points out 'the mother's house acquires a sweet and romantic memory. Its hardships and quarrels are easily forgotten, and the love of one's own parents appear tender and kind compared to the constant friction of the new home. It is generally considered correct for girls to go to the parents' house for important domestic events such as the ceremonies for the birth of children, marriages and funerals, for some of the chief festivals and to help in the more urgent work

of the fields. Husbands, especially young husbands, resent this, for it means one pair of hands the less to work in their own house. Girls are not always very tactful in the enthusiasm they show at returning to their old homes and some girls make a regular habit of going there far too often for the comfort of their husband'. (Elwin, *Maria Murders and Suicide*, 119-20).

17

CO-WIVES

I THE CAUSES OF PLURAL MARRIAGE

'IN OLDEN times', says Kolean Haram, 'Santals used to have only one wife and no one ever had two. Now-a-days if a man is so lustful as to have two or three wives, Santals do not think it good'.[1] This view is still widely held and a number of proverbs record 'the dubious joys of plural marriage'.[2] 'A pair of dogs always bite', 'A co-wife pricks like spear grass', 'Pecking hens never agree', 'Sparks fly from a co-wife like an ebony branch flaming in the rains'. In the folk-tale Siṭ and Lakhan,[3] the story ends with the moral, 'There is no controlling a second wife and they are hard to get on with. First wives are the best and they are obedient and agree with the opinion of their husbands'. What are the circumstances then in which co-wives are taken?

The most frequent occasion is when a Santal and his wife have no children. The man himself may be very anxious for a son. His wife realises that children will be of help in their old age and if they are fairly well off, a second wife may be taken with the hope that she will bear a son.[4]

A Santal of Sarauni failed to get children so at his wife's suggestion he married her sister.

Jagan Tudu of Bhalke had no children from his wife, so with her consent he took a second, had children by her and both wives lived happily with him.

Dhapra of Taldangal had similarly no children. He took a second wife, got children and both wives were happy.

Not all co-wives, however are taken with a view to getting children. Sometimes a first wife becomes diseased or sickly. She cannot attend properly to the house work and there is no one to cook her husband's food. When this happens the husband brings a co-wife to act as a house keeper and to help her in the running of the home. In such cases there is often no estrangement and the second marriage is simply for convenience.

If these considerations sometimes result in a second marriage with relations the presence of a wife's younger sister or her frequent visits to the house may lead to her induction as a co-wife.

The wife of Damdhar Murmu of Belatari brought her sister to help her in house work. The younger sister fell in love with her brother-in-law and later on he installed her as his co-wife. The three are living happily together and each of the two sisters has now had several children.

In Boarijore, Kanhu Marandi was a servant in the house of Ram Pargana. While working there he married a girl of the village and had a daughter by her. Sometime later he became friendly with his wife's younger sister and used to meet her in the fields at night. One day he decided to take her as a co-wife and brought her to his house. The two sisters are now living happily with him at his own village.

But besides the younger sister another relation is often taken as a co-wife.

If an elder brother dies, his widow often remains a part of the household. She may already have allowed her husband's younger brother access to her person. If he takes her as a co-wife, the terms of marriage excuse him from paying a further bride price. There is the advantage of common cultivation. Her children remain to assist in the house and if his first wife likes her company, the household continues as a smoothly working unit. Even if his first wife is opposed, their conventional intimacy may prompt him to instal her as a wife.

Rasik Marandi of Nawadih married Sona Hansdak'. Sometime later he married her younger sister and after his first wife had died he took his elder brother's widow as yet another co-wife.

Phogor Hembrom of Sildhawa was married and had

children. His elder brother died leaving a young widow and children. Phogor was afraid that she would desert the children and marry some one else. So in order to have a woman to mind the children, he installed her as his co-wife.

In Telgama, Sakla Soren was married and had a son and daughter. His elder brother died leaving a widow who also had a son and daughter. The two brothers were separate but after some time Sakla became intimate with the elder brother's wife and made her pregnant. Sakla's wife did not approve of their intimacy and Sakla sometimes beat her for remonstrating with him. He then began to live openly with his elder brother's widow and when the child was born he accepted the paternity. The widow has now been accepted as his co-wife but the two wives are living separately.

If the presence of relatives accounts for certain plural marriages, position in tribal society also sometimes prompts a Santal to indulge in several wives. If a Santal is wealthy or holds a high office such as that of a pargana he sometimes keeps co-wives for his personal and tribal prestige. In Asanbona Lakhan Tudu had seven wives 'because he was pargana'. In Mahulbona the manjhi took a second wife 'so that he might boast of his wealth'. Chotrai Deshmanjhi describes how during the rebellion Sido and Kanhu collected girls as they went through the country. 'Wherever they camped, they made the boys and girls of the village dance and if a girl caught their fancy, their orderlies would place a cloth on the girl's head and say she had become the Thakur's. The girl was then put on a palki and taken to them. In this way both Sido and Kanhu got numbers of girls. Any one's daughter or daughter-in-law became theirs if their eyes fell on her and their clothes were put on the girl's head. If a man said anything he was shown 'the pod of a pea', and their orderlies slew him. So from fear not a word was said'.[5] At that time, Sido and Kanhu were establishing themselves as Santal rulers and it is evident that they regarded a large number of wives as necessary for their new authority and prestige.

If the taking of a co-wife is often at the first wife's instance, yet another cause of plural marriages is friction between husband and wife.

Baghrai Hembrom of Sildhawa had a wife who always

quarrel with him. He did not divorce her but brought a co-wife.

Barka Hembrom of Machidanr had constant friction with his wife so he also brought another.

Moreover in certain circumstances a first wife may be constantly deserting her husband or avoiding relations with him. The husband may not want to divorce her. In fact his sole wish may be to secure her permanent return. When in spite of constant trying, he fails to win her back, he sometimes takes a co-wife as a substitute.

Leko Soren was the first wife of Hode Murmu of Astakandar. Every year she used to leave him and go to Burdwan for paddy cutting. Hode wanted her to stay in his house and did not want to divorce her. In the end he did not do so but brought a girl as a co-wife.

Yet another cause of double marriages is infatuation with a stranger.

Jalpa Marandi of Bagnol was married and had children by his first wife. He fell in love with another girl, and eloped with her to Chittagong. Later he brought her back to the village and installed her in his house. His wife did not like it and in the end he had to build the second wife another house. Similarly, Bhokta of Bawa became friendly with a girl while he was away from his first wife and was working in the coal mines. When he came back, he brought the girl with him. His wife was very angry but did not divorce him and the village accepted the second girl as his co-wife.

Finally the need of a wife in the world to come may sometimes impel a Santal to take a second wife. Chota Murmu of Lakhibad was first married to a girl who had been once divorced. Later he decided that he must also have a dangua or unmarried girl as his wife in order that he should not be alone in the after world. His wife's younger sister was still unmarried and he therefore took her.

In Jitpur, a wedding had been arranged between Kadu Tudu and the elder daughter of Alma Kisku. Before the marriage took place another man put *sindur* on the girl and thus made her his wife in hanapuri. The girl, however, declined to marry him and it was finally decided that Kadu would marry her in sangha form. He accordingly first married the elder girl and then celebrated a dol bapla with her younger sister.

II THE CLAIMS OF THE FIRST WIFE

Once a Santal desires a second wife he usually seeks his first wife's approval. Lack of consent however does not prevent a second marriage and if the village accepts the second wife, the attitude of the first wife is immaterial.

If, however, a first wife cannot stop a second marriage the bringing of a co-wife entitles her to certain definite reliefs. She is entitled in the first place to receive either a cow or five rupees as hirom baiha. This is given to her partly as a means of purchasing her consent and partly as compensation for the loss of her married prospects. According to earlier custom a first wife would wait with a broom, a load of firewood or a ladle until the second wife appeared and would then beat her out of the house. To purchase entry, hirom baiha was given. But it is not in every case that the cow or money is claimable. The first wife must either be actually living with her husband at the time of the second marriage or if she is living apart, it must be against her will and by the fault of her husband. If she has gone away and refuses to return in spite of her husband's efforts no hirom baiha can be claimed. The test in such cases is whether the husband or the girl's parents have made attempts to bring them together. If the girl's parents have approached the husband and said 'Why are you not taking her? She is willing' ; and if he has still refused, hirom baiha must be paid. But if he himself has been rebuffed, nothing can be demanded. Finally, if the co-wife is the elder brother's widow no hirom baiha is payable.

Surju Hansdak' of Bokrabandh had a wife who always deserted him. All his attempts to bring her back failed and finally he brought another woman as a co-wife. His first wife claimed hirom baiha but the village declined to sanction it as they said that she herself was to blame.

Similarly, when all the attempts of Kalu Hembrom of Kheribari to get his wife to live with him had failed another girl was brought as his co-wife. His first wife claimed hirom baiha but in this case also the village refused to sanction it.

Once hirom baiha has been paid in cash, or a cow has been reserved, it acts as a permanent insurance against further marriages. If the husband takes a third wife or a fourth no further payment is required and the payment covers all his later experiments. Such hirom baiha is confined to the actual animal shown and all its offspring and if the animal dies before it is claimed, the husband is not required to give another animal in its place.

But besides enabling a first wife to claim hirom baiha a second marriage is a valid ground for divorce and if the first wife decides to leave her husband, she can claim not only hirom baiha but her full chadaodi or divorce money.

Such award of divorce money, however, is not entirely automatic and the claims of the wife are determined by her own conduct. If her previous desertion is responsible for her husband taking the co-wife, she can still demand divorce but is not entitled to divorce money or to hirom baiha. On the other hand if she is living with her husband or has been deserted by him she can claim divorce and both payments are admissible. If, however, she avails of this ground, she must avoid giving her husband any cause of action. If she elopes with a lover, her husband's rights remain and he can still claim a double brideprice. Similarly, if after living with her co-wife, she deserts her husband but for reasons not connected with the co-wife, the husband can claim return of bride-price if he also is not to blame. Her own conduct does not affect her right to divorce but it determines the terms on which it will be granted.

III HIROM CETAN BAPLA

While a wife cannot prevent a second marriage, her attitude has important bearings on its method. The marriage in whatever form it occurs will be known as a hirom cetan bapla—the taking of a co-wife but if the first wife has agreed to a second and the girl has not been previously married there is nothing to prevent a full dress celebration by the village. Similarly, if her opposition is so extreme that she refuses to live with her husband, the result is tantamount to a divorce and a full dress wedding is again quite possible. Equallyif the second wife is a divorcee and there is either consent or desertion by the first wife, a public ceremony in sangha form may be observed. In all such cases active village celebration depends on the absence of conflict with the first wife. If, however, the latter does not leave the village and presses her objection the village will suit its action to the case. For example, if a childless wife objects, sympathy will go on the husband and a full dress wedding may go on even though the first wife sulks in a room. But if the first wife has sons, is of good character and is hard working, the village may accept the marriage but refuse to celebrate it.

IV THE POLYGAMOUS HOUSEHOLD

The attitude of the first wife similarly determines the way in which the household will actually adjust itself. In certain cases the act of keeping a woman in a separate house with the knowledge of the village may have been the only circumstance behind a village acceptance of the woman as a second wife.

In other cases if general unwillingness and dislike has made a full dress wedding impossible, residence in the same house will also be difficult. In that case also the second wife may be given a separate house in the village. When Ghata Marandi of Ghanti married a second time he already had children by his first wife, there was no full dress wedding and he installed the girl in his father's house lower down the village lane.

On the other hand, when there is no undue opposition, the second wife may be brought to the same house and either share a room with the first wife or have one to herself.

Singhrai Marandi of Karmai was a big cultivator with a large house. He had five wives and all of them lived with him in the same courtyard. Nimai Murmu of Rajpokhar also had five wives and kept them all in a single house. In Titria Bhadu Murmu had four wives and they too lived together.

This household adjustment is made by the husband, and if friction developes it is he who is held to blame.

In Sagra Hopna Kisku had been married fourteen years but had no children. He then married a second wife with the consent of the first and for a year all three lived happily together. As he was anxious for a son, he slept most nights with the second wife. When the second wife became pregnant, Hopna began to sleep with his first wife again. One night in the hot weather he was sleeping with her on a cot while the co-wife was lying on another. The co-wife could not bear her isolation any longer so she threw a heavy stone at the first wife and hurt her. Hopna took the matter to the village the next day. At first the co-wife denied having thrown the stone. Then she admitted it but added that since she had started to be big in her body, Hopna had turned his eyes from her. The village council blamed Hopna for every thing and he was told to pay the cost of the meeting, to look at both his wives with equal eyes and to sleep with both of them in the same room. A few days later the co-wife gave birth to a daughter and the friction ended.

Similar action was taken by the villagers of Chhota Haripur when the co-wife of their manjhi Gora Soren complained that his senior wife was always abusing her. Gora was held responsible and the villagers reprimanded him for failing to keep order in his house.

V THE RIGHTS OF A CO-WIFE

When a woman becomes a co-wife or chutki, what are her rights?

If she has married with the approval of her batki (the first wife or her husband) she is given a cow, some ornaments or some land as monrofa.* This gift is also an insurance against friction and like hirom baiha is designed to protect the co-wife against a break down of the union.

The son of Bariar Baske of Sahri was married to a girl who was still a child. With the approval of his wife's parents he brought a chutki and showed to her as monrofa. Sometime later he brought his first wife. The two did not get on well so he kept them in separate houses. His first wife was then grown up and as he neglected his chutki the latter left him and demanded the calf. The boy refused to give it but the village held that the chutki was not to blame and awarded monrofa to her.

*In the Jamtara area this is termed jai jant.

When Sital Hembrom of Jambar brought a second wife his first wife acquiesced and Sital showed the co-wife three bighas of land as monrofa.

In cases where land is given the gift operates from the break-down of the union or from the time of a partition. If, however, the marriage fails from the co-wife's own fault, all claims to monrofa lapse. Moreover, monrofa is given only when the first wife accepts the marriage. If the co-wife comes in the teeth of her opposition, nothing is set apart for her. 'She has come with her eyes open. Why should her husband give her any thing?'

Once a co-wife is installed, she acquires the same civil rights as a first wife. She is entitled to food, drink and clothing, and is as much her husband's wife as her batki. The fact that she may not have been married with a full dress wedding matters nothing. In Santal society there is no institution of the kept mistress, for once a mistress is kept and the village acquiesces, she at once becomes a wife, while on the other hand if the village does not acquiesce, she is no longer kept.

There is however, a difference of economic position according as the co-wives live separately or jointly. If they share the same courtyard and kitchen they have equal rights in everything. The batki usually supervises the household while the chutki looks to all the outdoor work. If however, the co-wife is given a separate house and kitchen, certain movables are allotted to her and it is only in respect of these that she acts as custodian. Similarly when the husband dies, movables are inherited on the basis of the household. All sons inherit their father's lands equally, irrespective of whether their mother was a first, second or third wife, but each son inherits only those movables which were in his mother's household, when his father died.*

The right of a co-wife to maintenance continues for as long as she affords her husband no valid ground for divorce or

*This principle is followed throughout the District except in the Godda Subdivision where the accepted rule is that all sons share their father's movables irrespective of whether their mothers are joint or separate.

until she passes the age beyond which divorce is disallowed. If her husband tires of her, he must still arrange to keep her and if she has passed the age of divorce and he declines to live with her, he must allot her sufficient land to keep her in food and clothing.

This parity of status is further reflected in the treatment of children. When a daughter by one wife is married, all her father's wives are entitled to a mother's itat or present. Her own mother receives a cloth but each of her co-mothers gets one also. If a co-wife dies, her children become the responsibility of her husband's other wives. They must act as foster mothers and rear the children as if they were their own. The latter cannot however claim any share in their property.

Finally, a co-wife can demand a due share in her husband's affections. Not every plural marriage ends in failure and when a husband unites with both his wives each night, he is on the way to achieving domestic happiness. It is when passion for one wife leads to the exclusion of the other that 'the dogs begin to bite'.[6]

REFERENCES

1. *Horkoren Mare Hapramko reak' Katha*, 99.
2. Verrier Elwin, *Maria Murder and Suicide* (Bombay, 1943), 105.
3. Bompas, op. cit., 238-240.
4. In the Folk-tale, Not to be had for Money, this situation is vividly depicted: "When the girl at last understood that she could not any longer hope to get children she cried every day, and because she was grieving over this, she wasted away . . . 'Chando has not given me a child. What can I say? That is my grief. Therefore I am wasting away. It may go so long as my strength lasts. But some day in the future, when my husband and become old who will support us, who will take care of us? It is on account of these anxieties that I am crying and wasting away'." (Bodding, *Santal Folk-Tales*, I, 363-367).

   In many cases the unmarried sister of the first wife is chosen since both the women know each other and are likely to live happily. When this happens however it is due to personal preference and there is no tribal law which confines selection to a sister.
5. W.G. Archer, The Santal Rebellion, *Man in India*, XXV (1945), 233.

6. Geoffry Gorer gives an interesting note on Lepcha practice. 'If after a number of years of marriage' he says 'a man's wife is sterile, he has a right to apply to his wife's family for a second wife, providing his first wife agrees. In theory it is only permissible to take a second wife from the first wife's ptso, and ideally this second wife should be the first wife's real or classificatory younger sister. This is recognised in the terms with which co-wives are always referred to; the Nepali words jethi and kanchi meaning 'eldest sister' and 'youngest sister' are always used: Lepcha has no equivalent terms to indicate the position of a child in the order of birth. In the great majority of cases the ideal conditions are observed and the two wives, if not actual sisters are of the same ptso and use kinship terms. In cultural theory the co-wives have already an established habit of co-operation and co-habitation which only needs to be renewed, and the situation of co-wife is meant to be an agreeable one. This expectation is not always justified; occasionally co-wives quarrel; but the majority are glad for the companionship of a close relative, and the lessened work which their presence means. The husband is meant to spend alternate nights with each of them.' (Gorer, op. cit., 166).

18

WIDOWS

Rajas and emperors
Mount flags on their elephants
Manjhis and paraniks
Plant flags on their horses
Widows, widows
Put flags about their beds.

—*Bir Seren*

I THE STATUS OF WIDOWS IN SANTAL SOCIETY

IN HIS paper 'Some Remarks on the Position of Women among the Santals', Bodding describes a widow as 'a piece of masterless property, utterly destitute except for what people may give her or for what she may be able to earn through her own work.'[1] It is impossible to say how far this description was ever generally true but at the present time it has no resemblance at all to Santal theory or practice. Today a Santal widow has a number of exact rights and these are determined by whether she is young or old, and with or without children. If a widow is young, it is inconceivable that she will stay unmarried long. 'A widow neighs like a tethered stallion'. 'A woman and rice land do not lie vacant'. Even if she has children but is still young she is usually remarried and it is only when a woman is old that she tends to stay a widow.

II THE EFFECTS OF REMARRIAGE ON A CHILDLESS WIDOW

If a childless widow remarries, the first result is to sever her connection with her dead husband—his family, his land and movables. She can take to her new house all the personal property which she owned as a married daughter and she will also retain any land which she has either acquired herself or in which she possesses rights of taben jom. If however, her first husband has any kinsmen or female relatives, they will inherit all his land and movables and only in default of all other heirs whether male or female and subject to her staying in the village will the widow keep his property. In this latter case, children by her second husband are allowed to inherit her first husband's land after the widow has died—provided the matter is taken to the village and the inheritance is approved. If the village so likes it can withhold this approval and the land is then treated as village stock and settled with a villager. If a widow remarries a younger brother of her dead husband, she does so as an ordinary widow and the only difference is that her father cannot claim a further brideprice.

III THE EFFECTS OF REMARRIAGE ON A WIDOW WITH CHILDREN

When a widow has children and then remarries, the position is much more complicated. If there are no other heirs and no other guardians of higher priority she will herself remain in charge of the property and if her children are all daughters she herself will first inherit it.

If there are sons by her first husband, such inheritance by a widow will be only temporary and when they reach majority they will themselves take over as their father's heirs.

If there are other guardians with stronger claims, but without priority as heirs the custody of the land and movables passes to them until the children reach majority. They also take over the persons of the minors unless by private agreement the widow continues to keep them. If the widow's first husband has left an heir with higher priority such as a brother, paternal uncle or paternal nephew, he becomes the guardian of the children and also in certain circumstances the final heir. If all the children are girls, he himself inherits the land and movables but must keep the girls in food and clothes, meet the expenses of their death and sickness and arrange for their tattooing, initiation and marriage. If he fails in these duties, the widow can request the village to revise the arrangement but otherwise the husband's near kinsman inherits to her complete exclusion.

If a widow remarries but her husband has left sons, a near kinsman again intervenes but this time merely as custodian of the property and in no sense as an heir. He can again administer the land and movables as he thinks fit but is charged with the maintenance of the children and the performance of their ceremonies. When the sons are old enough to manage the land themselves they have the right to take over their father's cultivation as well as any movables which still remain.

IV THE PERMANENT WIDOW IN A JOINT FAMILY

If this is the position when a widow remarries what are her rights if she does not take another husband but remains a widow?

In such cases she is virtually a substitute for her husband. She steps into his place, acts as his representative and exercises almost all his rights and duties.

If her husband was joint with his brothers she will continue to live in the family and the situation will not differ materially from what it was in her husband's lifetime. Her right to maintenance will continue and if her husband's family neglects her without cause she can demand sufficient land to keep her. If there is a complete family partition the widow and her children will get the share which would have gone to her husband had he been alive.

V THE PERMANENT WIDOW WITH SONS

If her husband was separate from his brothers the position will be somewhat different and I will first discuss the rights which accrue if her sons are major, and then describes those which she obtains if all of them are minor.

If the sons are major and already separate, the widow will get her dead husband's share of the family land as well as his movables. If she has major sons and they are still joint, she will act as head of the family until she gets too old for active decision. The eldest son will then gradually take over the management of the joint household or if the married sons desire they will demand and effect partition. During this period the land and movables will be owned jointly by all the sons, and the widow will have no rights in any of the property. Her sons will hold it, subject to the obligation of maintaining their mother and unmarried sisters and if they neglect her, she can demand and get the separation of sufficient land and movables to keep her. If her sons die unmarried she inherits the property until her death or remarriage.

When all the sons are minors, the widow inherits all the land and movables exactly as if she were their father. She supervises the cultivation, administers the movables and runs the joint household as if her husband were still alive and directing the affairs. She must not however leave the village and if she does, her rights lapse. When her sons grow up and marry, they can demand and effect a partition and the widow's rights are the same as those which her dead husband could have claimed. She will keep sufficient land and movables to maintain herself, and if she is old she will live with one of her sons and link her share with his. If, however, her sons remain joint, after reaching manhood, the land and movables continue to be the widow's property and it is only at her death that her sons' rights mature. The position in fact is that while a son is his father's ultimate heir, his minority makes a 'substitute' father necessary and once this 'substitute' father has taken over in the form of his mother it is as if a second father had come between him and the property. His final rights are in no way affected but they have now to be deferred until his 'substitute' father dies or he himself marries.

During this time a widow is expected to take due care of the family movables and to sell them only for food, clothing and for cultivation expenses. If she begins to waste the movables the villagers can interfere and as a last resort, can appoint a manager to administer the lands and movables for the widow and her children.

VI THE PERMANENT WIDOW WITH DAUGHTERS OR NO CHILDREN

These principles determine the case of a widow with major or minor sons. But her husband may have died leaving no sons but only daughters, what are the rights of a widow in such circumstances ?

In all these cases, the widow again acts as a 'substitute' for her husband. She inherits all his land and movables subject to the condition that she must remain in the village and must not remarry. If she leaves her husband's house and goes to another village, her action amounts to abandonment. Similarly if she taken another husband within the village her rights normally lapse and only if there are no other heirs can she keep his movables and land.

If the widow has daughters who are still unmarried, her inheritance is subject to the duty of maintaining the daughters, meeting the expenses of their death or sickness and arranging for their tattooing, initiation and marriage. For this purpose as well as for her own maintenance she can sell her husband's movables but if she wastes his property, the village can intervene and appoint a manager.

This role of 'substitute' husband is even further extended. Like her husband, she can convert a son-in-law into a ghar jawae by agu mit'. She can marry a daughter in ghar jawae form. She can adopt a son for her dead husband. If her daughter dies, she can marry her serving son-in-law to another girl and keep him as a ghar jawae. In all these cases she must obtain village approval but provided the community agrees it is immaterial whether her husband's agnates approve or object.

Finally, when she dies it is as if her husband had again died but this time without a widow. Whoever would have taken his land and movables but for his widow's presence now inherits them. If her husband's father is still alive, he takes it and if his father is dead, his brothers inherit. In essentials, the inheritance of a widow's property is the inheritance of a widower's.*

VII

How does widowhood affect the private life of Santal women?

If a widow marries again it is as if she eloped and all her rights in her dead husband's lands and movables lapse. If she is detected in an act of sex the adjustment depends on whether she can prove the use of force. If force is proved the Santal responsible is fined by the village and out of the fine a share is given to the widow as la jao marao or khiti puran.

Jhopar Marandi of Sugnibad had forcibly connection with a widow of his village. Jhopar was fined twenty rupees and out of this five rupees was paid to the woman.

In Kharbari Durga Murmu had forcible connection with the widow of Utra Soren. The village fined him ten rupees and half of this was paid to the widow.

In such circumstances since the woman was not at fault the incident does not affect her status in respect of her dead husband's lands and movables.

If on the other hand, she colludes with a lover her husband's kinsmen can intervene. Her act is then equivalent to a second marriage and she must leave the house and property.

Finally the woman's relation to her husband's bongas is also affected. As a wife she secures access to them but only in a subordinate role. She cannot herself make offerings and perform sacrifices. On her husband's death, she is debarred from acting for him and can at most assist such kinsmen as are qualified. If she has sons, she will guide and assist them in this function but if she has daughters only or is childless she must either prevail on kinsmen of her husband to perform the worship or allow the service to lapse. It is this latter contingency

*This applies only to property inherited by the widow. I have discussed the disposal of self-acquired property or land held by her as a taben jom in Chapter 15.

which darkens her closing years for unless the household bongas are appeased and the recent dead are honoured there is no escape from the anxieties of death.

REFERENCE

1. P.O. Bodding, Some Remarks on the Position of Women among the Santals, *J.B.O.R.S.*, II (1916), 242.

19

MOTHERS

I

ONCE a Santal girl has settled in her husband's house her first desire is to become a mother.

When the sal trees are in leaf
On the mountain
How lovely they look
Wealth in the house
A door in the doorway
But without a child
All beauty fades.

—*Don Seren*, 2107.

Similarly when her children grow up her chief ambition is to be a grandmother for it is through the rearing of children and grandchildren that a Santal woman best fulfils her nature. When marriage takes a daughter from her, the void in the home is paralleled in the heart.

Holding the eaves
Sitting at the door
Why are you weeping, milk tree?
Why should I not weep?
Why should I not mourn?
For nothing, girl
I reared you.

—*Don Seren*, 2058.

What are the exact rights of a mother in tribal law?

II

Although a child satisfies one of its mother's deepest needs, it is only while the child is still unweaned that it is in any sense her property. Even then she holds it only in trust and unless she is married to a ghar jawae its actual owner and tribal guardian is its father. As a mother she can insist that its father does not evade his responsibilities but beyond that she has no rights and if her marriage fails she must surrender the children.

If her marriage is stabilised and the children grow up with her she can demand and exact obedience so long as they are little. But we have seen that however lazy or unruly a daughter may be her parents can only expel her if she sins with a Diku though they may sometimes resort to expulsion if their sons are disobedient.

Similarly it is only at weddings that her mother's status receives formal or public recognition. When a daughter is married a mother receives part of the brideprice in token of her share in rearing her. When a son is married, he bids good-bye to his mother on the outskirts of the village. He pretends to suck her breasts and gives her one rupee as nunu taka. If the bridegroom arrives in a palki, the bride's mother can demand five rupees from him as jhili ladu or sweets.

It is when her children are grown up and she herself is in middle age that a mother's rights become important. From her daughter she can expect help in illness and if her husband is dead she can arrange with the village to marry her daughters to ghar jawaes or to bring a married daughter's husband to her house by agu mit'. She cannot, however, demand that a married daughter should keep her neither has she the right to intrude in a married daughter's house.

From her sons on the other hand she can demand much greater rights. If her husband is alive, the two can require their sons to maintain them and to treat them in sickness. If her husband dies after his sons are adult, a mother can require a son to keep her and should she be estranged from all her sons, she can demand and get her husband's share of land,

and movables. With village approval, she can also adopt a son for her dead husband.

Moreover, provided a mother does not remarry and remains in the village, she has certain rights of inheritance. If a married daughter dies leaving no son, daughter, father nor major brother her mother inherits her land and movables. She also inherits her land if her daughter is unmarried and there are no more highly qualified heirs. In the case of sons a mother who does not remarry and remains in the village is also in certain circumstances an heir. If a son dies leaving no son widow, father, brother, nor brother's sons, his mother inherits his land and movables. This however is subject to provisions, for if she subsequently remarries or leaves the village, she loses all land or movables which she has previously inherited.

Finally, at a mother's death, her sons and after them her daughters have first claim to all her land and movables.

III

If a mother's status depends on her sons, a grandmother's position is equally dependent on her grandsons. As a Santal woman grows older there is a greater danger of her being thought a witch. On the other hand, it is grandmothers whose views are valued in settling weddings, whose store of tribal knowledge assists in educating the children, whose knowledge of folk-tales and riddles contribute to village amusement. At a wedding both the grandmothers receive a share in their granddaughter's brideprice in recognition of valuable part which they have played in rearing and training the girl.

So far as the inheritance of property is concerned, a grandmother occupies the same place in relation to a boy or girl's paternal uncles as a mother does to their brothers. Her sons, in other words, have a prior claim, but if there are no sons, a grandmother takes precedence over her husband's brothers. The order of inheritance is

son, if major
son of major son, if major
widow, if not remarried and in the village
son if minor
son's son
father
brother
brother's son
mother, if not remarried and in the village
grandfather
paternal uncle
paternal uncle's son
grandmother

As with a mother all rights of a grandmother in inherited property end if she remarries or leaves the village. When a grandmother dies her son's sons have the first claim to succeed provided their fathers are already dead, after that her daughters, after them her daughter's sons and finally her daughter's daughters.

Mothers and grandmothers are not an important subject of Santal law but the functions implied by the relationships are some of the most basic in Santal society.

20

SISTERS

I

WE have seen that in Santal society the life of a woman hinges on her father, and her sons. Yet we must not on that account ignore her status as a sister. A girl is often an object of great admiration to a brother. There is little conflict of interest between them. The two often help each other in their love affairs. It is her brother who escorts her to *melas* and markets and after her marriage fetches her to their parent's house. Between an elder and a younger sister the relationship is often like a mother and a daughter. The former is the younger's natural confident, her senior companion. It is the elder sister who teaches her much that makes her a Santal woman. Moreover in certain circumstances, a sister has exact rights and duties. While her parents are living, these are as it were submerged. It is when her parents die that they reach the surface and influence the life of the family.

II

If an unmarried girl has a grown up brother and their parents die, she is first entitled to his guardianship and protection. Her father's duty of keeping her in food and clothes, tending her in sickness and arranging for her tattooing, initiation and marriage devolves on her brother. He must respect her private property and if his sister dies unmarried, he must bear the expenses of her funeral.

If a girl has several brothers, their responsibility is joint and while their sister usually lives with only one of them until her wedding, the duty of keeping her is shared by all.

If a brother dies and there are no widows, sons, brothers, mother, male agnates or daughters, an unmarried sister inherits his lands and movables as a last reversioner. The guardianship of her person and property is taken over by a villager and the brother's property is administered for her until her marriage.

If a girl has sisters and no brothers, she will act as a little mother to those that are her juniors, and will herself be guided by those who are older. Their guardianship will first vest in an agnate of their father but if an elder sister is married, she can in certain circumstances become the guardian of a younger. If there are no brothers or mother and the father has left no agnates, an unmarried girl shares her father's property with her sisters.

III

When a girl is married, her brother ceases to be a guardian but the tie of brother and sister is not abruptly snapped. In certain cases, a sister is given land by her brothers as taben jom so that she may keep a footing in the village and visit their houses from time to time.

Moreover, to a young unmarried brother she is often a deputy mother. In certain cases, she becomes his legal guardian and in others by arrangement in the family, she may take him to her house.

If a brother dies without any other heirs, she and her other sisters whether married or unmarried share the land and movables.

IV

Finally, if a sister is divorced or her husband dies without land, she reverts first to her father or mother and after them to her brothers' keeping. She can again demand maintenance and if they shirk this duty she can claim sufficient land for keeping her.

V

These rights and duties do not bulk largely in Santal life for it is rarely that circumstances bring them into actual play. Yet they are not without importance. They act as safeguards to the life of children. They cement the ties of blood. They maintain the family as a source of mutual aid.

21

GHARDI JAWAE

'I IGNORE the absurd argument that there is a difference between a ghardi jawae and a ghar jawae'—Mr. Deputy Commissioner E.S. Hoernle.[1]

I INTRODUCTION

The house husband or serving son-in-law is a common figure in almost all the tribes of Middle and Eastern India. Among the Kharias he is known as a ghardamad or ghar jiaa, among the Uraons as a ghardi joa while the Gonds and Baigas refer to him as the lamsena.

Among Santals he appears in two important but widely different forms. The first or ghardi jawae is a temporary house husband who serves for a fixed term of years and goes away at the end. The second or ghar jawae is a permanent house husband. He goes to his father-in-law's for life and is the catalyst by which his wife inherits her father's lands. Both these social forms are obviously of very great significance since they influence the inheritance of land, yet of all Santal institutions there are none which have been more widely misunderstood. J.F. Gantzer in his Settlement Report states :

> 'According to tribal custom, it is permissible for a man with daughters and no sons to take a son-in-law into his house as a ghar jamai and to give him thereby all the rights of a son. The adoption of a ghar jamai is a formal proceeding leaving no room for doubt as to the father-in-law's

intention and resulting in the ghar jamai cutting off all connexion with his own family as far as his rights to property are concerned, and becoming to all intents and purposes the son of his father-in-law. When such adoption has been formally made the ghar jamai can succeed as a son and oust other male relatives. It is of importance to note that a ghar jamai can be adopted only by a deliberate public act in the presence of the village community at the time of the marriage, and that according to tribal law a father-in-law cannot at a later stage convert an ordinary son-in-law into a ghar jamai. A widow cannot in any circumstances create a ghar jamai. There is a distinction between a ghar jamai and a ghardi jamai. In both cases the bridal party goes from the bride's house to fetch the prospective husband and no dowry (pon) is given, but whereas the ghar jamai is adopted permanently as a son, a ghardi jamai merely lives and labours in his wife's home for a previously stipulated period which may extend upto five years. He thereby works off the debt due on account of the non-payment of pon. A ghardi jamai is not entitled to get anything from his wife's family, but the woman herself is usually given a small present (arpa) annually at the harvest season, and this is utilised for setting up her new home. At the expiry of the stipulated period, the ghardi jamai is free and may return to his own home with his wife.'[2]

This statement must have influenced many decisions of Settlement Courts yet out of ten sentences, not less than seven are incorrect.

II PREVIOUS ACCOUNTS

The earliest description of the Santal house-husband is in *Horkoren Mare Hapramko reak' Katha.* In this account, only one term, ghardi jawae, is used but it is obvious from the concluding sentences that the institution was already branching out into a second form. Kolean Haram's account is as follows :

'If a man has no son or has very young ones who cannot work then such people if they have grown up daughters keep a ghardi jawae. Only the poor and orphans become ghardi jawaes. A ghardi jawae does not have to pay pon or any kind of payment, everything is paid by the bride's side. The marriage is performed like a regular marriage. The ghardi jawae works at his father-in-law's house for five years in order to win his wife. He does not get any wages for that, he only gets food and clothing. When they take in a ghardi jawae they show him a calf. If the girl does not get on well with the boy and the five years are not completed, the boy goes back with the calf. At the time of the marriage, the daughter's parents give her a calf. For five years she gets ir arpa. She can give this 'ir arpa' paddy out on loan to any one she likes. After the five years is up if they like, they can stay there on wages or they can leave the house.

If the girl's parents have no son and if their daughter and their son-in-law look after them until their death, the pair will get the house, all the lands and half the cattle and goats. The other half goes to the girl's father's relatives. The ghardi jawae and his wife have to meet the expenses of the *bhandan* ceremony. If there are two or three ghardi jawaes they share.'[3]

This latter paragraph is unfortunately very far from clear and in the next account by C.H. Bompas written between 1900 and 1906 it is noteworthy that the second term ghar jawae has now been coined but that the two terms are still used as if they were synonyms. Bompas's note is a summary of Kolean Haram's statement and runs as follows :

> The ghardi jawae or ghar jawae—the son-in-law works for five years for his father-in-law without wages after which he can leave the house with his wife. The husband pays nothing in the way of marriage expenses. If the wife has no brothers and the ghardi jawae stays on in the house and works for his father-in-law till he dies, then the ghardi jawae inherits all the immovable property and half the movable property, the other half of which goes to the relatives of the deceased. If there be more than one ghardi jawae they divide the property.[4]

This summary is obviously a distortion of Kolean Haram's meaning for the Santali nowhere states that the ghardi jawae alone inherits. Kolean Haram's actual words are—'*Ar kuriren engat apat kora gidra bako tahentakin khan, ar ghardi jawaetekin kin asul—duruc' le kin khan orak' duar ot barge joto kin nama ar mihu merom adhakin namkoa'.* Here the use of the dual kin in the phrase ghardi jawaetekin makes it clear that if the ghardi jawae inherits, it is only along with his wife and it is not one but both who take the land. But even correctly translated, the statement obviously raises far more issues than it solves. It seems to assume that the girl and the ghardi jawae will always be a pair. But obviously one must die before the other and even after they have got the land, they may not always live together and one may divorce the other. If both have inherited, a divorce would seemingly involve a division of the property. Similarly on the death of one, the other would presumably take all. But even this does not dispose of all the difficulties for if the ghardi jawae secures his wife's share, who then succeeds to the ghardi jawae? If there are no sons or daughters, what 'rule of inheritance' applies? Does the land go to the ghardi jawae's father, brother or uncles or do the uncles of the girl succeed? On all these crucial points, Kolean Haram is silent.

The next account is in the first edition of the District Gazetteer. This was published in 1910 and was written by L.S.S. O'Malley from notes supplied by Bodding. In this account O'Malley says :

> Ghardi jawae is the name given to the custom of obtaining a bride by service, just as Jacob served for Rachel. The bridegroom pays nothing for his bride, but lives with his father-in-law and works for him without wages for five years. He then gets two buffaloes, some rice and some agricultural implements, and sets up house for himself and his wife. This form of marriage is usual when a girl is deformed, ugly or unattractive and also if a man has only daughters or grown-up daughters and infant sons. Only a poor Santal will consent to becoming a bridegroom in this way.[5]

In this note, there is no reference to an inheriting son-in-law and the term 'ghar jawae' is also absent.

The first detailed attempt to define the two terms was made by Bodding in 1916. In his article on 'The Position of Women among the Santals', he begins by emphasising that Santal women had originally no right of inheritance or occupancy with regard to cultivated lands. He then goes on to say 'Formerly it did not much matter, a girl would when married have a husband to support her, she would with such an one be just as well provided for as if she had inherited her father's land. Now-a-days it is becoming different. There may be personally acquired property, the possession of which will give prospects of maintenance.

Now it has never entered their heads, that daughters should inherit land equally with sons; but they are willing that daughters whose husbands come and live with their parents-in-law should get a little of their land; and they are anxious, if there are no sons, that one or more of the daughters should get all the land of the father in preference to some more or less distant relations stepping in perhaps to oust their own flesh and blood from what might support them.

They have found a way to effect this; they let a daughter inherit through a male intermediary; they marry their daughters and give the husband the position of a son; provided he lives with his father-in-law.

An ordinary marriage among the Santals is performed at the house of the bride, with feasting here and at the house of the bridegroom, the expenses being paid by each party.

If a man gets a husband for his daughter for the purpose just mentioned, he goes about it in a little different way, and gets what is called a ghardi jawae.'[6]

Bodding then explains the difference between an ordinary marriage and a ghardi jawae one, although he does not make it clear whether his account refers to the marriage of a ghardi jawae or of a ghar jawae. He then adds :

> As will be understood, a ghardi jawae as such is not entitled to anything more than his wife, and is not in himself an inheritor of his father-in-law's lands.[7]

Finally he deals with the problem of inheritance.

'If a man wishes his ghardi jawae to become his heir, this

has to be specially arranged and publicly declared, and such is done at the time of marriage.

A marriage is, of course, a public affair, the village people, specially the headman and other officials, have to be present. What is done has their consent, and they would not ordinarily think of opposing any agreement made at the time of marriage later on.

A man with only daughters (also in case he has had sons who have died without issue) will generally arrange for one or more ghardi jawaes and also for these becoming his heirs. Such son-in-laws, will, so long as they remain, have the position of sons, they will support and take care of the parents-in-law when they get old; and on the death of these they get everything, except half the cattle which the brothers of the father-in-law are entitled to.

In quite recent years it has become the custom to call such an inheriting ghardi jawae a ghar jawae, a term introduced by outsiders.

Nominally it is the son-in-law who inherits, not according to any other right, but according to an oral will (if one may use such an expression) executed at the time of marriage. Actually it is the daughter who becomes inheritor, but as she is debarred from performing certain duties in the village, she has to have a representative, who is her husband who stands as tenant and owner. The expectation is that the sons of the pair will be born to take up the inheritance. But if the ghardi jawae in his turn should have only daughters, he will be permitted to arrange himself with a ghardi jawae in exactly the same way.

That it is the girl for whom this arrangement is made and who is the actual heir, should not need any demonstration. If a ghardi jawae leaves, he loses his rights, his own relatives have no rights of inheritance in his father-in-law's lands. If his wife dies, he may have a life interest there, provided he does not remarry. The children of the ghardi jawae are in this case the real inheritors and owner.'[8]

This article obviously goes a long way to clarifying the position and particularly in its closing paragraph, it states what is virtually the essence of the whole position. Unfortunately not all of Bodding's phrases are clear and some of them are contradictory. If 'the ghardi jawae is not in himself an inheritor of his father-in-law's lands,' how is it that 'nominally it is the son-in-law who inherits?' If 'actually it is the daughter who becomes the inheritor' how is it that 'the daughter inherits through a male intermediary?' Is it the daughter or the intermediary who inherits? If 'she has to have a representative, who stands as tenant and owner' who is the owner—the daughter or the representative? If it is the daughter, then in what sense does the husband inherit? What in fact is nominal inheritance as against actual inheritance? Moreover, if the ghar jawae dies before his wife, who inherits? If in his lifetime the wife is the actual but not the nominal heir how can she become the nominal heir at his death? If at his death she is the nominal heir, why is she not also the nominal heir in his lifetime?

Later, in 1928, Bodding wrote the following note re-explaining the two terms :

> Ghardi jawae is a man who when marrying pays the bride price by serving his father-in-law for, as a rule, five years, instead of giving money. Except for the applying of *sindur* (which has to be done by the man) the bride, or rather her father, acts as if she were the husband, takes the lead, so to say. I mention this because it is of some importance to understand the position. Ordinarily a man will, when his years of service are over, leave his father-in-law's house taking wife and children with him. He may naturally also stay on, in this case a servant for wages.
>
> In cases where a man has only daughters and no sons to inherit his land and he, as is natural, wishes to secure this for his daughter he may arrange for this in the following way. He procures a ghardi jawae for his daughter and arranges with him that he will stay with them, taking care of his parents-in-law so long as they live, the son-in-law will act as if he were a son and have a son's rights and duties; to mention only one thing he will have on the death of his father-in-law to perform the ag muk, which is always supposed to be done by the principal heir. Such an inheriting or it might even be called an adopting son-in-law (the Santals do not, however, use such a name) has been

> called a ghar jawae. It is a name of fairly recent date; when I came to the country, it was not in use, so far as I know; the traditions of the Santals as first edited by the late Mr. Skrefsrud do not mention this name, but include all under the name of ghardi jawae. I am under the impression that the term ghar jawae was brought in during the last settlement. It was felt to be needed to have a separate word for an inheriting son-in-law. Another cause for coining a fresh name might be, that such a ghar jawae might have been married to a daughter of the man in question in the regular way, without there being at the time of the marriage any thought of the son-in-law coming to settle in his wife's old home, but then the sons of the father-in-law died or anything happened to make it desirable to bring a son-in-law there for the purpose stated. Such cases have happened. Here another name than ghardi jawae would fit in, although this name was formerly the only name used.
>
> A condition for becoming a ghar jawae is that the agreement is public, that is to say, done with the 'official knowledge of the village headman and community' but I do not think that anybody's permission is required.

This note obviously takes the matter much further and it is of particular value in showing that a son-in-law need not have been a ghardi jawae in order to become a ghar jawae. Yet the former confusion is still present for while making it clear that the object of a ghar jawae is to secure the father's land for the daughter, Bodding again uses the term 'inheriting son-in-law'. If the first statement is correct, the only adequate term would have been 'an inheriting daughter'.

Bodding's last words are given in *A Santal Dictionary* published in 1934. Here he made only one entry ghardi jawae and wrote :

> 'Ghardi jawae—a son-in-law who instead of paying for his wife or giving clothes to his wife's female relatives goes to his wife's home and pays for his wife by working five years with his father-in-law. People who have grown-up daughters and sons or only small ones will marry their daughters off in this way. In the case of only daughter. this is the way

> of letting a daughter inherit the land which a daughter in the usual way cannot inherit. A ghardi jawae who in this way comes to his wife's home and stays on there for good is now-a-days called a ghar jawae, a term recently introduced by the settlement officials.'[9]

This is only a brief summary and obviously excludes many points. Yet its omissions are significant. There is no mention of the son-in-law inheriting. There is no allusion to any 'oral will' or a 'nominal inheritor'. The ghar jawae is seen to be simply 'a way of letting a daughter inherit the land'.

What then is the essence of these two institutions?

III THE GHARDI JAWAE

If we examine the actual working of village life, we find that the ghardi jawae is essentially an expedient for meeting a temporary situation. A Santal father finds himself growing older. His daughters are grown up but his son is only a child. In such circumstances, a temporary house-husband is a convenient solution of his difficulties. A poor or over-crowded family supplies a boy who needs a wife while the father-in-law secures a temporary assistant to help him in his work.

Ponda Kisku of Dighi had two grown up daughters and one small son. He found it difficult to manage his fields so he brought a ghardi jawae for the elder daughter. The ghardi jawae worked for five years until the boy was bigger. After that he took his wife away and went to another house.

In Simaldhab Jadu Tudu had five children. The first four were daughters and the last was a son. As the son was little he took ghardi jawae for the second daughter.

In certain cases a man has daughters only but has still a hope of getting a son. He does not want to make any permanent arrangement but he needs help in his cultivation. In such circumstances a ghardi jawae is again a convenient solution for he lives in the house for a term of years and then goes away.

Moreover as Risley pointed out :

> 'when a girl is ugly or deformed and there is no prospect of her being asked in marriage in the ordinary way', the

mode of marriage, ghardi jawae, is sometimes resorted to and he instances a case 'in which a girl who had on one foot more than the proper number of toes was married in this fashion'.[10]

Since the institution is based entirely on mutual convenience, a man is not restricted to the number of ghardi jawaes whom he can bring. He can bring only one ghardi jawae for one daughter but if a man has five daughters and desires to bring five ghardi jawaes, there is nothing in tribal law to prevent him doing so.

Baghrai Tudu of Kasalpahar had five daughters and no sons. He brought two brothers Raghu and Jholan Murmu from Chandpur as ghardi jawaes. When their terms were ended, they stayed on for some years in the village but after Baghrai had got two sons, they took their wives and returned to Chandpur.

There is similarly no bar to a widow bringing a ghardi jawae for her daughter. Rani Soren of Ranipur had three daughters and brought a ghardi jawae for one of them. She would have liked to have installed him as a ghar jawae but as her other two daughters objected she did not press this at the village meeting.

In Agiabandh Baijnath Soren died leaving a widow, four daughters and a small son. In order to assist her in the house the widow brought a ghardi jawae for one of the daughters.

IV PRELIMINARIES TO INDUCTION

When a Santal needs a ghardi jawae, his first step is to talk it over in the village. He mentions it to his brothers or uncles or if they are no bad terms, he goes direct to the manjhi. He explains his difficulties and seeks village approval. When the agnates agree, this approval is given at once but if they object, the village talks it over in a meeting, considers their objections and then decides. The fact that the brothers are against it may often lead to village disapproval but their objection is not in itself a bar to the arrangement. It is the villagers as a whole and not the agnates who decide whether a ghardi jawae may be brought.

Baila Hansdak' of Guhiajuri had only one daughter and no son. He wanted to marry her to a ghardi jawae but his brothers opposed him, the villagers did not overrule them and in the end he married her in ordinary form.

On the other hand, when Ramai Marandi of Dalabor who had three grown up daughters and a young son proposed to bring a ghardi jawae for his second daughter and was opposed by his brother the villagers sided with Ramai and in spite of his brother's opposition a ghardi jawae was approved.

Similarly, when Nimu Marandi of Darbarpur wished to bring a ghardi jawae for his only daughter, his brother who had two sons opposed this proposal. The matter was discussed in the village and Nimu was allowed to bring a ghardi jawae.

After approval in principle, negotiations start. A boy has first to be found and when he has been chosen, the terms of the wedding are worked out. These terms are always very precise and they are decided in a village meeting at the girl's house which the manjhi of the boy's village attends.

V THE TERMS OF SERVICE

The first essential term is the length of service. This is almost always five years though it is sometimes fixed at seven.

During this period, the ghardi jawae must work in the house, help in cultivation and must in fact do everything that a paid servant should do. At the end of his term he reverts to his father's house and land with the same rights as if he had never been away. He can claim maintenance or partition like any other son and when his father dies, he is entitled to a son's ordinary share.

Since he is only a temporary house-husband, his children are named as in an ordinary marriage, and his wife has also only the ordinary rights of a married daughter.

In return for his period of service, he receives the following concessions. He gets his wife free of bride price. He is kept in food and clothes by his father-in-law. He is tended in sickness.

Finally, when his term ends there are certain animals and articles which are payable to him. These may consist of a pair of bullocks, or buffaloes, a bale of paddy, an axe and a kudi (mattock)—the basic equipment which he needs for starting a house and the exact terms are settled at the commencement of his service.

In Jagudi a certain Suna had two small sons, so he brought in Bhim Soren as a ghardi jawae. Bhim served for five years and then with the approval of the village stayed on another five. At the end of this time, Suna's elder son was grown up and Bhim went back to his village. He took with him a pair of bullocks and a bale of paddy.

Sometimes a plough, a yoke or a dao are also given or a cow is settled in place of the bullocks. The animals and articles are shown to the parties at the time of settlement and it is only these shown animals and articles which are given later. If a cow or bullock dies during the five years, the ghardi jawae cannot demand another in its place. Gopal Kisku of Beoa was shown a cow but nothing else when he was taken as ghardi jawae of Munia Hembrom. The cow had a calf but both the animals died before the five years were up. When he went back he took with him only a bale of paddy.

During all this period the wife of the ghardi jawae continues to earn her share in each year's harvest (ir arpa), and at the end of the term she is entitled to take all of it to her husband's house. This ir arpa is given for every day she or her husband works and while the ghardi jawae himself has no claim to it, his work sometimes qualifies his wife to receive it. Moreover, occasionally a father allots his daughter a little land, 'mit pati jumi', for the period of her husband's stay. The two cultivate this land jointly but its produce belongs to the girl and is added to her ir arpa or share in harvest.

VI BREACH OF CONTRACT : THE FATHER-IN-LAW

When a ghardi jawae is taken, it is in the hope that all will go smoothly and the contract will be kept. But circumstances sometimes prevent this and a crisis may develop in the family itself. The ghardi jawae may not prove as docile as his father-in-law would like or may not work as hard as the family requires. In that case, the arrangement obviously fails and the father-in-law expels him from the house.

Musuc' Marandi was a ghardi jawae in the house of Jalpa

Baske of Kharu-kadma. He worked for three years but as he did not work as his father-in-law wanted and often disobeyed him, he was expelled and sent home.

When this situation arises a village meeting is called and adjustments are made.

If the ghardi jawae does not want to lose his wife, he pays his father-in-law a proportionate bride price and the brother's due and unless this is paid or excused or unless his father-in-law agrees, he cannot take his wife with him. He does not, however, have to recompense him for the cost of the wedding but he forfeits all claim to the implements, animals or grain which would have come to him at the end of his term. If there is friction with the wife as well as with the parents-in-law, the ghardi jawae merely goes away and the marriage is dissolved.

In Bhagmara Chunu Murmu was brought as ghardi jawae to a girl of Itahari. He served his father-in-law for about a year but as he proved very lazy his mother-in-law drove him out. His wife did not want to go with him so he was sent away with nothing.

Mongal Soren of Bichkora brought a ghardi jawae for his daughter. He did not satisfy them and after two years the boy and girl were divorced and the ghardi jawae sent back. For the two years the boy had worked he was given ten rupees.

When there are children, they stay with their mother until they are weaned and after that they follow their father to his home.

VII BREACH OF CONTRACT : THE GHARDI JAWAE

A variant of the same situation is when the father-in-law is satisfied but the ghardi jawae revolts.

In such cases if the ghardi jawae goes away he is given nothing and if he wishes to keep his wife, he must pay the brother's due and a proportionate bride price. If he does not want his wife, he can leave her and chadaodi or divorce money can be claimed from whichever side is to blame.

If the ghardi jawae is at fault, his wife can demand this money, but if she herself is to blame, the girl's father can be made to give it to the ghardi jawae.

Durga Tudu of Talkhora was a ghardi jawae. His wife

stopped talking to him and he went away. There was a village meeting and the girl's father had to give a bullock to the boy as divorce money.

VIII THE DEATH OF THE FATHER-IN-LAW

It is possible, however, that while the household is on smoothly working terms, disruption may suddenly ensure from death.

When the father-in-law himself dies before the term is up, two consequences are possible.

If there is a minor son, the ghardi jawae is expected to stay on and complete his term. 'The father needed help. The son will want it also.'

Similarly, if there are daughters only and the mother needs him the ghardi jawae must stay, 'for the house is his duty'. If, however, the mother is dead and the father's brothers desire a change there is an end of the contract.

The position, therefore, is that the family can demand the completion of the period and if it does so, the ghardi jawae must stay. If it decides to end the contract, it must give the ghardi jawae all the dues he would have got at the end of his term. It is not, however, required to give him any compensation for the last years.

IX THE DEATH OF THE DAUGHTER

If the death of the father-in-law abruptly releases the ghardi jawae from his contract, the death of his wife has a similar dissolving effect. The ghardi jawae is free to return to his house and can claim all the implements, animals or grain which his father-in-law would have given him, if the term had been completed.

Mangal Marandi of Sembari brought a ghardi jawae for his daughter but she died before the term was up. When the ghardi jawae left the house his father-in-law gave him a bale of paddy.

Another Mangal Marandi of Bichkora brought a ghardi jawae for his elder daughter. Before the term was up the girl died leaving a baby daughter and Mangal suggested that the ghardi jawae should remain and marry his second girl. The daughter did not, however, want him so the ghardi jawae returned to his home. He took with him two bales of paddy and forty rupees.

If the father-in-law requires the ghardi jawae to remain in his house, he can insist on his completing the term but on condition that he provides him with another wife. In such circumstances, his period of five years' service does not start afresh but is counted from the date he married the first wife.

Potol Chunda Murmu of Kamarsali brought a ghardi jawae for his elder daughter. The girl died and her father then married the ghardi jawae to his second daughter.

In Baramasia the sister of Kalu Marandi was married to a ghardi jawae. After they had lived together for three years she died and Kalu then retained the ghardi jawae's services by marrying his younger sister to him.

In certain cases in order to retain the ghardi jawae's services a girl from another family is brought.

Mandal Murmu of Malipara brought a ghardi jawae for his daughter. The girl died and Mandal then arranged another girl for the ghardi jawae. The ghardi jawae completed the term and at the end he left with his second wife and all his dues.

X THE DEATH OF THE GHARDI JAWAE

Finally, there is the chance that death may remove the ghardi jawae himself. If he dies leaving children, the responsibility for maintaining them and his widow devolves on his father and brothers. The position in fact is the same as if the ghardi jawae had been married in ordinary form and had lived and died in his father's house.

Moreover, any movables which were payable at the end of his term now become payable and when his widow goes to his father's house she is entitled to take them with her in trust for her son or daughter.

A Santal of Darbarpur brought a ghardi jawae from Bardaha. Before the five years were up, the ghardi jawae died and then his widow with their little son went to the house of his father. The widow was given all the movables which were due to the ghardi jawae.

If the ghardi jawae dies leaving no children, his widow cannot claim maintenance from her father-in-law but remains with her father. Another ghardi jawae is then brought for her or her father marries her again in sangha form. If her father is dead, her brother or paternal uncle or nephew arranges her second marriage.

Ram Marandi of Kauadhap brought a ghardi jawae for his sister. The ghardi jawae died after two sons had been born. The father of the ghardi jawae did not claim the children and Ram Marandi then brought a second ghardi jawae for his sister. Ram was the village manjhi and in consultation with other villagers he settled some waste land with the two sons of the first ghardi jawae.

XI THE COMPLETION OF THE TERM

What is the position when the term runs its full course?

The first and ordinary course is for the ghardi jawae to return to his village. He has not lost his rights in his father's family and his right to a share in the lands is intact. In that case, the village five are called to his father-in-law's house and given rice beer 'as witnesses'. The father-in-law declares the period is over. The ghardi jawae receives the agreed animals, implements or paddy. His wife gathers her ir arpa and any other private movables and they go to his village.

Girl, your husband sulks
Like a palm tree
With few leaves
O tell me what he wants
Father he demands
Two sheaves of paddy bales
He demands
A pair of buffaloes.

It is possible, however, that his father-in-law may want to keep him in the village. In that case if the ghardi jawae agrees he allots his daughter a few bighas of land and the two go on living there. The ghardi jawae is no longer a house-husband but his wife is part of the village. The land is hers for taben jom and the ghardi jawae cultivates it for her.

Barka Tudu of Dudhuakol for example took in a ghardi jawae because his only son was small. The ghardi jawae completed his five years and Barka gave his daughter a little land in the village.

Thakur Murmu of Dula brought a ghardi jawae for his daughter. When the term of five years was up he approached the villagers and some land was settled with his daughter. The ghardi jawae and his wife then remained in the village and cultivated the settled land.

In Sitasal Basia Murmu was brought as a ghardi jawae. When the term was over his wife was given five bighas of land by her mother with village approval and Baria remained at the village and cultivated the lands for her.

Finally, if both sides approve the term of service is extended for a further five or seven years and either the contract is again worked out in the village or the ghardi jawae merely goes on living in the house.

Father,
You took me as a ghardi jawae
Five years have passed
And you are bidding me farewell
O you true one
Tell him you will stay
And who will send us out?

In such cases, as the ghardi jawae has already worked off his wife's bride price and bare itat, full remuneration is necessary and this is decided when the term is extended.

Lopsa Hembrom of Machidanr brought a ghardi jawae for his second daughter. The ghardi jawae completed his first term of five years and then by agreement stayed on for a further four years. At the end of this time he was given a bale of paddy and some money for bullocks in payment of his first dues. Besides this, he was given forty rupees for the four years of his extra service.

In Bokrabandh Yanga Choto Tudu completed his five years' service as a ghardi jawae in 1945. As his wife's brother is still too young to plough, the term has been extended for another five years and Yanga Choto Tudu will be given five rupees a year in return for his services.

If there is no formal settlement the ghardi jawae and his wife continue as members of a joint household. Their expenses are met by the girl's father and they are given separate movables at his discretion.

Maisa Tudu of Gamuria was brought as ghardi jawae in the house of Pandu Hembrom of Sohorghoti. Pandu had two sons and two daughters. One son is grown up but as the family are all content Maisa is still in the house although his term is long since up.

Occasionally, the father-in-law rationalises the position by changing the ghardi jawae to a ghar jawae. If that is not done, the son-in-law's position is precarious. His wife will only have the rights of a married daughter. If her father dies and his agnates intervene, the issue hangs on their kindness. They may give the girl a little land for her maintenance, or they may send her to her husband's village. 'What can a ghardi jawae expect?—A little something for his wife; for himself—nothing'.

REFERENCES

1. Deputy Commissioner, Dumka, Title Appeal No. 17 of 1927, Bali Tudu and Others—versus—Padi Tudu and Others.
2. J.F. Gantzer, *Final Report on the Revision Survey and Settlement Operations in the District of Santal Parganas, 1922-35* (Patna, 1936), 23.
3. *Horkoren Mare Hapramko reak' Katha*, 94-5.
4. H. McPherson, *Final Report on the Survey and Settlement Operations in the District of Santal Parganas*, 1898-1907 (Calcutta, 1907), 124.
5. *Gazetteer* (first edition), 135.
6. Bodding, op. cit., 244-45.
7. Ibid., 246.
8. Ibid., 246-47.
9. P.O. Bodding, *A Santal Dictionary* (Oslo, 1934), II, 528-29.
10. H.H. Risley, *The Tribes and Castes of Bengal* (Calcutta, 1891), II, 230.

22

GHAR JAWAE

I ANTECEDENTS

IF a ghardi jawae solves a temporary difficulty, a ghar jawae is essentially a way of meeting a permanent situation and there are four needs which may result in his induction.

The first and most important is the need for an extra man to look after the land—not merely for five years but for the rest of a lifetime. A Santal may have several daughters but no sons. His chance of getting a son may seem small but he needs a man to help him in his cultivation and look after him in old age. Or again, his son may be small and it may be ten or more years before the boy can plough. He may not want a ghardi jawae, but a man is necessary.

Moreover, if a Santal with no sons marries his daughters in the usual way, all of them must leave his house. They will go to their husbands and all their children will grow up in another's house. They will be named according to their husband's families. If there is only one son, he will be named after the husband's father and only if there is a second will he take the name of his maternal grandfather. To avert the loneliness of old age and to fill the house with children a ghar jawae is brought.

But besides a wish for children and to insure against the stresses of old age, love for particular daughters may also induce a Santal to induct a ghar jawae.

Mausa Tudu of Jibanpur had two daughters. He married the first to a ghar jawae but when he realised how much he loved his younger daughter, he brought a ghar jawae for her also.

The widow of Rengha Hansdak' of Susania had four daughters. The second was her favourite and although the first was unmarried, she brought a ghar jawae for the second girl, so that she might continue in the house.

Similarly if a daughter is crippled and there is little chance of securing a husband for her in the ordinary way, a boy is sometimes procured by taking him as a ghar jawae.

A daughter of Duglu Marandi of Bhadria had a deformed leg. Her father could not get anyone as an ordinary husband for her so he brought Dhambo Murmu of Kutam as a ghar jawae.

Dharmae Hembrom of Mahuatanr had two sons and a daughter. The daughter had folded ears, so her father married her to a ghar jawae. Dharmae was joint with his brothers and in order to secure a husband for her he separated ten bighas from the joint stock and settled the girl on them.

Moreover if a girl has an illegitimate child and paternity is unproved, a ghar jawae marriage is sometimes resorted to as a way of procuring a husband.

Finally there is often the wish to keep certain land in a family.

Pitho Marandi was manjhi of Ranipahar. He had two daughters. One of them died and the other he married to a ghar jawae. The ghar jawae deserted her and he then negotiated for a second. While he was doing this Pitho called his relatives and the villagers. His own brothers were much opposed to the proposal and insisted that they themselves would keep Pitho. But Pitho and his old wife did not trust them. They said, "We are only ourselves and this girl. Anything we possess we have got by our own work. Why should another enjoy them? Why should we drive our daughter out? Because of this we are bringing in a ghar jawae." The agnates still opposed but the villagers agreed and Pitho brought a ghar jawae.

II GHAR JAWAES IN ONE FAMILY

To all these needs the ghar jawae is a multiple solution and it is perhaps for this reason that when a ghar jawae is to be brought, the bringing is not necessarily confined to any one daughter in a family but several or all the daughters, if need be, can each be married to ghar jawaes.

Mohon Marandi of Damma had four daughters and no sons. He had vast lands and brought ghar jawaes for each of his daughters.

A Santal of Ranidih had three daughters. The two eldest, Mako and Bale Hembrom, were married to ghar jawaes. Then the ghar jawae of the middle daughter married the youngest by kundal napam. His first wife did not like this so she divorced him and brought for herself a second ghar jawae. The third daughter's marriage was then recognized as in ghar jawae form and when the father of the three girls died, his land was inherited by each of them equally.

Narain Hansdak' of Barakarela had land in two villages and four daughters. The first two were married in dol form and for the third and fourth he brought ghar jawaes and reserved for each daughter some land in separate places.

Ramai Hembrom of Murgabani brought a ghar jawae for his eldest daughter but when she and her husband neglected him, he converted his other daughter's husband into a ghar jawae.

In Khatangi Khudu Murmu had one son and three daughters. When the son died, he converted the eldest daughter's husband into a ghar jawae. Then when the husband of his second daughter went to the war, he brought her back and when the husband was discharged, he also became a ghar jawae.

III INDUCTORS

This general elasticity is further seen in the variety of relatives who can act as if they were a father and arrange the marriage of a girl in ghar jawae form.

A grandfather for example, can arrange a granddaughter's wedding in ghar jawae form.

Budan Murmu of Kalajor had a grown-up granddaughter and a small grandson. His son died and there was no one to help in the house. In 1943 he brought a ghar jawae for his granddaughter and when I visited the village in March 1944 the wedding was about to be performed. Budan has holdings in two villages and his granddaughter will get one of them and his grandson the other.

Similarly, Pitho Soren of Pipra had no sons. So in order to be looked after in his old age he brought a ghar jawae for his granddaughter. He had a paper written saying that he had done this and that his granddaughter would inherit all he had. Jitu of Amgaiti also brought a granddaughter and married her to a ghar jawae.

In certain areas, as for example, near Godda it is doubtful if the village would approve if there were other grandchildren. In Baromasia circle, also, the general sense is that only if a daughter herself has been married to a ghar jawae can a grandfather take a ghar jawae for a granddaughter. But these are only local views which may influence particular decisions. Provided the village agrees, a grandfather is fully qualified.

In a similar way, a paternal or maternal uncle or a paternal aunt can bring a ghar jawae for a niece.

Babna Baske of Bathani had no children but his elder brother died leaving an only daughter. Babna's old father was still alive and Babna brought her to their house. He married her to a ghar jawae who died and then in 1943 he brought a second ghar jawae. The girl will inherit not only her father's but also her uncle's lands.

Sabru Tudu of Kunji was left alone with neither any children nor any agnates. With village approval he brought a ghar jawae for his sister's daughter and the girl will inherit all his lands.

Equally a brother can bring a ghar jawae for a sister and a sister already married to a ghar jawae can bring other ghar jawaes for her younger sisters.

Dubrai Hansdak' of Parsoti was a widower with an old mother and a sister. There was no one to help him in the house so he married his sister in ghar jawae form and she and her husband looked after him until he died.

In Chota Darma Kanhu Marandi was blind, so with village approval, he brought a ghar jawae for his sister and the two lived in his house and kept him. This sister had already been married once in ordinary form but had been divorced.

Madhu Soren of Adaro had three daughters. The eldest was married to a ghar jawae from Gadel and later she brought a ghar jawae for each of her younger sisters.

Moreover where an only daughter has been widowed, the uncles may marry her again to a ghar jawae and a widow also can bring a ghar jawae for her dead husband's daughter or granddaughter.

In Manglapara a widow with a widowed daughter had a minor grandson. As the boy was too small for cultivation the widow married her daughter again to a ghar jawae whom she brought from Jamtara.

In Kolarkonda Hisi Besra was a widow with one daughter. The two brothers of her husband agreed to a ghar jawae being taken and she brought in Sibu Murmu. When she died the two brothers tried to oust the daughter but as the village had fully approved of Sibu coming the daughter kept the lands.

Rubani Murmu of Dhokra was a widow with four daughters and a son. She married three in ordinary form and then in consultation with the villagers she brought a ghar jawae for the remaining daughter. The fourth daughter and the son have since shared equally.

In Jamalpur Naran Hembrom died leaving a widow and a son. Sometime later the son died leaving a daughter and Naran's widow then brought a ghar jawae for her granddaughter from Sirampur.

Equally a girl who has been once married to a ghar jawae can herself bring another husband as a ghar jawae while in certain cases a Santal can arrange a ghar jawae for an adopted daughter or granddaughter and with village approval the girl concerned will inherit land.

Matlu Hembrom of Benagaria married a widow with a daughter by her first husband. He had two sons by her and adopted the daughter as his own and married her to a ghar jawae. When he died the sons were small and the adopted daughter shared equally with the sons.

IV THE APPROVAL OF THE VILLAGE

Once a Santal decides to take a ghar jawae, the matter goes to a village meeting and whether his brothers, sons or other agnates are first consulted depends on their relations. If they are on friendly terms, consultation is natural and normal. If they are on bad terms consultation is very unlikely and the matter is left to be fought out in the meeting. In this meeting, the particular situation is examined and if the village thinks it is reasonable for a ghar jawae to be taken, it gives its approval, even though all the agnates oppose. If on the other hand there is no case for a ghar jawae it declines to give assent.

Lotho Soren of Bichkora had eight sons while his younger brother had two daughters. The brother wanted to bring a ghar jawae but Lotho objected on the ground that if he wanted a boy, he should adopt one of eight sons. The village considered Lotho's viewpoint to be reasonable and no ghar jawae was brought.

In Nawadih Dabra Marandi had a son, Barka, by his first wife. His wife died and he married again. By his second wife he had two daughters of whom the first was married in the ordinary way and for the second he decided to take a ghar jawae. Barka was very much against it but the village overruled him and a ghar jawae was brought.

In another case, Phoce Hansdak' of Baghsol had two daughters while his elder brother had three sons. When Phoce proposed a ghar jawae his brother strongly objected. Phoce replied 'I am not giving my daughter your land. I am only giving her my own'. The village supported him and the ghar jawae is now ploughing his lands.

In all these cases, village sanction was sought and a decision was emphatically given—in one case against the bringing of a ghar jawae and in three cases in his favour. In certain cases, on the other hand, the village takes a middle course and where the agnates are very assertive and hold a strong position in the community, village sanction is sometimes made conditional on a compromise.

When Lal Hansdak' of Mahuadangal was married as a little

boy in ghar jawae form, his wife's agnates demanded five bighas of land for curuc' cawale as the price of their consent. This was approved by the village and the sanction was given subject to this grant.

Similarly when Kunduc' Tudu of Sugapahari brought a ghar jawae for his daughter, the agnates induced the village to make it a condition that only half the land would go to the daughter and the rest be reserved for the agnates.

The position, therefore, is that while village approval is the final sanction and while in most cases, no conditions are attached, the meeting may make whatever settlement it thinks fit. If no conditions are expressly stated, the claims of all agnates are extinguished.

V ELIGIBILITY

When village approval has been given the next step is to choose a daughter and arrange a boy who will marry her.

So far as daughters are concerned, there are scarcely any restrictions and almost any daughter can be married to a ghar jawae.

A daughter with brothers is eligible and neither the brothers nor other ghar jawaes have any power of veto. One or more daughters can be given ghar jawaes and there are cases in which every daughter has been married in this way.

Moreover the fact that a daughter has been married once in the ordinary way and has then been divorced or widowed is no bar to a second marriage in ghar jawae form. If there are no sisters and a widowed daughter is alive, she can herself arrange a ghar jawae provided the village agrees.

Equally almost any boy can be taken as a ghar jawae. It is of no consequence whether he is a bachelor, a divorcee or a widower with children and provided he is already married in the same family, even a married boy can become a ghar jawae.

Jalpa Tudu of Dundin was married to a girl of Turka. His wife's younger sister became a widow and Jalpa was then married to her in ghar jawae form. Jalpa and his two wives then lived together on his second wife's land.

VI INHERITANCE BY A GHAR JAWAE MARRIED DAUGHTER

How then does the bringing of a ghar jawae affect a daughter?

The first effect of the marriage is that so far as her father's lands are concerned, the daughter becomes a son. During her father's lifetime she cannot claim a partition but on his death she inherits his land to the exclusion of all the agnates and her mother. She must however keep and clothe the latter and in fact her mother's maintenance is an essential charge on her property. If she has a brother, the normal rule is that she shares equally with him—'The two are brothers. They will share alike'—and it is only if a smaller share is expressly allotted to her at the induction of the ghar jawae that she inherits less.*

Lengra Murmu of Chhatarchua had a daughter and a son. He brought a ghar jawae for the daughter and on his death the lands were shared equally by the brother and sister.

Fudan Hansdak' of Bhagnadih had two daughters and no son. He married one to a ghar jawae. Then his wife died and he married again. From his second wife he had a son and now the ghar jawae married daughter and the son have shared his lands equally.

In Hathwari Juha Marandi had four sons and one daughter. He married her to a ghar jawae and when he died each son and the daughter got a fifth-share. Later, two sons died and the daughter and her surviving brothers got a third share in their land.

On the other hand in Talbola the paranik, Tibru Baske had one son and many daughters. He married a daughter in ghar jawae form and at his death his son inherited land paying rent of Rs. 10 while the daughter got land with a rent of five rupees.

If a brother inherits with her and then dies without sons or

*In the Godda subdivision the normal rule is that a ghar jawae married daughter receives only a half share.
Manka Kisku of Dalabor had a lame son and three daughters. He brought a ghar jawae for the youngest daughter and on his death, his son inherited two-thirds of his property while the ghar jawae married daughter received a third.

ghar jawae married daughters, his widow will hold his land till she dies, remarries or leaves the village but after that the ghar jawae married sister will inherit. If there are several ghar jawae married sisters they share equally. If a ghar jawae married daughter inherits with a brother, she can demand a partition and separate her share.

In respect of a paternal uncle's lands, a ghar jawae married daughter is almost but not quite a nephew. If her father or any other paternal uncle is alive or has left a son these latter inherit to her own exclusion.

Kishun and Sital Soren were two brothers of Sanmoni. Kishun married his daughter to a ghar jawae and when he and Sital died the girl claimed both their lands. There were several agnates and while the girl inherited her father's land her claim to the lands of her uncle was disallowed.

If however there are neither sons, brothers nor nephews the ghar jawae married daughter inherits exactly as if she were a nephew.

If these define her rights in land her marriage to a ghar jawae makes her in respect of movables, if not a full son, at least a semi-son. If she has a brother she will share equally unless a smaller share has been expressly allotted to her. If she has no brother but her father has left agnates she will inherit all the movables but if the agnates perform her father's funeral, they are entitled to whatever movables are sufficient to cover the expenses. Where there are no brothers or agnates, the ghar jawae married daughter inherits all her father's movables.

Moreover her status as a son in respect of her father's land invests her also with the right to adopt a son or daughter. She can only do this, however, with village approval.

Maran Baske of Dhanjuri was married to a ghar jawae but had no child. She then adopted one of her husband's nephews as posu putra and after their death the posu putra inherited Maran's land.

VII THE EFFECTS OF REMARRIAGE OR DIVORCE

Throughout this process, the ghar jawae acts only as a catalyst.

He himself has no right of inheritance in his father-in-law's property but is merely the means by which his wife secures these rights. As soon as a ghar jawae has been brought the girl becomes a son and even though she divorces her husband her rights as an inheriting daughter continue. She must, however, remain in her father's house and on his lands. If she were to leave his house and property, she would cease to be a son, her function as a ghar jawae married daughter would end and she would be no different from a daughter married in a husband's house.

If her husband dies and the girl re-marries, she must, therefore, take another ghar jawae as her second husband.

Provided she does this, her status remains but if she marries again and leaves the village, this second marriage in a different form cancels her status and she again becomes a daughter.

Mani Hansdak' of Tilaki was married to a ghar jawae and inherited her father's lands. The ghar jawae died and when she married again she brought a second ghar jawae and kept all her rights in her father's property.

The daughter of Bondo Tudu of Baramasia was married to a ghar jawae. After she had inherited her father's lands her husband died and when she married again she brought a second ghar jawae and retained all her land.

Similarly when Phedge Murmu of Ghagri was married to a ghar jawae she inherited her father's land. Later she divorced her husband and gave him chadaodi and when she married again she brought a second ghar jawae and kept her lands.

On the other hand, in Dugubathan, Dhani Hembrom who had inherited her father's land after a marriage to a ghar jawae did not like her husband and later the boy left her and went back to his village. She then married a boy of another village in ordinary sangha form and lost all her rights in her father's property.

Similarly the daughter of Bhusan Soren of Kaludi was twice married in ghar jawae form but failed to keep either of her husbands. She was then married a third time to a boy in another village and when she left her father's house she lost her rights in his land.

In Burhikura the eldest daughter of Rambai Soren was

first married to a ghar jawae but after his death she married a boy in another village. When she left her father's house her status as a ghar jawae married daughter ended.

In taking a second husband, the widow of a ghar jawae is not required to induct a younger brother of her dead husband but if the family agrees and the village approves, she can bring him to her house and announce him as her husband. As in other cases of a widow marrying a younger brother-in-law no further ceremony is strictly necessary and the installations with village approval is all that need be done.

Kulodi Hembrom of Kelahi was married to Barka Kisku in ghar jawae form. They lived with her father and had two daughters. When the ghar jawae died his younger brother was brought to the house to look after the cultivation and children and since then he has been living with Kulodi in her house. There was no formal ceremony but the village has accepted the union as a hilitet' sangha and Kulodi has retained all her rights as a daughter married to a ghar jawae.

In Gopaldih Motha Hembrom was taken as a ghar jawae for a girl in Jordiha. The boy died and after his death the girl brought a second husband. The second marriage failed, and after divorcing the boy the girl brought the younger brother of her first husband as a ghar jawae. There was no village meeting and the boy has been living as her ghar jawae husband by general consent.

In Kodlo Ainthu Marandi brought a ghar jawae for his sister. The boy died and his younger brother was then brought in his place. In this case also there was no formal ceremony but the second union was announced to the village.

VIII RIGHTS IN CHILDREN

But it is not only in these respects that the status of a daughter is changed. If the girl becomes a son in respect of her father's land, she is also to a great extent a father in respect of her children. Any children she has by her ghar jawae husband are brought up in her father's house and if she divorces her husband, they remain in her custody. If she is originally married in ghar jawae form, they are named as if she were a son. The first son is named after her father and it is only her second son who takes the name of her husband's father.

Pitho Tudu of Telo brought a ghar jawae for his only daughter. The girl gave birth to three sons and two daughters. The first was a daughter and was named Bumbuc' after the girl's mother, the second was a son and was named Pitho after the girl's father, the third was a son and was named Dukhia after the ghar jawae's father, while the fourth was a daughter and was named after the ghar jawae's mother.

Similarly after a son-in-law has been converted into a ghar jawae the naming of the children switches over to this new principle. He may already have had children who were named after his father and mother. Any new children, however, will be named in the order of a ghar jawae. A converted ghar jawae if he has had no daughter earlier will therefore name his first daughter after his wife's mother while his first son after the conversion will similarly be named after his wife's father.

Pratap Hansdak' of Thari had a son and a daughter. His son died leaving a son who also died. His daughter had been married in ordinary form to Dugu Marandi, but when the son died, Pratap converted his daughter's husband into a ghar jawae by agu mit'. Later his daughter had a son and she named him Pratap.

There is however one important respect in which the girl remains a mother. Her children take the sept and sub-sept of the ghar jawae and while her sons can worship her ancestors they must take the abge or sept bongas of the ghar jawae. If their father dies without telling them the names of these bongas they must learn them from his brother and failing that they will go to a man of their sub-sept, give him a cloth and take the names from him at a lonely river during the festival of Sohrae. For her children a ghar jawae married daughter is a father for every purpose except their sept.

IX RELIGIOUS CONSEQUENCES

While a girl becomes to a great extent a son in respect of her father's property, there remain certain matters in which she continues to be a daughter. For religious purposes she is linked to her husband's bongas and in respect of her father's bongas, she is no different from any married daughter. She cannot, for example, worship the household bongas and once she has had *sindur* from her husband, she is debarred from entering the shrine in her father's house or assisting at his sacrifices. Since her husband is of a different sept, he is equally debarred from assisting his father-in-law and when the latter dies it is necessary to arrange for the worship of the house and abge bongas by one of the agnates. Moreover, at his death the father himself joins the family ancestors and unless he also is worshipped his anger is liable to blast the house. Frequently one of the agnates does this service freely. If, however, its free performance is not forthcoming, the ghar jawae married daughter is expected either to provide the rice and fowls each year or to set aside some land as curuc' cawale to have the sacrifices done. The grant of such land lies purely within her discretion and none of the agnates can demand it as of right. It is made after her father's death when the occasion first arises. If it is not given the agnates can at most refuse their services and murmur at the girl's impiety. Occasionally at the time of according its approval to the marriage the village may specify how much land should ultimately be given and I have already noted a case in which an excessive quantity was allotted as the price of agreement. More usually curuc' cawale is only a few kathas. 'It is given to the dead father. It is for him.' An agnate holds it for his lifetime and after that it merges in his property and is taken by his heirs.

X FUNERARY FUNCTIONS

In respect of her father's funeral, the role of a ghar jawae married daughter is less distinct. She must meet all the costs but if she has a son, it is he who will put the fire in his grandfather's mouth. If there is no son, and her father has left any brothers, paternal uncles, or nephews in the village, one of these will officiate. If, however, there are neither sons nor agnates either the daughter herself or the ghar jawae will perform the office. Each is qualified to do so but each will do it only in the last resort.

Bhondo Soren of Langidih died leaving brothers and also

a ghar jawae married daughter with children. At his funeral ceremony the son of the daughter put fire to his mouth.

In Raniganj Ratu Hembrom died leaving a ghar jawae married daughter with sons. A son would normally have done the ag muk but as during his lifetime Ratu had expressed a wish that his daughter should do it the girl herself put fire to his mouth.

Shankar Marandi of Kusumdih died leaving a ghar jawae married daughter. In this case, the girl and her husband were both alive and the ghar jawae himself performed the ceremony.

Mangal Marandi of Masanjore circle had brought a ghar jawae for his daughter. The daughter died leaving a daughter and when Mangal himself died there was neither a grandson nor any agnate to perform the service for him. At his funeral ceremony therefore the ghar jawae did the ag muk for him.

In Anguthia Kandna Murmu died before his ghar jawae married daughter had born a son. In this case, no agnates were available so the girl herself put fire to his mouth.

XI THE RIGHTS OF THE GHAR JAWAE

If a marriage in ghar jawae form converts the girl into a son and gives her a number of special rights, it also converts the boy into a semi-girl. While the girl virtually becomes a husband, the boy to a great extent becomes a wife. It does not, however, change his character as a son in relation to his own father and he remains throughout a member of his father's sept.

The first respect in which he resembles a wife is that he leaves his father's house and goes to live permanently with his father-in-law. He becomes a part of his father-in-law's household in the same way as a girl who is married in the usual form becomes a part of her husband's establishment. Just as a wife is custodian of all her husband's movables, a ghar jawae is a manager of land, first for his father-in-law and later for his wife. Similarly just as a wife transports her ir arpa and private movables to her husband's house, a ghar jawae takes all his private belongings, his dancing gear, clothes and private ornaments to the house of the girl. In return for these functions, he has a wife's status in the household. He is entitled to maintenance in food and clothing and treatment in sickness and when he dies the family must meet the expenses of his death. If for any reason friction develops with his wife but she does not divorce him, separate lands can be allotted to him for his maintenance.*

A same role of wife is filled when questions of divorce or breaches of contract arise. Just as a wife in a joint household compels her husband to separate if she cannot tolerate her mother-in-law, a ghar jawae who finds the household insufferable first tries to induce his wife to abandon her father and return to his home. If his wife agrees, she forfeits her status as a ghar jawae married daughter and the ghar jawae takes her to his house. If his father-in-law is responsible and the two are unwilling to go, they are either turned out together or the village forces the father-in-law to keep them. If they are turned out, 'they must manage till their father dies. After that the girl will inherit'.

If friction develops between the girl and the ghar jawae and divorce becomes necessary, it is the ghar jawae and not the girl who is sent home to his parents while if the fault is with the boy, the girl can claim chadaodi or divorce money?

Balea Kisku of Baghmara brought a ghar jawae for her youngest daughter. The boy did not like living with her and when he deserted the girl, he was made to pay her seven rupees as chadaodi.

In Katikund Matal Murmu brought a ghar jawae for his daughter who was deaf and dumb. After two years the ghar jawae left her. He was made to pay a bullock worth seven rupees as chadaodi.

In Basoha Phagu Murmu was taken as a ghar jawae in Khijuria. He did not get on well with the family or his wife

*Phagu Hembrom of Susni was taken as a ghar jawae in Hathia. He was always loafing and although his wife tried to make him work he never listened to her. In the end, the girl lost patience with him but instead of divorcing him she built a small house on an adjoining plot of land and has made him live separately from her.

and after four years, he was sent home like a girl and given a cow as chadaodi or divorce money.

If the ghar jawae deserts the girl for a second wife no claim arises for hirom baiha but if his desertion is due to the girl, the ghar jawae can claim a sum as compensation. This is paid in cash or kind and is regarded sometimes as chadaodi, sometimes as chadaodi and a bride price, and sometimes only as an indemnity for his years of service in the house.

Somari Soren of Dhobna was a ghar jawae. His wife quarrelled with him and brought another boy as second ghar jawae. Somari did not wish to lose his status and at the village meeting he was awarded eight maunds of paddy as divorce money and compensation.

In Guhiajuri Jorwal Marandi brought a ghar jawae for his daughter. The girl did not like him and in the end he was divorced. At the meeting he was awarded a pair of bullocks, a dhoti and a turban as compensation.

Pradhan Murmu of Baghmara was married as a ghar jawae to a girl of Kajha. After sometime the girl did not like him and when he was sent back he was given twelve rupees as a bride price and seven rupees as chadaodi.

If a ghar jawae is like a wife, has he any rights in his wife's person?

As I discuss later, a ghar jawae wedding exempts a bridegroom from the bride price and the brother's due. If therefore another Santal goes to his wife, he cannot claim a double bride price 'for there is nothing to be doubled'. All he can do is to make the incident a ground for separation, claim divorce money and compensation and return home. If he decides to stay he can only demand celan gitil from the adulterer. If his wife permanently instals another man, he can only advance these claims and if he himself has deserted her, no formal ceremony of divorce is necessary before the girl can marry again. If the girl is ravished, the same principles apply as in other cases. The woman herself can get lajao marao and the offender give a fine and celan gitil.

XII THE DEATH OF THE GIRL

What is the ghar jawae's position if the girl dies?

Here also the analogy of a wife continues and at the girl's death it is as if the ghar jawae becomes a widow. If his children are all daughters, he is entitled to hold his wife's lands and movables and to maintain them and perform their marriages from the proceeds. Like a widow he inherits the land for life subject to the performance of these duties and it is only if one of his daughters is herself married in ghar jawae form that she can demand a separation of her share on reaching maturity. If the children are minor sons, the ghar jawae has similar rights. He holds the land like a widowed mother and if there is a partition he gets a share sufficient to keep him according as the village decides. If his sons are major, they inherit subject to the duty of maintaining him. If there are no children he inherits all land and movables for life. If his wife has left a widowed mother, he must maintain her from the property. In all these cases his rights are subject to his remaining on the land and not remarrying without the approval of his sons or his wife's reversioners.

Buka Tudu of Kumarpur married a girl of his village in ghar jawae form. The wife died without children and although she had agnates all of them had left the village and migrated across the Ganges. As none of them claimed the land Buka inherited it and has since brought another girl as his wife.

In Gamharia Chandrai Besra was brought as a ghar jawae to Kurumpahar. His wife died leaving a son and a daughter. Sometime later, these also died. There was no agnate or other heir and Chandrai then succeeded to all his wife's land and property. Later he brought his nephew Barka Besra to his house and adopted him as a posu putra. When Chandrai dies Barka will inherit all the lands of Chandrai.

To enjoy all these rights, the ghar jawae must continue to act throughout as a ghar jawae—to cultivate the lands and assist in the rearing of the family. Otherwise like a widow, who deserts her husband's village, his rights lapse and his function as a ghar jawae is ended.

XIII THE RE-MARRIAGE OF A GHAR JAWAE

What are the implications of re-marriage?

If he remarries without the approval of his father-in-law, his own sons or the father's agnates, he becomes like a widow who similarly remarries. If he has children, the agnates may make their own custody a condition of maintenance for unless the marriage is approved the ghar jawae cannot remain on the land and it is only his children who can stay.

Birsin Murmu of Singa was taken as ghar jawae in Babupur. When the girl died he brought another woman to his wife's house but the girl's agnates did not approve of the marriage, they drove him from the village and he lost all connection with his former wife's land.

Similarly in Kulaipara the wife of a ghar jawae, Chatur Soren, died leaving three daughters. Chatur wanted to remarry but the girl's family objected and in the end he had to leave the lands and marry in his village. The three daughters remained behind and later the agnates married one of them to a ghar jawae.

Equally if he remarries and is to stay in the family, his marriage must be done in circumstances similar to those which would enable a widow to remain in her husband's house. Just as if a widow is to be kept, she must marry either a younger brother of her husband or a boy who is adopted as his brother, a ghar jawae must either marry a sister of his wife or his father-in-law must induct a girl to act as a substitute for her.

If his father-in-law is dead, this function devolves on the nearest relations, and unless they have given their consent a second marriage by a ghar jawae annuls his status.

When a second marriage is duly approved it is either with a sister of the first wife or with a girl specially inducted for the purpose. If it is with a sister-in-law, the marriage gives her the status of a ghar jawae married daughter and she and her children then inherit one share in her father's land, while the children of her dead sister inherit another and an equal share.

If a girl is inducted from outside, it is unusual for her

to be formally adopted in the sense of changing her name, sept and bongas and her status depends on what is announced at the time.

If she is given all the status of a substitute daughter her rights are those of a ghar jawae married daughter and her children are named as if they were her predecessor's. If the first wife had no children, the first son and daughter by the second wife will be named after the first wife's parents, the second son and daughter after the ghar jawae's parents and only a third son or third daughter will be named after the parents of the second wife. Moreover, if there are children by the first wife, children by the second wife will inherit as if their mother was the same. The second wife becomes as it were an extension or replica of the first.

A Santal of Saldali brought a ghar jawae, Tula Soren, for his daughter. The daughter had a son and then died. The parents-in-law were fond of their son-in-law so they made him stay on and brought him another wife. When the marriage was being settled, the parents of the second wife said, 'We are giving our girl to him but where will our grandchildren have their land'? The father-in-law said, 'They will share with his first son.' This was approved by the village and the sons by the second wife will inherit equally with the son by the first.

A Santal of Tengic' Beda brought a ghar jawae for his only daughter. The girl died without any children. The ghar jawae went on living with him and a few years later his father-in-law brought him another wife from Targhara. The ghar jawae is still with his father-in-law and has now got four children. At the marriage it was made clear that his sons by the second wife will inherit his father-in-law's land.

If, however, no announcement is made the assumption is that the ghar jawae will retain his right to maintenance in his father-in-law's household but that all children by his second wife will inherit his own father's lands and not those of his father-in-law. Similarly on his death his widow will revert to his father's land.

The Pargana of Mandro Bungalow I had two daughters. He married the younger to a ghar jawae but she died leaving a son. The ghar jawae went on living with him and some years later he married him to another girl. The ghar jawae got a son by the second wife but it is only his first son who will inherit. The other son will have no claim to the pargana's land but will inherit land in the ghar jawae's village.

Similar principles determine the taking of co-wives. If a ghar jawae takes a co-wife against the wishes of his wife, the latter can divorce him and make him leave the house. If, however, the second wife is brought with the first wife's approval children by the second wife inherit according as the first wife announces at the marriage. If she herself is childless and the object of the second marriage is to gain a son, she may agree to regard the co-wife as a replica or deputy of herself. In that case, the first child will be named after the first wife's parents, and they will have the same rights as if the first wife was their mother.

Lalu Marandu of Dhanbad was a ghar jawae in his own village. His wife had no children and then with the wife's approval he took a co-wife. At the time of the marriage his first wife announced that if the co-wife had children they would inherit her land.

If on the other hand, the first wife expressly reserves these privileges, children by a second wife will inherit land only in the family of the ghar jawae himself.

Dhugru Kisku of Karijori was married as a ghar jawae in his own village. He had several children by his wife. After his brother's death, and with the wife's consent, he brought his sister-in-law as a second wife. His first wife reserved all rights for her children, and when her husband and the second wife died, she expelled the latter's son from her house.

XIV RIGHTS OF A GHAR JAWAE IN HIS FATHER'S FAMILY

How does a ghar jawae stand in relation to his own family? Here also there is the same reversal of roles and the normal rule is that a ghar jawae retains a son's rights in his father's land and movables. So long as his father is alive, and there is no partition, the ghar jawae will cultivate only his father-in-law's lands. If, however, his father dies or the lands are partitioned, he secures a son's share in his father's lands.

Similarly if at his marriage he is already a widower with

children, his sons retain their inheritance in his father's land and nothing in the marriage contract can defeat their rights.

Rajmat Hansdak' came as a ghar jawae to Chuka Buju Marandi in Jirua. His father has died and he now cultivates his wife's lands in Jirua and his own in Majdiha.

Rupai Hembrom of Karhabel was taken to Dhamna as a ghar jawae by agu mit'. He did not cultivate his lands in Karhabel but kept his rights in them.

A boy of Kolha was married in ghar jawae form to a girl in an adjoining village. He was living in the house but the girl was still very young. For a time he went back to his house in Kolha and while he was there he fell in love with a village girl. The affair was discovered and the girl's father demanded a bride price. The boy had three brothers and there had been an equal partition—the boy retaining his fourth share while being a ghar jawae outside. But the total amount of land was very little. At the village meeting, the boy and the girl wanted to marry but the elder brother refused to pay the bride price as he said it would mean another girl to feed, a greater strain on the land and giving up the ghar jawae form in the other village. If the boy stuck this out, he and everyone else would be better off, so the bride price was not paid and the matter ended with the payment of lajao marao and a fine.

In Dudhani Ramu Kisku was one of two brothers. He was taken as a ghar jawae but on his father's death he inherited half his land.

The only circumstance in which this rule is departed from is when the parties make a declaration at the wedding either restricting the boy's share or eliminating it altogether. When this is done, the restriction is conditional on his status as a ghar jawae remaining, and if for any reason he leaves his father-in-law's house, and returns to his father, his full rights as a son are revived.

Finally in religious matters it is to his father's family that a ghar jawae belongs and he can neither sacrifice to his father-in-law's bongas nor learn their names.

In Ghatiari the father of Bhagmat Kisku was a ghar jawae. The ghar jawae's father-in-law told him the names of his bongas and Bhagmat's father worshipped them. No action was taken by the village in this matter but none of the neighbouring Santals approved of it. It was against all known custom. 'It was wrong'.

Similarly while he can usually* share his father-in-law's sacrificial meat (except the head) he can only do so in respect of sacrifices within the house and is debarred from sharing the meat of animals sacrificed outside it. We have already seen that only in a last resort can he put fire to the mouth of his father-in-law. If in the greater part of his functions he is like a wife it is in religion and land that he remains the son of his father.

XV CONCLUSION

What is the Santal attitude to the serving son-in-law?

There can be no doubt that the transference of roles always begins by putting the ghar jawae at a disadvantage. He is treated as a girl not only at his wedding but in the daily work of the house. He is ruled by his wife and must obey her like a servant. He can spend only with her approval and can visit his relatives only with her consent. Accordingly it is usually only poor boys who accept the contract and since their motives are mainly economic, a ghar jawae wedding is inevitably regarded as a poor man's choice. Equally among girls a ghar jawae is treated as the last resort of a girl long past her prime.

In a troop we girls had gone
To gather cowdung in a rice field
My girl friends tell me
Karam twig you are still unmarried
Never mind
We will get you a ghar jawae.

—*Don Soren*, 2207.

*Cigi Tudus, for example, are debarred from sharing any sacrificia meat with any other sept.

In Santal practice the ghar jawae is the official refuge not of the unmarried mother but of the unmarried girl.*

If this is the standard attitude, however, the post is very far from lacking all compensations. Unlike the same institution in many other castes and tribes cohabitation starts from the time the wedding is settled. The ghar jawae both serves for his wife and lives with her. Moreover when his induction is due to lack of servants, he may come in time to exercise a dominant voice in the counsels of the family. In Santal law he will remain technically a wife but in actual practice his position may differ little from that of an ordinary husband. If the couple get sons, the practical difference will be even slighter. Moreover as I show later a ghar jawae saves himself not only the major expenses of a wedding but, also the bride price and the brother's due. If he must pocket some of his pride, the resulting benefits must often far outweigh the loss of dignity. Finally the vitality of the institution and its wide prevalence suggests that the stresses are far more apparent than real.

In the present the ghar jawae is a valued means to family adjustments. In the past he was the agency by which Santal society developed a new view of women's rights.

*Contrast the Baiga lamsena (Elwin: *The Baiga*, 288).

PART FOUR

THE LAW OF MARRIAGE AND DIVORCE

23

THE DEFINITION OF A SANTAL MARRIAGE

I THE SANTAL LAW OF MARRIAGE

BEFORE a boy and girl live publicly together and are known as man and wife a number of meetings are considered necessary. Even when the marriage is by capture, intrusion or elopement at least one meeting is held while if the union is negotiated a series of meetings precedes the final celebration. On all these occasions expenditure is necessary. Moreover each marriage is of necessity the transfer of a person. Usually it is the girl who is given to her husband but occasionally as in the wedding of a ghar jawae it is the boy who goes to his wife. Each of these transfers is a vehicle for claims—public, exact and rigid.

The function of the Santal law of marriage is to control and regulate these claims and charges. It enunciates ritual and concedes rights. It controls expenditure and imposes standards. Finally it defines the conditions which accord a Santal union the status of a marriage.

I will begin therefore by defining a Santal marriage in terms of tribal law and will then review the various types of union which are included in the term. One of these—jawae kirinok' bapla—I have already discussed in the chapter on The Illegitimate Child—and a second—hirom cetan bapla—is examined in the chapter on Co-Wives. I will end by describing the bride price, the brother's due and the law of divorce.

II THE DEFINITION OF MARRIAGE

Like many tribes of Middle and Eastern India, Santals possesses a flexible and intricate system of tribal marriages.*

It is not a case of one type of marriage being alone valid with the rest more of less irregular. There is rather a congeries of unions, all of which are sanctioned by law and all of which are valid.**

It will be convenient if I follow the example of Verrier Elwin*** and first describe them in tabular form.

1. Dol bapla	a full dress wedding celebrated with dancing and drumming in the two villages.
2. Golaeti 3. Tunki dipil	public celebrations but on a smaller scale. Golaeti, an exchange of brothers and sisters, tunki dipil a poor man's wedding.
4. Sangha	weddings of divorced girls and widows.
5. Jawae kirinok' bapla	marriage by the purchase of a husband for an unmarried mother.
6. Hirom cetan	the public induction of a co-wife.
7. Iputut'	marriage by the forcible smearing of a girl with *sindur* or its substitute.
8. Or ader	marriage by capture, when a boy or girl 'pulls' the other into a house.
9. Nir bolok'	marriage by intrusion, when a boy or girl force themselves into a family.
10. Kundal napam	'meeting at bedtime.'

*The Murias for example, possesses six different types of marriages, the Birhors ten, the Dudh and Dhelki Kharias five.

**This is fully paralleled in Chenchu practice where 'the social status of the marriage partners and their children in no way depends on the form in which their marriage was contracted' (Haimendorf: *The Chenchus*, 139). Among the Reddis also 'once a couple is settled as man and wife their social status is in no way dependent on the circumstances in which the union was brought about'. (Haimendorf: *The Reddis of the Bison Hills*, 125).

***Compare *The Muria and their Ghotul.*

11. Apangir	elopement
12. Ghardi jawae	the taking of a temporary serving son-in-law.
13. Ghar jawae	the induction of a permanent serving son-in-law, the wedding being celebrated as in a dol bapla but with certain differences and the roles of boy and girl reversed.
14. Agu hatar	a ghar jawae wedding by anticipation.

Besides these fourteen types, there are certain 'cross' arrangements. Each of the first twelve, for example, can be converted into a ghar jawae marriage by appropriate ceremonial while in certain cases the ghar jawae union is 'anticipated' by resort to nir bolok' or kundal napam. Similarly the term hirom cetan covers all the ways of inducting a co-wife whether by dol bapla, or ader, or by simply installing her in a separate house, while the distinctive ritual of sangha is sometimes availed of in the later stages of or ader, nir bolok' kundal napam or apangir.

All these ways of marriage differ widely in method and detail but there are two basic conditions which all of them require. The first is the negative principle that the union shall not break the rules of exogamy, ignore prohibited degrees of relationship,* nor offend the canons of tribal integrity.

If these rules are broken, the boy and girl are punished and their union can never be recognised as a marriage.

The other principle is that the union must be approved by the village. In many forms of marriage this is secured by the appointment of a match-maker and by prior consultation with the villagers. In others, the boy and girl first come together and approval is taken later at a village meeting. In yet other cases, there is neither prior consultation nor explicit approval but if the two live publicly together as husband and wife with neither village intervention nor tribal punishment, local acquiescence validates their union.

In Santal law any union is a marriage which fulfils these two conditions.

*I have discussed these fully in my report on *Bitlaha*.

24

THE STANDARD FORM OF WEDDING DOL BAPLA

I INTRODUCTION

If a Santal marriage is to excite general admiration it must preferably be celebrated by a wedding in dol or sadai form. This involves a series of intricate negotiations, a formal expression of approval, the public granting of *sindur* and a feast and dancing in the two houses. The ceremony not only unites the boy and girl but fuses the two villages in a ritual act.

II THE MATCH-MAKER

The first step in this form of marriage is the appointment of a raebaric' or match-maker. This envoy is often an old and respected friend who can be either a man or a woman and who represents either of the two families.[1] During the course of the talk it is necessary for a number of dates to be fixed and on all these occasions the boy's father must bring the match-maker and the village officials together and give them rice beer. Similarly, when dates are considered by the girl's family the officials of her village are consulted and they and the match-maker are given rice beer in the girl's house. At the end of the marriage when all has been successfully accomplished the match-maker is given the customary presents.

III THE FIRST INSPECTION

When the match-maker has been chosen, his first task is to scour the countryside for scent of a suitable girl. In most cases the family already has a girl in mind and if no girl has actually been inspected a few eligible girls are often known of from before. The match-maker, therefore, selects a family and first secures their agreement to consider the proposal. After that a date is settled for a first inspection by the families.

This first view is arranged at a market, a *mela* or under a tree between the two villages. In some cases it takes place in the jogmanjhi's house at the village of the girl and almost all the families of both villages attend the inspection. Each person is saluted by the girl and the boy, and the villagers subject them both to a critical scrutiny. If the first inspection is held at the house of the jogmanjhi and the first response is favourable, the boy's party sometimes go on to the girl's house, drink rice beer, eat a meal of rice and then return.

Normally however neither side commits itself to more than a polite neutrality and a day or two later the match-maker ascertains their views. If either is insufficiently impressed, they tell the match-maker that they did not find a good omen and the negotiations go no further. If both sides are willing, they accord provisional approval and the match-maker then arranges for a fuller view.

This full inspection is known as orak' duar nel, the viewing of the household, and is sometimes held at the boy's house and the girl's, sometimes first at the one or first at the other and sometimes only at the boy's house or only at the girl's. When it is done at the boy's the match-maker brings the girl's father, her uncles and aunts and the manjhi and paranik of her village and the whole party is shown the boy's house and are conducted round the lands. If the boy's family can afford it the party are given rice beer and a meal of taben, khajari and gur and later in the day they are given more rice beer and a meal of rice with meat. If a visit is made to the girl's house, similar formalities are followed but the lands are not inspected.

When a party has returned to its village, they again consider the proposal and inform the match-maker. If they are not impressed they politely withdraw their provisional approval but otherwise, they confirm the original agreement.

When the visit is to the girl's house or to both the houses similar action is taken and views are similarly exchanged.

If at this stage either side withdraws, no claims arise, for the matter is merely being explored.

IV THE BETROTHAL

After 'the viewing of the household', the families decide whether to perform the wedding quickly or to postpone it to a later date. If they do not want it immediately they arrange for a formal betrothal to 'block the way'. This ceremony usually takes place at the girl's house and is then followed by a visit to the boy's but in certain cases, the boy's house is visited first and the girl's later. If an early wedding is desired, the visit to the boy's house is all that takes place.

Each of these visits is known as horok' cikhna or 'the recognition by clothes' and the subject of the first is to give a bahu bandu or cloth to the bride.

The boy's party consisting of the male members of his greater family together with the relatives on his mother's side go to the girl's house. They take with them the manjhi and paranik of the village and also a few villagers. The party often consists of men only but sometimes of women also. In the girl's house they are given two meals, the first of rice beer with taben, khajari and gur and the second of rice beer with rice and a goat or pig. The girl's father seats them in the courtyard and the girl is taken up by each of them in turn. The boy's father gives her a piece of cloth and the other members of the party make small gifts.* When the giving is over, the presents are counted by the officials of the two villagers.

The object of the visit to the boy's house is to give a jawae

*These presents whether at the girl's house or at the boy's are often determined by what each villager received from the father of the girl or boy when one of his own children was married. In the case of ordinary villagers, the present is often of only one anna.

dhuti or cloth to the bridegroom. The girl's party goes and is given similar entertainment. They take the boy on their knees, kiss his right ear and give him small presents. The girl's father gives him a cloth and the other members of the party present him with either a bangle, armlet, necklace or small sums of money. The articles or money are then collected in a basket and the officials of both the villages make an account.

These visits for horok' cikhna whether to the girl's house or the boy's are either with a large or a small party. If large, the party goes with drums and horns and is called dahar ten ko, those who go by road. If it is small, no drums are taken and the party is called suruc' hor ten ko—those who take a short cut. When both the families are well-to-do, large parties always go and the expenses are correspondingly great. When the houses are poor the expenses are kept lower and only small parties make the visits. Each party goes in nearly equal numbers and the cost of the two visits is kept, as far as possible, the same.

As soon as a date for the first visit has been settled, both families are committed to the subsequent wedding and if one party withdraws from the proposal without the other being to blame, the other side can claim all the expenditure it may have incurred since the viewing of the household. If the proposal is broken between the fixing of the date for giving the bride a cloth and the actual visit, the girl's family can claim the cost of all its preparations. In the hot weather and the rains, rice beer takes three days to brew and in the cold weather six to seven days. If, therefore, the girl's family have already started to brew rice beer they can claim the cost of whatever rice has been wasted. They cannot, however, demand the cost of the rice, taben, khajari and gur intended for the meal nor the price of a goat since these are not perishable and can be kept and eaten later. Similarly if the boy's side resiles from the agreement after 'the visit for the bride's cloth' and the girl's house is not to blame the girl's father can claim all the costs incurred during the ceremony.

The same principles apply in the case of the visit to the boy's house for 'the bridegroom's dhoti'. Here also if a date for the visit has been settled and the boy's house has made its preparations they can claim the cost of any rice beer that is wasted by the conduct of the girl's family. Equally when the ceremony itself has taken place and the girl's family breaks off the proposal, without sufficient cause, the cost of their entertainment in the boy's house can be demanded. Moreover, if the boy's side breaks off the proposal after both the bride's cloth and bridegroom's dhoti have been given, the girl's father can claim all the costs of entertaining the party when 'the bride's cloth' was given.

In all such cases, it is not what a party has received but what it has spent which forms the basis of a claim. The aggrieved party can claim all the expenditure it incurred as a result of the promise to marry and the party at fault cannot claim any set off either for the presents it gave or for the entertainment it provided. Similarly, if a party is itself at fault it cannot claim its costs and it is immaterial whether the proposal is broken by the party itself or by the other side. If neither side is obviously at fault, the expenses are estimated and whichever side has spent more is given sufficient to equalize its loss.

In Kusumba the marriage of Lal Kisku was arranged with the daughter of Ladum Soren of Daldali. The 'giving of the bride's cloth' was dispensed with and 'the recognition by clothes' was done at the house of the boy. After the ceremony was over the boy's family learnt that the girl's brother was a leper. They did not relish a connexion with such a house and therefore, broke the proposal off. In this case, the girl's family had given the boy a dhoti but had not undergone the expenses of 'the bride's cloth'. The boy's father did not claim the cost of 'the recognition by clothes' as the girl's father was not entirely to blame. Since the girl's family had also received entertainment, they did not make any demand for the cloth.

In Amtala Chotu Ramu had negotiated the marriage of his son in Jamni. 'The recognition by clothes' was done in his house. Then he went with a party to Jamni but the girl's father refused to give them food. There was a tremendous quarrel and they went back in a huff. After that, Chotu Ramu broke the marriage off. When he told me about this he said that he could have claimed the cost of 'the recognition by clothes'. He did not, however, do so and it is possible that he himself was partly to blame.

Mandal Baske of Patardih had arranged his son's marriage in Haldidih and 'the bridegroom's cloth' had been duly given in his house. Then the girl came to know that the boy had six toes on each of his feet and she refused to go on with the marriage. Mandal claimed the expenses of 'the recognition' but these were disallowed since the fact of the boy's deformity had been suppressed. The girl's side were, therefore, not at fault and nothing was awarded.

In Durga, a marriage had been arranged between Hopna Murmu and Hendi Soren. The bride's cloth was given in the girl's house and a few weeks later, a party from the girl's side went to the boy's house for giving the bridegroom's dhoti. A good deal of merry-making took place and the women of both parties smeared each other with oil and turmeric. During the merry-making, the mother of the girl got excited, stripped herself of her clothes and started dancing naked. This conduct disgusted the mother of the boy and a few days later, after the party had left, the match-maker was instructed to suspend the negotiations. The girl's mother was very angry and her husband attempted to recover the cost of entertaining the party. Since, however, they themselves were at fault, the boy's father declined to pay and in the end they got nothing.

Suna Marandi of Chhatani had arranged the marriage of his son and the ceremony of the bridegroom's cloth had been celebrated. The girl's presents then withdrew without good reasons and Suna was awarded forty rupees.

Gobind Soren of Mohonpur Amdangal had settled the marriage of his son in Chapria. The bridegroom's cloth had been given in his house but before the bride price was paid the girl's father refused to give his daughter on the ground that the boy's family were too poor. In this case, the girl's family were held to be at fault and sixty rupees was paid to the boy's father on account of the expenses.

In yet another case, Saklu Murmu had betrothed his son to the daughter of Japla Marandi of Pandanpahari. 'The recognition by clothes' was duly performed in Saklu's house and seventy rupees was spent in feasting the bride's party. Some months later Japla postponed the wedding and later his daughter eloped with a man of Asanbani. When the marriage failed, Saklu demanded his expenses and the pargana and five manjhis awarded him the full seventy rupees.

But apart from claims for actual costs a jilted party can in certain circumstances claim compensation even though it has not provided entertainment.

The daughter of Mangal Hembrom of Gandhrab was engaged to a boy in Bichipahari. 'The recognition by clothes' had taken place at the boy's house and then the boy refused to marry her. He gave no reason, so the villagers made his father pay ten rupees to the girl's parents for 'not keeping his word'.

Finally once a 'recognition by clothes' has been performed the boy and girl are technically betrothed and can live together as if they were fully wedded. The girl does not permanently leave her father's house but it is quite normal and even proper for her to go on a visit of a few days to the boy's house and share a room with her proposed husband.

In the case from Morga, Hendi Soren paid a short visit to Hopna's house after the bride's cloth had been given. She slept with him for a few nights and the match-maker then took her back to her parent's house.

Similarly in the case from Pandanpahari, the girl stayed at the boy's house for several nights following 'the bride-groom's dhoti' and when she went back the boy went with her and lived with her at her house for a further week.

If after sleeping together the marriage breaks, no claim for damages or lajao marao arises and it is only if the connexion leads to pregnancy that notice is taken.[2]

V THE PAYMENT OF THE BRIDE PRICE

When the ceremonies of 'recognition by clothes' have been completed, the next stage is taka cal or the payment of the bride price. For this purpose, the boy's parents with the village officials and their wives and a few others go to the girl's house.* They take with them their own food for a morning meal but are provided with fuel, leaves and earthen

*In Pakaur Subdivision, the delivery of the bride price is done by the match-maker only and there is no formal visit by the boy's side.

pots. When they arrive rice beer is drunk and the bride price is finally decided. It is also settled whether the girl's brother will receive an animal as his bare itat or brother's due or whether this will be paid in cash. After the settling of the bride price the boy's father gives the girl a present and then makes over the bride price to the jog manjhi of the girl's village. This bride price is known as panja ten and is paid either in full or in part. When it has been paid the boy's party is given rice beer, a meal of rice and a goat or pig. The following morning, after drinking more rice beer the party returns home. On this occasion, the match-maker usually receives five pais of taben and khajari from the girl's mother in addition to his meals and rice beer.

If the marriage is broken off between the date of fixing the payment and the actual visit for giving the money the same principles apply as in the case of 'the bride's cloth' and 'the bridegroom's dhoti'. If the girl's family is not at fault they can recover the cost of any rice beer that is wasted. Similarly if the proposal fails either during the visit or after it, the girl's faimly can demand the actual cost of the entertainment given. In addition, they can claim whatever cost was incurred at the ceremony of the bride's cloth. 'If on the other hand, the girl's side is to blame and the boy's party breaks the proposal at any time before, during or after the payment of the bride price, they are not responsible for the costs of the girl's side and can themselves recover whatever was expensed at the recognition by clothes.' Moreover if the bride price has been paid and the girl's family are at fault the boy's father can recover all the money he has given.

If however, the girl's side are free from blame and the marriage is broken by the boy no refund of this money can be claimed, but if the boy's party is at fault and the girl's father breaks the proposal, the bride price must be given back.

Morol Hembrom of Beora had betrothed his son to a girl of the same village but a different tola. The bridegroom's cloth had been given, and a date had been fixed for payment of the bride price. Four days before that date the girl's father heard that a kisar bonga was in the boy's house and broke the marriage off. In this case, no expenses were awarded but the girl's father refunded thirty-five rupees in lieu of a ring, a pair of saris and some trinkets, which the boy's side had given.

In Bhodai Charan Kisku had settled the marriage of his younger brother with a daughter of Pandu Hansdak' of Rajabhita. All the stages had been completed and a bride price of fourteen rupees had also been paid. Before the wedding took place, however, the girl refused to marry the boy. In the settlement which followed the girl's father returned the bride price and also gave nineteen pailas of rice in lieu of the four pots of rice beer which the boy's family had brewed on the occasion of jawae dhuti.

Sakla Hembrom of Mirzapur had agreed to marry his son to Churki Tudu of Dumaria. Half the bride price was paid but the day following the payment Sakla refused to marry his son to Churki and demanded her younger sister instead. The girl's father did not agree and the marriage failed. Sakla demanded the return of the bride price but as he himself was to blame, the claim was disallowed.

VI THE WEDDING

When the bride price has been wholly or partly paid the way is open to the wedding and a date is then settled by the match-maker. This is usually in March, April or May when the trees are coming into flower and there is little work in the fields.

For one, three, five or seven days before the wedding, the boy and girl are each rubbed with oil and turmeric.

A dak' bapla or water marriage is performed in each village and both parties make offerings at their majhithans to secure the blessings of the founders.

Before the boy leaves for the girl's village his mother pretends to suckle him and receives a rupee as nunu taka or 'the price of her breasts'.

The boy then goes with his party down the village street and over the fields to the village of the girl.

In this village he is taken round from house to house and given gur, while a mock battle rages between the two opposing camps.

Oil and turmeric are then put on the boy. He is washed

and given a new dhoti and pichauri and the girl herself is given a cloth from the boy. He then rides on the shoulders of his babre or Brahmin while the bride's younger brother comes mounted on a relative. The two meet and then the boy ties a turban on his new brother-in-law, and they spit some chewed rice on each other's cheeks.

This act of family union is an immediate prelude to the Sindurdan.

'The bariat is once more marshalled and headed by the Dom musicians, proceeds to the bride's house, and waits outside in the street. Those chosen to carry out the bride, generally the bridegroom's brothers, enter the house and as a beginning are served with liquor. The bride, attired in her marriage raiment, steps into and seats herself in a large new shallow flat basket known as a bahu daura. The bearers then lift and bear her out into the street, where the bridegroom awaits her sitting astride on the shoulder of his brother-in-law, or uncle. The bride in her basket is raised to the level of the bridegroom, and each sprinkles the other three times with water by means of a sprig of a mango tree. The fathers, uncles and aunts of the couple then salute each other in the fashion peculiar to their new relationship. Some *sindur* in a sarjom leaf is then given to the bridegroom, who with the little finger of his right hand marks the bride five times on her forehead, and what of the *sindur* remains on the leaf he wipes off on her brow. The bride is then lifted out of the basket by the bridegroom and the upper garments of the two are knotted together so that where one goes the other must follow.'[3]

This is the crux of the wedding—the act which finally makes the boy and the girl man and wife.

After that they sit together and share a joint meal. The circling ceremony of gidi cumaura is then done and women of both sides give presents to the pair. The girl's mother usually presents the boy with a pair of bangles and the girl with a neck ornament. The other women of the village also perform the ceremony and give small money presents to the boy and ornaments or money to the girl. The bride then goes to the boy's camp where she goes round saluting each member of the party and receiving small presents of money. Feasting and farewell addresses follow and the next morning the boy returns to the village taking the girl with him.

At his house, the brother's bullock is shown to the bride's brother. The boy and girl again sit together. The circling ceremony is again performed, small presents are given and the village is feasted.

The girl's party then go home but after five days they return and take the boy and girl to the girl's house for a visit of two days. Rice beer 'for dismissal' is drunk in the two villages and with this drinking the wedding ceremonies end.

VII THE CUSTOMARY GIFTS

To the bride and bridegroom this ritual is a long process of nervous exhaustion. It surrounds them with unaccustomed homage. It subjects them to strange forms of behaviour.

But to the two families, the strain of a wedding lies chiefly in its expense.

This expense is neither arbitrary nor accidental. Part of it is dictated by custom while the greater portion is planned and approved by the two families before the wedding day arrives.

The cost falls into two classes :

(i) gifts or payments to members of the two families, the wedding assistants, and the manjhis and jog manjhis of the two villages ; and
(ii) the cost of entertaining the villagers, erecting the mandwa or marriage shed, hiring musicians and palkis together with minor miscellaneous items.

Of these groups, the first accounts for far less expenses but is of great importance for the success of the wedding. It is far more rigidly determined by custom and the failure to meet any of the dues may provoke an angry remonstration.

TABLE 24.1 : **Standard* gifts or payment made by the bridegroom's side**

Recipient	Gift
(1) Bride's side :	
Bride's father	Gonon pon or bride-price.
Bride's brother	Bare itat or brother's bullock (animal or cash).
Bride's younger brother.	One turban.
Bride herself.	One new cloth.
Bride's elder sister	Two rupees as taram gande (if not already married).
Bride's younger sister	One anna 'for opening the door' after *sindurdan*. One pice for 'releasing the crab' when washing the bridegroom on his second visit to the bride's house.
Babre Era	The bridegroom's cloth discarded by him at the formal washing prior to the *sindurdan*. One pot of rice beer, four pice, one leaf cup of rice, one leaf cup of khajari for her services at the washing, four annas for cak puraini or cow-dunging the base of the centre pole in the girl's marriage shed. One pice for 'releasing the crab' when washing the bridegroom on his second visit to the bride's house.
Gate Kuri	One anna as son chadaoni.
Manjhi	One rupee.**
Jogmanjhi	Four pice at the formal washing of the boy before the *sindurdan*.
(2) Bridegroom's side :	
Lumti kora (or best man)	One turban.
Babre	One cloth (5 cubits).
Bridegroom's mother	One rupee (nune taka).
Bridegroom's younger sister	One anna 'for opening the door' in the house on the return of the bariat.
Babre era	Four to six annas as cak puraini or cow-dunging the boy's shed.

TABLE 24.1 (*contd.*)

Recipient	Gift
Three tetre kuriko***	One pice, one leaf cup of khajari, one leaf cup of rice.
Jogmanjhi (bridegroom's village)	One pice at dak' bapla, or turban (if marriage is of the first or last child in the family).
Women who cook the feast	Four annas (culha jharauni).
Barber	Four annas.
Match-maker	One cloth, two annas as karpa kudi (for wearing out his shoes) 9 annas.
Bride	One calf or brass bowl and plate or one rupee 'to make her eat' when the bridal sit for a joint meal at the bridegroom's house. Out of this she keeps 8 annas and gives the rest to the members of the bariat.
Bride's father's elder brother (gongo) Bride's mother's elder brother (mama)	One to two cloths or five to sixteen rupees. In return he gives the bride-groom's party taben and rice beer at his house and the bridegroom a cow or bullock (gongo salaka or mama salaka).
Women who cooked in bride's house	Two annas (culha jharauni).
Jogmanjhi	One anna as gupi or puchia kundi for 'shepherding the girl' for every year between the horok' cikhna and the wedding.

*In the Rajmahal subdivision these payments are often on a more lavish scale according to private agreement. For example, the babre era is given a rupee by each side, for cak puraini instead of four annas. The tetre kuriko are often given four pice each instead of one pice. The bride's younger sister gets one rupee instead of one pice for 'releasing the crab' and so on.

**If he keeps the whole rupee, he must give the boy's party a meal of rice and a goat or pig or a pot of rice beer and some taben.

***Village girls who act as 'maids of all work' in addition each is often given two skeins of thread.

On the bride's side there are similar customary gifts although they are considerably fewer in number.

TABLE 24.2 : **Customary gifts and payments made by the bride's side**

Recipient	Gift
(1) Bride's side :	
Lumti Budhi (or chaperon)	One anna.
Three tetri kuriko	One pice, one leaf cup of khajari, one leaf cup of rice each.
Jogmanjhi	One pice, one cloth (if the marriage is of the first or last child).
(2) Bridegroom's side :	
Bridegroom	One dhoti, one pichauri.
Bridegroom's younger sister	One anna for releasing 'the grip of the crab' when washing the bridal pair on their return to the boy's house.
Match-maker*	Seven annas.
Optional Payments	
(1) Bridegroom's side :	
Bridegroom	One calf or brass bowl and plate or one rupee 'to make him eat' when the bridal pair sit for a joint meal after the *sindurdan*.
Lumti kora	One todor (wristlet) or turban.
Father	Enhanced bride-price with obligation to make return gifts and gonon taraoni.**

*These are the standard payments to the match-maker but there are a number of local variations which I record below :

Area	*Boy's side*	*Girl's side*
Jamtara	One cloth	One cloth
Narainpur	One cloth Four annas	One cloth Two annas
Kundahit	One cloth Eight annas	One cloth Six annas
Nonihat	Nine annas	Seven annas
Poreyahat Chandna	One cloth Nine annas	Seven annas
Pakaur subdivision	Any amount fixed by private negotiation.	
Raksi	One cloth One rupee	One cloth Eight annas

**See Chapter 33.

IX THE WEDDING COSTS

These customary gifts rarely account for more than a third of the total costs and the bulk of the expenses are comprised in group II.

In this group a major item is the entertainment of both villages to meals of rice and rice beer. It is this which is the aim of every family and it is only if their resources are weak that entertainment is confined to rice beer only. When however a feast is approved, the decision is not announced in public but a mandwa is merely erected in the courtyard.

This shed or marriage booth consists of a canopy of sal and mango branches covering a central pole or khunti. The khunti is made of a sal branch planted with a mahua branch and a little mound of earth or cok khunti is heaped up at its base.

When it is erected it is put up one, three, five, or seven days before the wedding and the boy and the girl are rubbed with oil and turmeric from the day of its erection. For making the booth the services of the village boys are impressed and in return for their work they are given a meal of rice each and a pot of rice beer to share. A mandwa sacrifice must also be made in the sacred grove. The priest takes three fowls—one brown and two white, two pais of rice and a pot of rice beer. At the grove he says, 'Jaher era, in the name of the mandwa I am offering a fowl. Look on it with favour. When we go to the girl's village as the bridegroom's party, may there be no trouble or danger on the road or in the forest. May there be no stumbling and fumbling. Let nothing be broken. Let no one be bewitched. Let every trouble be removed to the left and right of our path. When we eat and drink, let no one have an ache in belly or head. Let the two families be of one mind. May there be no quarrel, no accusations, no checks or hindrance. May this wedding reach its end in calm and peace.' He then offers the brown fowl to Jaher era and with similar invocations sacrifices the two fowls to Maran Buru and Moreko Turuc' Ko. As far as possible, this sacrifice is done either on the day the booth is erected or on the day following the end of the wedding. If the wedding overstretches the family's resources it is sometimes postponed to the erok' festival when it is included in the erok' sacrifice. During each day of the mandwa, the three tetre kuris or 'Maids of all work' attend the bride or bridegroom, assist in the annointing and are given their meals each day. The jogmanjhi also supervises the ritual and is given food and drink for every day the mandwa stands.

But besides these incidental charges, the erection of the mandwa is of great importance for it commits each family to a village feast. In the girl's village, her family must entertain the whole village with rice beer and a meal of rice and also provide the bridegroom's party with a similar meal. In the boy's village his family must give the villagers a feast on the return of the party with the girl and her friends. On the side of the villagers, it assumes cooperation in the gidi cumaura or circling ceremony and the giving of small presents to the boy and the girl.

If for any reason these expenses cannot be incurred a camda or simple shed is put up instead. No sal or mahua branches are erected in the courtyard and there is no cok khunti or earthen mound. The boy and the girl are not given turmeric in its shade and at the circling ceremony only the family intimates attend and the present giving takes place in the privacy of a room. No sacrifices are necessary and the village boys can claim no feast. Rice beer, however, is brewed and the village drinks and dances.

XI MINOR CHARGES

If rice beer and a feast of rice and meat are the main charges, a few other items also involve cost.

The boy's party must send ahead a set of 'sacrificial things'. These consist of a goat, a pot of rice beer and some pais of rice together with a little tobacco, salt and oil as a present to the bride's party.

If the wedding is to be done in fairly ordinary style, five Dom musicians must be hired to accompany the bridegroom. These are usually given their food and drink, two rupees in cash, twenty pais of rice and a goat or pig. If the family is well-to-do, they are also given cloth.

If the families are of rather more than average position, the boy is carried to and from the girl's house in a rahi or palki. This is hired for one, two or three rupees and the bearers are often paid one rupee per kos as well as their food and drink.

In certain areas, if the boy's side goes with a palki, the girl's mother can demand jhili ladu or sweets and the boy gives her a cloth with five rupees tied up in it. In return she gives him a cow and calf.

XII BOR HORO

All these expenses are met by the party concerned but if the girl's family is poor, a special type of loan known as bor horo, is sometimes advanced by the boy's father to assist the bride's parents in performing the wedding. The loan is often as much as ten maunds of paddy and is repayable without interest any time in the next few years. It is advanced against the security of the brother's bullock and until the loan is repaid the animal is kept by the boy's father.

Dasmat Tudu of Chandarpura gave one bis of paddy to his son's father-in-law. The bride's father repaid it after two years and then the brother's bullock was taken.

Jetha Murmu of Madhusingha borrowed a maund of paddy when he married his daughter to Jhari Hembrom of Talberya. Two years later he gave him sixty bamboos as the equivalent of its price.

This loan of paddy is only advanced to the bride's side and is an important means of easing the wedding burden and spreading its strain over a number of years.

XIII LAST CLAIMS

When the wedding is over no formal record of its cost is preserved. Each family knows its own expenses and the costs are often a source of gossip in the village. But if the marriage succeeds they have only a passing interest and are not remembered except as standards for future weddings. If, however, the marriage fails, the costs may suddenly acquire significance.

It is possible that although the boy and girl may have seen each other, they are not in fact willing parties to the marriage and in deciding on the wedding their parents may have overruled their wishes. In such cases, particularly, if they already have their village friends, the boy or girl may resort to or ader, nir bolok', a pangir, or iputut', and stage a sudden wedding of their own. Moreover, at any time immediately before, during or after the wedding, facts may come to light which may make the marriage unsuitable. The girl may be discovered to be pregnant by another boy or the boy himself may be found to be undesirable. In such circumstances, the marriage may break either between the fixing of the date for the wedding itself or in the period immediately following it. When this happens the party at fault is liable for all the expenses the other side has incurred. If the breach occurs before the actual wedding meals have been cooked the party at fault is liable only for the rice beer that is wasted, but if the wedding is in progress and more expenses have been incurred, it must meet their cost.

When a marriage breaks in the closing stages, the status of the boy is unaffected but the girl becomes a semi-divorcee. If the mandwa has been put up but the oil and turmeric have not been applied she is called a mandwa chadwi. If the oil and turmeric have been given but the *sindur* has not been applied she is called a susun sasan chadwi. This does not prevent her from being wedded later as an unmarried girl or dangua. But she loses the fresh status of a girl who has never been formally connected with a boy.

Bharat Marandi of Baramasia was due to marry a girl of Bhangabandh. When his party reached the girl's house the boy was in a palki and the girl's mother demanded jhili ladu. The boy's party had not brought any sweets with them and in a huff the girl's family broke the marriage off. In the settlement which followed the boy's parents were awarded sixty rupees.

In Phulbaria Nuka Murmu had arranged his daughter's marriage with a boy of Birdhan. Before the mandwas were erected the girl fell ill and the boy's family were asked to postpone the date of wedding. They did not pay any attention to their request and went in a party to the girl's village but as the girl was still ill no mandwa had been erected and the wedding could not be celebrated. The bride-price had already been paid but as the boy's party were sent back the marriage broke. Since the boy's side was at fault the bride-price was not returned.

In Ichaghati Ram Kisku had arranged the marriage of his son in Balichur. On the wedding day, the bride's party reached the girl's village bringing the bridegroom in one palki and his father in another. The palki with the father was set down at the entrance to the bride's house and this led to a quarrel between the two families. The bride's father refused to go on with the wedding and the girl became a sunum sasan chadwi. The girl's father refused to attend a village meeting or to refund the bride-price and other expenses. Ram Kisku accordingly went to court and was decreed one hundred and thirteen rupees including costs. This decision was approved by all the local Santals and as the girl's father was responsible for the break down he has since been debarred from employing a match-maker for his daughter and the girl will now be married only if a match-maker from the side of a boy approaches her father.

In another case, Phudan Besra of Murgabani had settled his daughter's marriage with a boy of Khairoa. When the boy's party came to the village a quarrel arose at the time of the mock battle (daram-dak') and a fight took place between the two villages. The wedding ended in confusion and the girl became a sunum sasan chadwi. At the village meeting it was held that the girl's side were to blame and her father was made to pay twentyfive rupees to the boy's father as bride-price and expenses.

In Baliari Tursa Kisku had two twin daughters. The elder was Sita and the younger Kapra. The marriage of Sita was settled at Khairbani and that of Kapra with a son of Damdhar Murmu of Belatari. When it had been settled that the two marriages should follow one another, the boy's family at Khairabani pleaded that they could not perform the wedding that year owing to lack of funds. Damdhar Murmu on the other hand was ready for the wedding. There was then a meeting of the three parties and it was agreed that since the elder daughter's marriage had been finally settled Damdhar would not be required to pay Sita taram gande (or the elder daughter's fee for permitting the prior marriage of a younger sister). Tursa accepted this decision but when the party of

Damdhar's son reached the house and Kapra was about to be raised in the basket he again demanded taram gande for the elder daughter.

Damdhar refused to pay. There was a complete deadlock and the boy's party went back without performing the wedding. In the settlement which followed the villagers awarded one hundred and forty rupees to Damdhar to cover the cost of the bride-price and his expenses and Tursa was made to pay this sum. Kapra became a sunum sasan chadwi but when she was later married to another boy, she was lifted in a basket and given *sindur*.

In yet another case the marriage of Randhon Hembrom of Atgaon had been arranged with a boy of Bostadiha. The boy's party reached the village but when the bridal basket was taken into the girl's house and the girl was about to enter it, some *sindur* was detected inside it. The villagers of Atgaon declared that as the basket was polluted the girl could not be lifted in it, and the boy's party were sent away. In this case, no claim was made as on the journey back the boy's party found another girl and married her there and then.

REFERENCES

1. Of Lepcha match-makers, Geoffrey Gorer notes 'All the real marriage negotiations are carried on between two bek-ku (between men) representing each side. Any experienced and tactful man with the exception of the spouse's father who knows the correct things to say and the correct way to say them and has a sufficient vocabulary of tang-bor may take this role'. (Gorer, op. cit., 317).
2. There is a parallel to this practice in Lepcha society of which Geoffrey Gorer notes: There are two stages in Lepcha marriage, *asek* or betrothal and *bri* or bringing home the bride. *Asek* is actually the validating ceremony at which the formal gifts from the family of the groom to that of the bride are presented. These gifts are called 'the price of the bride' and once they are accepted the groom has full access to his bride and all children born after '*asek* are considered as legitimate. (Gorer, op. cit., 154).
3. A Campbell, 'Santal Marriage Customs', *J.B.O.R.S.*, II (1916), 315.

25

TWO METHODS OF ECONOMY
Golaeti and Tunki Dipil

I TUNKI DIPIL

IF A dol bapla is the best form of Santal marriage, the cost of all its stages may sometimes render its performance impossible. Economies are then essential and recourse is had to a cheaper wedding, to tunki dipil or golaeti.

The first of these cheap weddings is 'bearing on the head a small basket'. In this form, a match-maker is employed and the officials of both the villages are consulted but the number of visits is greatly curtailed. 'The viewing of the household', 'the recognition by clothes' and the 'payment of the bride-price' are often finished in one visit. There are no Dom drummers, no large feasts and no marriage booth or shed is erected but the usual bride-price must be paid and a bullock given to the bride's brother.

If at any time the proposal fails after a date is fixed for either horok' cikhna, payment of the bride-price or the actual celebration, the claims of the parties are decided on the same principles as in a full-dress wedding. The party at fault must bear its own expenses and it must also compensate the other party for all the costs it has incurred.

The wedding itself is celebrated with a bare standard and the two families perform only as much of the standard ritual as their means allow. In one important way however the ritual varies from that of a standard wedding. The boy does not go to the girl's house and the *sindurdan* is done in the house of the boy.

Hendu Kisku of Kusumba wedded Nani Hansdak' of Katikund in tunki dipil form. The viewing of the household and horok' cikhna were done in one visit to the boy's house, and then on the wedding day itself, the match-maker took six men to the girl's village. The bride's family gave them food and the match-maker paid the bride-price to the girl's father. He gave the manjhi a fee of one rupee, the bride herself a cloth and the babre era a few annas. After that the bride put on her cloth and set out walking with the party for the house of the boy. A few relations went with her and all her private possessions were carried with her in a tunki or small basket. When they reached the house, the boy was washed and given a dhoti and pichauri by the girl. After that the girl was lifted in a basket and *sindurdan* was done. There was no marriage booth or shed at either house and the ceremony ended with a little quiet feasting. The next day a small bullock was given to the bride's brother.

A similar simplicity marked the wedding of Sauna Hembrom of Amtala with Paklu Marandi. Both parties had widowed mothers and were very poor. The viewing of the household and horok' cikhna were completed in a single visit to the boy's house and two-thirds of the bride-price were sent to the girl's mother through the match-maker. After that the wedding itself took place and a party of five went to bring the girl. They took with them two pots of rice beer, a cloth for the bride, a 'sacrificial goat' and their own food for one meal. When they had brought the girl back she was lifted in a basket and *sindurdan* was done. A circling ceremony was performed inside a room but only the relatives and village officials attended and gave presents. The boy's mother gave the villagers rice beer, and the wedding ended with general dancing through the night.

In both these tunki dipil weddings there was no adherence to a strict pattern, but the costs were kept low and the essential ritual of doing the *sindurdan* at the boy's house was followed.

II GOLAETI

If tunki dipil is one means of effecting savings, an even more radical method is golaeti. In this form a boy and girl of one family are exchanged for a boy and girl of another. Many of the standard expenses are halved and the two negotiations are telescoped into one.*

There are, however, certain conventions which slightly limit its use. In each case the boy and girl on one side must be children of the same father and as far as possible an elder sister of one family should marry an elder brother of the other. Similarly, a younger sister of one family should marry a younger brother and the younger brother should also be younger than the boy whom his elder sister marries.

When Jata Kisku of Siripur performed the marriage of his two children in golaeti form the girl was aged thirteen years and her brother ten. The elder daughter was married to Mansing Soren of Kadma while her younger brother married Mansing's younger sister. Mansing was aged fourteen and his sister ten.

This convention, however, is at most a counsel of perfection and in many golaeti marriages an elder brother and a younger sister in one family marry an elder brother and younger sister in the other. Campbell indeed goes so far as to say that in golaeti marriages 'the sister must be younger than her brother otherwise a marriage of this sort cannot take place.' This is not at present the accepted principle in the Santal Parganas though it is often followed in the actual conduct of such weddings.

Ram Charan Soren of Malipara married the younger sister of Biswas Marandi of his village while Biswas married the younger sister of Ram Charan. Similarly, Pagla Hansdak' of Sitasal married the younger sister of Kuryo Hembrom of Sirsa while Kuryo married the younger sister of Pagla.

At the present time the only essential conditions for golaeti weddings are that both the families should each have a marriageable boy and girl.

*Golaeti marriages are not very common as many Santals regard them as unlucky and likely to result in the early death of one of the parties.

If these conditions obtain, negotiations follow a simple course. The inspection of the two families is confined to the first meeting and the viewing of the household. But instead of two separate visits, one for each boy and one for each girl, a single visit to each house is made for both.

If the viewing is satisfactory, both sides give their words and the date of the weddings is decided. There is occasionally a further betrothal by 'recognising clothes' but this is optional with the parties. As the claims to bride-price cancel each other out no bride-price is paid and none of the various brothers is allotted a bullock.

During this period no costs are incurred and if the marriages fail before the wedding date is fixed, neither side can claim expenses.

A similar telescoping is observed in the marriage ceremony itself. The party of the eldest boy moves first and goes to his bride's house. *Sindurdan* and the circling ceremony are performed and the bridegroom presents a turban to the bride's brother as well as a cloth to the bride. The party of the eldest boy then returns home taking the girl with him and is followed shortly after by the party of the girl's brother.

A second *sindurdan* and circling ceremony are then performed in the house of the first boy.

In this way one wedding follows on the heels of another and since the halving of costs is itself a major economy, the entertainments of the villagers and the customary payments are frequently on the same scale as in a dol wedding. These expenses are divided by the two families and the costs are kept to an agreed level.

If the two weddings break any time between the date of their fixing and the first *sindurdan*, the party at fault must reimburse the other side for its costs. Similarly, if one of the weddings breaks after the other has been performed the whole procedure has to be reviewed. If the side of the first boy is at fault, or if his sister runs away, his father must pay the other side a bride-price and brother's bullock and indemnify him for any extra cost involved in the second wedding. If, however, the side of the first bride is to blame and her brother refuses to take her husband's sister, the father cannot then claim a bride-price or a brother's bullock or any extra expenses. The jilting of the second girl is held to cancel all claim to a bride-price for the girl who is married first. Similarly, if either of the marriages breaks down after both have been performed, the matter is adjusted as if there had not been any exchange. The bride-price and brother's due become payable in respect of the girl whose marriage continues while in the case of the broken marriage the claims are settled as in ordinary divorce.

Bhado Tudu of Bhawani married his son and daughter to Khade Kisku and his sister. Three years after the two marriages Khade's sister refused to live in Bhado's house and the marriage ended in divorce. Bhado then realised a bride-price and brother's due in respect of his daughter who had married Khade.

26

THE FORCIBLE MARRIAGE
Iputut'

I THE EFFECTS OF SINDUR

IN THE celebration of a Santal marriage *sindur* plays sometimes a significant and central part. It is not an essential requisite of a valid marriage but until a girl has received it she is technically still a virgin and is attached to her father's bongas. 'Her base may be cracked but her head is still intact'. Once the *sindur* has been given this status is immediately altered. All her religious duties to her father are transferred to her husband. She is now in touch with the latter's bongas. She can clean his private shrine, cow-dung a place for his offerings, fast and make the flour for the sacred cakes. Above all the first *sindur* marries her for ever. Even though her earthly marriage fails and divorce ensues, she is now the wife of her husband in the after world and must live with him for ever. It is these attributes of *sindur* which explain the *sindurdan* ceremony in negotiated marriages and the consequences which follow when a boy applies *sindur* to a girl's head by force.* This latter action is known as iputut' and if the girl consents it has the full value of a formal marriage.

What are the circumstances in which this form of marriage is attempted?

*Mud, earth, sand or grit, if so applied to a girl's head, are also treated as substitutes for *sindur*.

II ANTECEDENTS : OPPOSITION BY PARENTS

In the great majority of cases, the girl fully consents and the most normal situation is when a Santal boy and girl desire to marry but one or other of their parents is unwilling.

Tibu Tudu of Baskia was due to marry a girl of Duaria. The households were inspected, the clothes shown and the bride-price had been paid. Then Tibu's father suddenly died and the girl's party said 'There is a bonga in his house. We will not marry her.' The matter dragged on. Tibu used to meet the girl when she went for gathering mahua. Both of them wanted to marry but the girl's parents kept refusing. Then the boys of Baskia told Tibu to itut her. They made their plans and at the Gamra hook-swinging the boys of Baskia all surrounded the girl, shut her in a ring of arms and Tibu rubbed *sindur* on her head. Then they rushed away. After that the two villages met, there was no further delay, the claims were settled and the iputut' was celebrated with a dol bapla or full dress wedding.

Similarly in Saharghati, Sital Marandi wanted to marry a Soren girl but the boy's parents objected as the girl was older than the boy. Sital did not listen, so on the jale morning of Sohrae, the two went inside the jogmanjhi's house and Sital put *sindur* on her. They told the manjhi's wife and Sital then took her home. At the meeting Sital gave two goats and paid the manjhi five rupees and later there was a dol bapla, the bride-price and brother's due were paid and the girl was lifted in the basket.

III IPUTUT' ON IMPULSE

A second circumstance is when a boy does iputut' more or less on impulse.

Such a case occurred at Sibtala on 18 April, 1944. There was a wedding in the village and a girl from Chandapura and a boy from Dhankutar had come to attend it. Both had relatives in Sibtala. Both knew each other and a marriage between them had already been settled. Suddenly the boy put *sindur* on her and dashed away.

In another case of Simaljore, the brother of Singrai Murmu was a ghar jawae in Dhamna. Singrai was in love with his sister-in-law's younger sister, Gondo, but the girl's mother was objecting to their marriage. Singrai went to Dhamna on the morning of the Baha festival. The girls were throwing water on the men but as Singrai was of another village they did not throw any at him. Then on the spur of impulse Singrai picked up some mud and rubbed it on Gondo's head. Sibu and Mohon Hansdak' pounced on him and said 'Why have you done it on her head? Why did you not do it on her body?' So they gave him a thrashing and took him to the manjhi. Next morning they sent Singrai with a villager to the manjhi of Simaljore to report and fix a date. On the day in question the villagers of Dhamna went to Simaljore with axes, arrows and drums and when the manjhi said, 'Why have you come,' they replied 'A leopard of your village has scratched one of our calves'. Then they all sat round and Singrai was asked, 'Did you do it?' He answered, 'I picked up a little mud and put it on her head'. This was held to be iputut' and two goats were killed. Singrai was told to pay a bride-price of twelve rupees, to give the brother's due and pay the manjhi five rupees 'for saving his head', and a fine of five rupees as jobrani, for doing it by force. Then the villagers went back and Singrai gave a goat in Dhamna 'to clean the axe'. A date was settled for dol bapla and a match-maker was appointed.

The matter did not, however, end there, for a little later Gondo's mother changed her mind. The wedding meant a second marriage with the same family and she believed that one or other of the girls would be sure to die. So she said, 'I will not give her'. She did not press for payment and the matter dropped. Sometime later, Gondo was married in Jobalda as a divorcee and there was no dol bapla or *sindur*.

IV OUSTING A RIVAL

A third situation is when more than one suitor is in the field.

In a case of 1944, talks had started for a girl in Paharpur.

The boy's parents had inspected her at a market and a proposal had been made through a match-maker. The offer had not been rejected but the clothes had not been seen. Meanwhile a boy from a well-to-do family of Dundua met her at a market, took her off with him several times and decided to marry her and the matter was broached through various friends. The girl and her parents thought the Dundua boy would be a better match but the difficulty was the talks that were going on for the first boy. As the girl's parents had not said 'no' at first, they did not like to say 'no' later. So they finally suggested that the Dundua boy should settle matters by putting *sindur* on the girl. He did so and the two were married.

Finally it may happen that a boy is wildly in love with a girl but the girl and her parents are hesitating. In such circumstances, iputut' forces the issue. It is not entirely against the girl's will nor entirely with her consent. It is a way of precipitating a decision.

V COERCION FOR MARRIAGE

If consent is usual, however, it is by no means invariably given and iputut' is sometimes done when the girl is quite unwilling.

Budhrai Murmu of Kurumpahari wanted to marry Bale Marandi a girl of his village. The girl who was much taller and bigger, however, did not want him and preferred to wait for marriage in another village. The boy did not change his mind, and one December morning he went with three friends and surprised the girl in a paddy field. His friends held her down and the boy put *sindur* on her head. The girl was very angry and refused point-blank to go with him. The village met and Budhrai's father gave three goats. Budhrai tried to persuade her but Bale was completely adamant. Budhrai failed, and in the end Bale stayed with her parents.

VI REVENGE

Marriage, however, is not the only object of iputut' and

although cases are rare, the act is sometimes an outrage and is done for revenge.

Paklu Kisku of Phulapani had gone with her husband and son to her father's house for the marriage of her brother. When the wedding was over her husband went back and she and her son stayed on. Four days later there was another wedding in the village. Paklu went to it and as she was coming back Chotka Hembrom took out some *sindur* and rubbed it on her forehead. A villager caught him but the man got away. Then they went and told the manjhi. The manjhi tried to hold some meetings but Chotka did not come. In the end Paklu went to court, Chotka was fined and Paklu got forty rupees as compensation. In this case the man was an unsuccessful lover and had done the iputut' in order to spite her. Paklu had at first agreed to go with him and leave her husband but later she had taken another lover and ignored him. Paklu's husband did not divorce her and the two are still together.

VII THE AFTER LIFE

A last case arises from the Santal view of the afterlife. If a Santal is married to a divorced girl or a widow, his wife will be parted from him after death. To secure a wife for ever he must, therefore, put *sindur* on a still unmarried girl and iputut' is sometimes done for this purpose.

Sibu Hansdak', the old guru of Dhamna, was once partly responsible for such a case. Sadho Hansdak' who was a divorcee of Kurua had become pregnant by Mandal Marandi of Dhamna. She wanted him to marry her but Mandal said he would first wed an unmarried girl so as to have a wife in the world to come. The girl did not want a co-wife, so she consulted Sibu. Sibu suggested that the boy should secretly itut the girl's unmarried sister. The boy and the girl agreed, so one day they took her sister to the forest and the boy secretly put *sindur* on her and a little later married Sadho.

VIII ADJUSTMENTS : MARRIAGE

Once the iputut', in one or other of these forms is over the girl tells her father, and certain consequences follow. The matter is discussed first in the girl's village and then at a joint meeting in the boy's. If the incident is proved and the boy and girl desire each other the settlement is as follows.

If both are unmarried the boy pays the girl's father the usual bride-price and the brother's due. He gives the villagers two goats and pays the two manjhis one rupee for summoning the meetings. Out of this sum each manjhi takes eight annas and if the villagers decide a further one anna is realised for payment to the boy's jogmanjhi. In the Jamtara subdivision and in the Paraiyahat, Pathna and Nonihat areas the boy must also pay his own village manjhi five rupees 'for saving his head'.

If the girl is unmarried but the boy is either a widower or has been divorced the same sums are realised but instead of two goats three are taken. Similarly in addition to all the other payments, the village can also impose a further fine called jobrani, 'for doing it by force'. This additional penalty is normally not inflicted but if the village resents the boy's behaviour it is sometimes imposed.

Mansa Murmu of Huralpahari had been widowed once and divorced twice. At the Sohrae festival he forced some *sindur* on Tetaromoni Hembrom who was still unmarried. At the village meeting the girl agreed to live with him but the boy was made to pay three goats, five rupees 'for saving his head' and a sum of sixty rupees. The latter included a bride-price, the brother's due and a further sum for force.

Finally if the girl has been divorced or widowed the boy must pay her father the usual bride-price for a girl of that status and also the brother's due if claimable.*

He must also give the villagers two goats** and pay the two manjhis their joint fee of one rupee.*** No extra sums for 'saving his head' or 'fining for force' are realised.

IX ADJUSTMENTS : SEPARATION

It is not in every case, however, that the boy and girl agree to

*See Chapter 34.

**In the northern part of the Rajmahal Damin where the bride-price is unusually high only one is payable.

***In the Dumka Damin eight annas.

marry. The boy may have given *sindur* with the girl's consent but may change his mind between the act and the village meetings. He may suddenly discover that the girl is already pregnant, and in that case the iputut' will seem only a disastrous mistake. The boy will blame the girl for making him do it but the girl may insist on going to his house.

> Juri,
> Before the village and the country
> You forced the *sindur* on me
> If now
> You do not keep me
> I will bring a case
> In Godda Court
> I will sell you up
> Down to your little loin cloth.
>
> —*Don Soren*, 1964.

More usually, however, it is the girl's refusal that prevents consummation; but her parents or the village may also intervene.

A Tudu boy of Sadhudih did iputut' to a Besra girl of his village. The matter went to a meeting but the villagers said that such a marriage would be breach of custom. Although the girl was willing to remain, the marriage was disallowed.

In all such cases, since the boy has acted by force he must pay a sum large enough to act as a deterrent to others. He must pay his own manjhi five rupees for 'saving his head' and give the villagers money or goats as if the girl had gone to him. Besides this he must pay to the girl's father a sum which is sometimes a bride-price, sometimes a fine for force and sometimes both a bride-price and the brother's due. Occasionally there is an even further charge for 'wiping off the *sindur*'. When it is not one claim, the extra sum is another. Yet its intention is invariably the same. It is a compounding of the outrage in a way which will both punish the boy and compensate the father of the girl.

X IPUTUT' TO A MARRIED GIRL

If the girl is a married woman, there are two alternatives. Her husband may decide to keep her and if she has not gone away with the man or had relations with him, he can claim a sum as sindur urani for 'wiping off the *sindur*'. This is in addition to the five rupees which the man must pay the manjhi 'for saving his head' and the money or goats he must give the villagers as if the girl had stayed with him. Sindur urani is normally between five and fifteen rupees according as the villagers decide. If, however, the girl has actually been with the man and her husband takes her back, he can claim not only sindur urani but an extra sum as celan gitil, 'for cleaning the pot'. This latter sum also varies from five to fifteen rupees according to village discretion and the custom of the area.

Her husband, however, may not wish to keep her and in that event he can also claim from the boy a double bride-price and if the marriage has been recent he may also be awarded the costs of the wedding.

Jetha Hembrom, a married boy of Kathla fell in love with a married girl of the same village. He put *sindur* on her at a hook-swinging and paid her husband sixty rupees.

Hari Kisku of Sagra did iputut' to a married girl. He also had to pay her husband sixty rupees which included a double bride-price and the cost of the wedding.

In certain cases, however, the boy who does the iputut' also does not want to keep her. This does not make any difference for 'the act has made the girl his wife'. He must pay her husband a double bride-price and in certain circumstances the cost of the wedding. He must also give the girl divorce money.

In all these cases, the payments are in addition to the five rupees which the man must pay the manjhi 'for saving his head' and the money or goats he must give the villagers.

There is one other claim. According to Santal custom, no boy or girl can be married unless their caco chatiar or initiation ceremony has been done. This usually occurs when the child is seven or eight years old but it is sometimes put off until later. If a boy ituts a girl and her initiation has not been done, it is as if he has married her without her first becoming a full Santal. Iputut' makes this ceremony immediately necessary and the boy has, therefore, to give all its costs.

Bhusan Soren of Benagaria was picking mangoes with Bidhni Marandi of the same village when he did iputut' her. Bhusan was seven years old and Budhni five. At the village meeting the boy's father gave two goats and paid sixteen rupees which included five rupees for 'saving the boy's head'. In addition, an extra five rupees was realised from his father for performing the initiation ceremony of the girl.

XI THE RESULTS OF IPUTUT'

These are the consequences for the boy, but for the girl the most important effect follows from the *sindur* itself.

If the girl is still unmarried and goes to live with the boy iputut' is, as it were, a telescoped version of a full-dress wedding. It qualifies her to assist in the service of the bongas in the same way as a dol bapla with *sindur* would have qualified her. It gives her the complete status of a fully married wife though it may also be only a preliminary to a fuller celebration. When Singo Marandi of Dhamna was ituted by Jongal Baske of Dudhani on the Sakrat morning of Sohrae, she said 'I will go with him but they must lift me in the basket', so a dol bapla with *sindur* took place later.

If a girl is married by iputut', lives with her husband and is later on divorced, it will be by a tearing of the leaves and if she marries again it will be as a divorcee. Because she was still unmarried when the first iputut' was done, she will also be her husband's wife in the afterworld.

But a still unmarried girl does not always go to the boy and in that case her iputut' has the effect of a marriage and divorce. The *sindur* puts her into contact with the boy's bongas but her denial cancels this relation. She becomes a divorcee, a bohok 'chadwi.' 'Her head is divorced but her tail is intact'—and only if she belongs to certain septs and khunts can she secure a fresh bonga relation.* Moreover even if she marries

*See Chapter 27.

later, her husband will be only 'for this life' and in the afterworld she will go to the boy who put the *sindur* on her.

But the girl may already have been married and then divorced. In that event, the iputut' will affect her according as she has had or not had *sindur* earlier. If she has been married without *sindur* and then divorced, she is still the equivalent of a girl not yet married and the *sindur* gives her all the qualifications. She will not belong to her 'first husband' but will go in the afterlife to the boy who did the iputut'.

If, however, the iputut' is not a first but a second *sindur*, the result will depend on her sept and khunt and in almost all cases, the position will be as follows. Her first *sindur* will have given her a special relation to certain bongas—those of her first husband. The tearing of the leaves will have cancelled this but having once acquired this relation by *sindur*, she cannot acquire a new one. Her 'contact' with one set of bongas disqualifies her from 'contact' with any others. If, therefore, she goes and lives with the boy who ituts her the second *sindur* scarcely differs from the *sindur* given at a baha saoha. This is a kind of fake or symbolic *sindur* which I describe more fully later. It enables her children to be married with *sindur* at a dol bapla but it does not qualify her otherwise. Only in the case of the Cilbinda khunt of Hansdak' and a few others is the second *sindur* like a first *sindur* and carries with it all the privileges.

There is a similar complication in the case of a married woman. If she has already had *sindur* from her husband, she is already in relation with his bongas and the second *sindur* abruptly breaks this connection. A married woman who stays on with her husband, therefore, is reduced to the position of a divorcee. She can no longer assist him in the ceremonies or clean his shrine. Since she has had *sindur* she is like a divorcee with whom a husband has done baha saoha. Her children can have a dol bapla with *sindur* but that is all.

Similarly if a married woman has iputut' and goes to the man the position is the same. She is like a divorcee who is married in sangha form.

XII THE SANTAL ATTITUDE

What is the final Santal view of iputut'?

To a boy this wild act is a form of excitement, a source of danger, a style of romance. He may get a beating but he has either made a girl his own or ruined her. He has either defied his parents, had his revenge or won a girl for ever. The cost may ruin him for a few years but the penalties are only money.

To a divorcee or a widow also, the results are slight. Both are anxious for remarriage. Each can no longer expect a fresh bonga relation. Iputut' is neither necessary nor damaging and it is usually only by accident or in the excitement of a wedding that iputut' is done to a divorcee or a widow.

> Thinking it was fresh
> I took a cooked bel fruit
> Thinking she was not yet married
> I rubbed some *sindur* on a chadwi.
>
> —*Don Soren*, 1859.

It is to a married or unmarried girl that iputut' is disastrous. In the one case it deprives her of her right to assist in the offerings of her husband. In the other it attaches her to his bongas and links her to a man in the world to come. The damage is not 'for a day' but for ever. To a married or unmarried girl, it is moment's disaster which 'an age of prudence can never retract'.

27

WIDOWS AND DIVORCEES
Sangha

I INTRODUCTION

ONCE a girl has been given *sindur* in a full-dress wedding 'the brief glory in the lifted basket' can never return. If her marriage ends in divorce she is still her first husband's property in the afterworld and it is only as a temporary wife that she goes to a second husband. If she remarries, it is for 'the mutual comfort the one of the other' and the marriage is for convenience rather than for ever.

We must bear in mind, however, that not every married girl receives *sindur* and if her union is a 'copse marriage' the death of her husband or their divorce may leave her previous status unaffected. 'Her base will be cracked but her head will be intact'. While in legal fact she will be a widow or divorcee, religiously it will be as if she had never been married. Never having been lifted in the basket or given *sindur* she can still be lifted at a second marriage and if her second husband gives her *sindur*, it is he who will possess her in the afterworld. Such cases do not involve any different rights and claims from a dol bapla or full-dress wedding* and it is only when a woman has already received *sindur* or the circumstances preclude a dol

*Phalia Marandi of Seldana was married. When her husband died, Cere Hansdak' of Mohanpur married her and since she had never had *sindur*, the wedding was in dol form.

bapla that her marriage is performed in the manner known as sangha.*

II DIVORCEES

Once a girl has been divorced, the range of her husbands is greatly narrowed and although a fresh unmarried boy is greatly prized, it is usually only with widowers or with boys who have themselves been divorced that marriage is arranged.

In certain circumstances, however, a divorced girl secures an unmarried boy as her husband. If, for example, a girl is beautiful or a boy and girl have fallen in love the fact that she is a divorcee does not prevent their wedding.

Choto Soren was a servant in the house of Ramdas Hembrom of Saraipani. The daughter of Ramdas had been divorced. Choto fell in love with her and after commencing their union by 'meeting at bed time' they were married in sangha form.

Kailu Marandi of Katikbhita was still unmarried. He met a divorced girl of Hijri and because she was very beautiful fell in love with her. He induced his parents to accept the marriage and the two were married in sangha form.

If a boy is poor and is still unmarried he sometimes marries a divorced girl in order to save the expenses of a dol wedding or to marry in a rich family. Mangat Hembrom of Bokoa was very poor and still unmarried. He could not afford the ordinary marriage expenses so he married a divorced girl of his village.

It is when her first husband is a ghar jawae for her father agrees to bring a ghar jawae that a divorced girl stands the greatest chance of securing a husband who has never been previously married. Here the prospect of comfortable living with adequate lands outweighs the disadvantage of possessing another man's previous wife.

*In the Godda sub-division, this term is applied only to the marriage of a widow with her husband's younger brother. Other marriages of divorced girls or widows are known as chadwi randi bapla or dol bapla.

Unmarried boy
If you will keep me
Although I am a chadwi
I will give you
Twelve bighas of land
Unmarried boy
If you will take me
Although I am a chadwi
I will keep you
Like a Babu of Jamtara.

—*Don Soren*, 2034.

Bhutal Hembrom of Telbhita had two daughters. He married the elder in dol form but after she was divorced he brought a ghar jawae for her.

Similarly Dulhi Murmu a divorced girl of Udalbani secured an unmarried boy by taking him as a ghar jawae.

III WIDOWS

The same factors influence the marriages of widows. When a widow remarries it is only rarely that she secures a husband who has not previously been married. As with a divorced girl her greatest chance is when a still unmarried boy falls in love with her or a boy is so poor that he cannot afford a marriage with an unmarried girl.

Ladhru Marandi of Seja fell in love with a widow of his village who was 5 years older. He himself was still unmarried but because he was in love he married the widow in sangha form.*

In Barkunri Siru Hembrom was an unmarried boy who used to live by daily labour. He fell in love with a widow of his village and after she had become pregnant and given birth to a child, Siru first married a plantain tree by putting *sindur*

*In the Kundahit area when an unmarried body marries a divorcee, he first puts *sindur* on a plantain tree. The plantain represents an unmarried girl and the rite converts him into a divorced boy.

on it and then celebrated the marriage as a divorced boy with the widow.

In Ghangraband Bhulu Marandi could not afford the expenditure of a dol wedding for his unmarried son. There was a widow in the village and on account of poverty he married his son to her.

Similarly if the widow's dead husband was a ghar jawae or if her parents agree to bring a ghar jawae as her second husband an unmarried boy can sometimes be secured.

Jata Murmu of Jhantipahari had married his daughter in dol form. He had a son but after his daughter's marriage the son died. Later his daughter became a widow and Jata then secured an unmarried boy of Phasiedangal and married his daughter to him in ghar jawae form. Similarly, Barka Murmu of Bichgarha had married his daughter in ghar jawae form. Her husband died and Barka then brought the dead husband's younger brother as a second ghar jawae. Prior to his being brought this boy was still unmarried.

In Dhamna Sibu Hansdak' brought a ghar jawae for his daughter. The ghar jawae died and after that he brought a boy who was not only still unmarried but was also considerably younger. There is an air of solid contentment about Sibu's household and the husband has not regretted the widow.

But besides these circumstances there is one further practice which sometimes leads to a widow's marriage with a still unmarried boy.

Under the terms of her first marriage, a younger brother of her dead husband can marry her without paying an extra bride-price. This right is usually exercised when the widow is liked by a brother-in-law but it cannot be enforced against her will. If the widow does not like any of her brother-in-laws, and refuses to marry them her rights are not affected. As between brothers who have got wives and those who have not the latter have ordinarily the first claim while as between brothers in the same class, the eldest has a preferential claim over the others. If, however, two or more brothers wish to take her and the widow likes one more than the other, she will marry the one she likes. If two of them like her and the widow has no particular preference, the elder of the two will get her. After a younger brother has taken her, all the brothers who are younger than her dead husband will continue to call her hili (elder brother's wife) but only those who are younger than the second husband can licitly have access to her.

Lodheya, Tursa, Jetha and Chhotka Tudu of Hathi-Hariyar were four brothers. Tursa, the second brother died leaving a widow and one child. Lodheya as elder brother was debarred from marrying her and Jetha had already a wife. Chhotka was still unmarried and took the widow in sangha form.

In Ulatari the elder brother of Dodo Hansdak' died leaving a widow and two sons. At the funerary feast to his brother, Dodo declared her to be his wife and sometime later a son was born. Dodo died and his younger brother then kept the widow as his wife.

IV THE YOUNGER BROTHER OF THE DEAD HUSBAND

When a widow remarries a younger brother of her husband, a village announcement with drinking of rice beer is usually all that is necessary and the union is known as doho ruar. If the woman has already been associated with the bongas of the family by receiving *sindur* from her first husband, no further *sindur* is applied.

Chunda and Bhadu Murmu were two brothers of Dugubathan. Bhadu was a widower and when Chunda, his elder brother, died he married his widow by calling the villagers and giving them rice beer.

In Nimakalan Bhuju Hansdak' was left a widow with a daughter. At the funerary feast of her dead husband the villagers collected and it was declared that she was remarried to her husband's younger brother. The meeting then drank rice beer.

In certain cases, there is even less formality and if the widow goes on living with her brother-in-law in the same house the village tacitly recognize them as man and wife and terms their union doho saoha, hilit era sangha, or asul sangha.

Iswar Baske of Santaldih was already married when his elder brother died. He liked his elder brother's widow and began to live with her as her husband. His own wife did not approve of the marriage and left him. Iswar continued living with his elder brother's widow and had children by her. He did not, however, summon a village meeting or give rice beer. Similarly Pagla Murmu of Kalajhore kept his elder brother's widow as his wife and did not call a meeting or give rice beer. In both these cases, however, the villagers recognized the union as a marriage. In a case from Dhawadangal Ramu, Kisto, Raju and Anpa were four brothers. The second brother died and the youngest brother then married the widow without announcing the union in a village meeting. This union is also valid and the widow is accepted as Anpa's wife.

V BAHA SAOHA

If a widow or divorcee is married outside her first husband's family,* a match-maker is appointed and the procedure follows, in summarised form, the negotiations of a full dress wedding.

The match-maker first locates a suitable widow or divorcee, reports to his patron and then broaches the proposal. The woman's father then 'views the household' and if he is satisfied, he agrees to perform the marriage. The village manjhis are informed and a date for the wedding is settled. Prior to this date neither party has incurred any expenses and if the proposal fails no claims of any kind arise. But once the date is fixed, each side is committed to the wedding and if either side breaks it without due cause, the other must be compensated for all its costs.

When the wedding day comes, a small party from the bridegroom stays at home and his family or village goes to the woman's house with the bride-price. After eating a meal, paying the money and giving the woman a cloth they return bringing the woman with them.** The bride and bridegroom are then taken into a room and in the presence of the two manjhis and jogmanjhis and a few villagers, the central rite of baha saoha is performed.

This rite consists in essence of the bridegroom smearing *sindur* on a flower and inserting it in the woman's hair. There is, however, considerable variation in the ways in which this is done.

When Khade Kisku, the famous dihri of the Dumka Damin

*See also Chapter 22, Ghar Jawae.

**The bride-price is sometimes paid a few days earlier.

hunt, took a divorced girl as his second wife he put *sindur* on a dimbu flower with his left hand. Then again using his left hand he took the flower and put it in the girl's hair above the left ear. This use of the left or unclean hand symbolised the soiled nature of the newly taken wife.

On the other hand when Lokhan Hansdak' of Mohuadangal married a divorced girl, he put *sindur* on a dimbu flower but used his right hand in putting it in her left ear. He avoided the left hand as since he himself belonged to the special khunt of Cilbinda Hansdak' his second wife had all the privileges of a first and was not 'soiled' by her former connexion.

These two weddings followed traditional practice but in the Pathna and Barhait bungalows, the custom of applying *sindur* through a flower is no longer in vogue. The couple sit together and the man rubs *sindur* on the woman's forehead with his right hand.

Similarly at Boarijore the two stand on leaf plates facing each other and the boy puts *sindur* on the girl's forehead with the little finger of his right hand. At other places in the neighbourhood, the girl sits on the jogmanjhi's lap, the boy mounts on his father's knees and from there he puts the *sindur* on her head with his right hand.

In the Chorkata area the practice is for the boy to put the dimbu flower in his left hand, take some *sindur* between the thumb and little finger of his right hand, smear it on the flower three times* and then taking the flower in the left hand to put it in the girl's hair above the left ear. After this is done, the boy's mother puts *sindur* on the boy's head and then on the girl's and the other women put *sindur* on her head as well.

In the Poreyahat police station, the boy holds a dimbu flower and with his left hand smears some *sindur* on the girl's hair where she knots it on the top of her head. If her hair is cropped he smears the *sindur* on her left ear.

If a dimbu flower is not available, a dimbu leaf or twig is sometimes used or a gulanj, mati or raj baha is employed instead.

*In the Rajabhita area the flower is smeared with *sindur* five times.

At the time the flower is given the witnesses shout '*Hari bol*', as in a dol wedding.

If the marriage breaks between the payment of the bride-price and the performance of the ceremony, the price is forfeited if the man was at fault. But if the widow or divorced girl is to blame, the price must be returned.

Similarly if the bridegroom is jilted when his preparations are advanced, he can claim the cost of whatever food and rice beer is wasted.

At the end of the ceremony, the match-maker, manjhi and jogmanjhi are given presents at half the rates current in a dol wedding.

VI CONCLUSION

The effect of this ceremony is to confirm a widow or divorced girl in the full status of a wife. In the case of certain sub-septs:

Sub-sept.	Sept.
Cilbindha	Hansdak'
Rok butur	Marandi
Goda	Marandi
Manjhikil	Marandi
Kuari	Hembrom
Khanda	Soren

The *sindur* extinguishes the bonga relationship with her previous husband and once she has had a male child by her second husband, she is fully qualified to assist him in the worship of his bongas.

In the case of other sub-septs, however, the *sindur* has only very limited implications. It enables the woman's daughters to be lifted in the basket and given *sindur* in dol form on the occasion of their weddings. It does not, however, qualify her to assist her husband in serving his bongas. It is at most a hollow substitute, a means of conferring a superficial dignity and it is public recognition rather than the *sindur* which makes her a valid wife.

28

MARRIAGE BY INTERCOURSE
Kundal Napam

I INTRODUCTION

WE HAVE seen that when a boy resorts to iputut', and the girl agrees to stay, their union is regarded as an abrupt breach of tribal order, a valid but inferior form of marriage. But besides iputut', there are three other forms of Santal marriage which are 'mundu bapla', 'copse marriages', 'jungle weddings'. These are also performed without the formal approval of the families or village. If there is consultation it is behind the scene. There is no match-maker, there are no formal meetings. The boy and the girl first come together and when their union is an accomplished fact, the 'offence' is brought to the village and the marriage is adjusted.

The first of these forms is known as kundal napam or 'meeting when lying down'. This term is sometimes loosely applied to a couple when detected together in the open. Doman Murmu of Simbra met the daughter of Jolha Kisku of Balia Khora at a hook swinging festival. They went to the festival together and when the night came they slept together near the hook swinging field. In the morning, people of their village found them together and jokingly said 'this is kundal napam'. The boy and the girl then went home and sometime later a match-maker was appointed and they were married in dol form.

In Babupatojoria, Bhagmat Tudu was found sleeping in the

open with Mukhi Soren of his village during a Sohrae festival. Both of them wanted to live together, so the jogmanjhi acted as a match-maker and the village approved their wedding by kundal napam.

More strictly, however, the term is applicable to continued meetings and a common circumstance is when a boy and girl are away from their village working with a labour gang. Here also they may meet at night and this nightly meeting is in course of time accepted as a marriage by kundal napam. Mangal Hembrom of Jaipur met Sanodi Tudu of Bhurundia when both of them were working at the Jainty Colliery. They began to sleep together at night and when Mangal left the Colliery he took the girl with him to his village. Their union was kundal napam, and the village has accepted it as a marriage.

The most common circumstances, however, which give rise to such weddings are when a boy lives in a house as a servant and contracts relations with his master's daughter or a girl servant; or when a mistress of the house is widowed and the servant sleeps with her. In Chiriapathar, Munshi Kisku was taken as a servant. He fell in love with the daughter of the house and the two met at bed time. The girl gave birth to two children and Munshi was recognised as her husband by kundal napam.

Dugu Marandi of Litipara kept Kato Hembrom as a servant. Dugu's daughter fell in love with him and they used to meet at night and sleep together. Later their kundal napam marriage was celebrated as a formal wedding and the servant worked off the bride-price by becoming a ghardi jawae.

In Nawadi the widow of Manu Soren kept a servant. He began to sleep with her. In the end the matter came to the village and their union was recognised as a marriage by kundal napam. In Bahan also Ramdi Murmu, a widow, kept an unmarried boy as her servant. They began to sleep together and the village accepted their union as marriage by kundal napam. They lived in the widow's house for ten years and then the boy took her to his village.

If the daughter of the house is adult and her marriage has been over delayed or if her parents have 'shown her like grains in the market' but no one has asked for her, they sometimes hire a boy servant and allow the two to meet. In such cases, the parents of the girl connive at sexual relations and the boy and girl meet at night with their express or tacit encouragement.

Chunka Hansdak' of Khijrum who was a chadwi with no children. He was not getting a husband for her so he brought an unmarried boy to his house as a servant and when his daughter and the boy began to sleep together he called a village meeting and their union was accepted as a marriage by kundal napam.

Yet another circumstance is when a girl is living in a house as a servant and sleeps at night with a boy servant or with her master's son. Hopni Kisku of Godhaidhab was the eldest of four sisters. She went to Bagjori as a maid servant in the house of a widow, Sumi Marandi, and there the widow's son, Ranga Soren, fell in love with her. Hopni became pregnant and had a son, Somai Soren. This marriage also was by kundal napam and was accepted by the village.

II ADJUSTMENTS

When in this way a boy and a girl commence relations the matter is brought to the village and if the parents approve the union there are three lines of possible action. If they decide to regard the 'meeting at bed time' as merely anticipating a standard wedding, they inform the village and fix a date for its celebration. No match-maker is employed and the stages of viewing the households and recognizing the clothes do not normally arise. The bride-price, however, must be paid and the brother's dues must be given. If the boy is a servant and the girl is the daughter of his master, the boy is either converted to a ghar jawae or is allowed to take the girl away. In arranging the celebration the principal object is to secure the public gift of *sindur* to the girl and the wedding is either in dol or tunki dipil form as the means of the parties allow. If the boy is taken as a ghardi jawae or ghar jawae, the wedding follows the procedure for those forms.

When the union merely anticipates a formal wedding the 'offence' is condoned by the village and the subsequent celebrations absolve the parents from paying any fine. If, however, a standard wedding is not proposed, the parents inform the village manjhi and the matter is brought before a meeting. It is decided what bride-price and brother's due will be paid and the parents of the house announce that, the two have come together and are man and wife. A goat is killed and distributed to the meeting. If the boy is a servant with a guardian the latter provides it. Otherwise the master of the house gives it for him. The costs of the sitting are then realised and with its proceeds the meeting drinks rice beer in recognition of their union.

Bodoc' Hansdak' of Ambajora was a servant in the house of Gopal Kisku of Mahualo. He worked there for five years without receiving any pay. Gopal had a daughter and Bodoc' used to sleep with her at night. On the day when the five years were up Bodoc' took her quietly to a friend's house. A village meeting was called and it was held that Bodoc' had earned twenty-five rupees. Out of this, twelve rupees were accounted for as bride-price, six as the brother's due while the girl's father gave seven rupees in cash for a goat. The union was recognised as a marriage by kundal napam and Bodoc' and the girl then went to Assam.

In Pokharia Bado Marandi and Salho began their marriage by kundal napam. Their union was sanctioned at a village meeting and the two lived together for 15 years without any further celebration. When the eldest of their children was about to be married Bado gave his wife *sindur* by baha saoha.

Lobin Besra was a servant in the house of Harma Marandi of Dahua Simra. His master's daughter was a chadwi and the two began to sleep together by kundal napam. A village meeting was then called, their union was recognised as a marriage and the girl's father gave the meeting rice beer. Later on there was no further celebration but the girl's father had much land and he gave the daughter fifty bighas as taben jom and the two remained in the village.

Finally in certain cases the formal summoning of a village meeting is dispensed with, there is no formal announcement and the union acquires its sanction only by village acquiescence.

Munshi Marandi of Kadhara had two daughters and a small son. To help him with his cultivation he brought in Hodo Soren, a boy who lived across the road. Hodo began to sleep with his elder daughter Putu and when Munshi heard of it he was at first very angry, gave Putu a beating and sent the boy home. The girl, however, was very much in love with him and moved across to his house. The matter came before the village but nothing was decided. Some months later a child was born and Munshi agreed to have a dol wedding provided Putu did not live with the boy until the wedding was over. Putu did not agree to this so the wedding was given up. Months went by and at last her mother induced Munshi to bring them back and in 1944 they had been living for seven years in Munshi's house. They had then got two daughters and as Munshi's son was still quite small, Hodo was doing all the cultivation. In this case the village had at one time decided that there would be a dol wedding but when this broke down the union was accepted as a marriage by kundal napam, and no further meeting was held.

There are finally two circumstances which may from time to time arise. If a dol wedding is contemplated and for that reason no meeting is held and if for any reason the negotiations fail and the marriage ends, the initial agreement to replace the union by a dol wedding is taken as an admission by the family that the kundal napam was a marriage. In that case the boy and girl are treated as married from the date of agreement and if the boy resiles, he is liable to give the girl's father the bride-price and brother's due and to pay the girl divorce money. If the negotiations have involved the girl's father in any legitimate expenses the boy is also liable for their cost. Similarly, if the girl's father resiles from the agreement and the boy's side has been put to monetary loss the girl's father will have to reimburse him for the same expenses.

If and when the liaison is first detected the girl's parents do not approve of the union or if the boy himself declines to regard the girl as his wife the matter is taken to the village. If it is the boy or his parents who are declining to accept the union as a marriage and if the girl is neither pregnant nor has had a child by him he is made to pay lajao marao of five rupees to the girl's family and a fine or two goats to the villagers. If, however, the girl is pregnant or has had a child but the boy does not wish to live with her any longer he must pay the bride-price and the brother's due, give the girl divorce money and also pay the villagers a fine at the same rates as for a marriage by or ader. He must also accept the paternity and pay the usual charges in respect of the child.* If on the other hand the boy is willing to live with the girl as her husband but the girl's parents reject the union, lajao marao and a fine to the village are all that need be paid.

29

MARRIAGE BY CAPTURE
Or Ader

I CAUSES OF OR ADER

IF kundal napam is a 'copse marriage', another and even more common form of 'jungle wedding' is or ader or marriage by 'pulling in'. This is normally resorted to when a boy and girl are already in love and an ordinary situation is when the two families approve of the union but find it difficult to solemnize it with a standard wedding. In such cases, they anticipate a formal wedding by a year or two and with full family approval the boy captures the girl and takes her to his house.

Ganesh Kisku of Amjora had arranged the marriage of his son with the daughter of Nimbai Besra of Gauripur. The ceremonies of jawae dhuti and bahu bande had been performed but owing to lack of money the girl's father could not perform the wedding the same year. By agreement between the parties, therefore, the boy took the girl to his house by or ader. Similarly Boro Chandrai Hansdak' of Bodachapor found it difficult to perform the wedding of his daughter with Saona Soren of Kusbona. With the approval of the parents, therefore, and the sanction of the village Saona married the girl by or ader at a Sohrae festival, and two years later a formal wedding was performed.

If the family circumstances do not improve, such a union

sometimes becomes a permanent substitute for a formal wedding.

A second circumstance is when a boy and girl have met as lovers and the girl becomes pregnant. In this case, the matter goes to the village and if the boy and his parents are willing the matter is adjusted by the girl going to his house. Here also 'pulling in' may merely anticipate a later wedding or may simply form the approved basis of the union.*

If consultation with the families is sometimes a prior condition, it is even more common for 'pulling in' to be resorted to without their approval.

The boy and girl may be anxious to have their relations recognized but the girl's parents may be opposed to the wedding. The boy may possibly be a divorcee and the girl's parents may desire to marry her with a boy not previously married. Similarly the boy may come from a poor family and the girl's parents may be doubtful of her happiness. In the alternative the girl's parents may dislike the boy or merely not approve of him, or the boy's parents themselves may not be willing. In such cases capture is a way of circumventing the disapproval of the parents.

Dundo Baske of Mehdip met a girl of Ronchura at a wedding in his village. He fell in love with her and some months later he met her in Borio market and went to her village. The girl was willing but her parents disapproved so from there he took her to his house and 'pulled her in'.

In Kalipathar Hapai Marandi wanted to marry Mokhadi Murmu. A match-maker was appointed but after 'the boy's house had been seen' the girl's father withdrew from the proposal. A month later, Hapai met the girl at Dalahi market and persuaded her to be his wife. He took her to his house and although the girl's father still opposed, the girl remained with the boy and their union was recognized by the village, as a marriage by or ader. They have since had two children.

In Semra Ram Soren was in love with Thurgi Murmu. Since the boy and the girl were of the same village the girl's parents did not approve of the marriage. With the girl's approval, therefore, the boy took her to his house and they

*For examples of this adjustment, see Chapter 5.

have since had four children. In this case, there has been no wedding in dol form and their union has remained all along a marriage by or ader.

Other cases occur in which the two families may not be opposed to the union but they are merely not consulted.

Thakur Hansdak' and Balhi Murmu of Dhanukdih had both been married once to other partners and been divorced. They used to go about together and one day at the Kundahit market they drank rice beer together and decided to get married. When they reached their village and without consulting their parents, Thakur took the girl to his house. Although they had not been previously consulted the two families had no objection to the union and a formal wedding was celebrated later.

Finally, a boy may be in love with a girl and the girl herself be quite unwilling to go with him. In such cases the boy sometimes takes the help of friends, surrounds the girl at a mela or market and forcibly drags her to his house.

Or ader, however, is by no means confined to boys only and girls also occasionally resort to this expedient and capture boys instead. The most usual circumstance is when the boy's parents are known to disapprove of their union and in order to compel the boy to face their displeasure the girl induces him to live temporarily at her house.

Maiya Tudu of Jaraki 'captured' Jhago Hembrom a boy of her village and after she had 'pulled' him into her house, his parents agreed to accept their marriage.

In Tarajuri Mandri Soren, a divorced girl, fell in love with Mandal Murmu, a boy who was still unmarried. As she knew that his parents would not relish a wedding with a divorcee, she 'captured' him and kept him in her house for two weeks. When the villagers asked him why he was living here the boy said he could not help it as the girl would not let him leave the house. The marriage was then approved by the village.

In other cases, a widow formerly married to a ghar jawae may 'pull' a boy into her house and thus commence a second ghar jawae union by or ader.

III ADJUSTMENTS

When a case of 'capture' occurs, the adjustment depends on whether it was done by family agreement or the action precipitates a village meeting. If the 'capture' was merely in anticipation of a formal wedding, the villagers will know the circumstances and no formal announcement or meeting will be necessary. Similarly, if the 'pulling in' has resulted from the girl's pregnancy, the meeting itself will have made the necessary adjustment and no further steps will be needed. The wedding is then performed later or the boy and girl live together without any further ceremony. If no *sindur* is given and they later desire to marry their children in dol form, they sometimes resort to a delayed form of sangha wedding. At the wedding of their child the couple go inside the house, sit on a mat and the husband gives his wife *sindur* on a flower.

If, on the other hand, the boy abducts the girl from her village without her parent's knowledge, the following steps are taken.

The girl's family first informs the jogmanjhi and this official with a few villagers goes ahead to scout. He asks cowherds if they know where the girl is and in due course he learns the village to which she has been taken. He then meets the manjhi 'Where do you come from? You are stranger in our village.' 'We come from such and such a village.' 'You never came before. What matter has brought you?' 'It is nothing to be scared about. Two days ago a weak and thin goat was left by the herd and is missing from the fields. A leopard carried her to your forest. We tracked it and it came this way. There is blood on the trail'. 'I will call the jogmanjhi and he will search for it. Perhaps the leopard has dragged it somewhere near. These days leopards are very bold and snatch their prey from under one's very eye'. The jogmanjhi of the boy's village then comes and the manjhi says, 'Jogmanjhi, our friends say that a leopard has brought one of their goats into our forest. Is this so?' The jogmanjhi says, 'Yes, I heard yesterday that somewhere in the lower part of the village a leopard brought a goat. I will ask about it. Wait till I return'. The jogmanjhi then tells the boy's family that the jogmanjhi and some others have come in search of the girl. He then returns and confirms that the girl is in the boy's house. The boy's father or guardian also comes and a date three or five days later is fixed for a joint village meeting for adjusting the matter. If the girl has been taken forcibly the jogmanjhi of the village brings her back. Otherwise she is left with the boy and the party returns.

On the day fixed the two villages hold a joint meeting. The boy and girl are asked to state how it happened and whether any force was used. When the interrogation is over, the manjhi or jogmanjhi asks the villagers to decide the matter. If the girl declines to stay, damages or lajao marao of five rupees are payable to the girl or her father. Each side must also give the cost of the sitting. If, however, the girl remains, her parents merely ask that the necessary dues should be paid and these are as follows.

If the girl is not a married woman and is not engaged to be married the boy's father pays the correct bride-price and the brother's dues. If the boy brought her by force against her will but the girl has agreed to stay, the boy's father must pay the girl's father an extra two rupees if the boy is unmarried and an extra four rupees if he is divorced.

Besides these payments the boy's father must provide the meeting with goats according to the status of the boy and the girl. These must be given irrespective of whether the girl was forcibly captured or came of her own accord. If both had never been married he must give two animals. If the boy is either married or divorced and the girl is a divorcee he must give one while if the boy is either married or divorced and the girl is unmarried three animals must be given. In addition he must pay one rupee to the two manjhis to share as their mandla or fee and each side must also pay the local costs of the sitting.

When Chunda Tudu of Dhansaria married Chunki Hembrom by or ader he himself had been divorced but the girl was still unmarried so apart from the bride-price, the brother's due and the cost of the sitting he gave three goats.

When the daughter of Hugu Kisku of Basha was pulled in by Panchu Soren of the same village neither the boy nor the girl had been previously married so the boy paid the meeting two goats.

These goats are distributed as follows.

If there are two villages and three goats, the girl's village takes two goats together with the head and a foreleg of the third. If there are two goats, it takes one and a similar fragment of the second.

If there is one goat or only one village, the whole meeting shares.*

If the girl was already engaged to be married to a different boy a stiffer penalty is exacted and the boy's father must also pay all the expenses incurred by her prospective bridegroom after 'the viewing of the household'.

If the girl is married the boy's father will have to pay the girl's husband a double bride-price and if the marriage was recent the expenses of the wedding. He will have to give his own manjhi five rupees for 'saving his head' and the bride-price of a divorced girl to the girl's father. In addition he must pay a fine of ten rupees to his village or give two goats.

When these details have been settled a date is fixed for payment of the dues. The girl stays with the boy and their union is accepted by the village as a valid marriage by or ader. Wherever possible all the dues are cleared in the first meeting; otherwise the father and mother's share in the bride-price is paid and the balance is sent at a fixed time within a year. If the boy's father defaults in clearing these dues the jogmanjhi of the girl's village is sent and if there is still failure the matter is brought before the villagers or the five manjhis.

*When Mangal Murmu of Kusma pulled in Pudi Tudu of Bhagabandh, both were unmarried and the penalty was, therefore, two goats or pigs. At the meeting, however, which I myself attended, the actual animals proved controversial, Mangal brought out two pigs, Pudi's father rejected them as he said they were too small and in the end Mangal paid ten rupees instead.
When Panu Soren of Silingi was 'pulled in' by a Santal of Bandkoe she herself had not been married but her husband had been twice divorced. On this occasion three goats were given.

30

MARRIAGE BY INTRUSION
Nir Bolok'

I CAUSES

IF MARRIAGE by capture is normally resorted to by boys, nir bolok' or intrusion is a common expedient of girls. 'This marriage', says Campbell, 'consists in a young unmarried woman intruding herself into the house of the parents of a young man upon whom she has set her affections, or with whom there may have been love passages and he has ceased showing her attention. Being hurt at the treatment she has been subjected to, she resolves to venture on the Intrusion marriage and thus assert what she regards as her right. It is always Leap year in Santalia and a Santal maiden need never pine away in single blessedness or sigh her heart out for the man she loves'.[1] In certain cases the girl is already pregnant by the boy and in order to ensure that he does not jilt her the girl forces herself into his family.

Such cases pre-suppose a certain unwillingness on the part of the boy. But in other cases, the boy himself may not be unwilling and 'intrusion' may occur if his parents are opposing, have arranged his marriage elsewhere, or are merely indifferent. The girl then resorts to intrusion with the approval of the boy with the object of inducing his parents to accept their union.

When Chotu Ramu of Amtala was a young man he met Gungi Hembrom of Choudhuri during the Dasae festival at the Katikund dibi. They met from time to time and three months later Gungi intruded in his house. His parents said, 'Have you come as a guest? What is your work?' She brought an extra cloth with her but no rice beer or leaves. The girl said, 'I have come to live with him'. Then they called some villagers and Chotu Ramu was asked if he had given her his word. Chotu Ramu said, 'I have told her she may come'. Then the villagers of Choudhuri came. A meeting of the two villages was held and Chotu Ramu's father paid the bride-price and the brother's due and the girl was accepted as a wife.

In Beldiha Dhunu Tudu was in love with the daughter of Pitho Marandi of Hathipur. Their parents did not approve of their union, so in order to win them round the girl forced herself into Dhunu's house. The parents were obliged to accept the marriage and in the end it was celebrated in tunki dipil form.

Ringti Hembrom a divorcee of Buradi was in love with Luda Marandi, an unmarried boy of her village. The parents of the girl did not approve of their marriage as they did not want to marry her in the same village. When the boy and girl saw that the girl's parents were obdurate the girl entered the boy's house. The village met and later a sangha marriage was celebrated.

In Dumdumi Suruj Tudu was in love with Lobai Hembrom of her village. The parents of Lobai brought another girl as his wife but the boy and girl did not give up their friendship. Lobai did not want his wife and in the end Suruj forced herself into his house. At the village meeting Lobai divorced his wife and his union with Suruj was accepted as a marriage.

In all these cases, the girl was either unmarried or divorced but in certain cases married women also resort to intrusion.

Sumi Soren of Patharcapa who was married in another village fell in love with Budan Marandi. The boy was of her home village and when the girl could bear her husband no longer she deserted him and entered Budhan's house. Budhan was a divorced boy and was willing to marry her. At the village meeting, therefore, he paid the girl's husband sixty rupees as double bride-price and the expenses of the wedding and later he celebrated the union by a wedding in sangha form.

But besides intrusion by a girl nir bolok' is also resorted to by boys and a common circumstance is when a widow is living alone and has either no agnates of her dead husband or has land in her own name.

Botua Tudu of Bando intruded in the house of a widow of his village. The two were in love and the village accepted the intrusion as a wedding. Batua already had one wife and after doing nir bolok' with the widow he lived with them in their two separate houses.

Similar action is taken when the parents of the girl approve the union but the boy's parents oppose. In such cases the girl may invite the boy to intrude in her house in the expectation that after some time the boy's parents will allow them to go to his house.

Kubraj Murmu of Dumdumi was in love with Sorno Hembrom of his village. His parents were opposed to the marriage, so the boy intruded in the house of the girl. The girl had no brothers and her parents were glad to have the boy. At the village meeting, their union was accepted as a marriage and after some time the boy returned to his parents taking the girl with him.

Finally nir bolok' is sometimes done by a boy if the girl has either been once married to a ghar jawae or serving son-in-law and then divorced or widowed, or her father is proposing to bring a ghar jawae as her husband.

Bangi Murmu of Amtala was the eldest of three sisters and had once been married to a ghar jawae. Her husband had deserted her and while she was gathering Mahua flowers, she met Sam Marandi of Salaipahari and began relations with him. The only member of Sam's family was a brother who had gone to Assam and he himself was a casual servant. While their love affair was progressing, Sam heard that the girl's father had started negotiations for another ghar jawae. That night he went to Bangi's house. Bangi's father said, 'Why have you come?' 'To work as your servant.' As the father needed a servant, he let him stay and a few days later he found them sleeping together. After that there was a meeting and the boy said 'I have come to live with her'. The girl said 'I told him he could come.' Then the boy was accepted as a ghar jawae and some time later he and the girl went to Assam.

In Parba a girl had also been once married to a ghar jawae but her husband had deserted her. One night a wedding was going on and the girls and boys were dancing in the village lane. A village boy had set his heart on the girl and fearing that others might take her, he decided to intrude. He went to her house, called to the girl and went inside. The two slept together and the next morning the villagers found them in her house. They asked the girl, 'Will you keep him?' The girl said, 'I will take him as a ghar jawae.' The boy's parents agreed and the boy stayed on.

II METHODS

When a girl decides to intrude she makes her preparations and these are described by Campbell as follows.

'A young woman having decided upon a bir bolok' marriage takes a few of her companions into her confidence and informs them of her design, and looks to them for their countenance and assistance. She prepares a large pot of handi or beer, and carrying it poised on her head goes straight into the inmost apartment and having disposed of her pot of liquor sits down to await events.'[2] She has, of course, chosen her time so that there is no one to oppose her entering. The action has been performed in daylight before witnesses and it soon spreads that such a woman has gone into such a man's house. The man's mother when she hears of it, is greatly incensed, but by the unwritten law governing such cases is precluded from ejecting her from her house by force. If she can by hook or by crook prevail upon her to come out herself she is at liberty to do so. Of course, a small crowd soon assembles in the courtyard, some of whom sympathise with the intruder, and others take the part of the man against her. The mother, however, sets to work resolutely to do her level best to drive her out. She carefully closes up all apertures by which air can enter and then flings a large handful of pepper into the fire, and shutting the door anxiously awaits the result of her strategy. A Santal house is generally divided into two apartments by a partition wall about five feet high, so that there is no obstruction to the fumes of the burning pepper, pervading every corner of it. The crowd in the courtyard are speculating as to whether she will be able to hold out or not, and the mother is scolding in her shrillest tones. When a considerable time has elapsed the spectators begin to urge the irate dame to open the door, as the fumes of the burning pepper must have in a large measure become innocuous. She, thus counselled opens the door and the girl is brought out into the fresh air, where she rapidly throws off the effects of the burning pepper. By the time she has recovered her breath her mother-in-law for now they stand in the relation to each other of mother-in-law and daughter-in-law appears with a quantity of janhe, with which she has mixed some oil. This she puts in the dhinki or large mortar and orders her daughter-in-law to pound it into flour. This of course owing to the presence of the oil is impossible, but a brave attempt is made and continued till the bystanders begin to indulge in uncomplimentary remarks directed against the older woman, and she feeling the force of them, or being ashamed to longer indulge her spite brings the exhibition to a close. She accepts the position and, as the story books say, all live happily together.[3]

At the present day, the battle of pepper rarely occurs, and the impossible tasks are also not inflicted. The girl merely goes to the boy's house, sits in the courtyard or on his verandah and finally explains her presence to the boy's parents.

If the parents do not relish the intrusion and the girl is of the same village, they call the villagers and try to coax her out.

While Bale Marandi, a divorced girl of Majdiha, was living in Amtala with her father's sister, she had a love affair with Maidan Murmu and decided to marry him. During the Sohrae festival she went and sat on his verandah. Maidan's parents asked her what she was doing and she said, 'I have come to live with Maidan'. The villagers intervened and said that as Maidan was still unmarried she had better go away. 'Even if he keeps you', they said 'he will take a fresh unmarried girl later.' In the end they coaxed Bale away and she returned to her village.

If, however, the girl is a stranger they make her over to the jogmanjhi and call the people of her village for a joint discussion.

III ADJUSTMENT

If the parents do not strongly object and the boy himself is anxious to keep her, the girl is allowed to stay in the house. If she comes from another village the jogmanjhi arrives with a party and tells the boy's manjhi 'A she-goat has run off with a he-goat from the grazing ground. It went towards your village. We have come to look for it'. The manjhi then takes similar action as in a case of capture and the two villages hold a joint meeting three or five days later.

Similarly, if the girl is of the boy's village, a meeting is held to adjust the situation. At this meeting the procedure is the same as for 'pulling in' and the girl is either retained by the boy or is returned to her father. If she remains, the boy's father pays the correct bride-price and the brother's due, the girl is formally accepted as the boy's wife and each side pays the costs of the sitting.

If, however, she is not accepted, she is put back in her father's charge. Provided she was not invited by the boy, no claim for lajao marao or damages arises, there is no penalty of goats or pigs and the failure to intrude leaves her status as it was.

If on the other hand the boy is proved to have encouraged her and then refuses to keep her he either gives a sum of lajao marao or is required to pay a fine to the village. In certain cases, he may also be required to pay both according as the meeting decides. The cost of the meeting is then taken from both sides and with their payment the incident is closed.

In Hathi Hariri the daughter of Dunbai Marandi intruded in the house of Matal Soren. At the meeting, Matal said that he would marry her but his parents refused to have her in the house. The meeting finally decided to disapprove the union and the girl was returned to her parents. As the boy had encouraged her to intrude his parents had to pay lajao marao of five rupees.

Champai Marandi, a divorcee of Tesjuria intruded in the house of Morol Soren. The boy's parents did not let her stay but since Morol had encouraged her to come the village awarded five rupees as lajao marao to the girl's father and fined the boy twenty rupees.

The daughter of Nunku Hansdak' of Thikuba did nir bolok' in the house of Ceda Soren of Dhundli. The boy and girl were both divorcees. After the girl had stayed in their house for some days the boy and his parents did not want to keep her and at the village meeting their union was not accepted and the boy was fined five rupees.

Similarly, if a boy intrudes, a meeting also adjusts the matter. If there is no objection on the girl's side, the intrusion is accepted as a marriage. If his presence is unacceptable he is asked to leave the house and may also be punished with a fine; both parties paying the costs of the village meeting.

Phudan Besra of Kerabari fell in love with a daughter of Jiban Murmu of Ghangrabandh and intruded in her house. The girl refused to marry him and her parents also did not accept him. Phudan was, therefore, driven out and the villagers fined him five rupees.

If a boy intrudes at the instance of the girl, and is later on rejected, the boy himself is awarded five rupees.

Keota Hansdak' of Baromasia was due to be taken as a ghar jawae by a girl of Borband. The girl invited him to intrude so he went to her house and stayed a night with her. The next night the girl went to a different boy. Keota complained to the village and he was given five rupees and went back home.

REFERENCES

1. Campbell, op. cit., 336.
2. Bodding notes that at the time of entering, the former practice was for the girl to go with a bundle of leaves in her armpit. (Bodding : *A Santal Dictionary*, I, 295).
3. Campbell, op. cit., 336-37.

31

ELOPEMENT
Apangir

I CAUSES

A FINAL type of jungle marriage is apangir or elopement. According to Bodding this term was originally used about 'elopement with a married person or with a relative who according to Santal law cannot be married. Formerly the husband tracked the eloped pair and cut them down where he found them and buried them on the spot. Every body passing such a place throws a stone or a Branch of dead leaf.' At the present time elopement is by no means confined to these cases although they still account for an appreciable proportion.

The most usual background to elopement is when a boy and girl are in love but one or other of their parents disapproves of the union. In certain cases, the two families may have quarrelled and there is, therefore, little hope of a marriage by family agreement. Moreover, the boy's family may be poor and the girl's family may object on the ground of his indigence. The girl may not wish to go to the boy's house and elopement may seem the best course in the circumstances. If their love is such that 'no wind can blow the leaves from the stem' they may prefer to seek a new home in a new country. If the difficulty is one of family disapproval, a temporary elopement may secure a family recognition of their marriage.

Kandan Soren of Dholpathar was in love with Manjhan Marandi of his village. Both of them wanted to marry but neither of their parents approved of the match. The boy's parents objected because the girl was older than the boy while the girl's parents said that they would not marry their daughter in the same village. When the boy and the girl failed to persuade their parents they decided to elope. They went away for three months and when they returned the boy's father paid a bride-price and the marriage was celebrated.

In Baratanr Hopna Tudu was in love with the daughter of Kasrae Murmu of Barapahari. Their marriage had been approved by their parents but when the girl's party was going to the boy's village for 'viewing the house' they saw some earth being dug in the way. They considered this a bad omen and the marriage was broken off. Later the girl's parents arranged her marriage with another boy and after completing the ceremony of horok' cikhna and taka cal, a day was fixed for the wedding. The girl was still in love with Hopna and on the day the marriage booth was erected the girl went to Hopna and the two eloped. After living together for a month they came back to the boy's house and their union was accepted.

In other cases elopement is often resorted to when a girl is married against her will or after being married becomes dissatisfied with her husband. She has either a previous lover or finds another boy and in order to avoid friction with her husband they decide to leave the neighbourhood and go elsewhere.

Finally in certain circumstances a boy and girl of similar septs or forbidden relationships may fall in love and decide to live together. Their union can never be legal, so long as these impediments are known. After suffering bitlaha or in anticipation of its performance, they leave their locality and elope to a distant country. In this new area they suppress their relationship, and appear simply as married strangers. They are 'married by the journey' and provided they abandon their parents' homes and never return, public acceptance by the area affords them a 'false' married status.

Badha Tudu and Kobyan Tudu of Khejurdenga were brother and sister. They fell in love and decided to live together. When the matter became public, a bitlaha was performed and the two eloped to another country. In Bokrabandh Prodhan Hansdak' was already married and fell in love with the daughter of his father's sister. One day his wife saw him carrying rice and water out of the house and being curious to know why he was doing this she followed him and saw him take it to the girl. The next day she reported the matter to the village manjhi and after the village had met it decided to consult the council of five manjhis. Before the council could meet, Prodhan eloped with the girl and nothing has been seen of them since.

II THE TECHNIQUE OF ELOPEMENT

When a boy and girl decide on this course, their elopement may be either local or to a distance. If it is local they get together some food and go a few miles off to the house of a relative or friend. After staying there a week or two they either return or are detected and brought back. When they return of their own accord they either separate and go to their own houses or the boy brings the girl to his own house.

Dudum Murmu fell in love with Talamani Hembrom and used to meet her in the fields. He was not certain whether his parents would approve so when she became pregnant he eloped with her to his brother-in-law's house in Banjhi Bunglow. The two stayed there for a week and when they returned to his house the village accepted them as married.

III ADJUSTMENT

If on their return the pair separate but the girl desires to have the boy as her permanent husband and the boy himself is willing, she induces her parents to negotiate a formal marriage for her. Since all the neighbourhood knows of the elopement, her parents usually resort to this course as it may otherwise be difficult to secure for her another husband. If, on the other hand, the girl is taken to the boy's house and her parents at last locate her, a joint meeting of the two villages is held. If the union does not involve outcasting the same adjustments are made as in or ader or capture. The union is recognised as a valid marriage by elopement and may either be supplemented by a full dress wedding in dol form or left by the meeting as it is.

If the boy desires to give the girl *sindur* but not in dol form, he may give her *sindur* on a flower by baha saoha.

If the adventure is accepted as a marriage, the correct bride-price and brother's dues must be paid and the goats, manjhi's fee and the costs of the sitting must be given according to the same scale as in a union by or ader.

Similarly if the girl is married or her wedding has already been settled her husband or prospective bridegroom must be indemnified in the same way as in a marriage by 'pulling in'.

If, on the other hand, either the boy or girl regret their short adventure or if their parents refuse approval the adjustment depends on whether their conjunction is proved or the girl has merely returned to her house after a short absence. If the elopement is proved the settlement depends on whether the girl was taken 'for ever' or for a day. If she can show that the boy has promised permanent marriage and while she herself is still willing to live with him the boy is resiling, her father can claim the bride-price and the brother's due and the girl herself can claim chadaodi or divorce money. The son of Basit Murmu of Jitpur eloped with the daughter of Ramu Marandi. They spent the night in the forest and next morning returned to the village. Both the boy and the girl wanted to marry but the boy's father threatened to expel him if he did so. The boy then lost his nerve and declined to take the girl. At the village meeting the boy's father paid twelve rupees as bride-price, two rupees as brother's due and chadaodi or divorce money.

If, on the other hand, the union was only 'an exploration of lovers' and either the girl or her father does not wish the marriage to proceed the girl's father can claim lajao marao for lowering her value as a bride and the boy must also give the village two goats.

Bhagrit Soren of Ranga eloped with a girl of his village to the house of his relatives. The girl's parents were not in favour of the marriage, so after discovering the couple they separated them and took the girl away. At the meeting the villages realised two goats from the boy and made him pay five rupees as lajao marao to the girl's father.

In Mahuatanr Jetha Hembrom eloped with Munia Marandi of his village. Eight days later they returned but their parents opposed their marriage and in the end the boy paid ten rupees for two goats and five rupees as lajao marao to the girl.

In Dhankutta Arjun Hansdak' was in love with Joba Kisku of Kurumpaghar. Their parents were opposed to the marriage, so they eloped during the Kali puja mela and went to Bengal. After three months they returned and the girl's father tried to get her back. When the village met he strongly opposed the marriage but finally agreed to accept it on condition that a dol wedding was performed and forty men went with him to the boy's house for jawae dhuti. The boy's father replied that he could not entertain such a large number and the villagers reduced it to nine. The girl's father did not accept this condition and the meeting dispersed without a settlement. Four days later they met again and the girl's father agreed to take only nine men and the ceremoney was then performed. Some time later, three persons from the girl's side came for taka cal and paid six rupees as half the bride-price. They promised to give the rest after a few days. The girl's father then said that six rupees should be set off as wages earned by his daughter in Bengal. A third meeting of the villagers was held and it was found that the boy and the girl had nine rupees with them when they started to return. Both of them fell ill and five rupees had gone in the expenses of their sickness. The meeting, therefore, decided that out of the balance of four rupees half should be taken as the girl's share and the boy's father must, therefore, pay eight rupees instead of six as the balance of bride-price. The boy's father agreed but the girl's father then refused to celebrate the marriage that year. Finally when she saw how much opposed her father was to the marriage the girl herself changed her mind and refused to go on with the marriage. Yet another village meeting was then held and the six rupees paid by the boy's father was treated as lajao marao and the matter ended.

In a similar way if the girl desires to stay but the boy is not willing the girl can claim lajao marao as damages, while if the girl is already married similar principles govern the adjustment as in the 'capture' of a married woman.

Barka Hembrom of Bansduma eloped with a married

woman of Siltha. They lived together for two years and then returned to the village. The elopement was accepted as a marriage and Barka had to pay the woman's husband a double bride-price and give the manjhi five rupees for saving his head. In Udalbani Mangal Baske eloped with the wife of Bariar Hembrom. They stayed away for four months but on return decided to part. Bariar did not divorce his wife and Mangal paid fifteen rupees as celan gitil and fifteen rupees as fine to the village.

In all these cases, elopement was either proved or not contested. If on the other hand, the boy and girl are not surprised together and there is no proof of their elopement, nothing can be claimed.

Chota Hembrom of Telo eloped with the daughter Dukhia Besra of Balajore. Three days later the boy deserted the girl and ran back to his house. The girl followed him but the boy denied that he had taken her away. As the elopement was not proved lajao marao was not paid.

In Amgachi Bhado Murmu eloped to Assam with a girl of Katikund. After one year, the boy came back alone but as there was no proof that the girl had gone with him Bhado paid nothing.

Similarly when the daughter of Rengta Soren of Atgaon eloped with Dhar, a servant boy in the village, they went to the boy's house in Dorai. After three or four days they returned, the girl going to her parent's house and the boy to his master's. There was no proof of their elopement so nothing was given to the girl.

Similar adjustments are made if the elopement is to a distance. In such cases, however, the couple make bigger preparations and usually stay away for several years. If their union is permissible negotiations are then made by go-betweens or the matter is reopened when they at last return to the village.

32

GHARDI JAWAE AND GHAR JAWAE

I GHARDI JAWAE

WE have seen that when a girl is married to a ghardi jawae, it is only after five years that her union merges in a standard marriage. This distinction is reflected in the technique of the wedding and while a formal match-maker is employed and the general ritual of a dol wedding is observed there are four important ways in which the bringing of a ghardi jawae differs from a wedding in dol or standard form.

The first is that the betrothal is done after the viewing of the house and unless both the parties expressly will it, there is no presentation of either a cloth to the bride or a dhoti to the bridegroom. After the two houses have been viewed the decision is taken and after that the two families move straight to the wedding.

Secondly the wedding takes place in the girl's house and instead of the boy's party going for the girl, the girl's father and some old villagers go for the boy. The boy is treated like a girl, and the girl's party which brings him is called the kora bariat, or the boy's train of followers.

Thirdly when the boy arrives with the party there is no daram dak' enec', in which the two parties face each other in war-like lines. There is no wild brandishing of sticks, and no final fusion and embrace. This is because the wedding is in no sense a marriage by capture. It is rather the delivery of a captive to the girl. The boy is merely brought to the village and after the girl has been lifted in the basket and he has given her *sindur*, he is quietly installed.

Finally there is no bride-price and no brother's due and while some of the minor payments such as the fees to the manjhi and jogmanjhi and the tips to the bride's sisters are often given there is no rigid scale and the only compulsory gifts from the boy's side are the basket, the *sindur* and the cloth for the bride.*

If such a wedding breaks the same principles as in a dol wedding determine how the claims shall be settled.

A brother of Ranghna Hansdak' of Kalkipara was due to be married as a ghardi jawae in Burhiduba. A date had been fixed for the girl's party to fetch the boy and rice beer had been brewed. The girl then eloped and Ranghna Hansdak' claimed and was paid the cost of the rice beer.

In Litipara Jitu Murmu had arranged a ghardi jawae for his daughter and the boy had actually reached the house. Before *sindur* could be given, however, the girl took a strong dislike to him and her father then broke the marriage off. The boy was given eight rupees to cover the expenses in his house and as compensation.

If the girl is divorced or a widow and has had *sindur* from her first husband, the wedding is in sangha form and differs from the standard ritual in that the ghardi jawae does the flower ceremony in the girl's house and not in his own.

II GHAR JAWAE

When a ghar jawae or permanent son-in-law is brought for a girl, his induction fulfils a number of important needs and involves radical adjustments in the girl's rights. It is not surprising, therefore, that the ways of conferring this status should be elastic and variable, and there are in fact seven ways in

*In the Rajmahal sub-division where the bride-price has now reached abnormally high levels, a reduced bride-price is sometimes taken from a ghardi jawae and when Jatu Soren of Mangrutikar was married as a ghardi jawae in Taljhari, he had to pay sixteen rupees.

which a son-in-law is made a ghar jawae and all of them are fully sanctioned by Santal law and practice.

III GHAR JAWAE IN DOL FORM

If the wedding is publicly celebrated, it closely follows the lines on which a ghardi jawae is wedded. There is the same engagement of a match-maker, the same viewing of the houses and the same betrothal without a recognition by clothes. If the families so desire, the girl's party visits the boy's house and gives him a dhoti but this is neither necessary nor compulsory. Similarly on the wedding day, there is the same fetching of the boy, his same installation in the girl's house and the same exemption of the bride-price and the brother's due. As in the wedding of a ghardi jawae the ghar jawae must bring the *sindur*, the basket and a cloth for the bride but there is otherwise great flexibility in the customary presents.

There is, however, one important addition to the ritual. On the morning after the wedding* the bridegroom is brought out jumi jaega lebet acur lagit—'for being taken round the lands'. The girl's father and the village officials conduct him through the fields and he is shown all the lands which he will cultivate for his father-in-law and his new wife. If there is already another ghar jawae or if there is an adult son, the new ghar jawae is shown only the share which he himself will cultivate. Similarly if at the time of his induction certain lands have been reserved for the agnates as curuc' cawale, these are excluded from the showing.

This inspection of the lands is in almost all areas a normal aspect of a ghar jawae wedding and it is everywhere a valuable indication of the ghar jawae's status. It is not, however, a *sine qua non* of a valid wedding. In some cases Santals do not do it 'because they forget'. In others they leave it out 'because it is not strictly necessary' while in certain villages it is reduced to a nominal gesture. When Chunda Soren was taken as a ghar jawae for the sister of the Sibtala manjhi, the manjhi

*In the Rajabhita area this is often done on the day before the wedding.

merely gave a jerk with his chin, Chunda looked over his shoulder and the showing was done.

If the negotiations fail at any time the claims are determined by the same principles as in a dol wedding and whichever side has wrongly put the other side to loss is responsible for indemnifying him.

Rengta Hembrom of Naraiangarh agreed to marry his daughter in ghar jawae form to the son of Mangal Murmu of Abhua. A party from the girl's side came to Mangal's house for jawae dhuti and Mangal incurred sixty rupees in giving them a feast. Six years went by and Rengta still did not celebrate the wedding. Finally Rengta took another boy as ghar jawae and broke off the match. When he heard this, Mangal claimed sixty rupees.

Similarly in a case from Ranga, Kunju Murmu betrothed his son as a ghar jawae in the house of Kandna Soren of Raghunathpur. The boy used to visit the girl and Kunju solemnized the presentation of the bridegroom's cloth by feasting the girl's party at his house. Later a rift developed and the girl's father broke off the match and took another boy as ghar jawae. Kunju then claimed one hundred and twenty rupees as the costs of the ceremony.

IV GHAR JAWAE BY AGU HATAR

If the bringing of a ghar jawae by a public celebration is the usual and best form, it is also permissible to anticipate a ghar jawae wedding by inducting the boy and celebrating the union later. Just as a dol wedding can be anticipated with a marriage by or ader, agu hatar enables a ghar jawae to precede his wedding by a period in his father-in-law's house. In such cases his status as a ghar jawae is confirmed by a village meeting and is fully accepted and if any of the parties die before the formal wedding is performed the status of the marriage as a ghar jawae union is in no way affected.

In 1945, Thakur Hansdak' of Ranidinda obtained the approval of his village to the bringing of a ghar jawae. By the time everything was settled the marriage season had gone by and Thakur Hansdak' was also short of funds. As he needed the ghar jawae for helping him in the fields he brought in

Munshi Tudu by agu hatar and in 1946 he performed the wedding.

In Rohra Sundar Hembrom arranged a ghar jawae for his daughter who was married and divorced. A match-maker was appointed and when everything was settled he brought the boy by agu hatar. This was in 1944 and no wedding has as yet been done.

In Sugnibasa the widow of Sibu Tudu brought a ghar jawae for her daughter Lukhi Tudu by agu hatar. The wedding was not performed that year but the taking of a ghar jawae was approved by a village meeting. The two lived together and got two daughters. But before the wedding could be celebrated, Lukhi died. Her death did not, however, affect the position of her husband and later his mother-in-law provided him with a second wife in place of her dead daughter.

If the marriage breaks between the boy's induction by agu hatar and a formal celebration, the boy can demand all that he might have earned if he had been a servant.

In Duarpahari Sakla Soren brought a boy of his village as a ghar jawae by agu hatar. Later he took a dislike to him and decided not to perform the wedding. The boy was, therefore, sent home but Sakla gave him three cloths and his pay as a servant at the rate of five rupees a year.

In Hariari Harma Tudu brought a boy of his village as a ghar jawae by agu hatar. Later on he got his lands cultivated by another Santal and when his son-in-law protested the two quarrelled. The ghar jawae appealed to the village and Harma was made to give him fifteen rupees. The boy then left his wife and went to his home.

V GHAR JAWAE BY CONVERSION OF A GHARDI JAWAE

A third method is when a ghardi jawae is converted into a ghar jawae. This usually occurs either when a minor son has died or when the term has been extended and the ghardi jawae is the main means for supporting an aging couple. It can be done either before or after the term has expired. In such cases, a village meeting is called, the matter is talked over and with village approval and the drinking of rice beer, the ghardi jawae is declared a ghar jawae. If the family likes, he is taken out and shown his father-in-law's lands.

VI GHAR JAWAE BY CONVERTING A KUNDAL NAPAM MARRIAGE

Yet another method is when a boy who has married a girl by kundal napam is accepted by his father-in-law and the village as a ghar jawae. This is often done when a servant boy has married the daughter of the house, and with a view to providing for the girl, her father decides to change their status. A declaration is made at a meeting and with village approval the son-in-law becomes a ghar jawae. At this meeting, he is often taken round the village and shown his father-in-law's fields and the meeting ends with the drinking of rice beer.

Ram Tudu of Simra for example had four daughters and no sons. He kept four servant boys and each of them married a daughter by kundal napam. Later there were village meetings and the four boys were all accepted by the village as ghar jawaes. In all these cases, a meeting with a declaration and approval was all that effected the change.

If the boy has not given the girl any *sindur* a full dress wedding in ghar jawae form is possible and instead of having only a meeting, the meeting approves and a wedding can follow.

VII GHAR JAWAE BY OR ADER

If a ghar jawae is sometimes taken by agu hatar, he can also be inducted by or ader. This is often resorted to when a girl who was married to a ghar jawae is left a widow. Provided she remarries in ghar jawae form she retains all her rights as an inheriting daughter and while the villagers are normally informed and given rice beer it is unnecessary for her to seek their formal permission or approval.

The daughter of Ana Marandi of Baraband was married to a ghar jawae. Her husband died leaving a boy and a girl and she then brought another husband by or ader.

VIII GHAR JAWAE BY NIR BOLOK'

A similar method is permissible when a boy decides to intrude.

If the girl is unmarried and her parents accept the union, the boy's intrusion may be accepted as a marriage and he himself converted into a ghar jawae by village ratification. A formal wedding may follow later but this is not compulsory.

Similarly if the girl is a widow who was formerly married to a ghar jawae intrusion by a boy may form the basis of a valid second marriage and with village recognition the widow may confer upon him all the rights of a ghar jawae.

IX GHAR JAWAE BY AGU MIT'

Finally when a daughter has been married in another village in any of the other forms but her father requires her presence at home, he can bring the girl and her family back and convert her husband into a ghar jawae by agu mit'. For doing this a village meeting is held preceded sometimes but not necessarily by a meeting in the son-in-law's village. Village approval is obtained and the girl's father then announces that he has inducted the son-in-law as a ghar jawae by agu mit'. As in other forms of ghar jawae marriage the concurrence of the greater family is unnecessary and all that must be done is to assemble the villagers and obtain their approval in a meeting. After the meeting the ghar jawae is often taken out and shown the lands. It is not necessary, however, to refund the bride-price and the brother's due.

Parbet Hembrom of Dhamdhamia had three daughters. He married one outside the village, another in it and the third in the village next to it. None were married in ghar jawae form but all three were in due course brought to the house for supporting the old couple and the husbands were recognized by the village as ghar jawaes by agu mit'. After the death of the old couple the three daughters inherited. In this case, village acceptance was shown among other things by the fact that one of the son-in-laws was appointed jogmanjhi and when he died the son of a second son-in-law succeeded him.

Mangal Tudu of Laijuri was not on good terms with his brothers. He was also finding it difficult to cultivate his fields. His daughter, Malo was married to Kalidas Besra of Jimuasole and had a small son. Mangal decided to bring them back. So he sent the same match-maker who had arranged the wedding and fixed a date for a meeting in Jimuasole. The village agreed to Kalidas going so Mangal took him to his house. His agnates did not like it but the villagers of Laijuri accepted the position. Kalidas cultivated Mangal's land and died in Mangal's house. After Mangal's death, his widow held the lands and when she died, Mali inherited.

In Amjhora Talan Soren had a son and daughter. He married the girl in ordinary form but five years later his only son died. A year later he brought the girl's husband as a ghar jawae by agu mit'.

In Karanpura Singhan Kisku married his daughter in ordinary form. Some years later he caught leprosy and as no one in his family would look after him he brought his daughter back by agu mit'.

33

THE BRIDE-PRICE
Gonon Pon

I THE SANTAL THEORY OF THE BRIDE-PRICE

WHILE a marriage is being negotiated or when it has become an accomplished fact, the claim which bulks largest is the gonon pon or bride-price. This sum of money is payable by the boy's father or guardian in all marriages except kirinok' jawae, golaeti, ghar jawae, ghardi jawae, and agu hatar. It is always referred to as a price yet it has no relation to the bride's economic value. It is rarely an indemnity for the expense of her rearing, it is not her capitalised value as a maid servant and it is only in joke that marriage songs refer to it as a motive for marriage.

It was you who said
We shall make money if we marry her
But if my girl had stayed
We would have had our leaves for curry.

Since I was little, mother
You hammered me with a stool
You spanked me with a fan
Now you are seeing the bride-price, mother
You are calling me parrot.

—*Don Soren*, 1739, 2024.

'The bride-price is a cheat' said Lokhon Hansdak'. 'The father never gains. The wedding ruins him. There would be no weddings if the bride-price were all'. The bride-price is in fact a highly conventional gift rather than an act of business. It confirms the family's responsibilities for the girl's fidelity. It is a way of formally recognizing a son-in-law. It stresses the conception of woman as property. 'The price is symbolic. It is a legal payment that acts as the foundation of the rights of the husband and his family'.[1]

II THE BASIS OF CALCULATION

In determining what amount shall be paid a number of factors play their part. If the marriage is negotiated the price is usually determined by local customary rates but in certain areas, particularly in the Rajmahal Subdivision free play is also given to private competition. In such cases the conventional rate is merely a starting point for negotiations and the final amount is reached after private bargaining by the parties. If, however, the marriage is first accomplished and the bride-price claimed later, the amount is decided by the custom of the area.

These customary rates vary considerably all over the Santal Parganas and sometimes also change from year to year according to local decision. The method of calculation however follows a uniform pattern and boys and girls are first divided into certain standard categories.

III THE CLASSIFICATION OF GIRLS

For this purpose a girl is any one of the following types:

1. Dangua—One who has either never previously been married ; or if married, has since been divorced and has never had *sindur*.
2. Cupi or penda dopot' chadwi—One who has either had an abortion after being known to be pregnant or has given birth to a child out of marriage, and has never had *sindur*.

3. Chadwi—A girl who has been given *sindur* and has left her husband. If she has been married and divorced but has not had *sindur*, she is known as chadwi but retains the status of dangua.
4. Bapla maejiu—A married girl whose marriage has not been dissolved.
5. Randi—A girl whose husband has died. If she has neither had *sindur* nor a child her status is a dangua's.

These groups are sometimes further subdivided according to the number of times a chadwi has been divorced and a widow has been widowed.

IV THE CLASSIFICATION OF BOYS

In a similar manner boys are also classified and every boy is a member of one of the following groups :

1. Dangua—One who has never given a girl *sindur* or has never lived with a girl in any form of marriage.
2. Chadwa—One who has either given a girl *sindur* or lived with her in marriage but has since been divorced.
3. Bapla kora—A boy who is still married.
4. Randi—One who is a widower.
5. Erwellet'—One who is the younger brother of a widow's husband.

These groups are also sometimes subdivided according to the number of times a widower has been widowed or a chadwa has been divorced.

V EVALUATION OF BOYS

In assessing the bride-price it is these groups which are borne in mind. In the case of boys the order of preference is fairly stable and while a widower is sometimes on a parity with a chadwa and sometimes slightly inferior, a dangua invariably ranks first. As he is deemed a much more desirable type of husband, he is required to pay a lower bride-price and it is only if a boy is the younger brother of a widow's husband that this position is affected. In this latter case no bride-price is charged as the widow is already in the family.

Tables 1 and 2 illustrate the influence of the boy's status on local rates.

TABLE 1 : **Dangua girl**

Dangua girls marrying	Litipara	Poraiyahat	Rajabhita	Nonihat
	Rs.	Rs.	Rs.	Rs.
Dangua	12	12	12	12
Chadwa I	16	14	14	14
Chadwa II	16	16	15	16
Chadwa III	16	18	15	18
Married boy	16	16	16	14
Widower I	16	18	14	18
Widower II	16	21	15	20

TABLE 2 : **Widow I**

Widow I marrying	Basetkundi	Poreyahat	Masanjore
	Rs.	Rs.	Rs.
Dangua	9	9	9
Chadwa I	9	7	7
Chadwa II	9	9	7
Married boy	9	9	7
Widower I	9	9	9
Widower II	9	12	9

These variations are based on several considerations. A chadwa for example is less desirable than a dangua, because he has already lost one wife. Even if he is not to blame it is thought his conduct first have been defective. It is, therefore, risky to give a girl to him and he must therefore pay her father more. If he has been divorced several times, the fault is more obviously his and the risk is correspondingly greater. A thrice divorced chadwa who marries a dangua girl must therefore pay more than one who has been once divorced. If the man is a widower, he is as much a source of danger as a widow for 'one wife has died and another may die also'. On the other hand, if the woman is a widow, these defects are to some extent set off by her own disabilities and accordingly less notice is taken of the extent to which a man is a chadwa or a randi.

VI EVALUATION OF GIRLS

If the order of preference is fairly rigid in the case of boys, there is a bewildering variety in the local ways of evaluating girls.

In many areas, girl is preferably a dangua, after that a chadwi and last of all a widow while a cupi or penda dopot' chadwi is sometimes classified as a dangua and sometimes as a chadwi. Moreover if the girl is marrying a dangua boy a twice divorced chadwi ranks lower than a once divorced one while a widow who has lost only one husband is preferable to one who has been widowed twice.

TABLE 3

Dangua boy marrying	Katikund	Nonihat	Chorkata
	Rs.	Rs.	Rs.
Dangua	12	12	12
Chadwi I	12	7	7/8/-
Randi I	9	7	5

Tables 4 and 5 illustrate the degrees of divorce and widowhood on local rates of pon.

TABLE 4 : **Divorce**

Dangua boy marrying	Masanjore	Pakur	Basetkundi	Poreyahat
Chadwi I	7	16	7	7
Chadwi II	7	14	5	5
Chadwi III	7	12	3	3
Chadwi IV or more	7	9	1/4	3

TABLE 5 : **Widowhood**

Dangua boy marrying	Pakur	Katikund	Torayahat
Randi I	16	9	9
Randi II	14	5	7
Randi III	12	3	5
Randi IV or more	9	3	5

These differences are explained by various considerations. Whoever gives a girl her first *sindur* makes her his wife not only for the present world but for hanapuri. A dangua is therefore bought 'for ever' while a chadwi or a widow is merely 'hired'. Moreover there is greater risk in marrying a chadwi II than in 'hiring' a girl who has been only once divorced. A first divorce can as well be due to the first husband but if the girl has failed with one man, she has obviously a trait of character which makes marriage with her difficult. In the case of widows the fact that one husband has died suggests that the woman herself is a source of danger and if two have died the danger is even greater.

If these conventions hold good in certain areas there are other regions in which the order is radically changed and while a dangua continues to rank first a widow comes before a chadwi.

TABLE 6

Dangua boy marrying	Area		
	Torai	Poreyahat	Karbindha
Dangua	12	12	12
Randi I	9	9	9
Chadwi I	7	7	7

Here the accident of death is regarded as less important than incompatibility of character and the bride-price is adjusted accordingly.

In yet a third group of areas all these values are reversed

and instead of a dangua ranking first, the highest price is taken for chadwi.

TABLE 7

Dangua boy marrying	Pakur P.S.	Amrapara	Taljhari
Chadwi I	16	16	19
Dangua	12	12	16
Randi	16	12	19

In such cases the principles which elsewhere prompt the lowering of a chadwi's value are replaced by two other considerations. A chadwi is of much greater practical use than a dangua. 'She is expert in the house. She knows her work. Her husband does not have to teach her.' 'It is this world not hanapuri that matters'. For this reason also a widow sometimes shares this inflated value. Moreover, if the bride-price of a chadwi is high, married girls will rarely leave husbands, and divorce will almost end. Chadwis in fact may actually be more useful but they are not to be encouraged. The higher bride-price therefore both discourages divorce and at the same time recognises the value of experience.

Finally in the Rajabhita area, all these distinctions are ignored and a dangua boy pays a standard bride-price of twelve rupees irrespective of whether the girl is a dangua, chadwi or a widow.

VII THE BALANCING OF STATUS

These local rates and classifications are the starting points for all discussions of the bride-price and the exact sum is fixed according as the status of one party offsets the status of the other.

The following Table illustrates the interaction of different types of boy and girl on the bride-price.

TABLE 8

Boy	Girl	Litipara	Karbindha	Chandna	Masan-jore	Taljhari
Dangua	Dangua	12	12	12	12	16-23
Chadwa I	Dangua	16	16	16	32	32
Married I	Dangua	16	16	16	16	32
Randi I	Dangua	16	18	18	18	16
Dangua	Chadwi	16-25	7	7	7	19-25
Chadwa I	Chadwi I	16-25	7	7	7	19-25
Married I	Chadwi I	16	7	7	7	19-25
Randi I	Chadwi I	16	9	7	9	19-25
Dangua	Randi I	16	9	9	7	19-25
Chadwa I	Randi I	16	9	9	7	19-25
Married I	Randi I	16	9	9	7	19-25
Randi I	Randi I	16	9	9	7	19-25

VIII OWNERS OF BRIDE-PRICE

When the bride-price has been settled, it is taken by the person who performs the wedding. This is either the girl's father, a relative, guardian or a friend. If the girl is not a dangua, the whole price is kept by the person who arranges the marriage but if the girl is a dangua it is divided into four shares. The girl's mother receives five rupees, her mother's mother (or here budhi) two rupees, her father's mother (or bonga budhi) two rupees while the balance is taken by her father. In addition if the girl's father has a co-wife, she is treated as a second mother and an extra share equal to the mother's is realised from the boy's father. Similarly if the girl's mother is dead and her father has married again, he can realise an extra half share for the dead mother as well as the full share for her stepmother. If the girl's mother was divorced before the wedding, she can claim only a half share and the balance is taken by the father himself.

In Ilaki Ledha Hembrom had two wives one of whom was dead. When he married his daughter he took Rs. 16/8/- as bride-price. Out of this sum Rs. 5 was his own share, Rs. 5 the share of the living mother, Rs. 2/8/- the share of the dead mother and Rs. 4 the share of the two grandmothers.

Ram Murmu of Dugubathan had two wives both of whom were living. When he married a daughter by his second wife he took Rs. 19 as bride-price. Each of the mothers got Rs. 5, he himself Rs. 5, the bonga budhi Rs. 2 and as there were two here budhis (grandmothers on the mother's side) Rs. 4 was taken for them.

These shares are due to various reasons. The grandmothers receive shares 'because they looked after the girl when she was little.' The mother has a larger share 'because she fed the girl with her milk'.

Such shares are the absolute property of the mother and grandmothers and although they are often merged in the general family funds they are separate claims. In return for her money however the here budhi must give the boy's party a pot of rice beer, five to twelve seers of khajari and two to four annas.

Originally the woman's shares were paid in cloth and both Campbell and Kolean Haram describe them as if the bride-price were the father's share only. Since the giving of cloth prompted incessant quarrels, the shares are now essential parts of the bride-price of a dangua and are paid in cash.

If the bride is a chadwi or a widow, the mother and the two grandmothers get nothing for 'their dues were paid in the first gonon'.

Similarly if the girl's mother and grandmother (bonga budhi) are dead their shares go to the father. If the here budhi has died, the claim descends to her heirs and in return for receiving her share they must give the customary presents in return. If there is no wedding and the marriage is by or ader, nir bolok', iputut' or apangir, the person who was previously maintaining the girl is entitled to the money. If she was living with one of several brothers, the brother with whom she was living will get the bride-price.

If no one was maintaining her and her father is dead, her father's nearest heir can claim the amount.

Narsing Hembrom of Sahari died leaving a daughter by a co-wife and a son Ragda by a first wife. The co-wife married again and took the daughter to her husband's home. Later she deserted him but the daughter stayed on in his house. Subsequently she went to the tea gardens and there she got married.

Her father's heir was Ragda and it was he who claimed the pon.

In such circumstances when the girl is a dangua and even though there is no wedding the claims of the mother and grandmothers remain and must be honoured by whoever takes the price.

The daughter of Ram Murmu of Dugubathan was married by or ader at Kapasbera. The boy had been divorced and there was no dol wedding. As the boy was a chadwa thirty two rupees was realised as bride-price. Although there was no wedding the two mothers of the girl received five rupees each and her grandmothers two rupees each.

IX RETURN OF THE BRIDE-PRICE

Once a bride-price has been taken the girl becomes her husband's property. But if the contract fails and her husband is not to blame, the bride-price must sometimes be returned. This claim must be met by whichever person received the money and if he is dead his nearest heir must pay it. If the girl was a dangua and shares were given to her mother and grandmothers, the whole sum is payable by the girl's father.

In a similar way, if there are any arrears of bride-price they are chargeable to the heirs of the boy's father and if the person who was originally entitled to the bride-price dies, the claims descend to his heirs.

Dutu Soren of Atgaon married a girl of his village by or ader. When Dutu's father died only goats had been given and Dutu as his father's heir then paid the bride-price.

In Kharbari Ramai Murmu had a son who died leaving a daughter. Ramai himself arranged the marriage of the granddaughter and took the bride-price. Ramai then died and the lands were inherited by his grandson. The granddaughter was then divorced by her husband and it was the grandson who repaid the money.

Ranjit Soren of Bhadra had a son and a daughter. At his daughter's marriage he took the bride-price but some time after his death, the marriage failed and the girl's husband divorced her. The girl's brother then returned the bride-price and also paid chadaodi.

X ENHANCEMENTS

When the basic price has been settled, the father has the option of increasing his own share by making certain gifts in return. This is usually done only in big families for reasons of prestige and Kolean Haram describes the presents as follows. 'If the girl's father takes three rupees, the bridegroom's party get nothing in return. If he takes five rupees the bridegroom gets a cow, a brass bowl, a pichauri and dhoti while his party gets a goat, a pot of rice beer, five pies of rice with salt and turmeric as gonon taraoni. If the father takes seven rupees, the bridegroom gets a cow and calf, a brass bowl, a plate, a pichauri and dhoti and his party get gonon taraoni of a goat, a pot of rice beer and seven pies of rice.'[2]

These return presents are now-a-days decided by local usage and private agreement and there are no longer any principles which are every where the same. In the Raksi area, gonon taraoni is a meal of rice, meat and rice beer given to the members of the boy's party, the exact number who receive it being determined by the number of rupees in the father's share in the bride-price. If the share is three rupees, three members of the boy's party are fed, if nine rupees, nine members, if sixteen rupees, sixteen members and so on.

In addition, presents are made to the bridegroom. For enhancements of two or four rupees, nothing is given but if the father's share is nine rupees as against a normal rate of three he must give the bridegroom a cow while if his share is sixteen rupees he must give a brass plate and bowl in addition to a cow.

In the Pathna area, on the other hand, while gonon taraoni follows similar principles, the minimum presents to the bridegroom are :

For a father's share of Rs. 5 and 7 . . . 1 brass plate
1 brass bowl

For a father's share of Rs. 9	...	1 brass plate 1 brass bowl 1 brass water pot
For a father's share of Rs. 16	...	The same as for Rs. 9, with one calved cow in addition. The exact number of presents is determined when the bride-price is settled.

XI THE SANTAL ATTITUDE TO THE BRIDE-PRICE

What is the tribal reaction to the institution of the bride-price ?

For the boy's father or guardian, it is a drain of household funds which may well exhaust his savings, but, know of no Santal who would like its abolition. 'If no bride-price were paid', said Meghrai Kisku 'there would be no limit to the wives a man would take'. 'It was approved by the ancestors', said Chotu Ramu. Even therefore if the bride-price spells ruin, it is part of Santal usage and has the full aura of an ancient custom.

It is for the girl that the bride-price is full of sinister meaning.

I

For how much did you sell me mother ?
For what did you give me ?
For five rupees, mother, you sold me
For a small bullock you gave me away.

II

The father took thirteen rupees
The mother a silken sari
The brother a bullock like a horse
But your husband

Took you for ever

The mother on the stool
The father on the chair
O you sit at ease
Across the five hills
You are selling me
Stay at your ease.

When I was little, father
The friends liked me
But without mercy
You took my price
Father, you do not like my love.

It is money you like
Sweet as sugar
Is the true honey.

To the girl the bride-price is the loss of her home, the brutal end of all that she has cherished 'the death of her heart'.

REFERENCES

1. P.O. Bodding, *A Santal Dictionary*, II, 467.
2. *Horkoren Mare Hapramko reak' Katha*, 40.

34

THE BROTHER'S DUE
Bare Itat

I DEFINITION

NEXT to the bride-price, the most important transaction at a marriage is the bare itat or brother's due. This is negotiated when the bride-price is fixed and may be either an animal or a sum in cash. 'Cattle is the rule', said Ranjit Hembrom of Kalhajore, 'but if a man is poor or has no cows, he pays in cash'. When cash is paid the sum is known as candla dangra and the rate is determined by local usage. In the northern half of Pakaur and in the Rajmahal Damin, for example, the rate is five rupees, in the Dumka Damin it is two, while in the areas around Narayanpur and Kundahit only one rupee is charged. If the bare itat is in cash, it is payable at the same time as the bride-price.

II THE BASIS OF CLAIMS

The extent to which this conventional present can be claimed is determined by the circumstances of the marriage. If the marriage is in gola eti form, no bare itat is paid since the essence of the contract is the exchange of two boys and girls. Similarly, if the marriage is in ghar jawae or ghardi jawae form no claim arises for the husband's service is in lieu of all such payments. Equally in the marriage of a kirinok' jawae, the purchase of the husband automatically exempts him from the payment of the due. In all other marriages, bare itat may in certain circumstances be claimed and must always be given. If the girl has not been previously married, it is always claimable. If she has been once divorced and her father has repaid the bare itat he can claim it once again. He cannot however claim its payment if the girl has been more than once divorced neither can he demand if he has once received it and has not at any time been forced to give it back. Similarly if the girl has been once widowed and bare itat has never been received, its payment can be claimed at her second marriage but if bare itat has been received or she has been widowed more than once, no claim arises.*

The daughter of Badre Soren of Khutana was divorced by her first husband and the bare itat was returned. At her second marriage in sangha form to Barka Hansdak' of Bhagnadih a bare itat was claimed and taken from him.

Muni Tudu in Dulu was divorced without her husband having paid a brother's bullock. When she was later ituted by a boy of Belpahari he was obliged to give a bare itat in addition to the bride-price.

III THE PROCESS OF RECEIPT

When the wedding is in dol or standard form, and the due is an animal there are two stages in its presentation. The first occurs at the bridegroom's house on the day following the wedding. The bridegroom's father says to the jogmanjhi at dawn—after the gidi cumaura and before bathing. 'Go and see if the bride's people are up.' Then the bridegroom's father, the bride's relations, the bride and the bridegroom, the manjhi of the bridegroom's village and some others go out to the cattle. The bridegroom's father shows a calf, a young cow or a small bullock to the bride's party and says 'This is for you. Keep it in your mind'. The bride's brother or his substitute slaps the animal on its back, does johar to it and then salutes the

*In the Nonihat area, there is a local custom of paying one rupee as bare itat in all cases of Sangha marriage irrespective of whether bare itat has been paid before or the girl has been married more than once while in the Taljhari area, if the girl is a chadwi or a widow and bare itat was taken at her previous marriage and was not returned a half bare itat can be demanded.

village manjhi and other villagers. All sit down and the manjhi says to the bride's relations 'In olden days they said that the bullock given to the bride's elder brother could only be yoked from the top of an ant hill but we can only give you this. May this be all that offends you.' The bride's party reply, 'Those who would have been offended have gone before to the Samae valley to tend the crocodiles in the small sand'. The manjhi then says, 'Our responsibility is at end. If it is lost, if it strays, if it wanders away and comes to any grief or harm you will be the loser. Take it with you'. The bride's brother then replies, 'No, keep it for me. Let it stay here for a while and if anything happens to it show me the horns and skull. If you do not show the horns and skull we shall say it is still alive'. After that both sides salute each other and go down to the water for the bathing ceremony.*

In certain cases the boy's father 'shows a cow' in proxy for a calf—the contract being to give whatever calf is next born to it. If the cow bears two calves, only one can be claimed and as between male and female calves, only the he calf is given. Should the cow die before calving, the boy's father must buy a calf in its place. If, however, a calf is born and dies before it is claimed the ordinary rules apply. Occasionally, the shown cow may not belong to the girl's father and in that case the 'showing' amounts to a contract to buy a calf.

When the brother of Ranjit Hembrom of Kalhajore married his son he had no cattle of his own and 'showed a cow' of Ranjit's. In this case 'showing a cow' was a promise to procure a calf and a year later he bought a calf for twenty rupees and made it over.

In certain cases 'showing' is even dispensed with and the boy's father says 'There is a bullock at the grazing ground'. This means that he does not wish to pay cash but as he has no animal at present, he will give one later. As soon as an animal is procured he shows it to the girl's family and this is taken as the brother's due. If there is delay in getting an animal, the girl's family can demand whatever price the two villages consider reasonable.

*In the case of marriage in or ader, nir bolok', apangir and kundal napam, the bare itat is shown when the bride-price is paid.

After the showing of the gift, the second stage is when the animal is actually received by the bride's family. It was formerly the custom for the girl's brother to wait until the Sohrae festival following the wedding. He would then go the bridegroom's house to bring his sister to their home for the festival and at that time he would take charge of the animal. This, however, was never more than a rule of convenience and once the animal has been shown the bride's family can claim it immediately or at any later time. It is usual for a few days to elapse, since the girl's brother is preoccupied with the wedding and does not have the time to bring the animal to his village. Moreover, the calf is sometimes very young and cannot be separated from its mother. For this reason there is almost always some delay between the showing of the animal and its actual delivery.

IV THE OBJECT OF THE BARE ITAT

As it name implies, bare itat is 'the brother's present' and if the bride has brothers it is always one of them who is shown the animal and who is sent finally to bring it. Santal sentiment consider that the girl's brother needs some consolation for his loss. 'It is a sort of bakshish' said Sagram Hembrom 'to comfort him and ease his mind'. Moreover, the girl may have received various kindnesses when she was small and in the myth which sanctions bare itat and accounts for its origin it is the protecting role of the brother which is stressed. 'A certain Santal had mislaid his plough share in his loin cloth. He searched every where but could not find it and when he was tired of looking he said 'Whoever finds my plough share may have my daughters'. Many tried but none found it. At last a tiger took up the quest. The man agreed to give his daughter and the tiger told him that the plough share was in his loin cloth. The man did as he had said and one day sent his daughter alone to the spring for water. The girl's younger brother said that he would go with her also and taking only a toy bow and arrow they went along together. The tiger was lurking behind an ant hill and when the boy saw it he stopped his sister. Then with his toy arrow he shot the tiger in the eye and killed it. Then his sister promised that when she would marry he would get a bullock as bare itat'. And since then whenever a sister marries, her brothers are given this present.

V OWNERSHIP

If however it is the brother who receives the bullock it is against the background of the whole family that the gift is made. The bare itat is given not to the girl's eldest brother but to all her brothers jointly. If they are separate the animal is sold and its price divided among them. If they are still joint the animal becomes part of the family cattle. Like other earnings of sons it becomes the property of their father and it is thus the family rather than the brothers who receive it. The brothers are, as it were, only the agents for receiving the animal and it is the head of the family who is the ultimate claimant. For this reason, if the bullock is withheld, it is the father as much as the brothers who can sue for its recovery. Similarly, the fact that a girl may have no brother in no way affects the liability of the bridegroom's father to pay bare itat. In the absence of a brother the girl's father will receive it.

The same principles apply when the marriage is performed by some one who is not himself the father. In such cases, the person performing the marriage acts as a father and his son is entitled to receive the present. If he has no son, the person who performs the marriage will himself take the present. When a stepfather arranges the marriage of a stepdaughter, her own brother being only a stepson can not claim the brother's present and it will go either to the stepfather's son or failing him to the stepfather himself.

Barka Murmu of Kalyan had one daughter and no sons. So when he married her to Harma Kisku of Amarpur he himself received the brother's bullock.

In Dulu, Sufal Murmu performed the marriage of his sister's daughter. The girl had agnates on her father's side but as her mother's brother met the expenses, he also was given the brother's present.

Similarly when Salkhu Murmu of Dalabar performed the marriage of his stepdaughter, his eldest son received the brother's due.

VI CLAIMS AND COUNTER-CLAIMS

After the animal has been shown, it stays at the bridegroom's house for some time and there are four situations which may then develop and give rise to claims.

In the first place, if the period is several months or more and the animal is a young cow it may itself calve and in that case there will no longer be one animal but more than one. In such cases the girl's family is entitled to both the original animal as well as to its increase and if the original animal dies after having had a calf, that calf will go to them.

Dukhia Murmu of Amtala married his son at Katikund and a young cow was shown. It grew and calved twice and three years after the marriage the cow with its two calves were taken to Dukhia's house as bare itat.

In the second place, before the girl's family have taken charge of it the animal may die. In such cases, the girl's family can not claim its replacement 'for it was at their own risk that they left it with them'. It is imperative, however, that the bridegroom's family should send then at least the skull and horns as proof that it has died, and either immediately or a little later, the hide as well. If they do not do so the girl's family can claim that the animal is still alive and can demand its current price. It is also a standard convention that in case the animal dies, one-third of its flesh should be sent to the girl's family though if this is not done no compensation can be claimed.

The manjhi of Kusumba had in his house the bare itat bullock which was due from the wedding of his nephew's wife. One night the animal along with another strayed out of the cowshed and both were killed by a leopard. The next morning he told the relatives of his nephew's wife about the kill and sent them the hide and the horns. Under village custom two-thirds of any animal killed by a leopard is shared by the village while one-third is eaten by the owner. Since the bare itat was being held in trust, one-third of the meat was, therefore, sent to the girl's family. With the sending of the hide and horns the matter ended. But if he had not done this, the girl's family would have claimed a new bullock from him.

Thirdly, cases may occur in which for some reason the boy's family withholds the animal and declines to give it when claimed.

The most common circumstance is when the girl's father has taken a loan of bor horo and has not repaid it. In such circumstances the boy's family is entitled to defer the grant of the bullock until the paddy is given back and if the paddy is never returned all claim to the animal lapses.

Bhogna Besra of Rajbali borrowed one maund of paddy as bor horo when he married his daughter to the son of Poto Murmu of Sitna. He repaid it after six years and only then did the boy's family give the brother's bullock.

In Karanpura Soban Kisku borrowed bor horo at the time of marrying his niece. He sent his nephew to claim the brother's bullock but the boy's father declined to give it saying he must first have back his loan. Soban then repaid the paddy and only after he had done so was he given the bullock.

A second common circumstance is when the bride herself is continually leaving her husband's house and remaining at her father's. In such cases, the boy's family can claim that unless the girl settles permanently in their house they will not give the present. If a deadlock is reached, the matter is taken to a meeting of the two villages and if the girl goes back to the boy the animal is given without further objection. If, however, the girl obstinately refuses to live with her husband the claim for the brother's bullock lapses.

The daughter of Dhiba Baske of Bhognadih was married as a child to the son of Somae Tudu of Kalyan. When she grew up she did not live with her husband, so when her brothers went to demand the bullock, Somae said that they must first give over their sister. In the end the girl was taken to the house and Somae gave the bullock.

Guda Baske of Gahanda also withheld the brother's animal on the ground that his son's wife was not remaining but after she had settled permanently in his house, he cleared the due without objection.

A different version of the same situation is when the boy's family withhold the present and the girl's family suspect that they are doing so in bad faith. The girl may then be withheld and not sent to the boy's house until the animal is made over.

In such cases, the claim is not forfeited since the fault is with the boy's family.

The daughter of Dhanai Hansdak' of Rakso was married by or ader in Mahadeo. Her husband promised a cow as brother's present but when after a year the man had still not given it, Dhanai detained his daughter at his house. After that a cow was brought and then he allowed her to return.

In other cases, the question of the girl not living with her husband may not arise and yet the boy's family may withhold the animal. When this happens the girl's family will formally demand the due in the presence of the manjhi or villagers of the boy's village and if on the intervention of the villagers the animal is still withheld the family will then sue for its return. If the animal was asked for but withheld and it then dies the market value at death can be claimed. If the animal and its off-spring are still alive at the time of the suit the girl's family may claim either the actual animals or their current market price. Similarly if the animal has been sold, the girl's father claim the actual sale price or the current market value at the time of the demand.

Dhawa Murmu of Dalahi was married in Karanpura. At the wedding 'he showed a cow' undertaking by this that he would give as bare itat the calf if it calved or would buy a calf in its place. He neither gave a calf nor bought one so the girl's family took her back. The matter went to the village meeting and the two were ultimately divorced. At the settlement the meeting ordered Dhawa to pay the girl divorce money as well as the price of a calf. He paid the divorce money but put off paying the price of the calf. Then as the girl's family did not press the matter it finally dropped. In this case, although the price was not realised the claim of the girl's family was fully acknowledged by the village.

Finally cases may occur in which the girl's brother or the relative who bears the marriage expenses dies before the present has been claimed. In such circumstances, the claim devolves on the nearest heir and the liability of the boy's family is not affected by the death. Similarly if there are two or more brothers and one dies the brother's present will be shared by the surviving brothers and his dead brother's heir.

Kalka Tudu of Kalipathar married his daughter to the son

of Mangal Murmu of Bhalko. Mangal promised a bullock as bare itat but for ten years he failed to buy one. Then Kalka and his only son died and although the promise was ten years old, Mangal gave a bullock to Kalka's two minor grandsons.

In a similar way the death of the boy's father or of whichever relative performed the marriage in no way affects the obligation to make the payment. The liability descends to the heir and the bare itat can be validly claimed from him.

Lakhan Murmu of Komo married the daughter of Pitho Hansdak' of Goradih. A bullock was shown but before it could be claimed, first Lakhan's father and then his mother died. Lakhan inherited his father's lands and movables and himself gave the bullock.

Finally the death of the girl herself in no way invalidates the contract. Once she is duly married, the brother's present is payable and it is immaterial whether the girl lives or dies.

Dhanu Hembrom of Kukurkatha performed the marriage of his sister's daughter. After two years the girl died and two weeks later he claimed and took the brother's bullock.

VII THE RETURN OF BARE ITAT

When bare itat is claimed and given, the occasion of the gift is the transfer of the girl from one family to another. So long as she is with her husband, her brother is entitled to retain this due. If, however, she is divorced in circumstances which render necessary the return of the bride-price, the bare itat must also be surrendered. Where the brother's due was an animal, the animal itself must be returned and if it has died or been sold its equivalent in the form of a new animal must be purchased and given in its place. All increase from the animal however remains with the brother and since one animal was received only one animal is given back. If the bare itat was given in cash the money itself is returned.

35

DIVORCE

I GROUNDS FOR DIVORCE

WHEN a Santal boy and girl are married in dol form, the manjhis of the two villages deliver farewell addresses. 'Sitting with Sin Bonga, Maran Buru and the spirits of the five hills', they say 'we have joined the chain and the ring. The bridegroom has won the family of the bride. The bride has gained the house of the bridegroom. The houses are now one'. In spite of these farewell sermons, however, by no means every Santal marriage is successful and at weddings I have often been struck by the large number of adult girls who were no longer married but divorced. Accurate figures are naturally difficult to get and without a number of random samples, figures would not be of great value. My impression, however, which is based on many talks with Santals is that not less than one first marriage in seven ends in divorce and that at least two wives in ten have had previous husbands before settling finally into life-long marriage. On the other hand the proportion of second divorces is extremely low and if a first marriage is prone to break, it is the experience of marriage and divorce which often promotes stable domestic life.

This position need occasion neither surprise nor censure. It is rather an index to Santal commonsense and the tribe's realistic view of domestic relations. For once a marriage has broken down, the effort of the tribe is to adjust the situation and no Santal would willingly condemn the two partners to a lifetime of misery. The main ground for divorce is in essence the unwillingness of one party to go on living with the other. This unwillingness may be promoted by many different causes and may sometimes be dissolved by village discussion. None the less if one side no longer wishes to stay with the other, it is this which clinches the matter. So long as a woman is of an age at which she can remarry, divorce can be imposed even against her will. If she is past the age for taking a fresh husband, does not want to end her marriage and is not herself at fault, divorce will not be sanctioned but her husband can make her live separately after giving her a house and lands. If a woman declines to live with her husband and demands divorce, it can be granted to her at any age.

II FACTORS LEADING TO DIVORCE

Among the causes of divorce there are six factors which bulk largest. The first is the existence of previous lovers, and this is by far the most potent cause in the break down of first marriages. After that, infidelity, sickness, domestic friction, sexual maladjustment, witchcraft and breach of taboos all play their part. Only one of these is sufficient to drive a wife and husband apart but sometimes two or more combine and the divorce is due less to one factor than to the impact of a whole situation.

III PRE-MARITAL LOVERS

In the first few years of marriage it is the existence of previous lovers which is the source of greatest danger. Usually Santal parents consult the boy or girl before arranging a marriage and if the boy or girl oppose the wedding, they do not often go on with it. But tribal convention favours marriage out of the village and if a girl has a village boy, any marriage that her parents settle must abruptly end this love.

I

You reared me like a pet parrot
You petted me like a tame pigeon
Father when did you give your word ?
From my friend's love you parted me.

II

Girl, your time has come
You must go
To your husband
Break the rope
Of your friend's love
Say good bye
To your friend.

In many cases, the boy and girl realize that their love can only last till marriage and that in choosing their final juris their parents' wisdom must prevail. But in others the stress is too great.

O my love do not weep
Do not mourn
I will come and go
And share your love.

Even when the wedding has gone through, the boy and girl may be quite unable to give up their village lovers.

In a litter, in a palki father
You brought me a wife
But though you brought her
I will not leave
My village lover.
O daughter-in-law
You whom we have brought
Why are you weeping ?
Your son goes still
To his village lover.

Similarly if a girl has a boy in her village she often leaves her husband's house and goes rushing home. 'If', said Dhunu Hembrom, the boy says 'Even though you are married, I will not leave you', the girl cannot stay. She has to leave her husband. It is only when she gets a child that the link is tight. It is then that they settle.*

Dasma Tudu of Haruadangal was in love with a village girl but his parents married him to a girl of Beda Chapar. They brought the girl but he would not sleep with her. He went on going with the village girl and would not leave her. In a year the village girl was pregnant. Then the parents of his wife came and took her away and the boy paid five rupees and a cloth. After that Dasma brought the village girl to his house and took her as his wife.

A boy of Jilwa was married to Sukhi Soren of Kalhajore. But he would not keep her and kept sending her back. He also had a girl of Jilwa and could not give her up. In the end, the girl's parents agreed to a divorce and the marriage ended.

In Jitpur Bhago Soren was married in Tilabad, but she too had a lover in her village and kept returning. She stayed a month with her parents and then she forced herself into her lover's house.

In Elajpahari Kebol Soren was only a small boy when his parents married him. His wife kept staying in her village as a boy was her lover. Kebol took her for a few days but she always went back. When Kebol saw that she did not want him, he decided to take another wife and divorced her.

*The importance of children for stabilising a marriage is also recognised by Lepchas. 'The preliminary years are passed in the married couple getting accustomed to one another and setting up the pattern of mutual rights and duties on which Lepcha affection is founded. It is extremely uncommon and is considered very disreputable for a husband and wife who have children to separate, or even to show marked preference for anybody other than their own spouse. Such behaviour is stigmatised as shameless. At the wife's first pregnancy the young couple acquire greater importance and responsibility and the second half of the pregnancy is, as has been described, a period of great care and watchfulness for both parties. With the birth of the child the couple become more important; now they are really part of the village and are carrying on the family line, and as a sign of this their names are changed and also their mode of address to their nearer kinsmen'. (Gorer : op. cit., 341).

IV LOVERS AFTER MARRIAGE

If a previous lover is the main factor in unsettling marriages a later lover is sometimes also a disintegrating factor.

A girl of Chota Durgapur was married in Sitapahar. One day Chitu Murmu of Jambar was caught with her in a dried-up stream. The girl's brother who was out with some other boys saw them and took them to the manjhi. The village met and the girl's husband divorced her. Chitu kept the girl and paid a double bride-price.

In cases such as this the wife goes from one man to another. Her infidelity snaps her marriage but her lover gives her a fresh married status.

If a husband is unfaithful, the wife herself may divorce him and the taking of a co-wife sometimes has the same result.

Maina Soren of Chota Durgapur left her husband because he took a co-wife. She herself had not given him a son and his object was to get one through another. Maina did not like it and left him.

V SICKNESS

Much more important than infidelity, however, is the illness of husband or wife.

When a wife is always falling ill or the family itself is always sick, the cause may seem to lie in the marriage itself. In Bandubera a boy divorced his wife. 'She was never coming to me', he said, 'because when she came, she always got ill.' In Kendpahari, Make Hembrom was divorced because all her children died.

In Bankati Rasika Marandi had married a girl of Ranidinda. She lived with him for three years but as there were many deaths in the house, she at last went home. She refused to go back saying 'If I go, I shall die.' Her husband claimed return of bride-price and the girl's father paid it.

In this case, there were also other factors. One night when her father-in-law was drunk, and was taking her home from Ranidinda he caught hold of her and spoke to her by name. This breach of taboo greatly offended the girl but it was ultimately the fear that she would die that made her break her marriage.

While I was camping at Ranga in 1944, a case which was semi-psychological came before me.

In Ghatiari Chambra Soren married the elder daughter of Bhucun Hembrom of his village. In 1943, she died and he took her younger sister, Sona as his second wife. He paid Rs. 22 as bride-price but postponed paying one rupee and the bride's present. He got a child by Sona but it died. Sona used to dream and three times during her dreams she bed-wetted. Chambra then took her to her mother and married a girl from Katara. Sona who was a fair good-looking girl asked for a divorce claiming divorce money while her father demanded the balance of the bride-price and five rupees as brother's present. Chambru paid these up during the camp and divorce took place. A day later there was a wedding in the village and Sona was dancing with the village women with complete non-chalance as if nothing had ever happened.

In another case of sickness, Demda Murmu of Sibnagar had met Saura Hembrom for the first time in 1942 at a hook swinging at Ghager. They at once fell in love, he took her home and they were very happy. It was settled he would pay twenty three rupees but he only paid sixteen. She became pregnant, was ill and could not work. Then her mother-in-law began to grouse at her. She gave birth to a boy but her parents-in-law did not pay for the birth ceremony. When she got back her strength they took her back. At the Kalipuja time she again fell ill. Owing to fever and not getting medi-cines her milk stopped and she had to go home again. They did not let her take the child. She got well but all the time she was ill none of them came to see her. As no one had come, her brother then sent the jogmanjhi to find out whether they were taking her or leaving her. The parents-in-law replied 'We are neither leaving her nor bringing her, let her stay as she is.' The girl had no parents but only an elder brother. She brought the matter to a meeting and was given a divorce. Saura paid the divorce money and arrears of bride-price but although the other claims were due he did not meet them and they lapsed.

Such cases of sickness are important not only because of

the disablement but because they frequently point to malevolence by bongas, and in a case from Kalhajore a bonga lover was the main cause of the divorce. Jhunu Soren had married a Marandi girl of Nawadih. On the day of the wedding both the boy and girl were ill with fever. The wedding went on and they were married with fever on them. The boy brought the girl home but the fever did not abate. She went to her father's house from time to time and once when the boy had gone to fetch her and they were washing at a stream, the girl said, 'Do not keep coming for me or one of us will die.' Sometime later, they were visited by a bonga. They heard a stick beating on the floor of their room. They woke and saw nothing. Again the fever came. This time both the boy and girl were so ill that they lost consciousness. The boy's father called the girl's parents and a jan guru was consulted in the presence of the village. Divination was done and it came out that the girl had a bonga lover. The boy's father said, 'she must not stay here any longer.' The girl's father sacrificed a ram and after this the boy and girl recovered. A meeting was held. The boy's father said, 'He must pay me back the bride-price. If he wants the money let the bonga pay him.' The money was returned and the two were divorced. Since then the boy has re-married but no one has dared to take the girl.

VI DOMESTIC FRICTION

If illness is a common cause, domestic friction in all its many phases is often responsible for later separations. Such friction may have its roots in bad house-keeping by the wife, or in petty pilfering, or extravagance. Above all the clash of incompatible temperaments may reduce a household to nagging misery.

In the folk tale, *The Divorce*, a Santal had reason to suspect his wife's faithfulness. He did not however wish to make this a cause of action but tried to discover another ground.

"Time passed and one day her mother went to visit the troublesome wife. As she was leaving her daughter asked whether there was any special reason for her coming. Her mother admitted that she had come hoping to borrow a little oil to rub on the cattle at the coming Sohrae festival but as her son-in-law was not there she did not like to mention it and would not like to take any without his consent. 'O never mind him !' said the woman and insisted on her mother taking away a pot not of cheap mahua or mustard oil but of ghee."

'Now a little girl saw her do this and the tale was soon all over the village; but the undutiful wife never said a word about it to her husband, and it was only after some days that he heard from others of his wife's extravagance. When it did reach his ears he seized the opportunity and at once drove her out of the house, and when a panchayat was called he insisted on divorcing her for wasting his substance behind his back. No one could deny that the reason was a good one and so the panchayat had to allow the divorce.'[1]

VII SEXUAL MALADJUSTMENT

Another cause, though this is much less common, is sexual maladjustment.

Samu Hembrom of Masanjore was married to Bale Murmu, the daughter of the manjhi of Sundipalán. Bale was a large girl and the same age as Samu. Samu said she was too big and at last by mutual consent they separated.

In Chirapathar a girl complained of her husband. 'He sleeps with me only like a brother or sister. He is listless. He has no penis. What use is he ?'

In Dhawa, Nunulal Baske was taken to Nawadih as a ghar jawae. He lived for two years in the house but always avoided going to his wife. At last the girl lost patience and forced her father to take it to the village. In the meeting the elders said to her 'Why do you not want him?' 'Because he never talks to me day or night. He never fills my mind. He has not got any penis. He is not a boy'. When Nunulal heard this he was very angry but as the girl no longer wanted him, a divorce was agreed to and Nunulal was sent home with three rupees like a girl.

In this case there was obviously some inhibition, possibly arising from the status of a ghar jawae, which made the boy impotent.

In Raksibandh Mondol Soren was married to a girl of Bindin. The girl stayed with him three months but the boy could not 'fill her mind'. So her father repaid the bride-price and took the girl away.

Such instances are very rare and although cases of impotence occur, from time to time, they are usually not permanent and do not always cause divorce.

VIII BREACHES OF TABOOS

In all phases of Santal life taboo plays an important part and while breaches of its rules are distinctly uncommon their very rarity often lends them a swollen horror. Moreover the breach of taboo may flog the bongas into a fury of spite and if a wife's action threatens the welfare of the house or village, there is often no alternative but to divorce her.

In Surjudih Lubia Soren's wife kept her menstruation rags in the grain bin. Lubia to his great horror found them there one day and at once moved the village to approve a divorce. If he had not done so, he believed that all his wealth would have gone.

In Kulaipura Barka Soren found his wife had eaten uncooked rice. Uncooked rice is offered to the bongas and if a Santal eats it, he pollutes a thing reserved for bongas only. The pollution enrages the spirits and they rain illness on the village. Barka Soren was appalled at what his wife had done and at once divorced her.

IX WITCHCRAFT

A last circumstance which is of overwhelming importance and makes divorce virtually automatic is the discovery that a wife is a witch. This strikes at the roots of all security and so long as the witch remains, family relations are tainted with a sense of impending disaster. The dread of witches is so great that once a husband is convinced of his wife's guilt, he returns her to her family without any more ado.

X DIVORCE BY SONS

In all these cases, divorce is either of a wife by her husband or a husband by a wife. The dread of witchcraft, however, goes so deep that when witchcraft is in issue, the sons themselves can divorce their mother.

In Murbhanga there was a bout of sickness and a number of children died. The villagers consulted a jan guru who detected an old woman of Mohonpur. She was a widow and had grown-up sons. After she had been detected some village girls made a full confession. They told the villagers 'When a child was ill we took out its lungs and cooked them under a sal tree. There was a spring with bongas. The old woman used to call the bongas and give them pieces of cooked lung. We ate the rest and fixed a date when the child would die. On that day, the child died. The old woman had brooms round her waist. She sang in the jungle. We heard her songs and could never forget them. We took off our clothes and danced the lagre with her. We ate five persons.' The girls then showed the villagers the actual sal tree with a heart under it where the old woman cooked the lungs. When the villagers heard this, they decided to expel her from the village. Her sons drove her from their house and sent her to her brothers. When I was told about this case in 1944 she was still in her own village of Mohonpur but living in lonely isolation.

XI DIVORCE BY PARENTS

Moreover, on occasion the parents can themselves take the initiative and cause the divorce of their children. Indeed if the parents insist on divorce, it is very difficult for the boy and girl to withstand them and even though the boy and girl may be unwilling, the parents can prevail.

In a case which I describe below, Chita Hansdak' of Churibad was married to Somae Marandi of Lakardamani. Their parents quarrelled and it was the boy's father who divorced the girl.

The daughter of Ludhia Murmu of Piplatanr was married to the son of Bonra Marandi of Lakhanpur. While drinking rice beer the two fathers quarrelled and in his anger Ludhia took his daughter to his house. The girl had already got two children but the two fathers were so angry that they insisted on a complete severance of relations. The boy and girl implored the village meeting not to part them but the two parents insisted and Bonra paid divorce money of twelve rupees and the two were separated.

In Moralai Ano Hembrom had married a girl of Salpatra. Sometime after the wedding the girl became pregnant and went to her father's house. Meanwhile the boy's mother died and the father did not invite the girl's parents to the final funerary feast. This led to a rupture of relations and the girl's parents refused to send the girl any more to the boy's house. The quarrel was not mended and in the end at the instance of the parents the boy and the girl were divorced.

XII THE RITUAL OF DIVORCE

When a divorce is mooted, the matter is reported to the manjhi and the husband and wife with their kinsmen attend a village meeting. The matter is talked over, the responsibilities are fixed and if a divorce is approved, one of two procedures is followed.

If the wife is not a witch and the man has given her *sindur* either in a dol, tunki dipil, ghar jawae, ghardi jawae, or golaeti bapla, tearing of leaves or sakam orec' is done. This is described by Kolean Haram as follows: 'The villagers meet together, led by the manjhis of the two villages concerned. A *lota* with water is placed on the ground, and husband and wife are made to stand facing one another, one on each side of the *lota*, the man facing the east'. The headman of the husband's village then exhorts the man as follows : 'By the grace of Sing Bonga, the five mountain spirits and the ancestors, we, the people took omens from the uric' bird on the right side and the ere bird on the left and tied you together and joined you together with marriage chains like the lar and the bando climbers. We did not join you together for one day, but for ever and aye, like stone and rock, till you become hoary and mossgrown. Now it is no fault of ours, but if you cannot be united, what can we the people do? Now, therefore, both of you think well and reflect carefully in your hearts; otherwise you may at some future days say that the people made you separate. You, if you really want to renounce her, call on Sing Bonga, the five mountain spirits, and the ancestors, and tear the leaves, or else tear them not.'

'The man is then made to stand on his left leg facing the sun and with his hands in a supplicant posture. Thereupon they give him three sal leaves. He takes them, and with his cloth twisted round his neck, salutes Sing Bonga and tears the leaves with a jerk. Then the turns round and kicks the *lota* over with his right foot, and renounces any further connection with the woman. The man salutes all those present, commencing with the manjhi; the woman does the same. If the leaves are not torn straight, there is an idea that the pair will come together again. If all the water in the *lota* is not spilt, the idea is the same. It is thought that there is probably still some love left. In any case, in spite of their being divorced in this world, they will meet again in the world to come.'[2]

In a divorce at Ranga at which I assisted in June 1944, the procedure was almost identically the same but there were minor variations.

Surai Murmu of Chota Ranga had married Sumi Hansdak' of Mahagama in 1939. The villages are about two miles apart. Sumi lived with him for two years. Then she became pregnant. Surai's father, Suphal Murmu, thought that she had got the child enec' halante by 'gathering it at a dance' and not from his son. He began to ill-treat her. Sumi had the child but it died in Suphal's house. She went back to her parents. Surai did not fetch her. Then a year later Suphal brought another girl for his son. Sumi tried to get it settled by the two villages but Suphal never went to the meeting. Finally she complained in camp and I sent the matter to the pargana. The pargana awarded her seven rupees as divorce money and her father five rupees for the brother's present. A day later sakam orec' was performed.

First Suphal paid five rupees to Sumi's father who dobok' johared all present. Then he put seven rupees in Sumi's hands. After this, Sumi's father paid one rupee to the villagers as deke chedi 'for unstiffening their buttocks' and Suphal, somewhat grudgingly, did the same. Suphal and Sumi now faced each other. Each took a single mango leaf and tore it down the middle vein. The manjhi said to them 'Before the village five you have both torn the leaves. From today you are apart. If you meet at a chata or a pata and are caught together, you will have to pay another bride-price'. After this, the two johared and went away.

This ceremony differed from the standard ritual in three respects. Mango and not sal leaves were used. Only one leaf was torn and not three. There was no *lota* and it was not kicked over. But the essence of the ceremony—the tearing of leaves—was done and it was this that solemnized the divorce.[3]

In other areas there are similar minor variations and I have known cases in which jamun leaves were used instead of either sal or mango.

If the marriage has been in any other form, or *sindur* has been given by baha saoha—not in the basket but on a flower—the leaves are not torn and the parties meet before the villagers, settle outstanding claims, pronounce the divorce and go away.

If, however the marriage is by or ader, kundal napam, nir bolok' or apangir and neither *sindur* has been given nor a bride-price paid a meeting is unnecessary. If the girl foregoes her claims, she can simply leave her husband and marry again. But if she presses her claims, a village meeting is necessary and the husband must be heard.

When claims arise or if *Sindur* has been given, the appearance of both the parties is necessary and cases have been known to drag on for months merely because a party, usually the husband, evades attendance at the meeting. Here the Santal view is that unless both sides are heard, and unless each tears the leaves, or confirms the separation the union cannot easily be ended.

In such cases if the husband does not come and village persuasion fails the girl usually comes to Court and if the husband still does not put in an appearance, the claims are decided ex-parte and the girl is deemed to be divorced by the court's order.

There is one last case. If the wife is adjudged a witch there is no tearing of leaves—even though she has been married with *sindur*. She is merely taken by villagers and her husband or sons and made over to her father or brothers. Nothing is claimed and nothing is paid.

XIII THE CLAIMS OF THE HUSBAND

The double bride-price and the expenses of the wedding

Once a divorce is settled certain dues become admissible and I will first describe the claims of the husband.

The maximum amount which a husband can claim is double the bride-price and the expenses of the wedding. This claim is conceded in the greater part of the District* but is admissible in only one circumstance—when the marriage is of short duration, the wife has either not lived with her husband or lived with him scarcely at all and has then either gone off with another man or been caught in intercourse with him. In such circumstances, the adulterer is a thief, and since her husband has derived little or nothing from his outlay he is entitled both to a double bride-price and the cost of the wedding. This claim must be met not by the girl's father but by the adulterer. When it has been paid, the 'thief' can take the girl with him but if she does not stay, he must still pay the claim.

A boy of Daldali was married to Gansa Soren's daughter. Shortly after their marriage she met Gopal Hansdak' of Gamra and on hatia days she used to lag behind her husband and lose herself in the jungle. One day Gopal met her at the hook-swinging field in Kalhajore and late in the night the villagers caught them in an act of intercourse. The two were tied together and taken to the manjhi. In the meeting Gopal paid eighty rupees to the girl's husband. Of this twenty four rupees was a double bride-price and the rest were the expenses of the wedding.

In Kusumba Jitan Kisku was married to a girl of Talbaria During the months following their wedding he took her to his house several times but on each occasion she ran home as she already had a lover in Talbaria. One night her guardian caught the girl with her lover and took them to the manjhi. Her

*In the Godda subdivision and the Nonihat area of Dumka, such awards have not as yet been made and only a double bride-price has so far been allowed in such circumstances.

husband claimed double the bride-price and the marriage expenses and the lover paid sixty rupees.

The double bride-price

A similar but reduced claim by the husband arises from adultery of a wife but in slightly different circumstances. In this case, the wife either goes to another man or is caught in intercourse with him. Her marriage, however, is not recent and she has lived for sometime with her husband. As the marriage is not recent, it is held to have been sufficiently consummated. The husband has received an adequate return for the cost of the wedding. No marriage expenses can, therefore, be claimed and the adulterer must pay a double bride-price only.

Maika Marandi of Sundarpahari was married to Sham Murmu of Rajbandh. She lived with him for some years and then fell in love with Musin Besra and began to live in his house. Sham Murmu had paid a bride-price of twenty rupees and eight annas and when he brought a suit the arbitrators decreed it for forty one rupees.

In Amoi Lusi Marandi was married to Lapsa Tudu of Pagrodih. After she had born him two sons she eloped with Nunku Hembrom, the Sardar of Mihijam, Nunku paid her first husband a double bride-price but as the marriage was some years standing the expenses of the wedding were neither claimed nor paid.

When the double price has been paid the girl is free to live with the adulterer as his wife. If, however, she changes her mind he cannot compel her to live with him. Neither can he claim from her first husband or her father a refund of the money.

Jiban Marandi of Majdiha was married for some years to his wife and then went to the First World War. He came home in 1918 and rice beer was being brewed in his house. His wife went out saying she would get some water but actually she met her lover Chendu Tudu and went to the forest with him. When she was late in coming her husband and other villagers went to look for her and surprised her with her lover in the jungle. The original bride-price was twenty-two rupees and eight annas and it was decided that Chendu must pay her husband forty-five rupees. He paid it and took the girl to his house. She stayed with him for three days and then went back to her parents. Chendu asked her first husband to repay him the money but he said, 'I gave you the girl. What have you done with her ?' Chendu then demanded it from the girl's father but her father said, 'I do not know how you got her.' Neither claim could be pressed and Chendu got nothing.

In another case, Manjhi Tudu of Patobandh brought a married girl to his house by or ader. The girl was of the same village but her husband lived at Karandih. At the village meeting Manjhi Tudu paid a double bride-price and was permitted to keep the girl as his wife. The same night when the meeting was over and the money had been paid the girl told Manjhi that she was going to her parents' house and would come and see him later. After leaving him she did not return and although the villagers asked the girl's father to return the girl to her second husband, he did not do so and the girl remained in his house. In this case also, all the money had been taken by the girl's first husband and no refund was possible.

If after paying a double bride-price, the adulterer loses his wife to another man, he can in turn claim from the second adulterer a sum double the bride-price which he himself has given.

Ram Marandi of Barisjora married a chadwi girl of his village and paid a bride-price of seven rupees and eight annas. The girl then eloped with Munshi Murmu who paid her husband a double bride-price of fifteen rupees. Sometime later the girl left Munshi and went with Bisu Tudu. The second adulterer then paid thirty rupees to the first as a double 'double bride-price'.

In Maithani the wife of Dugru Marandi deserted him in favour of Bhado Murmu. Bhado took her as his wife and paid her first husband twenty-four rupees. After six months the girl returned to Dugru and he then paid the adulterer forty eight rupees.

In yet another case from Atgaon the wife of Thota Murmu went off with another Santal who paid him a double bride-price of sixty rupees. She left the first adulterer for a second who purchased his rights for one hundred and twenty rupees. Finally Thota himself re-seduced her but in order to secure her as his wife he was forced to pay the second adulterer two hundred and forty rupees.

This rule by which a double bride-price is paid by the adulterer is departed from in only one circumstance—when the second marriage has been actually arranged or actively abetted by the girl's father or guardian. In such cases, the father or guardian is required to meet the claim and the second husband is not responsible.

Matla Murmu of Kalipathar married a girl of Ghat Parolia. The girl did not stay with him and although he brought her many times she regularly returned to the brother's house. After one year her brother gave her in ghar jawae marriage to a Santal of Babupur. Matla then claimed a double bride-price and since her marriage had been arranged by her brother, a double bride-price of fifteen rupees was paid by him.

When a double bride-price is claimable it is necessary that the form of marriage should be such that a bride-price could be paid. In all ghar jawae or ghardi jawae marriages no such claim can be made. Similarly in a kirinok' bapla the bought husband has no remedy. He can send his wife away but cannot get money from the 'the thief'.

Equally in a golaeti marriage a double bride-price cannot normally be demanded. A brother is exchanged for a sister and no bride-prices are paid. In such marriages adultery is very rare but if it occurs the remedy is sometimes a double divorce, the sister being brought back while the wife is sent away. If the sister does not wish to lose her first huband a bride-price is assessed and the husband is indemnified with a double bride-price from the adulterer. This arrangement, however, is discretionary with the parents and if one or other side does not agree the only solution is the separation of both the parties.

Mathura Tudu and his sister of Daldali were married in golaeti form to the daughter and son of Lakhan Marandi of Sinduri. Sometimes later, Mathura's sister eloped with another boy of Daldali and the two villages proposed the payment of a double bride-price to Lakhan's son. Lakhan Marandi, however, did not wish to continue relations with the family and instead of accepting a double bride-price he insisted on a double divorce. His daughter was in his house at the time and later he married her to a boy of Mahuatanr.

There is finally one last qualification. The double bride-price can be claimed by the first husband only when he himself is obviously not at fault and has neither neglected nor illtreated his wife. If either of these circumstances is present the first husband can claim only a single bride-price. The daughter of Sukul Hembrom of Nischinta was neglected by her first husband and began to live with Mangal Besra of Dudhuakol. When the matter was brought before the pargana and five manjhis of Taljhari bungalow it was decided that Mangal should pay only a single bride-price in view of the former husband's neglect.

In Dighari the wife of Dugru Murmu eloped with Jolha Soren of Lahartanga after she had lived for fifteen years with her first husband. In this case, Dugru also was held to be at fault and only a single bride-price was awarded to him.

The father's bride-price

In such cases when a adulterer brings the girl from her husband he must also pay the girl's father a bride-price. This is calculated on the assumption that the act has divorced the girl and accordingly the bride-price for a chadwi is payable. If it is not given the girl's parents decline to recognize the marriage. They will refuse to invite their daughter to weddings or festivals. They will treat her husband as a stranger and if the price is still not paid they can detain the girl or place the matter before the village and enforce the claim.

Hiramani Murmu of Amtala had married Bodoc' Marandi of Bitra. Bodoc' was always ill so after two years she returned to her father's house and within four months eloped with Munshi Kisku. Munshi paid a double bride-price to the girl's husband and at a village meeting the boy's father paid twelve rupees as a chadwi bride-price to Hiramani's parents.

In Kusma, Buguc' Marandi was married to a boy of Salhajor. The girl was older than the boy and became mature before her husband. As the boy was too young to live with her she met Suphal Kisku of the next village and one day the villagers caught them in the forest in an act of sex. Suphal was chased for a mile and finally ran to the house of the manjhi.

The girl was also caught and in the meeting Suphal said that he would marry her. A double bride-price was paid to the first husband and seven rupees was given to the girl's father as the bride-price of a chadwi.

The daughter of Chanai Tudu of Khirbani was married at Simaljori and then went off with another man. The first husband was paid a double bride-price but although the girl's father demanded the bride-price of a chadwi the adulterer did not pay it. Sometime later the girl tired of her second husband and returned to her father's house. The boy demanded the girl. As she did not wish to stay with her second husband her father did not demand a chadwi's bride-price and the family were content to use it as a valid reason for detaining the girl and breaking the second marriage.

In yet another case the daughter of Jana Hansdak' of Pipra was married in Murjora but was detected in act of sex with a servant boy. The boy was made to pay a double bride-price to her husband but when he went to the girl's house to take her away the girl's father drove him out saying that he did not know him and had received no bride-price.

The single bride-price and the costs of the wedding

A third claim by a husband is for return of a single bride-price and the marriage expenses and there are two types of circumstances in which this may arise. The first is when the marriage is recent and the girl deserts her husband. The boy may have fetched her three times but every time she has stayed only a day or two and then returned to her parents. The cause of desertion may be a previous lover but actual adultery is not proved. In such a case the husband has gained nothing from the wedding and is, therefore, entitled to the expenses of the ceremony as well as to the bride-price.*

The daughter of Padum Marandi of Guihajori was married to the son of Bhagmat Hembrom of Kalhajore. The girl did not stay with him and after four years the boy divorced her and

*This is conceded throughout the district except in the Godda subdivision and in the Nonihat area where only a single bride-price has so far been allowed.

was awarded sixty rupees as a single bride-price and marriage expenses.

But besides these circumstances there is a second type of situation when a single bride-price and the wedding expenses can be demanded. This is when the girl is already pregnant at her wedding and deception is practised on her husband's family.

Chaku Hembrom of Kalhajore was married to a girl of Kolha. At the end of the wedding some women suddenly said 'The girl is pregnant.' The girl was asked but denied it. Some days later the boy's mother called a Dom Budhi. The Dom Budhi bluffed the girl that her husband wanted to get rid of the child but nothing could be done without knowing how long it had been there. Then the girl said, 'Two months'. The Budhi said that the medicine would not work unless she knew the boy's name. On this, the girl named a boy of Majdiha. When the boy's family heard this, they called the girl's parents. There was a meeting at which the Dom Budhi was a witness and the girl herself admitted the pregnancy. The girl was then given back and the bride-price and the marriage expenses amounting to sixty rupees were paid.

In another case Chita Hansdak' of Ghoribad married Somae Marandi of Lakardamani. They took to each other but as they were still young the boy was sent to Lakrapahari M.E. School to continue his studies. A little later the two fathers quarrelled. The girl was returned, the bride-price taken back and a divorce announced. Two years later the fathers made matters up and as neither the boy nor girl had been re-married, the boy's father proposed a second marriage of his son with Chita in order to economise the costs. Chita's father agreed and as the girl was now a chadwi, there was no full-dress celebration, the bride-price was paid once more and the girl was taken to Somae's house. A week later, on the way to a hatia, Chita's cloth accidentally got loose and a woman of the village saw that she was pregnant. On another day she had come off a hill with a girl and was bathing at a tank. The girl asked her if she was pregnant and she said she was. When the news reached Somae's father, he again returned Chita to her father and demanded back the money. The villagers held that Chita's father should have disclosed the pregnancy before sending the girl and they held that the money must be paid. In this case as there was no formal celebration, costs of the wedding were not claimed but had there been another dol bapla, these would also have been admissible.

The bride-price and chadaodi

A fourth claim is for the bride-price and chadaodi or separation money. This is usually awarded either when the girl's behaviour is such as to unfit her to remain a wife or when a girl has deserted her husband after living with him and the husband himself is not at fault. Chadaodi is allowed because in such circumstances the grant of full wedding expenses would be excessive but the marriage is not of such a length that the husband should not be indemnified.

In Kusumpokhar the wife of Hari Murmu was not staying with him. She was asked by the pargana why she did not go to him but in reply said nothing. As they had lived together for sometime but she gave no reason for deserting him it was decided that her father must return the bride-price and brother's present and pay Hari seven rupees as divorce money. The father paid and then the two were divorced.

Hopna Murmu of Amtala was married to Naren Hansdak's daughter. They got two children and then she started stealing. She first stole fifteen rupees and then another five and had a necklace made from the money. Hopna complained to the villagers and in the meeting Naren Hansdak' had to pay him sixty rupees. Of this fourteen rupees was the bride-price and the rest was chadaodi and compensation.

In Kenduatanr Singo Hansdak' was married to Mangal Tudu of Rupundih. As Mangal and his parents were poor Singo declined to live with him and her father returned the bride-price and paid Mangal a bullock as divorce money.

In a case from Kundahit a boy of Gundhludih married a girl of Ronchapor. They lived together for five years but when the girl's brother died her father brought her back and demanded that her husband should become a ghar jawae. The boy declined and since a ghar jawae was necessary the girl's parents insisted on divorce. The bride-price was returned and the girl's father paid twelve rupees as chadaodi.

In all such cases, if a husband can validly claim a single bride-price he is also entitled to divorce money.

Cases sometimes arise, however, when a man has expelled his wife for extravagance, pilfering or flirtation but himself has not taken step to dissolve the marriage. Moreover in certain circumstances the husband himself may be partly responsible for the girl declining to stay. In such circumstances chadaodi is not always insisted on and only the bride-price is paid to the husband.

The daughter of Bhoto Murmu of Baghasol was married to the son of Khade Soren of Bichhiapahari. She lived with him for two years and although they slept on the same cot the boy could not 'fill her mind'. The boy did not want to lose her but the girl told her parents that she could not stay with him any longer. The matter was discussed by the villagers and the girl's parents repaid the bride-price and took her back.

In the Bankati case, Barki Hansdak' deserted her husband because of illness in his house. They had lived together for some years, so only the bride-price was repaid.

In another case from Kusumba Mohon Marandi, a widower married a second wife. She failed, however, to look after his son by the first wife and was caught selling paddy without his knowledge. He expelled her from the house and accepted a single bride-price in return for divorce.

In Dharampur Lakhan Baske found his wife flirting with other village boys so he returned her to her parents' house. When the matter came before the villages he accepted a single bride-price and the two were parted.

Chadaodi

A fifth claim is for the payment of chadaodi only. This arises when a boy has been taken as a ghardi jawae or ghar jawae and then through no fault of his own the marriage is dissolved. Since no bride-price has been paid and the boy's guardian has also had to bear no wedding expenses, the question of returning these amounts does not arise. In certain cases, the chadaodi is fixed at the normal rate of seven rupees but enhanced chadaodi is sometimes paid by agreement among the parties. In the case of a ghardi jawae whose marriage is dissolved without the boy being to blame, an enhanced indemnity which includes the animals and utensils payable to him on the completion of his service can be claimed. If, however, the ghardi jawae or ghar jawae is at fault, and on that account the marriage breaks no claim whether to ordinary or to enhance chadaodi arises and he is returned to his father's house without any payment.

Jatu Soren of Mansingpur took a boy as ghar jawae for his daughter. The girl did not like the boy and after two years the marriage was dissolved. Jatu paid him seven rupees as chadaodi and the boy went home.

In Palajori Kalhu Besra brought a ghar jawae for his daughter. Later he himself got children and as he did not wish the daughter to inherit he dissolved the marriage and returned the ghar jawae to his father. Since the ghar jawae was not at fault the village awarded him an enhanced chadaodi of thirty rupees.

Gupi Murmu of Bhurkundi was brought as a ghar jawae to Bikrampur. Sometime later his wife eloped with a man of the same village and the village awarded an enhanced chadaodi of twelve maunds of paddy and a pair of bullocks to the ghar jawae.

In Daldali Chandrai Marandi brought a ghardi jawae for his daughter. After a year the girl began to ill-treat him and the marriage was dissolved. In the meeting the village awarded the ghar jawae an enhanced chadaodi consisting of seven rupees and a bullock. Chandrai then pointed out that no bullock had been shown to the ghardi jawae and the meeting then reduced the amount and awarded seven rupees only. While going home the ghardi jawae seized a bullock and took it with him. Chandrai, however, followed him to his village, collected the villagers and after satisfying them that no bullock had been shown returned with the animal.

The return of the brother's due

A sixth claim is for the return of bare itat or the brother's present. This can be entertained only if the present has actually been given. If it was given in cash, cash can be demanded and if in kind, the animal itself must be returned or replaced.* The claim can be made whenever a single bride-price with or without other compensation can be demanded. Where a double bride-price is demanded bare itat, however, cannot be claimed.

In all these cases, it is the girl's father who must pay and only if there is adultery is a third party liable.

Lukhi Murmu of Bansbani was married as a child. Two years after the wedding the boy's father gave a bullock as bare itat. After ten years the boy went to fetch his wife but the girl's family declined to give her. A divorce was then settled and in this settlement Lukhi's father received the bride-price and the greater part of the marriage expenses, but as the bullock had died in the meantime, a sum of five rupees was paid instead.

Other dues

Finally, if any other dues are outstanding these must be cleared as part of the general settlement attending the divorce.

Bistu Tudu of Barmasia was shown a jaituk cow on his wedding day by his father-in-law. After two years when he divorced the girl, the jaituk animal was still with his father-in-law. The animal was given to him as part of the settlement.

XIV THE CLAIMS OF THE WIFE

Chadaodi

If these are the various dues of a husband, there are four claims which arise in the case of a wife.

The first is for chadaodi or separation money. This normally consists of seven rupees and includes two rupees for a cloth as bande onodon, 'to cover her nakedness'. This cloth is distinct from the annual cloth to which a wife is normally entitled since if she is not given the chadaodi cloth there is danger that her bonga will remain in the house and bring disaster on it. For this reason it is claimable irrespective of whether *sindur* has been given. The full chadaodi is always

*In the Rajmahal Damin, a bride-price is sometimes paid by the ghar jawae. In such cases if the marriage is dissolved through no fault of the ghar jawae the bride-price is also returnable.

payable when the wife is either not at fault or the husband is as much to blame and only if the husband is a ghar jawae or ghardi jawae does he escape this obligation.

Pandu Hansdak' of Bokrabandh married a girl of Dulu. After a time they quarrelled and Pandu beat her. The matter was taken to the village and the boy was divorced on paying seven rupees as chadaodi to the girl.

Durga Marandi of Shampur did not like his wife but could not specify any special fault. The village allowed him to divorce her and he paid her divorce money of seven rupees.

Panu Soren of Silingi was or adered by a rich chadwa. For some months all went well. Then he started to beat her and she left him. The villagers intervened and awarded her chadaodi.

In many cases, although the wife herself is at fault her husband does not press for a return of the bride-price and chadaodi and with a view to ending a difficult domestic situation tenders chadaodi of his own accord. In such cases, chadaodi is given to the wife by agreement among the parties and is not a claim which the wife herself can enforce.

The wife of Baijnath Soren of Gauripur stole some maize from a Santal of the village. The woman was at fault and Baijnath divorced her. He paid her seven rupees as chadaodi.

The wife of Bhagan Soren of Bichkora stole a hansuli from her mother-in-law. Bhagan divorced her but paid her chadaodi.

In Hathmari Bhadu Marandi had a wife who always pretended to be ill and was incurably lazy. He, therefore, divorced her and although he himself was not to blame he paid divorce money.

Khela Murmu of Phulbanga caught his wife flirting with a village boy in suspicious circumstances. He divorced her and although the fault was with the girl he also gave her chadaodi.

Birsingh of Daldali married a girl who never kept his house clean and always neglected the cooking. He paid her five rupees as chadaodi and sent her back to her father.

Hirom baiha

In addition to chadaodi a second claim arises if the taking of a co-wife is responsible for the separation. If a wife is with her husband and he brings a co-wife, she can claim five to seven rupees* as hirom baiha whether she stays with him or not. Similarly if she is willing to live with him, but her husband is not fetching her, she can claim hirom baiha and divorce money if he takes a chutki.

Equally if after marriage the co-wife finds it impossible to live with her husband and the fault is not her own, she can claim divorce money and the mon rofa which was shown at her induction. If after the second marriage, the first wife finds it impossible to remain, she can demand divorce, and claim divorce money and hirom baiha.

Dukhia Marandi of Dulu brought a second wife and showed a bullock to his first wife as hirom baiha. The two wives were constantly quarrelling, so in the end Dukhia divorced his first wife and paid her seven repees as chadaodi as well as her hirom baiha.

In Tilatanr Chadra Marandi took a girl of Kalhajore as his second wife. He already had one wife and when after a time he tired of her he divorced his second wife, paid her seven rupees as divorce money and gave her the calf which he had shown her as mon rofa.

Hopna Kisku of Latberwa brought a second wife and showed a cow as hirom baiha to his first wife. The first wife stayed with him for another year and gave birth to a son. She was not happy, however, with her co-wife and as a result of constant quarrels she decided to leave her husband. At the village meeting, she was granted a divorce and given five rupees and a cloth as chadaodi and ten rupees as hirom baiha in lieu of the cow.

In Danha Bake Hansdak' had a first wife who did not live regularly with him. He, therefore, brought a chutki and showed her a she-buffalo as mon rofa. After the chutki had been brought the batki returned and began to live happily with her husband. Balke then began to neglect the chutki and then she returned to her father's house taking the mon rofa with her.

*According to local usage.

The wife's property

A third claim is for any property which the wife may have brought from her house as well as for any articles which her husband or relations have given her as presents. These are her absolute private property and on the dissolution of the marriage she can take them from her husband's house.

When Dina Hansdak' of Mortanga was divorced from Guna Marandi she got divorce money of seven rupees and also took with her three goats, twelve fowls and one brass bowl which she had brought with her from her father's house.

Bare itat

Moreover if chadaodi is awarded, all arrears of the bride-price and brother's present must be paid.

In the case of bed wetting, one rupee from the bride-price and five rupees for bare itat were due. These were paid and then the leaves were torn.

In Tulsipur the daughter of Kandan Soren was married to a son of Sarkar Kisku. The boy refused to take her to his house and also did not pay the brother's due. When the matter went to the village a divorce was sanctioned and the boy's father paid divorce money of seven rupees and also the brother's present.

Arrear dues

Fourthly all other dues of the girl of her parents must be cleared.

The wife of Kuar Hansdak' had given birth to a child at her father's house in Dharampur. After the child was born she divorced her husband and in addition to chadaodi the expenses of the birth and naming ceremony were also paid.

A girl of Karanpur was married to Bodoc' Marandi of her village. She fell ill in her father's house and her father met the expenses of her treatment. Her husband deferred paying them and in the end decided to divorce her. In the general settlement divorce money was awarded to the girl and her husband was made to pay all the expenses of the illness to the girl's father.

XV CHILDREN

There remains, finally, the problem of children

If there are any by the marriage and it is not in ghar jawae form, they are made over to the father. They are his responsibility and when the mother leaves they stay on in the house. If a child is still at the breast, it stays with its mother but only for the period of its suckling. For 'the price of the milk' the mother is given a special sum. There is no standard amount and the village fixes it according to the means of the father and the circumstances. In most areas, the rate is between two and three rupees per month but when Panu Soren of Silingi divorced her husband, she was given twelve maunds of paddy for feeding her baby.

In special cases if the children are daughters and their mother wishes to keep them they are sometimes kept with the girl. In such circumstances, the mother voluntarily accepts full responsibility and foregoes all claims and the father relinquishes all his rights. The children then go with the mother and she becomes their guardian. The father cannot, however, escape a final responsibility and if anything happens to the mother, they revert to his custody.

XVI RESULTS

What are the results of divorce ?

For the children none except the emotional strain caused by the loss of their mother. Daughters and sons retain their usual rights and the children of a divorced wife have the same status as those of any other.

For the husband also there are few consequences. In Pandanpahari a Santal forcibly divorced his wife. They had got four children but always quarrelled. He said, 'I cannot live with her any longer.' But the woman did not agree and said she would stay. So he called a village meeting, paid chadaodi and divorced her against her will. After that he married again but sometime later two of the sons from his first wife got weak, spat blood and died while another fell from only a small tree. The villagers said, 'The first wife is eating them. She did not want to go but he made her. She went but she did not take her bonga away.'

It is only in exceptional cases, however, that this is thought to happen. Ordinarily his greatest loss is of a 'child producing house-keeper.' This he can remedy by another marriage though he may not always get a second bride with ease. 'A tasting ladle—for how long will he last ?' 'A chadwa—a tried drum'. As his first marriage has failed, he is less eligible than a boy who has never been married. But even so the initiative is his and if he wants a wife, he rarely fails to gain one.

It is for the wife that divorce has the worst consequences. She loses her children as well as half her enga itat, the customary present at their weddings.* She is deprived of her husband as a source of maintenance and is forced back on her father's house. It is true that the chadaodi or divorce money is her own to keep and if she has private movables, or land of her own, her title to these is unaffected. Moreover, once she is divorced her rights again become those of an unmarried daughter and the principles of lajao marao again apply. She becomes a charge on her father and his heirs and can demand maintenance as if she had never been married. In certain areas her divorce raises her bride-price. But she loses her status as a married woman and the respect which accrues to the manager of a separate household. In her father's house, she shares in the house work but always with the sense that her proper place is in a home of her own. It is not surprising that after divorce she has only one obsession—to get another man and to marry again.

For this reason the divorced girl, the chadwi, is always a source of romantic danger.

In the upper village
They were dancing lagre
I went and danced
But my luck was out
I met a chadwi

Large is the village
And with three parts

*Unless she is a witch in which case she forfeits it entirely.

And the two girls are chadwis
Do not call out as you dance
For the two girls are chadwis.

Little boy
Do not go down
To the lower fields
A chadwi girl
Is in the upper village
Suddenly
She may say to you
'Keep me'.

That girl
I thought she was unmarried
But she proved a chadwi Teli
Oh you Teli girl you chadwi
Like an oil press
You have turned me round.

The daily effort of a divorce girl is to get a husband come what will. 'A chadwi decks herself like a banded flute'. 'A chadwi girl and a green bulbul; they sing in a thousand ways'! 'A chadwi girl has the head of a maina'. It is always neat and preened. 'A chadwi girl and a codgoc' fish—they are never in one place'. She is always after boys. 'A partridge decoys and a chadwi deceives'. For the woman, divorce is an agony of frustration that can end only with a second marriage.

REFERENCES

1. Bompas, op. cit., 363.
2. *Santal Parganas Gazeetter* (second edition), 168-9.
3. This ritual is paralleled among the Gonds and Baigas—'The parties go before the panch and solemnly break a straw in half, letting the bits fall separately to the ground. An earthen pot is smashed, and a rupee also dropped on the ground, but quickly recovered by one of the members of the panch and used for their refreshment. The panch then declares husband and wife formally separated and with no further claims on one another. Any jewellery given to the wife by her husband should now be returned. When a wife runs away, one of the first things the husband does is to recover all orna-

ments he has given her. To see this in practice is sometimes pitiable indeed : the husband seems to have no concern about the loss of the partner, no jealousy for the supplanter, but is simply concerned to recover the few pathetically cheap and tawdry ornaments and to extract a few rupees from the man who has cuckolded him. But we must remember that we are dealing with people to whom the price of a cup of tea in a railway restaurant represents a whole day's labour; who think in terms not of rupees or even annas, but of pice and cowries, and to whom these things are of gigantic moment.' (Elwin: *The Baiga*, 284).

PART FIVE

THE RITES OF CRISIS

36

BIRTH

I

WHEN a Santal is born, his arrival in the world imposes on the family a new set of rights and duties. It ushers into the household a fresh claimant to family property. It subjects the village bongas to temporary pollution, and sets in motion a new train of ceremonies. Above all it involves the father in some immediate duties and exposes him to special costs. These expenses are not on the ruinous scale of wedding charges. They rarely exceed fifteen or twenty rupees, but they are of great importance in village practice. They are the necessary corollaries of birth and their payment is enforced by all the sanctions of the village.

II PRE-NATAL COSTS

The first of these expenses concerns the treatment of the mother in the days preceding birth.

Santal women do not usually experience difficulty in pregnancy but if a complication occurs, a budhi or midwife has then to be consulted. If the midwife is a Santal woman the rule is to give her a share in the family food for the day. If she is non-Santal she is given a pai full of rice with some dal, and a little salt and spices.

During one of her pregnancies, the wife of Bijoy Hembrom of Kalhajore found her thigh and waist hurting. A midwife of their village was called. She came and attended and Bijoy gave her a day's food to take away and cook.

In Amtala while the daughter of Chotu Ramu was pregnant the child got out of position and a Santal dai budhi of Jamini was called for consultation. 'She came and put it right and after four days the pains started in the night and a child came.' Chotu Ramu fed her in his house on the day of consultation.

If the midwife had not been called Chotu Ramu would have risked his daughter's life and would also have failed in his duties as a Santal.

In all such cases the immediate responsibility vests in the head of the household but it is the husband who must ultimately meet the charges.

III DELIVERY

When the time of a Santal girl draws near, she either stays in her husband's house or goes to the house of her mother. If the child is her first or she has only had one or two children she usually goes to her home. If, however, her mother is dead but her mother-in-law is alive she stays at her husband's house. If both are alive and her husband does not want her to go home, her mother is often called over. Whether the birth occurs, however, at her husband's house or at her parents', it is the husband who must meet all the expenses.

Similarly if a woman gives birth to a child in the house of a friend or relation the head of the house is expected to meet all the immediate costs but the woman's husband must pay all his charges.

A husband and wife were on a visit to their distant relative, Kanhu Marandi of Rakso. While they were there, the woman gave birth to a child, Kanhu paid for everything but the woman's husband gave him all that he had spent.

On the actual day of birth such expenses are usually quite light. If the delivery is normal the dai budhi is given her food for the day, she can also demand four pice for cutting the cord and a cloth (parhand) three cubits long. In lieu of the cloth she is sometimes paid four to eight annas according to the local usage and the sex of the child. This money is not paid to her on the day of birth but is kept for the hoyo ruar day which occurs five days after the 'cutting of the cord'. On that day, she and the barber who officiates at the name giving receive their food and a pot of rice beer each. Besides these payments the midwife is sometimes allowed a maund of paddy for a boy and half a maund for a girl and if she is not the family midwife, she is sometimes given an extra rupee. If the labour is difficult and the midwife has to pull the child from the womb, she is paid five rupees more.

The niece of Meghrai Kisku who was married in Parta was pregnant but the child died in the womb. When Meghrai saw that the body was swelling inside, he called a Domin to bring the child out. The Domin said that she would take five rupees and a goat. Meghrai and his wife promised to pay her and the dai budhi then brought out two dead twins and saved the girl. The latter had gone to Kalhajore because her mother was there and when the operation took place her husband Mangal was away from the area. Meghrai, therefore, paid the midwife five rupees and the girl's elder brother gave the goat. The husband later repaid five rupees to Meghrai but when he offered to replace the goat the girl's elder brother said that it was on their own judgment that they had called the woman and that they should, therefore, bear part of the cost. Although the husband was quite willing to give the goat, the elder brother did not take it. In this case, five rupees was the customary charge but as the midwife demanded the goat and the family were worried, they gave her a goat also.

IV NIM DAK' MANDI

Once a child has been born the bongas of the house and village become impure and it is this pollution which is remedied by the ceremony of nim dak' mandi. This is done either on the first, third, or fifth day of the birth, or if longer time is needed, on any odd day following. The most usual times are the third or fifth days but if it is the harvesting or cultivation season, or the village is about to celebrate a wedding or a festival, it is sometimes performed the same day.

Moreover if the child is born on the day before a new

moon the ceremony must be done at once so that all pollution is removed before a new month starts.

In such cases, C.H. Bompas notes, the following ceremony is also observed : After bathing the child they place an old broom in the mother's arms instead of the child; then the mother takes the child and throws it out on the dung heap behind the house. The midwife then takes an old broom and old winnowing fan and sweeps up a little rubbish on to the fan and takes it and throws it on the dung hill; there she sees the child and calls out 'Here is a child on the dung heap'. Then she pretends to sweep the child with the broom into the winnowing fan and lifts it up and carries it into the house; and asks the people of the house whether they will rear it. They ask what wages she will give them and she promises to give them a heifer when the child is grown up.

If this is not done the child will be unlucky when it is grown up; if it is a boy, however, often he may marry his wife will die and so, if it is a girl, her husbands will die.*

Khare Hembrom of Telni gave birth to a girl the night before the first day of the Sohrae festival. As the festival could not start so long as the village was impure the ceremony was performed the following morning and after that the festival began.

In Nimakalan the wife of Surai Hansdak' gave birth to a girl the night before a wedding booth was due to be erected. As this could not be done while the village was impure the ceremony was performed the following morning and after that the shed was made.

V THE COSTS OF THE CEREMONY

The ceremony of nim dak' mandi is the essential corollary to a child's birth but as I have already fully described it,** I will now analyse only the costs which attend its performance.

*Bompas. op. cit., 415-6.
**See Chapter 5.

These are normally made up as follows :

1. Rice flour for making coko pitha and the paste to be sprinkled on the chests of those present. For coko pitha, flour is baked in the fire in leaves. Some of it is then rubbed on the navel, ears, and cheeks of the baby, a little is thrown over the roof and the balance is eaten by the old women. Quantity of rice used—2 pailas.
2. Rice for mixing with water and nim leaves and preparing nim dak' mandi. Quantity of rice used—6 pailas.
3. Leaf cups for serving nim dak' mandi. Cost—nil.
4. Two shares of food and one bowl of nim dak' mandi to both the naeke and the barber for assisting at the ceremony.
5. A double ration of food to the midwife for her services at the ceremony.
6. Oil sent to the naeke on the day of birth and on the day of nim dak' mandi. This must be 'enough for his body' and is about a tenth of a leaf-cup full.
7. Oil for the village men and women who attend the nim dak' mandi ceremony. Amount used—two leaf-cups.
8. Food for the midwife and the barber on the hoyo ruar day. Rice for the two pots of rice beer presented to them on that occasion.

When a Santal family is well-to-do, this scale of expenditure is often exceeded and particularly if the child is a boy a feast is often given to the whole village. The barber in particular is sometimes given a maund of paddy if the child is a boy and half a maund if a girl.

Since the midwife is the central figure at the birth and the ceremony, she often stays in the house until the nim dak' mandi has been fully performed. If the ritual is done earlier than five days from the birth she stays until five days are over. During this time, she gets her food each day and unless the girl's relations willingly forego any claim the cost of this food is met by the husband.

If the birth occurs outside the village, a subsidiary nim dak' mandi must be performed after the mother and child have returned. The villagers are called, the midwife announces the name and does johar and nim dak' mandi is drunk by all who are present.

If his wife is away from home the husband must also pay the jom dare or cost of 'feeding the tree' during the days immediately prior to and after the delivery. During this time the mother cannot help in the house but once she is up and about nothing more is charged and the help she gives is treated as a payment for her food.

VI CLAIMS

All these expenses must be met by the girl's husband and if he does not pay them, the girl's parents can detain her in the house.

The daughter of Siru Murmu of Amlagachi was married to Jugal Marandi of Baramasia. The girl was delivered at her father's house and when her husband came to take his wife and child her father demanded all the costs. The boy refused to pay so the girl was detained by her parents. There was then a village meeting and the villagers decided that the boy must pay two maunds of paddy and nine annas in cash. Even then he did not pay and his wife and child remained in the village. Subsequently Jugal went to court thinking that he would get an order for return of his wife but the court upheld the village decision and ultimately the boy paid ten rupees and took back his wife and child.

In Amoi the wife of Pitho Kisku became pregnant. The girl's parents told her husband to send her to them for the delivery. Pitho wanted the birth to be in his house but in the end his wife went to her parents. At her father's place she gave birth to a girl and because she had gone against her will her husband declined to meet the cost. When he came to take away his wife and child her parents did not let her go and there was then a village meeting. At the meeting it was decided that her husband must pay the cost and when he eventually did so, his wife and child went with him.

Dhagun Hembrom of Amtala was pregnant when her brother brought her home for the Erok' festival. Her husband did not come and fetch her. So she stayed on and after some months had a baby. Word was sent to her husband but neither he nor his parents came. The nim dak' mandi was done by her parents. After some time her husband wanted to take her but they said 'give us first four pice for cutting the cord, 8 pialas of rice for nim dak' mandi, six for rice beer and the cost of feeding the girl for ten days till she could help in the house again'. 'We could have claimed six days' food for the midwife and food for the barber,' said her uncle, 'but we forget it'. When the girl's husband refused to pay, she stayed on but a little later there was a wedding in the village, her husband came over and while the girls relatives were busy in the ritual he took her away. In this case, the boy evaded payment but all the claim was valid and if the girl's family had pursued it the village would have awarded it to them.

In many cases, jom dare is not insisted on but if the husband tries to evade meeting the birth expenses, it can also be charged.

Tanti Soren of Hathi Hariari was married to a girl of Dipna. His wife gave birth to a child at her father's house and her father demanded all the cost from her husband. The latter refused to pay and the girl's father declined to let his daughter return to her husband. The manjhis and villagers of both villages then met and decreed all the costs of birth together with jom dare in favour of the girl's father. The girl's husband then paid up but as he was poor his father-in-law remitted the 'feeding of the tree'.

In Tilabad, Dubai Soren was married to a girl of Sundmara. The girl gave birth to a daughter at her father's house and her father then sent a man to her father-in-law to realise the cost. The father-in-law paid every thing and sent 20 seers of paddy, 5 seers of rice and a cloth for the midwife.

If a child's paternity is disputed, the nim dak' mandi is frequently performed by the girl's parents and its costs charged later to whichever boy is adjudged to be the father.

The daughter of Ram Kisku of Kasba became pregnant by Kishan Tudu of her village. When she gave birth to a child Kishan had not been finally adjudged the father and the ceremony of nim dak' mandi was accordingly performed in the girl's house and the expenses met by her father. The child was a boy and it was named Sagram Tudu after Kishan's father.

When the village finally held that Kishan was responsible he was required to pay all the costs of the birth and the naming ceremony.

Jagu Hansdak' was a servant in the house of the manjhi of Litipara. While serving there he became intimate with the daughter of Ramchand Kisku. Before the matter was regularised the girl gave birth to a child and at the final settlement the boy paid the cost of the birth and the ceremony.

37

NAMING

I BAHNA AND MUL NAMES

WHEN children are born from a Santal marriage they are given two names. The first is called bahna. This is the 'outer' or 'village' name by which the child is usually known. The second is the mul or 'inner' name which is formally announced at the child's name-giving ceremony. The bahna is left to the parent's fancy but the giving of the mul name is determined by elaborate rules. Although, I have never known Santals baffled by these rules I myself have always found them bewildering in their complexity. Yet there is scarcely anything of greater importance to a Santal. By his birth he does not re-incarnate an ancestor. A father is not reborn in a grandson. But the giving of a name perpetuates a memory. It is a gesture of respect, an act of homage to family loyalties. It affirms a tribal tradition of honour. It extends a Santal's life beyond his death.

> Yet meet we shall, and part and meet again
> Where dead men meet on lips of living men.

Above all it is the vital clue to many problems of inheritance to family intentions, to the status of children and of heirs.

II THE STANDARD ORDER OF PREFERENCE

The most important relations whom the rules honour are the child's grandparents and uncles on both the father's and the mother's sides. On the father's side they are the decisive elements in the Santal 'greater' family while on the mother's side they are the allies who rally when the family has failed.

Accordingly, in the case of children born in dol or sadai bapla, the mul name of the first son must be the same as the father's father (gorom baba), the mul name of the second must be the same as his mother's father (also gorom baba) while the third son must be named after his father's elder brother (gongo baba), and the fourth after his mother's elder brother (mama). If the father and mother are themselves the eldest of several brothers and sisters, the third son will be named after the brother next in age to the father (kaka) and the fourth after the brother next in age to the mother (mama).* If the father has no brothers, the third son will be named after any other relations on the father's side, and if the mother has no brothers, the fourth son will be named after any relations in her family.

There is thus an equal balancing of the claims of the two families. The male principle is given its customary stress but the mother's side is given almost equal prominence.

Similarly the first daughter must be named after the father's mother (gorom ayo) and the second after her mother's mother (also gorom ayo). With regard to the third and fourth daughters the order is less rigid but the third is often named after the mother's eldest brother's wife, and the fourth after her father's eldest brother's wife. If the mother or father are themselves the eldest of several brothers and sisters and third daughter is named after the wife of the brother next in age to the mother and the fourth after the wife of the brother next in age to the father. If either the father or mother has no brothers the eldest sister of the father or mother is chosen instead.

If there are more than four sons or daughters in a family

*If the father or mother have several elder brothers a son will normally be named after the eldest unless one of them is dead. In that case the dead brother takes precedence over the living one.

those who are born after the fourth of either sex will be named after any other relation on the mother's or father's side.

Family with seven sons

Lothon Soren
of Bichgeda (Phuljuri)—Jobe Murmu

Padum Baijun Samu Bhogon Barka Baghrae Mangal

These are named after the following relations :

1. Father's father
2. Mother's father
3. Father's next youngest brother (Lotho being the eldest of his brothers).
4. Mother's eldest brother
5. }
6. } Father's younger brothers
7. }

Family with six daughters

Chunka Marandi
of Fatehpur (Morrow)—Lakhi Murmu

Jhumri Sukum Sukhi Khando Makho Sagori

These took the names of the following relations :

1. Father's mother
2. Mother's father
3. Wife of father's elder brother
4. Mother's younger sister (Lakhi having no married brother or elder sister).
5. Father's elder sister
6. Mother's next younger sister.

III TWINS

These rules govern all normal cases but they are modified in various circumstances.

If twins are born and both are boys, the pair will be called Ram and Lakhan and after that one or other of the pairs :

Sido and Kanhu
Bhorot and Chatur
Bhim and Arjun
Kunda and Kusal
Shiva and Shankar
Chand and Bhairab
Arsa and Barsa

If they are girls, the first pair will be named Chita and Kapra, the second Hisi and Dhumni, the third Dangi and Pungi and after that either Agia and Kuila or Maino and Mati. If the first set is a boy and girl they will be called Lakhan and Kapra, Bharat and Hisi or Chatir and Dhumni. Dharma Hembrom of Jhili had boy twins and named them Ram and Lakhan. Manjhia Murmu of Amtala had twin daughters and named them Chita and Kapra. If twins are born to a man who was himself a twin, the naming is adjusted and the boy receives not his father's name but the name next in precedence. In Kalhajore Sidu Hansdak' had twins, a boy and a girl, and following the rule, named them Ram and Chita. Ram also had twins and as he himself was named Ram he did not name them Ram and Lakhan but called them Bharat and Chatur. Similarly if a man has already had a son, has named him after the correct relation and the name happens to be the one next in order for a twin, the next pair of twin names is resorted to. Salkhu Murmu of Dalabar had a son whom he named Ram after his father. He then had boy twins. As he had already employed a name from the first pair, he called them Bharat and Chatur. The same principles cover triplets and if two boys and one girl are born they are called Ram, Lakhan and Chita, if they are two girls and one boy, they are named Chita, Kapra and Ram, and if they are three girls, their names are Chita and Kapra with another added. A case of quadruplets occurred in Boda ten years ago but neither the mother nor the children survived. If they had lived their names would have followed the same order of preference.

The reason for this change of rule is that since Raja Dasarath had twins by Sumitra, Santals think it auspicious to associate twins with him. In the case of girls Chita is a Santal form of Sita, the wife of Ram. She is said to form with the others the six bonga sisters who with five bonga brothers comprise the Mareko Turuc'ko, the Five-Six.

IV OJHAS AND SHRINES

The second factor which modifies the ordinary rules is when a man and his wife secure a child after recourse to an ojha. Here the major service rendered by the ojha entitles him to the greatest honour a Santal can give. In such cases the ojha is entitled to have a son named after him and a daughter after the ojha's wife or in the alternative to choose the name to be given to the child.

Manku Murmu of Bangaliya was not getting any children by his first wife. He consulted Luda Hembrom an ojha of Ranidih. The ojha treated Manka's wife and when in due course a boy was born it was named Luda Murmu after the ojha.

Rasika Murmu of Poraiyahat and his wife, a girl of Jamra, had had no children. They then consulted Karijha Soren, an ojha of Jamni and when the girl had conceived the ojha said that if the child was a boy it must be named Karmu and if a girl Karmi. A son was born and according to the ojha's words it was named Karmu.

Parents, however, may contract out of the obligation by paying five rupees to the ojha if the latter so agrees. Bhado Marandi of Amtala was not getting any child, so he consulted Tura Hembrom, an ojha of Dalahi. Tura removed the bonga and a girl was born. Tura's wife was Lukhi and Bhado therefore, named his first daughter not after his father's mother but after Lukhi herself. After having this child Bhado's wife 'flowered' and they had three children without recourse to ojhas. These three children were named as if they were the first of the marriage; the first son after Bhado's father, and the first daughter after Bhado's mother. Bhado said he could not pay Tura five rupees and so he named his first daughter after the wife of the ojha.

In Kala Dumaria Bhuju Hembrom got a son after having recourse to an ojha, Lakhiram Tudu. Bhuju did not wish to name the child after the ojha so he paid him one goat, one dhoti and two rupees and with the ojha's consent he named the boy after the child's grandfather.

In portions of the district where Hindu shrines have local reputations recourse is sometimes had to Hindu deities and if a child results from a visit to the shrine it is given the name, not of the pujari but of the shrine itself. Gulu Murmu of Baghmara had no children so with his wife he went to the jaithan in Jiakara. He promised the deity a goat if he got a child and when within a year, a son was born he gave a goat and named the boy Jiaram.

Kesar Baske of Rakh had no children, so with his wife he went to the village debithan and made a sacrifice in the name of the deity Kalyaneswari. Within a year his wife gave birth to a daughter and he named the child Kalyan Baske.

V AID AT WEDDINGS

A third circumstance is when the parents are too poor to perform the marriage of a particular son and the marriage expense is met by the relations, such as a brother, sister or uncle. In such cases, the boy may express his sense of obligation by naming his first son not after his father's father (gorom baba) but after the relation who performed the marriage. Similarly his first daughter may be named not after his father's mother (gorom ayo) but after the sister or the wife of whoever did the ceremony. Once the first child of each sex has been so named the ordinary rules apply.

Bhagmat Himbrom of Kalhajore performed the marriage of his sister's son, Sibu Kisku. Sibu continued living with Bhagmat and when a son and daughter were born he named them after Bhagmat and his wife.

Surju Baske of Dharampur performed the marriage of his brother's son and the boy named his first son and daughter after Surju and his wife.

Here also the important nature of the service may entitle the relation to more than conventional honour. A similar case is when one of the parents is particularly devoted or indebted to a friend, an ancestor or a respected member of the family. A stepmother, for example, is sometimes honoured in this way and while it is unusual for the first son or first daughter to be named after such persons, the second son or daughter or other and more junior children may be given their names.

Pero Murmu of Mandra had a servant whose wife was also taken to this house. Pero's wife treated her kindly and by way of gratitude the servant named his third daughter after Pero's mother.

In Dulu, Suphal Marandi had four daughters. He named the first after his mother, the second after his wife's mother and the third after his stepmother, the chutki of his father.

VI DEVOURING BY LEOPARD OR TIGER

Finally, in a few areas* in the Santal Parganas, if a person is eaten by a leopard or tiger no one will be called after him. This is because a baghaut bonga resides in a leopard or a tiger and when a man is eaten it is believed to be the bonga which has attacked him. Since the bonga has eaten him it is still in him and three is every danger that if a child is given the dead man's name the bonga will seize him also. In the Fatehpur and Nonihat areas, this belief is generally acted on but if the partially eaten corpse is burnt on an ant hill and the bones are buried in another ant hill, the danger ceases and a child can be safely given the name. Pero Murmu of Godaikhap was eaten by tiger and none of his sons named any of their sons after him. Elsewhere the ban is not observed and after Siru Besra of Kairojori had been eaten by a tiger his sons did not hesitate to name their sons after him.

A similar reluctance is sometimes shown in cases of leprosy.

*Taljhari, Rajabhita, Nonihat, Fatehpur, Jamtara, Narainpur and Katikund.

Bijai Tudu of Teliadih named his second son after his mother's brother because his wife's father had become a leper.

VII GHAR JAWAE

These principles apply to all marriages in dol or sadai bapla as well as to those in golaeti, kundal napam, nir bolok', or ader, apangir and ghardi jawae. There are, however, some important modifications in the case of ghar jawae, hirom cetan, sangha and jawae kirinok' bapla.

In a ghar jawae bapla, the daughter is, as it were, transformed into a son and it is the girl's side and not the boy's which receives preference. In such cases, therefore, the first son is named after his mother's father (gorom baba), the second after the boy's father (also gorom baba), the third after his mother's elder brother (mama) and the fourth after his father's eldest brother (gongo baba). Similarly the first daughter is named after her mother's mother (gorom ayo) the second after her father's mother (also gorom ayo), the third after her father's eldest brother's wife and the fourth after her mother's eldest brother's wife.

In cases where a ghar jawae survives his wife, his father-in-law brings a second wife for him, the naming varies with the circumstances. If there are no children by his first wife, the first son and daughter are given the names of the first wife's parents (by convention their gorom baba and gorom ayo) even though their mother is the second. The second son and daughter take the names of the ghar jawae's parents (also gorom baba and gorom ayo) while the third are named after the parents of their mother, i.e. the second wife. The fourth revert for naming to the first wife's family and are called after the brother or sister of the first wife (by convention their mama or kaki).

If on the other hand, there are sons and daughters by the first wife, no child by the second wife will be given the same name but subject to this reservation, their names will first honour the first wife's family, then their father's and finally their mother's.

In cases where an ordinary marriage has subsequently been

converted into a ghar jawae marriage by agu mit the preference changes from the time of agu mit.* Thus if the girl has no children before being brought back to her father's house any subsequent children will be named as if the marriage were originally in ghar jawae form. If, however, a girl has a son and daughter before being brought back, they will already have been named as in a dol or sadai bapla. If she then has two sons and two daughters the first son will be named after her father (the child's gorom baba) and the second after her eldest brother (the child's mama). Similarly her first daughter will be named after her mother (the child's gorom ayo) and the second after her eldest sister (the child's kaki).

VIII CO-WIVES

In a hirom cetan marriage where a man takes a co-wife (chutki) for his batki or first wife all the children will be treated as of one father. Thus if a batki has two sons and after that two sons are born to the chutki, the batki's two sons will be named after her husband's father (gorom baba) and her own father while those of the chutki will be named after her husband's brothers (gongo baba or kaka) and the chutki's father (also gorom baba).

Hamai Hansdak' of Kusumdaha had no sons from his batki. He then married a chutki and the same year both the wives gave birth to children, the batki first and the chutki next. The bakti's son was named after Hamai's father while the chutki's son was given the name of Hamai's brother. When the chutki had a daughter she was named after Hamai's mother.

If on the other hand the chutki has a son before the batki the son will be named after his father's father and if the batki has a son later, he will be named after his father's brother.

If, however, a son by the batki has been named after his

*In the Godda and Jamtara subdivisions, a change in the order of naming is not always resorted to.

father's father and has then died, a subsequent son by the chutki can be given the same name.

Bipin Hansdak' of Taljhari had a son by his batki whom he named Raska after his father. The batki and her son died and when Bipin married a chutki, he named her first on Raska.

Even if the first son by a batki is alive, the first son by the chutki can still receive the same name. Tanka Besra of Mandhopara had two wives and named each of his first sons after his father, Mohon.

IX WIDOWS

There are similar complications when a widow with children marries and has children by her second husband. In such circumstances the names of these latter children will follow the ordinary rules as in a dol bapla but if a child by her first husband has already been named after the widow's father or mother her second husband's brother or sister will take precedence. The ordinary rules in fact apply, with the proviso that if a name has already been given it will be omitted and the next name in order of preference will be given.

X ADOPTION

There remains the cases of sons or daughters adopted as posu putra. If they are unmarried at the time of adoption or are married but with no children, their children are named as if they themselves were the natural offspring of their adopting parents. If, however, they already have sons and daughters and have not already named a boy and a girl after their adopting parents the next son and next daughter will take their adopting parents' names. Subsequent children will be named as in a dol bapla, omitting only those relations whose names have been used already.

XI THE ILLEGITIMATE CHILD

Finally in the case of illegitimate children the ordinary rules will apply if a bought husband is procured for the child's mother and kirinok' bapla is performed. If, however, there is no marriage and a man is merely bought to give the child his sept, the child is either given the name of its mother's father (gorom baba) or mother's mother (gorom ayo) or is named after the parents of the man who gave his sept.

The daughter of Indra Soren of Karamtola became pregnant while still unmarried. She named so many boys that the village could not decide who was the real father. Sauna Hembrom was, therefore, paid five rupees and gave the child his sept. He did not marry her but the child was named Mati Hembrom after Sauna's mother.

In Gohanda Dhangi Tudu gave birth to an illegitimate child. Juga Hembrom was paid money to give the child his sept and although Juga did not marry Dhani the child was named after Juga's mother.

Similarly in Dudia, Matla Soren was paid to give his sept to the illegitimate child of Bhansingh Murmu's daughter. He did not marry her but the child was named Chura after Matla's mother.

If the jogmanjhi is compelled to give the child his sept, the child may be named after the jogmanjhi's parents.

Maidi Hembrom of Bhatondia got a child while still unmarried. No one could be got to give the child his sept so the village jogmanjhi was caught and made to officiate. The child was a daughter and was named after the mother of the jogmanjhi.

38

SICKNESS

I PRELIMINARY

AS A Santal reaches youth his first necessity is health. A sick Santal can neither plough his fields nor supervise his cultivation. Festivals and ceremonies go on, weddings break the calm of the village, drums summon the dancers, but the sick man can only lie and wait. He is not only deprived of all that makes him a Santal. He is a drag on his household, a source of depression, an end to zest. Moreover its sudden unaccountable invasion invests all sickness with an element of awe and mystery. Illness is not merely the disabling of an individual, a crisis in his family. It is often an index to a larger system, a clue to the waywardness of bongas and the virulence of witches.

II TAKING THE PULSE

At the onset of an illness, therefore, treatment veers between the prescription of medicine and the appeasement of the powers.

The first step is to summon a guru in the hope that the ill is only physical. The guru takes the patient's pulse, identifies the illness and details the herbs to be gathered and applied.

These are often quite successful and if within a week the patient is well the bongas are absolved and only the body is blamed. If the illness persists and the herbs achieves little the suspicion grows that other forces are at work and the guru makes way for the ojha.

This healer also takes the pulse. "If the pulse comes towards the thumb or the index finger it is a sign that Bongas, the orak' bonga, or some of the other bongas are at work. If the pulse comes towards the middle finger the abge bonga is 'hungry', if towards the ring or little finger, a spirit of the fields or of the village outskirts is at work. The pulse is further supposed to reveal whether the complaint is due to 'sudden fright' to inflammation, to poison and so on".[1]

From this reading, the ojha diagnoses the disease and at once applies a mantra. If this is successful the sick person at once rallies and gets well. If it fails, the ojha resorts to a second expedient and proceeds to divine the cause by sunum bonga.

III SUNUM BONGA

This process of divination is one of the most expert tasks in Santal life. The ojha gets ready some mustard oil and water and begins by taking two sal leaves. He creases the leaves and intensifies their markings. After that he dips a finger and marks each section with a drop of oil, declaring, as he goes so, what source of illness each mark will stand for.

'The possibilities,' says Bodding 'are supposed to be found among four classes : natural causes, human beings, bongas and the ancestors."

The natural causes are mostly counted into two headings natural disease and disom duk, an epidemic with high mortality.

The human beings who cause disease are the witches, and as every woman is considered a potential witch, separate marks are put down for the women of the household of the patient, of the wife's father's household, and of the wife's mother's original household. Individual beings are not sought for at this stage, only the household in which a possible witch may be found. A mark, or several, may also be put down for the village households.

The bongas are several; the most commonly suspected are the family bonga of the patient, or of his wife's father, the sima bonga (the spirit of the village boundary), the bongas supposed to reside outside the village, those invoked in the rice fields and on the threshing floor.

The fourth class consists of the forefathers, hapramko. These are seldom brought in, perhaps mostly when the ojha has a suspicion that some recently dead persons in the family may have a grudge of some kind.[2]

When all the marks have been put the ojha picks them with his finger and conjures the oil to declare the cause of illness. He then puts the other leaf on top and presses and rubs the two together conjuring the leaves also to divine the cause. Finally he removes the covering leaf and examines the disposition of the oil. According as the oil has run, the ojha announces the cause. If a bonga is at fault he advises an immediate libation of water with the promise of a bird or animal in the event of recovery. He also warns the family that the diagnosis may be wrong and urges them to employ a second ojha in case witches are at work and the analysis has been faked.

IV CATCHING THE BONGA

The next stage is to catch the bonga responsible and induce him to forsake the sick person. The ojha takes a little arwa rice, sets it on the leaf, touches it with the patient's left hand and then runs it through his fingers. He then goes out in the field by the house, scratches his thigh and mingles the blood with the rice. He then locates the bonga and scatters the rice round him saying as he does so 'Bonga, you have attached yourself to this Santal. Today I have caught you like a fish and like a crab. Leave him from now on. May all disease and sickness go. Ease his pain and may he recover like spring water. You are my Thakur and father.' After that he scatters rice for the bongas of the boundary saying 'Gosae, now you are here, you are in the stumps and roots, you are in the water, among the creepers, those who can walk come here, those who cannot, adorn it from a distance'.

After invoking these bongas, he prescribes a medicine and gives it to the patient.

V THE OJHA'S DUES

If the conjuration of this bonga and the taking of the medicine still have no effect, the ojha is asked to invoke his own tutelary or saket bonga. He accordingly vows a goat, sheep, pig or pigeons to the bonga and beseeches him to cure the patient.

If the patient then recovers, it is usual to wait for two months and if there is no relapse to redeem the vow forthwith. The patient gets the promised animals, calls the ojha to his house and after giving rice beer to the family inmates and the manjhi and paranik, he asks the ojha to make the offerings. The animals are sacrificed and after dismemberment are shared as follows : The head, liver, and lungs are cooked in rice and eaten by the ojha, the manjhi, paranik and the head of the household. The remaining flesh is split up into three. The ojha takes one-third, the head of the house one and the village people the rest. The meat falling to the head of the house is cooked with rice and given to the company. Rice beer is then drunk and the ojha is paid a fee of five four-anna bits, one of which is passed to the manjhi.

If after this there is no relapse within a year the ojha is often given a final fee of five rupees as well as a loin cloth.

VI FURTHER STEPS

In many cases these steps procure recovery. If, however, after vowing a sacrifice to the Saket bonga the patient still does not recover consultation with more ojhas becomes necessary. The village headman 'arranges to send people to seek enlightment. The people thus send take sal leaves and a little oil with them, and go in pairs to a number of known ojhas in the vicinity, to make these consult the oracle and find out the cause of the disease.

When they find the ojha, they give him the leaves and the oil asking him to perform sunum bonga. The ojha asks in whose name he is to do this and thereupon does what is required, tells the messengers what he has seen in the leaves and gives advice and warning.'[3]

'When the messengers come back they that the ojhas have found the cause of the disease to be that some bongas are at work, being hurt or hungry, the family bongas a little, those of the outskirts very much. Or, they have ceased to worship a peculiar bonga which their father or grandfather specially worshipped, or they may have neglected one of the ancestors, and so on. The message generally ends with a more or less strong admonition to take the necessary and proper precautions at once. They must engage a first class ojha.

The assembled men then speak to the person responsible, saying that he now can see the result of their help; he must himself look after the family bongas, and not trust in the ojha alone. To the already engaged ojha they will address some words, instruction him to make sure of his saket and assuring him that they will be responsible for his getting the necessaries for his work. 'They will not let his legs be broken as they express themselves.'[4]

Finally if after further sacrifices have been promised there is still no improvement, the suspicion deepens that witchcraft is the cause. For localising the witch a jan guru is consulted and when the witch has been identified, she is either made to cure the patient or is punished.[5]

VII THE RESPONSIBILITY FOR TREATMENT

Who then is responsible for initiating treatment ?

In all cases of sickness, the responsibility rests firstly on the head of the household. The father or guardian is responsible for treating children, a husband for treating his wife, a son for his widowed mother, an adult grandson for his grandmother.

The same principles cover all who are permanent or semi-permanent residents in the house. When a daughter is married to a ghar jawae, he becomes part of her father's family and any expenses for illness must be met not by the ghar jawae or his family but by the girl, her parents or agnates.

Mangal Kisku of Rakso brought a ghar jawae for his daughter. The ghar jawae fell ill and went to his father's house for treatment. His father met the expenses but later his father-in-law repaid him one goat and two pigeons and all the money he had spent.

Similarly when a ghar jawae in the house of Siba Hembrom

of Ilaki fell ill he also went to his father's house for treatment. When he recovered, his father-in-law gave the ojha one rupee and one dhoti as his fees and one fowl, two pigeons and a goat for the sacrifices.

The manner in which the ghar jawae is serving does not affect his liability and a ghar jawae by agu hatar can claim the same treatment equally with a ghar jawae in any other form.

Samu Murmu of Rakso brought a ghar jawae by agu hatar. The ghar jawae fell ill in Samu's house and all the expenses were met by Samu's widow.

Babulal Murmu was taken as a ghar jawae by agu hatar. He caught small-pox, and his father-in-law, Matla Hansdak' of Karmo, engaged an ojha and paid all the expenses.

On the same principles since a ghardi jawae is also for the time being a permanent resident, he too is entitled to treatment at his father-in-law's expense.

Duban Tudu of Pipra was a ghardi jawae in Bokrabandh. Six months after his marriage he fell ill and all the expenses were met by his wife's family. In Tilaki Siru Soren, a ghardi jawae, also fell ill and his mother-in-law gave a rupee to each of the two ojhas and sacrificed a fowl and two pigeons on his behalf.

In a similar way if a boy has married a girl by kundal napam and is living in the girl's house the usual practice is for the girl's father to meet the expenses of the boy's illness. The boy cannot, however, demand treatment from his father-in-law and if the girl's father objects the cost must be borne by his parents.

In case of servants the responsibility for treatment is fixed at the commencement of the contract and I have given a detailed account of this in the Chapter on servants and their rights.

If a casual visitor falls ill while in the house, his host must give him 'first aid' and at once get in touch with his guest's relations. The latter must then remove him and while it would be a breach of Santal hospitality to demand the first few expenses the visitor or his relations must bear all major costs.

Biswanath Murmu of Agnia fell ill in the house of Bodo Soren of Dharampur. Bodo got him treated but Biswanath later paid him all his expenses.

VIII CLAIMS AND ADJUSTMENTS

When a wife is with her husband and falls ill, difficulties rarely occur for the husband immediately arranges for her treatment. If, however, she is ill and goes to her parents or falls ill while on a visit, questions of compensation at once arise.

The wife of Bijai Hembrom went to her parents' house in Dhamna and fell ill there. She was collecting mahua flower early one morning when a splinter from a snake's bone ran into her finger. The place festered and she developed blood poisoning. She remained senseless for five days and her body swelled, so her parents called an ojha from Kurum. He gave her medicines and pronounced mantras. After that the poison came out and she got well. The ojha then sacrificed a goat and two pigeons. This was done at Dhamna but the goat and pigeons were sent by Bijai who also gave the ojha his fee of five rupees on the day of sacrifice.

If she had not recovered, there would have been no sacrifices and no fee.

Similarly when the wife of Meghrae Kisku's son fell ill in Kalhajore her father-in-law sent her to her parents' home in Kirhi asking them to look after her. An ojha was consulted and she got well. Meghrae and his son then took three fowls, two pigeons, five pailas of rice and four anna bits. The birds were for sacrificing to the bonga in redemption of the ojha's offer while the cash was the ojha's fee 'for pricking his thigh'. This latter fee was charged because the case was not serious 'but if she had been taken in a litter it would have been five rupees'. The sacrifices were done at Kirhi where the cure was effected and rice beer was also brewed. Meghrae and son did not, however, supply it as his daughter-in-law's people insisted on giving it instead. They also took nothing for the girl's keep during her illness.

In these two cases the major costs for treating the sickness were borne by the girl's husband but as relations between the families were good some minor items were excused. If, however, feelings between the families had been bad or the girl's side had been poor the following expenses would have been claimed from the husband.

1. Her food at two or three rupees per month 'because she was ill and could not work'.
2. Cloth—if the girl was ill for a long time and a new cloth became necessary.
3. Medical treatment including the cost of roots and powders (if purchased), the ojha's fee and the value of the sacrificial animals.*

At the time of visiting parents-in-law for taking a wife back after illness, an account is struck and the husband must then meet it. If he does not, the girl's parents can detain her at their house and if the husband still does not pay the charges and take her to his house his conduct gives a valid action for divorce.

The wife of a Santal of Pakri fell ill in the house of her father, Lalu Pauria, at Banka. The girl was ill for two weeks and her father bore all the expenses of her treatment. No word, however, was sent to her husband and when he was asked to give the girl's father two goats, and five rupees as the cost of treatment, he flatly refused. There was then a village meeting and it was held that he could not validly decline to reimburse his father-in-law. In spite of this, however, he did not pay the money so the two were then divorced.

In a case from Pakaur Damin which almost ended in divorce Chunka Kisku of Chitlo had married Turi Soren of Nawadih. The wedding took place in 1938 and Turi lived with her husband for three years. Then she got ill and as he did not give her any cloth she went back to her father's house. There she got better but after sometimes she again fell ill and Chunka was asked to bring an ojha. He did not do so, so her father consulted one ojha and then a second. The ojhas treated her and when she was well he paid the ojhas five rupees each and gave them each a dhoti worth two rupees. He also sacrificed two goats, four pigeons and five fowls. Chunka was asked to pay this amount but did not do so and Turi remained with

*The ojhas fees are normally five four anna bits in minor cases and five rupees in major. Further fees, however, may be settled by private negotiation and the number of sacrificial animals also varies with the illness and the ojha.

her father for four years. Finally when all attempts at a settlement had failed Chunku's father filed a money suit. This was summarily dismissed by the Subdivisional Officer who did not know the law on the point. I noticed this case while keeping an eye on Santal suits and interfered in revision. Both the sides came before me at my camp at Dharampur and Chunka then admitted that he must either divorce his wife and pay chadaodi as well as the arrears or settle the account and take her to his house. He looked at his wife and decided to take her and two days later the parties came, the account was settled and Chunka gave her a blue sari and led her gaily away.

In Mahuatanr the daughter of Sagram Tudu was married in Gasidih. The girl fell ill for six months in her father's house and her father was obliged to sacrifice a goat and four pigeons, to spend ten seers of rice and two seers of flour and to give a dhoti to the ojha. Her husband at first refused to pay these costs but after the matter had gone to a village meeting six rupees were awarded and after paying it the husband took the girl.

Similarly when the sister of Hopna Hembrom of Jhapri was on a visit to her father's village, she fell ill and her mother met all the expenses of her treatment. He asked the girl's father-in-law to reimburse him but the latter refused. Hopna then declined to let his sister go to her husband. The matter was then taken to the village and in the end the girl's father in law had to pay four rupees for a goat, and some fowls, and give one rupee four annas as the fees of the ojha. After he had paid it the girl went back to her husband.

IX CONCLUSION

The treatment of sickness furnishes in fact a wide field for legal claims. It stresses the magico-religious view of existence which underlies all Santal life. It illustrates the dependence of women, and the responsibilities of fathers, husbands and guardians. It is a mirror in miniature of all those mutual rights and obligations which makes the family the fundamental unit for tribal law.

REFERENCES

1. P.O. Bodding, Studies in Santal Medicine and connected Folk-lore : 'The Santals and Disease', *M.A.S. Beng.*, X (1927), 13.
2. Ibid., 17.
3. Ibid., 32.
4. Ibid., 33.
5. For this account of Santal medicine, I have followed Bodding, *The Santals and Disease*, 1-44. For a detailed account of witchcraft, see my report, *Bitlaha*.

39

DEATH

I

WHEN a Santal dies his funeral ceremonies fall into four stages. The first is the consignment of his corpse to fire or earth, the second is bringing home of his soul, the third is a journey to the river and preparation for his life in the world to come, while the final stage is the appeasement of his spirit by the sacrifice of a cow and his final transmission to the realm of the dead. In all these stages, death is at once a social ritual and a private drama. As with other crises in Santal life it is a focal point for tribal law. It is not only the transformation of an individual but the readjustment of a household, not only the detachment of a person from his land and his property but the avenue to new claims and rights.

II CREMATION

At a Santal's death, the news is given to the village by a drum beating three times, Kerem debe debe debe. This is a call to action and while the women keen by the corpse, the village men assemble at the house. Until the corpse is carried away there must always be five men at hand.

If the dead person is of the village, his death pollutes the village bongas and the whole community becomes unclean. If the corpse is of another village or was the wife or widow of such a Santal the bongas of the village are not polluted but the taint is given to the village where it lived. News is, therefore, sent to the village concerned and the co-villagers must receive the corpse and arrange for the funeral.

When the villagers have gathered the corpse is laid out on a cot and the women rub the body with oil and turmeric, wash the hands and feet and drip some water on the mouth.* A little vermillion is dabbed on the forehead and the body is wrapped in a cloth. This cloth is often made of silk and only if the Santal is very poor is cotton used.

A little gear is then got ready—a winnowing fan, a leaf plate, a mattock, some charred cotton seeds, some charred paddy and a fowl. A handful of thatch is pulled from the dead man's roof and the end of a straw rope is kindled from a fire in side the house. When lighting this rope, no one may blow on it with his breath.

A number of articles are also sent with the corpse. If the dead person is a man, some of his personal equipment—his battle axe, sword, bow and arrow, stick, flute or drum—is placed beside him while if the deceased is a girl or woman a few of her bangles, earrings, anklets and other ornaments are set down on the cot. In addition the following articles must also be offered—a piece of cloth (new or old), a plate, bowl and lota (all of brass), and a little money which is knotted in the cloth.

Besides these presents which are the minimum dues of the departed; and must be given from the family stock each near kinsmanis expected to contribute a small token of mourning—a coin, a bowl or a plate. This is not compulsory but is given out of family regard.

When the gifts are piled on the cot, four men lift it and with two others carrying the lighted rope and winnowing fan they bear the corpse out into the street. Ahead of them goes a third mourner strewing paddy on the ground. The body is then taken down to a piece of water. If the dead man owned a tank or bandh, he is carried to its side. Otherwise, he is borne down to the bank of a river or stream.

Brands of firewood are then arranged and a pyre is built up to the height of a hip. No special wood is necessary and if

*This is some times done in the village street after the body has been taken out.

the village has rights in firewood, the wood is simply collected from the forest. If there is no forest, the Santal conducting the funeral must procure it either by stripping some branches from his own trees or buying it in the village or market.

When the pyre is ready, the chief mourner bathes and then with the same bowl used by the women, he washes the hands and feet of the corpse and sprinkles water on its mouth. All those present bathe in turn and with the same bowl each performs the same service to the dead.

The cot is now lifted by the four bearers who go three times round the pyre and then place the cot with the head towards the south. A man mounts the pyre and looking to the west removes the cot from the corpse and sets the body on the wood. The corpse is stripped of every thing except its silk shift* and all the presents are taken off the pyre and set on the bed.

For performing this service only certain Santals are qualified. Those of a naeke khil are debarred from making the pyre as also are members of the nij khunt of each sept. The best persons for the office are the kudum naeke, any Santals who are not kudum naekes but are qualified to be so, or any member of the dead man's family. If no one qualified is present any villager may perform the task.

The man who mounted the pyre now takes the fowl, circumumbulates the pyre three times and then pins the fowl through the ear to an end pole. He then heaps some logs over the corpse and makes all ready for the burning. In return for this service, he can claim two annas but is sometimes given the cloth or brass bowl which was presented to the dead.

III AG MUK

When this has been done the corpse is ripe for burning and the man who first washed the body now performs the ritual of putting fire to the mouth. A small fire is kindled from the lighted rope and when it is fairly ablaze, he takes in his right hand a burning stick and in his left a bit of sedge, wound

*If the shift is of cotton, this also is removed as cotton does not burn quickly.

round with threads from the deadman's cloth. He lights the threaded sedge with the burning stick and as the cotton smokes he averts his gaze and touches the mouth with the lit stalk. After that he lights the pyre with the thatch taken from the roof and then in the names of the dead man's kinsman, he throws one piece of wood after another on the pyre. Other villagers cast on bits of wood, the cot is put by the side and the pyre is set ablaze. As they throw, they urge the corpse not to detain them but to burn itself out quickly 'O dead body, do not dally now. Go like the wind. Burn like a flame. We have given you wood, and fire. Be consumed and go.'[1]

This ceremony which is known as ag muk is of the greatest importance for Santal law since only one who stands in the nearest and most intimate relation to the dead can normally perform it.

If the dead person is a male, the following precedence is observed among the kinsmen.

1. Son.
2. Son's son.
3. Son of a daughter married to a ghar jawae.
4. Father.
5. Grandfather.*
6. Brother.
7. Brother's son.
8. Father's brother.
9. Son of father's brother.
10. Son of a sister married to a ghar jawae.
11. Ghar jawae husband of a daughter.
12. Ghar jawae husband of a sister.
13. Daughter married to a ghar jawae.
14. An asul duruc' servant.
15. A villager (Sarkari sengel).

*In the Jamtara subdivision and south Godda, a grandfather is 9 in order of preference and comes after the son of a father's brother; while in Rajmahal and North Godda a father's brother takes priority over a brother's son.

If the deceased is a woman the following have the right to do this office.

Unmarried (Dangua kuri)

1. Father.
2. Grandfather.
3. Brother.
4. Brother's son.*
5. Father's brother.
6. Son of father's brother.
7. Paternal nephew.
8. Son of a sister married to a ghar jawae.
9. Ghar jawae husband of a sister.
10. Guardian.
11. A villager.

Married (Bapla maejiu)

1. Husband.
2. Son.
3. Son's son.
4. Son of a daughter married to a ghar jawae.
5. Father-in-law.
6. Grandfather-in-law.
7. Husband's father's brother.
8. Husband's younger brother.
9. Son of husband's brother.
10. Sons of husband's father's brother.
11. Sons of husband's sister married to a ghar jawae.
12. Ghar jawae husband of a daughter.
13. Ghar jawae husband of a husband's sister.
14. Daughter married to a ghar jawae.
15. A servant.
16. A villager.

If a woman is divorced, the order of priority is the same as for a dangua except that if she has a son, he may sometimes be allowed to do it. If a woman is a widow, the order is the same as for a married woman except that the husband if of course deleted. As between persons of the same groups e.g. sons, uncles or nephews, whoever is eldest takes priority. Similarly as among nephews if a son of a younger uncle is elder than the son of an elder one, the former will perform the service.

If a person of high priority is ill or absent, one of lower

*In Rajmahal, West Dumka and West Godda, a father's brother has priority over a brother's son while a brother has priority over a grandfather.

priority can perform the task and if all others are absent an ordinary villager can assume the office rather than leave the dead one unattended.

This order of officiation both follows and departs from the order of inheritance. The performance of ag muk, therefore, does not in itself make a person an heir any more than guardianship alone qualifies a man to succeed. It is at most an office which an heir often performs, which may on occasions throw valuable light on the status of a claimant but which never in itself constitutes a basis for succession.

IV TERMINATION

While the pyre is blazing the villagers squat at a distance and shave their cheeks, the head of the mourner who did ag muk being shaved completely.

When the blaze subsides and the body is consumed, the unburnt logs are taken out, the ashes are gathered, and water is poured on the embers. The man who did agmug then picks out three pieces of bone, one from the skull, one from the upper arm, and another from the collarbone. These are called the jan baha or 'flowers of bone', and as he holds them in his clenched first oil and a little milk and water are poured over them. He then knots the bones into a piece of cloth torn from the shift.

These bones are, as it were, the life index of the dead. It is here that the dead man halts and his soul is, for the time being, contained.

The burning scene is then tided up. Each pall bearer stands in turn on the winnowing fan and digs a hole round it. The bones are covered with the dug earth, and the tray is mingled with the ashes and dug into the hole.

The fragments of the cot are then broken and after purifying the whole scene by sprinkling cow dung with water on all the places associated with the rites, the charred cotton seeds and paddy are sprinkled at the spot where the end poles were stood.

V UM NARKA RAKAP'

The mourners now over to a tank or stream where all take

baths. When they have finished, the man who did ag muk sets out five leaves by the water's edge, puts a little earth used for soap and a tooth twig on each, ties the 'flowers of bone' into a cloth at his waist, enters the water and after bathing, squats before the leaves. He then sprinkles as little of the earth and addresses Maran Buru, Porodhol (the ancestors), Pilchu Haram, Pilchu Budhi and the dead man in turn. 'O Pilchu Haram, this man has fallen. He is dead and gone. Do not consign him to the ashes. Keep him in your care. Bathe and wash your hair'. 'O dead one, today in your name we have bathed and rinsed our hair. Do not dwell in the ashes. You have left your home, your children and your cattle. When all is ready we shall bear you to your home.'

If the corpse is of a child from three to eight years old, the bones 'are made to swim' the same day. When the man who did ag muk goes to bathe, he consigns them to the water and makes the offerings when he comes out.

After this, all the articles taken to the pyre are either sold at once or made over to a villager for later sale. The proceeds go to the village as a whole and swell the little stock of funds which are reserved for village feasts. If a barber is employed he is given two annas from the proceeds.

As the party enters the village, some resin is burnt, and the mourners inhale the smoke. Then they go to their homes. Later in the night some of the older men go to the house and console the family 'Do not sorrow all the time' they say, he has gone away. He is happy. We too shall one day have to go. If you weep too much your body will grow thin, You will not do your work. While we live we must eat and drink. Go about your work. Put your soul under a flat stone. People say if you cry night and day the one who has gone before will but his head like a young buffalo. In the next world they will say to him 'come and dance. They are singing for you.[2] Do not mourn for him or you will load him with care and grief.'

VI THE POT OF THE DEPARTED

As the party disperses, the man who did ag muk takes a small but new earthen pot from the dead man's house and puts 'the flowers of bone' into it. He makes a lid for the vessel with a piece of broken pot, bores a hole in the middle—for 'the dead one to breathe' and inserts the culm of a grass, (*Rollboellia perforata*, Roxb) 'for the dead man to go in and out on'. The lid is then glued to the pot with turmeric paste and the pot with the bones is put in a shallow hole under a tree beyond the village. The top remains above the ground and is protected with a little heap of stones.

For the next five days, the dead one will remain with whichever enemy has killed him for until rice bear is brewed and the house is ready for the dead, the enemy cannot be dislodged and the dead one must wait, dangerous and impatient, at the end of the village.

VII BURIAL

If cremation is the ordinary rule both for men and women, there are certain circumstances in which resort is had to burial. If a Santal dies from leprosy, small pox, phthisis, asthma or cholera his body must be buried and least the touch of ag muk should infect the chief mourner, or the smoke carry the disease through the village, ag muk is also forbidden. Similarly if a woman dies in pregnancy the foetus is removed from the belly and buried, but her own body is cremated. If a child dies 'before it learns to talk' it can not announce the cause of its death and it is buried without further ceremonies. Finally in areas where forests are thin, firewood scarce and cremation impossible, burial is resorted to as the only feasible means of disposing of the body.

When burial is done as a substitute for cremation, the corpse is taken to the grave in the same manner as for burning. Instead, however, of piling up brands of firewood the villagers dig a long hole three feet deep, facing north to south and with two slots in each of its walls. A cloth is laid in the grave and the body placed on it. After that a chick is pinned inside the grave and the chief mourner does ag muk. Branches are slid down into the slots, other branches are laid over them and the body rests under a canopy of twigs. The cot is hacked to pieces and laid on top and then the man who did ag muk picks up a handful of earth and casts it on the boughs. The villagers throw earth after him and then more earth is shovelled up and the grave filled in. Finally boulders are laid over the mound like a shallow cairn and a maze of thorns is built up over the grave to keep it free of amimals. When the scene is purified with cowdung and water the mourners move away.

VIII TEL NAHAN

Five days after the death, the ceremony of tel nahan (oiling and washing) is performed. The village men gather at the dead man's house, wrap up a pai of taben, a pai of rice, and three pieces of country bread, collect from the house sufficient rice for a village meal and then assemble where the pot of the departed was buried.

The man who mounted the pyre then disinters the pot with the 'the flowers of bone', takes out the culm and pours the bones into the hands of the man who did ag muk. The latter wraps them in their original cloth and a little fire is made at the place where the pot was buried. As the flames leap up, the men say 'The hut of the old woman is ablaze' and the party move down to the end of the village. Here they meet the women. Some ebony sticks are tied together and stood up like a tripod. The pot is set down on the top and the man who mounted the pyre goes round it three times, strikes the pot with a fourth stick and smashes it to pieces.[3] This dislodges whichever enemy has killed the dead one and who until now has dogged his soul. Then the man who did ag muk holds out the bones in his hand and the women rinse his clenched fingers with turmeric, milk and water. He then knots the bones into his waist and the men go on to the piece of water beyond the frontiers of the village.

At this water the man who did ag muk purifies a piece of ground, squats by the water, sets out five leaves and on each of them puts some taben and a piece of country bread. He then offers to Maran Buru, Porodhol, Pilchu Haram, Pilchu Budhi and to the dead, throwing into the water each leaf plate inturn and addressing them 'O Pilchu Haram, Pilchu Budhi, today we have brought the fallen one from the village. We are bringing him back to the shadow of his house. Do not let him linger outside. Do not house him under the eaves. Take him by the hand and guide him to his rest.' 'O fallen one, today we are bringing you to the shadow of your house. Do not dwell outside it. Do not linger under the eaves'.

The men then bathe and rub themselves with oil and after that, they buy some fowls or a pig with money given by the chief mourner. These must be bought outside the village boundaries and are eaten with the rice before the party returns. By consuming this feast, 'in the presence of the bones' the mourners associates themselves with the dead and coax him to return.[4]

While the men are away, the women also bathe.

After sun down, the men return to village and assemble at the dead man's house. Here the feet of the man who did ag muk together with those of his two companions are washed by the nearest female relatives and 'the flowers of bone' are consigned to a new receptacle. This is either the hollow handle of a new broom or a small but new earthen pot. The vessel of the departed is then taken inside a room and put up in the rafters beyond the reach of smoke.[5]

If the dead person has been buried, and there are no 'flowers of bone' the villagers begin the tel nahan day by going to the grave. The man who did ag muk collects a symbol for the bones by taking up a handful of earth from near the body. He then goes down to a place near water. There he burns the the earth and puts it in a new earthen pot. The villagers return and the pot is put down on a tripod of ebony sticks at the end of the village. The women then gather, the pot is smashed as if it were a pot with actual 'flowers of bone' and the burnt earth is held in the hand and rinsed with turmeric, milk and water. After that the burnt earth is used as a proxy for the bones and the ritual is the same as in cremation.

IX ELICITING THE CAUSE OF DEATH

The villagers now gather in the courtyard and the man who did ag muk assumes the role of the dead man while two villagers take the parts of Porodhol and Maran Buru. The actor for the dead one demands water from all the deadman's kinsmen and the inmates of his house and when he is offered it, he demands water from all the villagers. Maran Buru and Porodhol are also given bowls of water which they drink.

The three are then given bowls of rice beer and the man who did ag muk asks the dead man how he died. 'I went of my own will' Porodhol is also asked and he replies 'I was kept inside. I do not know'.

After that, the dead is asked if the future holds any danger. If there is danger he replies 'consult the ojhas and jan gurus. They will give medicines. They will prescribe the sacrifices, all will be well.'

The people than drink rice beer and go to their homes. The dead person is now, as it were, in transit. He has lost the enemy that killed him but he has not as yet been admitted to the ancestors. He is still at one with the 'bones of flower'. They are his temporary abode and he must now dwell for some time in his house until his kinsmen can arrange for his final passage.

With the ablutions of the people, the village bongas cease to be unclean and sacrifices can again be made to them. The house of the dead one remains 'in the shadow' but his kinsmen are at liberty to perform weddings and make sacrifices.

X THE ROLE OF THE JADUPATIA

While these ceremonies are proceeding and sometimes even on the day death itself, the house of the dead person is visited by a jadupatia.* This individual combines the roles of itinerant minstrel and funerary beggar. He brings a few scrolls of paintings depicting the Santal myth of creation, the baha festival, the life in Death's kingdom and sometimes the Krishna cycle and the goddess Kali. He squats in the courtyard, unrolls his pictures, entones a recitative and finally produces a sketch in which the dead person is shown with blank and sightless eyes. In the corner of the drawing is a picture of a cow, a fowl, a bowl or a brass plate according as the jadupatia assesses the wealth of the family. At the end he exacts the animal or utensils as his tribute for restoring sight to the dead and only when it is given does he put the eyeballs in the sketch and leave the house.

*This practice is usual throughout the eastern half of the Santal Parganas.

The jadupatia's tribute is paid either from the dead person's own movables or if he has left none, from the property of the joint household, his guardian or his heir.

XI THE JOURNEY TO THE RIVER

Some weeks after tel nahan, the chief mourner fixes a day for consigning 'the flowers of bone' to water. The villagers assemble at the house, drink rice beer and the dead man, Maran Buru and Porodhol are again evoked and questioned. 'Today, we are taking you to the river. May no ache of head or belly wrack us. Keep us from all harm in the way,' and the dead man replies, 'shall keep all harm away. Go and come like the wind'.

The man who did ag muk then takes out 'the flowers of bone' in their little cloth and women pour turmeric, milk and water over his clenched hand. The ears of a fowl are chopped off and the blood stains some rice. If a date for the feast has been settled a cow is reserved for sacrifice and the blood is got by cutting a slit in the ear. The blood smeared rice is then put in a leaf packet while in another leaf, a copper pice and some *sindur* are tied together.

The man who did the ag muk puts on a new dhoti and knots 'the flowers of bone' into his waist. The party now set out. The man who mounted the pyre carries the pot or drags the broom sweeping the earth as he goes. At the village end, the man who did ag muk squats on the ground and the man who mounts the pyre offers a fowl, tears off its head, and throws the head, and carcase away. The pot is then smashed or the broom thrown away.

If the former custom of taking the bones to the Damodar is followed, the man who did ag muk takes one or two villagers with him and goes on to the river.

If, however, this is not done (and it is now-a-days no longer usual to make such a long journey) the villagers go in a body to a river or stream. If the departed was the owner of a tank they go there while if there is no river close at hand, they scoop a hole and fill it with water. The man who did ag muk goes to the west, taking the bones with him and never looking back. At the water he buys the ghat with a pice. Then he mixes the bones with the blood besmeared rice and entering the stream consigns them to the water.

After the bones are immersed, offerings are made to Maran Buru, Porodhol, Pilchu Haram, Pilchu Budhi and to the dead himself. 'O fallen one, today we have washed ourselves in the great river. Do not linger out side the house. Do not dwell in the eaves. When I return I will arrange your last feast'. The new cloth is then discarded and abandoned. The offerings are eaten and villagers go back.

On the way they buy fowls or a pig from a village not their own and after eating a meal with rice, they wait till sun-down and return to the village. There the chief mourner gives them rice beer and they go to their houses.

With this ceremony, the dead one is released from his temporary shell—'the bones of flower'—and is now an acknowledge ancestor, a family bonga. But he is not yet fully of the dead neither has he entered the realm of Jom Raja. He must now dally in the bhitar or private shrine and await the feast when his kinsmen will take their last farewell and send him happy and honoured, to his long home.

XII BHANDAN

The final stage in the funeral ceremony is the bhandan or cow sacrifice. This can not be performed earlier than nine days after the return from the river but is permissible at any later date. It is celebrated for all except small children and if the initiation ceremony of coco chatiar has not been performed this is done as part of the bhandan.

The village men first bathe and shave and assemble in the house of the dead. They are given rice beer and a meal. Then the man who did ag muk again sustains a role of the dead man, his companion is possessed by Porodhol and a third enacts Maran Buru. The deadman is re-identified. 'It is I', he says. Then he demands water from all his immediate relations and after water is given he again declares the cause of his death. Finally rice is offered to him and the family say, 'Keep us in peace. Do not trouble us. Do not take anything away.' The three men then emerge from their roles and are given rice beer.

The jogmanjhi now erects a sal branch in the courtyard and the man who did ag muk sacrifices a fowl by clubbing it on the head. The cow with the nicked ear is then led in, tied to the branch and after dedication, it is felled by the jogmanjhi with the butt-end of an axe. After that the near kinsmen offer fowls, pigs or goats.

In cutting up the cow, the side on which it falls is carefully observed. The fore-leg of this side together with the head is allowed to the villagers, the necks is given to the barber and out of the rest three divisions are made. The first is cooked with rice and is eaten by all (i.e., the villagers and members of the house), The second is divided among the villagers who take the pieces to their homes. The third is kept by the dead man's family. The man who does the bhandan gets the hide.

The other sacrificial animals are divided as follows: A calf, goat or pig is split in two down the spine. One side and the head goes to the man who sacrificed it while the other side is cut up into three. Out of these one goes to the villagers one to the man performing the bhandan and one to the man who gave the animal. The last share is cooked then and there.

If a samdhi attends the bhandan of a samdhi he must take two animals for sacrifice, ten seers of taben, ten seers of rice and two pots of rice beer. He must also bring a dhoti or sari as a present to the widower or widow. One animal is sacrificed with the others and shared on the same principles while the other is killed on the day he returns. The head and foreleg of the second animal is left with the host and the rest of the carcase is taken by him. When he goes he is given five seers of taben, one pot of rice beer and five seers of rice.

If fowls are sacrificed, they are all cut up together and divided into three-one to the man performing the bhandan, one to be cooked and eaten by those contributing and helping and one for eating by the villagers.

A little later some cooked rice is brought out and setting before the branch the man who did ag muk offers it first to the dead and then to the grand parents. 'O deadman, today we have given you rice. Take and eat it gladly. Look to your children. Keep them from harm. Go your way gladly. Keep all sorrows or ill far from the house'. Rice beer is then brought and offered in the same way.

After this the flesh is brought out and the man who did ag muk again sits before the branch. He faces east holding a dismembered leg of the cow and the man then recites the traditions of the ancestors. This recital often lasts the greater part of the night and ends 'We have cleaned the head that was full of ashes and the mouth that oozed blood. He who was black as a crow is white as a swan'. This recital, the man who did ag muk is purified. The villagers drink more rice beer. Then they prepare and cook the flesh with rice. The village share is taken outside and eaten in the street while the family eat in the house. These later provisions are mandatory for the village share is known as kulhi sura—'the feast of the street'.

Once the bhandan is performed, the dead one is finally gathered to his ancestors. He takes with him all the animals that were sacrificed. He enter's death's kingdom and is allotted a round of daily tasks by Jom Raja. If he has given *sindur* to a previously married girl, their deaths unite them in hanapuri, and husband and wife resume their earthly conjugal routine. Children, however, are parted from their mothers 'for in the life on earth they sucked their blood'. For much of the day the ancestors must devote themselves to Jom Raja and to executing his behests. But they are often free from tasks and can come for short periods to their villages. Even when they are involved in various duties, they see and hear all that is happening and can hurriedly take leave and intervene. For a generation they take an active interest in village matters and it is only when a generation has completely replaced the old familiar figures and their names are lost to memory that they merge in the multitude of the venerable dead and intervene no more.

XIII THE SUBSTITUTE BHANDAN

When the bhandan is over the impurity which has hitherto dogged the household ends and the family can again sacrifice to bongas, drink rice beer, use *sindur* and celebrate weddings.

It is, therefore, of great importance that once a man had died his bhandan should be done promptly.

If for any reason a family can not do the ceremony quickly, a substitute bhandan has to be arranged instead.

On the day of return from the river, a fowl is offered by the man who did ag muk. It is cooked with rice and offerings are made to the departed and the grand parents. The dead man is asked to accept the food and so make way for weddings and the placation of the bongas. After this the man who did ag muk is declared finally pure. The people are given rice beer and go to their homes. Some months or years later, a full bhandan is performed so that the spirit of the dead may be finally appeased.

XIV MORA KARAM

In addition to the bhandan, a karam for the dead man is some times performed. This bears the same relation to the bhandan as a choral Requiem Mass does to ordinary Mass. It is an optional enhancement of the funerary ritual. It is never compulsory and is performed only by those Santals whose status gives them particular dignity or honour in the area. The celebration involves a long recital of traditions not covered at the bhandan, the drinking of rice beer and an additional feast to the villagers.[6]

XV THE FUNERARY DUES

It will be obvious that no scale of expenditure can be posited for a funeral for at each stage the costs are determined by the means of the dead man and his family and heirs as well as by the size of the village and its various households. It is necessary, however, to make clear on whom the costs fall, and how they are met under tribal law.

The obligation to perform the funerary ritual rests in the first instance on whoever is for the time being the head of the household. In a joint household it is the senior head of the family. In a separate household it is the father or the husband. If a woman is married, she becomes part of her husband's family and accordingly even if she dies at her father's village, her husband is responsible for all her obsequies. If for any reason delay occurs and the body is burnt or buried in his absence, he is required to collect 'the flowers of bone' and to take them to his village. He must also pay all the costs attending the cremation or interment. If the dead person is himself the head of the household his next heir is required to arrange his funeral, and meet all the costs.

If the next heir is absent, some one on the spot may make the arrangements and incur the expenses but the heir must repay him when he succeeds to the property.

If a man dies leaving several sons, ag muk is the privilege of the eldest but the responsibility for the funeral as a whole is joint. Accordingly if as sometimes happens one of several brothers performs the funeral, he does so not in his individual capacity but in discharge of a joint duty. He can, therefore, recoup from his brothers a proportionate share of the costs and this is done by allowing him to cultivate his father's fields for a season before partitioning them among the brothers.

Similarly if a relation who is not the next heir performs the rites he may sometimes be allowed to cultivate some lands to recoup his costs and after that the heirs succeed.

We have seen that certain articles and utensils of the dead must accompany the body to the grave or pyre and that a piece of the deadman's property is exacted by the jadupatia. These articles are normally only a fraction of the dead one's movables but the funerary costs are not a charge on the remainder. If the person performing the funeral is the next heir, he may recoup his costs by selling the movables or the produce of the dead man's fields. If, however, the dead person is a woman, her private property will go to her sons while her funerary expenses must be met by her husband. The person performing the funeral is often the next heir but the right to inherit and the duty to the dead are always distinct.

XVI THE RIGHTS OF THE DEAD

What are the last rights of the dead?

For a generation the sole demand of the dead is to be honoured and remembered and if this is done they remain the unseen well-wishers of the hearth and home. If, however, they are speedily forgotten or conventional tribute is withheld they are liable to intervene in worldly affairs and cause sickness, loss and care. Even little things may cause umbrage and, like Fortune in Dryden's translation, the dead often appear

> Still various and inconstant still
> But with an inclination to be ill.

For this reason the dead must constantly receive oblations and whether it is a time of drinking water or rice beer, eating, a meal, celebrating a festival, a birth or a wedding or placating bongas the recent dead must be given their small offerings.

At the Sohrae, Baha and Erok' festivals, special sacrifices must be made to the dead and at the Sohrae festival the village decides whether to do the Khuntao or 'play with the buffaloes and cows' according as death has visited the village. If some have died in the preceding year, a limit is set to jollity and the 'play' is not held.

If there is no male member of the household qualified to sacrifice, an agnate of the dead one must be charged with the duty and if necessary must be given some land for curc' cawale to enable him to do so.

How deeply held are these beliefs will be clear from two examples.

For two years Chotu Ramu of Amtala had not offered to his ancestors at Sohrae. Then, a little before the Mag festival, a bullock went astray. He searched for it for ten days and failed to find it. Then on the festival day a man became possessed and told him that the bullock was in Buski but he must offer his father a sheep and it was because he had neglected him that this misfortune had be fallen them. Chotu Ramu then went to Buski recovered his bullock and made the sacrifice.

Similarly Ranjit Hembrom of Kusma, had not offered to his ancestors for three years. Suddenly his mother began to have fits and when they asked the ojhas the latter said it was because they had not offered to the ancestors. Ranjit then arranged for his uncle to do the sacrifices and his mother recovered.

In this conventional homage is given, the dead do not intervene in human affairs. Yet in every phase of life their influence is seen. They are the 'unacknowledged legislators', 'the guardians of the faith,' 'the army of law'. Their views and acts are constantly cited. They are the honoured source of tribal traditions. It is 'with the ancestors' that the village sits to settle weddings, discuss affairs and adjudicate disputes. It is the dead who with the living are the makers and maintainers of tribal law.

REFERENCES

1. There is similar practice in Muria funerals but the significance of the rite is different. 'The flames shot up and the women broke into loud and moving lamentation. The men threw twigs on to the burning corpse, muttering. 'God to whom we vowed gifts has failed us. Let him take these twigs instead, for it's all he 'llget.' (Elwin : *The Muria and their Ghotul*, 148).
2. There is a close parallel to this in Muria views 'It is said that the soul of the dead hear all things on earth the wrong way round. Mourning sounds to them like merry making, and a song sounds like a wail. (Elwin : op. cit., 157).
3. Campbell notes that 'if it be broken to pieces it is supposed that there will be no more deaths in the family at present but should it not be shattered to pieces, one or more deaths may be expected in the near future'. 'Death and Cremation Ceremonies among the Santals' *J.B.O.R.S.*, II, 449-56.
4. Elwin records of the Muria 'In some villages in the Kondagaon Tahsil the Muria go to the nearest bazar to buy parched rice, gram and liquor. They walk round the shops scattering the rice and gram and then visit the grave of the dead man. Here they eat and drink a little and then go home saying to the soul of the dead 'come home with us'. They go into the room of the departed and it is believed that the soul follows them.

   The mourners go to a bazar. The women carry rice, bread and sweets in their basket and sit down near the market place but away from it. They pretend to have a bazar of their own and the men of the party go to them and pretend to buy. The widow or the chief female mourner, if the deceased was a man, comes and sits in the middle of the party; the Gaita offers fire and incense and the rest give her leaves and flowers. In some villages it is supposed that it is at this time that the soul of the dead man mixes with his ancestors. Then the widow leads the party widdershins round the bazar and comes home. On their arrival at the house the mourners say to her 'Now let us depart. You have had great sorrow for your life has left you. You have had great expense, but don't worry. Live happily and eat your fill. God has given you sorrow, but if you brood on this sorrow over much who will care for your children?' (Elwin : op. cit., 157).

5. Among the Murias of Bastar, there is a permanent pot of the departed in each house. 'Some time after death "the soul is brought back to the house". The people go down to a tank or river. The near relatives of the deceased then go into the water crying on the dead to come to them and try to catch any kind of living thing. Whoever first catches a fish or prawn or frog, whatever it may be is regarded as specially loved by the dead and is rewarded with extra drink and small presents. They put the fish into one of the pots together with a ring. Then a girl (daughter or daughter-in-law to the dead) lifts the pot, puts it on her head, carries it up to the house and puts it down bear the pot of the departed. Then they pour the water together with the fish and ring into the ground and tie the ring which represents the man's soul, from the roof above the pot of the departed. Sometimes the ring is tied to a broom. They hang the pot itself up to the roof of the house.' (Elwin : op. cit., 152-53).

6. For a full account of the ritual in Santali, see Stephen Hari Murmu, *Caco Chatiar ar Karam Binti* (Dumka, 1945).

PART SIX

40

THE TRIAL OF SANTAL SUITS

I THE SANTAL CIVIL COURTS

WE HAVE seen in Chapter 1 that Santal law derives its pattern and continuity from a series of tribal councils. These bodies administer by far the greater part of Santal civil justice and rely only on their own prestige and essential fairness to secure the acceptance of their awards. If, however, a Santal is dissatisfied with a local order, or flouts a tribal decision, the scene of action shifts from the village and the remedy is a suit in the official courts of the district.

These courts are known as Santal Civil Courts and are constituted under Act XXXVII of 1855. They are competent to decide all suits valued at Rs 1,000 or less and are governed by a simple code of procedure known as the Santal Civil Rules.*

In this last chapter, therefore, I will turn from legal principles to administration and will note some of the more salient points which Santal courts should bear in mind when trying Santal suits.

II THE TECHNIQUE OF TRIAL

The first important consideration is the venue of the trial. A court room is usually the worst place in which to try a Santal suit for the raised dais, the wooden railings, the heavy benches

*I have dealt more fully with these Courts in my essay. *Court Justice in Tribal India.*

all create an atmosphere of remote severity which is the very reverse of what is needed for Santal justice. It is always preferable, therefore, to try a Santal suit in camp for this not only encourages the whole village to attend but gives to justice the homely air of a tribal proceeding.

When a hearing commences, it is best to get each party to state its own case and if a plaint or written statement has been filed to check first that it correctly represents a case. Since most Santals are illiterate, it not infrequently happens that their petitions contain either incorrect or incomplete data. A plaint or petition should, therefore, be treated only as a guide to the suit and by no means as an exhaustive recital of all its issues. If a case as orally explained by a Santal differs from the case as noted in his plaint or petition, the latter should always be discarded and the Santals oral case should be treated as his claim.

Moreover even when a plaint or petition correctly states a case, it sometimes fails to request the correct reliefs. It is better, therefore, to treat the written version only as a tentative beginning and when all the facts have been heared for the court itself to decide the proper relief. In many cases this will be the same as what is claimed but sometimes it is less and occasionally it is more. If a Santal is entitled to fifteen rupees but has claimed ten, he should be asked whether he has deliberately given up the extra five, and if not the court itself should amend the claim and decree him all his dues. This is very necessary because the court's decision will be quoted in the surrounding area and will cause confusion if the sum decreed is not exactly correct.

The same principles apply to the impleading of parties. In hearing Santal appeals, I have often found that in certain types of suit, and particularly those involving ghar jawaes, a party is made a plaintiff of defendant when strictly speaking he has nothing to do with the suit. When the outlines of a case are clear, therefore, the court itself should verify whether all the plaintiffs and defendants are relevant, should exclude any that are unnecessary and should add any that are relevant but have been accidentally omitted.

When the hearing is over care should be taken that only the party who is entitled actually gets the decree and that no one is linked to the award who is not entitled to a share. A husband, for example, has often no place at all in a suit brought by a wife unless he happens to be the defendant. Similarly a father, for example, can claim a return of bride-price but he cannot sue for the divorce money of his daughter.

A woman, and in certain cases her father can sue for lajao marao but her husband is not at all entitled to such money. If the decree merges together certain parties who should be distinct, it offends the Santal sense of logic and discredits the courts in Santal eyes.

III THE VILLAGE OFFICIALS

In the hearing of a Santal suit, what should be the role of the village officials ?

We have already seen that in almost every stage of Santal life the village community is involved. In certain cases its explicit consent is necessary. In others it must at least have tacitly acquiesced in. Without such positive approval or implied acceptance many acts are quite invalid by Santal law. Moreover 'registration' by the village is often a necessary condition for validating an action. In almost all Santal suits, therefore, an essential step should be to summon the village officials as witnesses for the court. Such officials should include at the very least the manjhi, paranik, jogmanjhi and godet, while the jogparanik, naeke and kudam naeke should also, if possible, be heard. Independently of what the parties assert these officials should be asked what happened in the village. If a particular act such as the induction of a ghar jawae requires formal approval they should be asked if a formal meeting was held and approval accorded. If the act is one in which village acquiescence is sufficient, they should say whether the parties were in any way denounced or punished. In cases of paternity, marriage, divorce and compensation the same principles should be followed. In all these cases the history of the dispute is of great importance and to this also the village officials are the persons most competent to depose.

Whether in fact as exponents of village policy or as independent observers of facts, the village officials are indispensable for the correct decision of a Santal suit.

IV PATERNITY

When a suit is for succession to movable or immovable property, it is nearly always questions of law which are involved and only rarely that the relationship itself is disputed. Occasionally, however, cases arise in which paternity is questioned and I will briefly suggest the ways in which such cases can be best approached.

The first type of case concerns the birth of a child out of wedlock and usually arises in the months immediately succeeding its birth. In such cases the mother is entitled to certain reliefs for herself and the child but a court is sometimes required to determine who is the father. In such cases it is often quite impossible to do justice by applying strictly the Indian Evidence Act and it becomes essential, therefore, to decide such suits in terms of Santal assumptions. In almost all cases, the whole village knows which boy is the father of a girl's child. It is useless to enquire how exactly it knows this for it is only rarely that a boy and girl are ever caught together in an act of sex. Yet the interest of a boy and girl in one another, their constant association, the gossip of their friends does not escape village notice. If a girl's assertion coincides with village observation, and the boy can neither give reasons for the false indictment nor accuse and name another as potential father, the village does not shrink from fastening the paternity on him, We must also remember that in Santal eyes it is far more serious for a child to have no father than it is for a child to be wrongly fathered on a boy. The injustice to the child far outweighs the possible injustice to the parent. Accordingly in all such suits if justice is not only to be done but recognised as being done the greatest weight should be given to village opinion and if a meeting has once declared a boy to be the father, a court should be extremely loathe to disagree. Similarly if the village has declared paternity unproved, the court should be very cautious in accepting evidence to the contrary. The village officials should be asked why they took this view and only if the circumstances raise a doubt about their bonafides should the village view be overruled.

When such suits arise, they are almost always in the form of claims for maintenance. But maintenance is only one of several dues and when the case has come to court, it is better to investigate the whole situation and liquidate it completely rather than merely pass a money decree for a few months' keep. Once the essential issue of paternity has been settled, the court should arrange for the child's early transfer to its father's charge. If the father can be induced to marry the mother, that is often the best solution but if he refuses, all the mother's dues for herself and her child should be realised from him and a time fixed for assuming custody of the child.

The second type of suit involving questions of paternity arises when a father dies and his sons or brothers attempt to oust a son by another wife. In such cases it is necessary to investigate the nature of the father's supposed marriage bearing in mind the great flexibility of the Santal marriage system, the limited uses of *sindur* and the fact that the union may have lasted only a few months. In many cases the marriage may have been by or ader or apangir and village knowledge and acquiescence will be its only valid basis. Similarly the whole process of naming the 'son' should be traced from its beginning. If his sept tallies with his father's, it should be seen whose true name he bears, whether a naming ceremony was duly held, whether the paternity was disputed at the time, what was decided by the village and whether the Santal in whose name he was shaved expressly declined all civil liabilities. If there was no dispute at birth, no hitch over the naming ceremony, and no express reservations it should be presumed that his parents were duly married, and that the Santal is a fully qualified son.

V SUCCESSION AND PARTITION

During the period 1900 to 1930, when Santal law was in transition succession suits were not uncommon, Since, however, the principles of inheritance are now settled, such suits are likely to decrease and if any are now brought their decision should be simplified by reference to the foregoing chapters.

Partition suits are similarly very rare but it is necessary to bear in mind a father's or a husband's slightly privileged position, and that a son who insists on partition against the family will can legally demand only a fraction for his maintenance and not a full or equal share. Similarly if a mother separates from her sons or a wife from her husband (the two not being divorced), the claim is always for what is reasonable rather that for what is equal. It is only when there is general agreement in the family and then very largely on account of that agreement, that shares at a partition are strictly equal.

VI ADOPTION

We have seen that adoption is a well-established Santal practice going back to long before the Santal Rebellion. If adoption is alleged but disputed, two points need careful investigation—firstly whether formal approval of the village was given at a meeting and secondly, whether bonga tala was essential and was done. This latter ceremony with its attendant change of name and sept is indispensably necessary for certain types of adoption but absolutely impossible in the case of others. It necessary, therefore, to investigate the previous relationship, if any, between the adopting parent and the adopted child in order that this crucial point may be decided. If bonga tala was necessary but was not done, the adoption is always quite invalid. In addition to these points, enquiry should sometimes be directed to length of residence in the adopting family, which person met the marriage costs of the adopted child and how the latter's children have been named. These circumstances are relevant whenever there is conflicting evidence on the point of village approval but if the evidence is clear that there was no village meeting and no formal ratification, such circumstances prove nothing and are obviously irrelevant.

VII GUARDIANS

Suits for declaration of guardianship are never very common but are sometimes necessary if near relations disagree or if a minor child is neglected in its guardian's house. When such suits occur, it is nearly always the custody of the land which is in issue and since it is very risky to allow land to remain with a distant reversioner, the table of preference should be strictly followed unless a guardian has patently abused his position and forfeited his claim. As in other Santal suits, the best course for a court to follow is to heal the dispute by securing, if possible, an agreed arrangement. If the latter is impossible the law should of course be enforced.

VIII THE RIGHTS OF WOMEN

In Chapters Thirteen to Twenty-two, I have set out the various rights of women both as owners of property and as reversioners or heirs. These rights are now everywhere accepted as current Santal law and there should, therefore, be little difficulty in now deciding suits in which a Santal woman is a party. The most important ways in which the law has clarified itself are that subject to various conditions a widow has precisely defined rights in her husband's property, a mother has also certain rights in her son's property and agnates still exclude daughters from inheritance unless the latter are married to ghar jawaes. In hearing all such cases, therefore, it is only necessary to verify the relationship between the parties because when that is settled the decision follows automatically in terms of the prescribed law. It is when the husband of a girl is a ghar jawae that a suit may sometimes become a little complex. As I have pointed out in Chapters 22 and 32 the Santal law relating to this institution is by no means simple. Besides considering the case of a marriage in original ghar jawae form, a court may also have to adjudicate suits in which the ghar jawae status has been later secured by a village adjustment. In all such suits the evidence of the village officials is of great importance since no one can become a ghar jawae without village approval.

Moreover a number of circumstances attend the valid induction of a ghar jawae. Continued residence in his wife's house, and the naming of his children in a special manner are valuable pointers to the status; while in the case of a Santal who alleges an original wedding in ghar jawae form, the ritual of the ceremony and the exemption of a bride-price* may also raise presumptions in his favour.

*Or occasionally as in Rajmahal subdivision payment of a reduced bride-price.

So far as the rights of the ghar jawae himself are concerned, I have dealt with these fully and it is perhaps only necessary to stress the importance of his continued residence in his wife's village and the forfeiture of his rights if he marries without the approval of her family. The whole law, however, is so intricate that in any suit involving a ghar jawae and his claims, the whole of Chapter Twenty-two should be freshly studied.

IX MARRIAGE AND DIVORCE

In Santal suits affecting marriage and divorce, the subject matter is almost invariably a money claim arising out of the conduct of a party, the union itself, the process of negotiation or the ritual of a ceremony. In all such cases, the local rates of payment should be ascertained by consulting the parties and if they disagree the pargana and neighbouring manjhis should be asked for a ruling. Similarly in claims for a brother's bullock, for damages on account of wedding costs, the village officials are the best persons to testify the value of the animals and to state the actual expenses.

Although suits for divorce itself are very rare, suits for reliefs arising from a divorce situation are very common. These arise only when a man and his wife have either separated or are in process of separation. It is desirable, therefore, that before such suits are either decreed or dismissed the marriage itself should be reviewed. I myself have found on some occasions that an apparent break-down in relations was due either to the fault of the parents or to a petty misunderstanding. A talk with the parties or a discussion with the villagers could sometimes put matters right and the claim for divorce money or return of bride-price ended with the boy and girl returning together. On the other hand suits sometimes occur in which although divorce is not expressly asked for, it is yet the only way out of a disastrous situation. In all such cases, the court should explore the various solutions, discuss the situation with the villagers and then proceed to do whatever is necessary to end the deadlock. If divorce is decided on, the terms must be worked out according to Santal law. If one side has evaded the village it is of the utmost importance that the court itself should decide. If in such circumstances the villagers and one party agree that the marriage should end, and the woman is also not beyond the age of divorce, the court should be prepared itself to gave that verdict.

There is, however, one case that involving witchcraft when age may sometimes have to be ignored. We have seen that if a woman is a witch, that in itself is a valid ground for her divorce and that not only her husband but her childern also can enforce a separation. It is obvious, however, that a court must be extremely cautious in granting this relief though it should not shrink from doing so if the circumstances justify it. A woman who herself admits witchcraft or who after repeated warnings and continued diagnosis by several jan gurus is adjudged guilty by the village should be pronounced divorced if her husband's family demands it.

VOLUME TWO

BITLAHA

A
Report
on
Santal Criminal Law

Law, say the gardeners, is the Sun,
Law is the one
All gardeners obey
Tomorrow, yesterday, today.

Law is the wisdom of the old
The impotent grandfathers shrilly scold ;
The grandchildren put out a treble tongue,
Law is the senses of the young.

Yet law-abiding scholars write ;
Law is neither wrong nor right,
Law is only crimes
Punished by places and by times,
Law is the clothes men wear
Anytime, anywhere,
Law is Good-morning and Good-night.

W.H. Auden. *Another Time*

PREFACE

I

IN THIS report I have attempted to describe all those incidents in tribal life which Santals of the Santal Parganas regard as offences. No enquiry into tribal law, however, can stop at the simple cataloguing of crimes. In certain cases what is criminal to Santal is not immediately and patently wrong to those who are not tribesmen. The refusal of a woman to give animals for sacrifice would not to many people seem a crime yet in the light of the Santal theory of witchcraft this might easily be a grave threat to village security. A love affair between a Santal girl and a stranger to the tribe might at first sight seem only a form of rural romance yet in the light of Santal views of tribal pollution it is one of the worst offences a Santal can commit.

> The glacier knocks in the cupboard
> The desert sighs in the bed
> The crack in the tea cup opens
> A lane to the land of the dead.

Even the most ordinary occurrence may suddenly acquire terror and horror in its tribal context. In describing these offences, therefore, I have treated them as logical consequences of certain tribal attitudes. I have explained the Santal 'world-view', the Santal theory of bongas the tribal attitude to health for only through an understanding of these conceptions can we seize the significance of many Santal offences.

Moreover in considering tribal crime and punishment it is essential to regard them not merely in terms of their immediate background but in the light of tribal culture as a whole. This is particularly important when we consider a Santal punishment such as bitlaha for to those who know little of Santal society the conduct of this ceremony might seem merely a distasteful rite. Its true nature can only be appreciated when we recall the dominant characteristics of Santal culture—its passion for cleanliness, its insistence on neat living, its genius for domestic architecture, its zest for play, its ban on indecency. The significance of the punishment—its overwhelming force as a Santal sanction—lies precisely in the circumstance that at other times this is not how Santal act.

There is another circumstance which I should also stress. The law of a tribe is necessarily an expression of tribal values but it does not express all the values of a tribe. The Santal delight in song and dance hints at one of the most obvious of Santal values but this is not prescribed by tribal law.

A society might have an imposing code of rules and yet be dogged with dread and tainted with gloom. Yet the best of law is ultimately its ability to promote the happiness of those whom it orders and controls. To describe the tone of Santal society would involve discursions far beyond the merely legal. Yet it is this and only this which in the last analysis can validate a law. Santals in the Santal Parganas have a zest for life, a gaiety which would be impossible if their law were out of gear or did not fit their tribal nature. It is to this that any discussion of Santal Law should constantly return.

In three of my chapters I have discussed the administration of Santal law, its relation to the Indian Penal Code; its place in the judicial system of the district. No one, I think, would deny that a sensitive relation between official jurisprudence and tribal ways of justice is an urgent necessity, for an order passed in contravention of tribal rules whether by deliberate decision or in ignorance of practice is capable of causing a degree of tribal dismay out of proportion to what a court can realize. If the objection of administration is to secure conditions in which a people may be free to lead their own lives in their own way, the conflicts between external decisions and tribal assumptions should be as few as possible. For achieving this ideal the education of magistrates is one method, but an older more indigenous expedient may, I think, secure more lasting results. 'The systematic belittling or over-looking of the part played in the jurisprudence of India by unofficial bodies, W.V. Grigson has said, 'is something of very long standing dating back to the first establishment of regular courts in British India ; this will be clear to anyone who studies the history of the growth of the courts, and the failure, in the face largely of lawyer opposition, of sincere attempts to use panchayats to settle all petty village disputes, civil or criminal and of reference to arbitration panchayats of the issues in the more important cases'.[1] The panchayat system was in India long before the British came and may flourish long after they have left. The return of justice to the village is the method which is most likely to satisfy the needs of the tribes.

II

To the many who assisted me in making this survey I must express my gratitude. As in the case of Civil Law in Santal society, I wrote this report in 1945 and 1946, while I was on Special duty. My enquiries date, however, from 1943 when as Deputy Commissioner of the Santal Parganas I first attended a bitlaha. It was the experience of this ceremony as well as the prevailing ignorance of Santal usage which prompted me to investigate the Santal law of crime. In making these enquiries I was much assisted by Stephen Murmu and Seth Charan Hansdak' both of whom unravelled points of Santal practice and greatly aided me in understanding the Santals and their views.

Surveys of tribal life often suffer from the fact that only one investigator makes them and, however, scientific may be his methods, it is inevitable that many areas should escape his scrutiny. There is often also little scope for independent checking and it would be surprising if a final draft did not sometimes contain assertions which further enquiries would have modified. After prolonged tours among the Bondos of Koraput in 1945, Verrier Elwin wrote an account of these people only to find in 1946, when he again toured widely among them that many of his statement required revision. I myself have had again and again to modify my views on Santal institutions because my first enquiries were incomplete. In this present report, I have therefore avoided the weaknesses of a single person's investigation by enlisting the assistance of various officers and Santals. When I had written many chapters,

I analysed their contents and prepared a series of questions. These were put to the same Santals who attested Civil Law in Santal society and the final draft was written only after I had scrutinised their answers. While therefore I alone am responsible for the final presentation, the independent enquiries by ten officers at twenty centres throughout the Santal Parganas enable for greater correctness to be claimed for the facts than would ordinarily have been possible. To those who conducted these enquiries—Sashi Kant Sinha, Stephon Hidim Tudu, Hari Tudu, Ram Dutta Pande, Ajit Kumar Chatterji, Keshav Nandan Sahay, Rameswar Nath, Seth Choron Hansdak', Jacob Hembrom, Doman Sahu and Sushil Soren—I am deeply grateful.

Besides these assistants, I must acknowledge the great help accorded to me by various officers and non-official gentlemen. Pandit Binodanand Jha, M.L.A. favoured me with frank constructive criticism. Mr. A.R. Adair, I.C.S., who succeeded me as Deputy Commissioner of the Santal Parganas, read the account in draft and advised me on many points of detail. Mr. Syed Muhammad Naqavi, displayed exceptional understanding of many Santal problems, discussed many bitlahas with me and gave the report the benefit of his alert and detailed scrutiny. Uma Prosad Das and Sachindra Nath Moitra gave devoted assistance in the preparation of the typescript.

To Rameswar Nath I must make a special reference. This young Magistrate has earned the affection of many Santals by his knowledge of their language, his interest in their life and his friendly sympathetic dealings. In the work of collecting reports he was of the very greatest assistance while his intelligent cooperation shortened many hours of arduous analysis.

Above all I must note some, at least, of the many Santals who in the course of four years have discussed their way of living with me and instructed me in their culture. Sibu Hansdak' guru of Dhama, is a current embodiment of Kolean Haram—inexhaustible in his knowledge of Santal folktales, ritual and practice and displaying to the full that great guru's genius. Meghare Kisku jogmanjhi of Kalhajore is an expert on marriages and the control of youth. Chotu Ramu Murmu of Amtala has had more crises in his life than any other Santal I know but has remained alert intelligent and witty to the end. Dhunu Hembrom, dihri of the Nuni buru hunt, in the course of a rich and varied life, has also experienced almost everything that can befall a Santal but his zest for Santal living is unabated. It is these Santals who among many others have rendered this report possible.

W.G. ARCHER

REFERENCE

1. W.V. Grigson, *The Aboriginal Problem in the Central Provinces* (Nagpur, 1944), 388.

PART ONE

THE SETTING

41

CRIMINAL JUSTICE IN TRIBAL INDIA

AMONG THE tribes of Middle and Eastern India, the administration of criminal justice displays a wide variety of methods.

In the Lushai Hills, official justice is coterminous with tribal. Lakher chiefs 'have been left in exactly the same position as they before the Lakhers came under British rule and every effort is made to support their authority and to prevent the people from going to officials over the head of the chief. The chiefs therefore decide all cases except those of a very serious nature, as such as murder or rape'. 'Chiefs have full power of control over their villagers—they can punish them by fines, and in the last resort if a villager refused to obey the chief's order the chief can refuse to allow the offender to cultivate his lands any longer and can turn him out of the village.'[1]

Similarly, in the Naga Hills, criminal justice is very largely tribal but Magistrates take a somewhat greater share in its administration. 'Subject to a right of appeal to the Deputy Commissioner, the Sub-Divisional Officer finally disposes of all cases except those involving serious crimes such as murder. These latter are committed to the Deputy Commissioner who has powers corresponding to those of a Sessions Judge. The Indian Penal Code and the Code of Criminal Procedure are not in force in the Naga Hills, the Magistrates being required to administer justice in the spirit of the Codes and not by their letter'. J.P. Mills adds 'In the settlement of cases and disputes tribal custom is followed except where it is repugnant to our sense of justice. For instance, a thief is usually punished by being made to pay the customary compensation but an habitual thief who has expended all his own and his relations' property on payments of this kind, is no longer trussed up and left for the night on a bed of stinging leaves, he is sent to jail instead. Head hunting and such grossly cruel practices as torturing mithan and plucking fowls alive are forbidden but wherever possible the principle is strictly observed of interfering with local custom as little as possible. In dealing with disputes even the customary procedure is followed as far as possible. For instance, in an Ao village, cases, save when so serious as to make an immediate report to the Sub-Divisional Officer imperative, are heard and adjudicated upon by the council of elders—a practice which tends to prevent the decay of their authority and sense of responsibility. A case is ordinarily only brought to the Sub-Divisional Officer, if the council cannot settle it or if one of the parties is dissatisfied with the decision arrived at.'[2]

While the Indian Penal Code, therefore, is not entirely ignored and tribal law not completely accepted it is evident that to a great extent the best is made of two systems.

In the Chittagong Hill tracts, 'there is a not dissimilar compromise. All petty criminal cases are decided by the village headmen or by one of the three chiefs and it is only in respect of the following offences that their jurisdiction is excluded and the Commissioner, Deputy Commissioner or a Magistrate intervenes:

(1) Offences against the State, against person in the service of the Crown in India, or against public justice ;
(2) riots in which grievous hurt has been caused or deadly weapons have been used ;
(3) the following serious offences, against the person, namely, murder, culpable homicide, voluntarily causing grievous hurt, wrongful confinement, rape, abduction, kidnapping, and unnatural offences ;
(4) extortion, robbery, dacoity, lurking house-trespass, or house-breaking when the property taken exceeds Rs. 50 in value ;
(5) forgery ;
(6) offences under Chapter IV of the Chittagong Hill tracts Regulation 1900 ; and

(7) any other offences or class of offences which the Commissioner may specify in this behalf.'[3]

In the larger areas of the Central Provinces and in much of Chota Nagpur, on the other hand, tribal justice is at a discount and the tribes are all administered according to the judicial pattern of British India.

In the Central Provinces, Verrier Elwin has noted 'The wilder Tribes, like the Baigas and Marias, rarely approach the courts, but the Gonds are temperamentally suspicious, individualistic and fond of litigation. "Bad" Gonds disloyal to the findings of the tribal panchayat or indifferent to the demands of tribal opinion, go to the court where by the application of an alien law they can often win their case.

The matter is complicated by the fact that the system of aboriginal jurisprudence runs parallel to the Indian Penal Code and the Forest Act, by whose provisions a large part of tribal life is, of course, governed. But it is of the greatest interest to note how completely unimportant these provisions are in the moral and social consciousness of the tribesmen. No social stigma attaches to the thief—provided he does not steal from a fellow tribesman. He may even be regarded as a hero if he effects a successful theft from a Government Research Forest. Adultery is punishable under Section 497 of the Indian Penal Code, but it is not punishable among many tribes unless it has been committed within the prescribed relations or outside their endogamous divisions. Kidnapping or abduction of women is severely punished by Sections 365 and 366 of the Indian Penal Code, but tries which for centuries have practised marriage by capture are not likely to take such laws seriously. Yet in 1931 a Bhil was convicted and punished by a British Court for a breach of the I.P.C. which was in entire accordance with Bhil custom'.[4]

In the Ranchi district of Chota Nagpur, there is a similar application of the Indian Penal Code and an Uroan Munda or Kharia is automatically bound by all its provisions regardless of whether they run counter to his tribal values. The difficulties which arise from such an application, I will consider later but it is worth noting here the view of two important administrators. 'The Criminal Law of a civilized community', J.H. Hutton has said 'is often entirely at variance with what is felt to be just and proper by tribal custom,'[5] while W.V. Grigson has referred to 'the great difficulty of applying to the decision of charges against tribal offenders the general practice as to the appreciation of evidence, court procedure, the assessment of guilt and the imposition of penalties laid down in the commentaries on the Evidence Act, the Code of Criminal Procedure and the Indian Penal Code, all of which had been imposed on the tribal and other area of Bastar, as of the whole Central Provinces (in which Bastar State was then included), without any thought that any section in these enactments, framed for sophisticated India on European models, might perhaps not suit every part of India.'[6]

In the light of this experience W.V. Grigson inaugurated certain changes in Bastar State, under which 'the regular Courts were deprived of jurisdiction over the tribesmen for seventeen sections of the Indian Penal Code, including those dealing with simple hurt and assault, thefts of property upto five rupees, mischief, trespass and adultery. The panchayats were permitted to impose fines of not more than 25 and in marriage cases to allow expenses upto fifty rupees. An appeal lay to the pargana, manjhi and his panchayat which consisted of four headmen chosen from his group of villagers.'[7]

But beyond these seventeen sections the police and the ordinary courts retained undisputed sway and when Verrier Elwin investigated Bastar crime in 1943, the resulting picture was still of 'tribesmen deeply attached to their own ethical and penal system, still regulating their lives by their own laws of ownership, partition and inheritance but unable to invoke any sanctions to enforce them and compelled in time of need to turn to a foreign code that was made without any reference to their traditions and the conditions under which they live.'[8]

REFERENCES

1. N.E. Parry, *The Lakhers* (London, 1932), 249-50.
2. J.P. Mills, *The Ao Nagas* (London, 1926), 4-6.
3. Chittagong Hill tracts Manual.
4. Verrier Elwin, *Loss of Nerve* (Bombay, 1941), 22-3.

5. J.H. Hutton, *Census of India, 1931, India* (Simla, 1935), 1, 505.
6. Verrier Elwin, *Maria Murder and Suicide* (Bombay 1943) with foreword by W.V. Grigson, IX.
7. W.V. Grigson, *The Maria Gonds of Bastar* (Oxford, 1938), 296.
8. Verrier Elwin, op. cit., 36.

42

THE SANTALS AND THE INDIAN PENAL CODE

I

WHAT IS the position in the Santal Parganas ?

At a first view the Santals of this district would seem to be in the same position as the Gonds of Bastar and the Central Provinces. The Indian Penal Code is in force. The Code of Criminal Procedure has been applied. Like the Murias and Maria Gonds, Santals have their own system of tribal justice and there are thus two parallel systems each with its code of offences, each with its own sanctions and penalties. Such parallelism is in theory exposed to all the weakness which Verrier Elwin has stressed yet until recently friction has been notably absent.

What is the explanation of this apparent lack of conflict ?

A first circumstance which deserves great stress is the earlier association of Santal with the actual day to day administration of the I.P.C. Until 1943, the regular police system was in force only in Dumka Town, in the Deoghar subdivision and in those parts of the Godda, Pakur and Rajmahal subdivision which lie outside the 'Damin-i-Koh'. Elsewhere in the Dumka and Jamtara subdivisions and in the whole of the Damin the regular police had only advisory functions and police duties were performed by village headmen under Yule's Rules of 1856. The main principle of these rules was that the people should be their own police and for this purpose the headmen of the village communities were given certain police powers and duties and the villages were grouped together under parganas or sardars, such of whom corresponded to a thana officer.[1]

In 1943 this system was altered and it is now only in the Damin that the Santals are still their own police. To certain adjustments which these changes render necessary I shall return in my closing chapter but here I will only note the more obvious results of the system. By allowing Santals to be their own reporting agencies, crime was, as it were, defined in Santal terms. Cases which were not crimes by Santal standards or which were not so understood were often not reported and thus the possibility of doing injustice in the name of alien law was largely obviated. Moreover, in all cases in which the Indian Penal Code prescribes one penalty and the tribal code another the Santals have to a great extent been left free to apply their own procedure. There can be no doubt that this humane system has done much to keep justice in the Santal Parganas natural and vital and to reduce to a minimum the conflict of two parallel systems.

In the second place the actual form in which the code has been presented to the tribesmen has had important consequences. Under Rule 9 of Yule's Rules, only a short summary of the code was brought to Santal notice and the offences which village headmen were required to report were confined to the following :

Murder and homicide
Assaults with wounding or severe personal injury
Rape
Dacoity
Highway robbery
Burglary
Theft including cattle stealing
Affrays and riots
Arson
Counterfeiting or uttering base coin
Receiving stolen property

With most of these provisions, Santals have always been in full accord. As early as 1868, Hunter noted that 'among Santals crime is almost unknown.'[2] All the sections therefore which ban offences against property merely punish what Santals have always disapproved.

Similarly in the case of murder, although there may originally have been some conflict, Santals no longer regard murder as either necessary or desirable. The early practice by which if a Santal killed another in a hunt, the dead man's relative could shoot the slayer in return has long since been abandoned. The killing of an adulterer and the slaughter of a man who forcibly put *sindur* on a girl have now been replaced by the award of damages. The summary killing of human sacrificers has died out and the execution of Santals for forcibly taking others into their septs is now a part of obsolete tradition. It is only in the case of witchcraft and of children born from Dikus that murder is sometimes condoned. Even so, murders of any kind are extremely rare and in the ten years, 1931–40 among a Santal population of 789,830 in the Santal Parganas, murders by Santals numbered only 78.[3]

The causes of these murders were :

Witchcraft	16
Quarrels over property	12
Defence of private property	5
Insanity	4
Revenge	2
Family Quarrels	5
Sex	10
Alcohol	19
Exasperation	2
Others	3

Equally although Santals do not regard assaults as serious unless they cause major disablement, they agree that it is criminal to quarrel violently and the relevant provisions of the code are, therefore, in the main in accordance with Santal sentiment.

It is only in the treatment of rape, that Santal values are at variance with a major section. If a Diku were to rape a Santal woman, Santals would fully approve of extreme punishment but as among Santals themselves the offence in its various definitions is not regarded as a major sin. Among the various contingencies, sexual intercourse with a woman, without her consent 'or' with or without her consent when she is under fourteen years of age 'are possible ingredients of rape'. In Santal village society, where pre-marital relations are usual, scarcely a single Santal boy has not committed this offence. Similarly even if intercourse takes place, 'without consent', and both the parties are Santals, the act is regarded more as a civil misdemeanour than as the subject for a criminal complaint. With this one exception, therefore, the Indian Penal Code in its summary form has not in practice come in conflict with major Santal attitudes.

Yet a third factor which has obviated friction has been the prevailing Santal ignorance of all the sections of the Code.

A Santal boy who drags a girl from a dance, or is caught attempting to make love 'outrages her modesty' but scarcely any Santal girl is aware that she can complain under section 354. If the girl is annoyed, she takes it to the village and the boy pays her five rupees.

A Santal woman who deserts her husband and marries another commits an offence under section 494 but I doubt if any Santal knows that he can send her to jail. Instead he demands a double price and perhaps the expenses of his wedding.

A Santal who commits adultery transgresses Section 497 but there must be very few Santal husbands who either know or care whether jail awaits the offender. The receipt either of compensation or of a double bride-price is all that a Santal husband normally desires.

A Santal who elopes with a married girl or takes her to his house is guilty of 'enticing or taking away a married woman' but I do not know of any Santal who regards section 498 as the appropriate remedy or even knows that it exists.

Again a boy who takes a girl to his house may be only wedding her by the or ader form of Santal marriage but if a lady doctor declares that the girl is under sixteen years, the boy is guilty of kidnapping and under section 363 could be sent to jail for seven years. Santals as a whole would be aghast if such a thing were done but as most of them have never heard of the section, the tribal remedy is left to take its harmless course.

Similarly a boy who elopes with a girl who is under eighteen 'procures a minor girl' and is thus guilty under Section 366.

Santal parents who keep a girl in their house pending a tribal decision on whether the 'abduction' should be treated as a marriage commit offences under Section 368.

Such things occur every day in Santal society and no one is aware that they are offences under the I.P.C.

There are yet other sections of which Santals are normally quite ignorant and which nonetheless go counter to their ordinary assumptions. An old Santal woman who assists an unmarried girl to effect abortion and a girl who 'causes herself to miscarry' are guilty under section 312 ; yet if the pregnancy has resulted from a tabooed relationship, Santals to a man would say that they had taken the only correct or possible course in the circumstances.

Equally if a Santal girl has a child by a Diku, the child will never be accepted as a Santal and if allowed to live will grow up a despised and dishonoured outcaste. If its mother kills it at birth she commits murder, if she secretly buries its body, she offends section 318 ; while if she abandons it, she is liable under Section 317. Yet while most Santals would regard all these actions as desperate remedies, almost all of them would consider any of them preferable to allowing the child to live.

It is obvious that ignorance is not a very satisfactory way of reconciling potential conflicts but I have little doubt that this is what has largely contributed to the present lack of friction.

Finally it is important to realise that although the Indian Penal Code specifies certain major crimes and details many offences, a great number of these are to a great extent irrelevant to Santal life. Many sections cover offences which Santals would never think of committing. They do not for example counterfeit money or utter base coin. They have only once waged war against the state. Until recently they were very loath to give false evidence. They do not break contracts or counterfeit trademarks. They are not interested in cheating, forgery, criminal misappropriation, or in offences relating to the army and navy.

On the other hand many matters which the Santal regard as of the greatest importance are scarcely touched on by the code at all. Sexual relations with a non-Santal shock Santals far more than murder yet this is not a crime according to the Penal Code. To practice witchcraft is to involve a whole village in potential danger yet this also is not an offence by the official laws of the land. To plough a village street may enrage Manjhi Haram and result in a total failure of rain but there is no statute which punishes such a wilful threat to general welfare. One reason then for the lack of conflict is what can only be described as the irrelevance of much of the Code to much of Santal life.

We may summarise the Santal attitude to the I.P.C., therefore, by saying that its major provisions do not in the main conflict with Santal standards, that much of it does not impinge on Santal life at all, that many important Santal crimes are omitted, and that where potential conflicts exists, Santal administration of the Code as well as ignorance of many of its provisions has hitherto prevented the emergence of deadlocks or the infliction of grave injustice.

II

If such circumstances explain the comparative unimportance of the Code, what is the explanation of the great influence exerted on Santal life by the Santal code of criminal law?

A first reason for its major influence is the vitality of the tribal councils through which Santal justice is administered. In the formative period of the district following the Santal Rebellion of 1885, Santal tribal officials were as far as possible absorbed into the administration. Under Yule's Rules, the manjhi was recognised as a police officer for his village while the pargana or president of the council of five manjhis became the equivalent of a Sub-Inspector. Under the revenue laws, the manjhi became the official rent collector and in the Damin the Pargana was given the powers of a supervising tahsildar. This official recognition of tribal officers greatly strengthened their general prestige, and at the same time tacitly implemented their authority in purely tribal matters. Moreover under the Santal Civil Rules arbitration by Santals in itself might, in certain sections seem hostile to Santal values, the administration itself was generally sympathetic. Although, therefore, the tribal councils have never been empowered by rule or statute to enforce their decisions in Santal cases, the formal recognition of the Santal officials has rendered almost automatic the acceptance of their decisions. Since the tribal officials are the custodians and administrators of tribal law, this important practice has virtually given the law all the force of a statute.

Another circumstance which has gone far to maintain tribal law is the highly integrated character of the tribe itself. At the present day a Santal is still acutely aware of his tribal nationality. His sole wish is to be a Santal. He is proud of his traditions, his festivals, his tribal organisation, his language, his code of life and manners. Santal law is inseparable from his Santal existence. To flout its cannons, to resist the will of the officials is to endanger every thing that makes him what he is. In a tribe which has fully maintained its integrity and structure, adhesion to its law is assumed by all its members.

Finally the long adjustment of Santal criminal law to the Santal temperament has made its provisions as natural and inevitable to a Santal as the tribal way of agriculture or the ritual of life and death. Not only is it based on the wisdom of the ancestors but its provisions cover all those points at which the peace and welfare of the village are likely to be invaded. Santal criminal law exacts allegiance because it reflects all those things which Santals value and is based on the primal facts of tribal life.

REFERENCES

1. L.S.S. O'Malley, *Bengal District Gazetteers : Santal Parganas*, (First edition, Calcutta, 1910), 232.
2. W.W. Hunter, *The Annals of Rural Bengal* (London, 1868), I, 217.
3. S.M. Naqavi, 'Santal Murders', *Man in India*, XXIII (1943), 236-52.

PART TWO

THE SANTAL LAW

43

VILLAGE ORDER AND DISCIPLINE

I INTRODUCTION

WHAT IS the scope of Santal Criminal Law ? What types of tribal action does it seek to regulate and control ?

It will be obvious that in any society the primary needs are order and discipline, welfare and security. It is natural, therefore, that these should be important subjects of tribal law. Beyond that are the contact of individuals, the relations of the sexes, all the conventions which determine conduct within a tribal frame.

I will begin, therefore, by describing the rules of order and discipline, the types of conduct which influence welfare and security, and the menace of witchcraft. I will then discuss the code of sex with its corollaries in the regulation of food. I will finally review the Santal ways of punishing crime with particular reference to the major punishment of bitlaha.

II ORDER AND DISCIPLINE

If life in a Santal village is to preserve an even tenor and the ways of ancestors are to be honoured, it is necessary that certain conventions should be observed. The structure of the village whether as a system of agriculture or a way of social living must be fully respected. The orders of the village officials must be obeyed. Approved methods of public expression must be followed and the dues of the community must be promptly and fully tendered. Private and communal property must be respected. Quarrels should not get out of hand. No one should resort to force. Abuse should be restrained. On the observance of these rules depends the peace and good living of the village. The rules of order are less the expression of positive Santal values than the indispensable conditions for the whole Santal way of life.

III ENCROACHMENTS

What are the basic rules for agriculture ?

In a Santal village, each Santal holds certain land as his share. This land has specified boundaries and no one may encroach on the land of anothers. If a Santal does so the aggrieved villager will complain to the manjhi and action will be taken. If the encroachment is small or accidental he will be warned or punished lightly but if it is deliberate or large, the penalty is more severe.

Lokhan Marandi of Kumarpur overploughed the land of another Santal. The boundaries were not very clear and as he did so by mistake, the villagers made him restore the affected portion and both men paid one rupee each as the cost of the village meeting.

In Kusma Bandhu Kisku dug away part of a balk which separated his land from that of Ranjit Kisku. Not much damage was done as it was intentional he was made to pay two rupees and to restore the balk to its original form.

In Bokrabandh when Domna Kolha overploughed a fair-sized strip of Goda Hansdak' land the villagers held that the encroachment was deliberate, they fined Domna five rupees and he was made to return the land.

In Bhatonda Thakur Marandi annexed a large plot of land belonging to a Mochi. The village intervened, the land was restored and a fine of fifteen rupees was taken from him.

If the encroachment is on a village boundary similar action is taken. The two manjhis meet and if necessary the matter is settled by the pargana and five manjhis.

When Chunku Murmu of Banspahari began to reclaim some waste land in the next village, both the villages were called and Chunku was fined fifteen rupees and was made to take away the earth which he had thrown on the land.

IV COMMUNAL PROPERTY

The same principles apply in the case of village property itself.

Dhunu Hansdak' of Goradih encroached on village grazing land. He was made to remove the encroachment and was fined five rupees.

In Atagaon Choron Soren ploughed part of the burial ground belonging to the Momins of his village. The manjhi called a meeting, Choron was made to level the ground and five rupees were taken from him.

In Tilaki Durga Baske ploughed the boundaries of the sacred grove. The villagers told him to stop and he did so.

In Piplatanr Bhoje Kisku removed a tri junction stone on the village boundaries. All three villages met and Bhoje was made to erect a fresh stone and pay each village one rupee and four annas.

If the encroachment is on a road, the fine is sometimes stiffer.

Sido Marandi of Rajhari annexed part of a road and besides having to give up the land he was fined fifteen rupees.

V MISCHIEF

If the maintenance of boundaries is of great importance, the preservation of water channels is also a prime necessity. In a Santal village, the drainage of fields is regulated by custom while irrigation from a public stream or drain follows a prescribed order of preference. Accordingly if a Santal stops the flow of water or diverts it incorrectly, he causes considerable harm and mischief to his co-villagers.

In Banspahari, Parta Besra blocked a stream and diverted its water to his fields. This immediately deprived Nabia Marandi of water and as his lands lay in the natural course of the stream he was entitled by custom to avail of it. Parta was made to release the water and give the village a goat.

In Gharmora Diku, Muchiram Mandal, drained water from a channel belonging to Monu Murmu. The village met and he was fined five rupees.

Jolha Soren of Kusbadhia changed the course of a water channel and put Lokhon Murmu to considerable loss. Lokhan complained and five rupees were paid to him.

VI GRAZING

Of equal importance to village order is the protection of standing crops. If cows, bullocks, buffaloes or goats are found in a field they are taken to the manjhi and the owner is made to pay a fine and sometimes compensation.

In Borgama, ten sheep of Raisen Murmu strayed by accident into the Khesari field of a villager. Not a great deal of the crop was grazed, so Raisen was fined one rupee and four annas and nothing was awarded as compensation.

In Sabdahra eleven goats belonging to two Santals grazed the horec' crop of a Diku. The village met, fined them two rupees and eight annas and they were made to give three pais of horec' per goat by way of recompense.

If the grazing is deliberate the fine is enhanced while if it is by night an even stiffer penalty is imposed.

Khitu Kisku of Pakhria Janumghuta was caught one night with two of his bullocks and a cow grazing a paddy field. He was given a severe beating, taken to the manjhi, fined fifteen rupees, and was made to give two arhas of paddy by way of compensation.

VII PIGS

These rules concern almost all domestic animals but in the case of pigs, special rules apply. When the crops are getting ripe the manjhi warns the villagers to keep their pigs within bounds. If after this a pig is found in a crop, the cultivator is entitled to kill the pig and can chase and shoot it anywhere outside its stye. Once it has reached the stye, a rule of sanctuary applies and if it is shot later, the killer can be fined and made to compensate the owner. If the pig is killed in the field itself, the infringement of the rule is obvious and difficulties do not arise, but when the shooting occurs outside the crop, the killer must prove that the shot pig had in fact caused damage. This is not always very easy and if he fails to prove it, the pig's owner can demand due compensation and the killer may be fined ten to fifteen rupees.

Ganga Murmu of Bargania found a pig eating his paddy. He chased it and shot it in a field some distance from the crop. Munshi Tudu of Kandia did the same thing and in both cases the villagers held that the killing was correct.

On the other hand when Ramu Kisku of Baski killed a pig outside his land, he failed to prove any damage so the villagers made him pay a fine of fifteen rupees as well as give twelve rupees to the pig's owner.

If the pig escapes but damage has been done, the matter is decided like and other form of grazing offence.

When the pigs of Jugu Soren of Siltha spoilt one hundred plants of a maize, Jugu was fined five rupees and gave the owner a hundred maize cobs in return.

Similarly when the pigs of Dibi Hembrom of Chuchi grazed a Kesari crop, the owner followed the pigs to Dibu's house and at a village meeting Dibu was fined two rupees and was made to give a maund of Kesari as compensation.

When a pig has been shot for grazing, the carcase is dismembered and the head and a foreleg are sent to the manjhi. The manjhi retains the foreleg but gives three or four pais of rice for cooking with the head. A meat pudding or small Sura is prepared and out of this one-third is kept by the manjhi and two-thirds are given to the villagers. If the killer himself contributes rice, half the village share is taken by him. The rest of the carcase is offered to the pig's owner but if he does not claim it quickly, it is eaten by the villagers. These rules must be strictly followed and anyone who breaks them can be severely punished.

Bisu Tudu of Ero killed a pig which was grazing his crop. He did not tell the manjhi neither did he take the head and foreleg to him. On the contrary he waited till it was dark, took the carcase secretly to his house and divided all the flesh with his family. When the villagers learnt that he had done, they at once accused him of theft and fined him fifty rupees. As, however, the pig had actually caused some damage, its owner was not indemnified.

In Nachanguria Hindu Hembrom killed a pig in his field, and took the head and foreleg to the manjhi, the latter kept a greater part for Hindu, three others and himself and set aside only a tiny share for the other villagers. When the villagers learnt of this wrong distribution, they reprimanded the five men and made them give the price of a whole pig as a fine to the village.

These rules apply only to daytime and if a pig is found in a field at night it is treated as if it were a wild one and is shot at night. The whole carcase is taken to the manjhi, rice is added and all the village shares.

In Gudi Jhopa, Dewan Hembrom killed a pig at night in his field. The meat was dressed and all the villagers ate it.

Similarly when Nandu Murmu of Panchkathia found some pigs in his paddy field one night he shot two of them, called the manjhi and that night all the villagers including the owner shared the flesh.

VIII RESERVATION BY CONDKA

Besides the general convention that standing crops may not be grazed and the issue of a special warning in respect of pigs grazing is further regulated by the erection of small Condkas. A condka is a pole with a bunch of straw tied to the top and when it is erected it entitles a Santal to keep a plot under grass or stubble and to claim redress if it is grazed.

Pero Kisku of Bodacapar had reserved a fallow field for grazing. A Santal of another village grazed his buffaloes there and he was made to pay five rupees as fine and compensation.

In Ghatiari Bgagmat Kisku caught two men grazing their buffaloes in a plot which he had kept for grass. The two were each fined five rupees.

IX THEFT

But besides avoiding damage and mischief Santals are also enjoined to protect private and communal property. In this respect the tribal code runs exactly parallel to the Indian Penal Code and what is theft in official law is also theft by Santal standards. It is important to note, however, that even here the adjustment of loss is often regarded as of equal importance as the punishment of crime. Similarly unless the offender is habitual or is not immediately caught but belongs to another village, Santals see little point in invoking the pargana or the police. Like grazing offences, theft of property is an immediate threat to village order and it is more important to put it right quickly then to set in motion a remote and elaborate machine which may also involve the village in an invasion by strangers. Accordingly almost all cases of petty theft are dealt with by the village itself and it is only when the village feels that the case is beyond its powers or is of some gravity that it takes it to the pargana or police.

Phuca Hembrom of Atgaon was caught coming down from a mango tree with some fruit. The village fined him three rupees and out of this one rupee eight annas was given to the owner.

In Dulu a Santal discovered that sixty jack fruits were missing from his tree. He told the manjhi that he suspected two Santals of his village. The village officials searched their houses and recovered sixty fruits. The two were then fined fifteen rupees and the fruit was given back to the owner.

In Mathurakunri Madan Hembrom was caught at night taking three seers of fish from a trap. He was fined fifteen rupees.

Kandon Tudu of Amgachi stole a trap as well as fish. A search was made and the trap was discovered in his house. He too was fined and paid five rupees.

When Choto Madhu Soren of Sasondih was caught stealing some rice and oil from the house of a widow, he was made to give her double the amount and to pay fifteen rupees as fine.

Similarly in Dharampur when the son of Hakan Marandi of another village was seen tapping toddy from a tree belonging to Basu Hansdak', the Santals caught him, tied him up for the night and sent for his manjhi. When the two villages assembled they gave him a thrashing and fined him fifteen rupees.

In all these as the offender had not been caught before, so the village itself took action. It is when a Santal proves unamenable to the village that official justice is invoked and it will illustrate the circumstances which lead to police intervention if I record in detail a case from Lakarjuria.

Suna Marandi of that village was seen one day in Dumka market with a couple of goats belonging to the manjhi. The villagers asked him what he was doing with them and he said that the manjhi himself had asked him to sell them. When they went back to the village the manjhi complained that two of his goats were stolen and when Suna was confronted with the witnesses he admitted he had taken them. The villagers knew that he had stolen things before but even then they decided to deal with the matter themselves and they fined him twenty-five rupees. Out of this ten rupees went to the manjhi as the cost of the goats and the rest was drunk and eaten by the villagers. Some weeks later Suna Marandi stole ten goats from Bhurkunda and a week later he was caught by Manjhi Hembrom of Chihurbona with yet another goat. The villagers made enquiries and it came out that some one of the ten goats were still at the house of Suna's parents-in-law. On this the villagers lost patience. The thefts were reported to the police and Suna was sent to jail for three months. Even this did not deter him and after coming out of jail, he stole two bullocks from Thakur Besra of Khatangi. The villagers reported this also to the police and this time Suna was awarded two years' imprisonment.

X AFFRAYS

If these agricultural rules are followed, the annual routine of the village proceeds smoothly. But it is equally important that all quarrels of whatever nature should be kept within limits and that no one should resort to force or disturb the village peace. 'A quarrel or dispute' Geoffrey Gorer has said of Lepcha society 'is a menace to everybody's happiness ; half the pleasure is lost from a feast if there is a feeling of discomfort in the air. For the Lepchas quarrelling is not natural or inevitable, but a deplorable accident which it is everybody's business to stop.'[1] Similarly if two Santals come to blows, they are liable not only for any harm they may do to each other but are answerable to the village for ignoring the officials and disturbing its quiet.

Accordingly if one Santal is to blame he is fined for having fought and may also have to pay his opponent some money as dard mitauni—for easing the pain. If both are to blame and no compensation is taken, both are fined for breaking the peace.

Ragda Soren of Tarain accused Bhunda Hembrom of depriving him of rice beer at the Sohrae festival. A quarrel started and in the course of it Ragda hit his opponent on the head and made it stream with blood. The villagers intervened and at the meeting Ragda was fined twenty rupees out of which five were given to Bhunda.

In Lakarjhuria a quarrel arose out of baiting the bullocks at Sohrae. One family objected to certain members of a household joining in their play. The spurned family felt insulted and finally they went over to the attack and began to beat the others. Then a general fight ensued and the villagers broke in and parted them. At the meeting the first party were adjudged the aggressor, they were fined fifteen rupees and out of this five were given as dard mitauni.

When Chotu Baske of Pathardih was dancing at Sohrae, his brother struck him with a *lathi*. Chotu returned the blow and after a scuffle the villagers parted them. At the meeting both were held to blame and each had to give the villagers a pot of rice beer.

Finally, if friction develops between two families the village does not wait for enmity to end in blows. It investigates the causes and does its utmost to establish good relations.

In Dalabor two brothers, Ram and Hikim Murmu, were on such bad terms that neither of the families was speaking to the other. The villagers intervened, and they were all made to drink rice beer together.

XI ABUSE

This control of violence extends also to language and while certain forms of invective are permitted, others are strictly prohibited. Abuse in fact is carefully classified into terms which if used would be punished but which no one ever uses, terms which are often used and are sanctioned by convention and finally, terms which are sometimes resorted to and are visited with village punishment.

To a member of an industrialised community, the terms which Santals never use will appear astonishingly numerous. There are no religious oaths. Impotence is never referred to, and Santal would think it highly dangerous to invoke the bongas as grist to private quarrels. Homo-sexual expressions are similarly unknown. 'No Santal ever thinks of them' said Sagram Hembrom. Similarly while bestiality is sometimes the theme of Bir Seren, bestial terms may only be referred to on the ritual occasions of a hunt or bitlaha. 'No one' said Sibu Hansdak' 'would use them in a quarrel. The village is not the jungle or a dungar dance'. Equally animals are never referred to as an opponent's parents and it is important evidence of the value which Santals give to sex that threats of copulation with members of a rival's family are limited to single class—his mother. Unlike normal village practice in many parts of Bihar sisters, daughters, aunts and grandmothers are all completely safe from verbal attack.

On the contrary the terms which Santal men normally employ are often only threats of simple injury. Lebet mealan', I will kick you ; tapa mealan', I will slap you ; dal mealan', I will beat you ; nel mealan', I will see you. These threats are usually substitute for actual violence and cause no one any anxiety. The village takes no notice and no one is ever fined.

There are also two sexual terms which are often used with impunity. Engame—I will go to your mother—in a threat which never calls for any notice while endic'—offspring of a penis—is in the invidious position of sometimes giving moral offence and sometimes not. It is to some extent comparable to the Baiga term bhosri, which 'almost corresponds', says Verrier Elwin, to the western 'bloody' and has the same advantage—that nearly everyone has forgotten what it means. It actually refers to the male or female genitals and has a wide range of usage. It is often employed in the genitice and then means. 'You are born of a penis'—a simple affirmation of faith in physiological paternity which generally causes a quite disproportionate amount of rage'.[2] But endic' is not identical with bhosri. It does not have the same explosive quality. It has lost its explicit meaning and it is often used merely as a strengthener to talk'. Without endic' said Sibu Hansdak', 'a man's words have no blood.'

These terms are often used without penalty though if there is a quarrel it is sometimes risky to use them. No one, however, may in any circumstances use them to women or in their presence and if a man does so, he is liable to fine.

Siru of Kurum abused his mother saying, 'endic' ge engame

derowatam. You offspring of a penis, I will copulate with your mother.' His mother complained to the village and he was fined five rupees for using the word 'der' and 'endic' to a woman.

Certain terms of abuse are sometimes used by men but are always condemned. These fall into three groups. The first is the threat to kill your opponent, the second is to allege that he is a bidhua or bastard, a kämbro or thief and a bitol or permanent outcaste while the third is to state that a woman is a witch or a loose woman. If a man uses any of these terms the village almost always condemns him and he is punished with a fine.

Chaitan Murmu of Bargama was ploughing his field when by accident he overploughed his brother's boundary. At this his brother shouted out 'Bidhua bhuia engran, Chaitan do, Sima ge sikeda : That bastard Chaitan, he has over-ploughed my field.' A quarrel started and at the village meeting Chaitan's brother was fined one rupee and four annas.

In Raksi Barka Soren accused another Santal of enticing away his wife. 'Endic' Kombro engran, eran nondem oko akadea' he said 'You thieving son of a penis, you have hidden my wife here'. The charge was actually not true but because he had called him a thief Borka was fined five rupees.

In Telni when the widow of Sam Hansdak' was one day going to the well for water, she stopped to chat with a Santal of her village. Her husband's elder brother was slightly drunk and seeing her talking to a man he bawled out' Randi era bandhar Sədom, Chindar do dal bit mealan. 'Widows and rutting stallions. You strumpet, I will give you a good thrashing'. The girl was very hurt and annoyed so she told the manjhi and the villagers fined the man twenty-five rupees for calling her a loose woman.

While I was at Bokrabandh in May 1944 a quarrel involving the use of the term witch was still going on in Pipra. Two friends, Loksa Baske and Chunu Soren, had been going on a visit when they started to discuss the affairs of their village. During their Loksa said that Barki Hembrom was a witch. When the news got round to Barki she was very angry and asked for proof from a janguru. Loksa denied that he had said it and accused his friend. The matter then went to the pargana and five manjhis who fined Loksa one rupee and his friend eight annas. A week later Loksa went to Barki and called her a witch to her face. The matter again went to the manjhi and as Loksa could not prove it he was fined fifteen rupees and told to pay five of it to Barki. When I left Bokrabandh, he was saying he would pay her five rupees and give the villagers two goats.

Among women, a reference to urine is the form which abuse normally takes and this can be employed to either sex without offending village rules. If a boy pushes into a group of girls, one of them may say 'Adoekedam, you pisser'. If a woman is angry, she says 'Adoyan anjoman' piss me if I will hear you'.

In addition a woman can apply the following terms to either sex-kara, blind, hejelic', a slut and both of these are taken in fairly good part. If she is wild with fury, she can say, 'Even a bear or a tiger would not eat you' or 'A dog has eaten all your shame'. None of these terms involve any penalty.

If, however, she calls a person a kombro (thief) a bidhua (bastard) or a bitol (permanent outcaste) she is liable to the same punishment as if she were a man.

In Gardi, at the hook-swinging festival Kanhu Tudu caught the breasts of a girl. The girl rounded on him and called him a bidhua. At this the boy was so insulted that he told his manjhi. The villages were called and at the meeting they held that even the boy's advances did not warrant the girl's using such a term and it was the girl and not the boy who was fined one rupee and four annas.

Even stronger notice is taken if a Santal woman uses words such as 'Nel mean, I will see you', or 'Thuk me. May you burst'. Although a man can say to another 'I will see you', a woman cannot say this for every woman is regarded as a potential witch and there is great danger in allowing her to use phrases which imply the wish or power to kill.

Two brothers shared the same house in Dhamna. One day the children of the elder brother took water from a pot which the wife of the younger brother had filled. The woman lost her temper and scolded them saying 'Bidhua do babon lohomok' kana. Baben thuk' kana. You little bastard, you are not dying or bursting'. The children told their mother who reported it to the' manjhi and the wife of the younger brother was fined a rupee.

In Telni Durga Hembrom was ploughing his field when his buffaloes got caught up in some beans which Barki Kisku had grown. When the girl saw the damage she accused Durga of theft 'Am kara do cekate bam idiakada. Dingra mara do, bidhua do noate ge bam ar joet' kana, Met' ya thuk' tama. You blind one, of course you have taken them away. You wretch, you bastard so that is why you are not growing any. Burst your eyes'. 'Such a stream of abuse involving not only bidhua but thuk' tama was too much for the boy and he caught her by the hair and slapped her three times. The girl complained to the manjhi but when the boy narrated the invectives she had used, the meeting fined the girl two rupees and four annas while the boy had only to pay one rupee as the cost of the sitting.

Moreover no woman may in any circumstances call another a witch, and in this respect Santal usage is completely parallel to Baiga. 'I have listened' says Verrier Elwin 'to quarrels in which women have been getting along very bouncingly with the most violent reflections on their own honour and the morals of their families, in which the obscenest expressions have been used with entire good humour ; but no sooner has the fatal word 'tonhi' been uttered than there has been screaming, passionate tears, and the initiation of a life-long feud. For the word 'tonhi' is not only disreputable, it is dangerous ; witchcraft and its punishment are still far too real to be referred to lightly'.[3]

In Chutia Pagan Marandi called another Santal woman a witch while the woman retorted by calling her an out-caste. Both were fined but it was Pagan who paid fifteen rupees and the other only seven.

Again no woman may call another a besram, backar, chinar, saidhin, jhaeki. These are all terms which imply a number of lovers and strike at the roots of Santal assumptions about the home.

No woman also can use male abuse to men or indeed employ any sexual expressions in public.

Chunki Hembrom of Dasorae was a particularly quarrelsome person and after her husband had gone to the war she annoyed the whole village by continually abusing people in sexual terms. In the end, the villagers lost patience. The manjhi asked for examples and after hearing them, he fined Chunki five rupees.

XII DISCIPLINE

Finally, if village order is to be maintained, the authority of the village officials must be respected, if a villager is summoned to a meeting and does not attend it, the meeting is usually adjourned to secure his attendance and if he then comes and the case goes against him he is given an enhanced fine.

Gumda Hansdak' of Patomdih was abused by a married woman. The latter was called to a meeting but instead of coming she went off to the forest. The next day she was taken to a second meeting and was fined five rupees for the abuse. 'If she had gone to the first meeting' the villagers said 'we would have fined her only two rupees and eight annas.'

If after one or more summons, a villager still does not attend the meeting imposes the minor form of village outcasting.

In Dullu Kali Marandi complained that her son was ill-treating her. The man went to the meeting and denied the charge but the woman stayed away. The meeting concluded that her charge was false and as she had boycotted the meeting they outcasted her by pante begar. Later she paid five rupees and returned to the fold.

In Telni when Chota Peru Tudu accused Champai Tudu of using his field well and causing it to go dry, Champai was summoned to a meeting twice and did not go. The villagers then excommunicated him by pante begar.

In a similar way, if announcements are necessary they must follow approved conventions.

If a man dies the correct way of spreading the news is by beating the drum, kurum dubu dubu dubu. The death of a villager pollutes the village and if anyone uses this drum beat without there being a death, the village may fine him for disorganising its routine.

Singrai Hembrom of Sibtala heard that his son had eloped with a girl of the village. He was so angry that he picked up a drum and announced to the village that his son was dead. The next day he realized his mistake, called the villagers himself and paid them five rupees.

In the alternative when a death occurs the godet should be informed and asked to tell the village.

Soban Hansdak' of Sitasol told the godet that a certain child had died. In fact the child was still alive and Soban was fined one rupee and four annas making a wrong announcement.

Another significant drum beat is bedko bedem. This is a call to the dungar dance and can be used only at bitlahas and bir sendras. If it is used without cause, it disturbs the neighbourhood and whoever is guilty is fined.

But besides observing these conventions, village orders must be respected and if a Santal ignores a decision and does not appeal to the five manjhis or go to court he can be sent out of the line for want of discipline.

Above all the customary dues to the village officials must be promptly and fully paid. The correct time for annual payment is the Mag festival in February and every householder must then pay the manjhi the prescribed dues. The payment of this fee is essential to the office and if a Santal defaults he can be punished for his failure.

Daso Kisku of Bara Kerela did not pay three pice as bheja at the Mag festival of 1939. He was, therefore, outcasted by pante begar and was only taken back 'in the line' when he paid it a month later and gave the village meeting its costs.

In Rajabhita in Chandna bungalow, Pitho Marandi did not pay the manjhi and godet's fees for two years. The manjhi complained to the villagers and it was decided that in future Pitho's share in all village feasts would go to the manjhi. When Pitho found that he was getting nothing, he paid the dues.

Similarly if a matter goes to a village meeting, the costs of the meeting must be paid when the decision is announced. The costs are usually five four anna bits but are sometimes one rupee or even two rupees and eight annas. If a Santal does not pay this, he challenges the authority of the village and if he persists his act may involve his partial ex-communication.

REFERENCES

1. Geoffrey Gorer, *Himalayan Village* (London, 1938), 142.
2. Verrier Elwin, *The Baiga* (London, 1939), 72.
3. Elwin, op. cit., 73.

44

VILLAGE WELFARE AND SECURITY

I INTRODUCTION

IF VILLAGE order and discipline are maintained the way is clear for prosperity and welfare and these in Santal thought mean normally only two things—good health and crops. If there is no sickness and the harvest is good, there is a general sense of well being but if illness is raging or the crops fail, all that gives Santals their zest in life is threatened.

The two forces which most intimately threaten welfarea re bongas and witches. Only a fraction of disease is due to natural causes. The greater part derives from supernatural influences. 'They have an idea', says Bodding 'that a human being has a natural right to health and life, and that consequently he ought to live to old age. Disease is something foreign and inimical to man'.[1] If the bongas do not intervene, Santals therefore assume that the crops will, of their own accord, be good. Equally if the bongas do not send illness and witches neither eat victims, plant the seeds of sickness nor prevail on bongas to interfere, the village will maintain its health. To ensure welfare therefore malevolence by bongas must be averted while the greatest offence against security is for a woman to practise as a witch.

II THE BONGA WORLD

How then can bonga intervention be controlled? If the Santal world-view, spiritual forces fall into two groups. Thakur Jiu, the Supreme Being, is, as it were, a neutral president. He made the world and is the source of life but apart from allotting to everyone a span of life he no longer interferes in ordinary affairs.

Below Thakur Jiu are two worlds—the world of bongas or spirits and the world of men. For many bongas, the bonga world is no different from the world of human beings. Stones, boulders, trees, hills and pools are their residences and they move like wind or air across the fields and villages of men. Other bongas, on the other hand, live in a bonga world at one remove from human life. It is sometimes reached by entering a pool. The water hardly reaches the knees when the visitor finds himself on a dry road and is in a land where tigers are huntin dogs and snakes are footstools. This bonga kingdom is often only vaguely separate from actual hills and forests and although a nucleus remains distinct, it is never completely insulated. While bongas however have access to the human world, it is only in special circumstances that men can see or visit the bonga kingdom. Similarly although bongas can if necessary see all that men do, it is only in special circumstances that men or women can meet bongas or see them in the flesh. Although a portion of the bonga world therefore is distinct, it is, as it were linked to the human world by sensitive strings or feelers. Even therefore when bongas are in their own apparently dormant, human events can provoke them to action, while human intercession can sometimes influence them to cause or avert disaster.

The bongas in fact are a parallel or border race whose relations with men are in a constant state of fluidity. Certain bongas are benevolent for some of the time while others are harmful most of the time. They resemble invisible strangers some of whom are friendly G-men while others are suburban gangsters. But in one respect they are vulnerable. There is no code of bonga loyalty and if one bonga is actively malevolent, others can often be induced to cancel his career of evil.

Moreover they are never organised as armies and their forays are like those of small raiding parties which can never result in annexing a kingdom but can only cause harassment and petty loss. It is by placating particular bongas, by inducing others to intervene and above all by avoiding insult or injury that a village's welfare is secured.

III BONGAS

What is the bonga hierarchy ?

The first and greatest bonga is Sin or Chando bonga. This bonga is associated with the Sun, and was first worshipped when the Santals at least broke through the mountain which blocked their way and come out by 'the gate of the sun'. He is regarded as a source of good only and should be worshipped by each Santal once in his lifetime. He remains however remote from human affairs and apart from giving the blessings of morning and evening and heat and rain, he is not expected to intervene in times of trouble. At his worship, the Jom Sim bonga is also honoured. This bonga was discovered by a Santal after one of the sacrifices to Sin Bonga. As he returned to fetch his axe the Santal saw a bonga eating the sacrificial scraps. He said nothing but when his companions fell ill, he gave out what he had seen. They then made a separate sacrifice to the bonga and all recovered. Because of this the Jom Sim bonga acquired some of the majesty of Sim Bonga himself and is worshipped as his satellite.

The next most important bongas are Maran Buru, Jaher Era and More ko Turuc' ko.

According to the early traditions, Maran Buru or the Great Mountain was originally called Lita and taught the Santal how to brew rice beer and to practice intercourse. He also taught women witchcraft and men the art of ojhas. He is a genial, somewhat Bachannalian figure who move through all the myths as a kind and understanding father. Hunter, even regarded him as 'a symbol of the Everlasting and Unchangeable one'.[2] While Man suggested that 'were a Santal to hear the story of our Saviour's mediation for fallen men, it would immediately awaken his ideas of Maran Buru'.[3]

Only slightly inferior to him in status are Jaher Era and More ko Turuc' ko. These two bongas are the Lady of the Grove and the Five-Six and at the Baha Festival they share a single shed with Maran Buru. Their identity and relationship however are full of mystery. Buchanan writes 'the most common objects of their worship are Marang Burha, an old man, Marako his younger brother and their sister Jaher Burhi, and old good-natured creature, who never does them any harm'.[4] Man describes them as 'the five brothers and the one sister'[5] while Hunter writes Maniko for More ko Turuc' and describes him as 'the husband as well as brother of the female deity in the triad, Jaher Era'.[6] Neither Kolean Haram nor Bodding throw any light on the curious numerals which serve as name for More ko Turuc' ko but C.L. Mukherjea notes from Mayurbhanj ; 'Another village deity is More ko Turuc' ko who is now a single entity but addressed in the plural. The Santals believe that they were five brothers (more—five) who were wedded to six sisters named Dangi, Pungi, Sisi, Dumni, Chita and Kapra (Turuc'—six). They are supposed to preside over the welfare of the village. His younger sister, Gosae Era, constitutes a separate deity of the Jaher than ; Jaher Era, another sister of Moreko is the goddess of Jaherthan named after her'.[7] In the myths which I myself recorded, the Five-Six are either five brothers with Jaher Era as their mother, five brothers, plus five brothers over again, with Gosae Era, making six and finally five or Six brothers.

Associated with these three spirits but in a slightly inferior position are two other bongas. Gosae Era is a Kamar girl whom one of the five brothers wedded while Pargana Bonga is the first pargana who still rules the local region.

All these five bongas are kind and benevolent and in a folk-tale recorded by Bompas, a boy climbs a tree in the sacred grove because 'he knows More ko Turuc' ko would protect him there.'[8]

Slightly lower than these jaher bongas but of great importance to the village is Manjhi Haram. This bonga is either the original founder of the village or the immediate ancestors of the present headman. He is worshipped at the manjhithan and in the sacred grove, the village is in his charge and he acts as the spiritual advisor of the headman.

The remaining bongas are comparatively subordinate but they are also of some importance and it will be convenient if I describe them in a list :

The Abge bongas—these are the patron saints of the khunt or subsept. Their names must be kept strictly secret and communicated only at death. They are believed to give earthly blessing and to save in danger. They preside over the family and are the chief means of warding off distress.

Orak' bonga—the spirit of the house'.

Naihar bonga—the bonga of the father-in-law' which accompanies a woman to her husband's house and looks after her interests.

Sima bonga—the bonga of the village boundaries.

Bonga of the village itself—whatever bongas are resident in trees, stones, springs or pools within the village but not those which haunt the boundaries.

Bongas of the neighbourhood—bir or forest bongas, buru or mountain bongas, dadi or spring bongas and hunt khuntut-bongas in the stumps of trees.

Bonga lovers who marry human beings.

Retained bongas of ojhas through whose help a harmful bonga can be attacked.

Kisar bongas—'brownies' who steal for their masters.

The Bonga Ruji Bonga—this bonga delights in sex and it is only by her favour that animals are killed in a hunt.

The bonga husbands of witches through whose help their fell designs are accomplished.

Bonga of Hindu festivals adopted by Santals—Jatra bonga, chata bonga, pata bonga.

Such other bongas whose names and origins are unknown but who raid the human world and cause havoc.

Besides all these there is one further class of bonga being—the hapramko or the departed. When his bhandan or final funerary feast has bean performed a Santal joins the company of the tribal dead and becomes a ancestral bonga in the family which owned him when on earth. Ancestral bongas do not normally intervenes in other houses but are jealously sensitive to slights from their own families. Moreover they form, as it were, an invisible village community and for at least a generation they act as anxious spectators of the village scene.

When the village meets it sits with the ancestors and it is the sense of their ghostly presence which lends weight and dignity to village views.

IV TYPES OF BONGA

These bongas are not, as Bodding thought 'without exception evil and enemies of man.[9] On the contrary they comprise two distinct kinds—those who are normally benevolent or at least neutral and those whose habits is to cause havoc, disease and mischief. The Sin and Jom Sim bongas obviously fall in the first class. So also do the bongas of the sacred grove and Manjhi Haram. All of these need regular respect, but unless they are slighted all of them preserve and save. Similarly the abge bonga is the recognised protector of the household and provided it receives a pig or goat each year its effort is to ward off illness, danger or witchcraft. 'But if a witch overpowers the abge bonga, the family is doomed.' It is the Sima bonga, bongas of the village, the bonga husbands of witches, and minor bongas whose names and places are unknown who are the main sources of trouble. The Sima bonga is always anxious to do harm'. It makes snakes and leopards attack men in the fields and must be constantly placated with fowls'. Bongas within the village are also full of restless mischief while unknown bongas are often responsible for attacks of sudden illness.

Similarly the Kisar bonga is a constant nuisance as he is always pilfering crops. The orak' bonga is not at bottom in inimical but is like a fussy old person. It easily takes umbrage and unless it is quickly placated, it strikes men and cattle with disease. An orak' bonga is never known to aid a family but is rather a liability which each house inherits and must carry on.

It is on the success with which the malevolent types of bonga are kept at bay that welfare and security depend.

V THE FUNCTION OF FESTIVALS

For meeting this situation, two lines of action are open to the village.

The first consists of mobilising the 'forces of neutrality or benevolence against the forces of evil'[10] and it is through the annual festivals and ceremonies that this expedient is adopted.

The first Santal festival is Erok; when seeds for sowing are broadcast. The village priest offers fowls to the bongas of the grove, to Manjhi Harm, Sima bonga and the bongas of the village and as he offers, he says, 'Take this in name of the erok' festival. Where we sow, may twelve shoots come. Let there be rain and storm. May the fields be flooded. Let no illness, no ache of belly or head enter this village. Take all sickness away. Carry it on a pole of gold. Carry it with strings of gold. If there are widows and women of bad omen who tear and fold the leaf, who doom and mark down, frown on them and destroy their good omens. Show them no favour. If they lurk in hiding, save us from them.

, Keep us from all harm, May the cattle roam at will in the forest, the man forest. Protect them with your covering hood.

After Erok, 'the Hariar festival is performed so that the paddy may grow green. Fowls are offered as at erok' and the same invocation is made.

The next festival is Ir gundli. This is for eating the first millet after harvesting. No fowls are killed but the first millet is offered in the jaher and the manjhithan. The priest invokes the same bongas and prays 'May no ache of belly or head come from eating it. Keep all illness far away'.

A little later comes the Janthar. This is also a festival of firsl fruits. A pig or ram is chased for sacrifice and the priest offers it with first paddy to the pargana bonga. 'Accept this pig', he says 'May no ache of belly or head assail us as we eat. When we reap the paddy and thrash it, make it more than it is. Increase the bongas' share. If there are rats and mice, stop them from eating it.'

When all the harvest is in, the Sohrae is celebrated. This is a 'harvest home', a period of relaxation, a time of drinking and dancing. But there also the bongas are not forgotten. Fowls are offered in a rice field to the same bongas and the priest prays that the feast may pass 'without ache of belly or head and in coming and going, all danger may be far away'.

The next festival is Mag, for cutting thatching grass. The same bongas are given fowls and the priest prays that the thatching grass may be abundant.

Finally before any flowers are eaten or worn, the Baha festival is celebrated. This is a celebration of the sacred grove itself. Two sheds are put up one to Naran Buru Jaher Era and the Five-Six, and the other to Gossain Era. Fowls are offered and the same bongas are asked to free the village from sickness and witches and preserve the crops and cattle.

In addition to these festivals which are celebrated every year a special festival of Mak' More is performed whenever sickness is raging in the village. The manjhi vows animals to the jaher bongas in return for their removing the disease. When the disease stops, goats and fowls are bought with house-to-house levies and sacrifices are performed in the grove.

All these festivals aim at security, the winning of the bongas' favour, the neutralisation of harmful intentions. They are performed both by the whole village and for the village as a whole, and until the correct festival has been celebrated, no one can commence sowing, harvesting or thatching. Every Santal must participate and if fowls and grain are offered, each house must make its contribution. These levies are as follows:

At Erok'	1 fowl 1 pai rice A little salt and spice.[11]
Hariar	-do-
Baha	-do-
Sohrae	1 fowl 1 egg 1 pai of rice for rice beer. 1 pai of rice with a little salt and spice.
Iri Gundli	A little millet from a field at random.
Janthar	A pig or ram is chased and purchased from its owner by a house-to-house levy. A little paddy from a field.
Mak More	5 goats 1 pig 1 sheep 1 fowl 1 pai of rice with salt and spice.

All these contributions are compulsory and it is only in cases object poverty that a Santal is exempted from making them. If he fails to give them he is not only risking his own welfare. He commits an offence against security and the village fines and half-outcastes him until he pays.

In Dhawa, Copla Tudu refused to contribute to the Mag

festival. I shall be in Bengal; he said. He went away and did not pay but when he returned all the village boycotted him.

At another Mag festival in Piplatanr, Jetha Marandi also declined to give his share, because his brother had been fined for incestuous relations with a niece. At the Mag festival it is usual for the village children to make toy bullock carts out of thatch and to run shouting and laughing through the village. Jetha's children went to join them but because their father had refused to give his share, the villagers drove them all away. The next morning they fined Jetha one rupee four annas and at the Beha festival they levied from him a double contribution.

Chandu Tudu of Phate cut some paddy before the Janthar festival had been performed. The villagers were very angry as they said he had defied the bongas and invited their displeasure. They demanded from him a pig and five fowls for special sacrifices and when he did not give them they did the sacrifice themselves and subjected him to minor boycott or pante begar. Chandu stayed pante begared for two years and when at last he approached the villagers he had to reimburse them for the pig and fowls and also pay a fine of two rupees and eight annas.

In Dhundli, the whole village was threatened with small pox and to avert the disease they promised the Five-Six a Mak' More festival if the sickness lessened. The small-pox came to end and they then raised, five goats, one sheep and one pig for the sacrifice. One villager named Anpa Kisku however refused to give his share. The villagers performed the sacrifice without him and subjected him to pante begar. Anpa Kisku remained for three years in this state of boycott. Then the time came for doing the initiation ceremony of his son. The villagers refused co-operation and in despair Anpa then begged for pardon paid a fine of two rupees and eight annas, gave a goat and was taken back.

Similarly Bhaero and Jalpa Murmu of Lagdum declined to contribute to Sohrae. The villagers therefore did not let them share the feast and ultimately they fined them one rupee and four annas each.

VI THE RITUAL OF CRISIS

But besides performing the annual festivals and thus enlisting the good will of the major bongas, it is necessary that the correct ceremonies should also be performed—particularly at the crucial times of birth and death. The effect of both these crises is to pollute the village bongas. Accordingly so long as the necessary ceremonies are not performed sacrifices must be suspended and it is only when the bongas cease to be polluted that they can again be approached. It is for this reason that a Santal who delays a birth ceremony is liable to be fined for his remissness, for he has not only suspended all the village sacrifices but has risked bonga displeasure.

In Mahuadangal, a widow gave birth to a son and named a Santal as the father. He avoided coming to a meeting and for nine months the naming ceremony was delayed, the village bongas remained polluted and all the sacrifices were suspended. At last the Santal appeared, admitted the paternity and the naming ceremony was done but because of all the trouble she had caused the widow was made to give a large goat as fine to the village.

VII THE PROVOCATION OF BONGAS

If village welfare can be promoted through annual festivals and ceremonies, it is also necessary that all acts which might in any way incense or provoke the bongas should be strictly avoided.

These acts fall into two groups—those which women may on no account perform and those which men equally with women are debarred from doing.

If a person breaks these prohibitions, he commits an offence against security which is quite as serious as encroaching on land or stealing cattle. He must therefore offer special sacrifices in atonement and if he does not, the village itself will do the sacrifice, subject the culprit to a boycott and eventually inflict a fine.

VIII TABOOS ON WOMEN

In the case of women, taboos are in many cases based on

latent sexual symbols and accordingly no women may do any of the following acts:

Climb a tree in the jaher or break its branches. This is because the jaher trees are the dwelling places of bongas and 'the bongas do not like women on their heads'. 'If a woman climbed a jaher tree' said Santals of Rajabhita 'there would be no rain for as far as she could see'. 'A woman who climbs a jaher tree' said Santals of the Rajmahal Damin 'pollutes the village bongas. They will rain disease on men and cattle.'

Two women of Bodacapar broke the branches of a jaher tree and took them to their houses for fuel. One of them died within two days and the other within eight.

Two Kamar women of Dhodih cut some branches of a jaher tree. A few days later both of them went mad. A jan guru divined the cause and after a goat had been sacrificed they came to their proper minds.

Mount a roof for thatching it. 'Bonga dwell in the roof. They will not allow a woman to walk on them. They will stop rain and there will be no crops. They will fill the roof with snakes and scorpions'.

A boy of Jhunjko was thatching a roof and his mother climbed on it to help him. The villagers caught her and she was made to give goat for sacrifice at the manjhithan.

In the Simaltola of Manihari in Purnea district, there was no rain. The villagers consulted a jan guru who divined that two women had thatched a roof. The villagers then enquired and found that a widow and her daughter had mounted a roof and thatched it. Thereupon they made the two women put *lotas* of water on their heads and walk the village street from end to end. They also took a goat from the widow and sacrificed it at the manjhithan. Shortly afterwards heavy rain fell.[12]

In Dhankunda, a widow had no sons. So she herself thatched her roof. The villagers caught her but instead of taking a goat, they slit her right ear.[13]

Plough a field. This also is an act which may stop rain.[14]

The son of Ramsin Hansdak' of Simbra was ploughing when his mother brought him his early morning food. He left a bullock yoked but as he ate, the animal strayed and his mother fetched it. She caught the plough by its handle, drove the bullock back and in so doing she ploughed some land. The villagers took a brown fowl and a black goat from her and sacrificed them at the manjhithan.

In the Santal village of Mahuadangal a Kamar woman had an only minor son and as there was no one else to assist her she decided to plough her fields herself. She did so several mornings while it was still dark. Then the villagers heard what she was doing and the next day caught her as she ploughed. The woman ran and was chased for three miles. After that they took five rupees from her for a goat and the manjhi offered it at the manjhithan.

In certain areas, besides a goat for sacrifices, extra penalties are also imposed. In villages round Kundahit, for example, if a woman ploughs a field, 'she must be tethered like a cow and made to eat some grass' while at Rajabhita she must circumambulate the village carrying a leaking pot of water.

Touch the handle or carry other part of a plough otherwise than on her head. This also causes drought and sacrifices are necessary.

In Kala Dumaria the daughter of Anu Tudu carried a plough on her head and touched its handle. The village intervened and the girl was yoked to the plough and made to pull it five times round a field.[15]

In Katikund, the wife of Ludu Murmu, carried a plough from a field to her house. The villagers took a pot, made four holes in it and filled it with water. Then they dressed her like a man and sent her round the village watering the earth as she went. When it was over they took a goat from her and sacrificed it at the manjhithan.

Use a leveller of if she carried it then only on the head.

In Kalhajor the daughter of Hopna Kisku mounted a leveller while her father drove the bullocks. The villagers feared that the rains would fail, so they took a goat from Hopna and sacrificed it at the manjhithan.

In Majdiha a Santal was ploughing while his wife stood on a leveller and the buffaloes pulled her round. Here also the woman's husband was fined and had to pay twentyfive rupees.

Shave a person.

This is thought to be a male act and 'she who shaves a person a woman may grow a beard herself'.

When a midwife shaved a boy in a village of Bokrabandh, she was made to give a goat for offering to Manjhi Haram.

IX TABOOS ON WOMEN AND MEN

But besides women men also are required to avoid certain acts and neither men nor women may do any of the following things: Plough the kulhi or village street. 'the kulhi' is the chest of Manjhi Haram. There are bongas in it. They will leave the village if its surface is broken.

In Goradih Ragat Hansdak' drove a yoked plough across the village street. He was taken to a meeting and gave a goat for sacrifice.

Balea Soren of Bhatonda dragged a plough across the kulhi. Within a month murraine broke out among the cattle. There was a village meeting and he gave a goat for sacrifice in the jaher then and was fined two rupees and eight annas.

Plough the jaher or sacred grove. 'The jaher is the haunt of bongas. It is their territory and ploughing will disturb them. If a man ploughs the jaher, the bongas will plague the village with leopards and tigers'.

When the son of Raghu Murmu of Simbra dragged his plough across the sacred grove, no sacrifices were done and a little later his sister died suddenly.

Cut a jaher tree. 'The jaher trees are the houses of bongas'. If a man cuts a jaher tree, his house will catch fire and the fire may burn the village.

In Belbhita Galu Hausak' cut a tree in the jaher and used it for his house. About a year later in the rains the house was struck by lightning and burnt to ashes.

A Diku of Bhadria cut a jaher tree in Duarpahari. As he cut it the bonga in the tree cried out *Ke Ke* like a pig and that night the Diku died.

When Jogon Soren of Raksi also cut a jaher tree, the villagers called a meeting and he was made to give twelve fowls for sacrifice in the grove.

In yet another case Dukhu Marandi of Piplatanr cut a jaher tree for making into a plough. He did it on his threshing floor under a heap of straw. Suddenly the straw burst into flames and the whole heap was consumed. The villagers consulted a jan guru who divined that jaher tree had been cut. On this matter then came to light, Dukhu was fined five rupees and in addition had to give a goat for sacrifice in the jaher at the stump as well as provide five seers of rice with salt.

Drag a leveller along the village street. This also is an insult to Manjhi Haram.

In Kalhajor Jaba Soren did this and had to give a goat for sacrifice.

Chunu Baske of Daldali did the same thing and had to make the same requital.

In Telni Karu Hembrom dragged a leveller from his field along the village street. The following night jackals came and howled by the village and a few days later cholera broke out. The villagers consulted two jan gurus who said that Manjhi Haram was enraged at Karu's action and had therefore sent the illness. Karu then gave a goat and five pailas of rice. The goat was sacrificed at the manjhithan and the illness stopped.

Drag a thorny branch (Janum jhanti) along the village street.

The thorns scratch and wound the chest of Manjhi Haram. The penalty is a goat at the manjhithan.

Eat uncooked rice (berel cawale).

In the Dumka Damin and part of the Dumka subdivision this is strictly prohibited though elsewhere in the district it appears to be allowed.

In the Dumka Damin 'it is the food of bongas and if any one eats it there will be famine'.

The wife of Chotu Ramu Murmu of Amtola caught her daughter-in-law eating uncooked rice. The village met and the girl was fined two rupees and eight annas. They also warned her father that if she did it again the family would divorce her.

Cover a pot of oil with a lid of mud.

Keep a bale of mahua on a stone shelf (dhula).

Both these things, if done, will cause a drought which in turn can only be averted by sacrificing a goat to Manjhi Haram. The offender will also be fined five or ten rupees.

X CONCLUSION

If these precautions are taken and the annual festivals are

duly performed, village security is still not completely ensured for certain bongas may spurn the offerings while others may evade their monitors. Moreover the activities of witches remain. But the range of hostility is narrowed. The onus is shifted to the individual. The village can face disaster knowing it has followed the precepts of the ancestors and done everything within its power.

REFERENCES

1. P.O. Bodding, 'The Santals and Disease', *Mem. A.S. Beng.*, X, No. I.
2. Hunter, op. cit., I, 187.
3. E.G. Man, *Sonthalia and the Sonthals* (London, Calcutta, 1867), 43-44.
4. Francis Buchanan, *An Account of the District of Bhagalpur in 1811* (Patna, 1939), 265.
5. Man, op. cit., 43.
6. Hunter, op. cit., 188.
7. C.L. Mukherjea, *The Santals* (Calcutta, 1945), 162.
8. C.H. Bompas, *Folk-lore of the Santal Parganas* (London, 1909), 441.
9. P.O. Bodding, 'The Santals and Disease', *Mem. A.S.B. Beng.* X, No. I, 1925. In this connection, W.J. Culshaw has observed 'The early missionaries were prone to regard all the 'bongas as evil spirits but the truth would rather seem to be that the 'bongas' are somewhat unreliable. Like human beings, they cannot always be relied upon and it is important for the Santals to be in their good books . . . The Santals (certainly) do not live in perpetual fest of the 'bongas' and that the word has a neutral connotation is perhaps indicated by the following phrase which occurs in a song composed by a Santal Christian convict, *Jisu Mase Sari* bonga do (Jesus Christ is the true 'bonga')'. ('Some Notes on Bongaism' *J. R. A.S. Beng.*, V, 1939, 429-30).
10. Elwin, op. cit., 61.
11. Households which celebrate a wedding are subject that year to an extra levy at Erok' of 1 pot of rice beer
5 fowls
5 pailas of rice with spice and salt.
12. There is a similar prohibition among Kharias. Should a woman happen even to get up on the thatch of a house or hut, some serious calamity to the vilalge is apprehended and a 'rog-khedna' or 'calamity—driving ceremony has to be undertaken, and the offending woman is required to procure rice and prepare rice beer to expiate her sin'. (S.C. and R.C. Roy, *The Kharias*, I, 119).
13. Campbell in 'Superstitions of the Santals' (*J.B.O.R.S.*, I, 1925, 222-23) states 'If a goat climbs on to the roof of a hut the owner of the hut

snips a piece off each of its ears. A goat climbing on to the roof of a house presages sickness or death to the inmates; the cutting off of a piece of each ear counteracts the evil omen'.

14. An alternative reason recorded by C.L. Mukherjea is that 'in ancient times when a woman first took the plough, the cattle in the yoke went on straight ahead and she could not make them deviate, either to the left or to the right according to her will, when left and behold, out opened a mighty river from the furrows to the consternation of everybody' (Mukherjea, *The Santals*, 55).

15. The plough punishment is also sometimes resorted to by other tribes. Among the Pardhans, 'angry men punish idle or unfaithful women by yoking them along with a bullock to a plough and drive them round a field. (Hivale, *The Pardhans*, 189).

Similarly "the Dudh Kharias of the Ranchi district like the Uraons and Mundas are so jealous of any usurpation, however, temporary or accidental, by women of men's functions in agriculture that should a woman be driving the plough even for the nonce, she is fined and a ceremonial expedition to drive out the calamities that it is believed would otherwise overtake the village, is undertaken. This ceremony is known as 'rog-khedna' or 'disease-driving' or 'calamity-driving expedition'. Until recently the offending woman would also be required to expiate her sin by being yoked to the plough, she handled and by ploughing a few feet of ground, she was also made to eat some grass and to go round the village begging for rice with which a feast and drink had to be provided for the village elders to 'expiate her sin' and re-incorporate her into the tribe.' (S.C. and R.C. Roy, *The Kharias*, I, 118-19).

45

THE MENACE OF WITCHCRAFT

I INTRODUCTION

FROM THE earliest times, Santals have been obsessed by the menace of witchcraft. In 1792, Sir John Shore described three Santal ways of trying witches. Man noted in 1867 'no reasoning with them, nor ridicule can dissuade them of their belief in witches, and of the necessity of their being at once murdered'.[1] 'It is but a few months since that a girl near Simrah, was charged with witchcraft, and with having killed the child of another Santhal by convulsions. A punchayat of nearly thirty old men was summoned, and the girl while confessing her guilt as a witch, said she was taught witchcraft by a certain chief witch, termed Rohomonee, and that they had buried a spirit in a certain house. Rohomonee was summoned to take the spirit out ; and dug up a bit of clay in the floor. This was deemed sufficient for her condemnation, and her daughter being taken away from the house by the father who had bid his doomed wife goodbye, and the whole of her family leaving her, she was set upon by fire men picked out for the purpose and beaten to death, while the punchayat sat that night for three hours in solemn conclave outside listening to the cries and groans of the victim as in her agony and supplication she broke the stillness of the night'.[2]

Kolean says 'The greatest trouble for Santals is witches. Because of them we are enemies of each other. If there were no witches, how happy we might have been'.[3]

Chotrae Deshmanjhi in his account of the Santal rebellion describes how number of girls were accused of witchcraft in the rebellion and were shown 'the pod of the pea' and slain.[4] Even as recently as 1944 when I was camping at Sundarpahari, the manjhis told me 'Witches are still our greatest trouble. How are we to end them ?' Apart from the bongas, there is in fact no greater menace to Santal security.

In this chapter, I do not propose to offer any explanation of witches or their strange powers. I do not think that hallucination, by any means accounts for all these phenomena neither do I think that the theory of a fertility cult in any way explains the institution. I shall therefore state only what Santals declare are the characteristics of witches, and note the accepted methods of punishing the witch and ending her dreaded career.

II INITIATION

How does a Santal girl become a witch ?

The first account of this process in English is by C.H. Bompas in *Folk-lore of the Santal Parganas*.

'When girls are initiated into witchcraft', he notes 'they are taken away by force and made to lead tigers about. This makes them fearless. They are then taken to all the most powerful bongas in succession ; and are taught to invoke them, as school boys are taught lessons, and to become possessed (rum). They are also taught mantras and songs and by degrees they cease to be afraid. The novice is made to come out of the house with a lamp in her hand and a broom tied round her waist ; she is then conducted to the great bongas one of whom approves of her and when all have agreed she is married to that bonga. The bonga pays the usual bride-price and applies *sindur* to her forehead. After this she can also marry a man in the usual way and he also pays the bride-price. When a girl has learnt everything she is made to take her degree (sid atang) by taking out a man's liver and cooking it with rice in a new pot; then she and the young woman who is initiating a stew is completely proficient and can never forget what she has learnt'.[5]

This account is supplemented by the Santali description of Kolean Haram.

'The witches train many followers. They lead astray young girls so that the seed may remain when they die. They wander at night with lights, enter houses and take out girls for making them their followers and if they do not agree they say 'If you do not learn, you will die, or the tigers will eat you'. So out of fear they try their hardest to learn. Having brought out their followers they put on brooms and taking broken winnowing fan under an arm and a lamp, they go to the Sacred Grove. There they sacrifice fowls, cook rice, meat and bread and eat them. The followers are made to comb the fur of the tigers and if they are afraid and do not wish to do it, they say 'They will not harm you. Do not be afraid'. Then they teach them incantations and jharni songs and in order to confirm them in the art they say to them 'Eat your father or elder brother'. If they do not agree, they make them ill or mad. With pins of crab, they pull out their livers and lungs, and having cooked them they make the followers eat them first. From that day their pupils lose all tenderness. When they are angry, they eat their children, parents or relatives and they do not have any pity even for their own husbands. They eat them also'.[6]

These accounts are substantially corroborated by a number of statements which were recorded in 1946 and I will only draw attention to certain extra points of detail.

In many cases a girl is, as it were, deduced into learning the art. The best age for seduction is when she is publi bande oe panci bande, that is, when she first puts on a girl's cloth.

An old witch then dilates to her on the powers which witchcraft will give her. She tempts her to hear the songs. She tells her not to be afraid. She mesmerizes her with stories of other witches. The girl listens with fascinated horror and at last she yields. Then the witch begins to sing her the witches's songs. These songs are a remarkable tribute to the power of poetry in Santal society for 'When a girl hears them she can never retract.' She has in fact taken the first step and must either become a witch or die.

It will be obvious that such songs can be recorded only with the greatest difficulty and Man noted 'I have been unable to obtain a good witch song from any of their reputed witches. In only one instance did I find a woman willing to sing one, and I had placed her in hajut with her husband, for complicity in a witch murder. This young lady, to save herself, had accused a friend of having taught her the black art, and in consequence the unfortunate woman, thus charged, had been condemned to death and executed. The prisoner told me that she, with four others, had been put into a sleep by the victim, and then carried through the air in a winged chariot to the bottom of a lake near Burhait; arrived there, they saw beautiful houses and gardens and horses etc. etc. Although apparently willing to talk, she used to put off singing her incantation song from day to day with a kind of 'call-tomorrow' sort of manner. I resigned my hopes of ever obtaining the verses, for her husband had eyed me uneasily not seeming to like the daily interviews I was having with his bride. As the girl was young and pretty, and her protector imprisoned by me—recollecting that 'Caesar's wife should not even be suspected'—I resigned my pursuit of knowledge to the consideration of prudence'.[7]

I myself cannot pretend to have been much more successful but apart from obtaining several invocatory charms, I was able to secure two songs from Santals who had gone about with witches.

I

I have cut the plantain grove
I have taken off my clothes
I have learnt from my mother-in-law
How to eat my husband
On the hills the wind blows
I have cut the thatching grass
I have grown weary
Weary of eating rice.

II

The weapons are ready
The axe glitters
Over the smooth verandah
The wasps are swarming
O Bagru leave us
Kill the young servants
Kill the girls, the boys.

After the songs have been heard, the next stage is the introduction to the bongas themselves, for a witch must not only be married to a bonga but must learn from him the art of killing. This is sometimes a dangerous interlude since if the bonga husband does not like his bride he may sometimes kill her.

In Jhimoli Ragda Hunsdak' was grazing his buffaloes at night when he heard a child crying. He hid himself and from where he crouched he saw a woman with a little girl beneath a Simol tree. The woman was calling out to a bonga to come down and marry the child. The bonga was unwilling but at last he came, paid twentyfive rupees as bride-price and took the child. When Ragda heard the witche's voice he recognised her as his own wife and the child as his niece. A few days later, Ragda's niece fell ill and since the bonga had never wanted to marry her, there was little hope and very soon she died.

Finally a young witch must qualify for full membership by eating one of her own family. For this purpose she herself either assists in the killing or shares in the flesh after the killing has been done.

Rengta Kisku of Dumdumi was attacked and mauled by two bears. A jan guru was consulted and declared that Rengta's sister was under training as a witch with her husband's elder sister. To complete her course, they had marked down Rengta for killing and his sister had attacked him as a bear in order to eat his flesh. The two girls were severely beaten and Rengta's sister then admitted that she had tried to eat her brother and had become a bear for doing so.

In Rajpora, the little daughter of Juna Hembrom was selected by her two aunts for training as a witch. They decided that the girl must eat her own father and one day as Juna was going out to plough, the two women took the girl with them and felled him with the blunt end of an axe. The women then took out his liver and cooked and ate it behind a house. The little girl did not take her share but hid it under a stone. A little later her father fell ill and in remorse the girl told her grandmother all that they had done. A jan guru who was consulted confirmed what the girl had said and by applying special medicine Juna was saved.

III THE RITUAL OF MEETINGS

Once a girl has been initiated, she must observe the discipline of witches, and her first duty is to assist at the ritual and to attend the witches' gatherings. These assemblies take place either every night, on certain fixed nights, particularly on Saturdays and Sundays or at longer intervals. A godet bonga is deputed to summon the witches. He goes through the village carrying a black hen and as soon as the witches hear it they rise and hurry to their posts. Sometimes another bonga is also sent out with a drum to lull the village, to a trance and prevent anyone from seeing the revels. The place of meeting is either the manjhithan, the sacred grove, a lonely dale, a great tree, the end of the village or a cross road. In a folk-tale two boys suddenly see a light flaring by the river. The light stands still. Then it glides to a great bar tree and next day the boys learn that the tree is the haunt of witches.

As the witches leave their houses they strip themselves naked and put on girdles of brooms. Each leaves a broom on her bed and her bonga familiar transforms it into a dummy which is the image of herself.

As the witches gather, they bring their witches' lights and another folk-tale narrates how a boy who stayed behind at the manjhithan after the night's dancing was dazzled by their beauty. 'Suddenly he heard the sound of drums and set up with a start. At the end of the village he saw some green and blue flames. Near the manjhithan was a deserted house and he went to it to see who were coming. He saw a great crowd of women reach the manjhithan and climb a bar tree. The bar tree was full of streamers. Lotus flowers and leaves were hanging on it and on all the branches the buds of lotus flowers were flaring like glowing sticks. A blue light was coming from them. So much light was in the tree that those who were climbing could be clearly seen. In the tree were women of all castes. The bar tree was going six or seven cubits above the ground and below the tree grooms were standing, clad in the dress of rajas. Their uniforms were glittering in the light. Behind them was a tiger like a great ox, and on the tiger a bonga was mounted. The bonga looked like a pargana. In his hand was a costly stick which flashed in the light. The boy did not know who they were or where they went, but the old women told him they were witches and the hanging lights in the bar tree were diamonds. Such diamonds are always found with those who are true witches and they are called the witches' lights. But when there is wind or rain the lights do not shine'.

When the witches have assembled they honour their immediate superior—Pargana Bonga, if the meeting is in the sacred grove and Manjhi Haram if they have gathered at the manjhithan. This ceremony has also been described in a folk-tale and I will quote a short extract.

'Two boys lay in wait at a great bar tree. Night fell and the witches came trooping in with lighted flares. When all had come, a huge bonga stood in their midst. His beard reached to his chest. His teeth were like chisels and his eyes were as large as grain measures. He was the master of the bongas and witches and it was he who ordered which men they should eat'.

The assembly then settles its business. If it is an expedition to procure the seeds of sickness, the witches mount the branches and the tree glides through the air. If it is food and meat, they decide their next victim and either a witch is authorised to kill him or the council summons him to their presence. If there are novices they are made over to the bongas for instruction. If there is no particular business, the witches simply dance and then disperse. When their business is dancing two boys are employed as the witches' drummers and a folk-tale tells how two boys grew fond of the witches' company and every night performed this service for them, the witches dancing the Sohrae and Lagre dances from the manjhithan to the jaher and the boys dancing and drumming naked before them.

At a school in Narayanpur in Birbhum, a boy was always dozing in his classes. His teacher who came from Kanglapara in Pakur asked him why he could never keep awake and at last the boy confessed that every night he went out with witches to dance naked and to do the drumming at their dances.

IV 'EATING' BY WITCHES

Once a woman has become a witch, the village is at her mercy. She can induce sickness and cause death and there are five methods which lie at her disposal.

The first is to kill her victim by extracting, cooking and then eating the lungs, liver or heart. This is by far the most common methods and it will illustrate its details if I quote a folk-tale from Bompas.

'There were once a woman and her daughter-in-law, who were both witches. One night during the annual Sohrae festival the men of the village were going from house to house singing and getting rice beer to drink ; and one young man named Chandrai got so drunk that when they came to the house where the two witch women lived he rolled himself under the shelf on which rice was stored and fell asleep. Next morning he came to his senses but he did not like to come out and show himself for fear of ridicule so he made up his mind to wait till a party came round singing again and then to slip out with them unperceived.

He lay waiting and presently all the men of the house went away to join in the danka dance ; leaving the mistress of the house and her daughter-in-law alone. Presently the two began to talka nd an elder woman said "Well what with the pigs and the goats that have been sacrificed during this Sohrae we have had plenty of meat to eat lately and yet I don't feel as if I had had any". 'That is so' answered her daughter-in-law; 'fowls and pigs' flesh is very unsatisfying'. 'Then what are we to do ?' rejoined the old woman, 'I don't know unless you do for the father of your grandchild'. When he heard this Chandrai shivered with fright and hid himself further under the rice shelf, for he saw that the two women must be witches.

That day was the day on which a bullock is tied to a post outside each house and at noon the husband of the younger witch began to dig a hole outside the house to receive the post. While he was working Chandrai heard the two women begin to talk again 'Now is your opportunity', said the younger woman 'while he is digging the hole'. 'But perhaps the ojha will be able to discover us', objected the other. 'Oh we can prevent that by making the ojha see in the oiled leaf the faces of Rupi and Bindi-naming two gilrs of the village—and we can say that my husband had seduced them and then declined to marry them and that was why they killed him'. The old woman seemed to be satisfied, for she took up a hatchet and went out to where her son was digging the hole. She waited till he bent down to throw out the earth with his hands and then cut open his back and pulled out his liver and heart and brought them into the house. Her unfortunate son felt a spasm of pain when his mother struck him but he did not know what had hurt him and there was no visible wound. The two women then chopped up the liver and heart and cooked and ate them'.

In an account which I myself recorded in 1944, 'the witches of a village gathered at the manjhithan. They took a man from his house and went dancing to the sacred grove. In the grove they made him eat adwa rice. Then the manjhi's wife said 'Hammer him on the head with the back of an axe'. A witch felled him and they cut him up and gave the manjhi's wife two shares. Then they said 'At the full moon this man will die'.

This method is much the most fatal but at the same time it is fringed with certain stringent conditions. Only certain persons can be killed in this way and then only by the most strict observance of certain rites. The first condition is that although the witch may herself do the actual killing and may herself eat the man, she can only do so by powers derived from the bongas. Accordingly she must first take a bonga's permission before she starts her murderous work. She need not necessarily secure the approval of Manjhi Haram or Pargana Bonga but at least one bonga approved by Pargana Bonga must consent to the act.

In Rajdah Doman Marandi chanced to offend the wife of his eldest son. The woman was a witch and in consultation with the two others, she decided to kill and eat him. But they had first to secure the bongas' approval. One night therefore they entered Doman's house, lifted him on his cot and carried him to the manjhithan. There they asked Manjhi Haram to approve the eating. Manjhi Haram declined so they carried him to the sacred grove. There also Pargana Bonga refused but advised them to consult the ato bonga in the village pool. The women again picked up the cot and with Doman still asleep carried him to the pool and there the ato bonga gave them permission. After that they took him to the end of the village and between a jack fruit and a mango they cut out his heart.

A second and equally important condition is that at least one member of the victims' inner family must herself be a witch. In most cases the witch, already in the family, does the killing but if she does not actually strike the victim she must assist at the operation either by touching him with her hands or with a knife or by pointing him out with her fingers.

In Jordiha a band of witches took Barka Tudu to the sacred grove. There they tied a rope round his neck and marched him round the grove until he fainted. His daughter who was one of the witches then 'killed' and 'ate' him. Sometime later Barka fell ill and when the villagers accused his daughter of 'eating' him, she confessed that she had done so at the instance of her mother.

Hopa Murmu of Doba was in love with a girl who was a witch. He himself was a witch boy and used to play the drum when the witches danced. As he was married to another girl, the witch said 'I will kill her'. With Hopa's aid the witch and a friend split open the chest of Hopa's wife and took her liver, lungs and heart. They cooked them in flour and ate them and the next day the girl died.

If no member of the inner family or household is a witch, the killing is postponed until a girl in the family has been seduced and converted into one.

Mongla Soren of Mohanpur had two daughters aged ten and eight. Two old women and two young girls of the village were witches and one day they proposed to 'eat' the youngest of the two daughters. Since there was no witch in the family, they first seduced the elder daughter and having made her into a witch they induced her to touch her sister. The girl did so, the women extracted her heart, cooked it in a pot and a little later the girl died. The women then demanded Mongla himself but the girl refused to touch her father and on this the witches made her ill. As she lay on her cot, she told her father everything, the pargana of Katikund was consulted and the witches were warned that they would be beaten to death unless they cured the girl. A little later the girl recovered.

In Amtala, there were two witches—the wife of Mongla Murmu's nephew and a woman of the village. They decided they must eat either Mongla or his brother Chota Ramu, but no one in the family was a witch. They decided therefore that Mongla's daughter must be converted and one day they took her to the jungle. At first the girl refused to help but the two women then called a tiger, mounted the girl on it caught her by the legs and threatened to kill her if she did not surrender one of the two men. On this the girl agreed, the two women went to her house and there the girl folded her hands and pointed at her father.

When bonga approval has been gained and a witch secured in the family itself, the next stage is the extraction of the vital organs. This need not necessarily be done at night but the family witch must herself be present. Sometimes the heart only is extracted and at other times only the liver or lungs. When the viscera have been taken out, the wound is closed but sometimes other objects are inserted in their place.

In Kukurtopa, Keso Murmu combined the offices of manjhi and village priest. The Sohrae festival came round and on the night before it was due to start, Keso suddenly felt severe pains in his belly. The pains subsided and the next morning he performed the sacrifices. But a few hours later he again fell ill and everyone thought he would die. His son went to call his uncle and as he was telling him, his aunt cried out 'Why should not Keso have a pain ? He has never paid me my fee as match-maker ?' Everyone was alarmed when they heard her say this. The whole village met and the woman was told to cure Keso at once. She took some oil, massaged Keso's belly and the pains eased. A little later Keso defecated and a tuber cut flat on both its sides was found in the stool.

In Saharghati, the daughter of Mongal Soren opened her father's chest and belly, took out his lungs and liver and put a pestle and tatauni back in their place.

When her father fell ill the girl confessed she had done this and was a witch.

When the liver, lungs or heart have been extracted they are cooked with rice, a portion is offered to the bongas and the rest is then eaten by the witches. If the entire organ is completely consumed, the victim's Sone or jiwi can never return, the man is doomed and nothing can now save him. If, however, only a part of the organ is extracted or if a portion of it escapes the eating, the jiwi can sometimes be regrafted into his body, and the man saved.

In the case from Amtala, which I have already described, Mongla Murmu's daughter first pointed to her father and her cousin's wife then opened the man's chest and extracted a piece of his heart. The two women took it to the forests, cooked it in a new pot with arwa rice and ate it. As they cooked they invoked three bongas—Gar Naran, Indi Naran and Pahar Nangin and offerings of the pudding were made to them. They gave the girl a share but she hid it under a stone. Some days later Mongla fell ill and it was only after his daughter had confessed and the three bongas had been appeased that he at last recovered. If all his heart had been extracted or if all of it had been eaten, Mongla would have died.

In the case from Rajdah in which Doman Marandi was taken on a cot and operated on at the end of the village, the three witches took out his heart, cooked it with some rice, danced round the hearth and finally ate the pudding. They did not, however, completely eat it and the pot with its leavings was put back in a house. After that they carried Doman home and put him in his usual place. The next morning when Doman woke up he did not notice any pain but was vaguely frightened and disturbed. He suspected that witches had been tempering with him and when the villagers went to consult a jan guru about another case, he went with them and told the jan guru what had happened. The jan guru said that witches had eaten his heart, and that his son's wife was responsible. In this case Doman ultimately recovered but only because a part of his heart had not been eaten.

After the victim's organs have been eaten, it is only a question of time before he falls ill. The witches' usually select a date for his death and some days earlier the fatal sickness starts. Sometimes they kill him almost immediately while at other times they allow a month or two to elapse and then the crisis comes.

In the case from Rajdah, nothing happened for several weeks. In Asian, Doman's heart was eaten but his death was settled for the full moon day in Mag. It was not until two months had gone by that he fell ill.

When the sickness starts, only the prompt discovery of the cause and the chance that a part of the organ has escaped consumption can prevent the witch from accomplishing her object.

V Action through bongas

If a witch fails to secure the approval of Manjhi Haram or Pargana Bonga or if one in the victim's family can be suborned, the method of 'eating' has necessarily to be abandoned and she is forced on one of four other methods.

These differ from the first in that the witch herself is no longer the agent of murder and the victim does not necessarily belong to her family. She is merely its instigator and the work of destruction is done by a bonga instead.

The first of these methods is when a bonga is himself the death dealing agent and afflicts the victim with disease.

In an account by C.H. Bompas, a witch summons a bonga and says 'Brother-in-law Ramjit, there is something that you must do for me; my nephew is ill ; he must die on such and such a day ; that day I must see the smoke of his funeral pyre ; but you must save me from the witch finder'. 'On the day before that fixed by the witch, the invalid became unconscious and was at the point of death'.[8]

The second method is for the bonga not to do the killing himself but to provide a death dealing agent in his place.

Bompas, for example, has described how a witch was incensed by her brother-in-law and summoned a bonga from a pool. 'When the woman saw him her tongue flickered in and out like a snake's and she made a hissing noise, such as a crab makes. Then the woman began 'Dharmal Chandi, I have a request which you must promise to grant'. And when the bonga had promised she proceeded 'you must have my brother-in-law killed by a tiger the day after tomorrow' . . . and 'the bonga promised to do what she asked and disappeared'.

In Bewa the son of Jagan Tudu was bitten by a dog. Next night while he was making water he felt his grandmother touch his chest. The following day he died saying she was a witch who had killed him through the dog.

Occasionally the bonga transforms the witches themselves into animals and I have already noted a case in which two girls attacked their victim in the form of bears.

A third method is to localise a bonga in a stone and then to bury it in the house or cowshed of the victim. 'Such bongas' says Kolean Haram 'are called 'Thapna Bongas'. They are of two kinds, one is a white stone, on which *sindur* has been put and hair wound round, another is a silk cocoon with one end cut off and insite it a little of every kind of grain and a white stone marked with *sindur*'.[9] If anyone steps on the stone he steps on the bonga and is at once struck with disease or death.

Finally the seeds of sickness can be strewn in the village, buried in its lanes and at the manjhithan or sprinkled in wells and hollow horns. These seeds are sometimes brought from the Kundli tank near Barhait. 'All the witches of the world come to it', a Santal told me 'and there is a place where they assemble. In this tank the seeds of sickness are to be found and witches go there for getting their supplies. They put the seed in little earthen vessels or in the shells of water snails. For taking the seed away, they yoke rutting buffaloes to carts. When they wish to bring sickness to any country or village, they bury some of the seed at the end of the village street and at the manjhithan. Then when the time comes, the sickness from the buried . . . seed spreads. The people and animals of the village feel pain and die'.

In a folktale which I recorded in 1944, a boy actually witnessed the purchase of the seeds.

'One night a boy was stranded in the forest and climbed a tree. Presently all the women of the village gathered and began to climb it and in his fear the boy flattened himself against a branch like a lizard. Then an old woman who was the guru recited a mantra and the tree rose in the air. She recited a second mantra and the tree flew through the air like an arrow. In a little while they crossed an ocean and reached a place with a great bonga. He had a shop with all the pains and illnesses of the world. The women left the tree and discussed what seeds of illness they would buy. They checked their money and chose the seeds of colds, coughs, and itches and the foot and mouth disease of cattle. When they had bought the seeds of sickness, the tree took them to their village. The witches unloaded the seeds in the sacred grove and put them on the manjhi's cart. So heavy were the seeds of sickness that even two large buffaloes were worn out in dragging them along. At the door of every house they sowed the venom and the next morning sickness blighted the village'.

VI DIAGNOSIS

When a witch has been at work, the sign is illness. We have seen however that not every illness is due to witchcraft and an ojha must first diagnose that witchcraft is the cause before further steps can be taken. As soon as this conclusion is reached; the matter becomes an affairs of the whole village. It is not merely one household which is threatened. The whole security of the village is undermined. The task of diagnosing the actual witch is therefore undertaken by all the village.

This process has been fully described by Bodding and I cannot do better than reproduce his account.

'The village authorities are called in, and the headman, takes action. Followed by the village men he walks at evening through the village street, calling out at every house in a loud voice, 'Beware', so and so is ill ; may he recover. We have caught thee ; if he does not recover, we shall certainly not call you good'.

As will be observed, it is a threat at random. They have no doubt that a witch is at the bottom of it ; but they do not know, or have so far no 'proofs' whatever their suspicions may be, who may be the actual witch ; she may be in any house in the village ; it is consequently advisable and politic to warn all ; then possibly the guilty one may think better of it and leave off.

If the patient after this should recover, well and good. It is to nobody's interest to go further into the matter. Wife, daughter, sister or mother of any of the men of the village might be 'proved' to be a witch. The headman's wife is more often than not suspected.

If, on the other hand, there is no improvement, the headman sends men out in pairs, to get other ojhas to divine by leaves, what is the cause of the disease. If the verdicts do not agree, they next day send to other ojhas. If the messengers bring the same verdict of witchcraft from three different ojhas, all doubts are thrown away.

The next thing is to find out, or rather to 'prove' by divination where the witch is. There is likely not one of those concerned who does not suspect a certain person ; but suspicion is not enough, and as there is no possibility of direct evidence, they have to rely on divination again. But now it is not the sunum bonga that is brought into operation.

Under the leadership of the village headman they proceed as follows : Going to a place where there is water they plant along the edge of the water a number of fresh cut small branches. First of all they plant a branch in the middle as 'witness' then in succession one for the house-god (orak' bonga) of the patient's household, then one for the house-god of his father-in-law's household, then one for each of the several fraternal female relatives, one for daughter and for sister, one for the unrelated part of the village and one for disom duk (epidemic disease). The number of branches will vary according to the number of relatives, and they may sometimes plant one for each household, also unrelated, in the village. As each branch is planted, *sindur* is applied to it.

After having scattered adwa rice over the place the following invocation is made : 'Greeting then, Day-god of the heavens'. Thou art spread out, like a mat, thou hast overspread the four corners, the four words; here then, as thou seest, we have planted branches to ascertain the delinquent, what is guilty thou wilt pronounce guilty, let that dry up and wither—thou wilt bud fresh, thou wilt remain unaltered and sound' (this to the witness branch).

It will be observed that they have planted twigs also for bongas; even if the leaf-oracle has pronounced the culprit to be a witch, here the appeal is made to the Supreme Deity, and no possibility must, in justice to all, be left unnoticed. Hence these twigs. They also address these bongas, somewhat in the following strain :

'Take care then, if thou art a bonga, let this one dry up and wither, and if it be not thou, remain unaltered and sound. Thou wilt bring out witness.' This formula is repeated over each branch. Having done all this they return home. Some five hours afterwards (when they think that withering may have commenced) or if the 'planting' takes place in the evening, then early next morning, they return to have a look at the branches, whichever branch is dead, the one in whose name it was planted is understood to be proved responsible. If it is 'proved' to be a witch, the female occupants of as many households as the representative branches of which have died are considered possible witches.

To be adjudged a witch is a serious matter; they do not therefore rest satisfied with doing this twig-planting only once. They repeat it twice or thrice, and each time inside the boundary of another village. It may, of course, happen that the oracle gives a different verdict in the different places, in such cases there is to the Santal mind no doubt that the witches have been at work as to hinder them in finding out the truth. However, they continue, until they are satisfied.

As has been seen, the divination proceeds by eliminating the various possibilities. The whole has by this time been narrowed down to a certain household. The individual has not been singled out as yet, although there is pretty little doubt in their minds.

It should be specially noted, that the operations undertaken by the ojhas and the village people, namely, the sunum bonga and the other kinds of divination, do not profess to single out any individual (except, of course, bongas who are specifically mentioned when they consult the oracle). So far as human beings are concerned they do not go further than pointing out certain limits within which the culprit is to be sought. They do not attempt the responsibility of naming individuals.

To name the individual is the business of the jan. He is the man who 'knows', namely, by revelation. 'The jans', says Kolean from whose description much of the following is gleaned, 'are our High Court in witchcraft matters. Those which the jans pronounce to be witches, we deem witches. Whether they really find them out, or the whole is humbug—we believe that they find them out'.

If the patient or his relatives decide to carry the matter to a jan, they always go along in crowd. If the whole village is down with some disease, the headman will go along; if not, he only gives advice as to who ought to go. There are, as a matter of course, a couple of men representing the patient, the husband and male relatives of some woman clearly suspected, and half a dozen or so for the village people as witnesses. They go together and never lose sight of one another to prevent any one from secretly informing the jan about their business.

They will, as a rule, go to a jan living at a distance who

cannot be supposed to have personal knowledge of the matter or of the persons concerned. When they reach the jan's village, they camp outside and are careful not to tell anybody any particular as to why they have come or who they are. They go to the village headman and ask him to introduce them to the guru, which he does, whereupon the headman tells them to bring out the things necessary for divination, namely, one betel nut, one leaf-cup, some adwa rice, mustard oil, *sindur*, resin of the sal tree, and some leaves of the bael tree.

The jan tells them to come to him at a specified time, and they return to their camping place. If any one asks them any question, they either do not answer, or if they do, they purposely give wrong answer.

At the fixed time they return to the jan, who will transact his business with them either in his own house, in the jaher or somewhere outside the village. The clientele sit quiet and look on. The jan puts down small handfuls of the adwa rice in a number of places in the name of different bongas, puts alongside all these heaps of bael leaves, and finally, having mixed the oil and *sindur*, puts *sindur* marks in front of the rice. He then throws the resin on burning coals, blows the shell, sounds the bonga bell and worships his bongas.

Next he becomes 'possessed' by the spirit of divination and in this state commences to utter incessantly incoherent words. He ultimately first names the part of the country where they come from, then their village, then tells how the village street runs, the name of the headman, of the person at whose behest they have come, the names of his uncles, brothers, sisters, sons, daughters and how many they are. All to prove that he has knowledge, outside the ordinary.

It is very impressive and when the jan asks: 'Well, gentlemen, have I told you this right or not ?' They answer : 'Absolutely correct; we are convinced; now let us hear the oracle'.

The jan, however, first demands his fee, one rupee, and if they have made any vow before starting, then the full amount of this in addition. When he has received all, he tells them who is at the bottom of their troubles, a bonga or a witch, and also reveals the names of these.

To confirm them in their faith the jan next asks them, whether they have not planted branches in so and so many places, and whether they did it properly. The answer is, of course, in the affirmative. And the jan dismisses them saying: 'If you are not satisfied, seek confirmation with seven soothsayers. If any such should tell anything else than what I have told, I shall return you the fees you have paid'.

Hereupon the deputation returns home.[10]

This account by Bodding is representative of current procedure except that the branches are usually restricted to female members of the victim's inner and greater family and sometimes only one branch is set up.

In the Narayanpur area, for example, sal twigs are not set out in a line but a single branch with a number of leaves is set up. The 'witness' leaf is known as dhorom. One leaf is earmarked for a bonga, and the other leaves are confined to the various female members of the victim's household. Other households are not included since if a witch is responsible, she must obviously be one of the victim's household. If the dhorom leaf withers, the victim is doomed.

Similarly in the Pakur subdivision it is only the female members of the victim's family who are subjected to a test by leaves.

VII CONFIRMATION OF THE DIAGNOSIS

When a jan guru has confirmed the diagnosis of the leaves, a second confirmation is usually sought. If the second, third or fourth jan guru differs, the matter remains inconclusive. The woman will still deny the charge and even if her relations accept the diagnosis they are debarred from acting on it without a second guru's opinion. Moreover the woman herself can go to the jan guru, interrogate him and if necessary discredit his opinion.

In Bordoha, the son of Dibia Hembrom fell ill. Witchcraft was diagnosed and the jan guru declared that the child's own mother had 'killed' and 'eaten' him. The woman indignantly denied the charge, took all the villagers back with her and demanded to know how the jan guru had reached his decision. The jan guru was unnerved by the woman's protests and, very unwisely for himself, changed his ground. He said that the child had not been 'eaten' but that the woman had induced a bonga to harm him. The villagers were greatly enraged at this change of attitude, acquitted the woman and abused the jan guru so freely that he had to shift practice to another part of the country.

Similarly the woman herself may have other jan gurus consulted and if these reject the first guru's reading, she is virtually absolved.

If, however, any second jan guru confirms the decision of the first, the diagnosis is usually regarded as conclusive and no matter how the woman protests, she is now treated as a proved witch.

In Siankhuri the wife of Chitu Baske was detected to be a witch. She appealed to five jan gurus but all of them confirmed the diagnosis and after that there was no help.

VIII REMEDIAL ACTION

Once a witch has been identified, the action taken varies according as the victim is still alive or is already dead. If the victim is alive and quickly recovers, nothing more is done. The taint of witchcraft may remain but it is thought that either other witches have distorted the jan guru's diagnosis or the witch herself has thought better of it and of her own accord has cured the victim.

If the sickness continues, the victim's plight gives an intense urgency to the situation and the witch herself is made to intervene, confess her crime and take the necessary measures. These measures vary according as the witch has 'eaten' her victim or has merely stricken him through a bonga.

In the case from Rajdah where Doman Marandi was 'eaten' the leading witch was the wife of his eldest son. When Doman's condition grew critical, he told his children that there was no more time to be lost. They therefore seized the woman, kicked her, beat her, threw her on the ground and jabbed her with a stick. The woman then confessed everything, named her co-witches and that if some fowls, a pig, a pigeon, a sheep and a goat were sacrificed to certain bongas whom she named, Doman might still be saved. These sacrifices were done the same night but it grew to morning before Doman's jiwi had been brought back. The witch said that they must wait till evening and that one of her co-witches must be made to help her. One of the two was then forced out of her house, given a thrashing and compelled to assist. That night two witches took the villagers to the spot where the heart had been extracted. When it was dark and they could scarcely be seen, one of them took off her clothes and climbed a tree. While she was in its branches a bird flew out. A great while later she came down, put on her clothes and the two went straight to Doman's house. There they went to the sick man and put on his chest a piece of fresh heart. They then asked an ojha to complete the cure. The ojha added some spices, put the piece of heart in Doman's mouth and told him to swallow it. He did so, went off to sleep, at midnight felt better and by the next day was cured.

In Rajpara, Juna Hembrom was 'eaten' by his two sisters and little daughter. The child told her grandmother that she had kept her own share under a stone and had not eaten it. A jan guru was consulted and on his advice a pigeon and frog was sacrificed, their hearts were mixed with spice and Juna ate them. Shortly afterwards he completely recovered.

In such cases the witch herself or her male guardian is required to give the birds and animals and if she does not do so she is at once outcasted by pante begar.

If the sickness is due to a witch's action but she has not 'eaten' the victim similar steps are taken to appease the bongas.

In Siankhuri, a jan guru diagnosed that the wife of Chaitu Baske was a witch and that Chaitu's younger brother was ill because she had set up a bonga. When the villagers heard this, they beat the woman and Chaitu was made to pay five rupees and give a pig, a pigeon and a white fowl for sacrifice. When he did this, his brother recovered.

If a bonga has been buried by a witch, the first task is to locate its stone.

Geda Hembrom and his family of Haripur were ill. Two jan gurus divined that some bongas had been buried in their house and by means of a divining rod they located the two stones. When the stones were dug up they were found marked with *sindur* and tied in human hair. Geda then took them to a field, sacrificed a sheep, a pig and three fowls and burnt the stones and hair. After that all his family got well.

If seeds of sickness have been planted, these also must be

located and the usual methods are either to divine their presence by means of little rods or to beat the witch until she confesses.

In Gorkond Hambro Hembrom caught smallpox and when his family consulted the jan guru, the latter named five women of the village as the witches responsible. The witches admitted that they had planted seeds of sickness and after they had pointed out the places, the villagers dug up some little earthen pots.

The pots with the seeds were then burnt and the witches were made to sacrifice a pig, a goat, a sheep, a pigeon and a fowl outside the village.

In Jasaidih an epidemic broke out among men and cattle. A jan guru diagnosed that 'poison' had been buried at the two ends of the village. The villagers dug the earth and discovered some snail shells. They took them out and threw them away and after that the attacks subsided. The jan guru also identified the witches and each of them was fined twenty-five rupees and made to give a fowl, a pig and a goat.

IX THE CURE OF WITCHES

If the victim dies, shortly after the diagnosis or is already dead when the witch is named, preventive action is obviously out of the question and all that can be done is to prevent a recurrence of the evil.

In many areas the family first vent their grief by giving the witch a beating and after that a village meeting is called and the woman is punished with a fine.

Suphal Murmu of Kalipathar accused his father's elder brother's wife of killing him by beating him on the chest. A jan guru confirmed that the woman was a witch but before anything could be done Suphal had died. His father wanted to kill the witch outright but the others advised him to be guided by the village. In the end the woman was fined thirty rupees and the money was paid by her brothers.

If the witch has been suspected for sometime or the village doubts if of her own will she can now abandon the art, they proceed to disqualify her from further intercourse with bongas by causing her to drink a mixture of human excrement and urine.

No bonga will ever go near excrement and accordingly a witch who has once been so polluted is deprived of all her maleficent powers.

In Sapdiha, the wife of Burhan Hembrom was declared a witch. Her husband paid twenty-five rupees and she herself was neutralised by being forced to drink some human excrement and urine.

In Mahagama in Ranga bungalow, cholera broke out and for sometime four or five persons died each day. All the villagers became desperate and seeing no other remedy, they beat all the women in the village and made them drink human excreta. A little later the cholera stopped and since then there has never been an epidemic in the village.

If the villagers are disinclined to force the mixture into the woman, they sometimes adopt more furtive methods.

In Bhuibhanga, the wife of Surai Murmu was proved a witch. Her husband consulted Chotu Ramu of Amtala who agreed to prepare a neutralising mixture. He got together specimens of excreta of as many animals as he could and also of various men and women. He then wrapped them in some sal leaves and kept them under a stone in the forest. After that he sacrificed a pig and five days later went naked to the spot. There he recovered the packet, pounded up the excreta, mixed it with a sondhani root and gave it to Surai. Surai mixed it with his wife's food and since then all the bongas have completely boycotted her and no jun guru has ever diagnosed her as a witch.

Yet another recipe was employed when the wife of Anu Marandi in the Nonithat circle was found to be a witch. She was bluffed into giving a few drops of her own blood. A piece of hoof from a horse which had died on a Sunday was pounded up and the blood mixed with it. This was then dropped into some rice beer and the woman drank it without knowing. This polluted her so completely that no bongas have ever helped her since.

If for any reason excrement is not administered and in spite of fining, the witch still continues her fell pursuits, the final resort is expulsion from the village.

In Dumka, the wife of Khara Hansdak' has been repeatedly diagnosed as a witch. She was first fined two rupees and eight annas then five rupees, then ten and finally fifteen. The villagers have now decided that if she is again detected she will be sent back to her parents.

Similarly in Sukbari, the wife of Gangu Marandi was proved, time after time, to be a witch. She was an old woman but in spite of her age Gangu was compelled to interfere and he returned her to her parents.

In the case where Doman Marandi was eaten by his son's wife, no immediate action was taken but some months later the girl was returned to her family.

If the witch is a widow and is living in her husband's house, his relatives can act for the dead man and expel her from the village.

Such a case occurred in Gargawa where the widow of Dasmat Murmu was often declared to be a witch. She had two grown up sons, but in spite of this her husband's younger brother intervened and she was driven from the village.

X CONCLUSION

The significance of witches for Santal criminal law will need no emphasis. They undermine security. They wreak vengeance. They kill and injure. The fact that they use invisible methods makes no difference to their role. On the contrary because their attacks are invisible, they are, if anything, more potent and dreaded. The witch is an enemy of society—as ruthless as a murderer, as criminal as a robber.

REFERENCES

1. Man, op. cit., 29.
2. Ibid., 159-60.
3. L.O. Skrefsrud and Kolean Haram, *Horkoren Mare Hapramko reak' Katha*, (Third edition, Benagaria, 1928), 210.
4. Chotrai Deshmanjhi, *Chotrai Deshmanjhi reak' Katha* (Benagaria, 1938).
5. Bompas, op. cit., 423-24.

6. *Horkoren Mare Hapramko reak' Katha*, 211-12.
7. Man, op. cit., 152.
8. Bompas, op. cit, 439.
9. *Horkoren Mare Hapramko reak' Katha*, 227.
10. Bodding, op. cit., 39-42.

46

THE REGULATION OF SEX

I THE SANTAL ATTITUDE TO SEX

IN THE Santal code of criminal law, sex and its regulation account for by far the largest number of rules and conventions. This is not because Santals are at all obsessed with sex, for sex plays neither a greater nor a lesser part in Santal life than it does the with Uraons, Mundas, Baigas or Pardhans. The regulation of sex is rather based on the view that sex is of such importance that its values must at all costs be preserved. It is not only 'a need of the night', a passionate necessity which should not and cannot be denied. It is also capable of profoundly affecting the structure of families and the integrity of the tribe. Santal law accordingly aims both at providing the greatest freedom as well as at enforcing the strictest control. The rules of exogamy must be strictly followed. Paternity must be acknowledged or adjusted. Short of marriage, sexual relations may occur but they should neither be publicly recognised nor socially sanctioned. Moreover the value of sex lies in its intimacy and there is no clearer index to Santal sensibility than in the value which the tribe acts on public reticence. In the privacy of night or in the secret meetings of lovers the sexual technique of Santals is as developed as that of the Pardhans. In the day time it is as if sex were an abstract diagram or an arid machine. At only one festival, Sohrae, is this control slightly relaxed while at the annual hunt, sexual terms are freely used. For the root of the year, Santals lead a fully developed life but within the ambit of their tribal rules. By insisting on these rules and at the same time providing two occasions for relaxation, Santals maintain a standard of happiness and decency which can have few parallels in Eastern or Middle India.

II RULES OF LANGUAGE AND BEHAVIOUR

For maintaining this approach to sex, the tone of village life is of the first importance.

We have already seen that sexological expressions play only a small part in Santal abuse. This avoidance of sexual terms extends to the whole range of public village life.

A party of girls from Kurum were going to see the Dibi festival at Dumka. As they went through Gidni they were singing songs and one of them who was slightly drunk cried 'Deper, deper, copulate, copulate'. On this a man of Gidni at once caught her and only after her friends had given her some clothes and she had left her own as security was she allowed to go. Two days later there was a joint village meeting and the girl was fined five rupees.

In Dumarthan the men were getting ready for the annual hunt. While they were waiting, two co-wives began to quarrel and in the course of the argument the elder said, 'You are always going after him like a bitch in heat'. Everyone took offence at this breach of village conventions and the next day the woman was fined two rupees and eight annas.

The manjhi of Choudhury was drinking rice beer at the Sohrae festival when he said in public to a group of boys 'Won't you let me copulate with your sisters?' All those who heard him were disgusted and the villagers fined him fifteen rupees.

There is a similar control of public behaviour. In village dancing, gestures by the drummers are often frenzied but they are never directly sexual. In the village itself there are no sexual pantomimes and the wearing of mock gentalia, such as W.V. Grigson has described among the Maria Gonds is permissible only at the annual hunt and at bitlahas. Similarly neither men nor women may appear naked in public and a breach of this rule may lead to a complete severance by a fine. In a case which I have recorded in *Civil Law in Santal Society*, a wedding was broken off because the bride's mother took off her clothes and danced before the women.

A girl of Bodacapar made herself naked and dragged a boy with her down the village street. The villagers intervened and fined her seven rupees.

In Karandia, a man got drunk on the Sakrat day. He tore his clothes off and ran naked down the village. The villagers tied him up and next day, they fined him five rupees.

Kuar Kisku, the pargana of Chandna, was returning home from market a little drunk. He decided to take his clothes off and go on his way with nothing on. Many others were also going home and on the way he stopped an old woman and asked her to do him johar. The five manjhis met and he was fined twenty-five rupees.

Ronjon Tudu of Bhatka was drinking with some friends one afternoon when he decided to go to the tank and have a bath. He came out of his house, took off all his clothes, tied them round his head like a turban and went strolling down the street. Next morning the village held a meeting and he was fined five rupees. Ronjon begged for pardon and in the end the fine was halved.

At a village meeting in Rmabani Kandua Murmu got exasperated with the council and as a mark of contempt he bared his buttocks and showed them to the meetings. The council was greatly incensed and immediately fined him five rupees.[1]

It follows that sexual intercourse itself must never be in public.

Dudga Marandi of Ilaki was caught in actual intercourse with a girl of his village. The boy was fined ten rupees and the girl five.

In Dumarghati the daughter of Lodga Hembrom showed her thumb to seven village boys and defied them to copulate with her. The seven accepted the challenge and one day they dragged her to the forest and attempted to have their way. The girl repulsed five but the last two were successful. The matter came to the village and each of them was fined two rupees eight annas—the girl for making the challenge and the boys for accepting it.

A boy and girl of Rajabhita in Chandna bungalow were seen in actual congress. They were brought to a meeting and as they did not want to marry they were each fined one rupee and four annas.

In Basduma Khare Murmu induced a girl of another village to go with him. The villagers caught them in each other's arms and the village fined Khare fifteen rupees.

The same principles apply to attempts and preparations.

In Bodacapar Chundka Murmu was caught with his village girl. They were about to start intercourse when the girl's brother reached the scene. Chundka was dragged to the manjhi and was fined five rupees.

In certain cases even though the boy and girl are merely anticipating marriage, they are liable to be punished if they are caught engaging publicly in an act of sex.

In Siakhuri Nandhna Murmu was caught with his village girl in actual intercourse. The villagers gave them a beating and although the boy's father paid bride-price and the girl was then and there accepted as a wife, the boy was fined five rupees and the girl two rupees and eight annas.

III CONVENTIONS OF MEETING

Provided sexual terms are avoided, conversation in a Santal village is free and unrestrained. Boys and girls and men and women talk to each other without embarrassment and there is a general case and freedom of conversation and movement. Talk however is always a potential means to greater intimacy and this general freedom is circumscribed by three conventions. So long as girls are unmarried or divorced they can laugh and joke with boys outside their village but such boys must always be Santals. At markets and melas as well as at weddings in other villages, girls can strike up acquaintanceships but only with Santal boys.

In Damru a Santal girl was seen drinking liquor with Mandal Sundi, a Diku of the village. She said he was the family moneylender and as he had offered her a drink, she had taken it. As the villagers suspected that there was much more behind it, they fined her five rupees.

Similarly within the village also Santal girls can laugh and joke but only with Santal boys of the village itself or with Santal boys who are not strangers. If a stranger is caught in the village area with a girl, the boy is taken to the manjhi and both the boy and girl are almost always fined.

In Susni, a Hansdak' girl was washing clothes in a pond by her father's house. A boy from Majdiha came down to the pond and began to talk to her. The girl's father saw them, called his son and the two caught the boy and took him to their house. Two men of Majdiha were called and the boy paid a fine of five rupees.

Pande and Mundri Soren of Sibtala were caught in the fields one night talking at a well with two boys of another village. Their cousins suddenly came on them, drove the other boys away and brought the two girls in. At the village meeting each girl was fined one rupee and four annas.

One day in Manjhla Sarwa, Jasmi Soren went to the forest and began to talk to a boy of Boro Sorwa. They were standing by a stream and the boy was urging her to 'fill his mind' with her. Suddenly the girl's brother chanced upon them. The boy was dragged off to the manjhi and at the meeting the girl was fined two rupees and eight annas and the boy five rupees.

For the purpose of this rule the fact that the stranger has come in a wedding party makes no difference and if he is found with a village girl he is caught and punished.

Two drummers
Play your drums
Two dancers
Dance your will
But do not come too close
or they will fine you ten rupees.[2]

At a wedding in Merehidiha (p.s. Salanpur, Bengal), two boys from Amoi had gone in the bridegroom's party. The next morning they were found near a well talking to three of the village girls. They were taken to the manjhi and each was fined one rupee and eight annas.

When a girl is married, she can still talk to men and boys but except in the public circumstances of a dance, a wedding or a festival, she is not expected to 'laugh or joke' with them. If she is found flirting with a boy, her husband can divorce her.

If a woman is a widow, she must act like a married woman so long as she is in her husband's village but if she has left his house and lands and returned to her parents, she is free to behave like a girl who has been divorced.

IV BAHONHAREA AND AJHNAREA

But besides these conventions which surround ordinary talk and conduct, certain relatives are bound by special rules. These complicated conventions have been analysed by Bodding and I will summarise his account as simply as I can.

The relations in question are:

1. Bahonharea	1. A man and the wife of his younger brother.
	2. A man and the wife of his wife's younger brother.
2. Ajhnarea	1. A woman and the husband of her younger sister.
	2. A woman and the wife of her younger brother.

The terms 'younger brother' and 'younger sister' include also 'younger cousins'—their mutual age deciding the family position and not the fact that they are children of elder or younger brothers.

All these relations must honour each other by never using each other's names while a woman in the presence of the male relative concerned must observe a number of intricate rules.

She must not sit on a cōt in his presence and though she may sit on something else, she must not expose her person. During the night she may lie on anything except a cot if the male relative is in the room. She must not touch a cot or clothes belonging to him. The wife of a younger brother cannot touch the wife of the elder brother if the woman is carrying clothes belonging to her husband, neither can she help the other to get a burden on her head as she might then come in contact with something belonging to the husband of the elder wife. Moreover the woman must never touch the man himself and can therefore never perform the service of washing his feet when he comes on a visit.

She must not loosen her hair, neither must she let anybody free her of lice in the presence of this relation. If she is unmarried she must keep her breasts covered in his presence and she must not climb a tree or mount a ladder when he is near. If, for instance, two brothers with their wives are going somewhere and have a bullock-cart with them, the wife of the younger brother is not allowed to mount the cart, even if the elder brother is himself walking.

She cannot sit on the same mat with him or by his side; she must not touch his shadow (because it belongs to him); if the man is treading the dhinki, she must not keep the paddy or rice in the stamping hole; and she must not eat or drink anything left or touched by him or his wife.

If she should unawares sit on his bedstead or touch anything belonging to him, she must at once wash or pour water on herself, as well as on whatever she has touched belonging to him.

The male relative for his part may sit or lie on a bedstead, though not on hers, in her presence, but he must not touch her or her shadow, her bedstead or her clothes or anybody carrying anything of her wearing apparel. If two brothers are walking together the younger one carrying the clothes of his wife, and they begin to chew tobacco-leaves and lime mixed together, the younger one must, if he mixes the ingredients, put the clothes down while he does it; if the elder one does it, he must not touch the hand of the younger one when giving him the tobacco—but must merely let the stuff fall into his younger brother's hand.

He must not tread the dhinki for her, sit by her side, or squat on the same mat. Even when one of the parties is dead, they are prohibited from touching the dead body. Instead of washing the dead body, they pour water from a cup.

If he should unawares touch her the two must take water in a cup pour it over each other and do johar.

As the woman would feel ashamed if the male relative saw her in any of the prohibited situations, he usually makes his presence known by coughing before he enters the courtyard or the house, thus allowing the woman time to take her precautions.[3]

On the part of women who stand in this special relation i.e., a woman and the wife of her younger brother, the restrictions are much fewer and in fact there are no prohibitions concerning lying, sitting, shadows or clothes. The younger one, however, must not touch the elder one on the body, the only exception being, that she is allowed to take the elder one by the hand; the elder one may give the younger one massage, help the younger one to get a burden on her head, to get a thorn or the like out of her foot, but the younger one is not allowed to do any such thing towards the elder.[4]

These rules are of great importance for they protect a junior member of the family from exploitation by his elders and if they are broken at all the offender is liable to exemplary punishment.

In Surjudih, Saman Hansdak' had been drinking in his house when he went out into the street. As he did so, he chanced to knock against his younger brother's wife. The girl exclaimed when she saw him coming but it was too late and he blundered into her body. His relations saw the collision and next morning they called a village meeting. As Saman had not intended any liberty, the two washed each other's feet and Saman paid one rupee and four annas as the cost of the meeting.

In Hororaidih the jogmanjhi, Bhagat Marandi, touched his younger brother's wife. The villagers fined him fifteen rupees and when he did not pay it, they semi-outcasted him and removed him from his post.

A much more serious contact occurred at Kusma in 1935 when a woman was kicked by her husband's elder brother. The Santal who told me of the occurrence said, 'A kick by anyone else would not have mattered.' She would have said 'What is he up to? Does he want to make love to me?' But the special relationship made the kick intolerable. The matter went to the village and when the man did not pay the fine, he was completely outcasted and bitlaha was done.

V LANDA SAGAI

There is yet another set of important conventions which influence Santal conduct. With certain of their kinsmen, Santals are privileged to joke about sex and the following are protected by this 'joking convention'.

1. Husband	Wife's younger sister
2. Husband's brother	Wife's sister
3. Wife's brother	Husband's sister
4. Grandfather	Grandson
5. Grandfather	Granddaughter
6. Grandson	Grandmother
7. Granddaughter	Grandmother
8. Grandfather	Grandson's wife
9. Husband	Wife's grandmother
10. Son	Father's sister's husband
11. Daughter	Father's sister's husband

VI THE ACT OF SEX

Against this background we may now examine the rules and conventions for intercourse itself.

Among all the tribes of Middle and Eastern India, premarital intercourse is tacitly assumed. N.E. Parry says of the Lakhers 'Apart from the fact that discretion in love is essential there is no bar to the freest of intercourse between unmarried persons and no fine is inflicted merely because a young man and a girl have slept together.'[5]

Among the Pardhans, Shamrao Hivale states 'Before marriage both boys and girls live lives of almost complete freedom. Even little children of four or five years indulge in erotic play together and most boys and girls have had their first experiences long before puberty. Elder people are amused and tolerant of the sexual adventures of their children. They appear to object to any attempt to correct them. They take the line that such adventures did them little harm and that in any case youth is a time for freedom and experiment. Darbari told me how he once came home late and found his seventeen year old son with a Gond girl. He said nothing at the time, but next morning warned the boy: Eat and drink, but be careful. Don't show off or you will come to grief. Don't do it in the house or someone may see you'. But that was all; it was commonsense advice without moral indignation. As boys and girls become mature, their adventures are of a more serious character. It is safe to say that almost every Pardhan girl has several fairly serious love affairs before her marriage. The existence of the hymen is unknown, for every girl has had it gradually and imperceptibly destroyed. Marriage, as in so many other tribes, is not the beginning of sexual experience; it is only the beginning of its discipline'.[6]

Verrier Elwin has noted among Baigas that 'by her wedding night each girl is already an experienced lover,'[7] while of the Mundas, Sarat Chandra Roy has referred to 'the sexual liberty permitted to the unmarried of both sexes' and has described how 'bachelor and maidens often find their way to each other's dormitories'.[8]

Of the Uraons, Risley notes 'Among the mass of the people girls marry after they are grown up and the freest courtship prevails at dances, festivals, and social gatherings of various kinds. Young men woo their sweethearts with offerings of flowers for the hair and presents of grilled fieldmice, 'which the Oraons declare to be the most delicate of food'. Sexual intercourse before marriage is tacitly recognised and is so generally practised that in the opinion of the best observers no Oraon girl is a virgin at the time of her marriage'.[9]

Similarly Dalton in discussing the Bhagats, a sect of Uraons says, 'The Bhagats rather discourage the unrestricted intercourse between the youth of two sexes that their ancestors smiled upon, and do their best to keep their girls from joining in the dances, hut the youngmen heed not the injunctions of the elders on this point and the girls evade them as much as possible'.[10]

It is not surprising therefore that among Santals also from three or four years before a girl reaches puberty and until she is married (even in certain cases until she has had a first child), she is assumed to have a village lover, 'Only one girl in a hundred,' said Sibu Hansdak' has never had a lover before her marriage.

It is necessary, however, that all pre-marital relations should be private and secret. If a boy and girl are caught together, the offence is less in their relationship as in the fact that they have done in public what should only be enacted in private. If the relationship is converted into a marriage, goats are therefore exacted by the village and if it does not end in marriage the boy is made to pay a fine.

If their intimacy goes undetected the girl sometimes marries her village lover but more usually she is married out of the village. Once she is married she is expected to forget the earlier tie and although it is this which is the most powerful factor in the early break up of marriages, it is the previous experience of a lover which more than any other accounts for marital stability. By tacitly allowing boys and girls 'to explore their hearts' during their early years, Santals avoid the dangers of adolescence, they eliminate the worst forms of repression and by, permitting previous knowledge they undoubtedly lay the foundations for stable married unions.

The second rule is that intercourse should always be with the girl's consent. If a boy cannot win a girl by words or presents, he is not entitled to have his way by force. If he does so the girl can complain to the village and the boy will be fined.

In Nipania, five Santal boys had intercourse with a girl of their village against her will and by force. The girl complained to the manjhi and the leader was fined five rupees and the others two rupees and eight annas each.

In Sildaha, the manjhi's son attempted to take a village girl by force. He was wearing a garland and in the struggle the girl snatched it from him and rushed away. She showed the garland to the villagers and the manjhi was made to give them a goat.

The third rule is that if after marriage intercourse with another man is detected, the adulterer will either pay a sum as compensation celan gitil or will pay double bride-price and sometimes the costs of the wedding and either take the woman or pay her divorce money'.[11]

VII TRIBAL INTEGRITY AND KIN INCEST

The fourth rule and it is this which is the most important

rule in all Santal society is that whether before or after marriage sexual intercourse is only permissible with certain Santals.

A Santal may in no circumstances have relations with anyone not a Santal—with a Hindu, a Muslim, a Paharia—while among Santals themselves intimacy is completely forbidden between the members of certain groups. If intercourse occurs between these members or if a Santal goes with a Diku, the act does not merely scandalise society, but also pollutes the bongas.

The first of such groups consists of kinsmen related in prohibited degrees, and I will set out these relations in the form of a table.

I

Son	Mother
Father	Daughter
Son-in-law	Mother-in-law (wife's mother)

II

Brother	Sister
Nephew	Aunt (Father's sister)
	Aunt (Mother's sister)
Uncle	Niece (Brother's daughter)
	Niece (Sister's daughter)
	Niece (Daughter of paternal uncle's son)
	Niece (Paternal uncle's daughter)
Cousin	Cousin (Father's brother's daughter)
	Cousin (Mother's brother's daughter)
Stepson	Stepmother (Father's co-wife)
Brother-in-law	Younger sister-in-law (Younger brother's wife)
Father-in-law	Daughter-in-law (Son's wife)

Nephew-in-law	Aunt-in-law (Father's brother's wife) Aunt-in-law (Mother's brother's wife).
Cousin-in-law	Wife of younger cousin (i.e. son of father's brother or son of mother's brother if the man himself is younger).
Son-in-law	Sister of Mother-in-law
Uncle-in-law	Niece-in-law (wife of brother's son).
Step-father	Stepdaughter.

III

Stepbrother	Stepsister.
Cousin	Cousin (Father's sister's daughter) Cousin (Mother's sister's daughter)
Grandson	Grandmother (Father's mother) Grandmother (Mother's mother)
Grand nephew	Grand aunt (Father's father's sister) Grand aunt (Father's mother's sister) Grand aunt (Mother's father's sister). Grand aunt (Mother's mother's sister)
Father-In-law	Sister of daughter-in-law (sister of son's wife).
Grandfather-in-law	Grand daughter-in-law (grandson's wife)
Brother-in-law	Wife of brother-in-law (wife's brother's wife) Sister of brother-in-law's wife (sister of wife's brother's wife) Sister-in-law (mother of son's wife) Sister-in-law (mother of daughter's husband)

Father-in-law	Sister of son-in-law (sister of daughter's husband)
Uncle-in-law	Niece-in-law (wife's brother's daughter)
	Niece-in-law (wife's sister's daughter)

In addition to these kinsmen, all relations who possess the same kinship by comparative analogy are also banned. For example a Santal is debarred from marrying his grandfather's brother's granddaughter for she stands on the same level to him as uncle's daughter. A Santal cannot marry his father's brother's granddaughter for her relationship to him is that of a niece. Equally a boy cannot have intercourse with the wife of his father's brother's grandson for she too ranks as the wife of a brother's son.

Moreover once any of these relationships have been established, they last 'for ever' and neither death nor divorce, children nor lack of children have any effect upon them. Even if a younger brother dies and his wife remarries in another family, his elder brother will retain his tabooed status and if a son divorces his wife, the latter continues to be a daughter-in-law in relation to his father.

All relatives therefore who are either related in any of these ways, who stand on a parallel footing to them or have ever possessed these relationship are debarred from sexual congress.

To suppose however that all these forms of kin incest, are 'fingers of one hand', that they are viewed with equal horror and are punished with identical penalties would be unduly to simplify the tribal attitude. Verrier Elwin in *The Baiga* has emphasised that 'many differing degrees of guilt' are involved in such relationship. 'A connection between mother and son which is very rare, is regarded with real horror; it is almost as bad to have intercourse with your father's younger wife. In the same class comes intercourse between a man and his mother-in-law and a woman and her father-in-law. These are the major crimes. After them, comes a connection between father and daughter, between a brother and his younger brother's wife and between a man and his father's sister. Brother-sister incest is held to be bad, but not so bad as the relations I have just described. For a man to go to his mother's sister is regarded as a small fault easily condoned by a tribal feast.'[12]

In Santal society there are similar degrees of guilt and I have indicated their gravity by arranging the relationship in three groups.

Intercourse with a relation in Group I, is by far the worst type. It excites general horror. It is visited by complete excommunication and the ceremony of bitlaha, and there is no option of any lesser punishment.

Dewan Tudu was married as a ghardi jawae in the house of a widow of Pokharia. One night Dewan's wife discovered him in congress with her mother. She complained to the village manjhi and although Dewan and his mother-in-law both pleaded to be fined, the village called the people of the neighbourhood, both were completely excommunicated and bitlaha was performed.

In Patsara, the wife and son-in-law of Jolha Murmu were caught together. Jolha took it to a meeting and the two were not only excommunicated but expelled from the village.

Kuar Hembrom of Jhawali (p.s. Katihar Purnea) was suspected of relations with his own daughter. He was fined fifteen rupees and told not to misbehave. Later on the girl became pregnant, the village suspicions were confirmed and after complete outcasting bitlaha was performed.

In Beldiha, Chundu Soren married a widow with a daughter. The girl lived in his house and after sometime became pregnant. She named her stepfather and the village decided to inflict bitlaha.

After Group I intercourse with a relation in Group II is also very serious but while it evokes disgust and horror it does not carry with it quite the same intensity of disapproval and revulsion as a union in the former cases. It is often punished by immediate excommunication and bitlaha but this is by no means mandatory and a lesser penalty can also be inflicted.

In Khijuridanga, Badha Tudu, an adopted son, eloped with his foster sister, Koleyan Tudu. The two were excommunicated and bitlaha was performed.

On the other hand, when Barka Kisku of Kesa had relations with his sister as a result of which the girl became pregnant, the villagers imposed a fine of fifteen rupees and Barka was made to purchase a husband for her by giving two bullocks, twelve maunds of rice and twelve rupees.

In Kitajore, Kanhu Murmu had relations with his brother's daughter, Jasmi and was fined twenty-five rupees.

Sukol Murmu of Jorbhitha was caught with the widow of his younger brother and fined one hundred and forty rupees.

In Saraipani, Dula Hembrom had intercourse with his son's wife and was fined five rupees.

In Mokro, a nephew-in-law, Jatu committed incest with his father's brother's wife. At first the village gave them the option of a fine of fifteen rupees but when they did not pay it they confirmed their excommunication and bitlaha was done.

In Chondordhipa, the son of Mundra Tudu was caught with the elder sister of his own wife. He also was not immediately bitlahaed but was punished with a fine of seventy rupees.

In all these cases bitlaha could also have been performed but the villagers decided on the lesser punishment.

Finally breaches of Group III are regarded as comparatively minor and while excommunication and bitlaha continue to be valid, such punishments are not considered essentially necessary and the offences are normally visited with fines only.

A Santal on war leave said to Stephen Murmu 'There is not a single young girl in the village. But my wife's sister has a daughter and I shall try to make her willing'.

In Supaidih, Sundar Marandi committed incest with the daughter of his father's sister as a result of which the girl became pregnant. Sundar was fined twenty-five rupees and was made to buy a husband.

VIII CLASS INCEST

The third type of intercourse which Santals completely bar is with a tribesman of the same sept or clan. This is not as Malinowski said of the Trobrianders 'a figment of native tradition from which practice has since moved'. Far from the stringency lessening as kinship receded, the rule is a fundamental tenet of Santal life and carries the same penalties as those for kin incest itself.

This is very clearly illustrated in the three myths which explain its origin.

The first two Santals, Pilchu Haram and Pilchu Budhi, had seven sons and seven daughters. Pilchu Haram took his sons a hunting and at the night's camp he gave them different septs. 'Do not marry in the same sept' he said, 'If you marry outside it, you will all stay together: He said this so that Santals might not be like cattle, and go anywhere'.

In the Santal myth of the creation, Thakur Jiu discovers that the Santals are no longer heeding their septs and are' 'going with each other like cattle'. He therefore rains fire from heaven, destroys all mankind except a single pair and because 'brothers had lived with sisters' compels the race to start afresh.

In yet a third legend an old woman had five grandsons and one granddaughter. One day the middle boy brought from the forest a flowering tree and planted it where the water pots were kept. A beautiful tree grew up and its flower was a dazzling white. The middle boy said, 'Grandmother do not let anyone pick the flower. If anyone picks it I shall have to marry her'. One day the brothers were hunting and their sister gazed at the flower. She picked it and put it in her hair.

The old woman saw what had happened and said to the fowls, 'Chut, chickens, what are we to do if brothers marry sisters?'

The girl heard her and said, 'Grandmother, what is it that you said?'

The old woman replied, 'Now you must marry one of your brothers'. When she heard this the girl fled in shame.

When the middle boy returned from the hunt he saw that the flower was picked and said to his grandmother 'who picked it?' She replied. 'The little girl'. 'Then I must marry her' he said 'Where is she?' The boy caught the girl and married her. Then from shame the girl killed herself, and the boy also cut himself to death. Then the girl cried :

Father my blood
And the blood of my brother
They are not the same

and the boy cried:

> Father my blood
> And the blood of my sister
> They go their ways.

Their blood flowed in different directions and did not meet. The villagers made a pyre and set the two on it. Then the girl cried:

> Father my smoke
> The smoke of my brother
> They are not the same.

And the boy cried:

> Father my smoke
> The smoke of my sister
> They go their separate ways.

The smoke rose from their bodies and drifted apart and from that time Santals regard as bad all marriages between brothers and sisters'.

Because of this sentiment clan incest is virtually on a par with the types of kin incest which I have placed in Group II. Complete excommunication followed by bitlaha is always permissible and it is only as gesture of leniency that a lesser penalty is sometimes awarded.

Bhaya Murmu of Dalahi fell in love with Phudgi Murmu of his village. Both were of the same septs and sub-septs. One day they were caught in intercourse and the village outcasted them and also did bitlaha.

In another case from the Masanjore direction Bajo Hembrom was caught with Makhi Hembrom. Their sub-septs were different but their main septs were the same. They also were outcasted and were made to suffer bitlaha.

If the extreme penalty is not imposed, the lovers are sometimes given the option of a fine and separation, but if the girl is already pregnant, the boy must buy a husband for her.

Bhogon Murmu of Talberia fell in love with Ludgi Murmu of Jobo. The villagers defected their intimacy, they fined Bhogon fifteen rupees and the two gave each other up.

In Teljuria, Kali Murmu eloped with a married girl of his own sept. Three months later the boy's father tracked them down, brought the couple back and returned the girl to her husband. The boy was fined fifteen rupees and the girl's father five and the intimacy ended.

In rare circumstances, separation itself is not insisted on and two lovers of the same sept are very occasionally allowed to marry provided they pay a fine and the girl changes her sept.

In Lakhanpur, Raghunath Soren was in love with Duli Soren. Their septs were the same but their sub-septs were different. At first the villagers fined them and told them to separate. Raghunath paid the fine but did not leave the girl. Then sometime later, a child was born and the villager decided to accept the union and regularise it.

The local pargana was prevailed upon to give the girl his sept. Bonga tala was done and the girl obtained the new sept of Murmu. After that a wedding was approved and the two were married in sangha form.

Gare Marandi of Mirjapur fell in love with Kanku Marandih of Katangi. They eloped to Bengal and there a Murmu was induced to adopt the girl by bonga tala and to give her his sept. When this was done two got married and returned to Mirjapur. Since the girl's sept was now different, the villagers accepted the marriage and nothing further was done.

In another case Gaedo Murmu of Kalidaspur eloped with Lendom Murmu. Gaedo was fined forty rupees and Lendom fifteen. A man of the Besra sept then adopted Lendom by bonga tala, gave her his sept and the union was accepted as a marriage.[13]

Finally in even rarer circumstances and provided the sub-septs are different, the village may exact a fine and ultimately condone a marriage. This is only done when the boy and girl are so firmly in love and nothing will dissuade them and the choice is between approving their marriage or enforcing a tragedy. In such circumstances, the village hardens its hear and usually enforces the law but if its resolution weakens, as very occasionally it does, it ends by condoning the septs and permitting the marriage.

In Dhanghera, Manjhi Hembrom fell in love with Thakai Hembrom. Their septs were the same but Manjhi's sub-sept was Laher and Thakai's was Guha. Since the sub-septs were different and the two were patently bent on marrying, the villagers exacted a fine of fifty rupees and allowed the wedding.

IX OTHER TYPES OF FORBIDDEN RELATIONS

In addition to these persons between whom intercourse is 'incest', there is one further type of relationship which is also forbidden. Like other tribes Santals have the institution of ceremonial friendships, and among boys the most important are the phul friendship and the alliance known as Karmu Dharmu.

To inaugurate a 'phul' friendship two boys attend a shivrat mela with their friends. Each takes a brass plate with some sweets, a flower garland and a cloth. When the mela is over each garlands the other and give him all he has brought. The witnesses then ratify the alliance by soaring the sweets.

The tie of Karmu Dharmu on the other hand perpetuates a ritual act and is correspondingly rarer. At the Dangua Karam festival which is celebrated only once in five years, the jogmanjhik tells two unmarried boys of the same sept to erect the Karam branch. These two boys are called Karmu and Dharmu and continue in this role until they are married. When the festival is over they take the branch away, report themselves to the manjhi and are given a meal of cold rice. This meal ratifies their ritual partnership and inaugurate a tie of permanent friendship.

Both of these friendships have important consequences. They are primarily pacts of mutual assistance and are thus forms of insurance against crisis. If the occasion demand it, the friends share each other's wedding expenses, help each other in cultivation and lend each other plough cattle. They rally to each other's aid at birth, sickness or death and assist each other with loans that carry no interest.

Similar institutions exist for girls and as with boys the two main types of friendship are phul and karamdar. Two girls become phuls by exchanging presents, sweets and garlands at a mela in the presence of their friends, while the two girls who do the circling ceremony of the karam put leaves from the branch in each other's hair, are given cold rice by the manjhi and are then recognised as life-long karamdar. These girls' alliance are important both as emotional supports and as means to domestic aid. The friends give each other presents such as little rings or bangles, put flowers in each other's hair and sometimes exchange clothes. At a wedding, the bride gives her phul or karamdar a necklace of flowers or beads. After marriage the two visit each other, attend weddings together in their villages or go to each other with parents at Sohrae. If there is illness in her family, a phul takes help from her friend. The alliance represents an intimacy of the heart, a means of comfort. It adds a new zest to joys and assists a girl in facing sorrow.

But besides linking two friends, the alliance puts each of the parties into a new relation with the other's family. In the case of boys, the ritual gives each of them the status of brothers while the parallel alliance for girls has the effect of converting the partners into sisters. A boy who is phul or Karmu Dharmu to another boy is therefore debarred from relations with his friends' sister, mother, step mother, mother-in-law and so on and is exposed to the same penalties for a breach of this prohibition as if his friend were a true brother. Equally a girl who is phul or karamdar to another girl cannot have relations with the girl's brother, father, stepfather or with any of a true sister's prohibited relations. This new relationship does not extend beyond the parties themselves and does not act as a bar to the intermarriage of their children; but it is of great importance in ordinary life and creates in effect a supplementary code of exogamy.

X THE CONSEQUENCES OF INCEST

If a Santal breaks any of these five rules, his act is not merely a breach of tribal integrity but what is even more important it is a pollution of the village bongas. So long as these remains polluted festivals and weddings cannot go on and it is therefore necessary that out of the fine, a goat should be offered to Manjhi Haram. If this fine is not paid, the village itself must procure a goat and make the sacrifice. The offenders themselves do not invite any supernatural punishment but their act exposes the whole village to bonga displeasure. It is for this reason that when the code has been broken it is irrelevant whether the intercourse was by consent or force. The sin is in the contact and the bongas are equally polluted whether the girl has agreed to the act or been compelled. For this reason even when a girl or woman is herself is quite innocent, her husband or guardian is made to pay a fine or the family is even directly bitlahaed for the pollution which has befallen it.

In Sitakohbar, Rauta Marandi was acting as foster father to an orphan girl, Mangri Murmu. One day at noon, two Santals and two Gwalas of the village noticed a struggle under a palm tree and running to the scene they found that a Gwala boy of the village had just had intercourse with the girl. The boy got up and rushed away but the girl was caught and taken to the manjhi. There she admitted intercourse but declared it was by force. The villagers met and decided that even though it was by force the girl had been polluted and bitlaha must be done.

In Goradangal Suphal Tudu had kept a Kol as his servant. His own wife was almost forty and had already had two children. One day Suphal accused the Kol of being his wife's lover. The woman indignantly denied the charge and complained to the jogmanjhi. The latter warned them not to talk about it as it was a big matter. Sometime later at the Gando mela the Kol came home wearing the woman's cloth. Suphal asked him what he was doing with his wife's cloth and there was again a quarrel. When the year ended, the Kol left his employment and was engaged by Suphal's brother. Then on the night of the Mag festival, everyone was slightly drunk. Suphal was dancing in the village and his wife was at home. In the darkness of the night the Kol entered their house. The woman thought it was a thief and lit a lamp. Then she recognised the Kol. There was a scuffle between them during which her *sankha* (bangles were broken and some cooking pots were overturned. After that the Kol went away and the next day the woman complained to the manjhi. At the meeting the Kol said that he was drunk so the villagers decided to fine him fifteen four annas bits or three rupees and twelve annas. Twelve annas of the fine was allotted to Suphal for the broken sankha. The Kol paid three rupees, Suphal demanded his twelve annas but the villagers said he would get it later. The meeting then adjourned to drink the fine. Suphal, however was disgrunted at not receiving his compensation and as they were squatting at the liquor shop he accused two 'sharp axes' of having taken the extra twelve annas instead. A quarrel ensued during which Suphal said he would kick them and got as far as raising his foot. The two 'sharp axes' said 'Prove we have eaten your money and we will give you ten rupees. Otherwise pay us ten rupees for falsely accusing us.' After that they all went home. Next morning the two men were still incensed at Suphal's conduct and decided to call the five manjhis and discuss with them the threat of kicking. The manjhis met and soon everything was out. The kicking dropped into the background and they began to discuss the struggle between the Kol and Suphal's wife. They held that intercourse had been attempted, that in the struggle the woman had been intimately handled and they finally ordered that Suphal must pay a fine of fifty rupees for having had his wife polluted. Suphal did not pay and in the end he and his wife were bitlahaed.

In both these cases the women were comparatively innocent but the acts had contaminated the tribe and the penalties followed.

REFERENCES

1. Havelock Ellis has recorded numerous examples of this gesture from different parts of the world : 'In its most primitive form', he says, 'this exhibitionism is a kind of exorcism, a method of putting evil spirits, primarily and secondarily evil-disposed persons to flight. It is the most effective way for woman to display sexual centres and it shares in the magical virtues which all unveiling of the sexual centres is believed by primitive peoples to possess. In the sixteenth century to distinguished a thelogian as Luther when assaulted by the Evil One at night was able to put the adversary to flight by protuding his

uncovered buttocks from the bed. But the spiritual significance of this attitude is lost with the decay of primitive beliefs. It survives, but merely as a gesture of insult. Among the Arabs the specific gesture is noted, and a man to whom vengeance is forbidden would express his feelings by exposing his posterior and strewing earth on his head. It is in Europe and in mediaeval and later times that this emphatic gesture seems to have flourished as a violent method of expressing contempt. It was by no means confined to the lower classes and Kleimpaul, in discussing this form of 'speech without words', quotes examples of various noble persons, even princesses, who are recorded thus to have expressed their feelings. In more recent times the gesture has become merely a rare and extreme expression of unrestrained feeling in coarse-grained peasants. Zola, in the figure of Mouguette in Germinal may be said to have given a kind of classic expression to the gesture. In the more remote parts of Europe it appears to be still not altogether uncommon. This seems to be notably the case among the South Slavs, and Krauss states that 'When a South Slav woman wishes to express her deepest contempt for anyone she bends forward, with left hand raising her skirts and with the right slapping her posterior, at the same time exclaiming 'This for you'. '(*Studies in the Psychology of Sex*, III, 100-101).

2. Don Soren, 3331.
3. In this situation is expressly envisaged in two Santal Songs.

I

From the right and the left
Come my husband's elder brothers
'Do not stumble on this big thorn
Do not tıead on the little thorn.'

II

Dodging into the shed
You came, boy
Take care of your feet
Or you will kick me
Take care of your clothes
Or you will cover me with dust.

(*Don Soren*, 2446, 2064)

4. P.O. Bodding, 'On Taboos and Customs connected therewith amongst the Santals'. *J.A.S. Beng*), LXVII, Part III (1898), 1-24.
5. Parry, op. cit., 292.
6. Shamrao Hivale, *The Pardhans of the Upper Narbada Valley*, (Bombay, 1946), 160.
7. Elwin, *The Baiga*, 232.

8. S.C. Roy, *The Mundas and their Country* (Ranchi, 1912), 542.
9. H.H. Risley, *The Tribes and Castes of Bengal*, (Calcutta, 1891), II, 141.
10. H.H. Risley, *A Statistical Account of Lohardaga District*, (London, 1877), 291.
11. For a full discussion of these adjustments, see *Civil Law in Santal Society*.
12. Elwin, op. cit., 188-9.
13. For further details of this form of adoption, see *Civil Law in Santal Society*, IV.

THE SIGNIFICANCE OF FOOD

FOR maintaining tribal integrity, the regulation of food is almost as important as the control and discipline of sex. Christoph and Elizabeth von Fürer-Haimendorf have said 'The social importance of food among the Reddies cannot easily be exaggerated. Public condonation of social crimes is signified by the community's participation in a feast provided at the expense of the culprit, and the communal eating of food is the symbol of group solidarity. The man or woman guilty of a violation of customary law, and therefore at variance with the rest of the community, is debarred from sharing other people's meals. Socially, eating together is considered in much the same light as sexual congress; the acceptance of cooked food at the hands of a person of lower caste, like sexual intercourse with such a person, defiles the Reddi and necessities a purification ceremony, Food is, in the Reddi's mind, the main medium whereby defilement or impurity is transmitted'.[1]

In Santal society also there is a similar perception of the value of food and it is less what a Santal eats that matters than the person with whom he eats it. Santals eat, for example, rats, alligators, bears, leopards and jackals and until the last tiger was killed in the district, tiger flesh was eaten with the greatest relish. There is similarly no taboo on the cow and while Santals do not butcher cows or bullocks for meat for they are far too valuable, cow sacrifice is an essential part of the final funerary ritual. Moreover a dead cow or bullock is eaten without compunction. Santals also eat pythons and dhamans and there are two kinds of bull frog which they regard as great delicacies. If Santals do not eat other frogs and snakes, it is because they do not like them and not because of ritual objections. The only important general prohibitions are of monkeys, jhirni lizards, hyenas and certain carrion birds. Monkeys are forbidden because of their likeness to men. The jhirni lizard is thought to harbour a man's jiwi or soul while vultures, the jalo falcon and crows are forbidden because they feed on putrefying flesh. Such prohibitions do not weigh heavily on the tribe and while it would be an offence against integrity for a Santal to eat them it would not normally occur to any Santal to do so.

Besides these general taboos, certain septs and sub-septs observe totem restrictions. These are not of great importance because they are not in practice ever broken. They are also very few in number. The only important one is the taboo on Murmus from eating murmu or nilgai.

If the unthinkable happened and a Murmu broke this taboo, he would be required to feast the members of his sept.

It is the circumstances in which food is eaten which raises all the major issues. Eating with a person is regarded as a gesture of intimacy comparable only to an act of sex. It is therefore subject to the strictest possible control and the first rule is that no Santal may in any circumstances eat with non-Santals. In the case of women, this prohibition extends even to the separate eating of food cooked by a non-Santal. Men on the other hand can eat food food cooked by others provided the person is not a Jolha, Mohammadan, Paharia, Dom, Chamar, Muchi, Hadi Bauri, or Mahali, and provided also that they do not eat it from the same plate.

This rule is so widely understood and approved that no one would normally think of breaking it. If however a Santal girl were caught eating with a Diku or even consuming some Diku's food she would be punished as if she had had intercourse itself. If a man is caught he is liable to fine and pante begar.

Ledem Hansdak' of Gangapano ate rice cooked by a Mohammadan. He was pante begared and was only admitted to the line after he had given the villagers a feast.

The second rule concerns eating from the same plate. This is forbidden to the following relations:

1. Mamo-bhagna Maternal uncle and nephews or niece

2. Mami-bhagna	Maternal aunt and nephews and nieces.
3. Bahonharea	(a) a girl's husband and her elder brother.
	(b) a younger brother's wife with her husband's elder brother.
4. Ajhnarea	A girl's husband and her elder sister.
5. Honharea jawae gomke	(a) Son-in-law and father-in-law.
	(b) Son-in-law and mother-in-law.
6. Honharea (kumin)	Daughter-in-law and father-in-law.
7. Bocha Misera	Married younger sister and her elder brother and elder sister.
8. Balaya	Girl's father and her husband's father.
9. Balakora Balakuri	Girl's mother and girl's husband's father.
10. Balaya	Girl's mother and girl's husband's mother.
11. Haram budhi	Husband and wife.

If any Santal breaks this rule, he is liable to fine and pante begar while in the case of a husband and wife the act disqualifies the man for life from making sacrifices to the bongas. He has become a woman.

There are similar restrictions on leavings. Bohonharea, Ajhnarea, Balaya, Balakora, Balakuri and husband and wife cannot take each other's leavings but in all other cases the younger relation can take the leavings of the older. A niece or nephew for example can take the leavings of an uncle. A married younger sister can eat the leavings of her elder brother or sister.

In Dundua the elder brother of a girl's husband was taking his night meal in the dark when he noticed that he was eating leavings. A light was brought and the girl confessed that she had given him her left food. The family were disgusted at her conduct and at a village meeting her husband divorced her.

These restrictions affect tribal integrity in a number of important ways. They imply an order of honour within the family. They stress the respect due to seniority and age. They emphasise the authority of men. Moreover by excluding certain relations from the intimacy of common eating they reinforce the tribal code of behaviour. They are minor but necessary aids to that general control of sex on which tribal integrity ultimately depends.

REFERENCE

1. C. von Fürer-Haimendorf in collaboration with Elizabeth von Fürer Haimendorf, *The Reddies of the Bison Hills*, (London, 1945), 101.

48

THE PUNISHMENT OF CRIME

I MAJOR AND MINOR CRIME

WHEN a Santal crime has been committed, its punishment varies with the nature of the offence.

The great majority of crimes are comparatively minor and the sentence is a fine which rarely exceeds twenty or twenty-five rupees. But in the case of clan and kin incest and of intercourse with Dikus, of eating with forbidden kinsmen or touching tabooed relatives, the crimes are major. They excite intense and angry disapproval and the sentence is either a fine or a full and immediate outcasting followed by the ceremony of Bitlaha.[1]

II THE PUNISHMENT OF MINOR OFFENCES

For a minor crime a village meeting is called. All the circumstances are considered and the manjhi announces the decision. If the offender is guilty the punishment is a fine and he must either pay the amount or suffer from a limited excommunication. This is known as pante begar or separation from the line. When the village sits to eat at a festival, and is eating in one line, the offender will not be debarred from joining the feast but the villagers will keep him from the line. When a bullock dies and the whole village shares its flesh, the offender will have no part. If an offence is punished with a fine, he is deprived of any share. If there is a birth, wedding or death in the offender's house no one will assist at the ceremonies. Similarly if there is a birth, or wedding elsewhere in the village the offender will not be invited, and if there a festival his house will be ignored. He will also be excluded from communal drinking and dancing.

But apart from this, he has no disabilities. The offender can still eat and drink with the villagers in a private way. He is not deprived of fire. He can take water from the common well and springs. His restrictions convey the village sense of disapproval but his daily routine or way of life is unimpaired.

As soon as the fine is paid the matter ends, and the offender is free to join the line as if he had never left it.

In Sibtala the mother of Mundri Soren refused to pay a fine. The Sohrae festival was at hand so on the day for garlanding the cows, the villagers treated her cattle as if they did not exist. Similary on the jale day, they sang in all the other houses but left out Mundri's mother. This brought her to her sense and she paid a little extra money and came back into line.

In Telni Champai Tudu was pante begared for failing to pay a fine. At first he was defiant, but a little later he noticed that the village boys were always stopping his sons from playing on their flutes and were continually running off with their drums. His daughters went down to join the other girls in a langre dance but the line declined to open and the women drove them back. This broke Champai's spirit and at the Sohrae festival he went to the manjhi with rice and a fowl and begged to be taken back.

If a Santal is fined and contests its justice, he can appeal to a meeting of a pargana and five manjhis and if he is dissatisfied with their decision he can put his case before the local people at the annual hunt. These bodies hear the matter and their decision of the latter is final but pending the hearing the sentence is enforced.

III MAJOR CRIME : THE SUMMONING OF THE VILLAGE

When a case of clan or kin incest or of touching or eating with tabooed relatives is detected the matter is similarly considered at a village meeting and there are two circumstances which may lead to its summoning.

The first is when a complaint is made to a manjhi either by a villager or relation of the offender or the manjhi himself learns of the offence. Pani Soren was married to Prodhan

Hansdak' of Bokrabandh. Prodhan was a young man of twenty-two and sometime after their marriage he fell in love with the daughter of his father's sister's son. Prodhan was, therefore, an uncle and the girl was his niece. One day the two went to the jungle and it was late at night when they returned. Prodhan's wife had kept his food ready and had gone to sleep. Prodhan went inside the house, took the food outside and shared it with the girl. He then went in again, took a leaf cigarette and again went out. His wife by this time had woken and when he went out she saw her husband coming with his niece to the western tola of the village. Prodhan did not come back until the next morning and the same day Pani bitterly complained to the manjhi. It was on her statement that the manjhi called a meeting.

The other circumstance is when a boy and girl are surprised in an act of intercourse either by relations or the villagers. Bhunda Kisku was working as a servant in Borowar where he had returned from working in Bengal. During his stay in Bengal the daughter of his grandfather's brother had started relations with him. The two were warned to keep apart but did not do so. One night there was a wedding in the village and the two were seen to leave the dance and go to the fields. Three villagers followed them and the girl was caught lying on her back and the boy squatting by her side. The boy rushed away but left his cloth behind. The villagers began to take the girl to the manjhi but as they went, she dashed away. Then they left the boy's cloth with the jogmanjhi who fixed the next day for a discussion in the village.

Similarly in Khajuria the villagers knew that Khari Murmu, a young married girl, whose husband was a soldier had begun a love affair with a Sauria Paharia. They did not catch them for more than two years but they warned the girl's father that the Paharia's visits should cease. The father did nothing. Then one September night, when the Paharia was sleeping with the girl on a cot, some villagers burst in and caught them. The girl and the Paharia were tied together and taken to the manjhi, the other villagers were called and a council met that night.

In cases such as this the detection followed by the arrest of the offenders or the seizure of their property leads to a meeting of the village.

IV TRIAL BY A VILLAGE COUNCIL

When the villagers assemble, their first thought is procedure and if a matter is in its infancy or is known only to themselves, they often try to dispose of it in the village. 'Why should we bring in others' said the manjhi of Khajuria 'when we can settle this ourselves'? Moreover there is often great reluctance to expose the offenders to the full publicity or bitlaha and unless the offence is between relations in Group I the villagers are often inclined to adjudicate upon it themselves.

If they decide to confine it to the village they question the parties and hear the evidence against them. In many cases the offenders themselves admit their guilt, and it will illustrate their attitude if I give in full the statement of a boy. In the case from Borowar the boy told the jogmanjhi. 'It began in Bengal. The girl and her father were there. We were sleeping apart. One night the girl took my penis and made it stand. I went and lay above her. After that, I went to her each night. When we came to the village we went on meeting. We slept in our houses in seperate rooms. I used to sleep and the girl would come to my house and poke me with a pole. She would make me get up and I had to go with her. In the winter when the paddy was heaped and I slept at the threshing floor she would come and pull me out and make me have her in the field. I told my master that we had ended it last year and paid a fine, but the girl was making me go on. One day she said she would tie a string to her toe and sleep near the door. She put the end of the string outside and told me to come and pull it. For three nights she went to sleep with the string tied but I did not go to her. Then she came to my house and made me go outside.'

If the crime is admitted or proved,[2] the village then considers the attitude of the parties. If the offence is only a temporary lapse and the parties do not intend to repeat it, the village may administer a warning and inflict a petty sum as fine.

Babulal Hembrom of Dumaria began relations with his younger brother's wife. When the matter first came to the village, it had only just started and the villagers gave him a warning and fined him five rupees.

Similarly when Naeke Baske who was later hanged for

murder began to sleep with his younger cousin's wife, the villagers did not at first punish him but warned him to cease and took two rupees and eight annas as the sitting charge of the meeting.

When Dula Murmu of Chorkata Circle, fell in love with his father's brother's daughter, the villagers did not at first fine them but gave them both a beating.

If, however, the parties have been warned or the village is annoyed or outraged by their conduct, they often take a grave view and proceed to drastic action. But even then the attitude of the offenders is still of crucial importance. If they are submissive and swear that in future they will avoid each other completely, the village often shrinks from immediate outcasting and gives them the option of a fine.

If the girl is pregnant, by a forbidden lover, the latter cannot be recognised as the child's father and therefore, as part of the settlement, the guilty man is made to purchase a boy who will act as the child's 'false' father and marry its mother.

In Kerabani Mangal Murmu had intercourse with a girl of his own sept. The latter became pregnant and at the meeting they admitted their connection, promised to separate and pleaded for fine. The villagers took a goat and some rice from the boy and he was made to purchase a husband for the girl by giving five rupees.

This option of a fine is always discretionary with the village and even though the parties plead for mercy it does not always follow that a lenient view will prevail.

When Johol Marandi of Bara Harrakha installed a Marandi girl in his house, the villagers outcasted them and recommended bitlaha. Johol's mother pleaded for a fine but the meeting did not listen. The five manjhis accepted the recommendation and although Johol's mother again pleaded, they refused to permit any lesser punishment.

Moreover if the option of a fine has been allowed once but after payment the two resume their guilty relationship, no second option is granted and the village proceeds at once to outcasting and bitlaha.

Dharma Manjhi of Chitra began to live with a widow of his younger brother. He paid a fine of one hundred rupees and promised to give her up. Sometime later he again began to sleep with her and the villagers thereupon outcasted him and did bitlaha.

In Nimakalan, Ram Soren was detected in intercourse with a girl of his sept. They were given the option of a fine and separation but as they did not avail of it, bitlaha was performed in both their houses. Sometime later they separated, approached the villagers, were allowed to give penalty feasts and were readmitted into the caste. In spite of one bitlaha however they could not do without each other and after a while they again came together and resumed their love. On this the villagers met again, gave them no second option and proceeded to complete outcasting and a second bitlaha.

Finally if the boy and girl are rude and defiant the village may refuse to consider even the possibility of lesser punishment and will proceed at once to outcasting and bitlaha.

V THE FIVE MANJHIS

It is not, however, every case that is finally decided by the village.

When Dhunu and Doro Kisku of Amjora returned from work in Morang, it was reported that they had had relations with a girl of their own sept and kin. The villagers found difficulty in reaching a decision so they referred it to the Pargana who consulted five of the manjhis.

In the case from Pokharia, in which Dewan Tudu was discovered with his mother-in-law the two admitted their offence and requested the meeting to adjust it. The village held, however, that they could not take the responsibility of settling it and accordingly they summoned the neighbouring people to dispose of it with them.

In Gambhra, a widower, Suksan Murmu was living alone. His own daughter's daughter used to take his food to him in the fields and in course of time he seduced her and they had intercourse whenever they could. The girl became pregnant and when the villagers asked who had done it she named her grandfather. The villagers felt hesitation in deciding this matter so the manjhi referred it to the pargana and five manjhis. In the end Suksan purchased a husband for the girl and was fined fifteen rupees.

Similarly if there is friction in the village the five manjhis may be asked to interfere.

In the case from Borowar, where the main offender was the girl, the first meeting failed as after confessing before the jogmanjhi the boy ran away. The manjhi was the girl's father and told the accusers to produce the thief or suffer fine. When the boy came back to his house, the people surrounded it but while they were fetching the Choukidar the manjhi came with an axe and drove them down the street. After that, the boy again disappeared and finding the manjhi entirely obdurate the villagers informed the five manjhis who ordered outcasting and bitlaha.

Similarly when Chhotka Marandi of Daldali had intercourse with his own sister he was fined fifteen rupees but instead of paying it he preferred to let the matter go before the neighbouring manjhis. The manjhis upheld the conviction and enhanced the fine to twenty-five.

VI THE ANNUAL HUNT

When five manjhis have given a decision their order is normally final but in certain circumstances the matter is considered by the Bir Sendra or annual hunt. According to Kolean Haram, this assembly was formerly the only body which could sanction a bitlaha and the matters were therefore kept in abeyance until the hunt met. This practice has now been given up and now-a-days the annual hunt tries an offence either when the complainant or offender has failed to secure satisfaction from the five manjhis or the incident has occurred immediately before the hunt and the people elect to include it in the proceedings.

Baburam Hembrom of Dumaria began relations with the wife of his younger cousin, Barsa Hembrom. The grandfathers of Baburam and Barsa were brothers and the offence was accordingly analogous to an elder brother having relations with the wife of a younger. Matters came to a head and although Barsa's wife had born him four children, the latter divorced her and she went to live with Baburam. The Dumka Damin Sendra was about to be held and although she was now divorced Barsa placed the matter before the president. As neither Baburam nor the manjhi of Dumaria attended the hunt, nothing was decided and the dihri who presided called another meeting at Gopikandar. Here also no final decision was taken as Baburam and the manjhi did not attend. Finally at another bitlaha the matter was taken up and the people, adjudging Baburam guilty, decided to perform the ceremony.

If there is dispute between the officials of a village and the five manjhis, this also is taken to the hunt and decided by the people.

Mangal Tudu of Kolharia had been to Bengal with a divorced girl of his village and sept. The two stayed in Bengal for six or seven months and when they returned the people of Kolharia found them guilty of clan incest. The two did not, however, accept the decision, so a council of the neighbouring manjhis was called. This council met three times, upheld the conviction and sentenced each of them to pay a fine of fifteen rupees. Both paid and with the fine money the officials of Kolharia arranged a village feast. At this feast, they reserved the major part for themselves, gave a small share to the villagers and did not invite the pargana, deshmanjhi, or surrounding manjhis under whose orders the fine had been inflicted. The manjhis, therefore, held a meeting and fined the Kolharia officials a hundred rupees for not inviting them. The officials declined to pay and the matter went to the annual hunt at Sapchalla. The hunt decided in favour of the manjhis, and the Kolharia officials were again given a chance to pay. They did not do so and the three officials were then bitlahaed.

VII FINE AND OUTCASTING

When a fine has been imposed by the village or by the five manjhis the parties usually try to pay the sum at once. If, however, they cannot pay immediately and their attitude is not defiant, it is usual to give them time to collect the money. Delay, however, is always avoided for the parties and all of those who share their kitchen are completely outcasted. They can no longer borrow fire. They lose access to all wells dug by the village. No one will accept tobacco from them or allow them to use a pounder. No one will eat or drink with them. No one will allow them entry to their houses or go into their houses or courtyards. They are not invited to village councils and if they bring any complaints, no notice is taken of them. They are not allowed to join a hunting or fishing expedition. They cannot attend a dance, a wedding, a birth or a funeral and if there is any ceremony in their house no one will go to it. None of their members will be accepted as a servant and if one of them falls ill no ojha may attend him. They are disqualified from getting settlement of waste lands. No one will help them in cultivation while the village women will lose no opportunity of taunting and abusing them.

Moreover in some areas until the fine is paid or the date for its payment has expired the men of the village will gather each night beyond the village street, beat the bitlaha measures on the drums, play the bitlaha tunes on their flutes and sing bitlaha songs. When the people of their neighbourhood hear the sound they ask why the drums are calling to bitlaha. The manjhi explains what has happened and that a date has been fixed for payment of a fine. After that when a fine has been paid, a village feast is held, goats are bought and some of the flesh is given to each of the neighbouring manjhis 'for stopping their ears'.

If the fine has been imposed by the five manjhis they are entitled to full shares in the exculpatory feast and the failure to invite them is a breach of tribal discipline which may itself provoke a fine, outcasting and bitlaha.

When the fine is paid the matter ends and those who have heard the drumming ask no more about it.

It is necessary however that if both the parties have been fined, both should pay and if both stay in the area, payment by one and not by the other is treated as no payment at all.

In Kharua, Salo Kisku fell in love with his younger brother's wife. Salo was fined twenty rupees and the girl ten. The girl paid the money but Salo refused to give his share. The girl's fine had therefore to be refunded and after they had been outcasted bitlaha was done in both their houses.

Once the fine has been paid, a goat is sacrificed to Manjhi Haram 'to end the pollution', and a feast is held. After that the matter must on no account be spoken of again and the preach of this rule may even be visited with complete out-casting and bitlaha.

In Khajuria in 1944, a Mohammadan boy was caught with the daughter of Basta Hansdak'. Basta was fined fifteen rupees and the boy five. Both paid, the feast was held and the matter ended. Some days later, Basta abused the manjhi and the others for fining him. 'You offspring of a penis', he said 'you fined me I will burn down all your houses'. The manjhi took this very seriously and at once called a meeting of the village. Basta was summoned but refused to go, so the village decided to outcaste him and published it through a bitlaha. Basta then came to his senses, took all his words back, swore never to speak about it again, and the matter dropped.

If, on the due date, the fine is not paid, the village meets and reviews the solution. In extremely rare circumstances it grants a further extension but such postponments are always unpopular and are hardly ever given. Santals believe that justice should be prompt and sentence once given should be quickly executed. Moreover a pending sentence keeps the whole village in suspense and the Santal instinct is to end the tension as swiftly as possible. Accordingly if a fine is not paid, the offender's position as an outcaste is regarded as permanent and steps are taken to arrange bitlaha.

VIII FLIGHT

What is the position if after kin or clan incest is detected one or both of the offenders leave the village?

If the offenders abscond before the village has met, all action is suspended and if they return and later on separate the village will, as likely as not, take no further action let the matter drop.

It at all interferes it will hold a meeting and try the offence as if the offenders had all along been present.

The daughter of Yangla Soren of Danga fell in love with a boy of the same sept. The village was about to meet when they eloped to Bengal. After some years they gave each other up and returned to Danga. The villagers called a meeting but as the two had separated nothing more was done.

If, however, a meeting has been held and the offenders fined, their failure to pay the money will have resulted in the outcasting both of themselves and of those family members who share the same kitchen.

If a kinsman is himself the complainant and has thus set in motion the machinery of justice, he will not himself be outcasted provided he had built himself a new *chulha* or hearth and has ceased to eat or drink with the offender. If, however, the same joint kitchen is in use, all who avail of it are exposed to the penalty.

Supposing the guilty parties leave the village, what is the position ?

Provided a bitlaha has not already been announced, elopement or flight postpones all further action until their return. The sharers in the kitchen, however, must pay the fine and pending their return the offenders can be treated as corpses. 'It is as if they are dead'. 'The village is dead to them'. Throughout the Damin this is only a symbolic way of expressing the tribal attitude but in Jamtara, much of Dumka subdivision, parts of Godda and the eastern fringes of Rajmahal the 'death' is treated as entirely literal and the final funerary feast or bhandan can be performed.

In Sibapahar Pokle Soren eloped with a Mohammadan of Jihubara. Her father declared her to be dead and gave the villagers five rupees in lieu of a funerary feast.

Bodon Soren of Birajdih eloped with the daughter of his father's brother's son. This was in Jamtara subdivision and bitlaha was therefore performed. The girl's father gave a feast and returned to caste and three years later performed the final funerary feast of his daughter.

Prodhan Marandi of Hariari fell in love with the sister of his father's brother's wife. Fines of twenty-five rupees were paid by each but after abandoning each other for a time they again commenced relationship. The girl's father realised the consequences which would befall and in order to forestall bitlaha he expelled the girl he performed her funerary feast. Prodhan and the girl then left the village and went to Bengal.

In another case from Hariari, Phate Hembrom had two daughters one of whom eloped with a prohibited kinsman. Phate performed her final funerary feast and on his death, it was the other daughter who inherited all his lands.

When the bhandan or final feast has been duly celebrated

the offender loses all his rights in lands and moveable and ceases to be an heir. If he returns to the village he will not be admitted and if he is granted entry by his family the whole household will be outcasted for life.

This is the ordinary rule but in one circumstances the 'dead' offender can be re-admitted. A fresh birth ceremony must be held, he must be formally given a new name, he must be ceremonially 'reborn'. Only then will he be again admitted into caste, and will revive his former rights and be free to cultivate his lands.[3]

If a death ceremony has not been celebrated, and the offender returns, the situation at the time he left the village is at once revived. But it is important to note that action does not follow a single pattern, and there are two types of regional usage.

In the Jamtara and Pakaur subdivisions, the prolonged absence is itself regarded as a pseudo bitlaha and the returning offender is treated as if bitlaha had in fact been done. He must therefore give a feast and after that he is granted re-admission. If the offender is a woman she is sometimes pardoned with a feast and sometimes bitlahaed.

In the Rajmahal, Godda and Dumka Subdivisions, on the other hand, flight and absence make no difference and both offenders will be bitlahaed as soon as they return. Separation does not save them but if one has died the village may either recommend the bitlaha of the survivor or accept a fresh condonation.

If bitlaha has already been announced, and the two offenders now abscond, their flight in no way alters the performance. The countryside assembles and bitlaha is done.

Khara Baske of Gaepahari committed kin incest with his father's brother's daughter. Bitlaha was announced and although they fled the country, the ceremony was performed in both their houses.

Finally what is the position if one offender absconds and the other remains ?

If a bitlaha has not already been announced and the option of the fine has been granted, the party remaining is allowed to pay its own fine and the bitlaha of the absconder is kept in abeyance. If, however, the option of a fine has not been granted and an immediate bitlaha is ordered, the ceremony is performed in both the houses and the fact that one of the offenders has run away is of no avail. If a fine has been imposed and neither of the offenders pay it bitlaha is done to both.

IX FLIGHT AND THE CULPRIT'S FAMILY

How does the flight of an offender affect his family?

If a bitlaha has been ordered, all the members of his kitchen are excommunicated and only when the bitlaha is over and their own penalty feasts have been given can only again be admitted to the tribe.

If a fine has been imposed but the offender flees before it is paid, the members of his kitchen remain outcasted until they pay the fine. When it is given re-entry is sanctioned but small additional feasts are sometimes exacted.

When the feast has been given, the members of the kitchen are no longer out of the tribe but they must on no account have any dealings with the offender. If the absconder returns, he must be kept out of the house pending the final village decision and if he is granted access to his family they will again be treated as polluted and will be outcasted for life.

If the crime occurs outside the house and the offenders abscond without re-entering their houses, the shares in their kitchen are not polluted and accordingly escape outcasting.

In Bara Harrakha a Dom was caught in intercourse with the wife of Batu Hembrom. It was the day of the hook-swinging at Brindaban and the villagers came upon them lying together under a culvert. They tied them together, took them to the manjhi and the same night it was decided to outcaste the woman and recommend bitlaha. The two were allowed to go and the woman at once went home and collected up her clothes. She then left the house, went away with the Dom and has never returned. Since her husband had allowed her to enter the house after she had once been outcasted, he was himself outcasted and had to pay a fine for a feast.

X BITLAHA

When a fine has not been paid and one or other of the

offenders is in the area or if the offence is such that regional punishment is necessary irrespective of whether they are present or absent, the stage is set for bitlaha itself.

The ritual of the ceremony is one of the most impressive in the whole range of Santal life. It is performed by an enormous crowd. It is done to the thunder and roll of drums. The crowd advances on the house in long surging lines. Finally a ceremony of symbolic defilement is performed in the heart of the courtyard. In its disciplined expression of revolted disgust, its intense assertion of tribal values, its savage dignity, the ceremony is unique in tribal India.

I will first describe the preliminaries and then proceed to an account of the ritual itself.

XI THE SENDING OF THE DHARWAK'

The first step for holding a bitlaha is to secure tribal approval to the staging of the ceremony. The village manjhi must first inform the Pargana and tell him of the village recommendation and then request him to summon a meeting of the five manjhis. This body acts as a reviewing authority and until it has met, and confirmed the village decision no bitlaha can correctly take place. Just as a death sentence by a Sessions Judge cannot be executed until it has been confirmed by the High Court, bitlaha cannot properly be performed until the five manjhis have tested its propriety and signified their consent.

If a manjhi or a village ignores this procedure and himself announces the ceremony, the five manjhis demand proof that the bitlaha is justified. If the announcer shows that the circumstances warrant it they accept the decision and do not interfere.

If, however, they are unconvinced, they fine the erring manjhi or village a sum known as ojok' jalat! This is the same amount as the outcaste himself will have to pay in order to return to caste. If the bitlaha then takes place, the sum is given to the person who has been unjustly punished and with this sum he gives a feast and is taken into caste. If the bitlaha is for any reason averted the announcer can still be punished with a fine.

'When bitlaha has been duly sanctioned a date is fixed by the five manjhis and pargana—sometimes in consultation with the dihri or president of the annual hunt—and the manjhi of the village then sends either a dihri, the jogmanjhi, the original complainant or a villager through the various to show a dharwak and announce the ceremony. If a woman has complained against her husband or a relative, she herself is sometimes sent. This dharwak is a twig or branch of Sal wood, with its leaves stripped to indicate the number of days in which the bitlaha will be held. One of the leaves is folded into a cone to symbolize the penis and another is pinned into a groove to represent the vagina. The jogmanjhi then takes the twig or branch and carries it round the markets. As he goes people ask him what is he taking it for and he tells them the time and place of the bitlaha and invites them to attend. It is usual to give not less than five or more than ten days notice for the ceremony.

XII THE RECALL OF THE DHARWAK'

This exhibition of the branch has the full force of a tribal command. It announces a decision. It summons the people for a definite act and once it has issued, it is only with the greatest difficulty that the order can be recalled.

Possibly because of the inherent difficulty in briefing a huge area and countarmanding an order once issued, tribal usage has now crystallised into two distinct types of regional practice.

In the Dumka, Pakur and Rajmahal subdivisions where the country is rough, hilly and forested a branch once issued cannot be recalled and the people will invariably assemble.

In the Godda, Jamtara and Deoghar subdivisions, on the other hand, where the country is in the main more open and less wild, a branch can be recalled provided there is at least one market day before the scheduled date of the performance.

Accordingly if the pargana and manjhis consider that a mistake has been made or that the branch was issued without justification or authority, a counter branch can be issued to stop the ceremony.

In Chajora, Bhada Murmu circulated a branch, without

consulting his manjhi or the manjhis of the neighbourhood. His action was directed against a Santal who had stood as sureity for his door planks. These planks were attached by court for some certificate dues and when Bhada still did not pay, the planks were sold. In his anger at losing his doors, Bhada decided to expose the Santal to bitlaha. There was still sufficient time however to countermand the notice, so when it came to the manjhis, they sent out counter branches and nothing happened.

Similarly if in these particular areas the guilty parties approach the five manjhis and pay either the original or an enhanced fine, the branch can be countermanded.

As far as possible the man who circulated the first branch is made to go round with the second but if he cannot be found, manjhis are sent out to scour the markets and inform the people.

Samla Marandi of Kalhajore in Sundarpahari bungiow was married in Sunmara. His wife did not come to him and Samla learnt that she was having a love affair with a Mahali boy of her village. He deputed a friend to watch her and one night the Mahali was caught in her house. The pargana and five manjhis fined the girl's father and the Mahali one hundred rupees each. A date was fixed for payment and when they failed to pay, a branch was sent out proclaiming a bitlaha. Some days later the two fathers approached the pargana and paid the fines in full. There were still some market days before the date, so a second dharwak' was sent out and the bitlaha was cancelled. Out of the total fine, five rupees was paid to each of the manjhis of thirteen villages, fifty rupees was given to Samla and the rest was kept by the parganas.

In a village near Kundohit, Arjun Soren was fined thirty rupees for attempting intercourse with his daughter-in-law. He did not pay the money so a branch was sent out. Five days before the date he approached the bir manjhi who had authorised the ceremony. He paid him the original fine with ten rupees extra and the manjhi sent out a second branch, recalling the first. Out of forty rupees, the manjhi kept five and the rest was devided among all the villages of three circles each village getting two annas.

Similarly when Ram Tudu of Kitajhore committed incest

with the daughter of his father's sister, he left the village with the girl but the two parents were both fined thirty rupees. They did not pay and accordingly a branch was issued. A day or two later they paid the fine but because a bitlaha had already been announced, they were fined twenty rupees more. A second branch then went forth and there was no bitlaha out of the total fine of fifty rupees, twenty-five went to Kitajhore, fifteen to the pargana and the remaining ten was divided among the villages summoned by the branch.

This usage of recalling a branch on payment of the fine is confined only to the Godda and Jamtara subdivisions and elsewhere in the district it is neither approved nor practised.

XIII THE RECEPTION OF THE DISOM HOR

When a meeting for bitlaha has been summoned, the assembly gathers on the previous night. Men and boys from all over the countryside come trooping in headed by their manjhis or the latter's deputies. They carry sticks, drums, flutes and buffalo horns, and at the fringes of the village they are met either by the Santal who circulated the branch or by the person at whose instance the bitlaha has been summoned. This person is almost always the manjhi or jogmanjhi of the village but if the bitlaha is at the instance of a private person, it is he or she who meets the men of the neighbourhood and explains the reason for the assembly. If this person is absent, the manjhi or the village official is expected to act for him and if there is no one to meet the gathering the omission is treated as the worst possible form of area insult. In such cases the gathering may abandon its original purpose altogether and instead bitlaha the convener of the assembly or even his whole village.

The village manjhi of Noaekal sent out a branch announcing a bitlaha. After the branch had gone round, he lost his nerve and fearing that the assembly would decline to ratify the ceremony, he lagged back and did not go to meet them. The crowd got more and more impatient and in the end they punished him with fine of twenty-five rupees.

In Telgama a bitlaha was announced for two of the villagers but the bearer of the branch failed to welcome the gathering.

They were about to bitlaha the whole village when another villager came and acting as his deputy led the crowd to the house.

In Chinadangal, a dispute arose between the villagers and a widow who was acting as headman and had refused to share a fee which she had taken as the cost of a meeting. The jogmanjhi and a villager quite rightly insisted that she could not keep it but she declared that unless the disom hor themselves decreed it she would give the villagers nothing. Finding that all argument was of no avail the jogmanjhi and the villager took out a branch inviting the neighbouring people to assemble for discussion. Not to be outwitted the widow astutely went to the newly created police station at Ramghar and asked for protection. The Sub Inspector of police decided to handle the situation in his own way and took into custody the jogmanjhi and villager who had circulated the branches. Accordingly when all the neighbouring villagers gathered, there was no one to meet them. The crowd called for them but no one answered, and not a single person came. The Sub Inspector then sent a woman with a pot of water and ten rupees to ask the people to disperse. This enraged the assembly still more as it now appeared that they had been called on utterly false pretences while the jogmanjhi and villager who could have explained every thing were still under close arrest. By this time the assembly had lost all patience so they decided to bitlaha the whole village for having sent out no one to welcome them or to explain the summoning. They then swarmed into the village. planted branches at both the village ends and went from house to house urinating in the courtyards. This bitlaha which was due entirely to the crassly stupid interference by the Sub-Inspector would never have taken place if the jogmanjhi and the villager had been allowed to meet the people in the customary manner.

XIV RATIFICATION

As the crowd assembles, they settle down into small groups. Some of them light fires, some doze, while others gather into circles for discussion or entertainment. Two or nude joker appear on the scene and dance the danger dance. Folk tales with a strong sexual bias are recited and lewd songs are sung. Sometimes in the night the dihri or president of the local hunt arrives and the assembly then becomes a supplementary hunting council. Matters not connected with the immediate bitlaha are taken up and discussed and the proceedings are identical with those at a hunt or bir sendra. In parts of Dumka Subdivision, the dihri sacrifices fowls to the forest and mountain bongas 'to preserve the hunt from harms'. If the hunting dihri himself does not come, the pargana or a manjhi takes command as the president of the crowd.

The next morning, the godet is sent to call the offenders. If they come they pay him one anna each, otherwise the manjhi of the village gives the fee. The facts are then formally recounted to the assembly. This recital provides the ceremony with its full background. It invests it with dignity and significance. It acquaints the crowd with the tribal law and reminds them of the horror of incest. When the recital is over the assembly is asked to ratify the decision.

Since in almost all cases, the offenders stay away, this ratification is often only a formally. Occasionally however they attend and offer payment of the fine. If they do so, the assembly may, if it limes, accept the payment and disband without doing the bitlaha. It is not bound to do so however and in the Pakaur, Rajmahal and Godda Subdivisions, as well as in the Dumka Damin any such receipt is against custom and the suggestion is angrily brushed aside.

On the other hand in the Jamtara subdivision and in the greater part of the Dumka Subdivision, fines can be and are tendered up to the last movement. At a bitlaha at Haripur which I myself attended in 1946, the offenders were expressly invited to pay their fines and avert the performance but all of them declined.

In Churinbandh, a Santal girl eloped with a Muslim. Her father was fined twenty-five rupees and did not pay, so a bitlaha was summoned. When the crowd had gathered the Santal pleaded for mercy and tendered thirty rupees. The dihri accepted the money and the crowd dispersed. Out of this sum five rupees went to the girl's village and the rest was divided among the villages that were present in the crowd.

In Birodhin, a Santal girl was one day drinking some

country spirit at a liquor shop and making eyes at a Tamuly from her village. Their jocking got more intimate and the girl suddenly sipped some liquor from his pot. Santals saw her do it and the matter went to five manjhis. The girl's father was fined fifteen rupees and when he failed to pay it, bitlaha was announced. The man took no steps but when the crowd had gathered he tendered the money. The assembly enhanced the fine to twenty-five rupees and when this was paid and given to the villagers, bitlaha was abandoned and the crowd dispersed.

Similarly if the branch has been issued by an individual without the due authority of the five manjhis, the offenders can protest to the assembly against the bitlaha. They can point out the irregular procedure and can request a full investigation. In such cases, if they fail to convince the body that the decision was wrong, the bitlaha is ratified and the ceremony goes on. If however they show that the circulation of the branch was malafide in all subdivisions except Godda,[4] the circulator itself then becomes an accused. He is either beaten, fined, urinated on or is himself bitlahaed. If he is fined and does not pay at once, bitlaha is done in his house without delay.

A Santal of Litipara summoned a crowd for bitlaha without consulting his manjhi or the manjhis of the neighbourhood. He failed to substantiate his charges, the bitlaha was cancelled and the man himself was severely beaten.

XV THE BITLAHA CEREMONY

With its formal ratification all is now set for the ceremony. The convener or the dihri take a Sal branch. The leaves are pinned to represent a penis and vagina. He goes to the head of the throng and the crowd the starts its thunderous descent upon the village.

It will illustrate the course of events if I now describe in detail the bitlaha which I attended at Khajuria in 1944. This arose out of intercourse between a Santal girl, Khari Murmu and Sauria Paharia but as the procedure at the Santal's house was the same as if the parties had been Santals it will serve equally well as an example.

Khajuria is two miles south of Dumka with a village street shaded by large jack fruits.

The meeting place was an airy field five or six hundred yards from the village with great views across the uplands to furry hills on the skyline.

When I reached the scene, five hundred men had gathered and there was a great din of drums. Six rows of men dancers were backing and advancing. A dozen drummers were racing to and fro and boys with flutes and horns were dancing in the crowd. As the lines went backwards and forwards the dancers sang bit seren and as each song finished there was a great shout of 'der, der' and 'deper, deper'. As the dancers swang to and fro they thrust out their buttocks and jerked their penises.

A little later the recital of the facts began. The manjhi and villagers of Khajuria squatted round and a manjhi of another village expounded the law.

'Why have you summoned so many ?' he said.

'One is now two. The girl is a Santal. The boy is a Paharia. We caught them copulating. There were two and they were one'.

'Have Santal girls ever been one with Paharias ?'

'Never. From the seven ages, from the time of the earliest ancestors, Santals and Paharias have never come together Santal with Santals, Dikus with Dikus Bhuiyas with Bhuiyas Kamars with Kamars, Paharias with Paharias and Sahibs with Sahibs. That is the law'.

'For how long are they one ? Did you catch them ?'

'They were caught at night. For three years we have tried to separate them. They never listened. They never did what we said. They have not given each other up. So we have sent out the wedding knots. Even if they give one hundred rupees now we will not take it. Today we will marry them.' 'No longer are they with us. They cannot eat and drink with us. They cannot join in any village talks. There can be no wedding with them. We have put them apart. We will not come near them at any death or any trouble or any festival. We will not link anything to them. We will not take their girls or give them out boys. Today all the countryside will know of them. If any one joins himself to them he will go the same way. We will not mix with them. They will live alone like mongrels, Doms and sweepers. Until they came back by giving a hundred plates, they will have no peace with anyone. Hear what we have said'. 'And listen men of the countryside. Whatever is the custom we will now do. But we will do no damage, spoil nothing, harm nothing. But according to custom we will dance before the house and urinate in the courtyard'.

The manjhi of Khajuria then brought a lota of water and five rupees, begged pardon for the crime in his village and besought the assembly to spare his house. The five manjhis then took the money and exempted his house from entry and defilement.

More dancing and druming then started and for half an hour, the line jerked backwards and forwards. Two nude jokers began to dart like snakes among the crowd. One of them had a string of cream coloured flowers round his neck and head while a great red apron of hibiscus flowers flaped to and fro about his sex. As they ran they jerked their organs, grappled with onlookers and dashed at the dancers. Gusts and mirth swept through the crowd while the clear sound of flutes rippled in the air.

The manjhi of Khajuria then brought out a Sal tree branch with the leaves sewn to represent a penis and vagina, and a solid leaf plate stuck on the tip. He held the branch aloft and the dancer moved slowly behind him up the slopes to the village. Bir seren songs broke out. There was a great thunder of drums and again the cries went up of 'der, der' and 'deper, deper'.

When they reached the village they went to Khari Murmu's house. This was locked and deserted and the crowd went down the street. At the end they turned back, came back and finally swept into the courtyard. The manjhi pressed the branch into the roof, the dancers jerked to and fro and twenty of them went inside the verandah and made water on the walls. Again they did the sexual dance up and down the courtyard shouting, 'der' and 'deper' with a laughing fury. Then they left the reeking walls and the crowd streamed out of the village and back to the field.

Before the crowd dispersed the manjhi of Mortanga who was acting as dihri made himself naked and offered three fowls at the end of the village. Two were to Manjhi Haram and to Maran Buru on behalf of the whole assembly, while the third was to the Ronga ruji bonga on behalf of the nude jokers. As he made the offerings he said 'Manjhi Haram today the people of your village and the men of the countryside were gathered. We danced your village through and through. We were forced to do it. We did no harm or sin. We are giving you your due. Accept it in your pleasure'.

For the Ronga ruji bonga he marked a circle with his loin cloth, took pinch of charcoal, touched it with his organs and put it in the circle. Then he took some *sindur* and arwa rice, touched his organ with them and put them in the circle. Finally he took up the fowl, pressed it to his penis and cut its neck on the axe. Then he said 'Ronga ruji bonga, today we pulled our foreskins back and before the people we exposed our organs. We did it well. Let them no longer stay exposed. Let each penis return to its sheath. In gratitude we offer you this fowl. Accept it in your pleasure.' This sacrifice was done in case a woman had viewed the jokers for, if a woman sees a joker's organ and curses it, his foreskin will never go back and the tip of his penis will remain forever exposed.

When the sacrifice was over, the jokers resumed their clothes, and dance and songs ended and the crowd went quickly away.*

This bitlaha which was typical of many such ceremonies differed in only three minor respects from the standard ritual that there was no defecation, that no cooking hearth or earthen pots were cracked and the symbol on the branch were confined to 'the bride and bridegroom' and the soiled plate.

In all other ways it was representative of local custom and might have occurred anywhere in the Santal Parganas.

XVI THE SIGNIFICANCE OF BITLAHA

It will be obvious that much of the effect of this ritual is due to the hugeness of the crowd whose presence dwarfs the village and infuses it with awe and terror. Just as the effect

*In this case bitlaha was not performed against the Paharia as his house was out of the Subdivision.

of sculpture is inseparable from its size, a bitlaha would be nothing if only a dozen men took part. It is because it mobilises a whole area and focuses in one place the resentment of a region that it reinforces powerfully the tribal code.

But numbers alone are far from fully explaining its significance and there are four motifs which contribute to its power.

A bitlaha is in the first place a hunt in which the offenders are the quarry. 'They are like beasts. They must be tracked and hunted down'. For this reason the men carry the sticks of hunters, a dihri presides, and the dancing, the drumming and the flutes parallel the measures of a sendra.

Secondly, a bitlaha demonstrates the beast-like conducts of the culprit. 'We have made them cattle,' said a manjhi 'They have acted like the early ancestors whose conduct ruined the world'. They have rutted like buffaloes! For this reason also the songs dwell constantly on bestiality.

Father, what is that yelping
In the hole in the ridge
Grandfather, hush
He is coupling with a bitch.

In the plaintain garden
What is that noise
Of pheng pheng

A deaf old man
Is going with a bitch
'Ban ban' it sounds
'Hae hae' it whimpers
as he goes to it.

Across the river, Barsa
You are always at a sheep
I shall tell your father
But my father goes to girls.

It is these songs which give the act its setting. They reduce it to its ritual level. They show it for what it is a coupling with a beast.

In the third place, a bitlaha is an ato bapla, a wedding by the village. 'The bitlaha crowd is 'a wedding party'. 'The family did not marry them', Santals say, 'But the people did.' The village puts the two offenders together, exposes their secret relation and broadcasts it over the area. For this reason leaf emblems of a penis and vagina are made to dangle on a branch and impromptu songs bandy about the names of the guilty lovers.

At the Haripur bitlaha, the original offenders were Mangal Tudu and Sonodi Tudu and the men sang:

Mongol you pressed my body to you
And now you are smiling
But what a wrong you did me
For the courtyard is filling
with village relations.

The street is filling
With men from the country
What a wrong you did me
But you flirted, Sonodi
You flirted with me
And we are both to blame.

Mongol,
From the spring below the pond
Pick the blossom for me
Like bel fruits are my breasts
And you may take them
My vagina
Is like a lamp
And I will give it to you
Utterly.

These mocking songs enlarge the offender like shadows on a screen. They toss their names from lip to lip. They degrade their intimacy and rob it of all its feeling and romance.

But besides portraying the act by song and choreography a bitlaha is also a form of tribal punishment. In Santal society the sole wish of individuals is to remain anonymous and obscure to lead their lives quietly, not to attract attention to remain merged in their tribal setting like crustacea in a pool. Bitlaha reverses all this. It invests the offender with all the publicity which he most dislikes. It pulls him out of his obscure setting and dangles him before the whole region.

And I have known the eyes already, known them all
The eyes that fix you in a formulated phrase,
And when I am formulated, sprawing on a pin
When I am pinned and wriggling on the wall
Then how should I begin.[5]

In shining clothes
come the men of the country
In clothes to their ankles
Swagger the chiefs
Girl, it was you
Who brought me to this shame
Father when they come
The harm will be ended
The world is big
to east and west
To north and south
Hide us in a corner

It is the exposure to collective shame which is the essence of the ritual and which makes it far more dreaded than any physical torture or consignment to a jail.

Finally, bitlaha expresses the tribe's sense of defilement. Besides a sakri sakam or soiled leaf-plate, other objects—a worn out broom (tutki janok') and a burnt piece of wood (rongo tutkat')—are often tied to the branch. A broom is an almost universal female symbol, and Margaret M. Murray in *The God of the Witches* offers the following comment. 'The connection in the popular mind between a woman and a broom probably took its rise in very early times, the explanation being that the broom is essentially an indoor implement, belonging therefore to the woman; the equivalent implement for a man is the pitch fork, which is for out-door work only. This is the reason why in medieval representations of witch dances, the woman or witches often hold brooms, while the men or devils carry pitch forks. The broom being so definitely a feminine tool came to be regarded as the symbol of a woman. Until within very recent times cottage women in Surrey, when going out and leaving the house empty, put a broom up the chimney so that it was visible from the outside, in order to indicate to the neighbours that the woman of the house was away from home. In other parts of England until the last century a broom standing outside a door showed that the wife was absent and the husband at liberty to entertain his male friends'.

Similarly fire is sexual symbol and in a contemporary poem by David Gascoyne the same imagery is used.

> Supposing the sex
> A cruelty and dread in the thighs
> A gapping and blackness—a charred
> Trace of feverish flames.

Just as the character of the broom implies the degradation of the act, the burnt piece of wood suggests the sexual ruin which the wilful breach of rule has caused.

Moreover the overriding sense of defilement is stressed by the urination in the courtyard and this is often reinforced by defecation and by the pounding of excrement in a rice pounder. 'At certain stages of early culture', says Havelock 'When all the emanations of the body are liable to possess mysterious magic properties and become apt for sacred uses, the excretions, and specially the urine, are found to form part of religious ritual and ceremonial function. Even among savages the excreta are frequently regarded as disgusting, but under the influence of these conceptions such disgust is inhibited, and these amanations of the body which are usually least honoured become religious symbols.

Urine has been regarded as the original holy water, and many custom which still survive in Italy and various parts of Europe, involving the use of a fluid which must often be yellow and sometimes salt, possible indicate the earlier use of urine. Among the Hottentots, the medicine man urinated alternately on bride and bridegroom, and a successful young warrior was sprinkled in the same way. Mungo Park mentions that in Africa on one occasion a bride sent a bowl of her urine which was thrown over him as a special mark of honour to a distinguished guest. Pennant remarked that the Highlanders sprinkled their cattle with urine, as a kind of holy water on the first Monday in every quarter.

Even the excreta of animals have sometimes been counted sacred. This is notably so in the case of a cow, of all animals the most venerated by primitive peoples, and specially in India.

Moreover 'in the folklore of modern Europe we every where find plentiful evidence of the earlier prevalence of legends and practices of a scatalogical character. It is significant that in the majority of cases it is easy to see a sexual reference in these stories and customs. The legends have lost their earlier and often mythical significance, and frequently take on a suggestion of obscenity, while the scatalogical practice have become the magical devices of love-lorn maidens or forsaken wives practised in secrecy.

Among many primitive peoples throughout the world and among the lower social classes of civilised peoples, urine possesses magic properties, more especially it would seem the urine of women and that of people who stand or wish to stand in a sexual relationship to each other. In a legend of the Indians of the northwest coast of America, recorded by Boas, a woman gives her lover some of her urine and says 'you can wake the dead if you drop some of my urine in their ears and nose'.

Among both Christians and Mohammadans a wife can attach an unfaithful husband by privately putting some of her urine in his drink. This practice is worldwide: thus among the aborigines of Brazil, according to Martius, the urine and other excretions and secretions are potent for aphrodisiacal objects'.[6]

In the Santal ceremony of bitlaha, urination is partly a symbol of the act of the two lovers but it is even more obviously a symbol of the tribe's pollution. Just as the house is defiled by the urine or the foeces, the tribe has been defiled by the conduct of the offenders.

The images are an expression in symbolism of the whole situation.

XVII THE CONSEQUENCE OF BITLAHA

When bitlaha has been once performed the ceremony has three important effects and I will revive them from the angle of the offender, the village and the tribesmen.

Since the Santal offender is already outcasted whether from the date he was given the option of a fine or from the day he was sentenced to bitlaha, bitlaha itself is obviously not an out-casting ceremony. It is merely an announcement to the area that the offence has been committed. If the annual hunt is the Santal High Court, bitlaha is 'a publication of the act in the Santal gazette' and because of the manner in which the publication is done it is also a punishment.

There is however one important respect in which bitlaha has advantages for the outcaste. In numerous cases, outcasting is a temporary order pending the payment of a fine. If the fine is paid the outcasting gives no further and no other remedies are necessary. If the fine is not paid outcasting continues but once bitlaha has been done the original fine is blotted out and the village can offer fresh and lighter terms. If the first fine is beyond the offender's means and it is for this reason that he is bitlahaed, it can now be scaled down so that granted 'a change of heart' nothing may stop his re-admission. If bitlaha is a warning to society it is also occasionally an avenue to the culprits' redemption.

If however there is no 'change of heart' and the offender remains obstinate and aloof, all his disabilities as an outcaste are continued. If bitlahaed man and women have already inherited land or themselves acquired land, they do not lose their rights of ownership but if the outcaste is a woman it is only in Jamtara and west Dumka that she retains land given to her as taben jom. In Godda, East Dumka and Rajmahal she forfeits these rights and her father or agnates resume the grant. In Pakaur if she is living with a Diku she forfeits taben jom land but does not forfeit it if her partner is a Santal.

If property has not already been inherited the position varies with the sex of the offender and the nature of the sin. If the outcaste is a man and his final funerary feast has not been performed, he keeps his rights of inheritance and provided the crime is clan or kin incest a woman also does not forfeit her rights as an heir. If however the woman is bitlahaed for sinning with a Diku, and does not return 'to caste' she forfeits all her rights of inheritance and is treated as a corpse, dead to all future rights in Santal property.

The same disabilities attend the death of an outcaste. If the person has a son or grandson, either of these may put the fire to his mouth, but if another kinsman does this office he must first pay the village a fine or he himself will be liable to outcasting. Similarly the final funerary feast of bhandan can only be performed when the jom jati of the outcaste has been done. If this not celebrated vicariously after his death the dead person will loiter in his former dwelling—an ancestor only half way on the road that takes him to the company of the dead.

For the village itself bitlaha is comparatively unimportant. It does not of itself introduce a fresh pollution but at the most publicizes a pollution which already exists. We have seen that both clan and kin incest as well as intercourse with Dikus pollute the village bongas and until the culprits make amends this state of pollution continues. The bongas of the sacred grove—Maran Buru, Jaherers, More Ko Turuc Ko, Gossain era, Pargana bongas and Manjhi Haram—all these are defiled and can only be worshipped again after a sacrifice of a goat or fowls in the sacred grove and at the manjhithan. If a wedding follows on the heels of an offence the villagers must appease at least Manjhi Haram and if there are no goats at hand two pigeons can be offered. With this sacrifice the bongas are purified and other sacrifices can follow in the usual way.

Similarly until this purifying sacrifice has been done no festival can be celebrated and the village must either find the animals itself or compel the offender to give them.

Finally from the time of bitlaha until the offender again comes into caste no Santal of the neighbourhood may have dealings with him of any kind whatever. Prior to bitlaha the outcasting was, as it were, known only to the village. After bitlaha, it becomes the common knowledge of the neighbourhood. The act of publication widens the circle of boycott and ensures that not merely the village but the tribe itself shall enforce the penalty. If, after that, any Santal has any dealings with the outcaste, he himself is liable to excommunication. If the village itself resumes relations, the whole village may have to undergo bitlaha.

Dukhu Murmu of Shampur began to live with a girl of his own sept. They were outcasted and bitlahaed but they continued to live together out of caste. Recently (in 1946) an ojha of Roldih attended Dukhu in his illness. He prescribed medicines and received his fees. When the five manjhis heard of his action, the ojha was made to pay a fine of twelve rupees and only by paying this did he avert outcasting.

If a member of the outcaste's family resumes relations the penalty is even stricter. He is at once subjected to bitlaha and is sometimes permanently outcasted, is known as jonom bitol and is not again taken in the tribe.

Manu Tudu of Saroya had left his wife and family in charge of his brother's son. Sometime later his nephew began to have relations with his wife and one night his own daughter detected them in each other's arms. The villagers fined them five rupees each and adviced separation. The boy did not however leave the house and the matter was reported to the five manjhis. They were then outcasted and bitlaha was done. Sometime later Manu returned. His wife and nephew then eloped to Bengal and on their return some years later they were again bitlahaed. After that the nephew died and Manu again accepted the woman as his wife. She was by now a permanent outcaste and Manu also was declared jonom bitol for having taken her again.

To the tribsmen themselves it is the risk of contamination by contacts with the outcaste which is the main consequence of bitlaha.

XVIII THE RETURN TO CASTE : JOM JATI

If this is the punishment for major Santal crime how does an offender end his sentence and again become a member of the tribe ?

'Every infringment of the established order', Christoph Von Fürer-Haimendorf has said of Chenchu society 'gives rise to two sentiments on the part of the community ; anger at the disturbance created by the offender, which may result in immediate infliction of corporal punishment and the desire to reestablish the disrupted harmony and to settle the question in a manner which precludes any repetition of the incident. There is no crime in Chenchu society which can not be expiated and the customary manner of atonement for a violation of the law is the feasting of the responsible men of the community. The gathering together of elders is essential for rectifying the evil consequences of an offence and such a gathering must invariably be accompanied by a feast at the expense of the culprit. The Chenchu may talk of 'fining' an offender but that does not mean that a fine is paid to those who came to harm by his unlawful act, but that the culprit must pay for food and liquor to feast the elders forming the council. It is really the feast in itself—with the eating and drinking together of plaintives and accused which restores the social equilibrium and signifies the condonation of the offence![7]

In Santal society there are three conditions for re-admissions that the offender should not have been outcasted for life, that he should show penitence, and finally that he should make atonement to the community through the gesture of a feast. It is this latter ceremony which readmits him to the tribe.

If his resources are small, a small feast is sufficient but if they are ample, the feast may cost him a hundred rupees or more. In deciding how large the feast should be the offender's penitence is a deciding factor. The village does not normally wish to continue his outcasting longer than is necessary and provided the offender is fully contrite he is brought into the tribe with as little delay as possible.

For achieving this end, the common procedure is as follows:

The outcaste first arranges a feast, brews rice beer, invites all the villagers and then requests the pargana and five manjhis with one or two from their villages to attend the celebration. Pigs are shot in the early morning and a little later one to three goats and sometimes some fowls are given to the naeke for sacrifice. The village officials, pargana and five manjhis sit at the manjhithan and the naeke says, 'Manjhi Haram, johar. We are giving this goat to you in sacrifice for we have kept you dirty all these days'. The goat is then beheaded and the head and blood put on the manjhi stone. The naeke sprinkles some rice and water and all do johar to Manjhi Haram. The head and the rice are then put in a new basket and are placed in the naeke's house. This sacrifice is often sufficient to purify the jaher bongas also but if there are other goats or fowls the officials go to the jaher where other sacrifices are made.

All the rice and flesh are now cooked. The outcaste serves it to the gathering and at the meal the manjhi says, 'Hear me, manjhis of the neighbourhood, from today this friend is again with us. His sin has been washed away. Henceforth we can drink water from the same pot and chew tobacco with him. We can marry our daughters in his house. We can take his girls. Now all is clean like the water of the springs. If any one speaks of this matter, listens to it or speaks evil of him, we shall fine him a hundred rupees and a hundred plates for it is a crime against a brother'. The manjhis reply 'From today he is in us'.

At the end of the feast the pargana and five manjhis are given some cash, a ball of cowdung is buried and the offence is over. During the feast there is no singing or dancing and the ritual ends in solemn quiet.

To illustrate local variations I will describe three actual feasts:

When Mukhi Hansdak' of Bokrabandh was bitlahaed in 1934 for going with a Paharia, eighty persons attended the ceremony for readmitting her to caste. Three manjhis from nearby villages came with two or three of their villages. A single goat was sacrificed at the manjhithan while three goats were killed for meat. The girl herself cooked the rice and flesh and gave five rupees to her own manjhi and one rupee to the jogmanjhi, paranik and each of the neighbouring manjhis. Since she was a girl she could not eat with them but they accepted food which she had cooked and served with her own hands. By inadvertance the pargana was not invited and at the annual hunt the manjhi of the girl's village was made to pay him ten rupees.

In a case from Dumarsol the son of Baijul Tudu had intercourse with the daughter of his father's elder sister. At the jom jati, five fowls were sacrificed in the sacred grove while a goat was offered at the manjhithan. A pig was shot and the combined flesh and rice made up the feast. Before the sacrifices Baijal gave the naeke a bowl of water in which there was one rupee. The naeke washed his hands and feet in the water, took the money and made the offerings. Similarly before the feast the village manjhi was given a second fowl with five rupees. He also washed his feet and hands, accepted the money and dined first. When he had eaten, the neighbouring manjhis and villagers shared the feast and Baijal went round distributing salt to them with his own hand. Besides the sacrifices, feasts and presents, Baijal also paid five rupees as lutur tubet to the village women, as 'their ears had been soiled by the bitlaha singing'.

At another jom jati which occurred at Telgama Ram Soren gave ten rupees to the pargana, five rupees to his own manjhi and one rupee each to five manjhis of the neighbourhood, while he himself served all the officials and the villagers with rice and meat. The feast and presents cost fifty rupees in all and the same sum was incurred by Barku Soren who had been outcasted with him.

When, as sometimes happens, a whole village is bitlahaed the ritual is slightly different and I will describe in detail what happened when the village of Chinadangal was re-admitted into caste.

The villagers first approached the manjhi who had acted as dihri and in consultation with five other manjhis a date was fixed. Since a whole village was involved, only nominal sum was required and the twelve Santal houses each paid two rupees. A pig and goat were purchased and a pig was killed in the house of the village priest. The goat was then sacrificed at the manjhithan and some country spirit was also offered. The villagers then dressed the meat while five manjhis and forty others sat about in the street. A little later the dihri was given five rupees. Each manjhi then demanded one rupee but the dihri overruled them. Later in the night the feast was ready. A Murmu of the bitol sub-sept ate first, then the manjhis of the other villages and finally the outcaste village sat with the other Santals and shared the meal. There were no speeches or ceremonies and with the joint feast the village of Chinadangal returned to caste.

XIX THE SANTAL ATTITUDE TO BITLAHA

What is the attitude of Santal culprits to the custom of bitlaha?

When offenders have been sentenced their attitude varies from one of active or passive defiance to that of resignation or sullan despair. In many cases they suffer bitlaha because they cannot pay the fine and it is after days of patient effort that the expenses of the penalty feast are finally got together. But in a few cases the offenders prefer the ceremony of bitlaha to the alternative of abandoning their guilty relationship.

Dewan Tudu of Pokharia was bitlahaed for sleeping with his mother-in-law. The bitlaha took place in January 1945 but in July they were still sharing a cot while his wife slept in another room.

In the case from Pahar kole, Lodga Hansdak' who was a rich young Santal with two wives deliberately did not do jom jati because it would have meant severing relations with his sister's daughter.

In rare cases the offenders show active defiance and bitlahas have occurred in which instead of following the usual practice and going quietly from the scene the offender have remained to face the crowd.

In a sensational case of Dumka Subdivision an old woman got ready some pots of boiling water. When the party arrived she went to face them and threw the water at the leaders. Then when the pot finished she turned away. But the disom hor were so angry that they stripped her naked and marched her through the village touching her private parts with their penises.

At Dhamni in 1933, a newly married girl of seventeen was going to her parent's without her husband's consent. Her father-in-law went after her, forced her down and had intercourse. The girl complained to the manjhi and bitlaha was ordered. She herself was polluted and was therefore subjected to the ceremonies. Since however she herself was the complainant and was also the victim of force she attended the ritual and carried the branch of Sal leaves. The party observed the usual uproarious dancing, uttered cries of 'der der' and 'deper deper' and sang bir seren while the girl moved calmly ahead as if insulated from the scene. As they neared the house, her father-in-law rushed out and aimed a blow at her with an axe. The blow missed and the party rushed upon him and gave him a great beating.

In a third case, resistance led to death. A middle aged widow Fulu Tudu of Taldih fell in love with Bulai, the husband of her younger cousin. The matter leaked out, several village councils were held and the two were each fined seven rupees and eight annas. They did not pay the fines and it was then decided to bitlaha them. On 27th May 1940 the people assembled and the manjhi of Taldih led them first to Bulai's house and then to Fulu's. At Bulai's a branch was planted and the ceremony went off without event. When however, they reached the second house, Udru Murmu, a relation, resisted entry. A fight took place. The manjhi was struck on the head, first with a lathi and then with a heavy pestle. Others hit back at Udru. Finally the crowd swept in, broke two pitchers and urinated in the courtyard. The manjhi was dragged away unconscious and died the next day.

These cases are the only ones in which Santals have resisted bitlahas and the normal attitude is far more usually one of despairing submission. Indeed in the bitlaha songs which portray the reactions of the guilty lovers, it is anxiety and dread which dominate their minds. The songs show the boy and girl waiting the results of the first meeting and viewing with sick suspense the impending ceremony.

Boy, the door
Do not open it too quickly
They have written it on paper
They have played it on the flutes
At the hunt on the big mountains
They will take our matter up.

They describe the approach of the great crowd and the revolution of the lovers.

The singing of the bulbul
A boy's words

' And with my grown body
I did not feel ashamed
The land has gone dim
The raiders are on us
Girl, do not call me elder brother.

Above all the songs emphasise the sense of overwhelming shame at ostracism by the tribe.

By day the meeting
Is at the stony hill
At night they are meeting
At the pool by the kadam
Girl, the meeting
Is never going to end
Girl, the money for the goat
The money for the baskets of rice
Girl, the meeting
Is never going to end.

You, elder brother
Smiled when you had loved me
I elder brother
Was shamed before the country.

Brother under the bar tree
You held a karam
But you put me to shame
Before the men of the country.

Dikus and others
Fence themselves with thorns
But we, O elder brother
The local men have fenced.

These songs do not necessarily portray the feelings of actual offenders, but their significance is obvious. It is because bitlahas are believed to induce these feelings that they remain the most dreaded sanction in Santal life.

REFERENCES

1. Such grading of crime is common in all the tribes of eastern India. S.C. and R.C. Roy describe certain Kharia offences for which complete excommunication is the punishment and add 'Punishment for breaches of other taboos are proportioned according to their respective gravity in tribal estimation. Breaches of taboos next in order of gravity, to those like sexual union either with non-Kharias or within the clan or the exogamous group, or the killing of cows or bullocks, are generally expiated by the offender by the drinking of the blood of a white cock or he-goat sacrificed in the name of the sub-god and treating the Panch or rice beer. Comparatively lighter taboos are removed by offering a libation of rice beer to the ancestor-spirits or by sprinkling mixed with pounded or powdered turmeric on the person of the breaker of the taboo. The offence is considered as comparatively light if the breach of taboo was unintentional or done in ignorance. The breach of such minor taboos as that against giving away fire from his house to an outsider on the day on which a Kharia takes out paddy seeds from his house for sowing in his fields, affects only the luck of the individual or family concerned (for example, their crops may fall) and is therefore not dealt with by the Panch.' (*The Kharias*, I, 167-8).
2. I have discussed standards of proof in *Civil Law in Santal Society*.
3. In the Jamtara subdivision a 'dead' offender is treated as an outcaste but is not deprived of his lands.
4. In the Godda subdivision there is no investigation by the assembly and bitlaha is an automatic corollary to a summons. If the latter has been wrongly issued, it is investigated and adjusted after the ceremony.
5. T.S. Eliot, *Poems 1909-1925* (London, 1925).
6. Havelock Ellis, op. cit., III, 50-52.
7. C. von Fürer-Haimendorf, *The Chenchus* (London, 1943), 167-8.

49

THE BITLAHA OF DIKUS

I PRELIMINARY

IF the bitlaha of Santals is comparatively straightforward the punishment of sexual crime with Dikus[1] is perhaps the most difficult problem in the whole of Santal justice. It is not only that the offence is one of the gravest which a Santal can commit. The crime is also an act of aggression by one community against another, a wilful violation of tribal susceptibilities, a denial of all that Santals value most. It is not surprising therefore that when such a crime occurs, it revives ancient bitterness. It accrues to itself grievances both economic and social. It raises in the most acute form the whole question of Santal existence in the Santal Parganas.

In this chapter therefore I will begin by describing as objectively as I can the Santal attitude to Dikus for without this background the Santal treatment of Diku crime can not easily be understood. I will then state the manner in which such crime has been punished in the last fourty years and I will end by recording the attitude of Hindus, Muslims and Santals to the custom of Diku bitlaha.

II THE SANTAL ATTITUDE TO DIKUS

For several centuries the Santal attitude to Dikus has been one of coolness. In a statement dictated in 1871 Kolean Haram said :

'In the old days when Ram was the king all the Santals went with him to Lanka to fight and help in defeating king Ravan.

Because of that for a long time we had no quarrel with Dikus. They lived in the open land, we in the forests and mountains. But later we had many quarrels with them and even now they are still quarrelling with us. Wherever we have cleared the land, the Dikus have come and snatched it from us. Even today if the Sahebs had not helped the Dikus we would have driven them like dust across the Ganges. From Campa, the ancestors fled to Tore Pokhori Baha Bandela. There they stayed for a long time but later many Dikus got in and settled on the land, which they had cleared. From there also the ancestors moved on. Some say it was from fear of Musalmans. In this way they reached Bari Badwa forest.

"They stayed there for a time but could not settle so they went to Khaspal Bolaonja. From there people went in several directions. Some went to Sir, some to Sikhar and some to Nagpur. It is since then that most of us are under Dikus. He cleared all the forests of the Raja of Sikhar and under him many of us owned villages. But the Dikus drove us from there also and took away our houses and lands. From Sikhar some went on to Tundi and there was no other place to settle in. The ancestors had said, 'Never cross the Ajai river; for the children of those who cross shall be treated as polluted even in the womb because over there is the land of the Musalmans, a corrupt country.'

'But we did not listen to the word of our ancestors and because of hunger we went there. Then in the course of time we came to the Santal Parganas. We have come along eating our way like silkworms. We are still here now. One day we shall go elsewhere. We do not know why God has punished us like this?'[2]

This account is corroborated by Jugia Haram who continued dictating after Kolean Haram had died and who supplied an account of the Santal Rebellion.

'Owing to the trouble caused by the Dikus and the pangs of hunger and after crossing the Ajai river we gradually spread towards the north and east, to the hills and the banks of the ganges. At that time there was only forests with Bhuiyas here and there, and on the hills, Mar Mundas. At that time the Bhuiyas and Mar Mundas were kings. They gave out land by agreement and took very little rent. Under them we had no trouble. But day by day the Dikus entered for trade and at last settled as money lenders. They became the king's money lenders also. Having taken money and clothes from the money lenders, the kings pledged their lands with them. In that way the Diku money lenders acquired the whole land by fraud and became kings themselves while the real kings grew poor like us. The Diku Kings who were living near the hills encroached on the lands of the Mar.

'We cleared the hills and forests for these new kings by taking loans from the money lenders and in return these kings levied rent from us. The money lenders give little and take a great deal. They take the year's crop and we have then to take fresh loans from them. However much we pay they are never satisfied. If they are not satisfied with the year's crop they drive away our cattle. If the debt is not repaid even then we work at their houses with our women and children for one or two pais of rice. As there were no officers, to whom could we cry ? Then came Diku police. But they were own over by the white money of their own caste men and dismissed our cases. We had great trouble and they harassed the whole country'.[3]

This continuing grievance received expression in the Santal Rebellion of 1855 when the Santal leaders Sido and Kanhu ordered all Dikus to be slain. It was inevitable that this rebellion should eventually be suppressed, but far from inducing in Dikus a 'change of heart' it accentuated communal bitterness. 'The costs of conflict', Jawaharlal Nehru has said 'are always great and the heaviest of these costs is the trail of hatred and bitterness that follows'. At the end of the rebellion Jugia Haram noted. 'There were no plough cattle. There was nothing to eat and the Dikus laughed at us and once again the money lenders got us in their hands'.[4]

As a result of the rebellion, the Santal country was formed into a district and given a type of administration that was sensitives to local needs. The loss of lands to Dikus however was very far from checked and in 1871 Kolean Haram could still declare 'the Dikus deprive us of villages, encroach on our boundaries and cheat us of our lands. The Dikus enter like a needle, and drive forward like a plough share. They make us quarrel and snatch each others property. There is no peace wherever they are. By giving false evidence in court they are wresting every thing from us. If there had been no Diku cats among us how good it would have been for Santals'.[5]

Since the 1890's the loss of land to Dikus has been greatly checked and this has not only removed a major source of friction but by ensuring stability in land tenure has given to Santals a new sense of security. Little however has been done to control or replace the money lender and it is not for nothing that Santals still say 'Diku pusi' and generally refer to Diku 'sa' 'a bush of thorns'. If after ninety years there is no longer quite the same bitterness or despair there is still a certain frigid mistrust in Santal-Diku relations.

The reasons for this continued estrangement are various. It is obvious that a traditon of bitterness does not easily die out particularly when there is a rebellion to provide it with a date. There are marked difference in temperament between the two communities and understanding is, therefore, very far from easy. There is a natural simplicity in Santal values which ill assorts with greater sophistication. If Santals and Dikus are to come together, not merely a change of heart will be necessary but to some extent there will have to be a change of head.

There is yet another factor which makes friendship difficult. A Santal, a Brahmin and a Muslim has each in his own way a form of communal conceit. A Santal does not merely feel himself different from a Diku. He believes himself to be superior. The Diku attitude to Santals is precisely the same. Friendship is impossible when the only basis is conflicting views of individual superiority.

Yet another factor contrives to raise a wall between the two communities. Santals are intensely attached to their own language of Santali and do not learn or speak either Hindi or Bengali with ease or avidity. Dikus on the other hand are disinclined to learn Santali and it is a remarkable fact that in a district bar of more than one hundred pleaders whose self-interest, one would have thought, would have induced them to learn the language barely three can speak and understand Santali. In such conditions understanding collapses through the mere lack of a common language.

It would not perhaps matter if each community kept its opinion of the other to itself. A Diku might still regard a Santal as different but he might contrive to treat him as an equal. Unfortunately even in the last ten years Diku gestures of goodwill have generally smacked of uplift. Instead of fostering mutual understanding and respect they have aimed rather at imposing Diku values—Diku language, Diku manners, Diku ways of thought. If they have been 'inspired by love' they have rarely been 'guided by knowledge'. Santals and Paharias do not like each other. They have separate problems which require separate treatment yet with the best of intentions an uplift body was named Santal Paharia Sevak Sangh.

Recently the Congress party of Bihar has declared its determination to maintain tribal cultures in all their integrity. If this principle had been enunciated earlier, it might well have transformed Santal Diku relations. As it is Santal Diku relations are certainly not beyond remedy, but there is still much latent coolness suspicion and mistrust.

III THE INVESTIGATION OF OFFENCES

It is against this background that sexual offences must be seen. A Santal girl may have only laughed or joked with a Diku but Santals regard her gesture as a threat to their integrity. If she has gone further and drunk or eaten with a Diku, she has polluted not only herself but the tribe. If she has had sexual connection, she has degraded the tribe 'in the very womb'. When such intimacy occurs, therefore, Santals refuse to be complacent and two courses are followed.

If intimacy is detected and the Diku is caught, both boy and girl are beaten and brought at once to a village meeting. If, however, the intimacy is known but the Diku escapes the village sits in his absence and arraigns the girl only. To this meeting other Dikus including the boy's kinsmen are sometimes invited. Diku participation, however, is never essential for Santals say that since the offence is against a Santal, it is for Santals only to decide what counter steps should be taken.

In Dhodhi, Bhola Sahu was caught in intercourse with the daughter of Dhodih Manjhi. It was daytime and in the jungle and some Santal boys came suddenly upon then. A wild scene took place. The village boys were wild with anger and beat the Diku so severely that he defeated. He was then tied to his own dhoti and dragged to the Dhodih Manjhi. All the Santals and Dikus then sat together and the two communities jointly fined the boy sixty rupees and the girl ten. The fines were paid and nothing more was done. The Dhodih Manjhi, however, could not endure the shame and later on turned the girl out of his house.

When Debi Mandal of Hariari was caught with the wife of Manjhi Hansdak, the two were tied together and taken to the manjhi. The Santals sat alone and after the Diku had confessed and asked for mercy they fined him and the woman twenty-five rupees each. The Diku was told to pay the woman's fine and did so.

IV THE OPTION OF FINE

If sexual intimacy is proved the village either proposes the immediate bitlaha of the two houses or gives the offender the option of a fine . . . It is not bound to inflict and accept a fine neither is it bound to recommend bitlaha. In Santal opinion either course is valid and either may be taken according to the village wish. If immediate bitlaha is recommended the pargana and five manjhis are asked to meet and the branch is issued on their joint instructions. If the offence falls short of actual intercourse, the tribal penalty is a fine and only if it is not paid, is bitlaha sanctioned.

While, however, it is open to the village to advise early bitlaha, it is more usual to explore first a less drastic punishment and to attempt to close the incident with a fine. There are various reasons why this attitude is adopted. Although Santals utterly detest any kind of sexual intimacy with Dikus, they are averse to victimising an offender unless it is absolutely necessary. They would much prefer to live in peaceful calm and unless the incident is aggravated by other factors, they are loath to take the extreme step. The option of a fine is, therefore, usually given. If both the parties are punished, the Diku is made to pay a heavy fine while the girl is given a lighter one. At other times either the girl herself is not fined or the Diku is made to pay the fines for both.

When a Diku of Porca was caught in intercourse with Randhni Hembrom of Amboa, the Diku was fined eighty rupees and the girl ten.

When a Teli of Siltha was surprised with Charki Hembrom, he was fined a hundred rupees and the girl escaped with fifteen.

On the other hand when Adinath Bhagat of Mandro was found one night sleeping with a Santal widow of Banglia the woman was merely sent back to her father's house but the Bhagat was fined fifty rupees.

In a case from Maharajpur, Raghunath Sahu caught a Santal girl and forced her to have intercourse. The matter was detected and in a joint meeting of the Santals and Dikus, he was fined one hundred rupees and out of this, forty rupees was given to the girl, 'as he had taken her by force'.

When a fine is imposed and is pending for payment, the Santal girl and members of her kitchen remain outcasted but immediately the money is given they are brought back into caste. In most cases the fine is assumed to cover the exculpatory feast but occasionally it is credited to the crime itself and an extra feast is demanded for re-entry into caste.

In Kulhapathar, a Diku boy, Gundadhar Pal, was caught in sexual intercourse with the wife of Barka Soren. He paid a fine of three hundred rupees and the two were parted.

Dudhnath Bhagat of Rajbari was detected with a Santal girl of his village. Both paid fines and the matter ended.

In Botio, Ainpa Mian began a love affair with a Santal girl of his village. One day the girl went to his house and informed his first wife that she had come to stay. The first wife was furiously angry, called some Jolana women and they all beat the girl and drove her out. At the village meeting the girl was out casted and Ainpa was fined five hundred rupees and the cost of a feast for bringing the girl into caste. He paid them and the girl was told to leave him and never go to him again.

In Katikund, Basudeo Bhagat was surprised in intercourse with a Santal girl of Daldali. The two were arrested, given a beating and tied together for a night. The next day the boy paid a fine of twenty-five rupees and the two were separated and sent to their homes.

In Bhulti, a Diku, Bisu Manjhi was fined one hundred rupees for intercourse with a Santal girl. The girl absconded to Bengal and her brother had to pay five rupees for being taken into caste.

In Haripur a Bengali boy was surprised with a Santal girl of Kusbedia. The villagers referred the matter to five manjhis. The boy's father pleaded for mercy and in the end the girl was fined sixty rupees and the boy three hundred.

In Litipara Chananjoy Mandal was caught with the daughter of Pero Marandi. He paid two hundred rupees and averted bitlaha.

V THE CONSEQUENCES OF FLIGHT

If one or both the parties leave the village, the same principles apply as if both of them were Santals. If the matter has already been adjudicated, and bitlaha sanctioned it is performed in their houses, irrespective of their presence or absence. If fine have been imposed, their families must pay them or they too will suffer the extreme penalty. It is only if the matter has still not reached the village that elopement or absconding helps the offenders. In such circumstances, the Santal girl is sometime treated as dead and her funerary feast performed or in the alternative nothing is done until she returns. The matter is then immediately revived and justice takes its course. Occasionally the girl is treated as a permanent outcaste, and she is then allowed to leave the village and join Diku for ever.

In 1945 a Halwai boy was caught in Jamtara with a Santal girl of Bewa. The Santals of Bewa arrested him and it was only when he had paid sixteen rupees on behalf of the girl's family that they released him and he went away. In this case the girl went with him also and since she herself was outcasted for remaining with him the fine itself absolved only the members of her family. Her mother later performed the girl's bhandan or funeral feast and she has since been treated as dead.

In Rajbari Budhnath Bhagat eloped with a Santal girl of his village. Their fathers were outcasted and had each to pay fines. These fines duly absolved the families, but when the boy and girl returned, they were not covered and were still out of their castes. They did not give each other up and finally in despair they embraced Christianity. They are now employed by a mission to preach the gospel.

A Mahajan of Sakhbaro began relations with a Santal girl of Birajpur. One day the girl's family surprised them together, beat the mahajan and then ducked him and the girl in a ditch of water. Even this, however, did not cool their ardour and finally the matter had to go to the village. There the diku was forced to pay such a heavy fine that his business as a money lender was ruined. The girl was outcasted and she has since been living with the Diku as his permanent mistress.

VI THE CUSTOM OF DIKU BITLAHA

If the option of fine is given but the money is not paid or if immediate bitlaha is proposed, two courses are open to the village.

In certain cases, the girl's own family will intervene. She is 'dead', they say 'we shall never see her again. Do not do bitlaha. We shall perform her funerary feast.' If the village agree, bhandan is then done, an extra feast is claimed for re-admitting the outcasted family and the Diku is left to go his way—the despised lover of a fictitious corpse.

A Santal girl of Kobinda Saro was caught with Ghula Mandal, Ghuja Mandal, a Diku of Majhladih. The Diku boy was beaten and he and the girl were each fined a hundred rupees. Neither paid and the villagers were about to do bitlaha when the girl's father paid the money for a funerary feast and gave a goat and a maund and a quarter of rice for his own readmission. The villagers accepted the payment, the girl was declared 'dead' and nothing more was done.

If, however, the girl's family do not take this step, bitlaha is then performed in the two houses.

This is the rule throughout the whole of the Santal Parganas except in the Narayanpur area at the Southernmost tip of Jamtara subdivision. In this latter area, the girl is regarded as so completely and irremediably defiled by intercourse with a Diku that she is 'thrown aside like a soiled leaf'. Bitlaha is done in her house and while her parents may be brought back into caste after giving a feast, she herself is is expelled for ever. No action is taken against the Diku as 'this would be to recognise him as her husband'. This, however, is the sole exception and throughout the rest of the district bitlaha of Dikus is an immemorial custom.

The ritual at such bitlaha follows the same lines as at the bitlaha of a Santal but besides the symbol of Santal defilement the worn-out broom, the piece of burnt wood, the used leaf plate—the skull, bones or foreleg of a cow or bullock are sometimes hung up before a Hindu's door while the trotter or the carcase of a pig is suspended from the roof of a Muslim.

To illustrate this usage I will now record twelve cases covering the last thirty years.

At Sibapahar in the Ranga bunglow of Rajmahal, a Muslim Jolaha was caught with Chita Soren in 1910. An immediate bitlaha was sanctioned, ten thousand Santals assembled, and the ceremony took place in both the houses. At the Muslim's house, a branch was erected, a soiled leaf plate with the leaf emblem of the bride and bridegroom and a piece of burnt wood were hung up by the door and there was urination and defecation throughout the courtyard and verandah.

In 1920, Nitai Das of Khutana in the Siltha circle of Dumka was given the option of a fine of one hundred rupees and on his refusal bitlaha was performed. A bullock's hoof was hung up on the roof but no *chulha* was broken and there is no urination of defecation in his courtyard and verandah.

The same year another bitlaha occurred at Gandupara in the Surajbare bunglow of Pakaur. Ratu Rai, a Bhuiya had connection with a Santal girl as a result of which she became pregnant. A chulha in the courtyard was broken and there was urination and defecation round the house. A soiled leaf plate, a piece of half burnt fire wood and a worn broom were hung up on the roof.

In 1922, Raghubit Pandey, a Brahmin of Sijua in Banskuli circle of the Dumka subdivision had intercourse with a Santal girl of his village as a result of which the girl became pregnant. The parties were given the option of a fine and they did not pay bitlaha was performed. The crowd which numbered 10,000—entered the Brahmin's courtyard, danced the dunger dance, hung up a bullock's hoof at his door but did not break any chulha and there was no urination or defecation.

Three years later Durga Charan Napit of Nayagarh in the Maheshpur P.S. of Pakaur Subdivision was bitlahaed for illicit relations with a Santal girl. A small crowd of only 300 assembled, a Sal branch with the sexual emblems was planted in the courtyard, there was a little urination but no chulha was broken and no other symbols were used.

In 1927, a Teli of Masanjore in Gumro Circle of Dumka was bitlahaed for intercourse with a Santal girl. A crowd of about 10,000 gathered, there was urination in the courtyard and verandah but no chulhas were broken and there was no defecation. A bullock's hoof was hung up in front of his door.

In 1930, Kedar Keot of Sinjuri in the Salhanapur P.S. of Burdwan was bitlahaed by the Santals of the Santal Parganas for intercourse with a Santal girl of Kusbedia in the Mihijam circle of Jamtara. A crowd of 1,500 Santals assembled, a bullock's skull was tied to his roof and there was urination and defecation in his courtyard. In addition, a fishing net was torn to pieces.

The same year Kandarpa Manjhi, a Diku of Salkhia in the Amba circle of Jamtara was bitlahaed for raping a Santal girl. Urination was done against the wall of his house in the village street and a bullock's skull was suspended to his roof. There was no defecation in his house or courtyard.

In 1935, Bhagua Kahar of Gangarampur in the Godda P.S. was caught in sexual intercourse with the wife of a Santal. The boy was fined twenty-five rupees and the girl fifteen. The fines were not paid and both were bitlahaed. A bullock's skull was hung up in the Diku's house and there was urination in the courtyard and verandah.

At a bitlaha which occurred the same year at Raidih in the Danro circle of Dumka, a crowd of 6,000 visited the house of Parsadi Rai a Bhuiya. The customary branch was placed on his roof, a chulha was broken, urination was done allround the inside house and there was defecation in a rice pounder and in an inner room.

In 1938, the bitlaha of a Muslim, Kadir Mian, was performed

at Barkuri in the Mandro bunglow of Rajmahal. A crowd which was estimated at almost 60,000 assembled, the ordinary symbols were hung up but no pig's troter was exposed. Defecation and urination occurred all round the house and courtyard.

In 1938 Isri Sahu of Bania Kumardiha in the Kendua circle of Dumka was also bitlahaed. The crowd numbered a thousand Santals. The cooking pots and chulhas in his house were broken and urination and defecation occurred in the courtyard, verandah and entrance to his house. Some bullock's hoofs and pig's legs were hung up on the roof.

VII OFFENCES WITH DIKU GIRLS

What is the position if a Santal boy has relations with a Diku girl?

In Santal opinion this also is a serious offence but as it does not involve 'a Santal womb' it does not require such severe punishment as forbidden intercourse by a girl.

Accordingly a boy who goes with a Diku girl usually is usually given a small fine and no case has so far occurred in which bitlaha has been ordered. No action against the girl is taken by the Santals and she is left to be dealt with by her castemen.

In Monohardih a Santal boy fell in love with a Barian girl of his village. The girl became pregnant and in due course the boy was caught. The Barians of the village then outcasted the girl and the Santals fined the boy. The girl was not punished by the Santals and once the boy had paid the fine the matter ended.

In Sundarpur a Santal boy had relations with the daughter of Sokra Mian. The Santals fined the boy five rupees while the Mohammadans made the girl's father give a penalty feast.

VIII THE ATTITUDE OF DIKUS

What is the attitude of Dikus to this form of punishment?

There is no doubt that while Dikus, as a whole, dread its actual infliction, their attitude is by no means one of unqualified disapproval.

So far as Hindus are concerned, to be intimate sexually with a person of another caste is as much a crime as it is for Santals. It is not surprising therefore that many Hindus either adopt an attitude of tolerant neutrality or while disassociating themselves from the ritual they accord their approval to the custom. The Brahmans and Bhagats of Debinagar, for example, said to Mr. R.D. Pande, 'Bitlaha is a good custom. It should always be done when a Diku has relations with a Santal. It would be great cruelty to Santals to deprive them of this right'.

In the meeting which preceded the bitlaha of Isri Sahu the local Hindus fully cooperated and it was with their full concurrence that bitlaha was finally sanctioned.

Moreover a Hindu boy who commits this offence cannot normally expect much sympathy from his caste people. He is blamed for disgracing his community. He is himself outcasted by them. 'If the Santal girl is pregnant', said Hindus of Karbinda, 'we will never take him back.' If his casteman interfere at all it is only to ascertain that the allegation is correct, to plead that no substantial damage should be done and to see that the ritual is not misapplied for private ends.

The attitude of Mohammadans is also not dissimilar. At Raksi the Muslims said to Mr. S.C. Hansdak' 'sexual intimacy between a Muslim boy and a Santal girl is as bad as illicit intimacy between a Muslim girl and a Muslim boy. One who has illicit intercourse should be punished with eighty stripes. Mr. Burhanuddin Khan, M.L.A., with whom I discussed the attitude of Muslims also told me that to Muslims illicit intercourse is a crime, the Muslims would boycott the offender and would exact a penalty feast. If there is any difference, it is rather that Muslims are somewhat more prone to tamper with Santal girls—partly because they marry later. To both communities the act is abhorrent but individual Muslims flout their community opinion a little more than do Hindus.

Finally there is a type of view which is not confined to Hindus or Muslims only but in many areas is shared by both. In these villages, it is realised that the Santals were the original clearers of the forest and since they were the first to face the forest bongas and risk their hostility they possess a special relation to the land. Accordingly it is usual for Hindu and Muslim households in Santal villages to subscribe to Santal festivals, to give the naeke oil at births and deaths, and to be particularly careful not to infringe Santal rules. In this view, bitlaha is part of 'the custom of the Santal country; it is linked to the bongas and a Diku would flout it at his peril'.

IX THE SANTAL ATTITUDE TO DIKU BITLAHAS

What reasons do Santals advance for doing bitlaha in the houses of Dikus?

'We punish them as we punish the thieves—so that they may not not do it again' said Santals at Poraiyahat. 'Why should a Diku foul our blood? To keep our blood pure we do this to them'.

'Dikus' said the Santals at Nonihat, 'think themselves much higher than us. If we did not punish them for making our caste bad, they would utterly currupt us. Then they have have spoilt our caste, our only remedy is spoil theirs back. If we did not bitlaha Dikus how would they fear us? How would they ever leave our girls alone? It is for this that we hang up bullocks's legs and pig's trotters and do stools and make water. It is because of this that our girls are safe and can go everywhere freely. . . We can not shut them in our houses. We must send them out to work. We can not tend them like cows. Only bitlaha protects us'.

Similar views are held at Chotkatta. 'If Dikus steal our girls and make their caste go bad' the Santals said 'we bitlaha the girls and do bitlaha to the Dikus. If we do not do this they would spoil and destroy us utterly. They would do with us whatever they liked and there would be nothing we could do. The bitlaha of Dikus is with us from the very earliest times in the whole of the Santal country'.

The utter necessity of the practice is stressed in other statements also. "It is the custom' said Santals at Taljhari 'Once a Diku has done it, we must do his wedding'. There is no other way.

Similarly at Raksi "If a Diku spoils a Santal girl he is asking for punishment. We bring a 'marriage party' and perform the 'wedding'. This is the custom—that we must 'marry' them."

The same views find expression in the Pakaur subdivision. 'If a Santal goes with a Diku', we must dance in their courtyards whoever they are, said Santals at Litipara; while a gathering at Basetkundi declared 'Because he has made us bad, we must subject the Diku to the dancing'.

Yet another view comes from Masanjore.

'Dikus are grasping and full of greed. They despise Santals utterly. Therefore when Dikus steal our girls and make their caste go bad, we foul them in return. We punish them so that they well feel the shame and never do it again'.

At Kundahit, the Santals asked 'If a Diku does not like bitlaha why does he make a Santal girl his friend' ?

At Pathna the Santals asked 'Why do we do bitlaha ? To frighten Dikus so that they never 'marry' Santals'.

Finally at Katikund, the Santals of the Dumka Damin said 'If we do not do this to them, how will they have any fear or dread ? Dikus can marry girls of any caste. They see how beautiful our girls are. If they could get them they would seize and marry all of them. We punish Dikus so that their own caste men may catch them. We punish them to keep our self-respect'.

REFERENCES

1. The conventional meaning of this term is 'non-aboriginal' or 'foreigner'.
2. *Horkoren Mare Hapramko Reak*, *Katha*, 11-16.
3. Ibid., 250-1.
4. Ibid., 254.
5. Ibid., 170.

PART THREE

THE FUTURE

50

THE ADMINISTRATION OF JUSTICE

I SANTALS AND THE COURTS

IN A apaper 'On Justice', Herbert Read has given a vivid analysis of English judicial conditions which with minor changes might pass as a description of official justice in the Santal Parganas.

'We are in a court of law and a man is being measured against a code. It does not matter what kind of a man he is—a Messiah or a thief; for the moment he is a piece of evidence, a neat bundle of ascertained facts, and these only will be measured against the inflexible code. Thus Christ went to the Cross and Martyrs to the stake; thus millions were packed like cattle into trucks and sent to Siberia or Poland. It is always the same pattern—human values against the edicts of Authority, or of the State.

'In the Central Criminal Court the case is over. The wigs change place. The prisoners leave the dock. A new defendant takes their place, a negro is to be tried for man slaughter. It is all in a day's work—thieves and Messiahs, murderers and prostitutes, embezzlers and aborters. A cynic might describe it as society with the lid off, the whole seething cauldron of man's good and evil impulses. But here in the court we are present rather at a vast attempt to put the lid on—all these sinister figures in black and crimson robes being so many presiding witches. And that is, of course the exact and the melancholy truth. Here in this immense centralized cauldron the officers of the Crown are attempting brutally, if necessary, to suppress the horrid mass of pullulating sinners, and are only dimly aware that the scene is so concentrated that if the writhing mass were to be dispersed and given space and light it might be reanimated, rectified by the agencies of human love and divine grace, which operate where two or three are gathered together, but not in a crowd. Justice like every thing else is suffering from centralization from concentration and suffocation.

'Most people go through life without coming into immediate contact with the judicial system. The greater part of those who do not have a direct experience of its working are only concerned in minor misdemeanours which do not raise any questions of principle. For the most part, unless we are directly implicated, for all we know of it, the legal system might operate in another planet. Few people, unless they are implicated, attend the courts as disinterested observers, and nothing is done by ushers and other court officials to encourage the public to attend'.

'The independence of the judiciary is symbolised in various ways. By means of wigs and gowns, the participants are dehumanised to an astonishing degree. If by chance, in the course of pleading, a hot and flustered barrister lifts his wig to mop his brow, an entirely different individual is revealed. It is as if a tortoise had suddenly dispensed with its shell. The whole business is carapaceous, a shell of custom and formality against which life, plastic and throbbing, beats in an effort to reach the light'.

'In such a system human values are at a discount, in their endless variety they have to be passed through a sieve of predetermined pattern. If they are too large or too shaggy they get caught in the meshes'.[1]

In the Santal Parganas, criminal courts have much the same character and indeed to describe a Santal's reaction to a criminal case fought out in a official manner and in a official court one would virtually be forced to depict a surrealist scene. The court buildings with their robust gigantic masonry are themselves the negation of all that is a village. Their red brick walls glare across a compound where black-gowned lawyers strut like sinister mechanics in a strange [factory. The court room with its wooden docks, its table and dais, its long benches is itself a huge and menacing machine. Even the ritual hearing is calculated to heighten rather than diminish the sense of mystery and strangeness. To start a case, a piece of stiff white paper must be bought. A stranger sitting in the compound decides what section of the code should be invoked. A pleader addresses that court in a language which is not Santali. At the close, judgment is delivered and the decision is sometimes so strange that even the complainant is astonished. Often on technical grounds the accused is acquitted and the grievance which prompted a recourse to court remains unredressed. Occasionally 'the cat in the red house'—as Santals term a magistrate—springs on the complainant himself and should the twisted processes of trial have given his complaint a false complexion, he may himself be sent to jail. Finally it as if the certified copy of the final order itself clinches the air of unreality. With its unintelligible language, its stiff crackling paper, its strange brown stamp, it symbolises all those features of the system which make official justice a gamble and a marvel, a mystery rather than a remedy.

II THE CRITERIA FOR SANTAL JUSTICE

If the administration of justice is to satisfy Santal needs it is obvious that it must embody certain standards. It should not run counter to Santal values—unless these are patently against the public interest or policy. It should not impose a complicated—mechanism of trial if a simpler alternative exists. It should make the fullest possible use of indigenous agencies so that to the tribe itself justice may seem not merely a figment of alien invention but a function of Santals themselves. Are any adjustments or conventions possible so that current administration may approximate to this deal?

III SANTALS AND THE POLICE

We have seen that until 1943, police work in much of the Santal Parganas was managed almost entirely without the police. The 'Police Sub-Inspectors' were sardars and parganas and apart from staffing police stations in the Deoghar Subdivision and in the zamindari tracts of the Pakaur, Rajmahal and Godda Subdivision's regular police officers were employed only for advice and supervision. After 1930 the growth of dacoities and burglaries in Dumka and Jamtara (mainly as a result of incursions from other districts) compelled Government to abandon this indigenous system and police stations have now been established in all parts of the district except the Damin. In the latter areas, a small staff headed by three Santal Inspectors of Police has been posted to assist the Santal headmen and parganas. The extension of police stations had certain obvious advantages. It has enabled large scale crimes to be combated effectively (though it is noteworthy that it did not prevent a severe outbreak of dacoity in 1944). It has led to the apprehension of many dacoits and burglars and by establishing police stations in outlying areas, it has given the Deputy Commissioner sufficient striking forces with which to maintain order and security if and when they are threatened. But in other respects the development has been very far from salutary. It has subjected many areas to the petty tyranny of 'dacoits in uniform', as police Sub-Inspectors are sometimes termed. It has brought in an outsider staff new to the district, ignorant of Santal ways and innocent of their language. It has violently infected some areas with police methods which were never known before.

In a case which occurred in 1945 an Assistant Sub-Inspector and some constables visited a village close to Dumka, seized and bound some of the villagers, suspended them head downwards from a beam and then mercilessly beat the soles of their feet. One of the villagers who was a Santal was so wounded and humiliated that he threw himself down a well while another, a Bhuiya committed suicide by hanging himself from a tree. Other instances of harassment to parties have been alleged whereas complaints of this nature against sardars and parganas were previously very rare. Moreover, through their ignorance of Santal criminal law, and an 'over-departmental' view of the Indian Penal Code, friction between the two laws which previously was notably absent is now developing. In 1945 some Santals were arrested by a Sub-Inspector for having shot and consumed a pig. The pig had grazed a crop and all of them had acted strictly in accordance with Santal custom. In fact they had taken the carcase to the manjhi and with full village approval the pig had been duly consumed. The sub-inspector, knowing nothing of this custom, charged the men with theft, sent them to Dumka and they had already spent two months in jail before the trial opened and the facts in all their bleakness were revealed. It will be obvious that from a Santal standpoint these developments are disquieting but I have felt great difficulty in suggesting any feasible remedies. If part at least of the expansion of police stations was dictated by temporary exigencies, the position would be considerably improved by reducing the number of stations to a minimum and thus enlarging the area under each officer. The expediency of such solution would, however, obviously depend on wider considerations of internal security. Similarly the weaknesses of a stranger staff would be eradicated if more Santals were recruited as Assistant Sub-Inspectors and Sub-Inspectors. Tyranny due to ignorance of Santal life would then be avoided while investigation of Santal crime would not be handicapped by linguistic difficulties. The pig case would never have occurred if the officer had been a Santal. But beyond ensuring these obvious advantages Santal recruitment would do little more. It would not affect the impulse to aggrandisement for this is an aspect of a tradition rather than of individuals. When I once said to an exceptionally able Superintendent of Police that for a Santal Sub-Inspector to extort money from a Santal was, I felt, the last word in meanness, he said 'He would have no option. The other Sub-Inspectors would 'frame' him if he started discriminating.' It is not surprising therefore that among the various cases of police extortion which came to light in the last four years one Santal Sub-Inspector was charged with extorting money while another had made the lives of various villagers wretched by constant demands for fowls and eggs. When all the traditions of a system require its officers to act in this manner, vigilance by the Superintendent of Police and greater resolution by the public but not a change in recruitment may mitigate its harshness. If discomfort in tribal life is not to prevail two measures seem eminently, necessary. The first is to restrict the number of offences which the ordinary police may investigate and I will return to discuss this point immediately. The other is to maintain the no-police system in at least the fourth of the district where it still exists.

This system has been discussed by the Santal Parganas

Enquiry Committee in the following terms. 'The importance of maintaining intact the indigenous institutions of the district, their report says has already been stressed. Among these the parganaits in the Damin-i-Koh play a very important part. They were originally the tribal leaders of the Santals-settlers and have continued ever since to hold their position as heads of the community. They appear to have been recognised at an early date as fiscal heads of local areas. With the establishment of the Santal system they were recognised by Government and came to occupy a mixed position partly as leaders of the Santal community vested with social and tribunal functions and powers to decide disputes both civil and criminal partly as fiscal heads of the area who were responsible for looking after the collection of the revenue and settling down disputes; partly as police officials responsible to Government for maintaining law and order and for the reporting and investigation of crime. The parganait came to be the main channel of communication between the village community and the Hakim.

'The system is still necessary and well-suited to the requirements of the Damin-i-Koh where the vast majority of the population consist of aboriginals living in primitive conditions. The Santals are much attached to it and in time of trouble the parganaits are the people to whom they turn for guidance and leadership. We think that it would be a mistake either to abolish the system or to restrict the powers of, or to impair the position occupied by the parganaits, but we do consider that changes in the method of appointment and tenure of office are necessary. There is abundant evidence both official and non-official that the parganaits have not maintained their old traditions, and that the feeling of respect for them is diminishing. There is a growing volume of discontent and criticism against them in the Damin. This deterioration has been in progress for sometime and we think that it is partly due to a too strict adherence to the hereditary principle in appointing them. In theory the appointment of a parganait rests in the hands of the Subdivisional Officer and the Deputy Commissioner and the rules require that in making the appointment the wishes of the community should be ascertained. But the office is hereditary in origin and the rules prescribe that, if possible, the son should be appointed to succeed his father except in the case of a parganait dismissed for misconduct. In practice the son or the nearest relative of the last parganait is almost invariably appointed and the authorities have found it difficult to get rid of incompetent parganaits, because the rules provide for dismissal only for misconduct and not for incompetence. Strict adherence to the hereditary principle has been largely due to a reluctance on the part of the officials to interfere with old customs or to do anything which might impair the parganait's position in the community. But the parganaits have themselves in many cases gravely impaired their own position.

'We consider, therefore, that appointment to this office should no longer be either hereditary or for life and we make the following proposals :

(1) That appointment should be made by the combination of election and selection. Jamabandi raiyats of the bungalow should elect three persons, from whom the Subdivisional Officer would select one for appointment.

(2) Parganaits should hold office for seven years and should be eligible for re-appointment.

(3) Parganaits should be removable by the Subdivisional Officer for incompetence or for physical incapacity or for misconduct which includes neglect of duty, corruption and habitual drunkenness. An appeal would lie to the Deputy Commissioner.

(4) The existing parganaits should be required to vacate their offices by annual rotation extending over the next seven years and election should be held in one-seventh of the bungalows each year.

(5) Every parganait on appointment should undergo some elementary police training.

(6) Only Santal raiyats resident in the bungalow should be eligible for appointment as parganait'.[2]

This passage offers a balanced defence of long established arrangement and I will merely draw attention to some aspects of the system as I saw it in the last four years. Its main advantages are that it eliminates friction between the two laws and ensures that all Santal crime is investigated in a Santal manner. The work of the parganas is supervised by the Subdivisional Officer who in turn is assisted by officers of the regular police force. All these latter officers are Santals. The parganas are usually the first to receive information of whatever crimes are committed, they themselves investigate all minor offences and pass on major cases to the Santal Inspector of Police. Since each pargana is a cultivator first and a Sub-Inspector second, he has no interest in inventing or stimulating crime. Even if a 'bad' pargana extorts money a fairly low 'ceiling' is set on his rapacity, for Santals in the Damin do not hesitate to complain. Moreover although the Deputy Commissioner gives every support to the system, he holds no brief for individual parganas and one who became a gross tyrant would be quickly removed. Even from the point of view of major crime itself, figures which were collected in 1944 showed that crime was not only on a very small scale in the Damin but was under considerably better control than in the police tracts themselves.[3] In mixed areas outside the Damin 'the police yoke' is probably a necessity. Within the Damin regular police would merely be a source of friction and exploitation and like their predecessors in the nineteenth century might end by by provoking a Santal rebellion.[4]

IV THE TREATMENT OF MAJOR CRIMES

How then should different types of crime be investigated and tried? It will be obvious that for certain types of crime, the existing machinery of enquiry by the police and trial by magistrates is the only effective way of securing justice. The professional dacoit, the skilled house-breaker, the forger or cheat—these types of criminal require much more severe punishment than villagers can properly impose while for combating their forms of crime village defence parties can at most contribute one element in a complex scheme of detection and arrest. All cases, therefore, of dacoity, robbery, receiving stolen property, cheating, forgery and assaults with grievious hurt should continue to be investigated by the police and the accused tried in the official manner.

Besides these major crimes, certain types of theft are also of sufficient complexity to warrent enquiry by extra village agencies. Cattle theft, for example, is often very difficult for villagers to defect since the stolen cattle are usually at once removed from the neighbourhood. For such cases valuation is probably the best test. If the stolen property is worth twenty-five rupees or more the police should investigate the crime but if the value is less, indigenous justice should take its course.

In the case of homicide and murder, the gravity of the crime also requires an official enquiry and trial, but of only because of this gravity, more than ordinary case in investigation is essentially necessary. During my four years in the Santal Parganas police investigation in Santal murder cases was often disquietingly superficial. Time and time again the police prosecutor could find nothing in the case diaries to suggest a motive for the crime or even to make the murder intelligible to the Judge and the assessors. All he could do was to place the facts as the police had recorded them and leave the court to interpret them as it liked. These omissions were almost always due to ignorance of the tribal setting by the Investigating Officers, but their existence was obviously of grave significance to the accused.

Verrier Elwin has stressed these same difficulties in *Maria Murder and Suicide* and his remarks are so obviously relevant that I will quote them in full:

'The importance of anthropological knowledge for the proper evaluation of aboriginal crime hardly needs illustration. One of the most difficult things that a Court has to decide in a case of homicide is whether the deed that it is evaluating comes under any of the exceptions to section 300 of the I.P.C. Was the crime premeditated ? Was it provoked by a serious and unbearable insult ? The difficulty here, which every Sessions Judge admits, is that what seems an extreme provocation to him or the Assessors may hardly be noticed by the aboriginal, and incidents that seem quite trifling to the 'civilised' mind may rouse the Muria or Naga to a fit of homicidal rage. The matter is complicated by the fact that the tribes vary greatly from one to another. The Bison-horn Maria, for example are passionately concerned about female chastity, and a wife's infidelity is constantly a cause of murder. But in this their Gond and Baiga neighbours to the north have a much lower standard. Love is comparatively free. Divorce is easy and a wife's betrayal is readily compensated by small fines. It is obvious, therefore, that a Gond or Baiga who suspects his wife of infidelity is not put to any thing like the same degree of provocation as that suffered by a Bison-horn Maria under similar circumstances.

'Premeditation may be indicated by tribal customs. The Bison-horn Maria express the spirit of implacable revenge by certain dramatic symbols. They pull out their public hairs, they remove a few handfuls of grass froman enemy's roof; they whistle loudly the dreaded sui whistle. In any case where an accused is proved to have indulged in one or other of these acts it may be assumed that his crime was premeditated.

'A Bastar tragedy, the murder of Tati Hirme by her deceased husband's younger brother Doga, provides an interesting example of how a knowledge of local custom can explain an otherwise meaningless crime. According to tribal practice a younger brother has a right over his elder brother's widow, a right which extends not only to her person, but to her property. This right Tati Hirme refused to Doga, and there is evidence that for a long time the youth bitterly resented her behaviour. On the day of the tragedy he went to her house and asked her for some tobacco. She refused and he murdered her.

'At first sight there is precisely one of those motiveless crimes which have so often puzzled outside observers. It is true that there was hostility between the parties but the refusal of a small gift of tobacco was hardly sufficient for so disastrous a result. But in Maria practice to ask a woman for tobacco is a symbolic way of inviting her to sexual intercourse, and when the boy asked his elder brother's widow to have congress with him, he was only demanding his right and when she refused it, he found the provocation, both to his pride and desire, so great that he killed her.

'Research both by medical science and by anthropology may in time reveal how far the apparently motiveless homicides of aboriginals can be explained as crimes of exhaustion and fatigue. Again and again a man kills his loved wife in a sudden explosion of temper and for no apparent cause. It is probable that in many cases the real reason is not alcoholic intoxication, but extreme fatigue.

'A point that often troubles the courts is the time element in cases where provocation is pleaded as an excuse. It is often found that there is a lapse of some hours between the actual incident that gave provocation and the subsequent act of violence. It has too often been held that this lapse of time should deprive the accused of gaining the benefit from exception of section 300 of the Indian Penal Code. But there can be little doubt that an aboriginal's intelligence does not work so quickly as that of a more sophisticated person, but even in matters of everyday life it often takes an appreciable time for an idea to take root and effect a result in his mind. Laubscher's analysis of the psychology of the Tembu Negroes of South Africa is of some importance here.[5] 'The Tembu' he says, 'is not by nature blood-thirsty, but his aggressive instinctive or pugnacious propensities are excitable, easily roused and explosive. His aggressive libido flows outwards, becomes readily externalized, and sudden impulsive assaults, often fatal, are not uncommon. Careful study of the emotional reactions of the participants in stick fights, of course, initially playfully performed for my benefit, has shown me how quickly and explosively the native loses his temper and retaliates with death dealing blows at his opponent. Fatal blows are only avoided by the defensive skill of the opponent. Aggressive impulses are quickly evoked although there is no apparent bad feeling after such a stick fight. I came to the conclusion that once an emotional impulse is aroused and the stimulus continues to be present, the native just drifts along with the impulse and exercises little or any inhibitory power, unless this inhibition is brought about by the evocation of another impulse, opposite in aim to the first, such as a fear of consequences, but it must be fear stimulated by something present at the moment. Resultingly, the intellectual machanisms of foresight, judgment and self-control are readily submerged by the instinctive impulse'.[6]

In the Santal murder cases recorded by S.M. Naqavi there are a number of examples which illustrate this need for exact tribal knowledge.

'In two cases husbands caught their wives having intercourse with lovers.

'Padam Tudu an old man of 60 years, had gone to Chandna market with his wife, Luksi Marandi. Luksi left the market earlier and when Padam reached home he found her having intercourse with a man in the darkness of the village lane. The man ran away and Luksi declined to say who he was. This enraged the old man and he killed her.

'In another case Jitu Hansdak' caught his wife Barki Soren in the act of intercourse with a man in his house. He could not see who the man was and Barki also did not give out his name. They had a quarrel but that night he did nothing. The next day he took her to her father's house but on the way they again quarreled. Barki called Jitu bastard and an idiot. Jitu then killed her with a dao which he had brought with him in clothes.

'In both the cases' S.M. Naqavi observes, 'it was less the detection of the act than the refusal of the wife to disclose the lover's name that led to the murders. If the name had been disclosed the husband would have had his remedy in the village council. He could have demanded twice the marriage money (pon). But in the absence of the name his remedy was gone. He was confronted with infidelity and could do nothing about it. It was the inability to adjust the matter in the tribal way that caused the murders'.[7]

In the second case there can be little doubt that the use of the very provoking term (bastard) also contributed to the murder.

I do not think that any radical changes in Santal procedure are feasible but at least three safeguards are desirable. Wherever possible the investigating officer should know Santali and just as parganas record their case diaries in that language, the ordinary police when investigating Santal murder should record all statements fully and record them in Santali. This will ensure that small points which in their tribal setting may prove of great significance are not entirely ignored or omitted altogether. secondly the Superintendent of Police while supervising the investigation should direct his attention specifically to the task of making the crime intelligible and deciding how far it actually falls under Section 302 of the Indian Penal Code. A case which if fully understood is actually an offence under Section 326 or 304 should never be presented to the court as if it were a crime under Section 302 for to do this is expressly to invite injustice.

Finally before a charge sheet is ordered the case diary with the note of the Superintendent of Police should preferably be examined by the Deputy Commissioner and also by the Public Prosecutor. If the case is still not fully intelligible, further investigation might then be made and the services of a Santali speaking Magistrate could also be utilised if necessary. When everything relevant is known the appropriate section should be decided and only then should the case be sent for trial.

V MINOR AND OTHER CRIME

Another category of offences consists of petty thefts, hurt, mischief, grazing, trespass, insults, public misconduct and defamation-matters which are offences equally under the I.P.C. and tribal law and which Santals habitually deal with in their village councils. It is obviously desirable that this type of local justice should continue. For cases of petty thefts, for example, a summary search of the suspect or his house, a conviction by a village meeting, the return of the stolen property to its owner, the exaction of a fine as punishment—these are for more consonant with essential justice than the elaborate machinery of the courts. Similarly for simple hurt or cattle grazing or mischief, the summary infliction of a fine and the prompt award of compensation go further to restore order and repair damage than a series of exhausting journeys to a remote magistrate and the expenditure of money the lawyer's fees and petty costs. Moreover the appropriation of the fine by the villagers themselves associates them with the processes of justice and actively interests them in the maintenance of rights. All offences therefore, under Section 379 (when the value of the property is less than twenty-five rupees), 323, 352, 426, 447, 448, 500, 504, 509 and 510 I.P.C. should continue to be tried by the villagers subject to the ordinary tribal rule of appeal to the parganas and five manjhis, while if a complaint under these sections is filed in court, it should normally be sent back to the pargana for decision in a tribal way.

There remains one last category—the type of incident for which the Indian Penal Code provides a penalty, often a severe penalty while, according to Santal law; the matter is either no offence at all or is a matter of civil adjustment. As I have described in Chapter 2, these 'offences' rarely come before the police or in the courts and are almost always dealt with in the tribal way. The fact, however, that as the law stands they could be brought to court if a party so elected makes it desirable that certain conventions should regulate their treatment. Of the portions of the I.P.C. which are thus involved offences under Sections 341, 342, 354, 363, 366, 366A, 368 and 76 are cognizable by the police while the remainder, under Sections 312-16, 318, 494, 495, 497 and 498 are cognizable on complaint to a magistrate. Of these cases only rape could be termed a major crime and even within rape only those types which involve the use of savage violence, the infliction of lacerated injuries or a consequential loss of caste call for severe punishment. In other types, tribal adjustment is greatly to be preferred for it compensates the outraged girl, it sufficiently penalises the culprit and it avoids the harassment and degradation of an official hearing. In all these cases, therefore, investigation by police should preferably be excluded by a standing order. If a case is reported to a Police officer he should enter it in his station diary and send a copy to the Subdivisional Officer. The latter should then depute a Magistrate for a local enquiry and if all the Santals desire a solution in the tribal manner this should normally be approved. Only if the case involves an outrage on a Santal by a Diku or contains features of special brutality should the offence be brought to court.

Similarly in cases where a direct complaint is filed the matter should preferably be referred at once to the pargana and his council of five manjhis for decision and settlement and only when the tribal agency has been tried and has failed or when the case has special difficulties should the Indian Penal Code itself be invoked and the case tried out in court. The Code in fact should be held in reserve to support tribal justice rather than supplant it.[8]

As a corollary of these conventions, it would be advantageous if an earlier practice in the district were now to be revived. Under this practice a complaint by a Santal was treated only as a statement of facts and the court itself decided what section was appropriate. If, for example, the complaint had not been investigated by the village or the pargana, a reference to either of these authorities was made with a view to securing a speedy local settlement. If the root of the trouble was the inheritance of land the petition was treated as a plaint and either sent for tribal arbitration or decided by the court as a civil suit. It is desirable that this should again become the recognised convention and that magisterial action should aim at the liquidation of the grievance. Tribal agencies would then be fully explored first and only if these failed to end the trouble the court would impose an official remedy. With the new Santal Civil Rule 26 which enables the Subdivisional Officer to confirm the award of pargana's council and give it the effect of a decree there is now no reason why all civil disputes between Santals should not be ended in a tribal manner.

VI APPLICATION FOR MAINTENANCE

What should be the approach to applications for maintenances under section 488 of the Criminal Procedure Code ?

Here also it is desirable that the whole situation should be examined in the light of Santal law. If a husband is not maintaining his wife because of a quarrel, friction or misunderstanding, an order under this section is unlikely to make matters any better. The routine award of five rupees a month will almost always be far in excess of what the husband can pay. He will invariably default and after once experiencing the difficulties of realising the maintenance through court even the woman herself will abandon the attempt to enforce her rights. If the petition concerns a child, it is the clarification of paternity which is nearly always the fundamental issue.

It is obviously more sensible to consider how best to solve the matter permanently than to treat the application in a legalistic manner. Here also, therefore, the petition should be treated primarily as the ventilation of a grievance, the tribal machinery should be set in motion and only if the other side is recalcitrant or the Santal council fails, should the Criminal Procedure Code be inviked to impose a solution.

VII THE TREATMENT OF WITCHCRAFT

What should be the magisterial approach to witchcraft? We have seen that in the decade 1931-40 only 16 witches were murdered and it is obvious that witchcraft is no longer the serious administrative problem which it was a century ago. Now-a-days it is rare for witches to suffer even grievous hurt and it is rarer still for such cases to be brought to court. What are slightly more common are petitions alleging that injury has been threatened because the complainant is a witch and requesting a court to give protection.

The difficulty in such cases is that beating is often an essential part of the Santal curative process. The witch clings to her secret as long as she can. She is beaten. The beating forces her secret from her and the whole machinery of restoration is set in motion. Without her confession, without her naming of the bongas and the prescription of sacrifices, the sick-man would have no hope. He would sense his own doom and collapse in despair. 'No reasoning with them, nor ridicule can dissuade them of their belief in witches'. Where logic fails, violence at least is comprehensible.

It is this attitude which accounts for the dismay with which Kolean Haram viewed certain earlier decisions by the courts. 'The Englishmen' he said 'decide all matters well but why they are misled concerning witches, that we do not understand. The witches eat us and when we catch and belabour them, the Hakims send us to jail. Why, we do not understand. We do not know how good can come. We are puzzled what to do. Even when we explain things to the Hakims they do not believe us. They say, "if she is a witch, let her eat my fingers. Then I shall believe". But the witches can not do this, so they send us to jail. Witches do not kill with knives and pots. They send people to the other world through their inner powers. In olden times the manjhi and paranik used to control them and if a witch did not mend her ways the village five would drive her from the village in disgrace. But the days these Hakims have let them loose and all of us have hung our tails'.[9]

So long as witchcraft, therefore, is regarded by Santals as a cause of disease and the witch herself as the main agency of cure, beating will obviously remain a necessary remedy and official injunctions against violence will seem merely capricious acts of alien authority.

Can anything be hoped from education? Verrier Elwin has considered this possibility in the account of crime in Bastar, but has reached a pessimistic conclusion. 'It is sometimes debated' in Bastar 'he has said' whether anything can be done to wean the Maria from violence. I doubt it. For example, an important cause of murder is fear of witchcraft and magic. Eliminate this fear and the number of murders will decrease. But the belief in witchcraft can only be removed by education. And how is the Maria to receive this kind of education that will achieve this end ? Even if schools were opened all over southern Bastar, they would only be little village schools which would teach up to an elementary standard and be staffed by school masters, themselves semi-educated. In the last ten years I have had a wide experience of village school masters, and I do not know a single one who does not believe in magic and witchcraft as firmly as any aboriginal. Those acquainted with the small towns of Central India will agree that even university graduates and men holding responsible positions in Government service are equally affected by the belief. Education in fact, would do nothing to lessen the fear of witchcraft. It might, on the other hand, stimulate other kinds of crime. Not a few educated aboriginals take to blackmail, impersonation and cheating once they have gained the power that literacy gives them. This account applies with equal force to the Santal Parganas.

If there is little hope from education, are any measures possible within the framework of witchcraft itself?

In this connection T.B. Creagh Coen has recorded the results of some interesting experiments in the Dangs, a minor state to the north of Bombay.

'When some one falls seriously ill and a spell is suspected the procedure is to get a Bhagat to hold what is known as Bhagati or investigation. This consists in his accepting some offerings—grains, a goat and drink are usual—and then going into trance. In trance, the Bhagat reveals the name of the witch, or a description of her house.

'After the name of the witch has been revealed the next step is to compel her to remove the spell. This is done in a highly direct and practical manner by tying her upside down and beating her within an inch of her life, until she confesses that she is a witch and promises to remove the spell by counter-magic. It is well known that this is not permitted in the Dangs. There is a standing order on witchcraft forbidding it; and enquiries which I made suggest that in fact grave cruelty of this kind does not now-a-days occur here. The Dangis being an obedient folk. It does, however, occur in Khandesh, and Mr. Masood tells me that witches are often cruelly beaten there; and I am inclined to suspect that minor bullying goes on, even in the Dangs. The fact that we do not allow what is considered the proper treatment is, however, well known, and a grievance'.

'I learned from the Dewan afterwards, though no chief mentioned this—and I suspect that the system which I am about to explain does not work quite so efficiently and universally as the Dewan suggested—that a remarkable variant to beating has been devised, somewhat as we have in Dera Ghazi Khan (unlike Baluchistan) largely taught the Biloches to report adulterers to the Girga for fine compensation and imprisonment instead of killing them. This variant consists in reporting the witch to the Dewan. The complainant first gets the Dewan's permission to hold a *bhagtai*, which he gives on condition that there is no beating. The *bhagtai* is then carried out up to the revelation of the witch's name. The complainant then comes and tells it to the Dewan; the mere fact that it is 'out' is often to stop the mischief. If the patient does not at once recover the Dewan sends for the witch and severely warns her to remove her spell. This always works, he says: but I am sure the people feel that it is a pale second best to a good lambasting'.

'One of the doctors tells me that very occasionally, witches are reported to him instead of to the Dewan and he has had two such cases in two and half years. The Dewan gets about two cases a month. I understand that complaints to the Dewan are usually sent in, not direct, but through the local Forest Ranger.

'Clearly we have here a problem not only in administration but in psychology. It is not merely a question of saving a few old women from being ill treated, but of gradually teaching the Dangis to adopt scientific medicine. So long as they attribute all illness to magic, they will not use our doctors; and I am convinced that it is worse than unless simply to drum it into them that there in no such thing as witchcraft, and even if it were true (which is highly doubtful) that these magical performances have never any basis in fact. They will not believe us, but they will receive a further blow to their self respect and pride in their own customs, which will merely be driven underground.

'An essential element in our approach to the problem must be acceptance of the Dangi's point of view towards magic; and our aim should be to devise some substitute for torture which could satisfy their belief and wishes'.

T.B. Creagh Coen then goes on to suggest that 'on the analogy of the scapegoat, we might induce them to beat an image of the witch instead of women, again we might also get subsidised Government Bhagats to say that, infact, there was no witchcraft involved, when called in'.[10]

These suggestions are important less for their intrinsic worth—for a Bhagat who never diagnosed a witch would be liable to early discredit while to beat a scape goat would have to be demonstrably effective before any tribe would adopt it. Their importance lies rather in the eminent commonsense of their approach and the identification of the Government with the minds of the tribesmen.

By a curious coincidence an experiment of a not dissimilar type seems to have been carried out in the Santal Parganas itself.

'Although punishment never seemed to have a very great affect in stopping witch finders; Man records 'yet a certain Assistant Commissioner found a great deal of use in an electrifying machine. If a parent or husband would come up and confidentially ask his advice, with regard to a daughter or wife charged with witchcraft, this 'lighting case' or devil's box' was brought out with great awe by the servants who had been often experimented on, and the girl, toed to hold the handles. When the wheel was turned no result would take place, and, therefore, she was considered quite correct but on the same ordeal being put to the questioners, they generally used to dance for half an hour, a practical proof which would stay any further belief in the girl's guilt and procure the witch finder condign punishment. It was ludicrous to see the awe the box was held in and the careful manner with which the servants used to carry it about to catch lighting. They used to be convinced that it wanted a supply from heaven periodically to ensure its safe action and their delight consisted in seeing it used with full power on'.

It is easy to scoff at such an expedient and dismiss it as absurd. Yet we should not lightly ignore its underlying approach. What is significant in the experiment is its insistence on the crucial role of the witch finder, for obviously witches continue to exist partly because jan gurus continue to discover them. If jan gurus could be increasingly discredited—so far at least as the diagnosis of witches was concerned—fewer witches would be brought to light and belief on their omnipresent malevolence would be correspondingly weakened. If the prevalence of witchcraft among the Santals is to be reduced only equally irrational devices are likely to have any success.

When witchcraft cases come to court, I suggest the following approach. As far as possible the solution should be sought in the tribe itself. There is little point in holding a trial as this merely places the magistracy in a false position and exposes its decisions to the charge of gross injustice. It is better if such cases are referred at once to the pargana and council of five manjhis. The village council itself will have taken action already and it is, therefore, desirable that a higher court should intervene. The five manjhis should then investigate the circumstances and take whatever tribal steps are necessary for having the incident closed. If village discipline has patently exceeded all acceptable limits they will themselves imflict some tribal punishment on the assailant while if they are satisfied that the woman herself is to blame they will see that remedial steps are taken.

It is true that this convention if adopted would not attack the larger problem but that I believe is a matter which only a mental revolution on a province-wide scale is likely to accomplish. For the present we shall have gained something if official action avoids conflict with Santal views of justice and no longer masquerades as alien whim.

VIII THE EFFECTS OF IMPRISONMENT

How far is imprisonment an actual punishment at all for Santals? As we have seen, it is only Santal women who are debarred from eating food cooked by non-Santals, while in case of men, it is only a few castes whose touch defiles their food. Since a jail usually contains a variety of castes and food is invariably cooked by some one who is comparatively pure, Santal male convicts can normally take jail food with impunity. When they complete their sentences and return home, they are, therefore, not outcasted and in fact they are normally exposed to no tribal penalties whatever. Even a Santal who has committed murder and served a sentence of transportation regains his customary place as soon as he returns and without any feasts or sacrifices he is allowed quietly to resume his daily routine in the village.

In the case of Santals sentenced to imprisonment, loss of tribal society, dancing and festivals, the break with the home, the lack of rice beer, the enforced abstention from sex—all these deprivations undoubtedly constitute a punishment but only, I think, over the long period. For any period short of a year, a Santal is not, I think, unduly perturbed by jail.

It is true that the Diku jail staff invariably treats him as a harijan and he is normally compelled to clean latrines by way of rigorous imprisonment. But he does not have to work hard in jail as he would often be obliged in his village. Jail food is never less than what he would get at home and it is often much better. Compared with bitlaha or even with pante begar—forms of tribal action which stress a culprit's guilt and make him feel a criminal, imprisonment for a short period is hardly a punishment at all.

It is rather the offender's household which is punished by

his term in prison. Often there is no one left to plough the fields or supervise the cultivation and even if there are others the loss of one man's labour may well result in much less food in the ensuing year. While the offender eats in jail, his wife and children starve at home. It is for this reason that in many cases a summary beating by the villagers is often a more essentially just punishment than detention in prison.

IX BITLAHA

Experiments in suppression

Finally, there is the problem of bitlaha. During the last ten years various persons have favoured the suppression of this ceremony as a savage and nauseating practice abhorrent to civilized men. Experiments were, therefore, made largely in 1941 and 1942 and again in 1945 to give protection to persons about to be bitlahaed and as far as possible to suppress the practice. What is significant is that all these attempts failed.

In Khandahar in 1941, a Brahmin Dukhi Choubey, stood as custodian for the cattle of a Santal whose son was evading arrest. Very unwisely he kept the animals with the Santal's father who sometime later sold them. The absconding Santal then returned and Dukhi Choubey and his son caught him. In the struggle, the Santal's mother intervened and was pushed and handled. The next day out of anger at his son's arrest the father gave out that Dukhi Choubey had caught the breasts of his wife. A council met in January 1942 but did not hold the charges proved. They demanded, however, from Dukhi Choubey one rupee and eight annas as the costs of the sitting. Dukhi Choubey refused to pay and the next day Santal's father took out a branch in Bhagaya, Boarijore and Mandro markets. The Brahmin's son brought the news to the police and on the day of bitlaha the Subdivisional Officer and an armed force went to the Bazar. Attempts were made to stop the crowd from pouring in but all of these were useless and Santals in enormous numbers assembled. The Subdivisional Officer made the tactical error of detaining the Santal who had taken out the branch, while attempts at persuading the crowd to disperse went on. Suddenly at 3.30 p.m. the crowd rushed at

Dukhi Choubey's house and set on it. Tiles were smashed, floors were dug up, the door frames taken out, two palanquins were wrecked, pitchers broken and the 'devithan' defiled. A few places were set on fire and there was widespread urination and defecation. The Subdivisional Officer ordered the crowd to stop. No one listened, but some began to shoot arrows and throw bricks while others began to rush at the police. As it looked as if the party might] be overwhelmed the Subdivisional Officer ordered firing, first with buck shot and then four rounds of ball. Two in the crowd were hit and with the firing the crowd went slowly away.

In this case although the magistrate took armed police with him, their presence in no way deterred the Santals. The bitlaha was done and the only difference was that the houses were wrecked as well.

In Shyampur Dukhu Murmu began to live with Sande Murmu, a widow of his own sept. The village separated them but the man again came to the woman's house. Then the five manjhis intervened and a bitlaha was ordered for June 18, 1942. The Subdivisional Officer of Pakaur intervened and on June 17 imposed a settlement. He made the Santal give some rice and chura, two goats and two rupees and agree to give the woman up. But the next day about two thousand Santals from the Damin arrived for the bitlaha. They went to the village, were stopped and were told that the matter was finished. They became very angry at this breach of tribal procedure, danced the dunger dance outside the village and went back saying they would do bitlaha to the village. Nothing happened for some months but the matter smouldered on. Finally, the manjhi of Shyampur informed the Subdivisional Officer that he must do the bitlaha as the Santals of the Damin were still threatening the whole village. By this time another Subdivisional Officer had taken charge and the matter ended with an orderly bitlaha of the two offenders. In this case, the attempt to stifle the bitlaha by imposing a solution ended in failure. The Santals went back for the moment but they did not abandon their intention and although it took a year, a bitlaha had ultimately to be allowed.

In another case from Pakuria Police Station, the manjhi of Dumgi Baromasia announced a bitlaha for October, 1944.

The Sub-Inspector of police for some reason decided to stop it. He compelled the manjhi and the villagers to go to the police station on October 21 and kept them there the whole of the next day. Meanwhile the crowd began to gather and were greatly enraged when they found the manjhi absent. 'Why has he gone to the thana ? It is he who invited us. The village street is the meeting place, not the police station ? They were told that the Sub-Inspector had compelled the manjhi to go. 'Then you must punish the Sub-Inspector'. Ultimately the Sub-Inspector returned with the village people, abandoned his attempt at banning and a peaceful bitlaha took place.

Finally, the difficulties of suppression are illustrated by a bitlaha which occurred, in November 1945, in Barakiar in the Pakaur subdivision. Three Mohammadans of that village were adjudged by a Santal council to have persisted in relations with three Santal women. The manjhi informed the Sub-divisional Officer that bitlaha was proposed and thinking that only Santals were involved, he permitted the bitlaha and fixed a date. After the notice had gone out, it was suddenly realised that the date fixed fell on the third day of Bakar Id and that bitlaha of Mohammadans was also proposed. Thinking that bitlaha of Mohammadans was against custom, and not knowing that in Pakaur Subdivision a branch cannot be recalled, the Subdivisional Officer issued orderes under section 144 of the Criminal Procedure Code forbidding the bitlaha until further orders. After much argument he induced the local Santal officials to accept this decision but the problem of the surrounding people remained. The village manjhi said that as the branch had gone out, villagers from far and near would arrive and that in view of the orders forbidding bitlaha on the Mohammadans it was likely that he himself would be bitlahaed in their stead. Realising therefore that his order was unlikely to be obeyed, the Subdivisional Officer took another magistrate and a small police force. He spent the night in parley with the local dihri while a crowd of ten thousand gathered. Then at dawn suddenly and without notice the crowd swept into the village and wrecked the six houses.

In this case the Sal branch proved an infinitely stronger command than the order under section 144. The latter on the contrary seems merely to have enraged the crowd and contributed to the wrecking. The presence of a magistrate neither stopped the bitlaha nor prevented its violence. Police were present but from the topography of the village and the size of the crowd even a company of soldiers might not have prevented the houses from being overwhelmed.

X PROSECUTION

But besides the employment of force to check bitlaha, a number of prosecutions were also tried, and various Santals were convicted and sent to jail. It is true that in a few places prosecutions have undoubtedly had the effect of paralysing action. When I was camping at Durgapur in 1943, a Santal was openly living with a woman of his own sept. I asked the deshmanjhi why they had not bitlahaed them and he replied 'Government have forbidden it. Bitlahas are our life, our blood. If we do not do bitlaha, the whole tribe will be spoilt. It is by bitlaha only that we keep our ways. But Government have forbidden it and from fear we are doing nothing'.

But here also what is of more significance is that among Santals as a whole, the tribal, will to perform the ceremony has been entirely unaffected and in fact the Barakiari bitlaha is only the last of many bitlahas all of which reflect the Santal determination to protect their tribal integrity. Indeed far from suppressing bitlahas the prosecutions seem merely to have increased the will to do them and to have spread bitterness and disillusion. At Chorkata the Santals said, 'Wherever Dikus have taken our caste we have done bitlaha to them. But now the Hakims are siding with the Dikus and even when we follow custom they punish us. A Teli boy had intercourse with a Santal girl. The village found them guilty. They referred it to the manjhis' council. The council ordered their bitlaha. They hung a bullock's leg in the Teli's house and danced the dungar in his courtyard. Then the Teli brought a case and the Hakim fined the manjhi, jogmanjhi, the dihri and the leaders. *They had done nothing beyond custom.*

It may safely be assumed, therefore, that if the custom is now to be suppressed, force on a much greater scale than has neither been tried will have to be deployed. A number of massacres may be necessary—for it is doubtful whether even if the Santals are shot they will abandon the ceremony. Such firings will inevitably accentuate bitterness and will expose the Government of the day to bitter tribal criticism.

Before such a step is advocated we should examine how far the problem warrants such an extreme solution and whether any alternatives are possible.

XI ASPECTS OF BITLAHA

At the 1941 census, there were 793, 830 Santals in the Santal Parganas. Figures for bitlahas have never been systematically recorded but it is unlikely that bitlahas in which both the parties were Santals have been less than five or more than fifteen in any single year. Figures for the bitlahas of Dikus in the last 25 years were ascertained in 1940 and I am giving below a statement of bitlahas in which one of the parties was either a Hindu or a Muslim, I have omitted six bitlahas in which full details could not be ascertained and have also excluded all bitlahas in which one of the parties was a non-Santal but an aboriginal or semi-aboriginal.

It is possible that a few more Diku bitlahas may have happened and these have escaped record. But the table is in the main a correct index to the scale of the practice.

Of these Diku bitlahas, five resulted in damage to houses and property. The remainder involved the defilement of courtyards but no other damage. It is clear, therefore, that even allowing for the destruction of property in five cases the practice as a whole is not a major threat to law and order.

There is another important aspect of the custom. When Hindu-Muslim tension reaches breaking point, the communal riot which succeeds is liable to be an orgy of aimless violence, directed at all the opposite community. In a bitlaha on the other hand the attentions of the crowd are aimed only at the guilty parties. Even when bitlaha is directed against a Diku, it is only the particular Diku whose house is visited. However, much an incident may have fanned Santal resentment and awoken communal hostility, the ceremony has so far never resulted in any thing resembling a communal riot. Even when houses were damaged as at Barakiari, dwellings of the Santals suffered equally with the Dikus and only the houses of the offenders were harmed. The Barakiari bitlaha occurred in the area which saw the start of the Santal rebellion and only a few months after Muslim attitudes in the neighbouring district of Rajshahi had led to a Santal—Muslim clash. Even then, there was no anti-Muslim riot.

We must bear in mind, therefore, that when in rare cases the custom has been exceeded there was control and discipline even in the excess.

Yet another point is deserving of emphasis. In almost all the cases which resulted in damage to property, the immediate antecedents were such as to have strained Santal patience to the limit. In reporting in 1936 on the violent bitlaha at Lohandia the Deputy Commissioner, Rai Bahadur S.C. Mukherji wrote:

'From enquiries at various places, I am satisfied that the trouble is due to the misconduct of the Dikus of Bazars in and adjoining the Damin in their treatment towards the Santals. It will be seen that so far as the observance of 'bitlaha' at Pathargama in Mahabir Bhagat's house is concerned, the Santals of Madhuchak had a legitimate grievance. Mahabir Bhagat's son carried on an illicit intrigue with Mangal Manjhi's daughter and it was only just and proper for him to pay the amount of fine which the Santal panchayat imposed on Mangal Manjhi for the Santal feast to take back Mangal Manjhi and his daughter into the Santal community. At Lohandia Bazar, the Dikus particularly the Bhagats adopted a clever method to have the Santal girls in their clutches. They were paying 6 pice as daily wages to a male Santal labourer and eight annas as daily wage to a Santal female labourer. The reason is obvious. They wanted to attract the female folk of the Santals and drive away the male folk from labour. This was going on apparently for a pretty long time. At Siripur Bazar also it was reported that a Mohammadan was carrying on a liaison with a Santal girl for a pretty long time. The Santals were forced, therefore, to take the law into their hands. It is unfortunate that this was not looked into carefully and the grievances of the Santals redressed in time to admit of the

TABLE : Bitlahas (1920-45)

Approximate year	Sub-divisions	Thana or Bungalow	Details of parties	
			Name	Residence
1920	Pakaur	Bw. Dumaria	Girl : Duli Tudu	Patrapara
			Boy : Darbari Mandal	-do-
1920	Dumka	Th. Ramgarh	Girl : Phulia Hansdak	Khutana
			Boy : Nitai Das	-do-
1921	Pakaur	Bw. Surajhara	Girl : Gaura Tudu	Gondo Parta
			Boy : Ratu Rai	-do-
1922	Dumka	Th. Raniswar	Girl : Lego Kisku	Sijua
			Boy : Roghubir Pande	-do-
1925	Pakaur	Th. Maheshpur	Girl : Mati Soren	Naraingarh
			Boy : Durga Charan Napit	-do-
1930	Jamtara	Th. Kundohit	Girl : Pendo Santalin	Saluka
			Boy : Kandarp Majhi	-do-
1933	Godda	Th. Mahawan	Girl : Wife of Phudan Marandi	Mohanpur
			Boy : Dinu Mian	-do-
1934	Rajmahal	Bw. Mandro	Girl : Champo Murmu	Borkhuri
			Boy : Kadir Mian	-do-
1935	Godda	Th. Godda	Girl : Wife of Bhator Soren	Gangarampur
			Boy : Bhaga Kabar	-do-
1935	Dumka	Th. Ramgarh	Girl : Chita Soran	Rajadih
			Boy : Parsadi Roi	-do-
1936	Godda	Th. Simra. III	Girl : Rani Manjhiain	Lohandia
			Boy : Ramrit Bhagat	-do-

1936	Rajmahal	Th. Rajmahal	Girl : Pano Santalin	Nakti
			Boy : Ratorna Mian	-do-
1938	Dumka	Th. Sarajyahat	Girl : Churki Tudu	Kamardih
			Boy : Isri Sao	-do-
1940	Dumka	Th. Raneswar	Girl : Rani Manjhiain	Sijua
			Boy : Sanichara Dhobi	-do-
1945	Dumka	Th. Jarmundi	Girl : Daughter of Lodo Manjhi	Lebda
			Boy : Kesar Mandel	Chiknia
1945	Pakaur	Th. Maheshpur	Girl : Lakhi Tudu	Barakiari
			Boy : Sujat Ali Mandal	-do-
			Girl : Moni Tudu	-do-
			Boy : Israil Mandal	-do-
			Girl : Durgi Tudu	-do-
			Boy : Hujru Mian	-do-

situation gradually developing into its present state. The Santals are ordinarily playful. But once they come to have a legitimate grievance they proceed to redress the grievance regardless of the consequences. A real Santal officer is he who can proceed to the spot, talk with them for hours, get at the facts and then redress their grievances. If the method which Babu Nageswar Prosad adopted in dealing with the situation at Pathargama had been adopted in dealing with similar such instances of 'Bitlaha' which had occurred before, there would have been no occasion to deal with a situation like the present one.'

In the cases which led to the destruction of Muslim houses the 'predatory' attitude of rural Muslims towards Santal women and their tendency to regard molestation as a Muslim right undoubtedly provoked some, at least of the damage.

Again, before the custom is condemned outright it is necessary to evaluate its main achievement. As early as 1871, Dalton noted 'Santal women are represented by all who have written about them as extraordinarily chaste'.[11] I have already stressed the great value, even the excessive value which Santals attach to their tribal integrity and the corresponding dismay with which they view attempts by strangers to pollute their racial stock. Up to the present Santals have succeeded in asserting this value to a remarkable degree. If the custom requires any defence therefore its justification will be found precisely in the fact that through its existence Santals in the Santal Parganas have maintained their dignity and self-respect.

Moreover a comparison of the Santal custom of bitlaha with the plight of the parallel tribe of Mundas is not uninstructive. If the Mundas ever practised bitlaha the institution seems now to have decayed. But the result is not indifference but disorder.

In March 1936, the Mundas of Tapkara in the Torpa police station of Ranchi discovered that a Munda widow was living with a Mohammadan, Subab Khan. The widow's son found the Mohammadan sleeping with her, snatched a blanket from him and drove him from the house. The next morning, Subab Khan was called before a Munda council and admitted that the blanket was his, while the woman ran to her father's village and did not return for fifteen days. The day following her return, Subab Khan was dragged to a meeting of two hundred Mundas and after being roughly handled he again admitted that the blanket was his. He was told to pay Rs. 200 as a fine because he had made the woman lose her caste, but he said he could not give this money. The woman was then brought and after stripping her naked, the Mundas placed her on the ground with her legs apart. Pig's fat was then poured out and rubbed in her private parts. Subab was then stripped. His head was forced between her thighs and he was made to lick the fact. When he had done so, the Mundas paraded them round the village, proclaiming that now they were married. Subab was then told to take charge of the woman and the two were left together in his house.

The value of bitlaha is that it substitutes symbols for action and a dance for an outrage.

Finally we would do well to ponder some remarks by Kolean Haram. 'Unlike Dikus' he says 'Santals do not get angry quickly but when their hearts are hurt, their anger knows no bound'.[12] To maintain bitlaha is to maintain Santal peace and order. To attempt its suppression is to invite the anarchy of revolt.

XII THE CONTROL OF BITLAHA

It is conceded that in the present state of Santal society, bitlaha is a necessity, what are the points to which criticism can reasonably be directed ?

It is obvious that in the vast majority of bitlahas the punishment lies in the humiliation rather than the damage. The cleaning of a courtyard, the replacement of a chulha—the cost of such damage can be calculted in annas only. At the same time a few bitlahas have undoubtedly led to much greater damage. At Barakiari the damage to six houses was estimated at fifteen hundred rupees. A few bitlahas also may possibly have been malafide while a few did not strictly follow custom. Obviously if the practice is to continue, certain principles must be applied:

1. The ceremony should be done strictly in accordance with custom.
2. There should be no destruction of property (other than the symbolic cracking of a chulha).
3. It should be done only in true cases which have been fully tested by the pargana and manjhis.
4. In view of Diku antipathy to the ritual, the option of a substantial fine should ordinarily be given so that Diku offenders may, if possible, avoid this disgrace.

What official conventions are necessary to maintain these conditions and to eliminate the last rist of excess ?

It will be evident from what I have said that unless particular antecedents provoke the bitlaha crowd, the ceremony is normally done with marked restraint and discipline. If at Lohandia and Siripur, Diku dealings with Santals had been better the bitlaha might never had occurred. Obviously, therefore, a first precaution should be to ensure that ordinary day to day relations between Dikus and Santals do not generate into local repressed feuds. This can be secured by vigilance on the part of touring officials, a more regular contact of officers throughout the district and in the Damin itself by the itself by the appointment of extra Damin magistrates. If Santal discontent is detected while it is still embryonic and the Santal grievance are speedily redressed, it is very unlikely that bitlahas will be violent.

Secondly it is necessary that 'rules for the conduct of bitlaha' should now be drafted in Santali and circulated among Santals so that the correct procedure may everywhere be understood. These should prescribe the steps to be taken by Santals to keep the Subdivisional Officers informed and should fix certain responsibilities on the manjhis and parganas. It should, for example, be emphasised that Santal custom requires the sanction of the pargana's council before a Sal branch is issued and each manjhi should be made responsible for seeing that this is duly done. It should be stressed that in the interests of communal amity, the option of a heavy fine should always be offered to Diku offenders and bitlaha should be recommended only when that option is rejected.

Thirdly, the pargana should be brought boldly into the

picture. Immediately a Santal-Diku offence is submitted to a Pargana he should hold his council and if, after investigating the case fully, the council is satisfied that the Diku is at fault the pargana should see that a second option of immediate paying the fine is allowed before the council provisionally advises bitlaha. If the fine is refused, the pargana should report his decision to the Subdivisional Officer and the latter should immediately go to the spot, and meet the council and the offenders. If the Diku alleges to the officer that the charge is malafide, he should be asked to clarify his position before the council, and the Subdivisional Officer should see whether there are any grounds for holding that the charge is false or due to enmity. If it is clear that the charge is malafide, the Subdivisional Officer will have little difficulty in inducing the council to revise its opinion. If, on the other hand, the circumstances in no way suggest a 'frame-up'—the Subdivisional Officer should accept the council's verdict. It is essential that he should not himself go into facts for once it is clear that the charge is not malafide, it is for the council to decide whether it is proved or not. It is well known that village standards of evidence are often superior to those of a court and tribal ways of ascertaining truth are often a great improvement on the Code of Criminal Procedure or the Indian Evidence Act. The function of the Subdivisional Officer should be more that of a Judge in relation to a jury than that of a magistrate trying an original case.

If the verdict is bonafide, the officer should then himself urge the Diku offender to pay the fine and should even canvass the opinion of other Dikus so that the matter may be adjudged in this manner.

If, inspite of all these efforts, the fine is still not paid, the bitlaha should be duly approved, a date decided for its performance in consultation with the council and the council itself made responsible for its orderly performance.

The same conventions should also govern the bitlaha of Santals. Before a notice is issued, the pargana must inform the Subdivisional Officer, a magistrate should ratify the decision after satisfying himself that it is bonafide and a date should then be given for the performance of the ritual.

When the date of bitlaha approaches, if the offender is a Diku, the Subdivisional Officer himself should go to the village the preceding evening while if the culprit is a Santal the enquiring magistrate should be sent. On arrival the officer should see that the offender leaves the village and if there is any likelihood of his resisting the crowd or remaining at the spot, he should be taken into preventive custody. For this purpose, the services of choukidars, sardars or parganas should be employed, so that there is no risk of bloodshed.

It is of the utmost importance that no police force should be deputed for on every occasion that the police have intervened violence has either occurred or has been narrowly averted. In the Lihandia bitlaha the police only escaped after firing. At Chinadangal, intervention by a Sub-Inspector led to a bitlaha of the whole village. At Tarajore in the Dumka subdivision a bitlaha for clan incest was peacefully performed in 1941. A chulha was broken and there was no defecation. As the crowd was dispersing, a Sub-Inspector and some constable arrived. They stopped some Santals, as they said 'to find out what had happened'. The Santals thought they had been arrested. The crowd came back, overpowered the party, beat the Sub-Inspector and released their comrades. News was sent to Dumka. The Subdivisional Officer hurried to the scene, rescued two constables and brought back the wounded officers. Then the crowd went peacefully away. Even in other matters Santals always regard Police with great suspicion. The appearance of a Sub-Inspector and constables invariably puts them on their guard. They suspect that some form of aggression or interference is imminent and at the least sign they are only too liable to anticipate force by restoring to it themselves. A constable was sent to a Santal village to enquire about an absconder and happened to insult a Santal woman. The Santals arrested him and when a Sub-Inspector of police tried to get him out the Sub-Inspector lost his watch. A Sub-Inspector of Police engaged in supervising village defence parties decided to rouse up a Santal village in the latter hours of night. He did so but his uniform did not save him and it was only after he had written out an apology that the Santals let him go. Two armed constables, who were scrounging rations, tried to take rice without paying for it. It was a Santal village and they got away. But only after they had fired two shots and dodged a cloud of arrows.

Accordingly, if bitlaha is to be performed peacefully and according to custom, it is essential that the Santals should neither be opposed nor be given the impression of opposition. If police are at all deputed, it should be to silence opposition to the Santals and not to oppose the Santals themselves. It is preferable that only a magistrate should attend them and then only in the capacity of a friendly observer. He should remind the manjhis that the ritual should be done in the customary manner without violence or damage. He should tell them that there is no objection whatsoever to an orderly bitlaha and if they enquire why he is present he should explain that he has come to prevent obstruction to the due performance of the ritual. During 1943 and 1944 these principles were applied to more than twenty bitlahas and in every case the ceremony was performed in perfect order.

Finally if inspite of all attempts at peaceful celebration the last contingency should happen and damage be done, a judicial enquiry should be held and not a police investigation. The pargana and manjhis of the circle or bungalow should be held responsible for the outrage and should be required to collect from Santals of their area sufficient money to set right the damage and indemnify the sufferers.

In a bitlaha of two Santals which occurred in 1945 after I had made over charge, damage was done in one of the houses. S.M. Naqavi intervened. The local pargana and manjhis all conceded that the damage could not be justified and within a week they had collected four hundred rupees and paid them to the victim. If damage can be traced to certain main offenders they should be made chiefly responsible for this indemnity and if necessary bitlaha should be done in their own houses by way of punishment to them for their actions. Only if Santal public opinion itself favoured imprisonment would it be well to hold a trial.

REFERENCES

1. Herbert Read, 'On Justice, *Horizon*, XI (1945) 432-3.

2. R.E. Russell, *Report of the Santals Parganas Inquiry Committee*, (Patna, 1938), 66-7.
3. In the years 1941 to 1943 the Damin provided one-tenth of the total cognizable cases. In more than half these cases chargesheets were submitted, and the percentages of convictions were 74 in 1941, 73 in 1942 and 45 in 1943. The area outside the Damin is three quarters of the district but it accounted for nine tenths of the cases. In these cases, chargesheets were submitted in approximately one-third of the cases and the percentages of conviction were 58 in 1941, 52 in 1942 and 45 in 1943.

The following figures for dacoities and bürglaries need no comment :

Year	Dacoity		Burglary	
	Non-Damin	Damin	Non-Damin	Damin
1941	99	16	1436	59
1942	110	10	1091	60
1943	439	56	1761	48
1944 up to September	85	16	777	19

4. For a discussion of the Santal Rebellion of 1855, see E. Thompson and G.T. Garratt, *Rise and Fulfilment of British Rule in India*, (London, 1944), J.H. Hutton, 'Primitive Tribes' in *Modern India and the West* (London, 1942), R. Carstairs, *Harma's Village* (Pokhuria, 1945) and W.J. Culshaw and W.G. Archer, 'The Santal Rebellion' *Man in India*, XXV (1945), 218-19.
5. B.J.F. Laubscher, *Sex, Custom and Psychopathology* (London, 1937), 302.
6. V. Elwin, *Maria Murder and Suicide*, XXXIV-XXVII.
7. S.M. Naqavi, op. cit., 245-6.
8. These views are largely in accordance with those of W.V. Grigson who states of various areas in the Central Provinces 'For every village there are two or three elders or panchas commonly known as Sianadmi and for groups of from 10 to 40 villages a mukhiya, also called naike by the Uriya Gonds. Practically all Criminal, Civil and tribal disputes are tackled either by the Sian Admi or the mukhiya and few panchas. In tracts near the courts the latter are some times resorted to as a means of enforcing the tribal award in civil, matrimonial and criminal cases but else where the zamindar is appealed to, wherever he can be approached. The fact that there is some sort of appeal to a sethis or naike for a group of villages. . . should reassure legal purists who dislike the transfer of jurisdiction from the courts to 'uneducated' village headman and elders and should overcome the objection that in a small village one or other of the elders is likely to be biased for or against one

of the parties'! (*The Aboriginal Problem in the Central Provinces,* 391).

9. *Horkoren Mare Hapramko reak' Katha,* 210-11.
10. T.B. Creagh Coen, 'Witchcraft in the Dangs' *Man in India,* XXV (1945), 187-8.
11. Dalton, op. cit , 217.
12. *Horkoren Mare Hapramko reak' Katha,* 144.

VOLUME THREE

CIVIL JUSTICE
IN
TRIBAL INDIA

With
Special Reference
to
The Santal Parganas

51

SYSTEMS OF TRIBAL JUSTICE

I INTRODUCTION

THROUGHOUT the tribal areas of India the administration of civil justice has proved a difficult and complicated task. That the ordinary assumptions of Hindu or Muslim India could have but little relevance has been obvious enough yet the need of deciding disputes in a way which seems just to the tribesmen has sometimes been ignored and widely varying systems are still in force in different regions. In this essay I shall deal primarily with the Santal Parganas and the problems which arise from Santal litigation. I propose to examine the different types of court which hear and decide Santal suits, to review their procedure and to discuss how far the indigenous law is respected and applied. I shall then describe the settlement operations and their repercussion on tribal law and I will end by examining what steps are needed for making the judiciary a more effective instrument of tribal justice. The problems of one district, however, are often the problems of another and, for considering Santal justice in the Santal Parganas, the experience of other areas is instructive. I will, therefore, discuss the fate of tribal law in courts outside that district and in order to provide a setting for Santal problems, I will begin by describing the various systems which administer tribal justice in other parts of India.

II THE NAGA HILLS

Systems of justice in tribal India range between the employment of the tribe itself as its own judiciary and its complete effacement by official agencies, and for the most striking examples of the first method we must go to the Naga Hills in Assam and the Chittagong Hill Tracts in Bengal. In the first of these areas the tribal councils are the original civil courts while the Deputy Commissioner of the Naga Hills and the Subdivisional Officer at Mokokchung have a merely co-ordinating and appellate function. The laws administered by the councils are known to and accepted by all the tribe, while in deciding appeals the Deputy Commissioner and the Subdivisional Officer are aided by 'a staff of interpreters whose duty it is to translate the Naga dialects into Naga-Assamese, the lingua franca of the district and to advise on custom.[1] 'These interpreters', says J.P. Mills, 'are very carefully picked men and the posts are much sought after for though the pay is not high, the prestige is great. Care is taken that no tribal interests are overlooked' and 'at Mokokchung there are interpreters from every tribe in the Subdivision'.[2] This employment of tribesmen as legal advisers obviously assumes great integrity on the part of the interpreters but this assumption seems to have been fully justified in practice and the result is a smoothly functioning system, still completely oral but well adjusted to tribal needs. A further important feature is that no pleaders are allowed.

III THE CHITTAGONG HILL TRACTS

The Chittagong Hill Tracts have a similar delegation of justice—each headman in the 360 mauzas of the district being a court of original jurisdiction, while each of the three circle chiefs exercises revisional powers. These powers are specified in Chittagong Hill Tract Rule 40.

'Save as otherwise provided in this rule the mauza headmen shall adjudicate on all disputes which may be brought to them by persons resident within their mauzas. They shall decide tribal cases in accordance with the social custom of the parties with powers of fine up to Rs. 25, of enforcing restitution, and of detention until the orders of the Deputy Commissioner in the matter are received.

Save as otherwise provided in this rule the chiefs shall adjudicate on all disputes in their khas mauzas as headmen and shall try such tribal cases as are referred to them from the decision of headmen or by the headmen themselves.

The chiefs shall have powers of fining upto Rs. 50 of enforcing restitution and of detention until the orders of the Deputy Commissioner in the matter are received, in tribal cases, and their decisions shall, subject to the general revisional jurisdiction of the Deputy Commissioner, be final. In all cases in which the chiefs or the headmen are unable to enforce the penalties imposed, they may apply to the Deputy Commissioner for assistance.

No court fee shall be levied in tribal cases tried by chiefs or headmen. Fines imposed in such cases shall be allocated to the aggrieved persons, if any, and to the community as a whole in accordance with tribal custom. The chiefs and headmen shall be entitled to such share in the amount of fines allocated to the community as a whole as is permitted by tribal custom and no nazzar or other imposition under any pretext whatsoever shall be levied by them in connexion with the trial of such cases :

Provided that the chiefs or headmen may levy fees to cover expenses of trying the cases on a scale approved by the Deputy Commissioner.

The chiefs and headmen shall have no power to try under this rule any criminal or civil matters other than the tribal cases referred to in this rule except as the Governor may, from time to time, empower them in this behalf'.

If a party is dissatisfied with a headman's decision, he appeals to the chief and from the chief goes to the Deputy Commissioner in whom 'the general administration of the tracts in criminal, civil revenue, and all other matters is vested.'

If a civil matter comes before the Deputy Commissioner and it is necessary for him to intervene, the following four rules govern procedure :

1. The administration of civil justice shall be conducted in the most simple and expedititous manner compatible with the equitable disposal of the matters or suits.

2. The officer dealing with the matter or suit will, in the first instance, endeavour, upon the viva voce examination of the parties, to make a just award between them. Witnesses

should not be sent for, except when the officer is unable without them to come to a decision upon the facts of the case.

3. The record shall contain the following particulars, namely, the name of the plaintiff, the name of the defendant, the nature of the claim or other matter in litigation, an abstract of the plaintiff's case, an abstract of the defendant's case, an abstract of the depositions of the witnesses (where witnesses are examined), the grounds of the decision, and the order signed and dated.

4. No court-fees shall be payable on a memorandum of appeal in cases where a Chakma, Magh or member of any tribe indigenous to the Hill tracts is an appellant, nor shall such fees be payable by hillmen in the said tracts in revenue cases in respect of petitions for settlement or relinquishment of lands, remission of rents, mutation, demarcation and subletting of lands.

A court-fee of two annas only shall be payable on all petitions relating to miscellaneous matters including petitions praying for the time presented whether by hillmen or by non-hillmen in the said tracts.

If a point of tribal law is involved the Deputy Commissioner consults a chief or some village headmen and an analogy of the Naga system he followes their advice and disposes of the matter accordingly. Lt. Col. G.L. Hyde the present Deputy Commissioner, who has supplied with much of this information adds that 'tribal custom has altered little in recent years' and that he has rarely found really conflicting opinions. Where a civil suit is tribal in nature it is nearly always returned to the headman or chief for adjudication and the vitality of the tribal courts is thus fostered.

IV BASTAR STATE

These are the only two areas in Middle and Eastern India where delegation is virtually complete. But since 1932 a compromise embodying some of the Naga and Chittagong systems has operated in Bastar State. Here the former civil courts are still allowed to function but their jurisdiction is confined to certain types of suit and to those which are beyond a certain valuation. For simple money, grain and cattle claims upto Rs. 25 in value together with claims for civil damages arising out of certain criminal offences, the competent court is now the tribal village panchayat, 'the convening of which and the selection of the elders of which are left to the village headman'. 'Any person dissatisfied with a decision of the village headman and elders can appeal within a month to the pargana headman, who is assisted by a panchayat of four headmen chosen every year by the assembled headmen of the villages of the pargana before the Tahsildar'.[3] Beyond the pargana's council, there is no appeal and accordingly for all minor civil litigation the Murias, Hill Marias and Bison-horn Marias have now a set of tribal courts administering their tribal law. Since the law is known to all the councils, the question of codifying it has not arisen though the fact that suits of higher valuation are still adjudicated by the ordinary courts suggests that sooner or later such action may be necessary.

'The experiment', says Verrier Elwin, 'has more than justified itself during the past ten years. Occasionally, a bad headman has diverted too large a proportion of the fines to his own use. A few courts have had to be superseded, and the jurisdiction of the ordinary courts restored because they were tampered with by Hindu and Mohammadan traders in adjacent market villages; here foreign influence had perhaps already gone too far towards detribalising the village life. But on the whole, the courts have worked well and have lifted from the villagers not only the burden of police and court investigations, but the physical distress and nervous exhaustion of long journeys to the distant courts, the demoralising contact of lawyers, lawyer's touts and petition-writers, and the bewilderment of dealing with laws they do not understand and which often run counter to their own traditions'.[4]

V THE KOLHAN

In the Kolhan estate of Singhbhum district yet another type of system is in force among the Hos.

Under Regulation XIII of 1833, rules were framed by Capt. Wilkinson, an Agent to the Governor-General, and under these rules certain civil courts were constituted and are still functioning. The Kolhan Superintendent and his assistants, all of whom are Deputy or Sub Deputy Collectors, try civil suits up to the value of Rs. 300 while suits valued at over this amount are heard by the Deputy Commissioner of Singhbhum. Appeals from the decisions of the Kolhan Superintendent and his assistants lie to the Deputy Commissioner and there is a right of second appeal to the Commissioner of Chota Nagpur who is the High Court for the tribe. Appeals from original decisions of the Deputy Commissioner also lie to the Commissioner and for these too, his decision is final.

But besides empowering certain courts to hear and decide suits, the rules also give the utmost encouragement to decisions by panchayat. Rule 20 authorises a court to select three to five persons among those 'most conversant with the matter at issue', it provides for their speedy meeting and requires the court to pass a decree in conformity with their award. Such decrees are not appealable unless corruption can be proved against the Panchayat or unless the award is 'contrary to the common law of the country or the rules enacted by the Governor-General-in-Council'. Such panchayats can be constituted on the order of the court or at the instance of the parties while Rule 22 provides that 'as the decisions of suits by Panchayat is to expedite justice and for the general good all persons shall be liable to be employed on them'.

Finally under Rule 26, 'Wakeels shall not be permitted to plead in any of the courts within the jurisdiction but parties shall be allowed to conduct their business in the courts either in person or by Mookhtears or authorised Agents. Suits for the remuneration of Agents or Mookhtears shall not be heard or decided in any court. The object of this Rule is to discourage vexatious litigation which in the Regulation Province is greatly promoted by intriguing Wakeels and Mookhtears'.

As a result of these rules the Hos in the Kolhan are to a great extent associated with the administration of their civil justice. The tribal councils and officials are not constituted into formal or permanent courts, but under the Rule for arbitration, ad hoc tribal courts consisting of Ho Mankis are constantly being formed for making awards. If for any reason Ho parties oppose a reference to such a Ho tribunal, the court itself decides and understanding conventions if there is any doubt concerning the Ho law on a particular point, it consults leading Ho mankis. For the rest, all Hos are bound by Ho law; Ho law is taken to be 'the common law of the country', and all Hos and officers are presumed to know its principles and apply them.

VI THE MADRAS AGENCY

A variation of the Kolhan system is in force in the Madras Agency where W.V. Grigson describes the legal provisions as follows. 'Rule 46 of the Madras Agency Rules', he says 'allows a court if it thinks a suit or issue fit for arbitration, to refer the suit or issue to arbitration before a panchayat of three or five members, as the court may decide. The court itself chooses one member to preside and each party chooses one, when there are three. When there are five 'four shall be chosen by the parties having separate or conflicting interests in the subject in the suit in the manner prescribed by the court. The panchayat's decision is filed then in the court as a razinama petition. The court has to satisfy itself that the parties fully understand the razinama, and then passes a decree thereon but for recorded reasons, may reject a panchayat's decision, if it appears clearly unjust or inconclusive. Under Agency Rule 45 when there has been arbitration without the court's intervention any person interested in the award can get it filed in the court and executed, after the other parties have been given a chance of being heard, and unless the award is prima facie illegal or defective or tainted with fraud of either party, or corruption or misconduct of the arbitrator; a panchayat's award would come within the scope of this. Appeals do not lie in general from awards under Rules 45 and 46'.[5]

VII THE CENTRAL PROVINCES

Outside these areas there is no official recognition of tribal councils and in the Central Provinces all suits by tribesmen are decided by the Regular Civil Courts.

I will discuss later the typical constitution of these courts but it will give an idea of their working if I quote a passage by Verrier Elwin: 'Of all their contacts with the outside world', he says 'none is more destructive of the high and simple standards of the tribesmen and their belief in human nature than their relations with the courts and lawyers. This has been described so well by Forsyth and the picture he drew in 1871 is still so true and accurate today that I cannot do better than quote he says :

'Our administration of civil justice, while perhaps sufficiently suited to the requirements of settled districts, is practically a negation of all justice to the aborigine in his jungle. The courts sit at distant stations; and in the Central Provinces there is even a rule prohibiting the trial of cases by civil officers on tour, unless both parties live on the spot. It wants only the slightest acquaintance with the timid and suspicious aborigine to see that this really amounts to denying him a hearing altogether. He will never come to the station if he can avoid it by any payment within his means to make, and, if he does, the chances are against his succeeding in escaping from it, and the crowd of harpies who clog the wheels of justice, without leaving behind him much of his wordly substance. The apparent necessities of a Government which impoverishes its treasuries to cover the land with public works have led to an economy in its judicial establishments that inevitably leads to a very superficial investigation of small causes, and to a corrupt execution of the processes of the courts'.[6]

Verrier Elwin then goes on 'The loss of nervous energy caused by a long succession of hearings, the distance that must be travelled (often a hundred miles for each hearing—I know a case where the complainant and four witnesses had to tramp an aggregate of 3200 miles before their case was finished) the realisation that truth is a commodity to be bought and sold, the divergence between the official laws and tribal custom, is a shock to the tribesmen from which he does not recover readily'.

VIII CHOTA NAGPUR

Throughout Chota Nagpur except the Kolhan the same conditions operate and the ordinary Civil Courts governed by the Code of Civil Procedure and the Indian Evidence Act are the sole tribunals, for the litigation of the tribesmen. These courts consist firstly of Munsifs with power to decide all suits valued at sums which range from Rs. 1000 to Rs. 4000 (according to the Munsif) and secondly of Sub-Judges who decide suits valued at any sum. From decisions of a Munsif or a Sub-Judge, the first appeal is to the Judicial Commissioner provided the suit is valued at more than Rs. 5000. If it exceeds that sum, the appeal is to the High Court.

Parallel to these courts are the tribal councils of the Uraons, Mundas and Kharias but none of these bodies have legal powers and there is no prescribed procedure for referring tribal suits to panchayats. The only agencies through which an Uraon Munda or Kharia can obtain a legal decree are the ordinary Civil Courts of the Division.

As in the Central Provinces these courts are very far from being adjusted to tribal needs and I will briefly note some of the ways in which they press hardly on aboriginals.

At present the court languages include only Hindi, Urdu, Bengali and English and an Uraon Munda or Kharia who brings a suit must, therefore, litigate in a language not his own. It is true that most Kharias use Hindusthani as a second language but more than a quarter of the Uraons and half the Mundas know only their tribal tongue.[7]

In such circumstances errors may easily occur both in plaints and written statements and in the absence of vernacular terms, the tribal law itself may easily be misunderstood. Moreover the ban on there own languages itself creates a form of tribal depression and Elwin has listed this as a significant factor in aboriginal decline.[8]

Secondly the court officers who are drawn almost exclusively from the Hindu and Muslim communities are not at present required to understand any of the tribal languages. This does not necessarily result in injustice but it must obviously lend the proceedings an air of strange remoteness. Moreover with his Hindu or Muslim background and with the restriction of his work to a purely judicial routine an officer does not necessarily have any knowledge of tribal society or its assumptions and, however, careful and conscientious he may be, he is forced to approach a suit with non-tribal conceptions. No one would perhaps dispute that an Uraon or Munda case would be decided better if the court knew something of Uraon or Munda society.

Yet another way in which the courts are ill-adjusted to the

tribesmen is through the complexity of their legal procedure. This in many cases not only defeats justice but promotes moral and economic ruin. After a lifetime of practice in the Ranchi courts, Sarat Chandra Roy recorded the view that 'This complicated system of administration of justice has tended to impair the natural truthfulness and honesty of the people in many cases. By repeated painful experience the people have found that under the complicated and cumbrous Procedure Codes and a too technical Law of Evidence which are now in force and which are beyond their comprehension, their native straight forwardness and veracity is no match for the chicanery and falsehood and the many subtle tricks employed against them by many of their adversaries. And 'law-touts' and other petty-fogging 'advisers' are not wanting to induce them to adopt the ways of their adversaries. Such advice unhappily they now not unoften follow, though rather clumsily. But as is inevitable, the expensive system of litigation through one court after another—Courts of Original Jurisdiction, Courts of First Appeal and Courts of Second Appeal is ruinous for the poor aboriginal, who, in most cases, cannot fight up to the last, and even those who can, only find themselves in the end utterly ruined through the expenses and trouble of securing ultimate victory. In this way the complicated British Indian system of administration of justice has more often than not helped in ruining the aboriginals economically and in degrading them morally'.[9]

NOTES AND REFERENCES

1. It is interesting to note that Hindu law was at first administered by English Judges with the assistance of Hindu Pundits and it was not until 1868 that these official referees were abolished (D.F. Mulla, *Principles of Hindu Law*, 11).
2. J.P. Mills, *The Ao Nagas* (London, 1926), 406.
3. W.V. Grigson, *The Maria Gonds of Bastar* (London, 1938), 296.
4. Verrier Elwin, *Loss of Nerve* (Bombay, 1941), 26.
5. W.V. Grigson, *Notes on the Aboriginal Problem in the Mandla District* (Nagpur, 1940), 8.
6. Forsyth, *Highlands of Central India* (London, 1871), 162.
7. The 1931 census recorded the following figures:

Figures :

Tribe	Tribal language as Mother language	Hindusthani as Second language
Kharia	66185	61827
Uraon	375318	257424
Munda	383035	192605

8. 'A great many of the tribesmen are now bilingual and others have altogether lost their ancient form of speech. This has been a cause of aboriginal decline, for with the passing of the old languages there has gone a whole world of culture, and the tribesmen forced to deal in a speech not his own with officials, landlords and merchants, finds himself at a disadvantage which constantly results in his exploitation.' (*The Aboriginals*, Bombay, 1943, 7).
9. S.C. Roy, 'The effect on the aborigines of Chota Nagpur of their contact with Western Civilization,' *J.B.O.R.S.*, XVII (1931), 374-5.

52

TRIBAL LAW AND THE COURTS

I THE CENTRAL PROVINCES

IF JUDICIAL procedure has often proved inimical to tribal interests, how has tribal law fared in the ordinary Civil Courts ?

In the Central Provinces Verrier Elwin has stated 'It is not uncommon for subordinate courts, especially if they are presided over by Hindu magistrates, to settle problems of aboriginal partition and inheritance according to the rulings of the Mitakshara Code.[1] How great is the general ignorance on this point may be seen by a study of the Objects and Reasons which were put forward in support of a Bill by which it was proposed the C.P. Legislature of 1935, to apply to the Gonds the Law of Mitakshara, as interpreted by the Benares School of Hindu Law, in matters regarding succession, adoption, joint family and partition. The member-in-charge of the Bill declared that since the Gonds had already adopted the Hindu customs in these matters, the Bill introduced no real changes, but simply consolidated existing custom. 'Gonds generally believe in and talk the language of Hindu Law. Adoption is very common among them. Their living is almost on the lines of a Joint Hindu Family with a manager in the father. They partition the family property just as any Hindu does.'

But actually adoption, far from being common among the Gonds is almost unknown. Their practice of partition is entirely different: where a joint family exists it is on a different basis. They do not, except in the neighbourhood of the towns, talk the language of Hindu Law. The Bill, in fact, instead of consolidating existing conditions would, if passed, have produced farreaching changes'.[2]

The High Court of the Central Provinces, however, now generally recognises the distinction between aboriginal custom and Hindu Law. In 1933 the Privy Council upheld a judgment of the Court of the Judicial Commissioner at Nagpur which decided that a marriage between an aboriginal Tanwar and a Kawar can only be valid if performed in the manner usual among the Tanwars, since the imitation of the Hindu Kshattriya practice of performing the sword ceremony known as Katar had not been established as a custom. The *Nagpur Law Journal*, commenting on this, observed that 'it is necessary to draw attention to the confusion likely to be caused through Kawars being treated as Hindus. The members of the Bar at the several districts of the Chhattisgarh Division, specially the Bilaspur Bar, will please make a note of the fact that the distinction obtaining in the Central Provinces between Hindus proper and the aboriginal tribes should be stressed in cases cropping up later on.' A notification of the Central Provinces Government has declared that the Gonds are not subject to the India Succession Act, and the High Court has ruled that for legal purposes Gonds are not Hindus'.[3]

This difficulty, however, is only one of many, and W. V. Grigson after discussion with a very experienced Sub-Judge emphasised to the C. P. Government 'the difficulties to which a Gond ignorant of the courts is put so long as Civil Courts have not the duty of ascertaining the true facts but only of requiring the plaintiff and the defendant to put up such pleadings and evidence as they think fit to rely on or know how to adduce. 'Not only is the Gond,' he states, 'often ignorant, but his pleader, not knowing Gond ways will often persuade him to advance a plea based on Hindu ideas and clearly wrong. The difficulties are enhanced by the rulings of the High Court as to the civil law applicable to aboriginals, the absence of any authoritive exposition of their customs, and the consequent bewilderment of judge, pleaders and parties. The High Court has rightly ruled that Gonds are not Hindu and not governed by Hindu Law; they are also not governed by the Indian Succession Act. In any case, therefore, of adoption, disputed succession, claims to property, guardianship, divorce or marriage, Gond custom has to be proved. A Gond does not know how to prove a custom. His pleader or his opponent's pleader knowing nothing of Gond custom tries to prove by obviously unreliable evidence that the family concerned followed in the particular matter the Hindu Law.'[4]

II CHOTA NAGPUR

In Chota Nagpur, the position is even more disquieting. As in the Central Provinces, there is not at present any legislative enactment prescribing by what law a tribesman shall be bound and although the position is slightly better in so far as the works of Sarat Chandra Roy contain informative outlines of Uraon, Munda, Kharia and Birhor law, these are of no avail if the tribal law is not correctly pleaded.

In his judgement Manu Uraon and Others vs. Abraham Uraon and Others (1941, *A.I.R.*, Patna 146), Agarwala, J. stated :

> 'With regard to their rights after the death of Madra Uraon the learned Subordinate Judge, who had decided the appeal, referred to Mr S. C. Roy's book on *The Oraons of Chota Nagpur*, and by reference to that book found that there exists among the Oraons a custom that when a father has separated from one of his sons and retained a part of the property for his own maintenance that property devolves on the son with whom he lived in his lifetime. This custom was not pleaded by the plaintiffs and the only evidence of it is contained in the passage in Mr. Roy's book, Mr. Roy is alive and was, therefore, available as a witness to the custom, if in fact there be such a custom. The plaintiffs neither called him as a witness nor gave any reason for not calling him and did not adduce any other evidence with regard to this custom which they have not pleaded in their plaint. The learned Subordinate Judge's attention is invited to the decision in 1 B.L.J. 225, in which Mullick J. observed :
> 'I would invite the attention of the learned Judicial Commissioner to the observations of the Madras High Court in 12 Mad. 495, to the effect that reference to works

> of history at the appellate stage is irregular and to be avoided.'
>
> By referring to Mr. Roy's account of the history and social customs of the Oraons at the appellate stage the learned subordinate Judge has fallen in to the error of finding a custom which was not pleaded on evidence which was not admissible and his decision must be set aside.'

But an even greater danger to tribal law arises from the use of the term 'Hinduism'. In the Central Provinces this issue does not seem to have caused difficulties as it was taken for granted by the High Court that the Gonds could not be bound by the Mitakshara Code of Hindu Law. The Patna High Court, on the other hand, has had to adjudicate a number of cases in which the tribesmen (often on the advice of their pleaders) have described themselves as Hindus by religion, and since it has accordingly had to decide what legal inferences are to be drawn from such pleadings. These High Courts decisions are obviously of great importance and I will review a number of the judgments in detail.

The first important discussion at this issue occurs in a judgment delivered by McPherson J. in 1925. In this case (Kritibash Mahton vs. Budhan Mahtani, 1925, *A.I.R.* (Pat), 733) the parties belonged to the aboriginal tribe of Kurmi Mahto and described themselves as Hindus by religion. McPherson J. said :

> . . . the courts below considered the main question to be : Whether the parties are aborigines or Hindus.
>
> There they misunderstood the position, the question set out being as meaningless as would be the issue, 'Are the parties English or Christians ?'

The term 'aboriginal', at least in Chota Nagpur, denotes race only. It is in fact so used in Section 46(6) of the Chota Nagpur Tenancy Act. It implies nothing as to religion which may be even within the same tribe animism, a slight veneer of Hinduism, various intermediate stages of Hinduism, or Christianity. On the other hand, the term 'Hindu' has in Chota Nagpur reference only to religion.

Now it does not admit of the faintest doubt that the

Kurmi-Mahtos of the Manbhum District are racially an aboriginal tribe. They are the most numerous community (whether tribe or caste of that district from which they have overflowed into the neighbouring districts). They have no concern whatever except in the accident of name with the Dravido-Aryan agricultural and menial caste of Bihar proper.

This important and numerous aboriginal tribe of agriculturists has, however, moved substantially towards Hinduism and rather faster than the other great tribes of the district, such as the Santals and Bhumijas. There is of course a good deal of variation in the stages that have been reached in different parts of the district and neighbouring districts in respect of the adoption or rather superimposition of Hindu practices, and some areas lag behind. Notification No. 550 of the 2nd May 191 under Section 332 of the Indian Succession Act, 1865 which withdrew the Act with retrospective effect from among other tribes, the tribe 'known as Kurmis' (that is the Kurmi Mahto tribe of Chota Nagpur as distinguished from the entirely distinct Bihari caste of Kurmis) on the ground that they have customary rules of succession and inheritance incompatible with the provisions of that Act, indicates that the whole tribe at least had not then become Hindu: if all Kurmi-Mahtos were Hindus then the notification would have been unnecessary as the Act does not apply to Hindus.

The parties, though aboriginals, being found to be also Hindus, it was still for the plaintiffs to prove that succession was not agnatic as the defendants in possession contended that it was. It was for the plaintiffs to, establish that the Dayabhaga applied. The agnates wo uld inherit under the customary rules of succession and inher itance of all aboriginal tribes in Chota Nagpur which, though they sometimes allow the widow or mother of the deceased to remain in possession of the whole or part of the inheritance by way of maintenance, are adamant against succession by or through daughters or sisters. The exceptional case of the ghar jawae in backward areas may be left out of consideration. It is also never safe to infer that a tribe or a member of a tribe, merely because of the adoption or superimposition of some Hindu practices or even when it is practically Hinduised, is Hindu so as to be affected by the Hindu shastras in matters of succession. On the contrary it is at least consistent with experience and probabilities that the tribal customs as to succession should be carried on into and persist after the adoption of Hinduism. This is also the view of the late Hon'ble the Reverend Dr. Andrew Campbell, the highest authority on the aboriginals of Manbhum. Further the agnates would also inherit if on conversion to Hinduism, the parties had adopted the Mitakshara system. The court did not consider this point. The Trial Court presumed that inheritance was governed by the Dayabhaga system, 'as it prevails in this part of the country.'

After discussing the school of Hindu Law prevalent in Manbhum, McPherson J. then added : 'In point of fact aboriginals, with few exceptions, move towards Hinduism as a tribe or large section of a tribe in a particular area, and they certainly do not contemplate any change in the customary laws of inheritance and succession of the tribe. The onus is clearly upon the person who, alleges that these customary laws have been discarded and that the aboriginal adheres to a particular School of Hindu Law in the matter of inheritance'.

In the present case the points for enquiry were first, whether the general Hindu Law was substituted for tribal custom in respect of inheritance as a part of the personal law of the parties, and if so, whether it was the Dayabhaga form of the Hindu Law on the point. On both points the onus would be on the plaintiffs whereas if the parties had been persons unquestionably governed by ordinary Hindu Law, the onus in the first matter to prove a custom at variance with Hindu Law would be on the person who asserted its existence.

In cases relating to inheritance among aboriginals in Manbhum it is always necessary to enquire whether even if Hinduised (slightly, partially, or completely) they have abandoned the tribal custom as to inheritance (usually they have not, even where, as is unusual, Hinduisation is complete) and then if they have abandoned the tribal custom what particular school of Hindu Law they have adhered to. Both points of enquiry are in Manbhum questions of fact to be determined on the evidence. Insufficiently considered decisions of subordinate courts have in some measure been disturbing causes, but prima facie it would seem exceedingly improbable that a tribe when it establishes itself as a new caste, should discard a tribal custom of agnatic relationship as the criterion for inheritance, especially when the leading Hindu castes of the district and a large section of the immigrant Hindus retain it, and other tribes of the district indisputably carry into Hinduism the custom of lineal primogeniture in the male line'.

This exposition of the law failed, however, to commend itself to a later bench and in Ganesh Mahto and Others vs. Sibcharan Mahto & Others (1931, *A.I.R.* Patna, 305) Jwala Prasad and Kulwant Sahay J.J. took the opposite view that the adoption of the Hindu religion raised a presumption that the Hindu Law of inheritance and succession had also been adopted and that the onus of proving that the parties were still governed by tribal law must shift to whichever party asserted it. In the absence of full proof of tribal law, the parties would be presumed to be governed by Hindu Law.[5]

It is obvious that this identification of law and religion loads the scale heavily against tribal law but another judgment of the Patna High Court goes even further. This judgment (1931, *A.I.R.* Patna, 198, Doman Sahu vs. Buka & Others) was passed by Terrell C.J. and Mohomed Noor J. and contains some observations on aboriginals in general. In the course of this judgment their Lordships said : 'The question whether a Mundari woman is or is not a Hindu is not very easy to decide. But the authorities are to the effect that the term 'Hindu' can safely be applied to all those who claim to be Hindus and are regarded by the society surrounding them to be Hindus. Reference may be made to Gour's Hindu Code, second edition, Article 322 where the learned author observes as follows :

'Besides the Hindus, properly so called, and those who are commonly so called, there remain a number of people belonging to the aboriginal tribes, such as Gonds, Bhils, Kurds, Santals, Kochees of Assam, Aroras of the Punjab, Khatiks, Kumbars and the like, who have become absorbed into the Hindu society and who consequently consider themselves Hindus, and as such bound by Hindu Law. The test in their case is the same. How do they regard themselves and how are they regarded by the rest of the Hindu community?'.

This observation is based upon the numerous cases which it is unnecessary for us to refer to. In the present case sufficient is it to say that in the case of many aboriginal tribes there have been judicial pronouncements to the effect that they are Hindus. The learned author further proceeds and says :

> 'The test applicable is not the Shastric test which has ceased to be applicable to the most orthodox Hindu. The fact is that the Shastras never contemplated the absorption of non-Aryan plebian people into the Hindu hierarchy. But no Shastras could stem the tide of human progress, and the non-Aryan races were not slow to take advantage of the Hindu civilization to which they became attached, and in course of time assimilated'.

It is a question of common knowledge of which we can safely take judicial notice that in custom, worship, religious observation and other rites the Mundas who are aborigines are akin to other aboriginal races which inhabit this province and if in the case of some of them it has been held by the courts that they are Hindus we see no reason to hold that a Mundari woman is on a different footing. In a case like the present one of the safest courses is to look not so much to Shastric injunction but to the treatment of the society towards the person who claims to be a Hindu. It is in evidence that the defendants, the issues of Mangri, were treated as Hindus and this could not have been the case if Mangri was treated as a non-Hindu. There is no doubt that at present the tendency is to treat the Mundas as Hindus and they also regard themselves as such.

The most recent discussion of this issue is contained in a judgment by Ray J. delivered in September 1945 (1945, *I.L.R.* Patna, 727-741 Chunka vs. Bhabani) and I will quote some of his remarks in extenso.

In this case the plaintiff who was the daughter of a Santal from Manbhum claimed to inherit to the exclusion of her father's agnates. She pleaded that both the parties were Hindus and in matters of succession and inheritance were governed by the Mitakshara Code. The defendants on the other hand pleaded in their written statement that both parties were governed by the Dayabhaga School of Hindu Law. Issues were framed on these pleadings but ten months later the defendants filed a pitition stating that they 'never gave any advice to file a written statement to the effect that these defendants are governed by the Dayabhaga system and all their acts are done according to that School, nor is that fact true. Rather they are aboriginals and the parties have no concern with Mitakshara and any other School of Hindu Law. In fact the parties are governed by tribal custom. According to their custom females cannot inherit, only the wife gets the enjoyment of the properties left by the husband during her lifetime. And this is the advice they gave. The former statement is not correct. The trial court acceded to this petition and the points at issue then became whether the parties were Hindus and governed by the Mitakshara Code or being non-Hindus, a customary rule of agnatic succession excluding females obtained amongst them. On these issues, the trial court recorded evidence and held that while the parties were not Hindus the evidence proved a tribal custom under which a daughter excluded agnates.

This decision was uphled by the first appellate court but on different grounds—it being ruled that both the parties were Hindus and that both by the Mitakshara and by tribal custom as proved in the case a daughter could inherit. Against this decision the defendants appealed to the Patna High Court and in his judgment Ray J. summarised the pleadings as follows. 'The defendants have preferred this second appeal, and the learned Counsel, appearing for them urges in the main, that the parties belong to an aboriginal tribe called Santals, and are outside the pale of Hinduism. The evidence on record does not establish that the Santals, to which class the parties belong, have been converted into Hinduism. The circumstance that the parties worship ghosts is inconsistent with their being Hindus. The onus of proof lay heavily upon the plaintiff to prove either that they were governed in matters of succession and inheritance by the rules of Mitakshara School of Hindu Law, or that plaintiff as the daughter's daughter of the last male owner could succeed in preference to the agnates by custom obtaining in the tribe; that the plaintiff has failed to discharge the same. His other contentions will be noticed presently. The learned Counsel in support of his contention of agnatic rules of succession and female exclusion relies upon Risley on tribes and the judgment of McPherson J. in Kritibash Mahton vs. Budhan Mahtani.

The learned Counsel on behalf of the respondents urges, in reply, that the Santals are sufficiently Hinduised even though they retain some of the relics of their ante-Hinduism period, and are, therefore, governed by the Mitakshara School of Hindu law which is lex loci of the area in which the parties live. In his view what Risley wrote is merely of historical importance and the Santals have subsequently been absorbed into the Hindu community, and, therefore, the presumption is that they are governed by the Hindu law. He further urges that the issue raised by the defendents that, amongst the Santals, the females are excluded from inheritance has not been substantiated by them. He also contended that the matter is concluded by the concurrent findings of fact by both the courts below.

The material question, therefore, is whether the parties are Hindus and as such governed by the Mitakshara School of Hindu Law, in matters of inheritance and succession, or whether the plaintiff is an heir to her maternal grandfather in preference to the latter's agnates who are the defendants in the suit in accordance with any well established tribal custom.

Ray J. then continues 'Risley in his historical work on tribes says that the Santals are aborigines and are not governed by the Hindu Law in matters of inheritance and succession. In such matters agnatic succession is the rule. McPherson J. in the case of Kritibash Mahton vs. Budhan Mahtani cited above, says the same thing though his observations were not necessary for the decision of the case. It was conceded by the parties in that case that the Hindu Law of succession was applicable. Manohar Lal J. in Harakhnath Ohdar vs. Ganpat Rai holds the observations of McPherson, J. to be *obiter dicta.* He leaves the question open to be decided, in each case, on its own facts. It is, therefore, to be examined on the evidence adduced by the parties viewed in the light of authoritative pronouncements bearing upon the subject, whether the Santals of Chota Nagpur, to which tribe the parties belong, are Hindus, and as such, governed by the Hindu Law relating to inheritance and succession.

Ray J. then considered various aspects of this issue. He rejected the contention that a ceremony of expiation was necessary in order to make an aboriginal a Hindu and held that the issue must turn on how far the parties had become either Hinduised out and out, or sufficiently Hinduised in order to attract the principles of Hindu Law in matters of inheritance and succession. He then referred to the judgments of Noor J. in Doman Sahu vs. Buka and Jwala Prasad, J. in Gonesh Mahto vs. Shib Charan and summarised his conclusion as follows: 'To sum up, the position is that it is possible in law that aborigines of non-Hindu orgin can become sufficiently Hinduised so that in matters of inheritance and succession they are prima facie governed by the Hindu Law except so far as any custom at variance with such law is proved; that is for the purpose of Hinduisation any formal ceremony of conversion is not necessary; that the test as to whether people of non-Hindu origin have become Hindus out and out consists not in 'their following the religious rules of Srutis and Smritis or their completely giving themselves up to Brahmanical rules and rituals but in their acknowledging themselves to be Hindus and in adopting Hindu social usages, the retention of a few relics of their ante-Hinduism period notwithstanding'.

In cases where complete Hinduisation is proved, the parties are to be prima facie governed by the rules of the Hindu Law, and the burden of proving that any special custom obtained in the community either as a relic of their non-Hindu period or otherwise is upon the party who sets it up. The case of Narendra Narain Choudhuri vs. Nagendra Narain Choudhuri, affords some illustration of the tests to be applied for the purpose of determining Hinduisation of Non-Hindu tribes. In that case adoption of Hindu names, employment of priests, performance of Pujas, such as Durga Puja, Mansa Puja, Kali Puja and so on, offering of pindas, observance of mourning, performance of funeral ceremonies were held sufficient proof of family aboriginal in origin having adopted Hinduism in its entirety, and the nature of the oral evidence was, as in the present case, several witnesses saying the family is a Hindu family, that the members of the family are Hindus by creed.

Ray J. then proceeded 'to examine the evidence in this case in the light of the law laid down in the judicial pronouncements referred to above', and continued I have thought it proper to go into evidence keeping in view that the question whether a family or tribe of non-Hindu origin has been so far Hinduised as to attract the provisions of Hindu Law in matters of inheritance and succession is a mixed question of law and fact. On reading the evidence, I find the defendant no. 1 admitting that he belongs to the caste of Santal. The learned Judge, who decided the case in *A.I.R.* 1929, Cal. 577, observes that it is only the Hindus who speak of caste. The same witness, defendant no. 1 says that he along with other agnates performed the sradh and fed people on the occasion of the death of the plaintiff's mother's mother. He speaks of jointness in mess and property and separation as prevalent in Hindu Mitakshara family. He says :

> Defendants 3 and 4 are not joint with us in mess and property.

P.W. 3 deposes that if out of two brothers one dies, the other brother gets the property, but if they are separate and the deceased leaves a daughter the daughter succeeds. P.W. 1 in cross-examination says :

> We perform Durga Puja, Kali Puja and Badna Puja.
> D.W. 1 says :
> There are Bengalis in those neighbouring villages. We have to go to these villages. In these villages Durga Puja and Kali Puja are performed. We go to witness these festivals and dance there. We bow in front of the idols. Bhakta festival is done.
>
> He further says :
> 'We perform bhoj (pinda) at the time of death of anybody'.
> It is admitted by the plaintiffs as well as the defendants' witnesses that they engage priests, though of their own caste, for the performance of marriage ceremonies. It is further deposed that at the time of marriage the bridegroom puts vermillion on the forehead of the bride. The custom is observed in Hindu societies, vermillion being the sign of a married woman whose husband is alive. As to the applicability of the law of survivorship, P.W. 2 says :
> 'If two brothers live jointly and if one dies, his property devolves upon the other brother. If they are separate, the property devolves on the widow in the absence of a son.'

It also appears from the plaint and the memorandum of appeal that the parties have adopted Hindu names such as Bhabani (plaintiff), Pandu and Keshar (defendants 3 and 4), Ganesh, Mahesh, Jugal and Kali, sons of appellant no. 2 substituted on his death in his place.

After considering this evidence, Ray J. continued, besides the adoption of the above Hindu social and religious usages as spoken to by the witnesses examined in the case, we have the strongest evidence afforded as to the complete Hinduisation of the parties by the fact that the stage of framing of issues and till almost the very last stage of the suit both parties asserted that they were Hindus, the only difference being as to whether Mitakshara or Dayabhaga School of Law would govern the question of inheritance at issue. The amendment was an afterthought and not bona fide. With regard to the correctness of the first statement, defendant no. 1 deposes :

> I got the written statement written by Ramesh Babu. I told him that we are governed by the Santal custom. I cannot say what he wrote. I am illiterate.

No reliance can be placed upon this evidence which by necessary implication denotes that the pleader concerned in drafting the written statement went against the positive instructions of his client.

It is also asserted by the defendant that on the death of a male holder of a property, his widow succeeds and her right is a limited one as it is in Hindu Law. This evidence a departure from the rule of agnatic succession in their Hindu period. The plaintiff has exhibited a judgment in which the right of a female to succeed in preference to the agnates was upheld, while the defendants have adduced no evidence whatsoever to show that in a case of disputed succession, agnatic rule has been recognised by courts. Both the courts have concurrently found that succession by females such as widow's daughter and daughter's daughter is a well established rule amongst them. This militates against the defence case of agnatic rule of succession. This rather proves complete Hinduisation of the clan. I cannot view this rule of succession as a survival of their old custom. Either it is a customary rule of succession or a rule of

Hindu Law. It is more probably the latter when judged with other Hindu social customs and usages adopted by their community. Their pleadings denote their consciousness of their Hindu status. It has been brought to our notice that according to Manbhum Settlement Report by far the majority of Santals have been recorded as Hindus.

Ray, J. accordingly concurred with the lower appellate court and dismissed the appeal.

I have quoted this judgment in detail because it is likely to become a leading case on the subject. It also admirably represents the viewpoint of a cultured Hindu scholar. But I have little doubt that if a tribesman could understand its argument he would find himself perplexed and baffled while if he were asked to comment on the suit in all its complex length he would express bitterness and disillusion. What would be the reasons for his bewilderment and dismay?

In the first place, the principles of law which were finally applied in this suit run directly counter to those which are at present accepted by the main Santal community as applicable in such cases. In the Santal Parganas which is the principal centre of the Santals, a daughter can only oust her father's agnates if she is married to a ghar jawae. Nothing was brought on the record of the case to show that she had done so or on the other hand that the Santals concerned had left their community. Yet the issues between them were decided not in terms of Santal law but in terms of a Code which the main Santal community does not accept.

In the second place, a tribesman would almost certainly be surprised at the interpretation placed upon the term 'Hindu by religion'. Aboriginals as a whole have no term of their own with which to describe their religion and as the experience of the census shows they are often quite willing to term themselves Hindus for want of any better label. When a tribesman says his religion is Hindu, he often merely means that he is not a Christian or Mohammadan. He certainly never implies that he has shed all his tribal ways, that he has adopted Brahmanic practices, or what is of vital importance that he has exchanged the law of his community for that of another. Even if he adopts certain Hindu festivals, it is often because they afford him fresh excuses for jollity and because tribal religion is often as elastic as Hinduism. 'Nothing', says Verrier Elwin 'is so infectious as a celebration. We will not, therefore, be surprised to find the Baiga observing a number of their neighbour's feasts, or rather keeping festival on the same days. They often have a quite different idea of what the festival is and sometimes no idea at all, but they do not like to be left out. Thus the Baiga observes the Holi and Dasahra festivals of the Hindus, but they know nothing of Kamadeva's attempt to rouse Shiva's desire for Parvati they have no idea of propitiating Holika. The Dasahra gains its importance by being the occasion for the Baiga Bida ceremony; none of the Hindu rites or theories are associated with it. It is the same at Diwali. It would be more accurate to say, not that the Baiga observe Dasahra or Diwali, but that they observe a festival at these times.'[6] The fact, therefore, that a tribesman participates in Hindu festivals or even calls himself a Hindu should not be regarded as of very great significance. In ordinary tribal practice, it merely means that he has added some festivals to his own tribal ones and has adopted a convenient name.

Moreover 'Hinduism' itself throughout its long development has always been tolerant of variety and there is nothing in Hindu theory or practice to prevent a tribesman from retaining all his tribal practices and yet being accepted as a Hindu.

Professor Suniti Kumar Chatterji, for example, has defined 'Hinduism' as 'a religion without any formal or official creed. It is a federation of different kinds of religious experience, rather than a single type of religious experience excluding or denying all other types.

It does not pin itself down to the experiences and, opinions of any single individual—Incarnation or prophet although it reverences all. It recognises that the Ultimate Reality manifests itself in various forms, and that Truth is approachable by diverse paths, and as such does not insist upon or inculcate a particular creed which must be accepted by all and sundry. It believes that man can attain to the *summum bonum* in life through the best that is available in his environment followed in a spirit of sincerity and charity.

Some doctrines like Karma or man's action determining

his fate, and Samsara or transmigration, are almost universally believed in by Hindus (including Brahmanists, Buddhists, Jainas and others) but it is not required of everybody to subscribe to these as a compulsory creed.

Hinduism does not seek to lick into a standardised type with the 'Hindu' name all the various manifestations of the human mind and of humanity; it recognises diversity on the basis of unity, and seeks no imperialism on the spiritual plane'.

"Hinduism, as a faith, Jawaharlal Nehru has said 'is vague, amorphous, many sided, all things to all men. It is hardly possible to define it, or indeed to say definitely whether it is a religion or not, in the usual sense of the word. In its present form, and even in the past, it embraces many beliefs and practices, from the highest to the lowest, often opposed to or contradicting each other. Its essential spirit seems to be to live and let live. Mahatma Gandhi has attempted to define it: If I were asked to define the Hindu creed, I should simply say: Search after truth through non-violent means. A man may not believe in God and still call himself a Hindu, Hinduism is a relentless pursuit after truth. . . . Hinduism is the religion of truth. Truth is God. Denial of God we have known. Denial of truth we have not known'. Truth and non-violence, so says Gandhi; but many eminent and undoubted Hindus say that non-violence as Gandhi understands it, is no essential part of the Hindu creed, we thus have truth left by itself as the distinguishing mark of Hinduism. That of course is no definition at all".[7]

When a distinguished scholar such as Professor Suniti Kumar Chatterji and a great national leader such as Pandit Jawaharlal Nehru both emphasise the all-embracing character of Hinduism, it is little wonder that an aboriginal without intending in any way to lose his tribal law sometimes also calls himself a Hindu.

It is this essentially elastic character of Hinduism which should surely determine the legal use of the term and in fact there is much to commend itself in Verrier Elwin's view.

'The religion of the aboriginals, at least of peninsular India', he says 'should be regarded as a religion of the Hindu family, with a special relation to the exciting, dangerous, catastrophic Shaivaite type, but as having a distinct existence of its own. For purposes of the Census, all aboriginal should be classed as Hindus by religion, but separate returns of their numbers by race should be provided.'

Verrier Elwin then adds an important corollary: 'Yet aboriginal religion (with its cow-sacrifice, its worship of daemonic beings, its ceremonial use of blood and liquor) although it belongs theologically to the Hindu family and although politically the aboriginals should be classed with the Hindu community is a thing distinct and apart; and where there have been attempts to assimilate the tribesmen too rapidly into conventional village Hinduism (a thing very different from the lofty Hinduism of history) harm has often been done'.[8]

If the term 'Hindu' is applied to aboriginals, therefore, it should be used in a strictly tribal sense. That is to say; just as there are Rajput Hindus, Brahman Hindus, Gwala Hindus, each with their own distinctive cultures, a similar autonomy within the great Hindu federation should be accorded to aboriginal Hindus. Aboriginals should in fact be recognised as Hindus but in a sense which does no injury to their customs, involves no revolution in their values, imposes no alien formula on their law. The term 'Hindu' should describe a fact, not inaugurate a revolution.

I have little doubt that when a tribesman uses the term it is this which is in his mind. He is emphasising his vital unity with other castes of modern India and is claiming a place in a great federation. In that view, his culture and law as they exist are already Hindu and the question of imposing the Mitakshara on him cannot arise. Aboriginal law should rather be accorded the status of a local branch of Hindu Law. Just as the Mitakshara applies to certain Hindus and not to others and within the Mitakshara there are also local schools such as those of Benares, Mithila and Bombay. Santal law might be designated as the Santal School of Hindu Law. In such circumstances, a Santal could describe himself as a Hindu without either exposing himself to the abrupt application of shastric injunctions or endangering all the principles and traditions which in tribal society have moulded his existence and defined his very life.

But apart from the law applied to his case and the interpretation given to the term 'Hindu', there is another way in which a suit such as this would perplex a tribesman.

In the suit in question, after his written statement had been filed, a defendant alleged that it entirely misrepresented his case, and the trial court was sufficiently impressed that it amended the issues. At the time of taking evidence on Hinduisation a number of significant points were apparently omitted (for they are not referred to in the High Court judgment). It does not seem to have been asked whether the parties participated in the Santal festivals of the Baha, Mag, Erok', Gundli, Janthar and Sohrae none of which are observed by non-Santals and in all of which offerings are made to specifically Santal deities. It was not enquired whether a non-Santal can worship the major Santal deities, Maran Buru, Moreko Turuc' ko and Jaher Era, whether *sindur* is necessary for a Santal marriage or a union can be valid without it, whether the Santals observe the Rajput or Brahmanic usage of a marriage dowry or on the contrary pay a bride-price, whether Santals eat pork and beef and whether like Santals, Rajputs and Kayasths drink rice water mixed with nim leaves at a birth ceremony, whether they use rice beer in their religious offerings, whether the Santal order of naming children is the same as in Brahmanic society, whether a cow is sacrificed at the final funerary feast of bhandan and whether cow sacrifice is part of Rajput usage. None of these questions which might have revealed important differences with caste Hindus were asked at all.

Moreover, at the stage argument in the High Court, only the McPherson judgment and Risley were cited as authorities. No reference was made to Campbell's 'Rules of Succession and Inheritance of Property as observed by the Santals',[9] to Bodding's 'Some Remarks on the Position of Women among the Santals',[10] to Sir Hugh McPherson's *Final Report on the Survey and Settlement Operations in the Santal Parganas, 1898-1907*,[11] to J.F. Gantzer's similar report for the revision Settlement, 1922—35[12], to the High Court's own ruling in Chunka Marandi vs. Pani Murmu (an appeal decided by Ross and Das J.J. in 1928) and not a single reference was made to the Santali text, *Horkoren Mare Hapramko reak' Katha.*

If a Santal's final reaction to this suit were one of bewilderment and dismay, it is considerations such as those which might explain his feelings.

NOTES AND REFERENCES

1. This tendency is very general in other areas also. 'The customs which regulate the ownership, usufruct or transfer of land among primitive tribes are generally at variance with those observed by more sophisticated communities, and in the conflict between the two the tribal custom is normally superseded by a code which is neither valued nor understood by the tribe and in the application of which the tribe is deprived of its property, generally in the name of law; either by alienation to foreigners or by transforming the trusteeship of a tribal chief into absolute ownership of a kind quite foreign to the customs of the tribe' (J. H. Hutton, *Census of India, 1931*, I, 504).
2. Verrier Elwin, *Loss of Nerve*, 23.
3. Ibid., 24.
4. Grigson, op. cit., 6.
5. 'The question, then, is what is the law of succession governing the parties. Reference has been made to a number of authorities to the effect that once it is shown that a party is a Hindu it will be presumed that he is governed by the Hindu Law of Succession and the party who alleges a special custom, has to prove the same. In this particular case we have the admission on the part of the plaintiffs that the parties have now become Hindus and have adopted the Hindu religion. The presumption, therefore, would follow that ordinarily they would be governed by the Hindu Law of Succession. In Mokka Kone vs. Ammakutti the question was considered by a Full Bench of the Madras Court in relation to a community who were originally non-Hindus but had subsequently adopted the Hindu religion. It was held in that case that in the case of persons professing the Hindu religion, the Hindu law as expounded in the Smritis and commentaries prevalent in the province in which the dispute arises should prima facie govern the parties though it is open to them to show that the Hindu Law has been either modified by custom or that particular rules have not been adopted by the community who retained in that respect their original customs; and it must be presumed that the parties are governed by the Hindu Law except in so far as they prove any custom which is at variance with it. These observations apply to the facts of the present case and in the absence of evidence it must be presumed that the parties are governed by the ordinary Hindu Law of Succession.'

   The Allahabad High Court, on the other hand, have ruled [Raj Bahadur vs. Bishen Dayal (1882) 4 All, 343 (348)] that 'the mere fact that a man calls himself a Hindu does not bring him within the purview of Hindu Law', (N. D. Basu, *The Indian Succession Act*, Calcutta, 1941, 42).

6. Verrier Elwin, *The Baiga* (London, 1939), 62.
7. Jawaharlal Nehru, *The Discovery of India* (Calcutta, 1946), 73-74.
8. Elwin, *The Aboriginals*, 25-26.
9. *J.B.O.R.S.*, I (1915), 21-25.
10. *J.B.O.R.S.*, II (1916), 239-49.
11. Calcutta, 1907.
12. Patna, 1936.

53

TRIBAL JUSTICE IN THE SANTAL PARGANAS

I

WHAT IS THE position of Santal justice in the Santal Parganas?

In 1938, this question was investigated by the Santal Parganas Enquiry Committee and I will quote in extensor certain passages from its report. The Committee began by pointing out that 'there are two sets of Civil Courts in the district.'

(a) The Regular Civil Courts established under the Bengal and Assam Civil Courts Act of 1887 which deal with suits valued above Rs. 1,000. These courts are under the jurisdiction of the High Court at Patna, and are governed by the Civil Procedure Code. The suits are tried by the Subdivisional Officers or by Deputy Collectors specially empowered, who are vested with the powers of a Subordinate Judge. The Deputy Commissioner is, under Section 8 of Regulation V of 1893, the District Judge.

(b) The Santal Civil Courts established under Section 2 of Act XXXVII of 1855 which deal with civil suits up to a value of Rs. 1,000. These courts are not governed by the Civil Procedure Code but by a special set of rules—the Santal Civil Rules—framed under Section 1 (2) of Act XXXVII of 1855.

By virtue of orders issued under Section 14 of Regulation V of 1893, money suits of every description, and rent suits against raiyats only, up to a value of Rs. 200, may be tried by Sub-Deputy Collectors and suits valued above Rs. 500

are triable only by the Subdivisional Officer. The course of appeal is to the Deputy Commissioner and the Commissioner. The High Court of Patna has no jurisdiction and for these suits the Commissioner of Bhagalpore is the High Court.

The Committee after discussing the Regular Courts then proceeded to examine the working of the Santal Civil Courts.

'The existence of two sets of Civil Courts', it said, 'one under the High Court at Patna and the other under the Commissioner of Bhagalpore, and still more the exercise of civil jurisdiction by officers other than those of the judicial cadre has often been attacked. The general criticism made of the Santal Civil Courts is that the officers lack that training in civil law which is necessary to enable them to decide cases correctly, that their decisions are often arbitrary and summary and that the Santal Civil Rules under which they work are defective and inadequate. This leads to injustice and Government have often been urged, therefore, to abolish these courts and to place all Civil Courts under the rule of the High Court and the Civil Procedure Code. The legal profession in particular is opposed to the present system and all the Bar Associations in the district have suggested its abolition.

'Nevertheless we are of opinion that it is necessary to retain separate Santal Civil Courts. These courts with their simplified procedure possess very definite advantages for the poorer classes of litigants. Their working is based on the principles that the ordinary litigation of the cultivators and of the poorer classes which forms the vast bulk of the litigation coming before the courts, should be tried in the simplest, cheapest and the most expeditious manner and as far as possible by direct dealing between the parties and the court. The Santal Parganas is a poor district and an examination of the statistics shows that over 92 per cent of the total litigation consists of suits valued below Rs. 200. The vast majority of these suits are of a petty nature. Cheap and speedy justice is more important to the people than technical perfection. We believe that the simple procedure of these courts gives less cause for harassment, delay and expense to the parties, and in these courts a rich man has not the advantage over the poor man that he has in the Regular Courts. Injustice may and has occurred owing to the ignorance of officers or the adoption of too summary methods, but the Regular Courts also are not immune from the infliction of injustice; and we believe that the good features the Santal Civil Courts are so valuable to the great mass of poor litigants that they should not be abandoned. We agree that the Code of procedure under which these courts work—the Santal Civil Rules—is susceptible of improvement and we make proposals on that subject in Chapter VIII of the report. We also think that, if officers are retained in the district for longer periods and if the Deputy Commissioner and the Subdivisional Officers are given more time to supervise their work, it will be possible to improve greatly the standard of judicial work in these courts. These measures, we consider, should remove most of the substantial causes of complaint against the Santal Civil Courts and we, therefore, recommend that they be retained.

'We have next to consider whether the present limits of jurisdiction of the Santal Civil Courts should be modified. A number of witnesses including several of the Bar Associations take the view that if these special courts are retained, their jurisdiction should be reduced to suits of a value not exceeding Rs. 250 on the model of the Small Cause Courts in the regulation districts. The Santal Civil Courts are suitable for the ordinary litigation of the agricultural population and they should have a jurisdiction sufficiently wide to embrace this. But they are not equally suited to more complicated litigation and are unnecessary for money and title suits of comparatively high value in which aboriginals and cultivators are hardly concerned. There is no doubt that among the more advanced classes the Regular Courts and a right of appeal to the High Court would inspire more confidence. We are of opinion, therefore, that the present limit of Rs. 1,000 is too high. At the same time we think that it would be dangerous to reduce it as low as Rs. 250. It is generally admitted that an extension of the jurisdiction of the Regular Civil Courts is likely to lead to increased litigation; and if the limit of jurisdiction of the Special Courts is placed so low as Rs. 250 there is a danger that the more affluent plaintiffs or those who wish to attract the jurisdiction of the Regular Courts, will over-value their suits. This device may be exploited to the disadvantage of the aboriginals and the poorer classes. We think, therefore, that the limit fixed should not only cover all the normal litigation of the poorer classes but should also provide a sufficient margin of safety against the tendencies which we have just described. We think that both objects will be secured if the level is fixed at Rs. 500. It may be argued that even at this level over-valuation will not be avoided; but we think that the risk is small. We accordingly recommend that the jurisdiction of the Santal Civil Courts be fixed at Rs. 500 and that suits over that value should be tried in Regular Courts under the jurisdiction of the High Court and the Code of Civil Procedure'.[1]

II

How does Santal justice fit into this pattern ?

It will be evident in the first place that as with other residents of the district, Santals also have two sets of courts to which they can bring their civil disputes. The recommendations of the Committee have not as yet been fully implemented and at the present time all suits valued at Rs. 1,000 or below are still triable under the Santal Civil Rules. Since land is not saleable in the district, valuation is necessarily according to an ad hoc scale and the following valuation has been approved by the Bihar Government.

	Per acre
First class dhani land ...	75
Second class ,, ,, ...	60
Third class ,, ,, ...	45
First class bari lands, tanks and bandhs. ...	45
Second class bari lands, tanks and bandhs.	30
Patit	15

As houses on agricultural land are also not saleable, their value is only the market value of their materials.

Since Santal suits rarely involve more than 13 acres of first class dhani land, or 22 acres of first class bari, the great majority of Santal suits are, therefore, disposed of under this simplified procedure. A few cases, however, have been filed and decided by the Regular Courts and if their jurisdiction is lowered to Rs. 500, a considerably larger number will fall within their ambit. Even more would fall if the scale of valuation were to be modified.

But besides the official courts, there is also a flourishing system of tribal councils and the official courts are at most only alternative and parallel agencies which are invoked when a Santal dislikes or shirks a tribal decision or when he cannot get it implemented.

These tribal courts have as such no legal powers for enforcing their decisions and their authority rests only on the willing acceptance of their decisions by the contesting Santals. They are not, however, devoid of contacts with the Santal Civil Courts and there are infact two important links with official justice.

Under Santal Civil Rule 22 'cases may be referred to arbitration with the consent of both parties, each naming one and a third being named by the court', and 'an award when confirmed shall have the effect of a decree of the Court'.[2]

This rule does not empower a court to refer a suit to a tribal council *suo motu* but it associates Santals with the decision of suits, it enables tribal experience to be brought to bear and it has the important consequence of freeing decisions from the iron hand of judicial rulings.

Rule 26 on the other hand gives the tribal councils a definite place in legal justice and accords them virtually the status of original courts. The rule provides that

'In a dispute decided by a local tribal council consisting of a Parganait and manjhis and in which no suit has been filed in court, the Parganait as president of the council/or the party in whose favour the dispute has been decided by the council may apply to the Subdivisional Officer having jurisdiction over the matter for confirmation of the council's award. The Subdivisional Officer shall then obtain a statement of the dispute from the Parganait together with the award and after hearing the parties and the council may either confirm the award or pass such orders as he thinks fit. Such an award when confirmed shall have the force of a Civil Court decree. All such applications must be made within a period of one year from the date of the council's award'.

This rule which was made by Government in January 1946 is still in its infancy but its promulgation has been widely acclaimed by Santals and it should go a very long way indeed to giving tribal justice a legal sanction.

III

How far are the Santal Civil Courts adjusted to Santal needs ?

In his book, *The Importance of Living*, Yin Lutang, the Chinese philosopher has observed, 'The quality of the bride and bridegroom is more important than the conventions of marriage and divorce and the men administering or upholding the laws are more important than the laws themselves'.

This is obviously true of Santal courts, and if an officer has no instinctive sympathy for Santal work all the rules in the world will not make him a good Santal administrator. At the same time a system can and does affect its officers and there are various ways in which the orders of Government and the Santal Civil Rules go far to create a type of justice both simple and sensitive to Santal needs.

Under Government orders for example every officer posted to the Santal Parganas is required to pass a departmental examination in Santali within two years of his posting to the District. Before 1942 this rule had not always been observed but during the last three years 9 officers passed this examination by the Higher standard and a further 6 by the lower. The result was that in 1945 the majority of the officers holding Santal courts did in fact understand and speak Santali and Santals who came to their courts did not, therefore, feel that the machinery of justice was either strange or hostile.[3]

Moreover under orders which were passed in 1944 Santali was made an optional court language in the Dumka Subdivision and as a result all petitions, plaints and written statements in Santal suits could be filed by Santals in their own language. This provision was of great importance for in the district as a whole only eight per cent of the total number of Santals speak or understand any language other than their own.[4] The results were of great interest for in the twelve months following the order petitions in Santali almost equalled those in Bengali.[5]

It has now been proposed that Santali should be made an optional court language throughout the district and if this is approved, not only will the task of following the pleadings in Santal suits be rendered everywhere much easier but the risk of the courts misunderstanding the parties due to faulty translation into English, Hindi or Bengali will be obviated.[6]

Moreover the Rules for the trial of suits aim throughout at keeping justice, quick, cheap and personal. Plaints for example, may be either verbal or written and after a plaint is admitted the defendant is summoned for its early disposal. On the first date both the plaintiff and defendant are examined and if the merits of the case are fully disclosed, the court may pass orders forthwith. If further evidence is needed, the Court examines the plaintiff's witnesses the same day and only if the defendant so desires is an adjournment given for producing evidence in defence. If both the parties are Santals, lawyers are only allowed to appear with the consent of the court and then only for special reasons and in practice lawyers do not appear. The result is that the parties have direct access to the court and suits are tried and decided on a level that is plainly and patently Santal.

Finally it has always been an unquestioned assumption of the courts that Santal law is 'common law' for Santals in the Santal Parganas. J.F. Gantzer in his Settlement report states that 'The Hindu or Mohammadan laws of Succession do not apply to Santals'[7] and as the judgments in the case Chunka Marandi vs. Pani Murmu shows, this principle has been consistently applied. As a corollary the courts have always treated Santal Law as 'an Indian Law, unwritten but existent' and under Section 57 Indian Evidence Act have taken judicial notice of it without requiring the parties to offer any proof. There can be no doubt that this underlying assumption—that there was a Santal law and that it bound all Santals—went very far to satisfying the needs of the tribe.

IV THE REGULAR COURTS

When the valuation of a suit is Rs. 1,000 jurisdiction shifts from the Santal courts to the Courts of Sub-Judges constituted under Act XII of 1855 and subordinate to the Patna High Court. Until 1943, this shift of jurisdiction involved an abrupt change of legal system but except for the final appellate stage, it did not involve a change of judicial personnel. All the Subdivisional Officers were *ex officio* Sub-Judges, a Deputy Collector at Deoghar was Additional Sub-Judge while none of the Sub-Judges were officers of the judicial cadre. Moreover Deputy Commissioner was himself the District Judge. Accordingly on the few occasions when the valuation of a Santal suit conferred jurisdiction on a Sub-Judge, the courts which tried the suit and heard the first appeal were also Santal Civil Courts. This system gradually became unsuited to litigation by non-aboriginals. The increasing pressure of executive business made piece-meal hearing almost unavoidable and delays grew so common that by 1943 the trial of suits by Subdivisional Officer-Sub-Judges had almost stopped. Yet for Santal suits, at least, the staffing of the Sub-Judge courts by 'Santal' officers and the appeal to a District Judge, (who was also the Deputy Commissioner) had one important advantage. From the circumstances of their work as executive authorities all of these officers had frequent contracts with Santals and all of them had some understanding of Santal society.

In 1943, the collapse of the system led to two important changes. The Subdivisional Officers retained their powers as Sub-Judges and all preliminary steps continued to be taken through the agencies of their ministerial staffs. The actual trial of Sub-Judge suits (other than rent suits) was, however, vested in two additional officers of the judicial cadre and these were posted as Sub-Judges at Dumka and Deoghar. In addition an officer of the judicial cadre was in 1944 posted to Dumka as Additional Sessions Judge and was vested with the powers of an Additional District Judge. Since then the majority of Sub-Judge suits and appeals from Sub-Judge decisions have been heard by officers of the judicial cadre.

V

How does Santal law fare in these courts and how far do they satisfy Santal views of justice ?

I have already stated that Santal Sub-Judge suits have

hitherto been rare and I have in fact been able to trace only two which went in appeal to the High Court. The handling of both of these suits is very instructive and I will discuss both of them in detail.

The first case[8] was decided by the Subdivisional Officer-Sub-Judge of Dumka on 21 November, 1925, it was heard and decided in appeal by Sir Robert Russell who was then the Deputy Commissioner-District Judge and the final appeal to the Patna High Court was decided on 10 August, 1928 by a bench consisting of Ross and Das J.J.

In his appellate judgment which was a model of its kind Sir Robert Russell said 'the plaintiff has filed the present suit to obtain a declaration that she is entitled by the customary law of the Santals to inherit as widow the lands of her deceased husband and to regain possession of them by order of the court. She has in the alternative prayed for the declaration that she is entitled to maintenance. The defendants in their written statement while not admitting that she has a right to hold the property in lieu of maintenance are willing to maintain her so long she lives. They deny in toto that she has any right to inherit the property. This is the principal issue to be decided in appeal.

Sir Robert Russell then went on 'The case is one of great importance because it is the first occasion on which a claim by a Santal woman to inherit landed property has ever been made or decided in the courts established under Act XII of 1855. The claims made by the plaintiff contest the whole course of rulings on this point given and the view of the law held in the Santal courts during the last 70 years. The Subordinate Judge has held that where the husband and his other relations have separated the widow succeeds to the land for maintenance for her lifetime and that she is entitled to hold till she remarries or leaves her husband's house permanently. He has, as far as I can understand his judgment, disallowed the plaintiff's claim to inherit the property outright but has conceded to her a life interest in it : though his argument would seem to admit both her claims.

'It is necessary to examine the whole body of evidence on this question *ab initio*, because I consider that the Subordinate Judge has taken an entirely wrong view of the evidence before him. He has accepted the oral evidence of 13 Santals on a mattter which affects about three quarters of a million people. He has on the other hand attributed very little value to the course of rulings in the Santal courts or to published treatises on Santal law or recorded opinions of disinterested and expert observers.

'The law of succession among the Santals is not a written or a codified law. It is law based upon custom and tradition. That law has nowhere been reduced to writing by the Santals themselves. But we are not for that reason ignorant of what the law is. It has been administered in the Santal courts of the district for the last 70 years at first from the knowledge gained by the officers from among the Santals themselves and from the decisions of Santal arbitration courts which have always been freely used to assist the regular courts. Besides these we have monographs written by officers or missionaries residing in the district who have become acquainted with the customs of the Santals through long residence among them. We have lastly a detailed and fairly authoritative transcript of oral traditions regarding Santal custom and law collected by two European missionaries. From all these sources a definite course of rulings has resulted. This body of evidence is entitled to great weight.'

Sir Robert Russell then reviewed the papers by Bodding and Campbell, the note by Bompas in the McPherson Report, a literal translation of the passage in *Horkoren Mare Hapramko reak' Katha* and the trend of decisions by the settlement and Santal law courts. He then proceeded :

'The rulings of the highest Santal courts are not reported and courts established under Act XII of 1887 are not compelled to follow them in the same sense in which they must follow rulings published in the Official Law Reports. But it is impossible for this court to ignore them since they are authoritative decisions by competent courts on the points in issue.

'The effect of all this evidence is that all written records, the trend of rulings and all expert evidence controvert the claim of a widow to succeed to her husband's lands by inheritance. It is in fact settled law that she cannot.

'The plaintiff's case in argument is that whatever the original custom was, and it is practically admitted that the

Hapramko reak' Katha gives a correct statement of that custom, the custom has entirely changed within the last 20 or 30 years. It is a matter of recorded fact that there has been a movement among some of the Santals during the last decade or so to improve the position of women in the Santal community.

'The plaintiff has examined 13 witnesses to prove her contention that the present practice among Santals is to recognise the claims of a widow with daughters to succeed, specially if her dead husband was separate from his agnates. Several of these witnesses are men of importance in the Santal Community. 5 of them are Parganaits of the Damin-i-Koh. These men are headmen appointed by Government as Revenue and Police officers over a number of villages and have considerable power and influence among their people. Their statements are prima facie of importance. Actually they must be largely discounted. The men called are a very small fraction of the body of Parganaits; most of them are Christians, and they all belong to the educated and advanced section of Santals. They speak for a small minority and they do not represent general Santal opinion. They give 14 instances in which the claims of widows with daughters were allowed. A few of them are not parallel to the present case, but I have no doubt that most of them are true. But these are isolated instances of a tendency which is slowly growing and an established custom cannot in the light of the evidence be deduced from them.

'The fact that a portion of the people desire a change and that Santal arbitrators not infrequently carry out this desire in their decisions is a matter of importance. Nor is the growth of such a custom a matter which can be prevented or denied. It may be destructive to the old communal organisation and of the system of land tenure now in force. But the change will probably take place ultimately. If parties agree between themselves amicably to let widows hold the land there is nothing to interfere with them; where arbitrators on equity decide such disputes on equitable grounds in favour of the widow the courts usually have not interfered. But when the matter comes before the courts to decide the question the courts can only follow the established customary law and say that the law recognized no right of the widow to inherit'.

This decision was upheld by the High Court and I will quote a portion of the judgment.

'This is an appeal by the plaintiff, a Santalin, who claimed to inherit immovable property from her husband. The Subordinate Judge decided in her favour, but his decision was reversed by the District Judge. The learned Judge referred in the first place to the authorities, such as they are, on the customary law of the Santals. It is conceded that the law is customary law. These authorities though recent are consistent. They begin with the record made by a missionary named Skrefsrud fifty years ago at the dictation of an old Santal, one Kolean. There are also the opinions of Mr Campbell who was for many years a missionary in Manbhum and the Rev. Mr Bodding, for many years a missionary in the Santal Parganas and a note drawn up by Mr Bompas, the Deputy Commissioner for the guidance of the courts reproduced in the final Settlement report by Sir H. McPherson and acted upon by the Settlement Officers. All these consistently declare that woman does not inherit. The learned Judge then took into consideration the course followed by the Settlement Courts and the Santal courts and found that this leads on the whole to the same conclusion. In the Santal courts, however, many of these questions were referred to arbitration and a number of decisions given by arbitrators, supported the plaintiff's claim. But these, according to the Judge were the decisions of arbitrators of more advanced views, many of the most influential among whom were Christians who were in favour of a change in the customary law. And indeed the plaintiff's case in argument before the Judge was that custom had entirely changed within the last twenty or thirty years.

'Now on this material it seems to me clear that the only possible decision was that which the learned Judge has given. The customary law that women do not inherit being established and in fact practically admitted, that law could only be altered by a well-established custom modifying it, or by legislation. But the customary law has only been subject to recent variation in particular cases. That is not a basis on which the court can act in a matter of disputed succession. The custom is there and it has not been changed although in cases decided by arbitrators effect may have been given to more enlightened opinion.

The appeal must, therefore, fail and be dismissed but without costs'.

It is in some respects unfortunate that this important case arose in the nineteen twenties for as was in fact conceded by Sir Robert Russell himself Santal law was at the time still in process of achieving a new synthesis. But I am inclined to think that the approach of all courts was overinfluenced by conceptions of tribal law as posited by the Indian Evidence Act. The sanction of tribal law does not lie in custom but in the continuing acceptance of certain principles by the tribal community. Custom may for the time being reflect these principles but it is the will to continue their application to disputes which gives to such principles their sanction. Accordingly the initial assumption in the judgments that both parties were bound by Santal customary law was not I think strictly correct. Both were bound by Santal Law but the basis ofdecision was the current 'Common Law' of Santals rather than the previous trend of Santal rulings.

In this view of tribal law, the acute difficulty of deciding a Santal suit in a court constituted under the High Court becomes apparent. If 'Customary Law can only be altered by a well-established custom modifying it or by legislation', a suit alleging a new custom could conceivably succeed if sufficient evidence were laid. But when the law itself is not customary but is rather a set of principles accepted independently of custom the court must either itself already know the law or must have a means of ascertaining it.

If the court is staffed by an officer of the judicial cadre, only a tiny fraction of his work will be Santal and he will normally not have any means of obtaining this 'Common Knowledge' except by consulting 'works of authority' or examining witnesses. The evidence of the latter on the principles in current acceptance by Santals would presumably be relevant under Section 48 of the Indian Evidence Act which states that 'when the court has to form an opinion as to the existence of any general custom or right the opinions on the existence of such custom of right or persons who would be likely to know of its existence if it existed are relevant.' Evidence on these lines would give the court some basis for understanding the law but the taking of it would be open to various objections. It would impose an intolerably severe burden on the Santal parties. It would be of little value unless it was based on many areas. Much of it would in any case be unreliable since the circumstance of the suit would distort the character of the evidence and result in the production of interested witnesses. Finally it would force the Santals into the despairing position of having each time to 'choose and prove their law'. The only other source is through 'works of authority'. It is true that my own *Civil Law in Santal Society* aims at stating the current 'Common Law' of the Santals but unless there is a will on the part of the courts to accept its principles and apply them to suits, or in the alternative a legislative enactment there is no guarantee that this will be done.

Finally we have already seen that in their judgment (Doman Sahu vs. Buka and Others) Cartney Terrell and Mohammed Noor J.J. stated : 'in custom, worship, religious observation and other rites the Mundas who are aborigines are akin to other aboriginal races which inhabit this province and if in the case of some of them it has been held by the courts that they are Hindus we see no reason to hold that a Mundari woman is on a different footing.' They also referred to an extract from Gour in which Santals also were assumed to be Hindus. In Santal Sub-Judge suits in the Santal Parganas no parties have so far ever pleaded that they are Hindus or if Hindu are bound by the Dayabhaga or Mitakshara codes of Hindu law. But there is nothing to stop a party doing this if he is so advised in future. If he did, a Sub-Judge would I think be faced with a virtually insoluble problem. If both parties took this plea, he would still have to decide whether it was legally acceptable, and in the absence of any legislative enactment he would have no material at all on which to base a valid decision. If one party took this plea but not the other, a deadlock would be reached.

The other case is very recent and as it is still sub-judice I will describe it in general terms.

A Santal, A, who was recorded for certain lands was left a widower with a single daughter, B. B contracted relations with person of another caste and left the village. A then married a widow with 2 daughters for both of whom he brought husbands. To one of these, a daughter, E, was born later. E's father died and her mother remarried in another village. A then adopted his step-granddaughter as his daughter and with village approval married her to a ghar jawae. The ghar jawae died and A then brought a second ghar jawae for her. A died and his daughter B then claimed his lands. The village council disallowed B's claim and allotted the lands to E, and this was confirmed by the local officers in a revenue proceeding.

Against this decision, another Santal, D, the son of A's great grandfather's son's daughter filed a title suit valued at Rs. 1097/4 annas and making B and E defendants. He alleged that since B had been outcasted for her marriage with a non-Santal she had forfeited her right to inherit. He further said that E was a 'rank outsider' who was maintained as a servant girl by A out of charity. He himself had continually helped A with loans and had been allowed by him to build a house at a cost of Rs. 900 on one plot of land and to cultivate and enjoy the produce of another. He, therefore, claimed title and possession as A's heir.

This suit obviously raised a number of important and difficult issues :

1. Does permanent residence with a person of another caste disqualify a daughter from inheritance?
2. Was the adoption of the step-granddaughter valid?
3. In view of the fact that under Santal Parganas laws a house on agricultural land cannot be sold and its value is only the market value of its materials, was not the suit overvalued and if so had the Sub-Judge jurisdiction ?

Of these issues, the first was referred to in the plaint but issues 2 and 3 found no mention and were virtually suppressed.

We will now consider the course of the suit : Summon were issued on B and E who appeared and told the court that they were too poor to file written statements or in fact do anything that day. The Sub-Judge, therefore, adjourned the suit to another date for filing of written statement and for settlement of issues.

On that date B and E did not appear and the Sub-Judge then fixed a date for *ex parte* disposal. On that date B and E were again absent. D was examined and D's lawyers then demanded an *ex parte* decree. The Sub-Judge who was an extremely able member of the judicial cadre had had no previous experience of Santal litigation, was unaware of the High Court ruling or of any authorities and asked the pleaders to cite law. D's lawyers then stated that a female and heirs through females can succeed to properties under Santal custom and in support he referred to Gantzer's Report on the Settlement Operations (pp. 22-24). (This report at most shows that the former rule against female succession was breaking down but does not allege that a new rule had as yet taken its place. Both D's pleader and the report were silent on the point whether relations with a person of another caste did in fact result in disinheritance).

The position then at this stage was that neither all the facts, all the issues, nor all the law had been placed before the Sub-Judge and he was now required to pass orders. The Sub-Judge has since told me that if matters had rested there he would have had to pass orders on the material then on record, i.e. D's *ex parte* statement of the facts and the *ex parte* statement of Santal law made on D's behalf by his lawyers. If he had felt uncertain of the Santal law, he would have fallen back on Section 37 of Act 12 of 1887. This section runs

(1) where in any suit or other proceeding it is necessary for a Civil Court to decide any question regarding succession, inheritance, marriage or caste, or any religious usage or institution, the Mohammadan Law in cases where the parties are Mohammadans and the Hindu Law in cases where the parties are Hindus shall form the rule of decision except insofar as such law has by Legislative enactment, been altered or abolished.

(2) in cases not provided for by Subsection (1) or by any other law for the time being in force the court shall act according to justice, equity and good conscience.

The point regarding jursidiction would have escaped him since the Santal Civil Rules and the relevant Revenue Law had not come to his notice. Even if he had felt doubtful of the valuation, he would not have felt justified in rejecting the plaint unless the defendant had raised this issue.

At this stage the suit came to the notice of the District Judge who decided to transfer it to the Subdivisional Officer-Sub-Judge in view of the latter's knowledge and experience of Santal Law. Against the order of transfer to the Subdivisional Officer-Sub-Judge D moved the High Court and in respect of this order also the Santal women took no steps.

Later on the two Santal women were asked why they had not filed appearance and their reply is so illuminating that I will quote it in their own words : They said 'We went to court. We had no money. We saw the other party with his Diku pleaders. We did not like it. We went back home'.

I have referred to this case partly because it illustrates the inherent difficulties in administering tribal justice by a regular civil court but also because it throws much light on the attitude of Santals when confronted with a complex machinery. The demand of all three parties was at bottom a demand for Santal civil justice. Even D would not have asked for anything else. The two women saw stretching before them a hearing conducted by pleaders who knew neither their language nor their law before a judge who did not know Santali in a court room, the very antithesis of a Santal village. They knew that D was wealthy and that if he failed at Dumka he would go to Patna. They themselves had never left the Santal Parganas. They saw demand after demand for lawyers' fees. They saw no end to the hearing. They took one look. They did not like it. They went home.

No one, I think, will blame them but no one, I think, will call this justice.

NOTES AND REFERENCES

1. R.E. Russell, *Report of the Santal Parganas Inquiry Committee* (Patna, 1938).
2. Rules 22-4 run as follows :

   22 (1) Cases may be referred to arbitration with the consent of both parties, each naming one and a third being named by the court. Arbitrators named by the parties must be acceptable to the court.

   (2) The arbitrators named by the court preside and shall be in charge of the papers connected with the case. The arbitrators may

hold the enquiry where they please and in their own way, and shall report their award within a time to be fixed by the court, or ask for an extension thereof. The court may for good and— sufficient cause, withdraw the case at any time before the award.

(3) Nothing herein contained shall debar the parties to any suit from referring their differences to any person or persons mutually agreed upon by them.

23. At the request of the arbitrators the court may issue a summons to any witness to appear before them.

24. (1) The arbitrators shall give their award in writing and they may be summoned to explain it. Any explanation so given shall be recorded and form part of the record.

(2) An award, whether unanimous or not, shall not be confirmed if fraud is proved or it is on the face of it contrary to the statutory law or the record of rights. In such cases the court shall proceed to hear and dispose of the suit itself.

(3) Where the award is unanimous the court shall save in the cases mentioned in sub-rule (2) confirm it. Where the award is not unanimous, the court may if it disagreed with it on any ground other than those mentioned in sub-rule (2) refer it to the next superior court, which shall, after giving the parties an opportunity to be heard, pass such decision on the case as it thinks fit.

(4) An award when confirmed shall have the effect of a decree of the court.

3. That this was unfortunately not always the case is shown by a remark of Jugia Haram. 'The officers since they do not know our Santali language cannot judge right and wrong. They get taken in by the deceptive speeches of the Vakils, and do not give us justice.'

4. The 1931 Census recorded the following figures :

Speakers of :	Santali only.	761688
	Santali with Hindus-thani as second language.	10,027
	Santali with Bengali as second language.	50,783

5. The figures for all types of petitions were :

English	5724
Hindi	7930
Santali	1563
Bengali	1619

6. The great importance of conducting all Santal judicial proceedings in Santali has been emphasised by Booding :

'They were formerly a truthful and thoroughly honest people. They have learnt to lie from the others; they have seen how the others manage to gain their purpose; they try to imitate. As yet they have not learnt to stick to the lie; it is not difficult to find them out. They are, I have been told, especially lying when they use not their own, but the Bengali or the Hindi language. It is a pity that they have to learn a foreign language to get a little education.. (P.O. Bodding, 'Notes on the Santals', *Census of India, 1931*, I, III B, 105).

7. Gantzer, op. cit., 23.
8. Chunka Marandi vs. Pani Murmu.

54

THE SETTLEMENT AND SANTAL JUSTICE

I

IN HIS Report on the Revision Settlement of 1922-35, J.F. Gantzer writes 'The district of the Santal Parganas is settled under the provisions of Regulation III of 1872. The chief difference between this settlement and others lies in the fact that under section 25, the published record has the force of a Civil Court decree and is final and conclusive. Moreover in preparing this record, the Settlement Officer and his staff do not merely as elsewhere, record the existing facts. They have powers of regulation and control and when disputes regarding title arise are empowered to decide them on their merits. One of the most important of these powers is to check the alienation of land and thereby to protect a mainly aboriginal population from being exploited by outsiders. To enable them to perform these duties and exercise these powers officers of this settlement are vested with all the authority of the Santal Civil Courts, whose jurisdiction in regard to land or any interest in or arising out of land is ousted during the period of the operations. It is also to be noted that whereas in normal times the High Court has jurisdiction in respect of land suits exceeding Rs. 1000 in value, during settlement this jurisdiction is entirely ousted, except that under section 25A of the Regulation disputes regarding proprietary rights may be subsequently carried to the Civil Courts and thus if they exceed Rs. 1000 in value, fall within the jurisdiction of the High Court'.[1]

Since this was written there has been one important development. The Commissioner of Bhagalpur has been made a tribunal under the Government of India Act and has been authorised to correct material errors in the record-of-rights. Such corrections are made only after full enquiry by the Sub-divisional Officers or their staff and the number of corrections in any one year has so far been so few that the record has virtually remained final.

II

How far has the Settlement fulfilled the requirements of Santal justice?

It will be obvious that in its village-to-village investigation of rights and through its direct contact with Santals the methods of the settlement are almost ideal for the adjudication of tribal disputes. It is unfortunate, however, that at none of the previous settlements have any of the officers or their higher subordinate staff been required to learn Santali and that all the proceedings have been conducted either in Hindi, Bengali or English. Similarly all the records have been written in one or other of these three languages and as a result an undertaking which might have been of great value to the Santals lost much of its intimacy owing to the barrier of language.

Moreover in view of the temporary supersession of the Santal Civil Courts, a detailed knowledge of Santal law was obviously necessary if the Settlement Officers were to adjudicate issues of title on their merits. Yet although this is obvious enough today, little attention seems to have been paid to this vital matter at any of the settlements.

Section 23 of Regulation III of 1872 provides that 'for every village shall be drawn up a paper setting forth the custom of the village or tribe in regard to the following facts :

(a) the existence of the office of manjhi or other village headship and the duties and emoluments of each headman, and the customs of succession to the headship by inheritance election or otherwise.

(b) the removal or suspension of a headman for misconduct, and the appointment or election to a vacant headship.

(c) the devolution of the lands held by proprietors or

> under proprietors or headmen or cultivated by raiyats, any custom contrary to the ordinary Hindu or Mohammadan law being noted.

This section was not complied with at any of the settlements and McPherson in his Settlement Report of 1909 concedes that in view of the clause, Santal Customary Law 'should have been dealt with more fully in the settlement record-of-right of Santal villages than has been done'.[2]

McPherson's comment is obviously an understatement, for apart from a note by C.H. Bompas translating certain sections in *Horkoren Mare Hapramko reak' Katha*, Santal law was not dealt with at all.

This ignorance of the law naturally had a number of important consequences and in fact the McPherson and Gantzer Settlements are partly responsible for the replacement of early Santal law by the principles which we know today. In this early law an agnatic relation could exclude a widow, daughter or sister from inheritance and after referring to Bompas's note, McPherson declares that 'the principles set forth by Mr. Bompas were followed in disputes about inheritance that arose during the settlement in Santhal villages'.[3] Bompas did not, however, join the district until 1900 and although his note has not been preserved, it seems unlikely that it was written long before the close of the operations. In fact McPherson in a judgment referred to by Sir Robert Russell[4] states that when the Settlement Courts became acquainted with the Santal law they ceased to record women as the successors to jotes. Evidently before that time the settlement officers following the ordinary settlement rule had recorded whatever cultivators were found in possession and in so doing had noted Santal women for a number of holdings.

This development, however, unintentional, was of great importance. A settlement entry conferred an absolute title for life on the person whose name was entered. Even if a woman had only the conditional right of a widow, the unqualified entry of her name converted that right into a life interest. Only nine years after the settlement Bodding wrote 'It ought to be just mentioned that the courts and the settlement have in many cases permitted daughters to get a *life* tenure in agricultural lands and recorded them as raiyats'.[5] There can be little doubt, therefore, that the McPherson Settlement did much to foster later changes in the rights of daughters and widows.

Between 1906 and 1922, Santal practice increasingly departed from the earlier principles and when the revision settlement began the extent of the change was quite unknown. The authorities did not, however, investigate the Law but merely adopted an attitude of neutrality and J.F. Gantzer gives the following description of procedure.

'The relevant portion of Kanapuri Rule No. 46 reads as follows : 'If a female is the cultivator of a field her name should be accompanied by that of her father if she inherited the property from him, or by that of her husband if she inherited from him'. It may be assumed, therefore, that the revision settlement records have been prepared in accordance with the prescribed rule, but in the absence of any definite finding on the point at issue embodied in a dispute list or other order passed by an Assistant Settlement Officer, the value to be attached to the entry of a father's name or a husband's name, as the case may be, is open to challenge when the exact nature of the woman's title is under consideration in a subsequent suit. The position may be summed up in Mr. Dain's observation in his judgment dated 9th April, 1934 in Commissioner's Santal Parganas Settlement Appeal No. 128 of 1933-34 :

> Where a woman holds land, it has not been the practice in the Santal Parganas to make any entry indicating the exact nature of the right by which she holds it, and any observations made on the subject at this stage would not bind a court before which the issue may be directly raised at some future time.

'When a ghar jawae has succeeded to his father-in-law's estate the holding has usually been recorded in his sole name. In some cases, at the request of the parties, the wife has been jointly recorded with her husband'.

Gantzer then proceeds : 'The rules against female succession among Santals whether Christian or non-Christians are changing owing to the force of public opinion, and the rules which have been previously accepted, cannot be treated as hard and fast and binding for all time. The change which is occurring is in the direction of ameliorating the condition of women and giving them a more assured footing in the family. During the course of the revision settlement operations, the daughters of a deceased Santal have sometimes been recorded as his heirs not only without opposition from the agnates but at their request. In other cases it appears from title suit decisions, that arbitrators in Santal cases have found in favour of daughters. This is particularly so in the case of girls who suffer from any physical defects. In dealing with cases of this nature the custom adopted in a particular locality must be carefully considered. It would be unwise to force upon an unwilling litigant a decision in advance of custom. If a change in custom has been well established and generally accepted it will, of course, be treated as the customary law of the locality in mitigation of the harshness of the ancient tribal law.

'As a rule we have tried as far as we could legally do so, to record daughters in all cases where not to do so would have involved real hardship, e.g., where the male relations not only want to claim the land but refuse to maintain the girl. Where close male relations who obviously have a clear right under the law, have been suspected to be likely to desert the girl, we have recorded them, but have also endeavoured to record the girl in the remarks column of the khatian as khorposhdar until death or marriage.

'As regards widows, the entries have had perforce to be even less uniform. There have been not a few cases in which no objection has been raised to the recording of the widow in her own right, and in such cases she has been described as wife or so and so. As in the case of Hindu widows, this entry is intended to indicate that she has inherited the property from her late husband, and that when she dies it will revert to those male relations who would ordinarily have inherited it at once under Santal law. In other cases the widow has like the daughter been recorded only in the remarks column as a khorposhdar for certain plots sufficient to maintain her, until her death.

'To sum up it may be said that where a Santal woman has been recorded as wife of so and so, she holds a widow's right as if she were a Hindu widow. Where a Santal woman has been recorded as daughter of so and so she may be taken to have full rights of inheritance somewhat in the manner of a woman inheriting stridhan property under the Hindu law. The question of succession in such cases is still somewhat in doubt as the system is new, but there seems little doubt that if she dies issueless, Santal sentiment would prefer that the property should revert to her nearest male relatives'.[6]

In addition to these statements on procedure, J.F. Gantzer also discusses the rights of ghar jawaes and ghardi jawaes but as I have shown in the Report on the Civil Law in Santal Society almost everything he says is incorrect. Since these principles were widely applied, much injustice inevitably ensued. By treating the ghar jawae as an adopted son—a thing impossible by Santal standards since this would virtually accuse him of incest—many ghar jawaes were recorded for lands to which their wives alone were entitled and it was only 'in some cases at the request of the parties that the wife was jointly recorded with her husband.' These decisions ran quite counter to the true tribal law. They gave a number of outsiders permanent rights in villages in which they had not been born. They gave family lands to Santals of entirely different families and in many cases they placed 'inheriting daughters' at the complete mercy of their husbands. In the Mandro area one ghar jawae who had been thus recorded married another woman, expelled his first wife (who should have got the lands) and sent her wandering destitute through the country. Local Santals who were shocked by his conduct were even more shocked when the settlement appellate courts upheld the entry and thus completely legalised his action.

In one further respect the settlement often failed to distinguish permanent rights from conditional or temporary ones. In many Santal villages man or service lands are attached to the office of village officials. The tenure of these lands is conditional on the performance of duties but in a number of cases Santals were recorded for these lands without any note to qualify their rights. When I was touring in the Godda damin, the Santals of one village were very bitter because the naeke or village priest had had his service lands recorded in this manner and was now refusing to discharge his duties.

The main criticism of the Gantzer settlement is that in

realising that Santal rights in land were not always permanent but were frequently temporary and conditional it did not take into account all the possible cases and as a consequence in far too many instances Santals who had only limited rights were given permanent titles.

III

If the settlement is to become a more precise instrument for Santal justice, it is desirable that the following steps should be taken :

As a preliminary to the start of fieldwork, all gazetted officers, amins and peshkars deputed to Santal areas should be required to pass the departmental examination in Santali by the lower standard. A year later they should be required to pass by the higher standard. All records of Santal villages should be prepared in Santali and it should be prescribed by standing order that all enquiries into disputed rights should be conducted in that language.

In order that the exact nature of a Santal's rights should not be obscured, operations in any village with Santals should begin with the preparation of an initial report. The amin should meet the manjhi, whether handi manjhi or prodhan, and through his agency should convene a meeting of the Santal villagers. At this meeting, the following questions should be asked :

A. Men

Are any Santal men in possession of lands as :

(1) custodian for (i) an absent villager
(ii) an absent kinsman?

(2) guardian of a minor boy pending his majority?

(3) guardian of a girl pending her marriage?

(4) *ghar jawae* whose parents-in-law and wife have predeceased him leaving him the right to possess the land subject to his not remarrying or leaving the village?

(5) as a village official?

(6) in temporary occupation for recoupment of funerary expenses?
(7) orphan reared but not adopted by his foster-father and given land 'from pity'?
(8) *asul duruc' ic'* i.e. given land with village approval in appreciation of or as part of a contract for life-long services?
(9) master temporarily cultivating a servant's lands on *si-tora.*
(10) creditor illegally holding land in redemption of a debt?
(11) purchaser illegally holding land by virtue of an illegal sale?

B. Women

Are any Santal women in possession of lands as :

(1) childless widow of a dead husband?
(2) widowed mother of minor children?
(3) wife separated from but not divorced from her husband?
(4) widowed mother separate from her sons?
(5) *taben jom* gifted to her 'for life' by a father, brother, uncle or agnatic relation?
(6) *taben jom* gifted to her 'for ever' by a father, brother, uncle or agnatic relation?
(7) original settlement taker?
(8) daughter holding in default of father, brothers, grandfathers, paternal uncles and paternal cousin brothers?
(9) daughter married to a *ghar jawae* and, therefore, inheriting like a son?
(10) daughter whose husband has been subsequently converted into a *ghar jawae* in any approved way?
(11) in temporary occupation for recoupment of funerary expenses?
(12) guardian of a minor boy pending his majority?
(13) guardian of a girl pending her majority?

If the village includes any such cases, all the details of each case together with the plot numbers of the lands should be recorded. This report should be checked by the Inspector and the Assistant Settlement Officer. It should also be carefully verified at attestation and should form a permanent part of the record for later consultation. In all these cases, the person actually in possession (provided it is legal) should be recorded in the khatian but full details of his status in respect of the land must be given in the remarks column. The value of this entry and the conditions attaching to it under Santal law should then be briefly explained in the Settlement Report.

If these steps are taken, the settlement will again become what indeed it was always intended to be 'an operation to preserve to Santals the enjoyment of their lands'.

REFERENCES

1. Gantzer, op. cit., 2-3.
2. McPherson, op. cit., 123.
3. Ibid. 123.
4. R.E. Russell, District Judge's Title Appeal No. [illegible]9 of 1926, Chunka Marandi & Others vs. Pani Murmu and Others (Record Room, Dumka).
5. P.O. Bodding, 'Some Remarks on the Position of Women among the Santals,' *J.B.O.R.S.*, II (1916), 248.
6. Gantzer, op. cit., 22.

55

THE FUTURE OF SANTAL JUSTICE

I

TO THE value of tribal law to aboriginal society a number of writers have given eloquent testimony. 'The tendance of the dead' Verrier Elwin has said 'devotion to the soil, the power to stage a magnificent festival, the discipline of tribal law, are things which modern village religion should not willingly let die. In the spirit of economic fellowship and the tradition of communal living, some primitive villages are a hundred years ahead of the modern world'.[1]

'It is easy' Dr. J.H. Hutton has stated 'to see how a combination of anti-tribal forces is likely to create a condition of excessive discomfort in tribal life, the most serious aspect of which is the complete breakdown of the communal organisation. A tribe living in comparative isolation will usually be found to have developed an adaption to its environment which within certain limits approaches perfection, an adaptation which may have taken many millennia to accomplish, and the breakdown of which may be the ruin of the tribe, for it is likely to proceed at a far greater rate than either the gradual change in physical environment or than the still slower process of adaptation to that change'.[2]

J.P. Mills has stressed how 'realising that on the preservation of customs developed exactly to fit the environment and tested by centuries of use depend the whole fabric of tribal society, Government has been at pains to preserve them to the utmost limit possible and to ensure that such change as must inevitably come shall not be destructive in its suddenness'.[3]

To the Santals, tribal Law is not merely a valued heritage. It is a definition of their culture, an indispensable basis for their whole way of life.

What steps are necessary if justice in the future is to conform to Santal needs?

II

We have seen in Chapter 53 the acute difficulties which confront a Santal when he is obliged by rules of valuation to leave the Santal Civil Courts and to litigate in the Court of a Sub-Judge. We have also seen the difficulties which a Sub-Judge himself experiences in administering Santal law in the light of ordinary legal procedure. The presence of two sets of courts has another disadvantage. Since neither the Deputy Commissioner's nor the Commissioner's Courts are subordinate to the Patna High Court, the rulings of one set of courts are in no sense binding on the others. We have already seen the tendency of the Patna High Court to treat Santals as well as other aboriginals as governed by the Hindu Code of Succession. We cannot, therefore, exclude the possibility of two entirely different systems of Santal law developing—one based on local 'Common Law' and expressed in the rulings of the Santal Civil Courts and the other founded on interpretations of Santal law in its Hindu setting by the High Court at Patna. Such a development would not only spread confusion in the courts but would cause bewilderment and dismay throughout the Santal community. Moreover the division of jurisdiction on the basis of valuation is open to many objections. It encourages richer Santals to over-value suits so that their less wealthy opponents may be exposed to a more complicated procedure. The rules of procedure in Sub-Judge Courts require the Siristadar only to check that the court-fee paid is sufficient and do not warrant the return of a plaint unless it is, on the face of it, so overvalued as manifestly to fall outside the court's jurisdiction. The Code of Civil Procedure does not require the settlement classification of lands to be given in the plaint and accordingly the provisions of the Santal Civil Rules can easily be evaded by merely omitting these details. Unless the opposite party contests the suit and makes valuation an issue, a Santal can readily escape the jurisdiction of the Santal courts if it so suits him. But on wider grounds, the use of valuation for determining jurisdiction is open to criticism. If the Santal Civil Courts were deliberately established in order to provide a judicial system more suited to the Santal mind, it is surely unreasonable to deprive a Santal of their special procedure merely because the property in suit is worth more than Rs. 1000, for a Santal remains a Santal whether the property is great or small. In such cases, the employment of a more complicated procedure and the use of lawyers as intermediaries are only too likely to result in a partial presentation of the facts.

For all these reasons, therefore, it is desirable that a single set of courts should administer Santal justice and that all courts constituted under the Bengal, Agra and Assam Civil Courts Act of 1887, should be relieved of jurisdiction in Santal suits. This will involve an amendment of section 9 of the Santal Parganas Justice Regulation (V of 1893). This section at present runs : 'The jurisdiction of the District Judge or a Subordinate Judge extends subject to the provisions of section 15 of the Code of Civil Procedure, to suits of which the value exceeds one thousand rupees and which are not excluded from his cognizance by the Santal Parganas Settlement Regulation or by any other law for the time being in force. Provided that such jurisdiction shall not extend to any suit for money in which the amount claimed exclusive of interest, does not exceed five hundred rupees'. I recommend that the following words be now added. 'Provided further that such jurisdiction shall not extend to any suits in which both the parties are aboriginals'.

This alteration will involve a consequential amendment to Section 2 of Act XXXVII of 1855 which runs 'The administration of civil and criminal justice and the collection of the revenue not being permanently settled land revenue within the said districts are hereby vested in the officer or officers to be so appointed [i.e. under Section 1(2)]. Provided that all Civil suits in which the matter in dispute shall exceed the value of one thousand rupees shall be tried and determined according to the general laws and Regulations in the same manner as if this Act had not been passed.' I recommend that after the words 'all civil suits' the words 'excepting those between aboriginals' be added.

III

If this step is taken, the Santal Civil Courts will be the only courts having jurisdiction in Santal suits and their simple and direct procedure will give to Santals the type of justice they desire. Can the administration of justice be made even further Santal?

In a note recorded in 1932, Bodding stated : 'I believe it would be advantageous for all, if the village councils could be given some more power and work, naturally with certain safeguards so that their work could be controlled. I believe, it is a fact, that a good many cases are brought to court that a Santal would never dream of beginning in his own village. He goes to the court as a speculation thinking it may be possible to gain his end by the help of a pleader or by the lack of knowledge on the part of an alien judge'.[4] We have seen that Santal tribal councils have now a definite place in the official system and that a Subdivisional Officer can now give their decisions all the force of a decree. I believe that this principle of tribal decision could well be taken much further and on the analogy of the tribal courts in Bastar, the Naga Hills and the Chittagong Hills tracts, the manjhis' council under the presidentship of the pargana should now be constituted a court of first instance for all disputes valued at less than fifty rupees. The pargana should be the presiding officer, and on behalf of the council should have the power to execute its decrees. I do not recommend a higher valuation at present because it is necessary to see first how well the system works. If it is successful the valuation should be capable of increase and provision should, therefore, be made by statutory rules that where the working of a particular tribal council warrants wider jurisdiction the Deputy Commissioner may by order confer enlarged powers upto a limit of, say, two hundred rupees. Once a case has been decided by a pargana's council, there should be a right of appeal to the Subdivisional

Officer. If a suit has been filed in a Santal civil court, no suit should lie in a tribal court but the Subdivisional Officer should have power to transfer it to the tribal court if he thinks fit.

IV

If tribal councils are associated with the Santal Civil Courts, a large number of small disputes will be disposed of by the tribesmen themselves. What action is necessary for ensuring that when a suit is tried in an official court the courts shall in fact administer Santal law?

We have seen that there is so far neither any order of Government nor any legislative enactment prescribing the law by which aboriginals in Bihar are bound. The resulting confusion has so far affected Uraons and Mundas severely but in at least one case from Manbhum, Santals also have been touched. In the general interests of tribal welfare it is desirable that this obscurity should end. The question whether aboriginals are bound by Hindu Law or tribal law is virtually based on a confusion of terms and if aboriginals are now accepted as being virtually aboriginal Hindus, there should be little difficulty in recognising their law as an aboriginal school of Hindu Law. The requisite steps for ascertaining that law I will discuss immediately but meanwhile early action to relieve the aboriginals of the burden of choosing and proving their law is needed. I suggest a short Regulation or Act prescribing that in all suits in which both the parties are aboriginals, they shall be bound by the tribal law of the aboriginal community concerned, and shall be excluded from the provisions of the Indian Succession Act and the Mitakshara and Dayabhaga schools of Hindu Law.

V

If this principle is accepted how should aboriginal law be ascertained?

In this connection my own enquiries into Santal law are not irrelevant and I will, therefore, draw attention to some of the matters which arise from my work.

As I have explained in the Preface to the Report on Civil Law in Santal Society, I was placed on special duty to record current Santal law. This order was an executive act of the Bihar Government and since such a record of tribal law was not covered either by legislative enactment or by rules having the force of law, my work has only the authority of a report made by an officer of Government in the official discharge of his duties. As such it is in the same category as the Gantzer's Settlement Report or a work of authority such as Bodding's 'Notes on the Position of Women among the Santals' or Jugia Haram's *Horkoren Mare Hapramko reak' Katha*. It is not, as such, binding on the courts but under Section 57 of the Indian Evidence Act a court may, if it so wishes, take judicial notice of it. For courts constituted under the Bengal, Assam and Agra Courts Act of 1887 this is the utmost legal authority which my report possesses and if similar reports are to have legal force in future and thus to be binding on the courts it will be necessary to provide them with legislative sanction. This purpose can best be served by a short enactment which should preferably include the following provisions :

1. The Provincial Government may by notification appoint an officer to enquire into and record the principles of law which are accepted by an aboriginal community as applicable to its members in the decision of their civil disputes.
2. The Provincial Government may frame rules to prescribe the procedure to be followed by such officer and the manner in which the record of tribal principles shall be attested and published.
3. Such record of principles shall include a statement of the tribal rules determining the rights of men and women in the ownership and inheritance of movable and immovable property, adoption, marriage and divorce.
4. Such principles when recorded attested and finally published shall for the time being constitute the personal law of all members of the aboriginal community concerned.
5. The Provincial Government may from time to time direct a fresh enquiry into such principles and approve

their amendment after attestation and publication in the manner provided for in the Rules.

6. For validating my own report this enactment should preferably be given retrospective effect.

VI

Finally there is one last matter to which I should draw attention. I have already urged that at least in the Santal Parganas where there is already one set of courts adapted to tribal conditions it is anomalous to have a second set administering law in a far more complicated manner and wedded to lawyers whose motto might not unfairly be described as 'my client right or wrong'. In the districts of Chota Nagpur outside the Kolhan the ordinary civil courts are the sole arbiters in tribal suits. I believe that here also a radical reconstitution of the courts is necessary and that only by creating aboriginal courts on the lines of the Santal Civil Courts are aboriginal requirements likely to be met. But even if this is not attempted steps should at least be taken so that Munsifs and Sub-Judges the Judicial Commissioner and at least one High Court Judge, should have an intimate knowledge of aboriginal society. In an inspiring address delivered at Chapra on 22 April, 1946, Sir Syed Wazir Hassan, ex-Chief Judge, Oudh Chief Court, expressed his disapproval of a European Judge being called upon to decide intricate questions of Hindu Law 'as a judge must know the cultural, social and national background of the cases, he is called upon to decide'. If this is true of Hindu litigation how much more does it apply to aboriginal cases? For such suits only exact and detailed knowledge based on an intimate understanding of the tribesmen can possibly qualify a judge to administer justice. If no one with such knowledge can be found it is better to admit the unsuitability of the system rather than to allow ignorance to go on masquerading as wisdom.

Is it too fantastic to suggest that in the end the best solution will be found in the increasing delegation of civil justice to the tribesmen themselves?

REFERENCES

1. Elwin, *The Aboriginals*, 18.
2. Hutton, *Census of India, 1931*, I, 506.
3. J.P. Mills 'The, Effect on the Tribes of the Naga Hill District of Contacts with Civilization', *Census of India, 1931*, I, III B, 148.
4. P.O. Bodding, 'Notes on the Santals', *Census of India, 1931*, I, III B, 107.

APPENDICES

APPENDIX I

CHRISTIANS AND THE LAW

I

At the 1941 Census, 789,830 Santals and 23,205 Tribal Christians were recorded in the Santal Parganas. Of the latter not all were Santals and taking the number of Santal Christians to be approximately 20,000, it is evident that Christians were only 2.5 per cent of the total Santal community. Of these approximately 10,000 were adherents to the Scandinavian Mission of the Northern Churches, about 7,000 to the Church Missionary Society and the rest were either Seventh Day Adventists, Roman Catholics or Plymouth Brethren. Santal Christians are, if anything, slightly more litigious than non-Santals but even allowing for this greater interest in the courts it is obvious that the litigation of Santal Christians does not at present constitute a major problem.

The matter is still further simplified by section 3 of the Indian Succession Act, under which the Provincial Government is empowered to exempt races, sects or tribes from the operation of its sections. By Notification No. 550, Home Department (Judicial) Simla dated May 2, 1923, all Mundas, Uraons, Santals, Hos, Bhumijs, Kharias, Ghasis, Gonds, Khond, Kokawas, Kurmis, Mahegunis and Pans dwelling in the Province of Bihar and Orissa were exempted. In all matters relating to the ownership and inheritance of land and movables, Santal Christians are, therefore, governed by ordinary Santal law. While, however, the principles of tribal law, remain the same, Christianity has occasioned a number of adjustments in detail and since these concern questions of proof and evidence, I will summarise briefly the more important changes.

II

The main matter which divides a Santal Christian from other Santals is, as we might expect, religious. No Santal Christian may participate in tribal festivals, sacrifice to the bongas, placate his ancestors or indeed associate himself in any way with tribal religious practices. Accordingly when a Santal institution presupposes adherence to the bongas, it is, as it were 'debongaized' for Christian use and its place is taken by a form in keeping with Christian standards.

In addition almost all the missions have banned dancing and drumming as well as the drinking of mahua liquor and rice beer. The Roman Catholics have been rather less squeamish and have not hesitated to associate both drinking and dancing with the festival of Christmas. The C.M.S. have followed a middle line frowning on public drinking but extending a lukewarm approval to the more decorous types of Santal dance. The Mission of the Northern Churches on the other hand has taken a somewhat firmer line. Bodding states : 'I shall not say anything about other missions. It has been our desire not so much to get Santal Christians as to have Christian Santals. We have so far as possible let our Christians keep their social customs when there is nothing in connection with them that is immoral or combined with their spirit worship.

We have been obliged to set our face against drink, for the reason that a Santal drinks to become drunk; anything that does not quickly intoxicate is considered worthless.

We have also been obliged to prohibit certain dances among our Christians; the Christians themselves say that they feel ashamed, when they hear the dancing drum. Their most common dance, practically the only dance seen or heard in the villages on ordinary nights is what is called large; the dance itself is ordinarily innocent enough to look at, except the suggestive movement of the girl's bodies. What is especially objectionable in connection with this and some other Santal dances is the opportunity they give the sexes for meeting at night; the opportunity is very frequently used for illicit intercourse'.[1]

Provided, therefore, that the bongas are not involved and dancing and rice beer are not *sine qua non*, a Santal institution in its Christian aspect closely follows the institution in its normal tribal form.

III

In the light of this general observation I will now briefly review the more salient Santal institutions. The working of the inner and the greater family, for example, is obviously unaffected by these changes but the institution of adoption has had to be modified so far as it involves bonga tala. If a Santal Christian desires to adopt a child who is not already a member of his greater family, he must continue to seek village approval as in an ordinary case and must also make a solemn declaration before a village meeting that the child is adopted by him. If the child has already been converted, nothing further is possible but if it is not a Christian its adopting father can have it baptised and at the baptism can mutate the sept.

The rights of stepchildren, guardians, custodians and servants are unaffected by Christian practice and so far as illegitimate children are concerned, the putative father remains fully responsible. If he has got the child by a non-Christian girl he is responsible for the expenses of purifying the house and village as if he were not himself a Christian. If a Christian girl has a child and cannot prove its father a husband is arranged for her in the same way as for a non-Christian.

So far as the rights of women go, Christian practice is identical with tribal except that it does not sanction co-wives, yet even here we must distinguish the attitude of different Missions. The Roman Catholic Mission for example does not accept as a valid marriage any union with a person not a Catholic. Accordingly if a Santal is already married to a tribal Santal or to a Christian but of another mission, it is as if he is not married at all and can, therefore, take another Catholic Santal as his wife. This does not of course affect the rights of the first wife and if she is not divorced, she retains all the status of a senior co-wife by] tribal law. The other Missions in the district take a radically different view and once a Christian Santal has been married in any form whether tribal or Christian he is normally debarred from marrying again during the lifetime of his wife. There is, however, one important exception.

If a Santal woman has deserted her husband for a period of years and attempts to claim her have all failed, the Scandinavian Mission occasionally recognises a second marriage by the innocent party. This is not celebrated in Church but a prayer is said and a hymn sung and after that the two can live together without shame. Other aspects of women's rights do not call for detailed comment and the institutions of ghardi jawae and ghar jawae flourish equally among Christians as among tribal Santals.

IV

With regard to marriage, also, Christian practice reveals few differences. A service in church is substituted for all the religious rites, *sindur* is on no account given and in most Missions all dancing is omitted. The rest of the marriage process is substantially the same and a Christian marriage in a good style includes a match-maker, visits for the bride's cloth and bridegroom's dhoti, the sending of a bridegroom's party to bring the girl, and the payment of a standard bride-price of twelve rupees and a brother's due of one rupee. If claims arise they are decided in exactly the same way as in a tribal marriage. As regards possible partners, Christian Santals observe the same rules of exogamy and acknowledge the same prohibited relationships and although marriages with Christian Dikus are not expressly forbidden, they are in the main viewed with abhorrence. While the Santal party is not actually boycotted, there is normally a distinct cooling off in relations with other Santals.

If a Santal boy does iputut' to a Christian girl, the act cannot, of course, marry her but the methods of adjustment are the same as if she were a tribal girl and declined to live with him. The boy is made to pay a heavy fine for outraging her and the girl's father is indemnified. Similarly although the other forms of Santal marriage are not countenanced by the church elders, Santal Christians not infrequently resort to them and I know of cases which illustrate all the forms of 'copse marriage'. In such cases, the fact that the parties are Christians does not of course affect the validity of the unions and once the fact of living publicly together is recognised by the village, the fact that the parties have not been to Church is not of legal consequence. It may be that where its influence is particularly strong the Mission may speedily compel the pair to put matters right either by parting the two or by bringing them to the altar. But only if the village as a whole declines to accept the union by an express declaration or by a social boycott would the union fail to be valid. If a husband is already married and lives publicly with another woman and the circumstances do not justify even tacit recognition, the Mission itself may excommunicate the Santal but unless the local Santal community also withholds recognition, it cannot deprive the union of its married status.

V

The most sharp cleavage between Christian practice and tribal law is in divorce. When a Santal Christian is married, his wedding is solemnized under the Indian Christian Marriage Act (Act XV of 1872) and after that he can only be divorced by presenting a petition to the District Court or High Court under the Divorce Act (Act IV of 1869). Since, for the Santal Parganas, the Commissioner of Bhagalpur is the District Court, it is obviously impracticable for most Santals to employ this remedy and the result is that even though a marriage may be unmistakably a failure the two parties are tied to each other for life. A section of Christian Santals would undoubtedly prefer a modified version of the tribal practice. They would solemnize weddings by a service but not formally register them. They would then keep the power of divorce with the village community but associate the church elders with the ultimate decision. Once a divorce was approved, the two would part without rancour and be free to essay a more godly union later. As it is, without a petition to the Commissioner a Christian Santal must choose between his wife and his religion for it is only by discarding his Christianity that he can also discard his wife.

VI

There is an equal similarity with a difference at the great crises of Santal life.

When a birth occurs in a Christian family, the nim dak' mandi ceremony is held in order to purify the house. Villagers both—Christian and non-Christian attend. There is the same general bathing and shaving. The ghat is never bought but the naeke is employed and the village itself is purified.

At times of sickness, Christian Santals employ ojhas and gurus like other Santals. They do not publicly associate themselves with mantras or sacrifices and ostensibly employ them for their knowledge of herbs and country medicines. They cannot, however, avoid giving the ojha his saket and also the animals vowed by him for making the patient recover. They, therefore, give him the animals and money as a free and do not ask questions concerning the use to which he puts them.

When a Christian Santal dies, he is buried and not cremated. After the burial, the people of the house also wash and a funerary feast is given to the village. There is no sale of the dead man's things, no tel nahan, no pot of the departed, no journey to the river, no bhandan, but the village itself is polluted and the naeke is given oil with which to make it clean.

VII

Finally in general matters of Santal law, there is no difference. The ownership of livestock, hospitality, credit, hunting and fishing are governed by the same rules and with the exception that no Christian child would be name after an ojha or a shrine, the principles of naming are common. The children of a Christian ghar jawae for example are named on exactly the same principles as those of a tribal one. The only difference is that Christian Santals have usually two mul names. One of these is purely Santal and follows the order of naming in the family. The other is a Christian name which indicates conversion and is chosen at will.

There is one last point in which Christian practice deviates from the tribal norm. We have seen that on the many occasions when the village meets to approve a proposal or adjust a matter, the final decision is ratified by rice beer. Even in minor matters such as the induction of a servant the neighbours seal the contract by swilling a little beer. This nourishing and popular drink however is normally forbidden to Christians and since it is necessary to 'seal a decision' by a communal and friendly act, in ordinary Christian practice, the place of rice beer is taken by a cup of tea. This harmless beverage blends gently with the talk and although it arouses little Santal enthusiasm, it is not perhaps an other element in tribal life than the mill-made dhoti or sari or the khaki tunic of the returned soldier.

VIII THE FUTURE

In many parts of India the advent of Missions has proved a terrible disaster of the greatest magnitude. 'If the aboriginal becomes a Christian', Verrier Elwin has stated, 'he generally finds himself deprived of the moral and social sanctions under which he has grown up, of the free and natural recreations to which he is accustomed, and in many cases he sinks into moral and economic degradation'.[2]

'The invasion of missionaries', says Dr. J.H. Hutton, 'is liable to produce as much evil as good, if not more, for their conduct and objects are generally in extreme conflict with tribal religion and with tabus of all kinds, and their point of view readily comprehensible to an alien administration which understands the tribal position very vaguely, if at all, and backed as it so often is by influentially vocal societies at a distance, is much more likely to obtain the support of authority than tabus which are on the face of them unreasonable to all except those to whom they are the most vitally important things in life'.[3]

J.P. Mills has vividly described the impact on the Nagas of the American Baptist Mission.

'As religion plays a part in every Naga ceremony and as that religion is not Christianity, every ceremony must go. Such ceremonies as the great Feasts of Merit at which the whole village, rich and poor alike, is entertained and of which the religious aspect is far less important than the social, have not been remodelled on Christian lines, but have been utterly abolished among converts. This has been the fate, too, of all village sacrificial feasts. The place of these is not adequately taken by small parties meeting to drink tea. The suppression among Baptists of the ancient feasts in which all joined is not only a loss to the would-be hosts, but to the village as a whole and not least to the poor, who always get their full share of good cheer at Animist festivals. To abolish these feasts is to do away with the very few occasions on which the awful monotony of village life is broken. They are, too, the natural Naga and Kuki way of distributing wealth. I have heard a Baptist teacher boast that his granaries were so full of the store of years that some of the grain was black with age. Had he been an Animist that grain would not have been left to rot uselessly but would have been eaten by his fellow villagers.

'To anyone who unable to reject some of the most hallowed passages in Scripture, regards fermented liquor in moderation as not only harmless but beneficial, the strong prohibition policy of the Mission cannot but seem a grave mistake. Few of its advocates attempt to justify it from Scripture. They use the arguments which brought the Volstead Act into being. Such an obsession has abstention from fermented drink becomes among concerts that teetotalism is often regarded as the outstanding mark of a Christian. Among the Aos 'teetotaler' and 'Christian' are used as synonymous terms in ordinary conversation. The substitution of opium for rice beer is probably rare among Christians now, but as in America, secret drinking goes on, with results that are normally evil.

'It is at the big feasts that singing and dancing are indulged in and full dress worn. These have been entirely suppressed among the Ao, Lhota and Sema Christians, the men of whom wear no ornaments at all having stripped their beads from their necks, their ivory armlets from their arms and even the cotton wool from their ears. The women are more conservative and still wear their beads, though I doubt if a girl would actually wear her ornaments at a Mission school. Angami men too are difficult to dislodge from their ancient ways. The best of them do not give up their picturesque dress and are quite ready to put on all their finery and take part in the ceremonial singing parties which are such a feature of their village life'.

'The suppression of the wearing of all ornaments or tribal finery, of dancing, of singing (except hymns), of village feasts and of all artistic outlet is spreading an unspeakable drabness over village life. Old songs and old traditions are being rapidly forgotten. Told year in and year out that all the past history, all the strivings, all the old customs of his tribe are wholly evil, the Naga tends to despise his own race, and no night of the soul is blacker than that.

'The suppression of the Morung in which the young animists learn to be useful citizens is unwarranted by any good reason that I have ever heard. It is part of the tendency to abolish old things just because they are old, and substitute for the strong communal feeling which has enabled the tribes to survive for so long an individualism which is really foreign to them. Not only is this individualism wrapped up with the strong emphasis on personal salvation, it is also the direct and natural reaction against the destruction of all the old things that mattered in village life and all the old expressions of the artistic and social genius of the tribe'. 'My tribe has erred hopelessly' says the convert 'all through the centuries it has tried to work out its destiny. I will work out mine, and mine alone'. An animist puts his village before himself. A Baptist puts himself before his village. No Semas are as prone to disobey their chiefs as Christian Semas, and Christian Aos have often refused to take part in village-government to which their years and experience called them. A 'civilized' Naga is apt to call customary discipline restraint, and many of them are eager to leave their village and live free of all control.

'Times are changing and new influences and tendencies are appearing. Tribes and villages acting as units will be able to judge of them and resist them if need be. Individuals will find them too strong. Will the time come when these hills will be inhabited by scattered families, without pride in the past or hope for the future, without arts and without recreation, dressed in non-descript garments as drab as their lives, and busy only to win from the steep, rocky slopes enough substance to enable them to beget children and die?'[4]

What has been the effect of Christianity on the Santals?

It is obvious that since Christian Santals are only an insignificant minority, the tribe as whole has not been gravely affected by Christian impact. Santal festivals, dancing, tribal religion, the Santal way of life all these remain intact. Indeed the publication of *Horkoren Mare Hapramko reak' Katha* by the Mission of the Northern Churches while testifying to the Mission's most sincere desire that in becoming Christians, Santals should as far as possible stay Santals, also gave precisions to the ancestral way of life.

If the Missions have had little numerical effect their propaganda is undoubtedly responsible in part for the present position of Santal law. The current principles determining the rights of women are fully accepted by Santals as a whole but the earliest advocacy of these changes came from Christian Santals and was sponsored by the Missions. Moreover as pioneers in Santal education, the Missions are responsible for that tiny band of educated Santals who are now the only channel through which the tribe can voice its hopes and fears. It is to the fewness of Santal conversions that Santal Christians owe their present position in the Santal community. Unlike many tribes in which a rigid barrier divides Christians from non-Christians, Santal Christians have remained Santals first and Christians second, non-Christians eat and drink with them. They can freely avail of communal water. They can borrow fire and can count on village aid. If a non-Christian Santal has sexual relations with a Christian, he is not exposed to tribal excommunication though he cannot convert the connection into a union without an adjustment of religions.

In all human matters in fact the Santal community as a whole is benignly tolerant of its Christian members.

It is in matters affecting the bongas that Santal Christians are, as it were, demoted. Having themselves denied the bongas, they are no longer subjects of bonga interest. If a Christian Santal commits incest or goes with a Diku, the bongas assume complete indifference. The Santal Christian is already out of the bongas, and is therefore in all essentials out of the tribe. He is no longer a true Santal and nothing he can do can induce the bongas either to warn or bless. It is this indifference of the tribe to his moral and religious conduct which is his greatest deprivation. Again the training of the Missions while it may kill the fear of death, gives also in its place a fear of life. The Mission ban on song and dance, the substitution or the solemn hymn for the jolly song, the reverend walk for the hop and skip of the dance has not in fact checked the sexual intimacies which Bodding deplored but has produced instead a subconscious resentment, a respectful hatred of all that is a Mission. Some of the most educated Christian Santals have never forgiven the Missions for making them Christians and thus depriving them of all that gives to Santal life its sanction and cohesion.

REFERENCES

1. P.O. Bodding, 'Notes on the Santals', *Census of India, 1931*, I, III B, 107.
2. Verrier Elwin, *The Aboriginals* (Bombay, 1943), 25.
3. J.H. Hutton, *Census of India, 1931*, I, 505.
4. J.P. Mills, 'The Effect on the Tribes of the Naga Hills District of Contacts with Civilization, *Census of India, 1931*, I, III B, 148-9.

APPENDIX II

SPECIAL OATHS

If there is difficulty in finding out facts, Santal councils occasionally have recourse to special oaths. As these are often of great importance I will briefly record their form and substance.

(A) BANSMATI

The most common special oath is known as bansmati. A little mound of mud is made and a piece of bamboo is stood up on its end in the mud. The person taking the oath grasps the bamboo in his right hand and pulling it out repeats the words :

'Dhorom dhorom in roret kana. Bedhoromin ror khan hani cotre Chando bonga menaea unigey bichar katina ar bedhoromin ror khan do bans bos nirbosok' an.'

'I am speaking the truth. If I do not speak the truth Chando Bonga is above and he will judge me. If I do not speak the truth, may my family die out like a clump of bamboos.'

These words are recited by the manjhi and the man repeats them after him.

This oath is believed to draw its power from the nature of earth and bamboo. Just as a flowering bamboo kills all other bamboos in the clump a lie if told will cause the family line to die out. Similarly just as water when poured down mud makes it disappear a lie if told before the earth will make you wither away.

This oath is very widely used in village decisions and it is generally believed that no one can take the oath falsely and not suffer. Ranjit Hembrom of Kusuma told me with great glee that in the last settlement a Mahali falsely claimed a part of his land. The Mahali took the bansmati oath but other evidence was against him and the settlement court did not believe him. Then to everyone's delight, the Mahali died within a year.

A girl of Dalahi was married to Jore Hembrom of Ukharapahan. She used to go to his house for a day and then go back. There were 4 meetings to get the girl to stay. At the first three the girl said she would remain but never did so but at the fourth meeting she was asked to take the bansmati oath that she would go to her husband and remain with him. She took the oath and holding the bansmati stick went round and did johar to all in the meeting. After that she went to her husband, stayed with him but fell ill. She tried several times to stay but each time was ill. Then the two families decided that it was no use trying any further. The boy and girl were divorced and the bride-price was repaid. In this case, it was generally thought that as the girl did not want to stay it was the oath that made her ill.

(B) HOPON BOHOK'

A second oath in common use is called hopon bohok'. A man takes his own child pits his right hand on the child's head and repeats the following words :

'Nok'oc hopon bohok' capo kate dhorom dhoromin roret' kana. Bedhorom in ror khan hopongey gujuk' tin ma.'

'With my hand on my child's head I am speaking the truth. If I speak false, may my child die.'

A variation of the oath is lutur ar met jotet in which the ears and eyes are touched and the person says :

'Nok'oc lutur ar met jotet kate dhorom dhoromia roret' kana. Bedhoromin for khan, lutur ar met sea ar thuk' tin ma.'

'With my hands on my ears and eyes I am speaking truth. If I do not tell the truth, may I become deaf and blind.'

Jitu Marandi of Nawadih quarrelled with the youngest sister of his wife. Jitu claimed to be a ghar jawae while the three sisters of his wife denied that this was so. The ghar jawae then took the hopon bohok' oath by putting his hand on the head of his son while a witness for the three girls took a counter-oath by touching his eyes, ears and navel. Jitu Marandi was not in fact a ghar jawae and three months later his son died.

(C) OATHS WITH HINDU INFLUENCE

Certain special oaths derive from Hindu influence. The tulsi for example, appears in the tamba tulsi oath and vests it with super normal gravity. A spot of ground is cleaned with cowdung. Two balls of cowdung, a copper coin (tamba) some tulsi leaves a little dub grass and a lota of water are set down. Then the man offering the oath bows with folded hands to the sun and taking up the coin and the tulsi says:

'Nok'oc tamba ar tulsi sap' kate dhorom dhoromin roret kana. Bedhoromin ror khan Chando bonga bicharkatina.'

'Holding this coin and tulsi, I am speaking truth. If I tell a lie may Chando judge me.'

The cow of a Mohammadan of Nurgi was killed by an arrow near the house of a Santal boy, Boka Marandi. Dhunu Hembrom of the same village was with him at the time and the village meeting and both were made to swear by tamba tulsi that neither of them had done so. Two weeks later both of them fell ill and although they cured for the time being by an ojha, both of them caught tuberculosis and within a year both had died within two days of each other.

If at the time of taking the oath, a child touches the person's body it is the child and not the person who suffers if the denial is false.

Manki Besra of Kurwa was believed to be a witch. The villagers suspected that she had eaten her husband and they accused her of having done so. She declared that she had not eaten him and was not a witch. She was then made to take the tamba tulsi oath and at the time of taking it her son was seen clutching at her legs. Some of the villagers tried to snatch him away but Manki had taken the oath before they could do so. Within two days the child had died.

A variation of this oath is known as guric' terel. A person takes some cowdung and kend leaves in his hand and turning to the sun says that before Chando he is speaking truth. 'Nok'oc guric' terel capo kate dhorom dhoromin roret' kana. Bedhoromin ror khan Chando bonga bicharkatina.' If he is actually telling a lie the oath will kill him.

Another oath with Hindu influence is Lachminat or gai dea capo. A cow is brought and after placing his right hand on its back, the man swears that what he says is true. 'Nok'oc gai dea capokate dhorom dhoromin' roret' kana. Bedhoromin' ror khan, Chando bonga bicharkatin'a'. This oath is sometimes used in disputes between Santals and Mahajans.

In a case from Senduria a certain Satu Lal swore by lakshmihat that a Santal named Raghunath had not repaid a loan of two hundred rupees. The Santal declared that all the money had been given back but in the end the Mahajan was believed and the Santal had to repay four hundred rupees in all. Shortly afterwards the mahajan caught leprosy and died.

Another oath involving cattle is by gobordhon or cowdung. A piece of ground is purified with cowdung. Some cowdung balls are set out and the person taking the oath picks up the balls and says 'If I am speaking false may Chando judge me.' 'Nok'oc guric' guli halan kate dhorom dhoromin roret' kana. Bedhoromin ror khan, Chando bonga bicharkatina.'

Hupuc' Tudu of Simbra stole some paddy from the threshing floor of his elder brother. His elder brother told him that he knew of the theft but Hupuc' indignantly denied it and then a quarrel arose. The villagers intervened and at their suggestion Hupuc' took the gobordhon oath. He had actually stolen the paddy and within a week of the oath he was dead.

(D) OATHS BY SNAKE OR TIGER

Finally oaths by wild animals are still occasionally employed. The correct form of the tiger oath, for example, is as follows :

'Dhorom dhoromin roret kana. Bedhoromin ror khan

hor bir re kuli jomina.' 'I am speaking the truth. If I tell a lie, a tiger will eat me on the way in the forest.'

Another oath is by a snake. 'Dhorom dhoromin roret kạna. Bedhoromin hor te calak' re bine jomin ma.' 'I am speaking truth. If I tell a lie, may a snake bite me as I pass on the way.'

APPENDIX III

ATTESTING AUTHORITIES

Name of Centre	Date of Attestation	Attesting Santals		
		Name	Village	Bungalow, Circle, Police Station
Boarijor	August 8-10, 1945. (Seth Charan Hansdak').	Durga Kisku	Borio	Borio
		Balaram Hansdak'	Measi	
		Ambai Marandi	Harinchora	
	February 4-8, 1946. (Domon Sahu & Sushil Soren).	Lakhin Tudu	Bichpura	
		Kanhai Kisku	Sripur Bazar	Boarijor
		Dukhu Marandi	Itahari	
		Chadra Kisku	Kandaniya	
		Hambra Hembrom	Sakirkita, Rampur	
		Khela Murmu	Meghi	
		Mongol Kisku	Dhamni	
		Barka Tudu	Goradih	
		Lakhan Baskey	Daldaligopalpur	
		Chundu Baskey	Lakrakol	
		Pero Murmu	Lilatari	Mandro I
		Baijnath Murmu	Baramasia	
		Bhagmat Kisku	Ghatiari	
		Raghu Murmu	Bangliya	Mandro II

Appendix III (Contd.)

Name of Centre	Date of Attestation	Attesting Santals		
		Name	Village	Bungalow, Circle, Police Station
		Chandu Tudu	Bhimchak Barkhuri	
		Kisu Hembrom	Ranidih	
		Phurlai Soren	Dhanbasa	
Raksi	August 5-7, November 6-8, 1945. January 27-29, 1946. (Seth Charan Hansdak')	Ramsai Marandi	Barabandh	Kusma
		Ram Murmu	Dugubathan	
		Champai Murmu	Tilaki	
		Suna Hembrom	Gilaha	
		Ramu Hembrom	Ilaki	
		Daso Kisku	Kusma	
		Pradhan Hembrom	Labri	
		Jetha Murmu	Kusma	
		Dubai Hansdak'	Bhagnadih	Berhait
		Terok' Murmu	Kherwa	
		Babulal Tudu	Baramasia	
		Anu Soren	Rohra	
		Pancu Soren	Ranga	Raksi
		Silhu Hembrom	Kundli	
		Mirja Murmu	Simuldhab	
		Jogon Soren	Raksi	
		Mohon Hansdak'	Dumra	

		Mondol Murmu	Jhimuli	
		Mondol Soren	Khejurkhal	
Taljhari	August 11-13, November 12-14, 1945. January 30—February 1, 1946. (Seth Charan Hansdak').	Mongla Marandi	Bindin	Brindaban
		Phagu Marandi	-do-	
		Bhondo Murmu	Sahraidhab	
		Naran Hansdak'	-do-	
		Soban Kisku	Karanpur	Maharajpur
		Garbho Tudu	Taljhari	Taljhari
		Samu Hembrom	-do-	
		Korna Marandi	Madansahi	
		Sundar Hansdak'	Taljhari	
		Hikim Hansdak'	-do-	
		Ramsing Murmu	Nipania	
		Jagan Hansdak'	Khairbani	
		Kanhai Hembrom	Dudhuakol	
		Daso Soren	-do-	
		Ramu Hansdak'	Semalojri	
		Champai Hansdak'	Mongrutikur	Banjhi
		Sagram Marandi	Ranidih	
		Singrai Baskey	-do-	
		Jogon Murmu	Chota Bisunpur	
		Mondol Murmu	Khajuria	
Pathna	August 2-4, November 2-5, 1945.	Hopna Marandi	Atgawan	Ranga
		Surai Murmu	-do-	

Appendix III (Contd.)

Name of Centre	Date of Attestation	Attesting Santals		
		Name	Village	Bungalow, Circle, Police Station
	February 2-4, 1946. (Seth Charan Hansdak').	Kanhu Marandi	Kumarpur	
		Bogol Soren	-do-	
		Jhandu Hembrom	Chutia	
		Pagan Marandi	-do-	
		Rengta Soren	-do-	
		Karu Soren	Bara Ranga	
		Parbat Tudu	Atgaon	
		Badoc' Soren	-do-	
		Lakhan Hansdak'	Telbitha	Pathna
		Bhima Murmu	Dharampur	
		Kanhu Marandi	Kendua	
		Charan Marandi	Sitapahar	
		Mona Tudu	Modikola	
		Raghu Marandi	Mongladih	
		Singrai Hembrom	Dharampur	
		Lal Pauria	-do-	
		Chunka Hembrom	Majurjhuti	
		Chota Dalu Murmu	-do-	
Rajabhita	August 8-10, November 8-10, 1945.	Karu Marandi	Bhadria	Rajabhita
		Hopna Murmu	Tetariya	

	January 28-30, 1946. (Domon Sahu & Sushil Soren).	Baijnath Murmu	Kusbila	
		Chota Peru Tudu	Telni	Godda
		Prithi Hembrom	Tengar	
		Pradhan Hansdak'	Tardiha	
		Maha Hansdak'	Kalyani	
		Baijun Murmu	Bargama	
		Surju Tudu	Patharkani	
		Hari Hembrom	Kamardiha	Mahagama
		Manidas Murmu	Amdiha	
		Salkhu Murmu	Dalabar	
		Surai Hansdak'	Nimkalan	Simra I
		Baijnath Soren	Balajhor	
		Bisan Murmu	Mahuabathan	Simra II
		Baku Kisku	Bara Dhanabandhi	
		Chota Ram Hansdak'	Bansjori	Karmatanr I
		Nawab Chandra Hansdak'	Mahuatanr	Karmatanr II
		Bariar Marandi	Sundarmaue	
Chandna	August 5-7, November 5-7, 1945.	Sital Murmu	Telbhita	Sundarpahari
		Dubai Soren	Tilabad	
	January 25-27, 1946.	Tore Kisku	Amjora	
	(Rameshwar Nath).	Barka Tudu	Tesobathan	
		Mansingh Tudu		
		Barsa Hembrom		

Appendix III (Contd.)

Name of Centre	Date of Attestation	Attesting Santals		
		Name	Village	Bungalow, Circle, Police Station
		Sundar Hansdak'	Boroa	Chandna I
		Burhan Hembrom	Manspara	Chandna II
		Bhado Marandi	Chhota Sindri	
		Hopna Hansdak'	Rajabhita	
		Sido Hansdak'	Goradih	Bokrabandh
		Pardhan Hansdak'	Potondih	
		Balea Hansdak'	Bokrabandh	
		Dewan Murmu	Komopahari	
		Dewan Marandi	Puru	Dhamni
		Bhoga Hansdak'	Jobordoha	
Pareya	August 2-4, November 2-4, 1945. January 22-24, 1946. (Rameshwar Nath)	Lodo Marandi	Dalu	Godda
		Saisingh Hansdak'	-do-	
		Samchai Kisku	Amarpur	
		Rasik Kisku	Pandaha	
		Sundeo Soren	Godda	
		Sitaram Kisku	Sarkanda	
		Bhutel Soren	Gopladih	
		Dubai Murmu	Bhatondha	Pareya
		Siba Soren	Hathihariyari	

		Thakur Murmu	Raghunathpur	
		Bona Hansdak'	Pindra	
		Kalu Hembrom	Kelabari	
Pakaur and Torai	August 2-3, November 1945. January 20-22, 1946. (Ram Datta Pandey).	Mania Kisku	Malpahari	Pakaur
		Balea Hansdak'	Bhusko	
		Prithi Tudu	Kanupur	
		Kathia Marandi	Pokharia	
		Ram Charan Soren	Malipara	
		Chandrai Marandi	Kalidaspur	
		Jhongo Murmu	Maruapahari	
		Lal Murmu	Sonajori	
		Jadu Murmu	Durgapur	
		Sundar Hansdak'	Takatola	
Basetkundi	August 4-5, November 1945. January 28-29, 1946. (Ram Datta Pandey).	Ram Hembrom	Lakhipokhar	Pakuria
		Chota Salkhu Soren	Gadrasale	
		Rupai Hembrom	Rajbari	
		Gobind Hembrom	Lakdum	
		Nandlal Hansdak'	-do-	
		Surendra Besra	Junka	
		Shyam Hembrom	Rajbari	
		Gopal Hembrom	Dhekiduba	
		Bhado Murmu	Pathradaha	
		Lakhan Hansdak'	Salgapara	

Appendix III (Contd.)

Name of Centre	Date of Attestation	Attesting Santals		
		Name	Village	Bungalow, Circle, Police Station
		Raisen Hembrom	Barhabad	Maheshpur
		Parao Tudu	Akhrasol	
Litipara	August 9-10,	Amu Soren	Jordih	Dharampur
	November 1945.	Chatur Kisku	Garduara	
	February 1-3, 1946.	Kuar Baske	Bara Ghagri	
	(Ram Datta Pandey).	Masidas Hembrom	Chhota Ghagri	
		Fagu Marandi	Dharampur	
		Dharmu Tudu	-do-	
		Keshar Kisku	Dhanigora	
		Gupnath Hembrom	-do-	
		Alima Kisku	Kaldam	
		Chaitan Kisku	-do-	
		Gula Murmu	Bansjori	
		Hari Hansdak'	Hathibathan	
		Durga Hansdak'	Dumdi	
		Gumari Hembrom	Amtola	
		Domon Tudu	Madhuban	
		Domon Marandi	Chitlo	Surajbera
Amrapara	August 7-8,	Jelhai Murmu	Telopara	Dharampur
	November 1945.	Haridas Tudu	Bishunpur	Amrapara
		Muchia Murmu		

	January 29-30, 1946. (Ram Datta Pandey).	Barka Hembrom		
		Jhade Tudu		
		Jhangal Murmu		
		Kalidas Marandi	Bara Paharpur	
		Kanan Marandi	Kalkipara	
		Maha Murmu	Amraparā	
		Ishwar Hembrom	Amrapara	
		Matla Murmu	Pariardaha	Maheshpur
		Banoten Kisku	Pachaibera	
		Lakhan Hansdak'		
		Jadu Marandi		
		Mangal Murmu	Dumarghati	
		Baijun Hembrom		
		Jagannath Mareya	Dumarghati	Maheshpur
		Kharu Murmu	Pariardoha	
		Mangal Kisku	Udalbani	Surajbera
		Singrai Murmu	Taljhari	Hiranpur
Katikund	August 2-3, November 2-3, 1945.	Chotu Ramu Murmu	Amtala	Katikund
	(James Hembrom Kumar)	Ramjit Hembrom	Haripur	
	February 10-13, 1946.	Kanhu Soren	Bichhiapahari	
	(Stephen Hari Tudu).	Jugal Murmu	Bartala	

Appendix III (Contd.)

Name of Centre	Date of Attestation	Attesting Santals: Name	Village	Bungalow, Circle, Police Station
		Srimat Soren	Daldali	
		Harma Marandi	Amgachhi	
		Jalpa Murmu	Asanpahari	
		Durga Soren	Bhangahir	Kuskira
		Sitaram Hansdak'	Jitpur	Jhilimili
		Singrai Tudu	Aluara	
		Siru Tudu	Pipra	
		Manik Tudu	Tesparta	Saldaha
		Bagal Murmu	Sarasbad	
		Ram Hansdak'	Domonpur	
		Matla Murmu	Ghasipur	
		Jetha Soren	Lakrapahari	
		Kisto Murmu	Karudih	Karudih
		Bhagmat Hansdak'	Karipahari	
		Jhagru Marandi	Ledapathar	Narganj
		Rejha Marandi	Lakhanpur	
Nunihat	August 7-9, November 7-9, 1945. (Keshav Nandan Sahay)	Budhu Hembrom	Nawadih	Kamardiha
		Kore Kisku	Baghjhope	
		Baso Murmu	Kala Dumariya	
	February 5-7, 1946. (Stephen Hari Tudu).	Ganga Besra	Latberwa	Amarpur
		Kusal Murmu	Gardih	
		Keso Murmu	Kukurtopa	Lakrapahari

		Karan Hansdak'	Kusbediya	Jhopa
		Churka Hansdak'	Kordiha	Sukhjora
		Jalpa Baskey	Jhilua	Beldaha
		Sukhan Murmu		
		Rasika Tudu	Garhitanr	Sahara
		Barka Marandi	Domohani	
		Baijnath Murmu	Baramasia	
		Nandu Murmu	Dumaria	
		Mangal Hansdak'	Machla	
		Surai Kisku	Katanja	Phuljhari
		Loba Murmu	Madhuban	Kasba
		Thakur Hansdak'	Mahadevagarh	
		Barka Baskey	Bahinga	Parghadih
Karbindha	August 4-6,	Dhunu Hembrom	Kukurkata	Mahubona
	November 4-6,			
	1945.	Samla Tudu	Cheharbani	
	January 26-28,	Barsa Murmu	Konapathar	
	1946.			
	(Jacob Hembrom)	Lapsa Tudu	Ranidinda	Guhiajuri
		Bugai Murmu	Bansberwa	
		Lopsa Murmu		
		Utra Hembrom	Hatimarabelmi	
		Lumbai Soren	Bakua	Danro
		Chandrai Hansdak'	Duarpahari	
		Jugu Soren	Siltha	
		Bodho Hansdak'	Ambasol Kakani	Amrapahari
		Matla Soren	Jhanjhar	
		Ramdas Tudu	Kusbona	

Appendix III (Contd.)

Name of Centre	Date of Attestation	Attesting Santals Name	Village	Bungalow, Circle, Police Station
		Suku Marandi	Ambasol Kakani	
		Gora Murmu	Dhobni	Ramgarh
		Haridas Kisku	Dholkatta	
		Pirthi Tudu	Bara Ranbohiar	
		Dandu Murmu		
		Harcan Murmu	Susama	Dudhua
		Manu Baske	Gardih	
Masanjore	August 2-3,	Jitu Hansdak'	Bardaha	Masanjore
	(Peter Murmu &	Tebol Hansdak'	Saltala	
	Uma Prasad Das)			
	November 2-3, 1945.	Kuria Hembrom	Darbarpur	
	January 22-24, 1946.	Nandu Baske	Sagbari	Lakhanpur
	(Stephen Hari Tudu).	Bhogon Hembrom	Sitasal	
		Suku Tudu	Dumdumi	Gormala
		Dasmath Hembrom	Datiarpur	
		Kishun Murmu		
		Karan Marandi	Barahorkhi	Banskuli
		Jitu Tudu	Jagdispur	
		Tunuc' Murmu	Bhangahir	Rangamasalia
		Dandu Soren	Jhilua	

		Govind Marandi	Kusumdih	Kumrabad
		Dasmat Hembrom	Baglajuri	
		Khudi Ram Marandi	Latabuni	Sukhjora
		Khudiram Marandi	Ragdih	
Chokerata	August 5-6, November 5-6, 1945.	Kolyan Soren	Khayerbani	Singro
		Ram Chand Marandi		
	January 26-28, 1946. (Stephen Hari Tudu).	Monsa Murmu	Kumirdaha	
		Babulal Tudu	Harladangal	Phuljhari
		Chota Ram Besra	Lakarjoria	
		Balku Soren	Khatangi	
		Mongol Soren	Bichkora	
		Khudu Tudu	Lodhna	
		Dodho Tudu	Khatangi	
		Mahadeb Hembrom	Duma	Pargadih
		Lakhan Soren	Dhundli	
		Surju Hembrom	Dhorli	
		Mongol Hembrom	Saraia	
		Kandna Marandi	Dumaria	Haripur
		Ramjiban Murmu	Baradhuba	Jartal
		Chandrai Hembrom	Jamua	Jarmundi
		Surai Murmu	Bikrampur	Tasaria
		Harma Murmu	Simla	Gumro
		Suphal Murmu	Agwa	

Appendix III (Contd.)

Name of Centre	Date of Attestation	Attesting Santals		
		Name	Village	Bungalow, Circle, Police Station
Kundahit	August 11-13, November 11-13, 1945. January 26-28, 1946. (Ajit Kumar Chatterji).	Suku Baske	Jadudih	Kundahit
		Keshar Hembrom	Mahishpur	
		Ram Hembrom	Sankarpur	
		Chando Tudu	Asanjuri	Siyarketiya
		Matla Soren	Kalipathar	
		Bhutuk Hembrom	Saguna	Amba
		Babulal Hansdak'	Jaipur	
		Sudan Baske	Rakh	Kuldangal
		Mangal Hansdak'	Kucha Kunri	
		Manjhia Baske	Santaldih	Afzalpur
		Chando Hansdak'	Lakhiyara	
		Morol Soren	Jokpahari	Khajuri
		Jiban Marandi	Prasadpur	
		Chhoto Hansdak'	Lakhiabad	Karaya
		Hudu Marandi	Brindaboni	
		Rakhan Soren	Kalipathar	Bagdahri
		Nalini Hansdak'	Sugunibasa	
		Mangal Marandi	Kharimati Rampur	Kasta
		Majhia Marandi	Ghusrukata	
		Lubu Hansdak'	Bhuli	

Fatepur	August 8-10, November 8-10, 1945. February 3-5, 1946. (Sashi Kanta Sinha).	Ch[illegible]ola Murmu	Anguthia	Asna
		[illegible]na Hembrom	Kairabani	
		Chaitan Marandi	Lakartanga	
		Chhotu Hembrom	Maheshpur	
		Makan Hembrom	Dudhani	
		Bhim Tudu	Chhotadih	Dhasania
		Chanda Soren	Bhimpahari	Dhasania
		Chandrai Hembrom	Phulsahri	
		Majhia Tudu	Amgachi	
		Harma Soren	Duma	
		Bhutka Hansdak'	Salpatra	Tilaki
		Kistu Marandi	Paranpur	
		Dhamna Murmu	Parjapatiya	
		Bastia Murmu	Lakhiabad	
		Kistu Hembrom	Putaljor	
		Raghu Hansdak'	Baratanr	Dhadkia
		Sham Murmu	Sugnibasa	
		Lachhu Tudu	Laludi	
		Bhomra Kisku	Bahnadangal	
		Sukhi Marandi	Chapria	
Narainpur	August 2-4, November 2-4, 1945.	Alhan Kisku	Kurta	Narainpur
		Hopna Hembrom	Chirudih	

Appendix III (*Contd.*)

Name of Centre	Date of Attestation	Attesting Santals		
		Name	Village	Bungalow, Circle, Police Station
	January 29-31, 1946. (Sashi Kanta Sinha).	Khela Marandi	Jabardaha	
		Lakhan Marandi	Janhedih	Dakhinbahal
		Sado Hansdak'	Champapur	
		Lakhia Murmu	Putberiya	
		Karan Soren	Chandadi	Lakhanpur Ghati
		Chhoto Baske	Patardih	
		Khulu Soren	Mirga	
		Meghrai Marandi	Rupdih	
		Manjhia Besra	Bagrudih	
		Mangal Marandi	Guniadih	Marro
		Bonga Murmu	Charkipahari	
		Saban Soren	Murgadih	
		Patai Hansdak'	Tiloki	
		Jadu Marandi	Phatepur	
		Lakhiram Marandi	Jasaidih	Pindari
		Bijan Murmu	Teliadi	
		Nanku Soren	Rataniya	
		Karua Marandi	Barua	
Jamtara	August 5-7, November 5-7, 1945.	Nandlal Kisku	Bharchondi	Bharchondi

February 2-4, 1946. (Ajit Kumar Chatterji).	Nandu Marandi	Kanchanbera	
	Nanda Marandi		
	Morol Baske	Muchiadih	
	Sukal Hansdak'	Kalajharia	Kalajharia
	Baijal Marandi	Salaiya	
	Budhan Marandi	Lakhanpur	
	Surai Marandi	Piplatanr	Pabia
	Madhusudan Kisku	Talberia	Lodhna
	Jiaram Marandi	Ladhna	
	Jiaram Marandi	Mihijam	Mihijam
	Hopna Marandi	Rangasola	Geria
	Baseth Murmu	Sukhjora	Dhobna
	Balaram Hansdak'	Jitpur	Gaychhand
	Mangal Tudu	Pagradih	
	Lakhan Kisku	Bodma	
	Ludu Hansdak'	Pipla	
	Thulu Hansdak'	Beoa	Jamtara
	Nayan Murmu	Udalbam	
	Chhutu Tudu	Asanchua	

BIBLIOGRAPHY

Allanson, H. Ll. L., *Final Report on the Survey and Settlement Operations in the District of Sonthal Parganas 1898—1910* (Calcutta, 1912).
(Contains a detailed account of measures to keep the Santal on his land as well as notes on Santal village officials).

Archer, Mildred, 'The Folk-tale in Santal Society', *Man in India*, XXIV (1944), 224—32.

Archer, Mildred and Archer, W.G., 'Santal Painting', *Axis*, Autumn, 1936, 27—28.

Archer, W.G., 'Santal Poetry,' *Man in India*, XXIII (1943), 98—105.

——, 'Betrothal Dialogues', *Man in India*, XXIII (1943), 147—53.

——, 'An Indian Riddle Book', *Man in India*, XXIII (1943), 265—315.

——, 'Festival Songs,' *Man in India*, XXIV (1944), 70—74.

——, 'More Santal Songs', *Man in India*, XXIV (1944), 141—4.

——, 'The Illegitimate Child in Santal Society', *Man in India*, XXIV (1944), 154—69.

——, 'The Forcible Marriage', *Man in India*, XXV (1945), 29—42.

——, 'The Santal Rebellion', *Man in India*, XXV (1945) 223—39.

——, 'Santal Rebellion Songs', *Man in India*, XXV (1945), 207.

——, 'Santal Transplantation Songs', *Man in India*, XXVI (1946), 6—7.

——, *The Hill of Fleetes, Life, Love and Poetry in Tribal India, A Portrait of the Santals*, University of Pittsburg Press, 1974.

Bishwas, P.C., *Primitive Religion, Social Organization, Law and Government amongst the Santals* (Calcutta, 1935).

Bodding, P.O., 'On the different kinds of Salutation used by the Santals', *Journal of Asiatic Society of Bengal*, LXVII, Part III (1898).

——, 'On Taboos and Customs connected therewith amongst the Santals', *Journal of Asiatic Society of Bengal*, LXVII, Part III (1898), 1—24.

——, 'Ancient stone implements in the Santal Parganas, *Journal of Asiatic Society of Bengal*, LXX, Part III (1901).

——, 'Shoulder-headed and other forms of stone implements in the Santal Parganas,' *Journal of Asiatic Society of Bengal*, LXXIII, Part III (1904).

——, 'Santal Traditions', *Journal of Bihar and Orissa Research Society*, II (1916).

——, 'Some Remarks on the Position of Women among the Santals', *Journal of Bihar and Orissa Research Society*, II (1916), 239—49.

——, *The Traditions and Institutions of the Santals*. Second Edition of *Horkoren Mare Hapramko reak' Katha* with a foreword by P.O. Bodding (Benagaria, 1916).

——, *Materials for a Santali Grammar* (Benagaria, 1922).

——, 'A Chapter of Santal Folk-lore', *Journal of the Royal Asiatic Society of Bengal* (1924).

——, 'A plea for a standardized system of writing the Munda or Kolarian languages', *J.R.A.S. Bengal*, New Series, XXI (192:).

——, *Studies in Santal Medicine and Connected Folk-lore*.

——, Part I, 'The Santals and Disease,' *Memoirs of the Royal Asiatic Society of Bangal* X (1925), 1—32.

——, Part II, 'Santal Medicine', *Memoirs of the Royal Asiatic Society of Bengal*, X (1927), 133—426.

——, Part III, 'How the Santals live', *Memoirs of the Royal Asiatic society of Bengal*, X(1940), 427—502.

——, *Santal Flok Tales* (Oslo, 1925—29).

——, 'The meaning of the words Buru and Bonga in Santali', *J.B.O.R.S.*, XII (1926), 63—77.

——, 'A Note on the "Wild People" of the Santals,' *Journal of Asiatic Society of Bengal*, XXVII (N.S.), 241—63.

——, *A Santali Grammar for Beginners* (Benagaria, 1929).

——, 'Notes on the Santals', *Census of India, 1939*, I, India, Part III B, 98—107.

——, *A Santal Dictionary* (Oslo, 1932—36). A masterpiece of learning.

Bolton, C.W., *Notes on the Settlement of the Sonthal Pergunnahs (Zamindari Portion) 1874—79* (Calcutta 1880, Deputy Commissioner's Record Room, Dumka).

Bompas, C.H., *Folk-lore of the Santal Parganas* (London, 1909).

Bonnerjee, B., 'The Social and Ceremonial Life of the Santals,' *The Indian Antiquary*, LIX (1930), 100 seq.

Bradley-Birt, F.B., *The Story of an Indian Upland* (London, 1925).

Buchanan, Francis, *An Account of the District of Bhagalpur in 1810-11* (Patna, 1939).

Campbell, A., *Santal Folk Tales* (Pokhuria, 1899).

——, 'The Traditional Migration of the Santal tribes,' *The India Antiquary* (1894).

——, *A Santali English Dictionary* (Pokhuria, 1899).

——, 'Rules of Succession and Partition of Property as observed by the Santals', *J.B.O.R.S.*, I (1915), 21—25.

——, 'Superstitions of the Santals', *J.B.O.R.S*, I (1915), 213—28.

——, 'The Traditions of the Santals', *J.B.O.R.S.*, II (1916), 16—29.

A variation of the myth as recorded in *Karam ar Caco Chatiar* and *Horkoren Mare Hapramko reak' Katha*).

——, 'Santal Legends', *J.B.O.R.S.*, II (1916), 191—200.

——, 'Death and Cremation Ceremonies among the Santals', *J.B.O.R.S.*, II (1916), 449—56.

——, 'Santal Marriage Customs,' *J.B.O.R.S.*, II (1916), 304—37.

Carstairs, R., *Letter No. 1394 dated 8-7-1892 to the Commissioner, Sonthal Parganas, forwarding J.A. Craven's Settlement Report*, (Deputy Commissioner's Record Room, Dumka).

——, *The Little World of an Indian District Officer* (London, 1912).

An account of his work by one of the greatest of 'Santal' Deputy Commissioners).

——, *Harma's Village* (Pokhuria, 1935).

(A novel of the Santal Rebellion).

Cole, F.T., 'Santali Folklore', *The Indian Antiquary*, IV (1875), 257.

Craven J.A., Settlement Report (1892) (with forwarding letter No. 1394 dated 8-7-1892 to the Commissioner Santal Parganas from R. Carstairs) (Deputy Commissioner's Record Room, Dumka).

Culshaw, W.J., 'Some Notes on Bongaism,' *Journal of the Royal Asiatic Society of Bengal*, V (1939), 427—31.

——, 'Some Beliefs and Customs relating to Birth among the Santals', *Journal of the Royal Asiatic Society of Bengal*, VII (1941), 115—27.

——, 'Lars Olsen Skrefsrud, 1840—1910', *International Review of Missions*, XXXI (1942), 347—53.
(A biographical sketch of a missionary who was also a pioneer of Santal studies).

——, 'The "Folk Consciousness" of the Santals', *Essays in Anthropology presented to S.C. Roy* (Lucknow, 1942), 219—27.

——, 'Santal Songs', *Proceedings Asiatic Folk-literature Society*, I (1944), No. I.

——, 'Early Records concerning the Santals', *Man in India*, XXV (1945), 191—3.
(Gives extracts from early reports of the Freewill Baptist Foreign Missionary Society ranging from 1838 to 1847 and includes a vivid reference to Santal dancing).

——, 'The Santal Rebellion,' *Man in India*, XXV (1945), 218—23.

Dalton, E.T., *Descriptive Ethnology of Bengal*, (Calcutta, 1872).

Deshmanjhi, Chotrae, *Chotrae Deshmanjhi reak' Katha* (Benagaria, 1938).

Dutta, Kali Kinkar, *The Santal Insurrection* (Calcutta, 1940).

Elwin, Verrier, *Folk-tales of Mahakoshal* (Bombay, 1944).
(A brilliant collection of folk-tales with notes and references to Santal and other folk-lore).

——, *Loss of Nerve* (Bombay, 1941).

——, *The Aboriginals* (Bombay, 1943).

Gait, E.A., *Census of India, 1901, Bengal* (Calcutta, 1902).

Gantzer, J.F., *Final Report on the Revision Survey and Settlement Operations in the District of Santal Parganas*, 1922—35 (Patna, 1936).

Gausdal, J., *Contributions to Santal Hymnology* (Bergen, 1935).

——, 'The Khunt System of the Santals', *J B.O.R.S.*, XXVIII (1942), Part IV.

Grierson, G.A., *Linguistic Survey of India, IV, Munda and Dravidian Languages* (Calcutta, 1906).

Hearn, W.N., 'Notes on the Santals', *Census of India, 1931*, I, India, Part III B, 108-9.

Hoernle, E.S., *A Brief Introduction to the Administration of the Santal Parganas* (Benagaria, 1929).

Hunter, W.W., *The Annals of Rural Bengal* (London, 1868).

——, *A Statistical Account of Bengal : The Santhal Parganas* (Calcutta, 1872).
(Reproduces the section in Dalton)

Koomar, C.H., *Santal Parganas, Santal ar Paharia Koak' Itihas* (Pokhuria, 1937).

Lacey, W.G., 'The Santals,' *Census of India, 1931*, I, India, Part III B, 97-98.

——, *Census of India, 1931, VII Bihar & Orissa, Part I Report.* (Contains a survey of recent Santal migrations with notes on Santal astrology, musical instruments, agricultural implements, bows and arrows and the life after death from notes by P.O. Bodding).

Macphail, J.M., *The Story of the Santal* (Calcutta, 1922).
'Cycle of the Seasons in a Santal Village', *The Calcutta Review*, (New Series).

Macphail, R.M., 'Notes on Santals', *Census of India, 1931*, I, India, Part III B, 109.

Mc Alpin, M.C., *Report on the Condition of the Santals* (Calcutta, 1909).

McPherson, H., *Note on the Aboriginal Races of the Santal Parganas* (Calcutta, 1908).

——, *Final Report on the Survey and Settlement Operations in the District of Santal Parganas, 1898—1907* (Calcutta, 1907). (The fullest account of the history and administration of the district).

Man, E.G., *Sonthalia and the Sonthals* (Calcutta, London, 1867).

Martin, Montgomery, *Eastern India* (London, 1832).
(Contains a garbled version of Buchanan's note).

Majumdar, S.C., 'Some Santal Songs', *The Visva-bharati Quarterly*, III (1925), 67--69.

Mitchell, J.M. 'Santali Songs', *The Indian Antiquary*, IV (1875), 342-44.

Mitra, Kalipada, 'The Originals and Parallels of Stories in Mr. Bompas's Folk-lore of the Santal Parganas', *J.B.O.R.S.*, XII (1926), 560—84.

——, 'A Mikir Tale and its Santali Parallels', *J.B.O.R.S.*, XIV (1928), 139—43.

——, 'Originals and Parallels of Some Santal Folk Tales', *J.A.S. Bengal*, XXV (1929), 101.

Mitra, Sarat Chandra, 'A Note of Human Sacrifice among the Santals', *J.B.O.R.S.*, XII (1926).

——, 'On a Santali Folk-tale of the Hero and the Deity Type', *J.B.O.R.S.*, XII (1926), 140—46.

——, 'Santali Life in a Santali Folk-Song', *J.A.S. Bom.*, XIII (1926), 48—51.

——, 'On a Satya Pir Legend in Santali Guise', *J.B.O.R.S.*, XIII (1927), 145—47.

——, 'A Further Note on Human Sacrifice among the Santals,' *J.B.O.R.S.*, XIV (1928), 147—49.

——, 'Folk-tales of "Der Mannund Fuchs" Type', *Man in India*, VIII (1928), 209—18.

——, 'The Dog-bride in Santal and Lepcha Folklore', *J.B.O.R.S.* XIV (1928), 422—45.

——, 'The Caterpillar Boy and the Caterpillar Husband in Santali and Chota Nagpur Folklore', *J.B.O.R.S.*, XIV (1928), 426—28.

——, 'The "Magical Conflict" in Santali, Bengali and Ao Naga 'Folk-lore', *Man in India*, IX (1929), 173—80.

——, Further Notes on the Dog-bride in Santali and Lepcha Folk-lore', *J.B.O.R.S.*, XV (1929), 600—06.

Mukherjea, Charu Lal, *The Santals* (Calcutta, 1945).

Mukherji, C.C., 'Notes on the Santals and Kherias of Manbhum District', *Census of India, 1931* I, India, Part III B, 110—12.

Murmu, S.C., *Gam Kahani* (Dumka, 1944). (A collection of Santal folk-tales in Santali).

Murmu, Stephen Hidim, *Karam ar Caco Chatiar* (Dumka, 1944).

——, *Hor Bapla* (Dumka, 1946).
(An account of Santal marriages in Santali).

Murmu, Stephen Hidim and Archer, W.G., *Hor Kudum* (Dumka, 1944).

Murmu, Solomon, *Hor Gidra Enec'* (Dumka, 1946).
(A record of Santal children's games in Santali).

Naqavi, S.M., 'Santal Murders', *Man in India*, XXIII (1943), 236—52.

Oldham, W.B., *Some Historical and Ethnical Aspects of the Burdwan District* (Calcutta, 1894).
(Contains long notes on Paharias but nothing on Santals barring a short reference to early contacts).

O'Malley, L.S.S., *Bengal District Gazetteers : Santal Parganas*, First Edition (Calcutta, 1910). Second Edition Revised by S.C. Mukherji (Patna, 1932).
(Reproduces a section on the Santals from the first edition but adds extra paras by P.O. Bodding on methods of cultivation, musical instruments and weapons. Adds an inaccurate note on ghar jawae and includes some incorrect sentences on inheritance).

——, *Modern India and the West* (London, 1942).
(Contains a discussion of Santals by J.H. Hutton).

Rapaz, Reuben Rusen Kisku, *Harmawak' Ato* (Dumka, 1946).
(A Santali translation of *Harma's Village* by R. Carstairs).

Roussos, Th., 'Santal Marriage Customs', *New Review*, XVI, 148—59.

Risley, H H., *The Tribes and Castes of Bengal* (Calcutta, 1891).
(The section on Santals includes the first statement in English of the Santal law of inheritance).

——, *The People of India* (Calcutta, 1908).
(Reproduces the section on Santals originally published in *The Tribes and Castes of Bengal*).

Rowat, F., 'Other Notes on the Santals', *Census of India, 1931*, I, India, Part III B, 107-8).

Roy, S.N., 'The Conversion of Santals to Hinduism', *J.B.O.R.S.*, II (1916).

Russell, R.E., *Judgment in Deputy Commissioner's Title Appeal No. 42 of 1923*, Lachu Hansdak' and Others versus Mangal Hansdak' (Record Room, Dumka).

——, *Judgment in District Judge's Title Appeal No. 9* of 1925, Tunka Marandi and Others versus Pani Murmu (Record Room, Dumka).

——, *Report of the Santal Parganas Inquiry Committee* (Patna, 1938).

Sherwill, W.S., 'Notes upon a Tour through the Rajmahal Hills', *Journal of Asiatic Society of Bengal* (1851).

Shore, John, 'Some Extraordinary Facts, Customs and Practices of the Hindus', *Asiatic Researches*, IV (1795), 345 seq.

Skrefsrud, L.O., *Introduction to the Grammar of the Santali Language* (Benares, 1873).

Skrefsrud, L.O. and Haram, Kolean, *Horkoren Mare Hapramko reak' Katha* : the Traditions and Institutions of the Santals (Benagaria, 1887).

Skrefsrud, L.O. and Craven, C.H., 'Notes on Fraternal Polyandry among the Santals', *Journal of Asiatic Society of Bengal* (1908).

Soren, G.G. and Archer, W.G., *Hor Soren* (Dumka, 1943).
Don Soren (Dumka, 1943).

Sutherland, H.C., *Report on the Management of the Rajmahal Hills dated 8 June, 1819* (Deputy Commissioner's Record Room, Dumka).

Thompson, E. and Garratt, G.T., *Rise and Fulfilment of British Rule in India* (London, 1934).
(Contains a commentary on the Santal rebellion).

Waddell, 'The Traditional Migration of the Santal Tribe', *The Indian Antiquary* (1893).

Ward, J.P., *Letter to Board of Revenue, Bengal, dated 17 August 1827* (Deputy Commissioner's Record Room, Dumka).